ADVERTISING SALES MANAGER
Ann E. Smith

ADVERTISING SALES REPRESENTATIVE
Dean L. Bennett

DEALER SALES REPRESENTATIVE
Dawn Behnke

ADVERTISING SERVICES MANAGER
Sara Malin Everts

ADVERTISING SERVICES REPRESENTATIVE
Harriett Schmidt

QUALITY COORDINATOR
Mary Nicloy

EDITORIAL COORDINATOR
Sybil Harp

EDITORIAL ASSISTANTS
Jeanne Delgado, Christine Paul,
Maggie Pernice, Ethel Rowen

ART DIRECTOR
Lawrence Luser

STAFF PHOTOGRAPHERS
Chris Becker
Darla Evans, Jim Forbes

GRAPHIC DESIGNER
Kim Watnos-Olson

PRODUCTION ARTISTS
Kim Watnos-Olson, Therese Gantz,

PRODUCTION MANAGER
David Koteski

PUBLISHER
Robert L. Hayden, Jr.

VICE PRESIDENT SALES/MARKETING
Daniel Lance

ADVERTISING DIRECTOR
Fred Hamilton

Kalmbach Publishing Co.
Customer Service
(800) 533-6644

THE MINIATURES CATALOG (ISBN 0-89024-261-5) is published by Kalmbach Publishing Co., 21027 Crossroads Circle, Waukesha, WI 53187, (414) 796-8776. Circulation: Available from Kalmbach Publishing Co., miniatures shops, book stores, craft, hobby, and gift shops in the United States and Canada. Product Listings: Address all inquiries and correspondence for listings to THE MINIATURES CATALOG, Advertising Sales Manager, 21027 Crossroads Circle, Waukesha, WI 53187. ©1995 by Kalmbach Publishing Co. Printed in U.S.A. All rights reserved. Reproduction in part or in full is prohibited without the expressed, written permission of the publisher.

Note: THE MINIATURES CATALOG is not a mail order catalog. To obtain the products listed in this book, see your local miniatures dealer or write directly to the manufacturer or craftsperson. Additional ordering information and manufacturers' sales policies may be found in the Manufacturers Index in the back of the catalog.

PRINTED IN THE U.S.A.

THE
MINIATURES CATALOG

WELCOME TO THE MINIATURES CATALOG

Your complete guide to the fascinating world of miniatures

WHAT'S YOUR PLEASURE? Whatever your experience in miniatures, *The Miniatures Catalog* is designed to help you derive greater satisfaction and enjoyment from your hobby. It is not intended as a mail order catalog, but rather as a buyer's guide. Consider it a roadmap through the delightful, if sometimes confusing, world of miniatures.

YOUR TOTAL RESOURCE FOR MINIATURES

The majority of products listed in *The Miniatures Catalog* are carried by miniatures shops. To locate the shop nearest you, consult the Shop Directory in this catalog, listing more than 200 shops. We encourage you to visit miniatures shops whenever possible, where you can usually find knowledgeable assistance in planning and completing your miniature projects. If there is no shop in your area, consult the Manufacturers' Index in the back to contact manufacturers for retail information. Although the manufacturers do not sell directly to consumers, they will provide you with a list of retail sources for their products. Please remember to include a self-addressed, stamped envelope with your request.To ensure accuracy, all product descriptions are written by the manufacturer or handcrafters. The catalog numbers refer to the manufacturers' catalog or price sheet numbers and are included to make it easier to order items from your local retailer.

The Miniatures Catalog is not a mail order catalog insofar as products cannot be ordered directly from it; however, many of the companies included in it do have mail order catalogs available and will sell directly to the consumer.

In addition to 3,000 miniature product listings, *The Miniature Catalog* also includes sources for Tools and Building Materials, Publications, Plans, Shops, Museums and Miniatures Shows. The Manufacturers Index and Product Index are useful in locating a specific item or supplier.

COLOR SECTIONS

The color sections of the Catalog are presented by the editors of *Nutshell News*, Kalmbach Publishing Co.'s monthly miniatures magazine. The first color section looks back on the past 25 years, when miniatures grew from a little known type of collecting to a comprehensive and rapidly expanding hobby enjoyed by thousands. The section also includes an original Kit Rendering by *Nutshell News* author Ron Benson, who leads you step-by-step through the process of customizing a miniature furniture kit.

The second color section presents a memorial tribute to Chrysnbon Miniatures' founder Judy Berman, whose contribution to the miniatures hobby is immeasurable. A talented miniaturist herself, she made miniature furniture kits and accessories accessible to all. Thanks to the generosity of the Berman family, photos of some of Judy's own miniature rooms are shown in this pictorial tribute, along with two how-to projects employing Chrysnbon products.

MORE INFORMATION ABOUT MINIATURES

In the Calendar section, you'll find a list of miniatures shows scheduled in the United States, Canada, and England from August 1995 through 1997. Miniatures shows are held across the country all year round, providing opportunities to see and purchase fine handcrafted work, meet other hobbyists in your area, view exhibits of projects made by local miniaturists, and sometimes participate in hands-on workshops. For the most current information on shows, see the calendar section of *Nutshell News*.

The Museum Directory includes more than 50 North American museums displaying miniature exhibits from antiques to contemporary collections. Be sure to check this useful section before traveling.

The editors and staff of *The Miniatures Catalog* and *Nutshell News* wish you many happy discoveries in the wonderful world of miniatures.

TABLE OF CONTENTS

PLUS EXCITING FEATURE ARTICLES

25 YEARS IN A NUTSHELL — PG. 7

SEE PAGE 346 FOR UPCOMING EVENTS IN YOUR AREA!

Collectible Miniatures _280

Fashion Scale

Smaller Scales

Publications & Plans

JUDY BERMAN - THE ANGEL OF KITS — PG. 225

Tools & Supplies

Special Sections

MAKE A BABY GIFT BAG — PG. 234

RON BENSON KIT RENDERING — PG. 14

MAKE MINE COUNTRY! KIT PAINTING — PG. 232

Miniscules

N2059 Pine Beach Rd. S, Oostburg, WI 53070

These are just a few of our prepasted vinyl-coated **WALLPAPERS.**
Also look for our fine textured and patterned carpets.
All available at these fine shops:

CALIFORNIA

Bearly Big Enough
2314 Pacific Avenue
Stockton, CA 95204-5336
209-948-2088

D & J Hobbies
96 N. San Thomas Aquino Road
Campbell, CA 95008
408-379-1696

Hillary House Miniatures
1117 Vine Street
Paso Robles, CA 93446
805-238-4593

COLORADO

Kris Kringle, Ltd.
2403 West Colorado
Avenue
Colorado Springs, CO 80904
719-633-1210

CONNECTICUT

Dollhouses Plus
211 Coram Avenue
Shelton, CT 06484
203-924-6966

The Small Collector
199 Ethan Allan Highway
Ridgefield, CT 06877
203-438-1956

Sugar & Spice®
2 East Main Street, PO Box 718
Plainville, CT 06062
203-747-0414

FLORIDA

Connie's Crafts
Osceola Flea & Farmer's Market
Booth A 42 - 48
Highway 192
Kissimmee, FL 34744
407-846-9088

Haslam's Dollhouse
7208 South Tamiami Trail
Sarasota, FL 34231
813-922-8337

ILLINOIS

Little Dreams & Wishes
300 East Broadway
Alton, IL 62002
618-465-0058

MASSACHUSETTS

Enchanted Cottage
2512 Massachusetts Avenue
Cambridge, MA 02140
617-491-8818

Hometown Miniatures
36 Pittsfield Road
Lenox, MA 01240
413-637-4778

Little House Miniatures
459 Main Street
Indian Orchard, MA 01151
413-543-6016

NEW JERSEY

Fran's Miniatures
104 Main Street
Hightstown, NJ 08520
609-448-7955

Rose's Dollhouse Goodies
123 East Main Street
Moorestown, NJ 08057
609-778-1484

NEW YORK

Lady Melissa's Miniatures
7 King Arthur Court
Sarasota Springs, NY 12866
518-581-7677

Manhatten Dollhouse Shop
176 9th Avenue
New York, NY 10011
212-989-5220

Treasures by Paula K, Inc.
Village Plaza, Rt. 202
Lincolndale, NY 10540
800-899-7285

NORTH CAROLINA

Gingerbread House
of Miniatures
2170 Lawnsdale Drive
Greensboro, NC 27408
910-273-2831

OHIO

Calico Corner General Store
4652 East Liberty Avenue
Vermilion, OH 44089
216-967-4830

Jan's Dollhouse
6600 G. Dixie Highway
Fairfield, OH 45014
513-860-0595

The Miniature Peddler
2766 South Arlington Road
Akron, OH 44312
216-644-3020

PENNSYLVANIA

Doll House Decor, Inc.
Rt. 100
(1-1/2 mi. N Exit 23 Pa. Tpk.)
Eagle, PA 19480
610-458-5669

The Doll & Mini Nook
336 West Broad Street
Quakertown, PA 18951
800-591-6886

TENNESSEE

Miniature & Dollhouse
Shop
5204 Homberg Drive
Knoxville, TN 37919
615-584-1907

Suzanne Andrews Miniature Shop
3915 Nolensville Road
Nashville, TN 37211
615-833-5555

VIRGINIA

Just Imagine
1985 Landstown Road
Va. Beach, VA 23456
804-430-0903

Miniatures From the Attic
111 Park Avenue
Falls Church, VA 22046
703-237-0066

Troy Miniature Shoppe
201 South Main Street
Bridgwater, VA 22812
703-828-3983

WASHINGTON

Rose's Fascination Shop
624 Edmonds Way
Edmonds, WA 98020
206-775-2017

WISCONSIN

Hobby World Miniatures
216 East College Avenue
Appleton, WI 54911
800-438-3968

Miniature Village
1725 50th Street
Kenosha, WI 53140
800-383-0188

A PEEK THROUGH THE KEYHOLE

**By Sybil Harp
Editor, Nutshell News**

When you look through this Catalog or attend one of the many miniatures shows around the country, it's hard to realize that only 25 years ago there was virtually no miniatures hobby as we know it today. Certainly there were people collecting miniatures, as well as making them, but most of them didn't know about each other and had no means of finding one another. Miniatures shops didn't exist, nor were there any miniatures shows.

What was there, back then? A few companies were manufacturing miniature accessories or furniture, although most of their products were intended for children's dollhouses. A handful of artisans were producing fine handcrafted furniture and accessories in 1" scale for the few active collectors scattered across the country. The only American magazines publishing anything on the miniatures hobby were *Hobbies,* which ran a regular column devoted to miniatures, and *Creative Crafts,* with an occasional article.

Although there was little awareness of the existence of a miniatures hobby, two superb examples of the miniaturist's art had long been on public display in the city of Chicago. Colleen Moore's Fairy Castle had its permanent home in the Museum of Science and Industry, and the famous Thorne Rooms had been exhibited in the Art Institute of Chicago since the 1930s. As popular as those two exhibits were, miniatures were apparently not seen as a potential activity for ordinary folks until the early 1970s, when makers and collectors of miniatures began to discover each other. With the introduction of *Nutshell News* and the founding of the National Association of Miniature Enthusiasts (NAME) interest in miniatures began to expand rapidly until by the end of the decade there was a mature, cohesive hobby served by an industry composed of manufacturers and distributors, handcrafters, retail stores, and publications.

We who are involved in miniatures like to refer to "the wonderful world of miniatures." We often think of miniatures as a microcosm of the larger world, but without the "real" world's less troublesome aspects. The world of miniatures, we say, is a place where all the problems are little ones, both literally and figuratively. Although the miniatures hobby is not unique in providing an escape from everyday life, its devotees claim that it has a distinct advantage over other activities in that it can be pursued on several different levels and related to many other interests.

> The January 1995 issue of *Nutshell News* marked the beginning of the magazine's year-long 25th anniversary celebration. The centerspread feature, "Artisans Showcase," presented this whimsical scene intended to portray "25 Years in a Nutshell." *Nutshell News'* unusual name is based on a quotation from Shakespeare's *Hamlet:* "I could live bounded in a nutshell and count myself a king of infinite space."

On these pages we picture some ways miniatures have been presented in recent issues of *Nutshell News*. This is by no means a comprehensive view of the world of miniatures; it is, rather, a peek through the keyhole. For those who have yet to discover that world, we hope it will also serve as an invitation to begin exploring a captivating hobby.

What is an anniversary without a special cake? Some of the miniature world's outstanding artisans were asked to contribute to our anniversary gala, where cake and pink champagne were served. This elegant Victorian table set with sterling silver, porcelain, and crystal graced the cover of the January 1995 issue.

Nutshell News' "Artisans Showcase" is a monthly feature showcasing work contributed by professional miniaturists. This contemporary living room reflects a current decorating trend by including some antiquities with modern furniture and accessories.

Different historical periods resonate with different people, and *Nutshell News* tries to represent as many periods as possible. This mounted knight by doll artist Albina Herron, shown on the June 1995 cover anticipates the Medieval romance and pageantry featured in that issue.

Many people associate miniatures with Victorian dollhouses. While virtually every decorating style and period has been represented in miniature, the Victorian period continues to be a favorite. This rambling Victorian mansion, "Rose," was inspired by two Los Angeles mansions, and incorporates details from several other houses of the period between 1885 and 1891.

A highlight of events in the world of miniatures was the opening of the Carole and Barry Kaye Museum of Miniatures in Los Angeles in June 1994. The museum, located on Museum Row on Wilshire Boulevard, which was featured in the January 1995 issue of *Nutshell News*, exhibits a multitude of creations by internationally known miniaturists. Dominating the opening was a magnificent miniature rendition of Fountainebleau by British artisans Kevin Mulvany and Susan Rogers. The spectacular exterior staircase leading to the miniature palace's entrance is pictured.

The gala opening of the Carole and Barry Kaye Museum of Miniatures was attended by notables from both the miniatures world and the "real" world, including guest of honor Elizabeth Taylor, who was presented with this original porcelain portrait doll created by artisan Gina Bellous.

Another California museum housing a fabulous miniatures collection is Betty Martin's California Institute of Art, a 1" scale building constructed to exhibit her hundreds of miniature artifacts from around the world, the result of a lifetime of travel and collecting.

Nutshell News readers look forward to the instructions and plans for a ½" scale house designed by Frank Moroz and usually featured in the May issue. The 1995 plans were for this New Orleans double barreled "shotgun" house. The miniature house followed an authentic design and featured two side by side apartments that could be combined into a single family house if desired.

Brooke Tucker wraps Christmas in a sophisticated color scheme with just a touch of gold — and not a bit of tinsel. Brooke made a three-part roombox using a color scheme inspired by the pink and celadon print fabric she used throughout. The white carpet in the living room is bordered by the pattern of the carpet she used in the dining room. The dining room chairs are upholstered in the same print fabric as the wallpaper.

You can design a whole scene around a single piece — Brooke says these rooms were inspired by the John Hodgson blackamoors she used in the hall between the living and dining rooms. "And I could not have done this (hall) without Sandra Henry Wall's flower arrangements!"

Joann's Do-It-Yourself projects are one of NN's most popular monthly features. "A Room of His Own" was a June, 1995 Father's Day project that Joann Swanson designed, based on an article she found in the October, 1928 edition of *Better Homes & Gardens*. She decided that the occupant of her room was a writer and so provided him with a typewriter (remember this is pre-computer vintage), manuscripts, stacks of typing paper and of course, many many books. In the bookcase is a "surprise cabinet" which opens to a folding table and four stools!

A Neoclassical Commode

One day a wardrobe, the next a commode

By Ron Benson
PHOTOS BY JIM FORBES

Kit Rendering or Kitbashing: The art of turning a kit into something different than what it was originally intended to be.

It is not always possible to find that perfect piece of furniture to fit into that empty spot in your roombox or dollhouse "off the rack." However, with a little bit of ingenuity and some elbow grease, kitbashing can not only provide you with just what you are looking for, but with the pride in knowing you built it yourself!

Houseworks' #4004 Bowfront Wardrobe is the perfect jumping off point from which to create our Hepplewhite neoclassical commode.

Begin with parts #17, 18 and 19, the drawer front, sides, and back. Use my template to cut these parts down to size. Now add part #20, the drawer bottom and assemble the drawer. You may want to sand the cut off edges a bit when the drawer is glued together. This drawer will be the basis for further alterations. It is essential that you complete it first.

Now take parts #1 and 2, the sides, turn them upside down and slip in part #4, the drawer divider. Do not glue at this time. Set your completed drawer on top of the divider. With a pencil, mark a line just slightly above the drawer on parts #1 and 2 (see drawing). This will be your cutting line. Now you may cut both parts on these lines. Set these aside for later.

Using my template, cut two smaller doors from either part #7, or #6, the doors. In my kit, one of the doors had a nicer grain, so I chose it for my doors. This will also mean you will have nicely matched doors instead of the usual kit mis-match. These doors will be used to cut the bottom on parts #1 and 2, the sides. Notice on the drawing I cut these parts so that I could use part #4 on the bottom so that the doors could be hinged between parts #4. You may need to fool with this a bit to get a good fit.

You may use my template to cut down the back, part #3, or set all the parts we have completed together and cut the back to match. The latter method is suggested to get a good fit. Now you may assemble the basic body as shown in the drawing.

The top, part #6 may be left as it is, or cut down to fit flush with the front and sides. This makes a bit more upscale

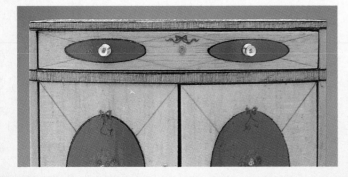

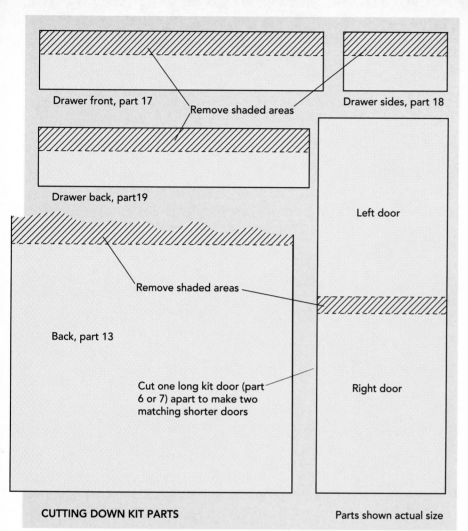

Drawer front, part 17

Remove shaded areas

Drawer sides, part 18

Drawer back, part19

Remove shaded areas

Back, part 13

Cut one long kit door (part 6 or 7) apart to make two matching shorter doors

Left door

Right door

CUTTING DOWN KIT PARTS

Parts shown actual size

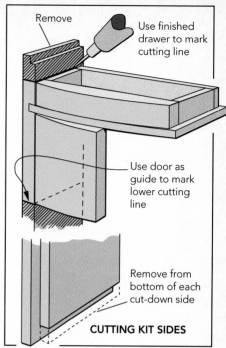

Remove

Use finished drawer to mark cutting line

Use door as guide to mark lower cutting line

Remove from bottom of each cut-down side

CUTTING KIT SIDES

Materials List

Houseworks #4004 Bowfront Wardrobe (see your miniatures shop)
Sandpaper
Micron PIGMA #005 pens, black & brown (art supply stores)
Oval templates
House of Miniatures clear finish
"Brasses" #D-116 oval escutcheons (2) (see your miniatures shop or write Black Diamond Designs, 1579 F Monroe Dr., #198, Atlanta GA 30324)
Water-based or enamel paints — Wedgwood blue, moss green, khaki green, maroon, red, white
Jeweler's saw

chest, but is not necessary. I left a bit of overhang in back. This was common to bridge the gap should the wall have a chair-rail. You may glue the top in place now.

I recommend you sand the entire piece as a unit. You should sand the front edges of the sides so that they follow the curve of the drawer and doors (see drawing). I found that the drawer had a slightly different bow than the rest of the piece. This is a good time to make it all match. By the way, don't install the doors yet.

I did the ovals and cross-banding with the black Micron PIGMA #005 waterproof pen. Do the ovals first. You may use my ovals as templates or buy a plastic template of ovals for this and future use. Start with the doors. Center the ovals on the doors and lightly draw a black line around them. These pens are fragile. Go around the oval several times rather than try to get the line in one go (see drawing). Set the doors aside for later.

Center another oval on the top, and

follow the same process. On the sides use my drawings as a guide to the placement of the "cross-banding" and center the large oval on each lower side. Note the "cross-banding" is in three horizontal strips. The top band follows the exact edge of the top, the second follows the lower drawer support, and the bottom band follows the base line.

I turned the chest upside down and ran the first line around the top. Do this lightly to save your pen. I put the unused part #5 where the drawer top would go (see drawing), and ran another black line around the edge. Repeat this process on the "cross-banding" at the top and bottom of the door openings. The lower line is created by placing the base flat and tracing around the edge as we did on the top. Now all you need to do is run these lines from there all the way around the sides (see drawings). I used the brown Micron pen to create the cross-banded effect (see drawings).

Our drawer ovals and side ovals can

be made by tracing around my template, or using the plastic template of ovals. Center each of the ovals above the lower ovals. Center in the spaces (see drawing).

Satinwood veneer on the doors of the original commode would have been pieced. Go from corner to corner (see drawings) and make "Xs" to each oval. Note that the drawer has a slightly different pattern.

Set the case aside while we alter the legs and base. Re-shape part #11, the apron, called "front stretcher" in the instructions. Use my small oval to use as a guide for the "inlaid" patera. This is created with the black and brown pens. Follow my drawings.

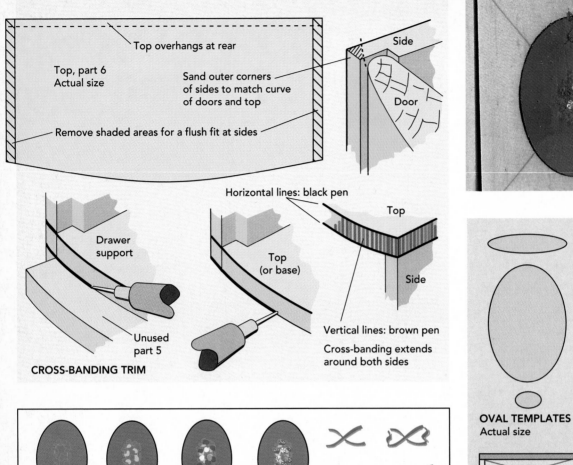

Top overhangs at rear

Top, part 6
Actual size

Sand outer corners
of sides to match curve
of doors and top

Remove shaded areas for a flush fit at sides

Side

Door

Drawer
support

Unused
part 5

CROSS-BANDING TRIM

Horizontal lines: black pen

Top

Top
(or base)

Side

Vertical lines: brown pen

Cross-banding extends
around both sides

Drybrush one
shade of green
over blue oval

Drybrush
second shade
of green

Paint large color-
ed dots over
green for flowers

Paint dots
over flowers
for "petals"

Paint con-
nected "X's"
to make bows

Paint inside of pulls white

Paint colored dots
to look like flowers

Remove darker areas from
front and side aprons

PAINTING AND LEGS

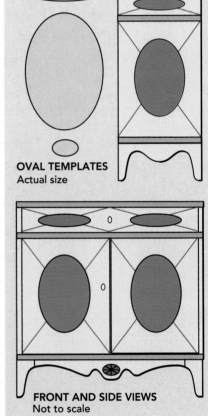

OVAL TEMPLATES
Actual size

FRONT AND SIDE VIEWS
Not to scale

Reshape the legs and side aprons, parts #9 and #10 as shown. The fronts will be a bit too deep since we sanded the front edges of the case. Sand these down to match with the case. I lightened the feet by cutting the sides to more of an angle and cutting a bit off the inside back (see drawing). Set these parts aside for later.

Now install the doors. Drill two new holes in the base for the pins. Once you have them in place you will need a small piece of scrap wood to use at the back as a stop for the doors (they will be non-

working). Once these are in place assemble the base as per the kit instructions.

Now we will do the painting. I painted the ovals a Wedgwood blue. I drybrushed two different greens for the foliage, using medium sized dots of white, red and pink to suggest the flowers. Use smaller dots of color on each flower to get the petal effect. Our bows are "Xs" connected as shown on the drawings. I used two shades of maroon.

I used the two pulls for the doors on the drawer. Paint the center white with dots of green and red or rose to give the

effect of Battersea enamel pulls. Use "Brasses" #D-116 oval escutcheons for the center of the drawer and the left hand door.

Finish with House of Miniatures clear finish. Paint the back and underside with mahogany stain which closely matches the so-called "Sheraton red" found on many neo-classical pieces.

While there are no period bow-fronted wardrobes, the kit is perfect for this Hepplewhite neo-classical commode, a first class edition to a formal late 18th century room.

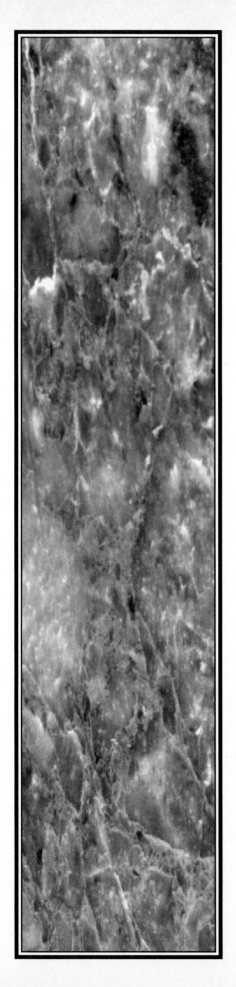

HOUSES & BUILDINGS

Colonial

CELERITY MINIATURE HOMES

Engelson Home

Stock No.: 1501 (kit); 1502 (assembled)
Price: See your local dealer for retail.
Dimensions: 32"H x 40"W x 24"D (includes porch)
Beautiful farmhouse with a large front offset and full-length front porch and steps. Three floors, nine rooms. Large rooms plus two stairways, movable partitions, chimney and all on a firm foundation. Decorated exterior as shown is a special order. This house can also be decorated in the Tudor style and is beautiful. Dado joint construction. Top quality 3/8" plywood.

VISIT A MINIATURES MUSEUM ON YOUR VACATION

DEE'S DELIGHTS, INC. HOMETOWN SERIES

CORONA CONCEPTS

The Willow Dollhouse Kit

Stock No.: 9305
Dimensions: 30-1/2"W x 16-1/2"D x 31"H; 1" scale
This classic colonial-style house features six spacious rooms for endless decorating possibilities. The downstairs fireplace centered between two built-in bookcases, master bedroom fireplace and shutters complement the authentic 18th century architecture. Other features include the ornate front door, gracious stairway and double-hung windows. Shingles and siding included! See your local dealer.

"The Colonial"

Stock No.: HOM400
Price: See your local dealer.
Dimensions: 26"H x 23-3/4"W x 16"D
Majestic two-column mansion features six rooms in an unfinished, assembled plywood dollhouse. Complete with five 12-pane windows, a solid panel door with classic pediment, interior staircase and chimney. Full foundation. Roofing and siding not included. Personalized dollhouse deed and finishing instructions.

CELERITY MINIATURE HOMES
Cindy's House

Stock No.: 1701 (kit); 1702 (assembled)
Price: Wholesale only. See your local dealer.
Dimensions: 28"H x 23"W x 19"D
A charming dollhouse. Three floors, six rooms. Kit includes nine main pieces plus railings, corner posts and turned posts, two stairways, chimney and movable room partitions. Great little house! Now available with room addition. Six main parts to create a charming kitchen! Size: 16" H x 11-3/4"W x 9-3/4"D. Dado joint construction. 3/8" plywood throughout.

Prices are approximate and subject to change

DURA-CRAFT, INC.

Colonial Miniature House Kit

Stock No.: CH300
Dimensions: 32"H x 28"W x 15"D
Eight rooms, one stairway, three floors. Split shake roof, hardwood flooring. Complete pre-cut kit including hardware (hinges) and plastic windows. Outstanding detail including windows, shutters, etc. See your dealer. Tongue and groove clapboard siding.

GREENLEAF PRODUCTS

The Jefferson

Stock No.: 8014
Price: $119.90
Dimensions: 29"H x 28"W x 16"D, two floors, four rooms
The Jefferson replicates the handsome simplicity of colonial American "saltbox" architecture. A paneled front door opens into a gracious hallway flanked by two large rooms, one of which includes a fireplace and built-in bookcase wall. The center stairs lead to another wide hallway and two big rooms, while a large third-floor attic partitions in two. Realistic window sashes add to the overall appearance of the house, as do windows silk-screened into divided panes. Rectangular shingles and durable clapboard siding are included in the kit and further enhance this affordable authentic dollhouse. Die-cut plywood.

HOUSEWORKS, LTD.
1/12th Scale Colonial Shell

Stock No.: 4101
Price: $225
Dimensions: 33"H x 33-1/4"L x 16"D
Kit includes 3/8" cabinet-grade plywood, front opening designs, step-by-step instructions, and a 3-in-1 Dollhouse Planbook for your reference. Write to Houseworks for information on the Houseworks Components Sets.

WALMER DOLLHOUSES
Montclair

Stock No.: 601
Dimensions: 36"H x 36"W x 23"D
A "neo-Colonial," part of our Sophistikit line of dollhouses, offers the following in the kit: All windows, front entry door, shutters, trims and porch, interior staircases, nine rooms in addition to hallways, third floor has ceiling for lighting. Companion product Montclair Siding (#6015) and Porch (#602). Montclair also features Walmer's dowel construction.

MODEL BUILDERS SUPPLY

Dollhouse "Brett"

Stock No.: AD003
Price: $121.60
Dimensions: 24" x 17" x 24"
An ideal traditional starter kit, but just as much fun as the larger homes. Four rooms plus attic, 3/8" walls, easy to assemble, unique ridge molding. Excellent quality, affordable price.

REAL GOOD TOYS

The Montpelier

Stock No.: M-1001
Dimensions: 32"H x 32"W x 18"D
3/8" thick exterior walls have clapboards milled directly into the plywood surface for an easy, one-step finish. Precision pre-cut parts, preassembled windows and door. A simple, lovely colonial home that is sturdy and spacious. Perfect for the discriminating collector. Three floors, 10 rooms with finely detailed staircases. A wide variety of porches and room additions can be added at any time.

FANTASY CRAFT

Contemporary

Fancy Forgery

WORKSHOP WISDOM

Here's how to antique those miniature paintings you cut from magazines! Spray with several coats of matte finish, allow each coat to dry. As the final coat dries, lightly rub a wad of dryer lint over it and, when totally dry, pick up the excess lint by dabbing the picture with a piece of adhesive tape. This technique dulls the picture, making it appear old and worn.

MARIBETH DURST
ST. LEO, FL

Workshop Wisdom Courtesy of *Nutshell News—3/95*

Craftsman Bungalow

Stock No.: HO6
Price: Kit $399.95, plus shipping
Dimensions: 28"W x 28"D x 26"H; 1" scale
Beautifully-detailed early 20th Century Craftsman home brings all the romance and charm of quiet tree-lined streets and childhood memories. Along with their Victorian sisters, many Craftsman Bungalows are cherished homes today. A delight to decorate and furnish! Easy assembly, 3/8" plywood, tongue-and-groove construction. Includes porch and dormer trim. Finishing kits, components and accessories available.

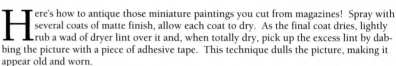

FANTASY CRAFT
California Contemporary

Stock No.: HO4
Price: Kit $1,159.95, plus shipping
Dimensions: 38"W x 36"D x 25"H; 1" scale
The latest in contemporary architecture—in miniature! Exciting two story home features: raised entry, curved stairs, living room, family room, dining room, kitchen with solarium wall and indirect lighting, laundry, two bathrooms, three bedrooms with mirrored wardrobes and two car garage with roll-up door. Enclosed four sides. 3/8" plywood, tongue-and-groove construction. Finishing kits available.

HOUSEWORKS, LTD.
Thornhill Shell

Stock No.: 9001
Price: $510
Dimensions: 36"H x 46"L x 28"D; 1" scale
A classic dollhouse designed with the most prestigious and spacious interior on the market. Kit includes all plywood parts pre-cut to fit, 14 spacious rooms, quoins (pre-cut, mitered corner blocks), dentil trim on front gable, chimneys, front steps, hinges and magnets. Write to Houseworks for information on the Houseworks Component Set.

Cottages &Cabins

VISIT A
MINIATURES SHOP
WHILE
TRAVELING

CELERITY MINIATURE HOMES
Hand Painted Cottage

Stock No.: 1102
Price: See your local dealer.
Dimensions: 18"H x 24"W x 19"D
This beautiful hand painted "Garden Cottage" is truly unique. Each house is numbered and signed by our artist, making each a collector house. Must be seen to be appreciated. Two floors, four rooms, made of 3/8" quality plywood.

CELERITY MINIATURE HOMES
Little Molly

Stock No.: 3901 (kit); 3902 (assembled)
Price: See your local dealer.
Dimensions: 32"L x 17"W x 29-3/4"H
(includes base); 1" = 1'
"Little Molly" enjoys her play time with this charming house. The living room, dining room and kitchen of this seven-room house are all on the first floor. Plus, there's an outside deck to play in the sunshine! Kit contains 14 main house parts plus railings, shutters, turned posts, movable partitions and interior stairway.

CELERITY MINIATURE HOMES
The Chalet

Stock No.: 203 (kit); 204 (assembled)
Price: See your local dealer for retail.
Dimensions: 29-1/2"H x 32"W x 16"D
Plenty of fun for the mini family that owns this home with front porch and patio deck. Three floors, six rooms. Details include stairway, movable partitions, shutters and flower boxes. Kit contains 10 main pieces plus scroll trim, railings and turned posts. A charming dollhouse for a beginning miniaturist. Decorated exterior as shown is a special order. Dado joint construction. Top quality 3/8" plywood.

CELERITY MINIATURE HOMES
The Cottage

Stock No.: 1101 (kit); 1102 (assembled);
1103 (decorated)
Price: See your local dealer.
Dimensions: 18"H x 24"W x 19"D
Small pioneers! The log cabin has two floors and four rooms with two movable partitions plus a stairway to a sleeping loft for your north woods get-away. Logs sold separately. The thatch roof accessory kit, #1101AK, contains a full-height chimney and window box to complete this model (thatched roofing not included). Top quality 3/8" plywood. Dado joint construction. Logs available.

FOR FAST SERVICE, VISIT YOUR LOCAL MINIATURES SHOP

CORONA CONCEPTS
The Aster Cottage

Stock No.: 9302
Dimensions: 16-3/8"W x 19-1/2"D x 20"H;
1" scale
The small, cozy atmosphere of this English Tudor style cottage will capture your imagination. The sleeping loft offers a romantic view of the large kitchen fireplace on the main level. Other features include a bay window, staircase, a Dutch door and silk-screened windows. The timber-style construction and side opening add character to this charming design. Stucco included! See your local dealer.

DURA-CRAFT, INC.

Ashley

Stock No.: AH130
Price: See your dealer
Dimensions: 16-3/4"H x 17-1/2"W x 12-1/2"D;
1"=1' scale
Two rooms, two floors, pine frame, 1/8" pre-cut plywood, knock-down construction. Fanciful cottage kit features front porch with benches, spiral staircase, fancy silk-screened windows, two dormer windows, bay window, working front door and two upstairs alcoves. Roof panels scored with shingle pattern.

DURA-CRAFT, INC.

Columbian Miniature House Kit

Stock No.: CB150
Dimensions: 23"H x 20"W x 13"D
Four rooms, two floors, pine frame, 1/8" plywood, knock-down construction. This delightful chalet style house has all the gingerbread charm of the real thing. Kit includes pine frame construction, silk-screened windows, stairway and real split shakes.

DURA-CRAFT, INC.

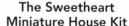

The Sweetheart
Miniature House Kit

Stock No.: SW125
Dimensions: 16"H x 17"W x 11"D
Four Rooms, two floors. Charming Tudor-style dollhouse kit will delight little girls everywhere. The cute little hearts, real stairs and flower boxes make it a sure favorite. Sturdy pine frame construction. KD 1/8" Lauan plywood, silk-screened windows, roof panels are scored with shingle pattern.

FANTASY CRAFT
Mountain Cabin Room Box

Price: $110.95
Dimensions: 27"W x 17"D x 14-1/2"H;
1" scale
Choose your favorite snapshot from your last camping trip to make your backdrop scene. Add backlighting and "trees" for a 3-D landscape. One-room cabin features a "shadow" window and a big country-style porch. Acrylic front, removable roof. Easy assembly, tongue-and-groove construction. Finishing kit $79.95, Backlighting Kit $74.95.

JUST GETTING INTO DOLLHOUSE MINIATURES?
If you have a question about dollhouse miniatures, stop by your local retail outlet and ask the expert behind the counter.

Subscribe to *Nutshell News* and learn how you can make miniatures yourself!
Call toll free: (800) 446-5489

GREENLEAF PRODUCTS

The Coventry Cottage

Stock No.: 8023
Price: $53.90
Dimensions: 20"H x 17"W x 17"D, two rooms, large attic
The Coventry snaps together with glue needed only for reinforcement and trim. It comes complete with shingles and 16 pieces of furniture. It has two rooms downstairs and a full "L" shaped attic plus a hanging swing for the front porch, two bay windows, flower box, gingerbread...it's all there in this charming dollhouse. Tab and slot assembly.

GREENLEAF PRODUCTS

The Storybook Cottage

Stock No.: 8021
Price: $39.90
Dimensions: 19-1/2"H x 19"W x 13"D
Shingles and nine pieces of die-cut furniture are included with this appealing dollhouse, and you'll find plenty of space to arrange it in the one large room and attic nook. You'll also find the customary Greenleaf charm—two bay windows, a flower box, sign and, of course, plenty of gingerbread trim. For ease of assembly, our designers have constructed the house to snap together into place, with glue needed only for reinforcement, shingles, trim and furniture. Two floors, one room, attic, tab and slot assembly.

MODEL BUILDERS SUPPLY

Dollhouse "The Cottage"

Stock No.: AD004
Price: $91.20
Dimensions: 21" x 15" x 20"
A four-room cottage ideal for first timers. 3/8" walls, two skylights, unique ridge molding, easy to assemble. Many different looks can be achieved. Excellent quality, affordable price.

GREENLEAF PRODUCTS
Vineyard Cottage

Stock No.: 8019
Price: $53.90
Dimensions: 14-1/2"W x 24-1/2"D x 20-1/2"H, 1"-1' scale
What began as a cluster of tents in 1835 on the Island of Martha's Vineyard became a community of Carpenter-Gothic cottages after the Civil War, measuring just 11' by 19' with their fronts bedecked in gingerbread and bargeboards. Our Vineyard Cottage captures the magic of these wonderful structures, featuring two first floor rooms, two dormers, a small nook above the loft, a staircase, Gothic bay and upper and lower front porches and Gingerbread trim. Shingles are included. Die-cut plywood.

OPENING SCENE REPLICAS
"Little House on the Prairie"

Price: See your local dealer or send for catalog.
Dimensions: 16"H x 25"W x 20"D
"Little House," the homestead of the Ingalls family, was the focal point of the most popular dramatic TV series ever. Our "Little House" kit includes windows, doors, batten siding, stone chimney, fireplace and foundation…even Caroline's little window box. Two front openings reveal the main room and loft nestled under a rustic exposed beam and rafter ceiling. The kitchen, which was added later, is revealed by a rear opening. This is the beginning of your Walnut Grove village. (See other Walnut Grove replicas in this section.) 3/8" and 1/4" cabinet-grade plywood.

Gotcha Covered

WORKSHOP WISDOM

Richard Waidelich did this for Beth. He glued three strips of wood together (a) to form a U-shaped channel and perhaps, added a strip of felt (b) in the lower one, then glued two of these channels to the front of her room box. Into the channels he slid a piece of Plexiglas (c) to form a dust-proof, transparent cover for her display, with a small Plexiglas finger-pull glued at the end (arrowed). It would be an advantage to glue a stop piece (d) at one end, faced with felt, and a piece of felt as an additional dust seal on the edge of the wall at the other. Did I mention that Richard is Beth's, obviously doting, father?

BETH MEYER
MARSHALL, MI

Workshop Wisdom *Courtesy of* Nutshell News—4/95

WALMER DOLLHOUSES

REAL GOOD TOYS
Adirondack Cabin

Stock No.: J-550
Dimensions: 19"H x 24"W x 16"D; 1" = 1' scale
Complete kit includes front porch and pre-cut plywood parts, windows, door, stairs, shingles and chimney. Log siding and trim is supplied in 26" lengths. Grooved sidewalls for easy assembly. Four rooms.

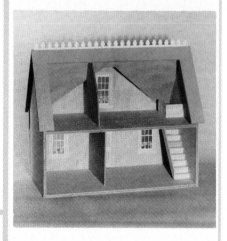

REAL GOOD TOYS
Blue Ridge Camp

Stock No.: J-500
Price: See your local dealer.
Dimensions: 19"H x 24"W x 12"D' 1" = 1' scale
Complete kit includes pre-cut plywood parts, windows, door, stairs, shingles and chimney. Log siding and trim is supplied in 26" lengths. Grooved sidewalls for easy assembly. Four rooms.

Kiwi Cottage

Stock No.: 448
Price: See your local dealer.
Dimensions: 20"H x 24"W x 14"D, 1" scale
The Kiwi Cottage is a three-room charmer complete with window boxes and flowers, gingerbread, windows, door and staircase. Constructed from 1/4", 3/8" and 1/2" cabinet-grade plywood. Assembly is fast and easy using our revolutionary dowel and glue assembly technique. Siding, shingles and custom components available separately.

Farm

Open Sesame

WORKSHOP WISDOM

When test fitting drawers in a dresser under construction, it can be difficult to pull them out if the drawer pull is not in place – especially if they tend to stick. Cut a piece of masking tape, double over one end, then adhere it to the inside of the drawer face to form a pull tab.

*DARLENE FOCAZIO
LEVITTOWN, NY*

Workshop Wisdom *Courtesy of* Nutshell News—*5/95*

CELERITY MINIATURE HOMES

The Little Farmstead
Stock No.: 2501 (kit); 2502 (assembled)
Price: See your local dealer for retail.
Dimensions: 18"H x 24"W x 19"D (includes porch)
"The Little Farmstead" is a quaint old place with its own special charm. The kit contains eight main pieces plus dormers, shutters, flower boxes, railings posts, stairway and movable partitions. Two floors, four rooms. Decorated exterior as shown is a special order. Dado joint construction. Top quality 3/8" plywood. Logs available.

CELERITY MINIATURE HOMES
The Old Homestead
Stock No.: 2801 (kit); 2802 (assembled)
Price: See your local dealer.
Dimensions: 28-1/4"H x 15"W x 29"D (includes 6" porch)
"The Old Homestead" is the perfect spot to sit and swing a while! This side-opening house does not require a turntable to enjoy the front and inside of its unique Old Country flavor. Kit contains seven main house parts, front porch, turned posts, foundation, stairways, full-height chimney and movable partitions. Three floors, six rooms. Top quality 3/8" plywood.

CORONA CONCEPTS
The Magnolia Dollhouse Kit
Stock No.: 9303
Dimensions: 33"W x 17"D x 22"H; 1" scale
This classic country farmhouse features long-pointed gables with decorative trim, double-hung windows (non-working) and four spacious rooms. Two sets of French doors leading to balconies and a cozy fireplace add to its country charm. Other features include a full porch, silk-screened windows and a curved staircase. Shingles are included! See your local dealer.

FOR FAST SERVICE, VISIT YOUR LOCAL MINIATURES SHOP

DEE'S DELIGHTS, INC. HOMETOWN SERIES

"The Farm House"

Stock No.: HOM 100
Price: See your local dealer.
Dimensions: 26"H x 23-3/4"W x 16"D
This assembled, unfinished Early Americana plywood dollhouse comes complete with wooden-framed windows, two-panel door, interior staircase, chimney, shutters and full foundation. Six-room floor plan includes two attic rooms. Roofing not included. Complete with personalized dollhouse deed and finishing instructions.

DOLL FAIRE'S VICTORIAN TIMES

Bee Tree House

Stock No.: 101
Price: See your local dealer.
Dimensions: 25"W x 32"H x 23"D, 1" scale.
This quaint eight room country farmhouse was one of the first to be built in Washington territory in the early 1800's. The original house was built near an accessible hive of honey bees, thus the unusual name. Our home is an assembled shell made of 3/8" birch plywood. Catalog $3.

DOLL FAIRE'S VICTORIAN TIMES

Cook Farmhouse

Stock No.: 102
Price: See your local dealer.
Dimensions: 33"W x 30"H x 22"D, 1" scale.
This nine room farmhouse is typical of many built before the turn of the century in the Pacific Northwest. Our miniature home was inspired by a home built in the Tillamook Forest in Oregon state by Henry Aloysius Cook. Our home is built of 3/8" birch plywood and is an assembled shell. Catalog $3.

DURA-CRAFT, INC. Farmhouse

Stock No.: FH505
Price: see your dealer
Dimensions: 32-1/2"H x 42"W x 33"D
"A country classic" only begins to describe the eight-room Farmhouse. A sweeping porch with curved steps, architectural ornamentations, moving windows and door, foundation and chimney brickwork, two elaborate fireplaces and hardwood floors enhance this splendid reproduction of country living. Finishing touches include split redwood shake roof, molded pine cornerposts, gutters and downspouts, silk-screen windows and molded pine tongue and groove clapboard siding.

REAL GOOD TOYS

New Concept Greenacres

Stock No.: NC-1700 or NC1700(FO)
Price: See your dealer
Three floors, 11 rooms, knockdown construction. Available front opening or rear open. an L-shaped farmhouse with spacious interior, the kit includes everything you need for a finished dollhouse. Easy construction with sturdy 3/8" plywood wall and floor panels, preassembled Houseworks windows and door, pre-cut clapboard siding and trim that you simply glue on to the basic house, fancy gingerbread trim and porch posts, foundation and wooded shingles. All wood 3/8" and 1/4" plywood.

JOIN A MINIATURES CLUB ... OR START ONE!

MODEL BUILDERS SUPPLY

Dollhouse "Walden"

Stock No.: AD002
Price: $167.20
Dimensions: 31-1/2" x 16-1/2" x 24"
Farmhouse with stained glass door and wraparound porch, two floors plus attic. Walls are 3/8" slotted wood, easy to assemble, unique ridge molding. Excellent quality, affordable price.

Prices are approximate and subject to change

REAL GOOD TOYS

The Simplicity™ Dollhouse

Stock No.: M-S700
Dimensions: 30"H x 26"W x 18"D
Features simple, quick and easy assembly! Beginners can do it! 3/8" thick exterior walls have clapboards milled directly into the plywood surface for an easy, one-step finish. Innovative, interlocking design and precision, pre-grooved parts guarantee a perfect fit. Preassembled windows, door, foundation and staircases. Optional porches and extensions are shown as well.

REAL GOOD TOYS

The Simplicity™ Plantation Porch Addition

Stock No.: M-S714
Dimensions: 28"H x 22"W x 7"D
Complete OnePac kit can be added to the Simplicity dollhouse at any time and includes completely pre-cut parts. The exterior wall has clapboards milled directly into the plywood surface for an easy, one-step finish that's ready to paint.

REAL GOOD TOYS

Victorian Gazebo Porch & Two-Room Addition

The Simplicity™ Dollhouse is shown above with the Victorian Gazebo Porch Addition & Two-Room Addition.
Complete OnePac kits can be added to the Simplicity Dollhouse at any time and include completely pre-cut parts.
S717 - Victorian Gazebo Porch - 16"H x 44"W x 24"D
This elaborate Victorian porch is a great place to gather on a hot, summer evening to enjoy good company.
M-S722 - Two-Room Addition - 19"H x 10"W x 15"D
Can be added to either side of the Simplicity Dollhouse. Pre-cut parts. The exterior walls have clapboards milled directly into the plywood surface for an easy, one-step finish that's ready to paint.

REAL GOOD TOYS
The Ponderosa

Stock No.: L1781
Price: See your local dealer.
Dimensions: 32"H x 37"W x 22"D;
1" = 1' scale
This log home comes as a complete kit, including windows, door, stairs, chimneys, wraparound porch and all finishing materials. Log siding and trim are furnished in 26" lengths and come with a special miter box. Eleven rooms.

REAL GOOD TOYS

The Vermont Farmhouse

Stock No.: M1401
Dimensions: 32"H x 32"W x 23"D
3/8" thick exterior walls have clapboards milled directly into the plywood surface for an easy, one-step finish. Precision, pre-cut parts, preassembled windows and door. The Milled Vermont Farmhouse, with its full length gingerbread trimmed porch, reflects the pleasant country living of Vermont. Includes all eave details and octagonal, hand-split wooden shingles for the finishing touch. Perfect for the discriminating collector. Three floors and 10 rooms with finely detailed interior staircases. A wide variety of side room additions can be added at any time.

WORKSHOP WISDOM

Noel collects many little clippings for the idea file, many of the clippings being small pictures. The problem was how to store and file them. The answer lay in the sheets of transparent pockets used by baseball card collectors. Each sheet has nine 2-1/2" x 3-1/2" (62mm x 87mm) pockets, and by punching holes in the margin of each sheet, they are nicely filed in three-ring binders.

NOEL ULRICH
FREWSBURG, NY

Workshop Wisdom Courtesy of *Nutshell News—12/93*

WORKSHOP WISDOM

Quick Cubes

Ice cubes, for that miniature party scene, are readily made by clipping a piece of that clear plastic canvas or grid used for needlepoint. Use a strong pair of shears to clip as shown, collecting the resulting cubes in a dish.

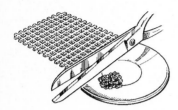

*GRACE WANROW
SEATTLE, WA*

Workshop Wisdom
Courtesy of *Nutshell News—5/95*

REAL GOOD TOYS

The Walton

Stock No.: M-1003
Dimensions: 32"H x 32"W x 23"D
3/8" thick exterior walls have clapboards milled directly into the plywood surface for an easy, one-step finish. Precision, pre-cut parts, preassembled windows and door. This classic colonial farmhouse is sturdy, spacious and includes the dormer detail, the complete gingerbread porch and octagonal, hand-split wooden shingles for the finishing touch. Perfect for the discriminating collector. Three floors and 10 rooms with finely detailed interior staircases. A wide variety of side room additions can be added at any time.

THE LAWBRE COMPANY

The Farmhouse

Dimensions: 27"H x 39"W x 18"D
Characteristic of the Midwest just before the turn of the century, the "Farmhouse" is suitable for early-American or Victorian decorations. Two floors plus attic, seven rooms. Trim parts and staircase are included. 3/8" cabinet-grade plywood. Assembled and unfinished, $245, plus options. Exterior finished as shown, $750. Crating and shipping extra.

THE LAWBRE COMPANY
The Galena Farmhouse

Dimensions: 32"H x 47"W x 21"D
Another Lawbre miniature house of great distinction, the all-time favorite farmhouse. We have used wonderful new original details and as always great attention to craftsmanship. Two floors plus attic, seven rooms. Available as an assembled shell or with completely finished exterior. Various options, too. 3/8" cabinet-grade plywood. Assembled and unfinished, $700, plus options. Exterior finished as shown, $2,245. Crating and shipping extra.

JOIN A MINIATURES CLUB ... OR START ONE!

SHOW SANTA WHAT YOU WANT FROM *THE MINIATURES CATALOG*

WALMER DOLLHOUSES
The Cherrydale

Stock No.: 453
Price: See your local dealer.
Dimensions: 25"H x 29"W x 18-1/2"D
Lilliput dollhouses are cute, easily assembled, sturdy and modestly priced. Third in the Lilliput series, the kit includes all gingerbread trims, wrap-around porch, pre-hung front door, Plexiglas windows and interior staircase. Two floors, four rooms plus attic. A wing addition, siding and shingle packs are available for upgrading and expansion. The front gable extension provides extra interior space and interesting decorating possibilities. 1/4" exterior walls and partitions, 3/8" floors.

Prices are approximate and subject to change

Federal

"The Federal"

Stock No.: HOM300
Price: See your local dealer.
Dimensions: 26"H x 23-3/4"W x 16"D
Clean, classic lines characterize the "Federal House" and make it easy to customize. Complete with five shuttered windows, solid panel door with classic pediment molding, interior staircase and two chimneys. Foundation extends 3-1/2" beyond front of house. Comes assembled, but unfinished. Roofing and siding not included.

Rustic Roofing

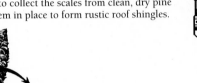

A n unusual idea for roofing miniatures is to collect the scales from clean, dry pine cones, trim them as shown, then glue them in place to form rustic roof shingles.

*DAGMAR M. NUTTING
AMHERST, MA*

Workshop Wisdom *Courtesy of* Nutshell News—5/95

REAL GOOD TOYS
Front-Opening Federal

Stock No.: FO-2201
Price: See your local dealer.
Dimensions: 32"H x 33"W x 22"D; 1" = 1' scale
This new Federal is completely front-opening. The FO-2201 deluxe kit includes windows, door, stairs and porch. The optional pre-cut finishing kit (FO-2201FK) includes pre-cut clapboard siding, shingles and trim. This 10-room house also features grooved sidewalls for easy assembly.

REAL GOOD TOYS
Williamsburg and
Williamsburg in Brick

Stock No.: DH86K
Price: See your dealer
Dimensions: 34"H x 32"W x 24"D
One of our customers' favorite designs, the Williamsburg comes with milled-in clapboard siding or with pre-painted "distressed" brick panels. Three floors, nine rooms. These complete kits, clapboard or brick, also include wooden shingles, preassembled windows, porch and roof rails, and interior stairs with railings. Cabinet-grade plywood.

THE LAWBRE COMPANY

The Chateau

Dimensions: 36"H x 57"W x 22"D
A French inspired country house of genteel proportion and detail, the "Chateau" is an ideal setting for a truly fine collection. Three floors, 12 rooms, 3/8" cabinet-grade plywood. Room sizes are generous, elegant architectural detail inside and out, even a curved staircase in the foyer and French doors in both wings. Assembled and unfinished, $685 plus options. Exterior finished as shown, $1,500. Crating and shipping extra.

Correct Ceiling Shrinkage

When restoring old dollhouses Teri found substantial gaps between the walls and ceilings, due to shrinkage. To compensate, she used a stippled finish, heavy paper called CEILING COVERAGE. This paper withstands the abuse of folding and repositioning, and was applied with a generous coat of Elmer's glue after inverting the dollhouse. Turn the edges of the paper down to overlap the walls 3/16" (5mm), as this will give a neat, seamless finish when the wall covering is brought up to cover the overlap.

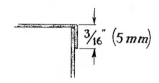

$3/16$" ($5\,mm$)

TERI HEREL
ELLINGTON, CT

Workshop Wisdom
Courtesy of *Nutshell News*—5/95

WALMER DOLLHOUSES

The Cranberry Cove

Stock No.: 452
Dimensions: 27-1/2"H x 24"W x 17"D
Lilliput dollhouses are cute, easily assembled, sturdy and very affordable. The six-room, three floor Cranberry Cove is the second kit in the Lilliput series. The kit includes all gingerbread trims, front porch, pre-hung front door, Plexiglas window and two interior staircases. Wing additions, siding and shingles are available for upgrade and expansion. Permanent nail and glue assembly. 1/4" exterior walls and partitions, 3/8" floors.

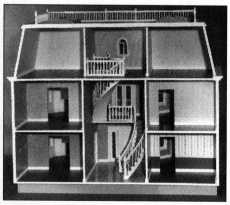

WALMER DOLLHOUSES
Foxhall Manor

Stock No.: 600
Price: See your local dealer.
Dimensions: 34"H x 42"W x 25"D;
1/12 scale
Unparalleled in the marketplace today, the Foxhall Manor offers all of the following: two-story bays open in front, curved balcony, dormer, two skylights, all windows, doors and trims, two sets curved staircases, curved landing rails, two-story foyer, 11 rooms in addition to foyer, rooms two-deep on first and second floors, 1/2" and 3/8" plywood and cabinet-grade solid wood. Woodworking skills helpful in assembly.

Faux Crochet

Doris loves the look of a crocheted afghan, but cannot crochet. To make an afghan with a crocheted look she bought a strip of flower trim and a strip of edging from the fabric store, sewed pieces of the flower trim together then edged it to create a very convincing crocheted afghan.

DORIS BROGDON
ANAHEIM, CA

Workshop Wisdom Courtesy of *Nutshell News*—4/95

Prices are approximate and subject to change

Southern Colonial & Georgian

ARCHITECTURALLY DESIGNED DOLLHOUSES
Hollyhall

A manor house with attached dependencies. The main house has three floors, nine rooms. Each dependency has two floors, two rooms. Completely front opening. House features four massive brick chimneys, curved portico with fluted Corinthian columns, one-of-a-kind cupola, rear entry with covered porch. Shown on a platform, fully landscaped. Cabinet-grade plywood.

FOR FAST SERVICE, VISIT YOUR LOCAL MINIATURES SHOP

DURA-CRAFT, INC.
Southern Mansion Miniature House Kit

Stock No.:SM700
Price: See your dealer
Dimensions: 31"H x 55"W x 27"D; 1"=1' scale
Ten rooms, three floors. This beautiful mansion kit has majestic columns, bay windows and balcony, representing an architectural style unique to the American South. Molded pine tongue and groove clapboard siding, windows, hardwood flooring (one floor) and shingles are included.

GREENLEAF PRODUCTS
The Beaumont

Stock No.: 8003
Price: $193.90
Dimensions: 26-1/4"H x 48-3/8"W x 20-1/2"D
New Southern Colonial Greek Revival Style. Serene and elegant, the Beaumont evokes the romance and refinement of the Greek Revival style in American architecture. With its grand portico, authentically proportioned turned wooden columns and airy sunroom, it's truly a masterpiece. Six room interior with large attic, elegant staircase and four fireplaces. Sun decks off the second floor bedrooms with traditional balustrades all around are the picture-perfect spot for white wicker and iced tea. Shingles and siding included. 1/8" die-cut plywood.

HOUSEWORKS, LTD.
1/12th Scale Georgian Shell

Stock No.: 4202
Price: $255
Dimensions: 33"H x 33-1/4"L x 21-1/2"D
Kit includes 3/8" cabinet-grade plywood, front opening designs, step-by-step instructions, and a 3-in-1 Dollhouse Planbook for your reference. Write to Houseworks for information on the Houseworks Component Sets.

THE LAWBRE COMPANY

OPENING SCENE REPLICAS
Tara from "Gone with the Wind"

Stock No.: T300
Price: See your local dealer or send for catalog.
Dimensions: 41"H x 42"W x 33"D
This unique replica captures the charm of the Old South and the drama of the Civil War era. The shell kit (shown here) plus specially selected component packages (sold separately) allow accurate replication of this most famous southern plantation house. Every room depicted in the original film classic is revealed from the original camera angles. Two massive chimneys, the imposing square columns, even the off-center configuration of the front windows, are all featured in this realistic depiction of Tara. 3/8" and 1/4" cabinet-grade plywood.

The Plantation

Dimensions: 31"H x 60"W x 22"D
"The Plantation" is an example of the classical line, proportion and balance that was the pride of the Antebellum South. Three floors, 11 rooms. 3/8" cabinet-grade plywood. Assembled and unfinished $985 plus options. Exterior finished as shown, $1,730. Crating and shipping extra. Photo and prices include the two optional wings that may be eliminated. Many options are available.

REAL GOOD TOYS
The Mulberry and
Twelve Oaks

M-1201 - Mulberry -
32"H x 32"W x 23"D
M-1210 - Twelve Oaks -
32"H x 60"W x 23"D
3/8" thick exterior walls have clapboards milled directly into the plywood surface for an easy, one-step finish. Precision, pre-cut parts, detailed porch columns and preassembled windows and door. The gracious "Mulberry" features a fabulous 2-story porch accessed by French doors. The unique additions can be added at any time to create the "Twelve Oaks," a true mansion for the discriminating collector.

THE LAWBRE COMPANY
Rosedawn Plantation

Dimensions: 37"H x 55"W x 26"D
"Rosedawn Plantation" is a bold and beautiful statement of the Southern Classical Greek Revival in all its elegant glory! Three floors, 12 rooms. 3/8" seven-ply cabinet-grade plywood. Assembled and unfinished $1,140 plus options. Completely finished, $3,625. Crating and shipping extra.

Prices are approximate and subject to change

WALMER DOLLHOUSES
Mulberry Lane
Two-Story Wing

Stock No.: 463
Price: See your local dealer.
Dimensions: 17-1/2"H x 10-1/2"W x 11"D;
1/12 scale
The Mulberry Lane wing addition opens
from the front and adds two full-sized
rooms. Windows and trims are included.
1/4" and 3/8" cabinet-grade plywood;
solid pine.

VISIT A
MINIATURES SHOP
WHILE
TRAVELING

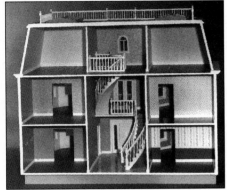

WALMER DOLLHOUSES
Foxhall Manor

Stock No.: 600
Price: See your local dealer.
Dimensions: 34"H x 42"W x 25"D; 1/12
scale
Unparalleled in the marketplace today,
the Foxhall Manor offers all of the
following: two-story bays open in front,
curved balcony, dormer, two skylights, all
windows, doors and trims, two sets
curved staircases, curved landing rails,
two-story foyer, 11 rooms in addition to
foyer, rooms two-deep on first and
second floors, 1/2" and 3/8" plywood
and cabinet-grade solid wood.
Woodworking skills helpful in assembly.

WALMER DOLLHOUSES
Mint Julep

Stock No.: 464
Price: See your local dealer.
Dimensions: 25"H x 24"W x 16-1/2"D; 1" scale
Traditional Southern plantation complete with portico
porch and fluted columns, second-story center balcony
with turned newel posts and balusters, gingerbread trims,
windows, door and interior stairs. Constructed using 1/4",
3/8" and 1/2" cabinet-grade plywood, the Mint Julep is
assembled using cabinetmaker fluted dowels and glue.
This revolutionary assembly is the fastest, simplest and
most accurate ever. Siding, shingles, wing additions and
custom components available optionally.

WALMER DOLLHOUSES
Mulberry Lane

Stock No.: 462
Price: See your local dealer.
Dimensions: 29"H x 24"W x 16"D; 1/12 scale
A front-opening Georgian kit, the Mulberry Lane
includes porch, pre-hung raised panel door, all
windows, chimney and gingerbread trims. The
interior features eight rooms including bathroom
and two halls, two sets of stairs and raised panel
landing rails. 1/4" and 3/8" cabinet-grade
plywood; solid pine.

WALMER DOLLHOUSES

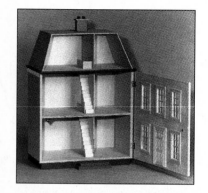

Southwestern

Georgie

Stock No.: 855
Price: See your local dealer.
Dimensions: 29-1/2"H x 19-3/4"W x 14"D;
1/12 scale
Part of the line of Miss Muffet Dollhouse Kits, the Georgie is a six-room, front-opening Georgian. Kit is complete with one-piece Georgian windows, keystone pediment, Georgian door, gingerbread dormers, chimney, steps and interior staircases. Companion products: Miss Muffet furniture.

FANTASY CRAFT

Courtyard

Stock No.: SW06
Price: Kit 129.95, Finishing Kit $219.95, Wiring Kit $72.95, plus shipping
Dimensions: 28-1/2"W x 22-1/2"D x 12-1/2"H; 1" scale
Beautiful Spanish or Mediterranean villa courtyard. Create an early California mission, Mexican restaurant, garden party or wedding reception. Backlight the windows and French doors. Easy assembly, 3/8" and 1/2" plywood, tongue-and-groove construction.

FANTASY CRAFT

Pueblo

Stock No.: SW07
Price: House Kit $199.95, Finishing Kit $175.95, Wiring Kit $75.95
Dimensions: 25"W x 18-1/2"D x 20"H; 1" scale
Top-quality, sturdy 1/2" plywood. Tongue-and-groove construction. Very easy to assemble and quick to complete! Features a patio entrance, grand room, beehive hearth, two upstairs rooms and a balcony. Open back. Authentic in design, this delightful Southwest house will be a sensational addition to your collection!

JOIN A MINIATURES CLUB ... OR START ONE!

FANTASY CRAFT
Santa Fe Roomboxes

Stock No.: MiniSW, SW03, SW03P
Price: Kit $26.95/$49.95/$69.95
Assembled $36.95/$59.95/$79.95
Dimensions: 10-3/4"W x 4"D x 8-1/2"H; 14"W x 10"D x 10-1/2"H; 20"W x 10"D x 10-1/2"H; 1" scale
Top-quality 3/8" and 1/2" plywood. Tongue-and-groove construction. Easy assembly. Complete this project in one weekend! Perfect room for Southwest miniatures! Acrylic top and front keeps your collectibles dust-free. Finishing kits available. Optional beehive hearth $19.95.

Prices are approximate and subject to change

FANTASY CRAFT
Villa & Villa Patio Room Box

Stock No.: SW04 and SW04P
Price: Kit $49.95/$69.95
Assembled $59.95/$79.95
Dimensions: 14-1/2"W x 11-1/2"D x 10-1/2"H; 20"W x 11-1/2"D x 10-1/2"H; 1" scale
Easy assembly. Top-quality 3/8" and 1/2" plywood. Tongue-and-groove construction. A proscenium arch frames the Villa. Add French doors and an arch-framed patio for a romantic setting. Paint flowers over the arches for a very special roombox. Acrylic top and front on villa; acrylic front on villa patio. (Doors extra.)

Town Houses

CELERITY MINIATURE HOMES

Deborah's Townhouse

Stock No.: 2401 (kit); 2402 (assembled)
Price: See your local dealer for retail.
Dimensions: 31-1/2"H x 23-1/2"W x 19-1/2"D
Welcome to "Deborah's Townhouse"! Three floors, five rooms. Kit contains 10 main pieces plus two stairways, two porches, shutters, flower boxes, railings corner posts, turned posts and scroll trim. Exterior beams not included in kit. Decorated model as shown is a special order. Dado joint construction. Top quality 3/8" plywood. Dimensions include porch.

GREENLEAF PRODUCTS
The Princess

Stock No.: 8900
Price: $299.90 (Kit)
Dimensions: 48"W x 18"D x 48"H; 2" scale
The Federal style Princess is in 2" scale to accommodate fashion dolls and their accessories. The second-floor French doors open to the balcony, and the attic has removable panels for storage. Shingles and silk-screened plastic windows included. Die-cut of extra sturdy 1/2" plywood.

REAL GOOD TOYS

Victorian Townhouse

Stock No.: J-818
Price: See your local dealer.
Dimensions: 38"H x 20"W x 20"D; 1" = 1' scale
This 10-room dollhouse kit comes complete with a scored novelty siding finish that's ready to paint. This complete kit includes windows, door, stairs, railings and grooved sidewalls for easy assembly. The unique interior is two rooms deep. The front is partially front-opening for easy access.

Beady-Eyed

WORKSHOP WISDOM

To quote Terry, "Here's an eye-dea!" Finding tiny eyes for equally tiny stuffed animals is a source of frustration, so she picked out a pair of matching seed beads and carefully sewed each to the animal with the thinnest monofilament available, using several neat, radiating stitches. She then carefully filled the hole with a small drop of black acrylic paint. When the paint was dry she then applied gloss varnish over the entire "eye."

TERRY LYNN UMLAH
MANCHESTER, CT

Workshop Wisdom Courtesy of *Nutshell News*—4/95

THE LAWBRE COMPANY

Chessington Plaza
Dimensions: 60"H x 30"W x 28"D
Five floors, 20 rooms
First floor shops, two three-floor apartments with studio gardens. Building is front and side opening. Quite an elegant limited edition building for the creative serious collector. 3/8" seven-ply cabinet-grade plywood. $6,850 finished, as shown, with variations. Crating and shipping extra.

THE LAWBRE COMPANY

The Bungalow
Dimensions: 32"H x 23"W x 35"D
This bungalow-style house was popular in the cities and suburbs of the 1920s. It is fully enclosed on all four sides. Two floors plus attic, nine rooms. Cabinet-grade plywood. Assembled and unfinished, $485 plus options. Finished, as shown, $985. Crating and shipping costs are extra.

SHOW SANTA WHAT YOU WANT FROM *THE MINIATURES CATALOG*

DURA-CRAFT, INC.

Tudor
Stock No.: TD200
Price: See your dealer
Dimensions: 20"H x 19"W x 12"D
Four rooms, pine frame, 1/8" plywood, knock-down construction. This Tudor house has an elegant bay window, real stairs, spacious rooms and delightful trim. Silk-screened windows and roof panels are scored with shingle pattern. This house will assemble easily and will delight the young ones. See our catalog for other models.

Tudor

GREENLEAF PRODUCTS
The Glencroft
Stock No.: 8001
Price: $99.90
Dimensions: 21"H x 25-1/4"W x 17"D, two floors, four rooms
Our cozy Tudor cottage reflects the designers' research into authentic English architecture. With its picket fence and half-timbered exterior, the house is a visual delight; it has silk-screened windows to simulate leaded glass and a flower box too. There are four spacious rooms, beamed ceilings, built-in bookcases, two window seats and two fireplaces. A winding staircase completes the mood of this wonderful English Tudor. Shingles included. 1/8" die-cut plywood.

GREENLEAF PRODUCTS
The Harrison

Stock No.: 8006
Price: $153.90
Dimensions: 31"H x 37-1/4"W x 21-1/8"D
Big rooms in this Tudor mansion! The Harrison uses movable partitions to create up to nine large rooms with six, count 'em, six bay windows to make the interior wonderfully bright and spacious. There's a hidden roof panel leading into a secret third-floor studio room with French doors opening onto an elegant terrace. Window boxes and diamond-patterned "leaded" windows complete the regal picture. Three floors, nine large rooms, tab and slot assembly. 1/8" die-cut plywood.

OPENING SCENE REPLICAS

"Wuthering Heights"

Stock No.: W400
Price: See your local dealer or send for catalog.
Dimensions: 38"H x 46"W x 29"D
All the eccentricities of rural gothic architecture are captured in this famous country estate set on the English Moors in the classic film "Wuthering Heights". Massive stone chimneys, interior archways, raised floors and rustic staircase are all faithfully recreated and revealed from the original camera angles. This is the perfect setting for your Jacobean furnishings and hunting trophies. Specially researched and selected component packages (available separately) complete the rustic stone exterior. 3/8" and 1/4" cabinet-grade plywood.

REAL GOOD TOYS

Front-Opening
Tudor Country Lane

Stock No.: CC15
Dimensions: 29"H x 14"W x 12-1/2"D
Pre-cut parts, hinges, windows, door and knob are included. The Tudor Country Lane is perfect for a child's first dollhouse. Includes all details shown, such as logs, stucco mix, chimney and octagonal, hand-split wooded shingles for the finishing touch. Three floors and five rooms.

Petal Pushers

Heather has found that dried flower petals will make fine wings for fairy dolls, and her choice is the petal of the pansy. Dried in a jar of silica gel (try your camera shop or Radio Shack), they have the satin feel of wings and retain most of their gloss. Apply to the back of the doll with a spot of quick-grabbing glue.

HEATHER COLBATH
ANCHORAGE, AK

Workshop Wisdom Courtesy of *Nutshell News*—1/95

Victorian

ARCHITECTURALLY DESIGNED DOLLHOUSES
Ceeweed Manor

Dimensions: 81"L x 36"H x 27"D
This three-floor, 14-room Victorian house can have as many as seven dormers. The house is fully enclosed with back opening. This is a gracious and stunning country home. Cabinet-grade plywood. Construction: Knockdown, glue/nail.

ARCHITECTURALLY DESIGNED DOLLHOUSES
New England Farmhouse

This is a partial front opening with open back. The house can be completely enclosed. Three floors, nine rooms. It has two entry doors onto the porch. The house is done in clapboard with cedar shingles and has five dormers. Cabinet-grade plywood.

CELERITY MINIATURE HOMES
Lady Kathleen

Stock No.: 1801, kits only
Price: See your local dealer for retail.
Dimensions: 47"H x 58"W x 24"D
Truly a Victorian lady's beautiful dwelling in miniature! Three-level Victorian roof line is accented with a six-sided tower, front projection and attached kitchen and nanny's quarters. This house features two porches with turned posts, movable partitions, two stairways, nine rooms, 10" ceilings and 8" attic. Kit includes house shell, railings, dowels, corner posts, turned porch posts and front steps. Dado joint construction. Top quality 3/8" plywood.

Prices are approximate and subject to change

CELERITY MINIATURE HOMES

Lady Emily

Stock No.: 4201 (kit); 4202 (assembled)
Price: See your local dealer for retail.
Dimensions: 34-1/2"H x 22"W x 23"L
"Lady Emily" would sit and write her poetry in the parlor of her beautiful old Victorian home. The kit contains all main house parts plus movable partitions with door openings, two interior stairways, turned porch posts, front steps, bay area in parlor, tower, attic knee walls and foundation. Decorative trims are listed in the instructions, but are not in the kit. Top quality 3/8" plywood.

CELERITY MINIATURE HOMES

Lady Jill Marie

Stock No.: 4301 (kit); 4302 (assembled)
Price: See your local dealer for retail.
Dimensions: 34-1/2"H x 22"W x 32-3/4"L
The Victorian "Lady Jill Marie" is a beautiful old historic house in Prescott, noted for its charming parlors. The kit contains all main house parts plus movable partitions with door openings, two interior stairways, turned porch posts, front steps, charming bays with roof top moldings, tower, attic knee walls and foundation. Decorative trims are not in kit, but are found in most local miniatures shops. Top quality 3/8" plywood.

CELERITY MINIATURE HOMES

Lady Kristine

Stock No.: 4001 (kit); 4002 (assembled)
Price: See your local dealer for retail.
Dimensions: 36-1/2"H x 22"W x 32-3/4"L
The Victorian "Lady Kristine" is a beautiful old home enhanced with three charming bay areas. The kit contains all main house parts plus movable partitions with door openings, two interior stairways, turned porch posts, bay roof top moldings, tower, attic knee walls and foundation. Decorative trims are not in kit, but are found in most local miniatures shops. Top quality 3/8" plywood.

CELERITY MINIATURE HOMES

Lady Melissa

Stock No.: 4101 (kit); 4102 (assembled)
Price: See your local dealer for retail.
Dimensions: 36-1/2"H x 22"W x 23"L
The Victorian "Lady Melissa" is a charming old home found on Main Street. The kit contains all main house parts plus movable partitions with door openings, two interior stairways, turned porch posts, front steps, bay area in parlor, tower, attic knee walls and foundation. Decorative trims are listed in the instructions, but are not in the kit. Top quality 3/8" plywood.

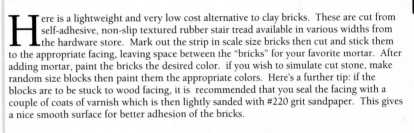

Tread On Me

Here is a lightweight and very low cost alternative to clay bricks. These are cut from self-adhesive, non-slip textured rubber stair tread available in various widths from the hardware store. Mark out the strip in scale size bricks then cut and stick them to the appropriate facing, leaving space between the "bricks" for your favorite mortar. After adding mortar, paint the bricks the desired color. if you wish to simulate cut stone, make random size blocks then paint them the appropriate colors. Here's a further tip: if the blocks are to be stuck to wood facing, it is recommended that you seal the facing with a couple of coats of varnish which is then lightly sanded with #220 grit sandpaper. This gives a nice smooth surface for better adhesion of the bricks.

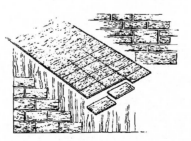

*HOLLY BURKE
KALAMAZOO, MI*

Workshop Wisdom Courtesy of *Nutshell News*—12/94

CELERITY MINIATURE HOMES
Second Empire Victorian

Stock No.: 2601 (kit)
Dimensions: 40"L x 52"W x 23-1/2"D
This huge Victorian mansion is a majestic dwelling in miniature. Three floors, 11 rooms. The three level mansard roof line is enhanced by the cubical central tower. The kit contains all main house parts plus railings, corner posts, turned porch posts, front steps, two stairways, movable partitions and firm foundation pieces. The house features 10" ceilings and 8-3/4" attic height. Model available without addition. Top quality 3/8" plywood. Dado joint construction.

CORONA CONCEPTS
The Orchid Dollhouse Kit

Stock No.: 9301
Dimensions: 21"W x 14"D x 21"H; 1" scale
This unique turn-of-the-century Victorian cottage features ornate trim, double-hung style windows (non-working), octagon-shaped dormer windows and a bay window. Each floor has a divider wall that can be placed where you choose, or left out completely for larger rooms. The detailed trim and decorative front porch add to its charming authenticity. Shingles are included! See your local dealer.

CORONA CONCEPTS
The Lily Dollhouse Kit

Stock No.: 9304
Dimensions: 30-1/2"W x 22-1/2"D x 28"H; 1" scale
This fashionable Victorian replica features seven full-sized rooms, one large hallway that can be furnished as an additional room, and a large elegant foyer featuring an exquisite double door. Open not only all across the back, but also on one side for easy access to all the stately rooms. The full wrap around porch leading to the back door adds yet another dimension for decorating. Its curved, mansard roof, ornamental trim and double-hung windows add grace and dignity to the architectural style. Shingles and siding included! See your local dealer.

DOLL FAIRE'S VICTORIAN TIMES

Lacamas Lake House

Stock No.: 104
Price: See your local dealer.
Dimensions: 34"H x 46"W x 23"D
Three floors, 12 rooms, partial tongue and groove construction, 3/8" plywood. This house was inspired by the Ledbetter home in southwest Washington state. Nestled on the north bank overlooking Lacamas Lake, it was fairly isolated in its day with roughly two miles to the nearest neighbor at Prune Hill. Presented as a wedding gift to a favored son and his wife, the building of the Ledbetter House was accomplished despite heavy timber growth in the area and poor roads. The house has large rooms, two porches (front and back) and bathroom addition. Assembled shell—Catalog $3.

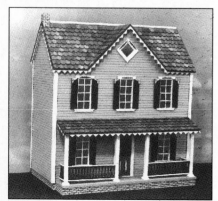

DEE'S DELIGHTS, INC.
HOMETOWN SERIES
"The Victorian"

Stock No.: HOM200
Price: See your local dealer.
Dimensions: 26"H x 23-3/4"W x 16"D
A delightful assembled, unfinished dollhouse that features scallop trim, attic window, shuttered windows, interior staircase, chimney and two-panel door and full foundation. Six rooms. Top quality 3/8" plywood. Roofing and siding not included. Complete with personalized dollhouse deed and finishing instructions. See your local dealer.

DOLL FAIRE'S VICTORIAN TIMES
Captain Joseph Angel House

Stock No.: 109
Price: See your local dealer.
Dimensions: 52"H x 48"W x 24"D
Three floors, 16 rooms, partial tongue and groove construction. 3/8" plywood. This miniature is a reproduction of a Victorian mansion that was perched high in the west hills of Portland, Oregon, in 1883. Among its features are 16 large rooms, open tower, front and back porches, attic, conservatory, and large entry hall. Assembled shell. Catalog $3.00.

DOLL FAIRE'S VICTORIAN TIMES
Elliott Bay Victorian

Stock No.: 105
Price: See your local dealer.
Dimensions: 52"H x 41"W x 23"D
Three floors, 14 rooms, nail and glue construction, completely assembled with removable partitions for ease of finishing the shell. 3/8" plywood. This beautiful Victorian house design was taken from a home built near Elliott Bay on Puget Sound. Striking points of this house are an open walk above the porch and a spacious tower containing a second-story sitting room. A miniature house of true heirloom quality. Assembled shell. Catalog $3.

DOLL FAIRE'S VICTORIAN TIMES

Park City House

Stock No.: 103
Price: See your local dealer.
Dimensions: 49"H x 31"W x 21"D
Four floors, nine rooms, nail and glue construction. 3/8" plywood. This smaller tower house is designed for those with limited space. It was inspired by many small Victorian houses in the old mining town of Park City, Utah, now a favorite ski resort for skiers all over the world. This eight-room house has a side porch that can also be made into a pantry or screened for an old back porch. (See Aug.'88 NUTSHELL NEWS.) Assembled shell.

DOLL FAIRE'S VICTORIAN TIMES

The Knapp House

Stock No.: 108
Price: See your local dealer.
Dimensions: 52"H x 39"W x 23"D
Three floors, 11 rooms, nail and glue partial tongue and groove construction. 3/8" plywood. You think pre-fab is new? This miniature house is patterned after a full-size Sears catalog house of 1910. The pre-cut kit cost was $2,500 and was shipped to your lot. All you did was provide a foundation and assemble the kit. This house has 11 large rooms, open tower and second-floor porch, wrap-around porch and traditional tower. Assembled shell. Catalog $3.

DURA-CRAFT, INC.

Alpine

Stock No.: AL200
Price: See your dealer
Dimensions: 23"H x 24"W x 19"D
Four rooms, one stairway, two floors. This charming design is full of character. It includes working windows, chimney, fireplace, under-stairway closet and balcony door plus realistic brickwork, gutters and down spouts, (one floor) hardwood flooring, split redwood shakes, stairway, silk-screened windows and molded pine corner posts and trim. The open interior allows for maximum interior design flexibility. Precision die-cut parts. Tongue and groove clapboard siding.

DURA-CRAFT, INC.

Cambridge

Stock No.: CA750
Dimensions: 43"H x 33"W x 22"D; 1"=1' scale
Nine rooms, three floors, two stairways. This classic curved mansard roof house features all the amenities including working windows and doors, split redwood shakes, brickwork, gutters and downspouts, (one floor) hardwood flooring, silk-screened windows, a sliding French door and molded pine corner posts. Precision die-cut parts. Tongue and groove clapboard siding.

DURA-CRAFT, INC.

Lafayette

Stock No.: LF140
Price: See your dealer
Dimensions: 20"H x 20-1/4"W x 14"D; 1"=1' scale
Four rooms, two floors, pine frame, 1/8" pre-cut plywood, knock-down construction. Unique house kit features front porch, window box, spiral staircase, working front door, silk-screened windows, gutters and down spouts, pine trim and brackets, starbursts, gingerbread trim, split redwood shakes and basement windows.

DURA-CRAFT, INC.

San Franciscan

Stock No.: SF555
Price: See your dealer
Dimensions: 43"H x 24"W x 20"D, 1"=1' scale
Seven rooms. This resplendent Victorian echoes the essence of the famous San Franciscan Painted Ladies. Complete with working windows with fancy silkscreened windows, realistic brickwork, real hardwood floors, gutters and downspouts, split redwood shakes, molded pine corner posts, and molded tongue and groove pine clapboard siding. Three floors.

DURA-CRAFT, INC.

The Crestview

Stock No.: CR250
Dimensions: 43"H x 22"W x 18"D
This elegant three-story dollhouse kit with seven rooms features a tower and peaked tower roof with finial. Comes with a large porch, bay window in the second level, three floors, two stairways and silk-screened windows on the front door. It features a sturdy molded pine frame and pre-cut pieces to make assembly easy. Includes real hand-split redwood shingles for all roof sections. Fish scale shakes for the perfect look included.

DURA-CRAFT, INC.

The Heritage

Stock No.: HR560
Dimensions: 29"H x 27"W x 20"D
Seven rooms, three floors. This Victorian Gothic-style house radiates elegance and grace. It features working windows and doors, fancy redwood shakes for the gables and roof, working attic access ladder, inside staircase with landing along with realistic brickwork gutters and down spouts, (one floor) hardwood flooring, silk-screened windows and molded pine corner posts and trim. Precision die-cut parts. Tongue and groove clapboard siding.

DURA-CRAFT, INC.

The Newberg

Stock No.: NB180
Dimensions: 27"H x 25"W x 18"D
This beautiful dollhouse kit has the authentic look that collectors and young ladies love. It features a sturdy molded pine frame and pre-cut pieces for easy assembly. Two floors, six rooms, one stairway and a garden window. Silk-screened windows on the front door and real hand-split redwood shingles for all roof sections. Fish scale shakes for that special look included. The main level includes a bay window.

WORKSHOP WISDOM

Accurate Circuit

Before drilling those foil strips for lighting, make a drill template — 1/8" (3mm) Plexiglas works fine. Dab a marker on the end of the plug's pins then apply them to the plastic to leave two circles. Use a sharpened nail or scriber to punch little dents dead in the center of each circle, then use a 1/16" (1.5mm) drill to make pilot holes before opening them out to the final required size. Check the spacing with a plug and, if correct, center the template over your foil and drill away. Every set of holes will be identically spaced. Pearl's are so accurate that she dispenses with commercial receptacles and uses Cir-Kit brass grommets, so her installation is less bulky.

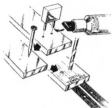

*PEARL RICH
NEW LONDON, NH*

Workshop Wisdom
Courtesy of *Nutshell News*—2/95

DURA-CRAFT, INC.

Victorian Miniature House Kit

Stock No.: VH600
Price: See your dealer
Dimensions: 40"H x 47"W x 21"D
Three floors, 10 rooms, two stairways. Authentic clapboard siding, split shake roof, hardwood flooring. Complete pre-cut kit including hardware, hinges and plastic windows. Outstanding detail including windows and shutters. Tongue and groove construction.

G.E.L. PRODUCTS

Lucinda & Amanda

All G.E.L. houses and extensions have realistic, trouble-free "no sand" clapboard siding cut directly into 3/8" outer walls. Dove-tailed grooves in walls and floors make assembly easy, fast, and secure. Wiring slots. Assembled window/door units and railings. Started nail holes. Styles include Victorians, farmhouses, capes, extensions, choice of porch styles. Written and/or Video instructions. Catalog and clapboard sample (dealers only).

DURA-CRAFT, INC.
Victorian Mansion

Stock No.: VM800
Price: See your dealer
Dimensions: 45"H x 52"W x 25"D
Four floors, 13 rooms, 1/4" pine. Authentic clapboard siding, split shake roof, hardwood flooring, two stairways. Complete pre-cut kit including hardware, hinges and plastic windows. New bay window construction. Outstanding detail. Tongue and groove construction.

FANTASY CRAFT
Country Victorian

Stock No.: HO7
Price: Kit $489.95
Dimensions: 36"W x 36"D x 30"H; 1" scale
Not just a dollhouse but a REAL house in miniature, this fabulous new Victorian is a reproduction of a rural home featuring a wraparound porch and an authentic floor plan. Living room, parlor, dining room, kitchen, sitting room, three bedrooms and bath. Enclosed on four sides. 3/8" plywood, tongue-and-groove construction. Finishing kits available.

JUST GETTING INTO DOLLHOUSE MINIATURES?

If you have a question about dollhouse miniatures, stop by your local retail outlet and ask the expert behind the counter.

GREENLEAF PRODUCTS

The Arthur

Stock No.: 8012
Price: $49.90 (Kit)
Dimensions: 23-1/2"H x 18"W x 13"D,
two floors, four rooms
A long-time favorite of our customers, the Arthur is a wonderful little house for the new collector. Features include silk-screened windows, a quaint front porch and four ample rooms. Gingerbread on ridge and roof make this cottage especially appealing to young and old. Pre-cut plywood, shingles included.

GREENLEAF PRODUCTS

The McKinley

Price: $115.90 (Kit)
Dimensions: 33"W x 9"D x 31"H,
three floors, six rooms
Any collector looking to display miniatures at eye level or in limited space will find his answer in the McKinley. This unique wall-hanging model is just 9" deep, yet with five large rooms, an attic cubby and a tower chamber. It has all the potential of a full-size house. Three latticed storage drawers beneath enhance the design and are perfect for storing accessories or hiding electrical components. Decorated in your taste, the McKinley is truly a piece of art which will be the focal point of any room. Tab and slot assembly. Pre-cut plywood.

GREENLEAF PRODUCTS

The Beacon Hill

Stock No.: 8002
Price: $219.90 (Kit)
Dimensions: 40"H x 32"W x 17"D, three floors, seven rooms
Dignified and grand, the Beacon Hill has become the "flagship" of the Greenleaf line. Its sophisticated exterior is enhanced by a curved Mansard roof, and no detail has been omitted, including even a little window in the cellar! The Beacon Hill has seven rooms, and it has two hallways that are large enough to be finished as rooms. Three fireplaces, three bay windows and winding staircase add to the elegance of this outstanding dollhouse. Pre-cut plywood. Shingles and siding included.

GREENLEAF PRODUCTS
Chantilly

Stock No.: 8008
Price: $93.90
Dimensions: 26"W x 19-1/2"D x 25"H;
1" to 1' scale
In the late 1800's the Palliser brothers designed American Homes available to the public through mail-order custom plans. We designed the Chantilly in their late-Victorian style that was popular for its great elegance, dignity, spacious rooms and modest price. The Chantilly features four rooms, a winding staircase, an attic with decorative beams, a chimney, three dormers, a bay window, a front porch, Gingerbread trim, a widow's walk and shingles. Die-cut plywood.

GREENLEAF PRODUCTS
The Garfield

Stock No.: 8010
Price: $289.90 (Kit)
Dimensions: 40"H x 41-1/2"W x 29-1/2"D
The Garfield is the largest model Greenleaf makes and one of the most impressive dollhouses to be found. Nathaniel Hawthorne hadn't seen it when he wrote "The House of the Seven Gables," but indeed our mansion has seven peaks as well as wrap-around porch, two balconies and two bay windows. You'll find easy access to the large rooms. In addition to the corner opening is a removable roof section and a lift-off turret atop the secret tower chamber. With its wonderful gingerbread trim and lovely detail, the Garfield is magnificent. Three floors, 10 rooms, tab and slot assembly. 1/8" die-cut plywood.

Prices are approximate and subject to change

GREENLEAF PRODUCTS

Emerson Row

Stock No.: 8007
Price: $83.90 (Kit)
Dimensions: 32-1/2"H x 24"W x 18"D
The Emerson Row, a stately and elegant Victorian as much at home in Back Bay Boston or Baltimore as it would be among the "painted ladies" of San Francisco. Features include full, separate entrance, basement living quarters that could be apartment or servant's space. Up above, four large rooms all with bay windows, and a full-sized attic comprise the main house. You'll love decorating all this space! The Emerson Row, a wonderfully charming and well-designed row home. Shingles included. 1/8" die-cut plywood.

GREENLEAF PRODUCTS

The Willowcrest

Stock No.: 8005
Price: $119.90 (Kit)
Dimensions: 33"H x 24-1/2"W x 18"D
A beautiful Victorian in the rich Mansard style with windows framed in ornate Second Empire molding, the Willowcrest features two bay windows, a third-story garret with curved front gable, balcony and two dormer windows. A front hall with winding staircase and three fireplaces complete the touches. In addition to the ample garret space, the Willowcrest rooms include a kitchen, living/dining room, bath and master bedroom. Shingles and siding included. 1/8" die-cut plywood.

GREENLEAF PRODUCTS

The Westville

Stock No.: 8013
Price: $99.90 (Kit)
Dimensions: 24"H x 25"W x 18"D,
two floors, four rooms
Look familiar? You've probably seen this house in real life someplace in your travels! Our Westville is a replica of a home sold by mail order catalog at the turn of the century. We spotted this one in the little hamlet of Westville, New York. Designed in the style of "Carpenter Gothic," the house features long pointed gables with elaborate decorative trim around the porch, balconies and roof. There are four large rooms and a spacious attic, as well as two bay windows and two balconies. We've included shingles and clapboard siding to fully capture the look of that "little house by the side of the road" for your trip down memory lane. 1/8" die-cut plywood.

GREENLEAF PRODUCTS
The Pierce

Stock No.: 8011
Price: $139.90 (Kit)
Dimensions: 33"H x 35-1/2"W x 25"D
The Pierce is a "Grande Dame" in its own right. One of our most popular models, the Pierce offers tremendous value at a most reasonable price, with lots of gingerbread and lots of Victorian charm. The house has six large rooms, an attic and a secret tower chamber along with an elegant curved staircase, silk-screened windows, two fireplaces, and a wrap veranda. There's a fine open feeling to this stately home and you're sure to be impressed by its grandeur. Three floors, six rooms, tab and slot assembly. Pre-cut plywood.

HILL'S DOLLHOUSE WORKSHOP

HOUSEWORKS, LTD.
1/12th Scale Victorian Shell

Stock No.: 4303
Price: $275
Dimensions: 33"H x 33-1/4"L x 22-1/2"D
Kit includes 3/8" cabinet-grade plywood, front opening designs, step-by-step instructions, and a 3-in-1 Dollhouse Planbook for your reference. Write to Houseworks for information on the Houseworks Components Sets.

New England Victorian

Price: Wholesale only. See your local dealer.
Dimensions: 32-1/2"H x 30"W x 14"D
Three floors plus attic, eight rooms. Made of 3/8", 5-ply birch-type plywood. Dadoed, pre-hinged roof, 1-1/2" foundation. Charming Victorian with a two-windowed tower, topped by a widow's walk railing and trimmed with post braces. The front section opens on hinges, the back is open with a hinged roof. The attic has a window in front dormer section. The peak and house front are trimmed with dentil molding. A front porch is in the recessed section. Also available with a wrap-around porch, with or without addition. Porch railings, interior stairs and stairwell hole railings are Timberbrook's.

JOIN A
MINIATURES
CLUB
...
OR START ONE!

MODEL BUILDERS SUPPLY

Dollhouse "Elgin"

Stock No.: AD001
Price: $182.40
Dimensions: 31" x 20-1/2" x 32"
Mid-size Victorian kit has 2 sets of stairs, three floors plus attic, divider walls and door openings on first two floors, walls 3/8" slotted wood. Excellent quality, affordable price.

OPENING SCENE REPLICAS
The Norman Bates House
from "Psycho"

Stock No.: N200
Price: See your local dealer or send for catalog.
Dimensions: 38"H x 28"W x 38"D
The original Norman Bates House exists as a 3/4 scale back lot movie facade. We have combined the effects created on individual sound stages within this sinister facade to recreate all the suspense of Alfred Hitchcock's classic film. The shell kit (shown here) can be completed with special component packages sold separately. The Old Grandville House (right) from "It's a Wonderful Life" also comes as a shell kit with separate component packages to achieve a new level of realism at an affordable price. Shell kits are of 3/8" and 1/4" cabinet-grade plywood.

Leather Jacket

WORKSHOP WISDOM

This dollhouse has a leather jacket hanging in the hall! Cut the thumbs from a pair of lightweight leather gloves, then sew them together at the back to create the basic jacket. Cut, trim and hem as required, gluing on pockets, buttons and even a sheepskin collar and cuffs if you are able. Finally, apply white glue inside to achieve permanent folds before hanging it on the coat tree.

cut

PATRICE A. WILL
LOUISVILLE, KY

REAL GOOD TOYS

The Hillcrest

Stock No.: M1016
Dimensions: 32"H x 51"W x 23"D
3/8" thick exterior walls have clapboards milled directly into the plywood surface for an easy, one-step finish. Precision, pre-cut parts, preassembled windows and door. The complete, Milled Hillcrest, features a roomy, full-length Victorian gazebo wraparound porch. This is country living at its best. Includes all eave details and octagonal, hand-split wooden shingles for the finishing touch. Three floors and 12 rooms with finely detailed interior staircases.

REAL GOOD TOYS

Mountain View Cottage

Stock No.: J-650
Dimensions: 19"H x 30"W x 18"D
This complete kit includes gazebo wraparound porch, windows, door, chimney, stucco and wooden shingles. The pre-cut plywood parts have grooved sidewalls for easy assembly. The railings, trim and laser-cut gingerbread are supplied in 16" - 26" lengths. Four rooms.

REAL GOOD TOYS

The Bostonian

Stock No.: M-96K
Dimensions: 41"H x 48"W x 24"D
3/8" thick exterior walls have clapboards milled directly into the plywood surface for an easy, one-step finish. Precision, pre-cut parts, Victorian windows and door. The complete, Milled Bostonian features an incredibly roomy interior and two story porch as well as the rooftop widow's walk. Includes all edge details, turned spindles and fancy porch posts, railings, brackets and wooden shingles for the finishing touch. Three floors and 13 rooms with finely detailed interior staircases.

REAL GOOD TOYS

The Sterling Estate

Stock No.: M-3216
Dimensions: 43"H x 51"W x 27"D
3/8" thick exterior walls have clapboards milled directly into the plywood surface for an easy, one-step finish. Precision, pre-cut parts, preassembled, fancy Victorian windows and door are included. The Milled Sterling Estate, with its roomy, Victorian gazebo wraparound porch, is perfect for the discriminating collector. Includes all eave details and octagonal, hand-split wooden shingles for the finishing touch. Four levels and 15 rooms with finely detailed interior staircases.

REAL GOOD TOYS

The Windy Ridge

Stock No.: M-1719
Dimensions: 32"H x 54"W x 26"D
3/8" thick exterior walls have clapboards milled directly into the plywood surface for an easy, one-step finish. Precision, pre-cut parts, preassembled, fancy, Victorian windows and door. The complete, Milled Windy Ridge features a roomy, Victorian gazebo wraparound porch as well as the Victorian two-room addition. Includes all eave gingerbread details and octagonal, hand-split wooden shingles for the finishing touch. Three floors and 13 rooms with finely detailed interior staircases.

THE LAWBRE COMPANY

Barstow Belle "Painted Ladies" Victorian House

Dimensions: 60"H x 28"W x 33"D
This is one of four "San Francisco Stick/Eastlake" style houses with Lawbre brackets, oriel windows, verge board, stick style windows and newel posts. Three floors plus tower, 13 rooms. 3/8" cabinet-grade plywood. Unfinished, $1,845. Finished $4,485. Crating and shipping extra.

THE LAWBRE COMPANY

Glen Cove Villa - Circa 1880

Dimensions: 41"H x 48"W x 26"D
A mansard turreted villa boldly detailed in the late-Victorian manner. Four floors, 11 rooms. Impressive two-story entry stair hall with split staircase and railings plus many interesting rooms make this house a decorator's delight. 3/8" cabinet-grade plywood except for mansard roofs. Assembled and unfinished, $1,090 plus options. Exterior finished, as shown (excluding greenhouse), $4,120. Crating and shipping extra.

THE LAWBRE COMPANY

Mariposa "Painted Ladies" Victorian House

Dimensions: 47"H x 28"W x 33"D
This is one of four "San Francisco Stick/Eastlake" style houses with Lawbre brackets, oriel windows and newel posts. Two floors plus tower, nine rooms. 3/8" cabinet-grade plywood. Unfinished, $1,325. Finished, $3,675. Crating and shipping extra.

THE LAWBRE COMPANY

Morley House "Painted Ladies" Victorian House

Dimensions: 34"H x 28"W x 33"D
This is one of four "San Francisco Stick/Eastlake" style houses with Lawbre brackets, oriel windows, verge board, stick style windows and newel posts. Two floors plus attic, nine rooms. 3/8" cabinet-grade plywood. Unfinished, $1,175. Finished, $3,445. Crating and shipping extra.

THE LAWBRE COMPANY
Amelia St. James House

Dimensions: 54"H x 65"W x 24"D
Both front and side opening, this wonderful Victorian house has the large rooms and high ceilings much sought after, yet requires a small amount of floor space. Two floors, 11 rooms, plus attic. Doors, windows and architectural details are by Derek Perkins and Daniel McNeil. Assembled and unfinished, $1,375 plus options. Exterior as shown, $4,230. Crating and shipping extra. 3/8" cabinet-grade plywood.

THE LAWBRE COMPANY
French Country House

Dimensions: 39"H x 64"W x 26"D
This splendid miniature house was inspired by the great manor farmhouses of Ile-de-France. The time period is the late 17th century. Three floors, 11 rooms, plus two rooms above wings. The detail is elegant and authentic, complete with oeil-de-boeuf dormers. The much requested large rooms are perfect for an elegant yet casual country decor. The first floor ceilings are 12" and the second floor, 11". There is a broad forecourt, perfect for a party. The windows and doors were designed especially for this house and are beautifully crafted. 3/8" cabinet-grade plywood. Assembled and unfinished, $1,340 plus options. Exterior finished, as shown, $2,935. Crating and shipping extra.

Prices are approximate and subject to change

THE LAWBRE COMPANY

Shadow Cliff Victorian House

Dimensions: 43"H x 32"W x 32"D
An outstanding Victorian house in the Queen Anne style, "Shadow Cliff's" rooms are arranged as they would be in a real house and are easily accessible from three sides. Three floors, 10 rooms. Includes full-enclosure walls. 3/8" seven-ply cabinet-grade plywood. Assembled and unfinished, $975 plus options. Exterior finished, as shown, $4,110. Crating and shipping extra.

THE LAWBRE COMPANY

Winchester "Painted Ladies" Victorian House

Dimensions: 47"H x 28"W x 33"D
This is one of four new "San Francisco Stick/Eastlake" style houses with Lawbre brackets, oriel windows, verge board, stick style windows and newel posts. Three floors plus attic, 13 rooms. 3/8" cabinet-grade plywood. Unfinished, $1,680. Finished, $4,255. Crating and shipping extra.

WALMER DOLLHOUSES

The Apple Blossom

Stock No.: 457
Price: See your local dealer.
Dimensions: 36"H x 29"W x 18"D
A romantic Victorian, a quality kit, at a great price from your miniature dealer. The kit includes gingerbread, windows, pre-hung raised panel door, wrap-around porch, gable, four-story tower large enough to furnish (and a secret room in the top of the tower!), six interior rooms, two interior staircases and raised-panel landing rails, three interior partitions. Available options are siding shingle pack and a two-story wing addition. The house can also be ordered built-up. 1/4" and 3/8" cabinet-grade plywood and solid pine.

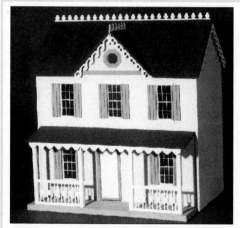

WALMER DOLLHOUSES
The Peaches 'N Cream

Stock No.: 450
Dimensions: 25"H x 24"W x 16-1/2"D
Lilliput dollhouses are cute, easily assembled, sturdy and very affordable. The Peaches 'N Cream was the first kit in the Lilliput series. Two floors with four rooms and third-floor attic. 1/4" exterior walls and partitions, 3/8" floors. Permanent nail and glue assembly. The kit includes all gingerbread trims, front porch, pre-hung front door, Plexiglas windows and interior staircase. Wing additions, siding and shingles are available for upgrading and expansion.

JUST GETTING INTO DOLLHOUSE MINIATURES?

If you have a question about dollhouse miniatures, stop by your local retail outlet and ask the expert behind the counter.

WALMER DOLLHOUSES
Miss Muffet Victoriana Dollhouse

Stock No.: 850
Dimensions: 25-1/2"H x 24"W x 14-1/2"D; 1/12 scale
A lovely Victorian with one-piece Victorian windows and door, charming gazebo, authentic gingerbread trims and interior staircase. Four rooms plus attic. Available with or without Miss Muffet furniture.

Children's Houses

WALMER DOLLHOUSES

The Nob Hill

Price: See your local dealer.
Dimensions: 36"H x 38"W x 26"D
Every aspect of this detailed home has "collector appeal," inside and out. The exterior window and door treatments, wrap-around porch, trims and rails are typically Victorian. The interior features eight spacious rooms, entry hall, two upstairs halls with stairs and a second-floor front hall. The kit includes all windows and trim, exterior doors, decorative rails and trim, wrap-around porch, outside steps and interior stairs. It is available with working or non-working windows. Pictured with asphalt shingles and pine siding, sold separately.

CELERITY MINIATURE HOMES
Welcome Home Kit

Dimensions: 12"D x 24-1/2"L x 22-1/2"H
A quality little playhouse with easy access to rooms and well designed for the younger child. The kit includes 13 house pieces plus a ladder. Animal figures are sold separately and add to the charm of this little house. See your local miniatures shop for ordering.

CELERITY MINIATURE HOMES

Annie's House

Stock No.: 4501 (kit); 4502 (assembled)
Price: See your local dealer.
Dimensions: 23"L x 15"W x 28"H; 1" = 1' scale
A charming front-opening house for "Annie"! This house is easy to assemble and easy to keep the pets outside! The kit contains nine main house parts plus three partitions and hardware. Very sturdy construction. A good house for children to play with. Stairways are sold separately.

CELERITY MINIATURE HOMES

Mandy's House

Stock No.: 4401 (kit); 4402 (assembled)
Price: See your local dealer.
Dimensions: 23"L x 15"W x 28"H; 1" = 1' scale
Excellent house for children, made of top quality 3/8" plywood so it is very sturdy. The house can be assembled easily in less than one hour. Kit contains 10 main house parts plus three partitions and hardware. Stairways are extra and can be added later.

REAL GOOD TOYS

Playscale® Country Farmhouse

Dimensions: 46"H x 26"W x 23"D; Playscale® Three to five rooms, three floors. Gingerbread porch, detailed shutters, full length closet and a 740 cubic inch storage drawer with divided compartments in the foundation. Playscale® Doll House kits are designed for dolls 8 to 12 inches tall and their accessories. 3/8" cabinet-grade plywood, grooved sidewalls, fancy octagonal wooden shingles and complete set of preassembled components to finish the exterior of the house.

REAL GOOD TOYS

Playscale® Estate

Dimensions: 45-1/2"H x 48"W x 24"D; Playscale®.
Five huge rooms, two spacious full length closets and two storage drawers offering an amazing 1,444 cubic inches of storage space with divided compartments. Playscale® Doll House kits are designed for dolls 8 to 12 inches tall and their accessories. 3/8" cabinet-grade plywood, grooved sidewalls, fancy octagonal wooden shingles and complete set of preassembled components to finish the exterior of the house.

REAL GOOD TOYS

Playscale® Victorian Townhouse

Dimensions: 58"H x 26"W x 22-7/16"D; Playscale®
Four to seven rooms, three floors plus tower room and two sun decks, bay front, full length closet, a 560 cubic inch storage drawer with divided compartments in the foundation. Playscale® Doll House kits are designed for dolls 8 to 12 inches tall and their accessories. 3/8" cabinet-grade plywood, grooved sidewalls, fancy octagonal wooded shingles and complete set of preassembled components to finish the exterior of the house.

REAL GOOD TOYS

Snow Country Chalet & Alpine Farmhouse

Stock No.: J-420 - Snow Country Chalet
J-430 - Alpine Farmhouse
Dimensions: 20"H x 19"W x 16"D
The exterior walls of this complete kit have clapboard siding milled directly into the plywood for easy, one-step assembly. Precision, pre-cut parts are ready to paint. Windows, doors, stairs, flower boxes, rails, laser-cut gingerbread, stencil and wooden shingles are included. These two-room, durable playhouses are perfect for a child's first dollhouse. Two floors and two rooms.

REAL GOOD TOYS
Playscale® Heartwood Cottage

Stock No.: 99151
Price: See your dealer
Dimensions: 33"H x 32"W x 19"D; Playscale®
For dolls, teddy bears or other 8" to 12" toys. Featuring laser-cut gingerbread and details. Easy assembly. Only hammer, glue and tape required. 10 sq.ft. of play space including spacious rooftop deck. Fully assembled windows and door. 3/8" cabinet-grade plywood. Now available in Playscale® or 1" scale.

WALMER DOLLHOUSES

The Cranberry Cove

Stock No.: 452
Price: See your local dealer.
Dimensions: 27-1/2"H x 24"W x 17"D
Lilliput dollhouses are cute, easily assembled, sturdy and very affordable. The six-room, three floor Cranberry Cove is the second kit in the Lilliput series. The kit includes all gingerbread trims, front porch, pre-hung front door, Plexiglas window and two interior staircases. Wing additions, siding and shingles are available for upgrade and expansion. Permanent nail and glue assembly. 1/4" exterior walls and partitions, 3/8" floors.

To A Tee

WORKSHOP WISDOM

Golf tees can be turned into really nice hat stands. Cut two or three to various heights, then glue a large round bead to the top of each and finish in your favorite color. If they fall over, just put a smear of Blue Tak under each. Liz also sticks golf ball markers to the wall of the bathroom and kitchen where they serve as very useful towel rails.

*LIZ MEATH
GLENS FALLS, NY*

Workshop Wisdom Courtesy of *Nutshell News*—3/95

WALMER DOLLHOUSES

Lilliput Wing Addition
Stock No.: 456
Price: See your local dealer.
Dimensions: 17"H x 10-3/8"W x 10-5/8"D
Lilliput wing for 449,450 and 454 Lilliput
dollhouses.1-1/2 stories.

WALMER DOLLHOUSES

Apple Blossom Wing Addition
Stock No.: 458
Price: See your local dealer.
Dimensions: 17"H x 10-3/8"W x 10-5/8"D
Two-room addition designed specifically for the
Apple Blossom dollhouse.

WALMER DOLLHOUSES

Strawberry Patch Wing Addition
Stock No.: 460
Price: See your local dealer.
Dimensions: 22-1/2"H x 10-1/2"W x 11"D
The Strawberry Patch dollhouse kit expands
beautifully with the addition of the two-story
wing. Like the house, the wing opens in the front.

WALMER DOLLHOUSES

The Apple Blossom
Stock No.: 457
Price: See your local dealer.
Dimensions: 36"H x 29"W x 18"D
A romantic Victorian, a quality kit, at a great price
from your miniatures dealer. The kit includes
gingerbread, windows, pre-hung raised panel door,
wrap-around porch, gable, four-story tower large
enough to furnish (and a secret room at the top of
the tower!), six interior rooms, two interior
staircases and raised panel landing rails, three
interior partitions. Available options are siding
shingle pack and two-story wing addition. The
house can also be ordered built up. 1/4" and 3/8"
cabinet-grade plywood; solid pine.

WALMER DOLLHOUSES

Georgie
Stock No.: 855
Price: See your local dealer.
Dimensions: 29-1/2"H x 19-3/4"W x 14"D;
1/12 scale
Part of the line of Miss Muffet Dollhouse Kits, the
Georgie is a six-room, front-opening Georgian. Kit
is complete with one-piece Georgian windows,
keystone pediment, Georgian door, gingerbread
dormers, chimney, steps and interior staircases.
Companion products: Miss Muffet furniture.

WALMER DOLLHOUSES

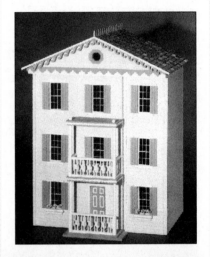

The Strawberry Patch
Stock No.: 459
Price: See your local dealer.
Dimensions: 33"H x 25"W x 17"D
The Strawberry Patch opens in front and is
another in the Lilliput kit series, which means it
assembles easily, is sturdy, playable and
affordable. The kit includes the two story front
porch, first floor window boxes with flowers,
gingerbread trims, shuttered windows, pre-hung
raised panel door, six full rooms with partitions
and two interior staircases with raised panel
landing rails. Available as options are a two-story
wing and a siding and shingle pack. The house is
also available built-up. 1/4" and 3/8" cabinet-
grade plywood and solid pine.

WALMER DOLLHOUSES
The Plum Pudding

Stock No. 454
Price: See your local dealer.
Dimensions: 27-1/2"H x 24"W x 17"D
Lilliput dollhouses are cute, easily assembled, sturdy and modestly priced. Fourth in the Lilliput series, the three floor, seven-room kit includes gingerbread trims, a two-story porch, pre-hung French and front doors, Plexiglas windows and two interior staircases. Wing additions, siding and shingle packs are available for upgrading and expansion. Permanent nail and glue assembly. 1/4" exterior walls and partitions, 3/8" floors.

Outdoors/Indoors

Mary prefers to see a window in a hatbox or closed-in room scene but is loathe to cut holes in the wall, so she offers this answer to her problem. She glues a suitable picture of an outdoor scene to the wall then constructs a window frame, complete with clear plastic glazing, which she glues over the picture. A set of drapes or sheers completes the assembly. Make the frame so that the glass stands about 1/8" (3mm) or more from the picture to give the illusion of depth.

WALMER DOLLHOUSES
The Cherrydale

Stock No.: 453
Price: See your local dealer.
Dimensions: 25"H x 29"W x 18-1/2"D
Lilliput dollhouses are cute, easily assembled, sturdy and modestly priced. Third in the Lilliput series, the kit includes all gingerbread trims, wrap-around porch, pre-hung front door, Plexiglas windows and interior staircase. Two floors, four rooms plus attic. A wing addition, siding and shingle packs are available for upgrading and expansion. The front gable extension provides extra interior space and interesting decorating possibilities. 1/4" exterior walls and partitions, 3/8" floors.

*MARY SIMONSON
SOMERSET, NJ*

Workshop Wisdom
Courtesy of *Nutshell News*—11/94

WALMER DOLLHOUSES
The Lemon Twist

Stock No.: 449
Price: See your local dealer.
Dimensions: 25"H x 24"W x 12-1/2"D
Lilliput dollhouses are cute, easily assembled, sturdy and very affordable. The Lemon Twist is the fifth kit in the Lilliput series. Two floors, four rooms plus attic. The kit includes all gingerbread trims, window boxes with brightly colored flowers, pre-hung front door, Plexiglas windows and interior staircase. Wing additions, siding and shingles are available as extras for upgrading and expansion.

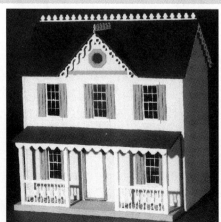

WALMER DOLLHOUSES
The Peaches 'N Cream

Stock No.: 450
Price: See your local dealer.
Dimensions: 25"H x 24"W x 16-1/2"D
Lilliput dollhouses are cute, easily assembled, sturdy and very affordable. The Peaches 'N Cream was the first kit in the Lilliput series. Two floors with four rooms and third-floor attic. 1/4" exterior walls and partitions, 3/8" floors. Permanent nail and glue assembly. The kit includes all gingerbread trims, front porch, pre-hung front door, Plexiglas windows and interior staircase. Wing additions, siding and shingles are available for upgrading and expansion.

WALMER DOLLHOUSES

Lilliput Wing Addition

Stock No.: 455
Price: See your local dealer.
Dimensions: 16"H x 9"W x 10"D
Lilliput wing for 452, and 454 Lilliput dollhouses.

Shops & Offices

CELERITY MINIATURE HOMES

CELERITY MINIATURE HOMES

The Corner Store

Stock No.: 601 (kit); 602 (assembled)
Price: See your local dealer for retail.
Dimensions: 27-1/2"H x 24"W x 15"D (includes porch)
"The Corner Store" kit contains 10 main house pieces plus movable partitions, interior stairway, exterior stairway with railing, two window boxes (Plexiglas not included) and turned posts. A unique design for two-sided display of the Corner Store. The corner entrance is enhanced by three turned posts. The store is on the first level with living quarters for the seamstress, florist or baker above. Decorated exterior as shown is a special order. Dado joint construction. Top quality 3/8" plywood.

CELERITY MINIATURE HOMES

General Store

Stock No.: 2701 (kit); 2702 (assembled)
Price: See your local dealer.
Dimensions: 19"H x 24"W x 15"D;
base 28"L x 19"W
"The General Store" sells a variety of wares! This kit contains six main store parts plus posts, store sign board and outside stairway. Here's the chance to be in business for yourself—in miniature! Two floors, three rooms. Tongue and groove construction. Top quality 3/8" plywood.

CELERITY MINIATURE HOMES

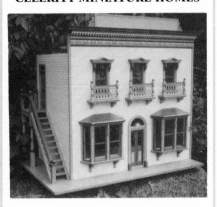

Victorian Antique Shop

Stock No.: 3801 (kit); 3802 (assembled)
Price: See your local dealer for retail.
"The Antique Shop" sells many exclusive items! The kit contains six main store parts plus sign board and outside stairway with posts and balls to complete. Decorative moldings and trims are listed in the instructions and are found in your local miniatures shops. Store: 19"H x 15"W x 24"L; base: 28"L x 19"W; store front: 25"H. Top quality 3/8" plywood.

GREENLEAF PRODUCTS
Brimble's Mercantile

Stock No.: 8022
Price: $95.90
Dimensions: 21-1/2"H x 18-1/2"W x 25"D
Your imagination will take over with the Brimble's Mercantile—we've seen it decorated as every kind of enterprise, from bakery to saloon. The kit has one huge room on each floor, which allows for a variety of shop or shop/apartment designs. It comes equipped with counters, display island, a whole wall of built-in shelves and extra-wide window ledges to serve as display areas. A little ingenuity and you're in business. Two floors, two large rooms, 1/8" die-cut plywood.

START A NEW HOBBY AND MEET NEW FRIENDS: JOIN A MINIATURES CLUB!

OPENING SCENE REPLICAS
Oleson's Mercantile from "Little House on the Prairie"

Stock No.: M040
Price: $269 (shell kit)
Dimensions: 29"H x 39"W x 36"D
This is a true, working replica of this famous general store. In addition to the store itself are the storage shed, upstairs bedrooms, plus a unique first-floor parlor companion piece or swing-out wing. The shell openings reveal every scene as it actually appeared in this popular TV series. Harriet Oleson herself would have been proud of the accuracy and realism of this unique shell kit and corresponding component packages (available separately). 3/8" and 1/4" cabinet-grade plywood.

OPENING SCENE REPLICAS
Walnut Grove Post Office from "Little House on the Prairie"

Stock No.: P020
Price: See your local dealer or send for catalog.
Dimensions: 28"H x 17"W x 31"D
This charming commercial establishment with its soaring front facade housed both the Post Office and Doc Baker's Office (in the rear), as well as the upstairs rental rooms. Front and rear openings reveal these separate enterprises just as you see them on TV. Special component packages (available separately) include clapboard and board and batten siding, stone foundation, wooden shake shingles, windows and doors, and, of course, the prominent Post Office sign. 3/8" and 1/4" cabinet-grade plywood.

REAL GOOD TOYS

Tube Tree Tub

WORKSHOP WISDOM

Need a sturdy base to support large trees in your landscape project? Cut off the end of a toothpaste tube as it is shown. Lisa actually recommends the top of those stand-up paste dispensers, but give them all a try. You can probably disguise the base with smaller plants or mini mulch.

*LISA FISCHER
HIGHLAND PARK, IL*

Workshop Wisdom Courtesy of *Nutshell News*—1/95

General Store

Stock No.: GS1
Price: See your dealer
Dimensions: 11-1/4"H x 15-1/4"W x 10-3/4"D
A complete general store with two walls of shelves, a counter, a ladder, Plexiglas windows, pine door, hinges, a sliding Plexiglas top and Victorian molding. One floor, one room. Includes an assortment of miniatures: barrel, butter churn, bottles, orange crates, old-time signs, checkerboard and more. The best low-end value we've ever made.

REAL GOOD TOYS
The Front-Opening Shoppe

Stock No.: FO-MK
Dimensions: 18"H x 24"W x 16"D
3/8" thick exterior walls have novelty siding scored directly into the plywood surface for an easy, one-step finish. Precision, pre-cut parts, hinges, windows and door are included. The complete Front-Opening Shoppe features an incredibly roomy interior and balcony. Includes all shelving, counters, turned newels, railings and wooden shingles for the finishing touch. Two floors with detailed interior staircase.

THE LAWBRE COMPANY

WALMER DOLLHOUSES

WALMER DOLLHOUSES

The Millwood Country Store

Dimensions: 38"H x 28"W x 24"D
Intended as a store, the large first floor is perfect for a variety of merchandise displays. One large room with a staircase that leads to a balcony that could be used as an office or additional display of goods. The Millwood is front opening, two doors and 1/2 of the roof are hinged for additional access. There are many exterior details and textures making this a very exciting little building. It is available as an unfinished shell with a separate pack of components or with a completely finished exterior. 3/8" cabinet-grade plywood. Assembled and unfinished, $800 plus options. Finished, as shown, $2,100. Crating and shipping extra.

Blueberry Pie

Stock No.: 461
Price: See your local dealer.
Dimensions: 32"H x 18"W x 17-1/2"D
The Blueberry Pie Townhouse is identical to the Blueberry Pie Shop. The front-opening kit may be built with or without the porch which is included in the kit. The 3-1/2 story kit is perfect for those miniaturists with limited space and unlimited imaginations. The kit includes all trims, windows, pre-hung door and front porch (not shown). Wing addition, siding, shingles and other components available for expansion. 3/8" cabinet-grade plywood.

Blueberry Pie

Stock No.: 461
Price: See your local dealer.
Dimensions: 32"H x 18"W x 17-1/2"D
The Blueberry Pie is a front-opening shop with 2-1/2 stories above for proprietor's living space, including separate bath. The ideal dollhouse for small spaces and big imaginations. Kit includes gingerbread trims, front porch, pre-hung front door, windows and three interior staircases. Wing addition, siding, shingles and other components are available for customizing and expansion. 3/8" cabinet-grade plywood.

WALMER DOLLHOUSES

WALMER DOLLHOUSES

The Old Village Shop

Stock No.: 519
Price: See your local dealer.
Dimensions: 36"H x 16"W x 17"D
Three floors, four rooms. This front-opening house features store window for display of miniature goodies and an exterior side staircase to the proprietor's quarters. A most popular choice. Kit includes exterior and interior staircases, top landing rail, doors, windows and porch steps. Easy illustrated instructions. 3/8" cabinet-grade plywood. 1/2" floors, sugar pine. Nail and glue assembly.

Ye Olde Curiosity Shop

Stock No.: 117M
Price: See your local dealer. Wholesale only.
Dimensions: 13-1/2"H x 20"W x 14"D; 1/12 scale
Ye Olde Curiosity Shop is spacious and curious—a place where anything goes! It is complete with large shop display window, front store, facade for sign, all architectural moldings and trims. The hinged front allows easy access to shop interior. Shelving is included. The shop is constructed using 1/2" and 3/8" plywood. Assembly is fast and easy, using cabinetmaking technology with fluted dowels and glue. Simplest and most accurate ever.

WALMER DOLLHOUSES
The Olde Firehouse

Price: See your local dealer.
Dimensions: 36"H x 18"W x 17"D
What little (and big!) boys' dreams are made of. This collector-quality kit includes windows, pre-hung entrance and garage doors, fire truck ramp, a blank sign over the door for personalization, interior stairs, railings and fire pole. The firemen share the three-story firehouse with sleeping quarters and a bath upstairs, mess hall on the second floor, office and fire truck barn on the first floor. Two sets of stairs, bathroom partitions, fire pole railings and, of course, a three-story fire pole for quick exit are all included. Furnishings are not included. 1/2" and 3/8" plywood and solid pine.

ALESSIO MINIATURES

Castle 101

Stock No.: 101
Price: $145
Dimensions: 13-1/2"H x 22-1/2"W x 22-1/2"D
Each castle is handmade, painted and grooved to provide you with a toy which will be realistic and sturdy. A very unique feature of our castles is the ability to separate their towers and walls, which provides for easy storage and hours of creative play and expansion. Pine and plywood. American-made. Sold separately.

Castles & Forts

ALESSIO MINIATURES
Western Fort

Stock No.: 202 (completely finished); 202A (kit)
Price: $124; $69.95
Dimensions: 7"H x 23"W x 23"D
The fort features cedar corners, pine posts and basswood ladders. It also has a four-hinge working gate. Extra ladders are also available. The fort is scaled for use with 1/32 Britains or any other 54mm miniature figure. All pine and cedar. American-made.

ALESSIO MINIATURES

Sir Edward's Castle

Stock No.: 301A (kit); 301 (completely finished)
Price: $69.95; $99.95
Dimensions: 12"H x 14"W x 14"D
Sir Edward's Castle is handmade and designed for hours of creative play. 1/2" pine. American-made.

Lotsa Swatches

WORKSHOP WISDOM

Sheila says that she "haunts" her local upholstery store until the owner gives her the old material swatches when the new samples come in. As a result she has obtained some really high-quality material samples which she had used for mini carpets, throw rugs, etc. She strongly recommends that you be considerate – telling the owner who you are and what you are doing. Like as not the owner becomes intrigued, especially if you show him/her some samples of your miniatures. Why not lend some roomboxes for a window display ... it could benefit you both.

SHEILA NICHOLS
WEST OSSIPEE, NH

Workshop Wisdom *Courtesy of Nutshell News—1/95*

ALESSIO MINIATURES
New Western Fort

Stock No.: 220
Price: $145
Dimensions: 12"H x 25"W x 25"D
American-made. Each pine fort is handcrafted to last a lifetime.
Seven ladders are included.

Miscellaneous Buildings

FANTASY CRAFT
Dan's Garage

Stock No.: RO5
Price: $126.95 (includes roll up door)-$146.95 assembled.
Dimensions: 14-1/2"W x 18"D x 11"H; 1" scale
Roll up the door in Dan's Garage and inside you'll find a door to the backyard. Look over the back fence and you'll see a neighbor's house! Backlighting gives the illusion of sunshine. Finishing kit includes wall studs, insulation, back door, fence, clapboard and asphalt shingles, $89.95. Wiring and backlighting kit, $67.95.

JUST GETTING INTO DOLLHOUSE MINIATURES?

If you have a question about dollhouse miniatures, stop by your local retail outlet and ask the expert behind the counter.

MINIATURES BY CHONG HWA
Oriental Dollhouses

Oriental Dollhouses - several designs available as kits or assembled shells. Hand painted oriental furniture and complete room sets; oriental accessories. Specializing in 1" scale oriental items.

Prices are approximate and subject to change

NORTHEASTERN SCALE MODELS, INC.
Dollhouse of a Dollhouse

Price: $13.75-$18.95
Dimensions: 1/144 scale
Choose one of our four miniature dollhouse kits for your dollhouse's playroom or child's bedroom. Parts are laser cut for precision, making assembly easy. Kits contain instructions, all basswood parts, windows and doors. Available are our basic dollhouse, log house, farmhouse and cottage.

OPENING SCENE REPLICAS
One Room Schoolhouse from "Little House on the Prairie"

Stock No.: S030
Price: See your local dealer or send for catalog.
Dimensions: 27"H x 15"W x 23"D
This quaint yet simple structure served as both school and church in Walnut Grove, and occasionally as the town meeting hall where pressing matters were hotly debated among the inhabitants of this rural Minnesota village. Special component packages (available separately) feature the rustic facade with exposed rafter ends, the church bell and beam, plus the little front porch. 3/8" and 1/4" cabinet-grade plywood.

PRECIOUS LITTLE THINGS

Deluxe Roadside Stand

Dimensions: 15-1/2"W x 9"D x 9-1/4"H
Handmade of wood with asphalt roof. Shown with store furnishings. Color catalog $3.50 or ask your local dealer.

Greenhouses & Gazebos & Gardens

Subscribe to *Nutshell News* and learn how you can make miniatures yourself! Call toll free: (800) 446-5489

DURA-CRAFT, INC.

Willowbrook Gazebo

Stock No.: WB900
Price: See your dealer
Dimensions: 16"H x 12"W x 12-1/4"D; 1"-1'
Ornate gazebo kit features fluted roof, vented cupola, two benches, molded pine brackets and intricate finial. It is made from 1/8" pre-cut plywood and framed with pine moldings. Ideal for weddings, park outings or as a bandstand.

AZTEC IMPORTS INC.

Town Square Gazebo

Stock No.: T7010-Kit, T7011-Assembled, T7012-Finished
Price: See your local dealer.
Dimensions: 16-1/2"H x 13"W x 13"D, 1"=1' scale
Easy to assemble kit with pre-shingled roof sections, preassembled rail and post sections, and preassembled base.

THE LAWBRE COMPANY
Greenhouse Kit

This is the ultimate greenhouse kit! It is generous in size and materials are high quality with all parts precision-cut to size. Easy to assemble with templates and complete instructions included. Basic kit is shown in example on the left. Greenhouse: 12"H x 10"W x 13-1/4"D. Potting shed: 14-3/4"H x 12-1/4"W x 7"D. Greenhouse kit, $69.50 plus shipping; with potting shed kit, $95.00 plus shipping.

GREENLEAF PRODUCTS
Arbor Kits

Stock No.: see below
Price: $7.90
Dimensions: see below
On a hot summer day imagine sipping a cool drink and enjoying a breeze under your arbor. These delightful arbor kits will add realism and charm to any dollhouse setting. 1" to 1' scale. 9017 (Heart-shaped arbor with settles, 8"H by 8"W by 5-1/4"D) and 9018 (Sunrise arbor, 7-1/4"H by 8"W by 4"D).

EMPRESS ARTS AND CRAFTS

Bell Top Gazebo (Windsor)

Stock No.: IWF161
Price: $50
Dimensions: 12"H x 8"W, 1" scale
Hand-soldered iron wire gazebo. Four other gazebos to choose from. More than 200 wire furniture items to select from our Windsor collection. Stem flowers and potted plants available also. Wholesale only.

REAL GOOD TOYS

The Gazebo

Stock No.: G-12
Price: See your dealer
Dimensions: 16"H x 13-1/2"D
Let your imagination run with miniature wicker furniture, bench seats, swings, planters or foundations. Use flowers, dolls or stuffed animals to create your own style. The Gazebo kit includes pre-cut, gingerbread trim, octagonal wooded shingles, foundation and front step. Step-by-step instructions are simple and easy to follow.

THE LAWBRE COMPANY

Gazebo Kit

Stock No.: Price:
Dimensions: 18"H x 9-1/2"W x 9-1/2"D
To create a garden fantasy or furnish as a separate display, this quality-made kit has most parts cut to size. Templates and full instructions are included. $48.50 (kit); $95.00 (assem./unfin.); shipping extra.

N.A.M.E.
Join a club and share!
The National Association of Miniature Enthusiasts.
130 N. Rangeline Rd.
Carmel, IN 46032
(317) 571-8094

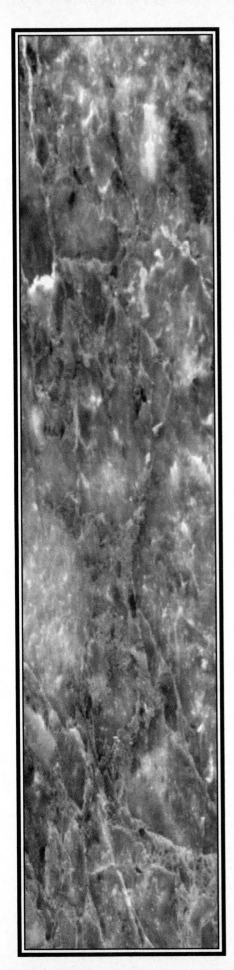

DISPLAYS for MINIATURES

Display Cabinets Boxes & Lamps

ARCHITECTURAL ETCETERA
Corner Shelf Unit & Room Setting
Stock No.: 275 - 279; 281
Price: $40 - $55; $165 for room setting
The corner cabinet has three clear, adjustable shelves and is lighted from above. It's designed for display of your collectibles and is available in white or walnut woodgrain.

AZTEC IMPORTS INC.

Shadow Boxes
Price: See your local dealer.
A variety of sizes and styles available, some with glass doors. Available in walnut and oak finish. T7060/20-1/2"H by 18"W; T7904/14"H by 11"W; D3106/4"H by 6"W; D6050/17-1/2"H by 1-1/2"W.

CELERITY MINIATURE HOMES

Porch Box Kit
Dimensions:
14"L x 8-3/4"W x 3-1/2"D
Each kit complete in one box. No decorating material in kit. May be found in your local miniatures shop. Dimensions above exclude roof section.

CELERITY MINIATURE HOMES

Room or Wall Boxes
Price: See your local dealer for retail.
Small box: 19"L x 8-3/4"W x 3-1/2"D
Large box: 27-1/4"L x 8-3/4"W x 5-1/4"D

COLLECTOR'S DISPLAY CASE CO.

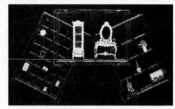

Clear Display Case
Price: $10; four or more, $7.95/ea.(plus S&H)
Dimensions: 9" x 12-1/2" x 1-3/8"
Strong, clear, lightweight plastic cases allow perfect viewing from all sides. Each collectible is suspended in its own compartment, protected from dust, damage and theft. Can be wall-mounted, or locked together when stacked. Dealer inquiries welcome.

Flattened Out

WORKSHOP WISDOM

This is a really easy method of ironing the kinks and wrinkles out of very narrow ribbons. Instead of trying to push the steam iron across the ribbon, try pulling it from under the iron in the direction of the arrow. It really works.

*SUSANNE RUSSO
FT. LAUDERDALE, FL*

Workshop Wisdom Courtesy of *Nutshell News*—3/95

Dollhouse Turntables

FOR FAST SERVICE, VISIT YOUR LOCAL MINIATURES SHOP

PAUL'S SPECIALTIES
Electric Collector's Turntable

Price: $36 - $40
Dimensions: 16"W x 16"D; 12"W x 12"D; 8"W x 8"D
Turntable complete with wiring. Connect to electrical system of any 12V dollhouse. Designed by a collector. Rotates 360 degrees with no tangled wires. Non-electric collector's turntable also available, $17 - $20. Same dimensions and material.

Glass Domes & Showcases

Home Sweet Home

WORKSHOP WISDOM

These neat miniature bird houses were made from a miniature turned wooden apple – which came already painted – and an acorn. Joan added the apple leaves from thin wood, then drilled holes for the entrance and for the perch which was made from the thin end of a toothpick. Why not add a Fimo robin to finish off? Incidentally, if you need really thin but strong wood for small details, such as the apple leaves, pick up a sheet of 1/64" (0.4mm) wood from a model or hobby store. One sheet is a lifetime supply and is ideal for small details. Can be cut with scissors, too.

JOAN CHANCE
MT. HOPE, KS

Workshop Wisdom *Courtesy of* Nutshell News—3/95

PAUL'S SPECIALTIES

Glass Domes

Dimensions: 5-1/2"W x 11"H or 8"W x 12"H
Glass domes with lazy Susan base. It is a hardwood base made of either oak or walnut. The lazy Susan rotates easily, allowing viewing from all angles.

Novelty Displays

BODEGA

Shadow Box

Stock No.: 506
Price: $19.50 plus shipping
Dimensions: 20-1/2" x 15-1/2"
Excellent quality, custom stain, made in America.
Several sizes and styles available. Any "state"
collector box available. Perfect for your miniature
collectables! Wholesale only.

OMNIARTS OF COLORADO

"Short Stories" Kit

Stock No.: 1193
Price: $22
Dimensions: 9"H x 7"W x 3-1/2"D
A display box that looks like a book to showcase
your own "short story." Made of hardboard and
custom-milled pine. Acrylic cover inside book
cover protects scene.

JUST GETTING INTO DOLLHOUSE MINIATURES?

If you have a question about
dollhouse miniatures, stop
by your local retail outlet
and ask the expert
behind the counter.

Room Boxes & Vignettes

ARCHITECTURAL DETAILS J.M. OGREENC

Roombox Details and Accessories

Dimensions: 1" and 1/2" scale
Designed especially for roomboxes and vignettes.
No opening required. Add a new dimension to
your next project. More styles available.
Made in USA.

ARCHITECTURAL ETCETERA
James River Library Roombox

Stock No.: 100; 110
Price: $2,800 - $3,200
This finished roombox includes a mahogany
floor, micro glass in the French doors and
exquisite cornice and molding. There is an
installed valance lighting system in the front
of the room and in the terrace area plus wall
plug outlets below the built-in bookshelves.
All the materials and workmanship are top
quality for the most discriminating collector.
The case is hardwood veneer, finished in
brown mahogany, with a removable glass
front. Interior dimensions are 23"W x 16"D x
12"H. Exterior size is 27"W x 21"D x 15-1/2"H.

ARCHITECTURAL ETCETERA
Custom Design Roomboxes

Price: $500 - $10,000 plus shipping
Custom room reproductions in 1" or 1/2" scale. We can construct a historical room setting in any period or an actual room from your own home or office. Each room setting is installed in a custom-finished case. Custom furnishings and accessories are also available. We have done well over 100 rooms in all sizes and price ranges over the last 20 years. Contact Architectural Etcetera for further details about past projects or obtaining a quote on your room.

ARCHITECTURAL ETCETERA
Period Room Box Kit

Stock No.: 120 - 130
Price: $400 - $950
Dimensions: 17-3/4"W x 8"D x 10-1/2"H - Interior; 19"W x 10-1/2"D x 11-1/4"H - Case Dimensions
This smaller box is available finished as you see it on the right or as a kit shown at left. The finished box has lighted cabinets, a complete fireplace, planked floor and painted walls and ceiling. A 12V fused and switched transformer is included. The exterior is covered in leatherette with a wood frame and glass front. Furnishings and light fixtures are not included. The kit box is assembled but with all the decorating parts loose and unfinished. It just takes your finishing ideas and labor to complete the project.

ARCHITECTURAL ETCETERA
Custom Walls

Complete walls in many designs. Made to your requirements. However, smaller dimensions will limit content. Wall with fireplace and recessed shelf units lighted and undecorated is approximately $295. Library wall, as shown, with adjustable shelves and wood finish is approximately $450.

FANTASY CRAFT

FANTASY CRAFT
Vanishing Stairs Room Box

Stock No.: R07
Price: Kit $54.95; Assembled $69.95
Dimensions: 20"W x 12"D x 13"H;
1" scale
Delightfully versatile roombox featuring stairs leading to a "shadow" room above and an outdoor patio area. Stairs are sold separately with a choice of bay window ($89.95) or French doors (69.95); picket or wrought iron fence with gate $25.95 each. Backlighting kit $74.95. Easy assembly, beautiful 3/8" birch, tongue-and-groove construction.

Porch and Parlor Roombox

Stock No.: R10
Price: Kit $109.95; Assembled $129.95;
1" scale
Dimensions: 16"W x 16"D x 16"H;
Decorate the porch in your favorite style. Room has a solid back wall, both sides are acrylic. Door and picture window in front wall. This also works well as a shop or general store. 3/8" birch with foundation. Finishing kit - $99.95 includes clapboard and all porch trim to finish like our Craftsman Bungalow.

FANTASY CRAFT
Small Shadow Hall
Large Shadow Hall

Stock No.: RO2S and RO2L
Price: Kit $49.95/$54.95
Assembled $59.95/$64.95
Dimensions: 12"W x 12"D x 10-3/4"H; 15"W x 16"D x 10-3/4"H; 1" scale
3-D hall. Perfect for any room that opens onto an indoor hallway or the great outdoors! Small features single-door opening; large features double-door opening. Wiring is available for backlighting hall. Beautiful 3/8" birch. Excellent for staining or painting the outside. Easy assembly. Tongue-and-groove construction. Acrylic front.

FANTASY CRAFT
Shadow Hall with Window
Shadow Hall with Room

Stock No.: RO3 and RO4
Price: Kit $59.95 each; Assembled $74.95 each
Dimensions: 17"W x 16"D x 10-3/4"H;
1" scale
Beautiful 3/8" birch is excellent for staining or painting the outside. Easy assembly. Tongue-and-groove construction. Both feature a "shadow" hall, one with a window to view a 3-D outdoor scene and the other with a "shadow" room. Both create the illusion of an actual room within a house! Acrylic fronts.

FANTASY CRAFT
Jan's Garden Roombox Series

Stock No.: RO9
Price: Kit $23.95 /$43.95;
Assembled $36.95 /$53.95
Dimensions: 1/2" or 1" scale
Easy assembly. Tongue-and-groove construction. Beautiful 3/8" birch is excellent for staining or painting. "Jan's Garden" with its graceful proscenium arch is now available in five sizes. Decorate a room or create an outdoor scene using a color photocopy as a backdrop. Perfect for doll or teddy bear displays. Acrylic top and front.
Mini - 10-3/4"W x 4"D x 8-1/2"H
Mini-D - 10-3/4"W x 6"D x 8-1/2"H
Mini-V - 8-3/4"W x 4"D x 11-1/2"H
Midi - 14"W x 6"D x 10-1/2"H
Original - 18"W x 8"D x 12-1/2"H

OLDE MOUNTAIN MINIATURES
Harvey Wallhangers

Price: Kits/Dealer Availability — Finished price starting at $125
A unique system incorporating a pine and plywood 'perspective style' vignette set up PLUS a selection of ten finishing kits that are fun and challenging to complete your own room settings. Choose from Santa Fe, The Shoppe, The Williamsburg, Irish Cottage, Mercantile Shop, The Proscenium, Sloanes Barn, Shaker Room, The Manfred and The Wethersfield. Can be hung on the wall or placed on a shelf. Great class projects. Unlimited possibilities.

OPENING SCENE REPLICAS
Addams Family Parlor and Vestibule

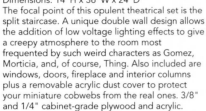

Stock No.: S6T1
Price: $189 (includes components)
Dimensions: 14"H x 36"W x 24"D
The focal point of this opulent theatrical set is the split staircase. A unique double wall design allows the addition of low voltage lighting effects to give a creepy atmosphere to the room most frequented by such weird characters as Gomez, Morticia, and, of course, Thing. Also included are windows, doors, fireplace and interior columns plus a removable acrylic dust cover to protect your miniature cobwebs from the real ones. 3/8" and 1/4" cabinet-grade plywood and acrylic.

SHOW SANTA WHAT YOU WANT FROM *THE MINIATURES CATALOG*

OPENING SCENE REPLICAS
Jessica's Kitchen from "Murder She Wrote"

Stock No.: S10T2
Price: $159 (includes components)
Dimensions: 12"H x 25"W x 14"D
Here is where Jessica Fletcher wrote her popular murder mysteries in the little New England fishing village of Cabot Cove. The kitchen is accurately laid out to accommodate the cabinets, the dinette, even the little corner potbellied stove. The screened porch and garden are enclosed in a removable acrylic dust cover. Also available is Jessica's Parlor (right) featuring the unique front exterior with its tiny vestibule. The parlor features foyer step down, parlor fireplace and bay window with cozy window seat. 3/8" and 1/4" cabinet-grade plywood and acrylic.

OPENING SCENE REPLICAS
Collinwood Great Hall from "Dark Shadows"

Stock No.: S2T3
Price: $179 (includes components)
Dimensions: 17"H x 27"W x 27"D
This typically English great hall with its gothic arches and grand staircase includes the angled wall where Barnabas' ancestral portrait was prominently displayed. This unique theatrical set also includes the front exterior with its massive columns and statuary niche. Also available is the Barnabas "Old House" (pictured right) and the infamous Collins Mausoleum. 3/8" and 1/4" cabinet-grade plywood and acrylic.

THE LAWBRE COMPANY
Bookshelf Display Case Kit

Stock No.: 1200 and 1201
Dimensions: 10"H x 19-1/2"W x 10-1/2"D
Display box that takes little space, is easy-to-build and looks great. Front and top removable. Shelves in bay window also removable. Ideal for bookcase shelf or table top. Includes two bay windows and door. Available as a kit or assembled/unfinished as shown in photo. Custom finishing available. Plywood, pine and Plexiglas. $54.50, kit; $96.00, assembled/unfinished; plus shipping.

WALMER DOLLHOUSES
Porch For All Seasons

Stock No.: 440
Price: See your local dealer.
Dimensions: 19"H x 18"W x 7"D
Make our porch a centerpiece for miniature fun in your home. Change accessories and furnishings with the holidays and seasons. Even the house interior can be decorated, giving a hint of the season indoors. The Porch For All Seasons may be hung on a wall or placed on a table or shelf. The custom kit is complete as shown with siding, shingles, unitized shuttered window, turned posts and rails, pre-hung Victorian oval-light door, trims and removable back. The kit is available with or without interior curio light.

WALMER DOLLHOUSES
Roombox

Stock No.: 117S/117D/117L/117CD/117CL
Price: See your local dealer.
Our roomboxes are the perfect showcase for special displays and themes. They are available in three sizes. Three of our five models feature a Plexiglas front which slides out as shown in photo. Two models have a Plexiglas front and top. Choose the design and size best suited to your space and miniature collection. 1/4" plywood and pine moldings.

WALMER DOLLHOUSES
Perspective Room Box

Stock No.: 117P
Price: See your local dealer.
Dimensions: 12-1/4"H x 24-1/4"W x 11-3/4"D; 1/12 scale
Imagination and creativity make anything possible in this versatile room box kit. There are two outdoor spaces to illuminate and decorate, standard window and French door openings, removable top and Plexiglas front. 1/2", 3/8" and 1/4" cabinet-grade plywood; solid pine.

Waxing Poetic

M elissa puts it very nicely – wax adhesive is to the dollhouse what Post-It-Notes are to the paper pushers of business. She uses little pieces of it to hang pictures, drapes, mirrors, etc., so they can be changed at a whim. She also applies it to the bottoms of lamps etc. so that they do not slide off the tables when the dollhouse is moved. To hang rodded drapes, for instance, she digs out dots of wax, applies them to the window frame, then presses the ends of the rod into it.

MELISSA BAILEY
NEWARK, NJ

Workshop Wisdom Courtesy of *Nutshell News*—12/94

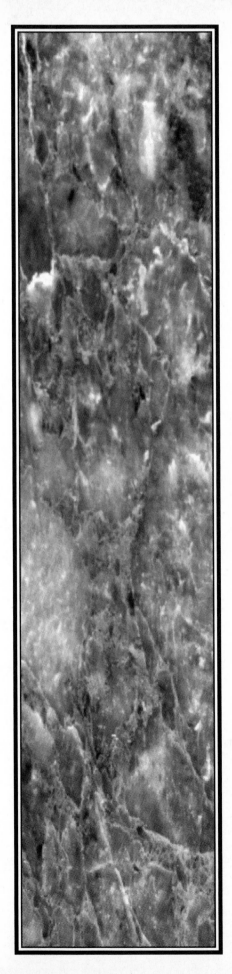

BUILDING
COMPONENTS
&
EXTERIOR
SUPPLIES

Architectural Components

ALESSIO MINIATURES

Dormer With Working Window

Stock No.: 400
Price: $14
Dimensions: 6"L x 3-1/16W x 5-1/4"
        bottom to peak
Classic dormer with working window. Affordable quality. American-made.

ARCHITECTURAL ETCETERA

Arch Frame

Stock No.: 250 & 251
Price: $35
Dimensions: 9"H x 8"W (O.D.)
Arch as fine detailing on all faces. Wraps around wall edges. Template provided. Columns available separately for archways of different widths. Specify 3/8" or 1/2" wall thickness.

ARCHITECTURAL ETCETERA

Chimneys

Stock No.: DPC2
Price: $48
Dimensions: 9-1/4"H (max.) x 3"W x 2"D
Chimney looks and feels like aged brick and mortar. Authentic design and scale. Can be cut with hand tools. White with brick stains provided. Molded special composition material developed for this project.

ARCHITECTURAL ETCETERA

Brackets, Border Squares and Miscellaneous Small Detail

Stock No.: 500 - 545
Price: $2.50 - $5

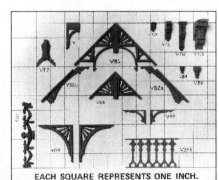

EACH SQUARE REPRESENTS ONE INCH.

ARCHITECTURAL ETCETERA
Architectural Components

Price: $2 - $5.50
Finely-detailed, high-quality moldings. I will also custom mold your originals. Other moldings included in our catalog.

ARCHITECTURAL ETCETERA

Vergeboards, Finials and Pedestals.
Stock No.: 550 - 567
Price: $2 - $12

ARCHITECTURAL ETCETERA

Columns, Capitals and Door & Window Pediments
Stock No.: 570 - 594
Price: $3.50 - $10

ARCHITECTURAL ETCETERA

Quoins, Fencing, Courtyard Stone and Chippendale Planter
Stock No.: 600 - 645
Price: $2.50 - $20

ARCHITECTURAL ETCETERA
18th Century Chinese Chippendale Fence

Price: $12
Two patterns form an intriguing design. Use in garden as a fence or as sides of a bridge. Also can be used as roof trim. Package has four fence sections (two each style) and five posts. Can be cut to fit. Each section: 2-1/8"H x 3/16"D x 3-1/16"W. Each post: 2-1/2"H x 1/4"D x 1/4"W. Total width 13-1/4".1" = 1' scale.

CLASSICS BY HANDLEY

Apex Trim
Stock No.: CLA70224
Price: $1.98
Dimensions: 4-5/8"W x 2-3/4"H
Made of unfinished wood with intricate detailing to add a great aura of style to your Victorian dollhouse. For 45 degree angle. One per package.

CLASSICS BY HANDLEY

Apex Trim, Small Fan Design
Stock No.: CLA70243
Price: $6.00
Dimensions: 5-1/4"W x 2-3/4"H
This lovely trim adds flair to any dollhouse. Designed for a 45 degree sloped roof.

CLASSICS BY HANDLEY

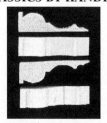

Fancy Brackets
Stock No.: CLA70261
Price: $2.49
Dimensions: 3/8"D x 1-3/8"H
These wood brackets add a special touch to eaves, bookshelves and other areas of your miniature creation. Four to a package.

CLASSICS BY HANDLEY

Large Apex Trim, Sun Design
Stock No.: CLA70245
Price: $8.98
Dimensions: 7-5/8"W x 4"H
This sun-designed apex trim is a welcoming accent. It is intended for use with a 45 degree sloped roof. Trim made of unfinished wood.

CLASSICS BY HANDLEY

Porch Lattice

Stock No.: CLA70250
Price: $12.00
Dimensions: 1-1/2"H x 12"L
These wood lattice panels come fully assembled and are proportioned for exactly 1" scale. Three panels per package.

CLASSICS BY HANDLEY

Hanging Store Sign

Stock No.: CLA70234
Price: $4.25
Dimensions: 2-1/2"W x 3-1/2"H
This sign is perfect for a country store or shop. Has gold tone chains to hang sign. Sign made of unfinished wood.

CLASSICS BY HANDLEY

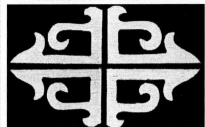

Porch Trim

Stock No.: CLA70223
Price: $2.69
Dimensions: 1-1/16"W x 1-5/8"L
This wood trim reflects the beauty and grace of the Victorian era. Four per package.

CLASSICS BY HANDLEY

Victorian Brackets

Stock No.: CLA70217
Price: $2.39
Dimensions: 9/16"W x 1"L
These wood brackets add a special touch to eaves, bookshelves and other areas of your miniature creation. Six per package.

CLASSICS BY HANDLEY

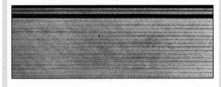

Wainscoting and Chair Rail Trim

Stock No.: CLA70239; CLA70240
Price: $10.98; $1.39
Dimensions: 3-1/4"H x 12"L and 24"L
This lovely wainscoting and matching chair rail give an elegant, distinguished look to any miniature room. CLA70239 has four panels per package.

DESIGN TECNICS MINIATURES

Authentic Brackets

Dimensions: 1" scale
Laser-cut wood bracket kits in 1" scale are derived from real prototypes and are designed by Fred Stephenson, architect and author of "The Architect's Angle" in Nutshell News. Parts may be painted different colors before assembly to produce precise paint edge definition. Nine different bracket designs are available.

CLASSICS BY HANDLEY
Dormer with Working Window

Stock No.: CLA70219
Price: $14.00
Dimensions: 3-5/8"W x 6-3/8"H x 6-7/8"D
This traditional dormer creates a classic look to any dollhouse. The working window adds an authentic touch.

FOR FAST SERVICE, VISIT YOUR LOCAL MINIATURES SHOP

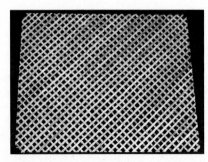

HANDLEY HOUSE
Lattice Work

Stock No.: HH322; HH513
Price: $8.95
Dimensions: 6" x 8"; 5" x 6"; 1/2" scale
Made of walnut veneer, each panel contains more than 270 glue joints. Easy to cut, fit and paint. Great for gazebos, room dividers, flower trellises and foundation lattices.
Handmade in the USA.

Prices are approximate and subject to change

HOUSEWORKS, LTD.
Assorted Brackets and Trim

Stock No.: 7058; 7059; 7028; 7026; 7027

7058 - Apex Trim - 45 degree pitch trim with elaborate waves of detail. Fits most roof apexes. Size: 3-5/16"L x 3-5/16"L x 4-3/4"W. 2 pcs./pkg., $2.95.

7059 - Porch Trim - this subtly ornate trim works well on any part of your dollhouse exterior. Size: 1-5/8"H x 1/8"W x 1"D. 2 pcs./pkg., $1.50.

7028 - Post Brackets - exterior decorative brackets used for Victorian detailing. Size: 1-11/16"H x 11/16"W x 1-5/16"D. 4 pcs./pkg., $3.95.

7026 - Ornate bracket used in the top corners of open interior doorways or for exterior detailing. Size: 1-1/4"H x 3/16"W x 1"D. 4 pcs./pkg., $5.95.

7027 - Eaves Bracket 1-3/16"H x 11/16"W x 1"D. 4pcs./pkg., $3.60.

HOUSEWORKS, LTD.
Traditional Dormer

Stock No.: 7002
Price: $11.75
Dimensions: 5-1/8"W x 5-11/16"H x 6-1/8"D
Assembled and ready-to-be-dressed out with your choice of windows. Designed for 45 degree pitch roof. Accepts #5004 window. Fits irregular opening: 3-7/16"W x 7-1/8"H.

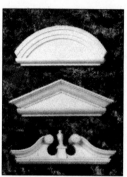

HOUSEWORKS, LTD.
Pediments

Stock No.: 7071; 7070; 7072
Price: $4.95; $4.95; $10.50

7071 - Federal Circle Pediment - this original design will give your windows a look never seen before. Style matches any Federal dollhouse design. 2 per pkg. Size; 1-3/8"H x 3-1/8"W x 5/16"D.

7070 - Federal Hooded Pediment - sleek, intricate detailing in this pediment will give you an easy way to enhance your dollhouse exterior. 2 per pkg. Size: 1-3/16"H x 3-1/2"W x 13/32"D.

7072 - Deerfield Pediment - now all of your windows can match your Deerfield door. This pediment boasts a delicately scrolled design with the most intricate detail ever seen in a pediment. 2 per pkg. Size: 1-1/8"H x 3-1/2"W x 13/32"D.

LASER TECH

HOUSEWORKS, LTD.

Large Dormer Unit

Stock No.: 7017
Price: $14.95
This dormer was designed to accept Houseworks single glazed windows #5038, 5039 and 5040. Size: 4-1/16"W x 6-29/32"H x 7-3/8"D. Covers roof area: 4-1/16"W x 9-3/4"H x 7-3/8"D with a 45 degree pitch.

HOUSEWORKS, LTD.

Chimney

Stock No.: 2404
Price: $7.95
Dimensions: 4-1/16"H x 1-15/16"L sq.
This solid wood chimney is topped with a detailed ornamental chimney hood. 45 degree pitch at base. Two per package.

Do you want to list your items in

The Miniatures Catalog?

Call

(800) 446-5489 for listing information.

Laser Cut Apex Trims

Stock No.: see below
Price: see below
Made of 3/32 basswood with intricate detailing to add a welcoming accent to your Victorian dollhouse. Intended for use on a 45 degree slope roof. Top to bottom: AT-001-$8.30; AT-002-$8.15; AT-003-$8.25.

LASER TECH

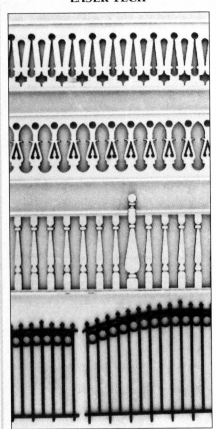

Porch Railings and Fencing

Stock No.: see below
Price: see below
Made of 3/32 basswood with intricate detailing to add a welcoming accent to your Victorian dollhouse. Railings come with top and bottom handrail. Top to bottom: PR-045 (12")-$16.75; PR-040 (12")-$16.75; PR-041 (8-3/4")-$12.55; F-137 (gate)-$6.05; GF-138 (6")-$17.75/(2).

PRECISION PRODUCTS

Plastic Veneer Styrene Sheets

Price: $7 per sheet
Dimensions: 15" square
20 styles in 1" scale; 30 styles in 1/2" scale.
Made in USA.

THE FRETWORKER, KIRK RATAJESAK

Scroll Work

Price: $.55-$3
Now you can get the quality finished dollhouse you've always wanted with authentic scroll trim from the Fretworker. These styles of porch and eave brackets are also available in 1/2" scale. Birch plywood.

WORKSHOP WISDOM

Those very small Christmas tree ornaments, which are about 1/2" (13mm) in diameter can be converted into neat mini oil lamps. Carefully extract the cap and wire loop, then soak the ball in a solution of 2 tablespoons of chlorine bleach to two cups of water (unfortunately, Dannie did not say for how long). Then with a small Q-Tip soaked in nail polish remover, wipe the coloring from inside. It only remains to use super glue to assemble the globe, a large brass rivet, a suitable jewelry finding or earring, and a shortened brass nail to make the lamp.

DANNIE LARSEN
MERTZON, TX

Workshop Wisdom
Courtesy of *Nutshell News*—6/94

UNIQUE MINIATURES
Wainscotting

Stock No.: WC-1, WC-2, WC-3, WC-4, WC-5
Dimensions: 11-3/4" to 12-1/4"
x 2-3/8" to 2-1/2"
Excellent trimmings that cover uneven wallpaper applications or spaces between the wall and the floor. They certainly make attractive borders for all walls.

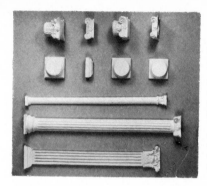

UNIQUE MINIATURES
Half Columns

Stock No.: see below
Dimensions: see below
These polyester resin cast column halves can be cut down and fitted together to construct any size column. Use alongside a door opening or to frame an archway. Adds the ornate trim needed to doll up a miniature room. Available in three styles: CO-1, 11" by 1/2"; CO-2, 12" by 1-1/2"; CO-3, 11" by 2". All are sold in pairs. The CS-1 and CS-2 are 3-dimensional and can easily form a column by using a 1" dowel. The CS-3 is a half column top (pilaster) and base. Send $3 for catalog. Made in the USA.

WALMER DOLLHOUSES

Large Corbel

Stock No.: 5450
Price: See your local dealer.
Dimensions: 2"H x 1"W x 13/16"D; 1/12 scale
A Designer Home Architectural Accent, this exquisitely detailed corbel is an elegant addition to an impressive facade.

WALMER DOLLHOUSES

Apex Trims

Stock No.: 5252; 5251
Price: See your local dealer.
Dimensions: 5-1/4" x 7-5/8"; 1/12 scale
Trims add interest and elegance to any structure. See our Designer Home catalog for other trims.

WALMER DOLLHOUSES

Grand Paces Wall Panel

Stock No.: 5452
Price: See your local dealer.
Dimensions: 1"H x 3"W; 1/12 scale
A Designer Home exclusive, the wall panel may be used on interior or exterior in a variety of ways.

WALMER DOLLHOUSES
Skylight Kit

Stock No.: 2097
Price: See your local dealer.
Dimensions: Fits opening 5" x 6-5/8"; 1/12 scale
Add a skylight anywhere. They are an interesting and attractive addition to any room. Part of our Designer Home series. Catalog available.

WALMER DOLLHOUSES

Grapeleaf Ceiling Medallion

Stock No.: 5455
Price: See your local dealer.
Dimensions: 1-7/16" diameter; 1/12 scale
Delicate and intricate design makes this Designer Home original an attractive addition to any room.

WALMER DOLLHOUSES
Single-Light Dormer
(45°Roof)

Stock No.: 2094
Price: See your local dealer
Dimensions: Fits roof opening 6"H x 3-5/8"W; 1/12 scale
This dormer is designed to accept Designer Home single-light windows, Traditional, Colonial or Victorian. Window openings are 2-15/16"H x 2-9/16"W. Windows are not included with dormer. Designer Home catalog available.

WALMER DOLLHOUSES

American Eagle

Stock No.: 5460
Price: See your local dealer.
Dimensions: Wing span 2-1/4"; 1/12 scale
Americana, Colonial, patriotism—all are conjured up by the addition of this beautifully-crafted symbol of American freedom. Another Designer Home original.

WALMER DOLLHOUSES
Store Display Window Kit

Stock No.: 2033
Price: See your local dealer.
Dimensions: Fits opening 5-9/16"H x 9"W; 1/12 scale
Exclusive Designer Home product. Interior window sill is more than 1" deep for display of shop wares. Designer Home catalog available.

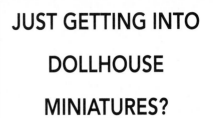

JUST GETTING INTO DOLLHOUSE MINIATURES?

If you have a question about dollhouse miniatures, stop by your local retail outlet and ask the expert behind the counter.

WALMER DOLLHOUSES
Dormer Window
(45°Roof)

Stock No.: 2095
Price: See your local dealer.
Dimensions: Roof opening 8-5/8"H x 3-5/8"W; 1/12 scale
Dormer accepts any standard size Designer Home windows. Window openings 5-1/16"H x 2-9/16"W. Window shown (#2017) not included with dormer. Designer Home catalog available.

WALMER DOLLHOUSES
36-Lite Bay Window

Stock No.: 2096N
Price: See your local dealer.
Dimensions: Fits opening 5"H x 6-3/4"W; 1/12 scale
Bay window has removable panes for easy finishing. Send for complete Designer Home catalog.

WALMER DOLLHOUSES

WALMER DOLLHOUSES
24-Lite Colonial Window

Stock No.: 2034
Price: See your local dealer.
Dimensions: Fits opening 5-1/16"H x 6-13/16"W; 1/12 scale
Lovely Colonial window is a companion product to items in Designer Home Colonial collection. Removable pane. Send for Designer Home catalog.

Dormer Kit

Stock No.: 2098
Price: See your local dealer.
Dimensions: Fits opening 4-7/8"H x 2-1/2"W; 1/12 scale
Part of Designer Home components, this uniquely designed dormer fits a 12-1/2° sloped roof. Catalog available.

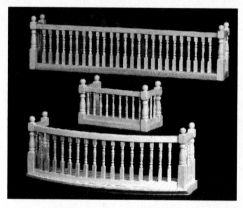

WALMER DOLLHOUSES
Designer Home Balconies

Stock No.: 5421; 5422; 5423
Price: See your local dealer.
Dimensions: 1/12 scale
5421 - Arlington Balcony;
5423 - Window Balcony;
5422 - Curved Balcony.
Assembled or kits. Designer Home
catalog available.

WILLO MINIATURES

Gatorfoam

Stock No.: JAS-G-1 thru 5
Price: $.03 - $.15 per sq. inch, plus shipping.
Dimensions: Custom cut to size
Superior construction material. Performance
features: rigid and durable, excellent strength to
weight ratio, highly moisture resistant, easily cut,
lightweight. Thickness available from 3/16" to 1-1/2".

WALMER DOLLHOUSES

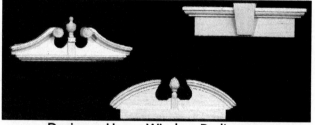

Designer Home Window Pediments

Stock No.: 2051; 2052; 2057
Price: See your local dealer.
Dimensions: 3"W at base; 1/12 scale
Customize our #2029 or #2030 Traditional windows with a unique Designer Home pediment:
#2052 - Keystone (exclusive design); #2052 - Ashton (companion product #1020 Ashton door);
#2057 - Broken Bonnet (exclusive design).

VISIT A MINIATURES MUSEUM ON YOUR VACATION

Brick & Stone Supplies

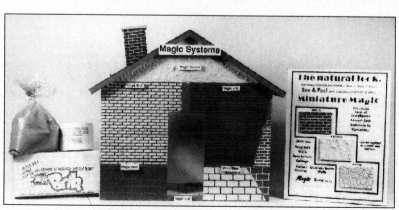

DEE'S DELIGHTS, INC.
Magic Systems Textured Surface Kits

Price: See your local dealer.
Lets you create realistic walls, patios, foundations,
fireplaces, ceilings - anywhere! Each kit contains dry mix,
self-adhesive patterned tape and complete instructions.
Very easy to install. Available in different patterns and
kits to cover 2 to 8 square feet. Magic Brik in white and
red, Magic Sla´t, Magic Stucco in white and red, Magic
Ston, Magic Bloc in white and red.

HANDLEY HOUSE

Mini Brick Mortar

Stock No.: OR599W (white); OR599(gray)
Price: $4.95
Dimensions: 18 oz.
For applying all types of miniature brick (both sheet and bulk), as well as stone and slate. Color can be changed by adding a good latex paint to OR599W.

HANDLEY HOUSE

Stucco/Adobe Mix

Stock No.: HH340; HH341
Price: $5.98; $9.49
Dimensions: 2-1/2 sq.ft.; 5 sq.ft.
Handley House Stucco Mix is our own formulation blended so miniaturists can achieve the correct scale, pattern and grain. Easy-to-work (complete instructions included), long lasting and economical.

HOUSEWORKS, LTD.

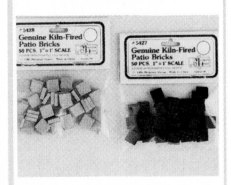

Patio Bricks and Common Bricks

Stock No.: 8205; 8204
Price: $1.25
8205 - Patio Bricks - 50 pieces of genuine, square clay bricks. All pieces are loose and polybagged. Brick size: 3/8"L x 3/8"W x 3/32"D.
8204 - Common Bricks - 50 pieces of genuine clay bricks. All pieces are loose and polybagged. Brick size: 23/32"L x 1/4"W x 3/32"D.

HOUSEWORKS, LTD.

Assorted Bricks

Stock No.: 8206; 8201; 8202; 8207
Price: $7.50; $7.95; $7.95; $5.25
8206 - 1/12 Scale Joint Common Brick Sheets - approximately 63 square inches. Styrene plastic. Sheet size 11-3/4"L x 5-1/2"W; brick size 1/4"W x 11/16"L x 1/8"D.
8201 - Common Bricks - genuine clay, mesh mounted. Each sheet covers approximately 72 square inches. Sheet size: 12-1/8"L x 5-3/4"W; brick size 23/32"L x 1/4"W x 3/32"D.
8202 - Patio Bricks - genuine clay, mesh mounted. Each sheet covers approximately 72 square inches. Sheet size: 12-1/8"L x 6-1/8"W; brick size: 3/8"L x 3/8"W x 3/32"D.
8207 - 1/12 Scale Common Joint Brick Corner - 3/4"W x 3/4"D x 11-1/2"L. Styrene plastic.

MINIATURE HOUSE

Checkerboard Bricks on Mesh

Stock No.: MH5421; MH5423
Price: $9.50
Kiln-fired ceramic bricks are available in black and white (MH5421) or red and white (MH5423). Pre-mounted on mesh backing, each covers 72 square inches.

MINIATURE HOUSE

MINIATURE HOUSE
Polystyrene Red Brick Panel

Stock No.: MH5320
Price: $5.95
Dimensions: 10-3/4"W x 16-3/4"L
Three-dimensional Polystyrene red brick panel is completely finished with grey mortar color. Accurately scaled 1"=1'. Easy to use and apply. Cut with scissors or razor.

Kiln-Fired Ceramic Brick

Dimensions: 72 square inches
Both patio and standard common brick shapes are available in 1" scale, on 72 sq.in. mesh-mounted sheets
or as loose brick (50 per package).
MH5400 - Mesh-mounted standard red, $7.95;
MH5415 - Mesh-mounted patio red, $7.95;
MH5417 - Mesh-mounted patio white, $8.50;
MH5405 - 50/bag standard red, $1.50;
MH5425 - 50/bag patio red, $1.50;
MH5426 - 50/bag patio white, $1.69;
MH5427 - 50/bag patio black - $1.69.

MODEL BUILDERS SUPPLY

3-D Plastic Sheets

Price: $3; $5.70; $9.08
Dimensions: 7" x 12"; 7" x 24"; 14" x 24"(roof)
MBS's highly realistic vacuum-formed sheets look absolutely real when painted with acrylic paints and mortar filled with tinted spackle. Fast and easy. Apply with MBS "Fast Fix" adhesive, RTV silicone or double-sided tape. Fieldstone: grey; Brick: red; Split Shakes: grey; Clapboard: white; Dressed Stone: grey; Interlocking: grey, red; Spanish Roof: red.

MODEL BUILDERS SUPPLY

Decorative Accent Brick

Price: $6.80
Dimensions: 7" x 24" sheet
This sheet of brick accents comprises surrounds for a Palladian window and door plus two styles of corner brick detail and four sets of sills or "eyebrow" headers. Requires trimming from sheet with knife, then fits over MBS brick. Preferred adhesive is MBS solvent cement. Available in sandy grey or red brick.

MODEL BUILDERS SUPPLY

Printed Paper Finishes

Price: $2.85
Dimensions: 8" x 10"
These patterns are a fast, economical way to show brick, stone, tile, pavers, marble; there are 64 designs on heavy paper. Apply with "Fast Fix" adhesive or double-sided tape.

MODEL BUILDERS SUPPLY

Rough Brick

Price: $5.70
Dimensions: 7" x 24"
The new 3-D pattern with its irregular texture and interlock matching ends is easy to make very realistic using thinned acrylic paints with subtle variegations and tinted spackle wiped in for grouting. Apply with MBS "Fast Fix," RTV silicone or double-sided tape. Brick red.

PRECISION PRODUCTS

Plastic Veneer Styrene Sheets

Price: $7 per sheet
Dimensions: 15" square
New brick, rough brick, coursed stone, random stone, stone block and cobblestone.
Made in USA.

Stained Glass

WORKSHOP WISDOM

Rebecca noticed that alcohol-based permanent art markers work very nicely on transparent plastic. So — after first drawing her stained glass window design on paper (a), she tapes a piece of window plastic (b) over the design, then colors it in using fine point markers. The leading can be done with a fine black drawing pen or better still, and more realistic, 1/32" (0.8mm) wide gray chart tape from the art store. The tape also serves to hide the "squiggly" edges to your lines.

REBECCA HILL
ORLAND PARK, IL

Workshop Wisdom Courtesy of *Nutshell News*—7/94

THE LAWBRE COMPANY
"Iron and Brick" Gates and Fencing

Stock No.: 0450 - 0465
Price: $12 - $120
For the complete landscape. These components can be used in many ways and combinations. Available finished or in kit form. Resin and metal castings.

THE LAWBRE COMPANY
Slate, Brick and Stone

All Lawbre brick, stones and slate are cast in Hydrocal cement, and all except the slate are supplied in natural white that can be colored easily with acrylic tints and paints. Slate is tinted medium gray when it is cast but can also be colored with acrylics. Package includes instructions and finishing suggestions. From left to right: 1026 - Slate flooring kit, covers 36 sq.in., $9.95; 1001- Rusticated Stone Blocks - (small), covers 25 sq.in., $6.95 (54 pieces); 1000 - Rusticated Stone Blocks - (large), covers 25 sq.in., $6.95 (29 pieces); 1002 - Field Stones - covers 35 sq.in., $6.95; 1016 - Lannon Stone - (6 pieces), covers 54 sq.in., $9.95 (also 1017, 26 pieces, covers 234 sq.in., $32.95); 1011 - Lawbre Brick - (6 pieces), covers 66 sq.in., $9.95 (also 1012, 26 pieces, covers 286 sq.in., $36.95).

WALMER DOLLHOUSES
Designer Home Flexible Brick

Stock No.: 5520/5521
Price: See your local dealer.
Dimensions: Sheets 11-1/2" x 5-1/2" x 3/32"; 1/12 scale
Designer Home brick is flexible, pliable and cuts easily with scissors. Corners interlock. Apply with any type adhesive, mortar with tile grout, paint or "age" as desired. Another Designer Home exclusive!

Door Kits & Parts

CLARE-BELL BRASS WORKS

Door Knocker

Stock No.: 1763100
Solid brass door knocker. Catalog, more than 200 items, $2.
See your local independent miniatures dealer.

Prices are approximate and subject to change

Doors, Working

CLARE-BELL BRASS WORKS

Door Plates and Knob

Stock No.: 1762-100 Threaded two-piece assembly. Fits 1/8" to 1/4" door. Solid brass. New! Glue-on (non-threaded) knob also available. Catalog, more than 200 items, $2. See your local independent miniatures dealer.

NOONMARK

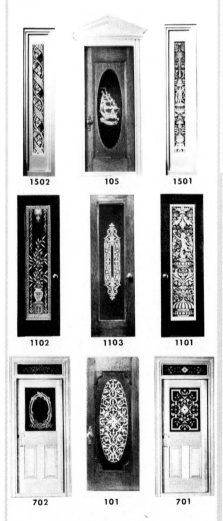

1502   105   1501

1102   1103   1101

702   101   701

Etched Door Glass

Price: $2.50 - $17.50 per pair, plus shipping
Our door lights are beautifully etched on real 3/64" micro-glass. The designs are sized to fit popular door components and are also suitable for scratch building. Other designs are available. Numbers shown refer to glass only.

JUST GETTING INTO DOLLHOUSE MINIATURES?

If you have a question about dollhouse miniatures, stop by your local retail outlet and ask the expert behind the counter.

UNIQUE MINIATURES

Appliqués

Made of polyester resin, these uniquely styled applique's have unlimited uses to accent your room decor. Apply to wood to decorate doors, wainscots, walls or even furniture and see them become handsome ornate creations. Each bag contains between two and four applique's. Send $3 for complete catalog. Made in the USA. Many other styles from which to choose.

ALESSIO MINIATURES

Classical Door

Stock No.: 456C
Price: $11.90
Dimensions: Fits opening 3" x 7"
Six-panel, flat classical door. Affordable quality. American-made.

ALESSIO MINIATURES

Classical Six-Panel Door

Stock No.: 457C
Price: $13.60
Dimensions: Fits opening 3" x 7"
Beautifully styled. Classical, six raised panel door. Affordable quality. American-made.

ALESSIO MINIATURES

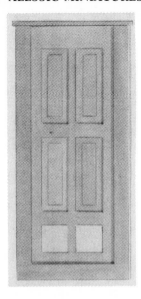

Front Door

Stock No.: 458
Price: $11.60
Dimensions: Fits opening 3" x 7"
Four raised panel front door. Two glass panels. Affordable quality. American-made.

ALESSIO MINIATURES

Classical Front Door

Stock No.: 458C
Price: $13.60
Dimensions: Fits opening 3" x 7"
Beautifully-styled, classical front door. Four raised panels, two glass. Affordable quality. American-made.

ALESSIO MINIATURES

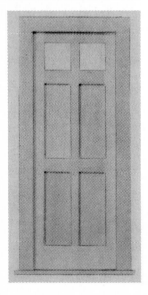

Interior Front Door

Stock No.: 459
Price: $9.90
Dimensions: Fits opening 3" x 7"
Four-panel flat interior front door. Two glass panels. Affordable quality. American-made.

ALESSIO MINIATURES

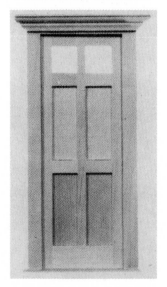

Classical Front Door

Stock No.: 459C
Price: $11.90
Dimensions: Fits opening 3" x 7"
Four-panel, flat, classical front door. Two glass panels. Affordable quality. American-made.

ALESSIO MINIATURES

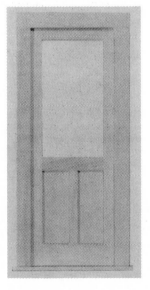

Front Door

Stock No.: 460
Price: $10.20
Dimensions: Fits opening 3" x 7"
Front door. Two raised panels with glass. Affordable quality. American-made.

Prices are approximate and subject to change

ALESSIO MINIATURES

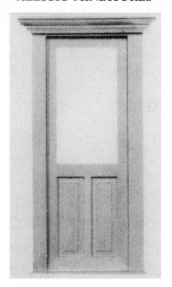

Classical Front Door

Stock No.: 460C
Price: $12.20
Dimensions: Fits opening 3" x 7"
Lovely classical front door. Two raised panels.
Affordable quality. American-made.

ALESSIO MINIATURES

Front Door

Stock No.: 450
Price: $11.70
Dimensions: Fits opening 3" x 7"
Front door with classic style. Affordable quality.
American-made.

ALESSIO MINIATURES

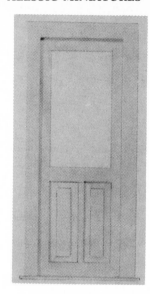

Interior Front Door

Stock No.: 461
Price: $10.20
Dimensions: Fits opening 3" x 7"
Interior front door. Two flat panels. With glass.
Affordable quality. American-made.

ALESSIO MINIATURES

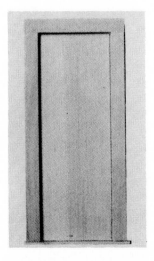

Interior Door

Stock No.: 451
Price: $7.30
Dimensions: Fits opening 3" x 7"
Interior door with clean, simple lines. Affordable
quality. American-made.

ALESSIO MINIATURES

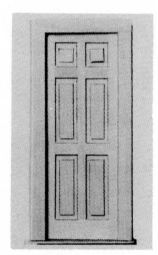

Interior Six Raised-Panel Door

Stock No.: 457
Price: $11.60
Dimensions: Fits opening 3" x 7"
Interior six raised-panel door. Affordable quality.
American-made.

ALESSIO MINIATURES

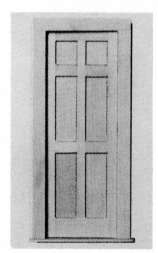

Interior Six-Panel Door

Stock No.: 456
Price: $9.90
Dimensions: Fits opening 3" x 7"
Interior six flat-panel door. Affordable quality.
American-made.

ALESSIO MINIATURES

Six Raised-Panel Door
Stock No.: 454
Price: $14.50
Dimensions: Fits opening 3" x 7"
Elegant six raised-panel door. Affordable quality. American-made.

ALESSIO MINIATURES

Six Raised-Panel Door With Glass
Stock No.: 455
Price: $14
Dimensions: Fits opening 3" x 7"
Elegant six raised-panel door. Two panels have glass. Affordable quality. American-made.

ALESSIO MINIATURES

Six-Panel Door
Stock No.: 452
Price: $12.50
Dimensions: Fits opening 3" x 7"
Classically-styled six flat-panel door. Affordable quality. American-made.

ALESSIO MINIATURES

Six-Panel Door With Glass
Stock No.: 453
Price: $12.50
Dimensions: Fits opening 3" x 7"
Classically-styled six flat-panel door. Two panels have glass. Affordable quality. American-made.

ARCHITECTURAL ETCETERA

Cast Exterior Doors
Stock No.: 300 - 319
Price: $6 - $60
Our cast doors are carefully made to achieve the finest detail possible. Cast in a urethane resin material, two castings per item, with the exterior piece and interior piece moving in or out ("telescoping") to adjust for varying wall thickness. All stock items come painted white but walnut wood finish is available upon request. All doors are supplied with removable clear micro glass. Etched glass in available at extra cost. The doors are all pin hinged with a one-piece interior trim. Instructions for painting, staining and installation are included.

ARCHITECTURAL ETCETERA

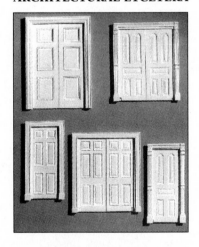

Cast Interior Doors
Stock No.: 320 - 339
Price: $20 - $35
These interior style doors are similar in construction to our exterior doors pictured elsewhere. Single doors will be hinged to open to the right unless specified otherwise. Wall thickness is 3/8" to 7/16". The door in the upper left is a false door, flat on the back, that does not open.

Prices are approximate and subject to change

ARCHITECTURAL ETCETERA

Wood Exterior Doors

Stock No.: 400 - 429
Price: $12 - $40
Our wood doors have been made to match those found in historical homes. Careful attention has been given to size and scale as well as reproduction of detail. We use clear pine for the wood parts and cast urethane resin or metal for some of the curved pediments and arched fan lights. The doors come fully assembled with assembled window muntin grids for both inside and outside. They are made to fit a wall thickness of 3/8". All doors have micro glass panes and complete interior & exterior moldings. Order our catalog for dimensions and wall opening sizes.

Subscribe to *Nutshell News* and learn how you can make miniatures yourself! Call toll free: (800) 446-5489

CLASSICS BY HANDLEY

Classics Victorian Outside Door

Stock No.: CLA71040
Price: $13.39
Dimensions: Fits opening 3-1/16"W x 7-3/16"H
This Victorian door, with matching molded interior trim, is a beautiful style exemplifying the Victorian era.

CLASSICS BY HANDLEY

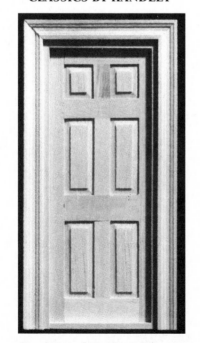

Traditional Six-Panel Door

Stock No.:CLA71380
Price: $9.50
Dimensions: Fits opening 3"W x 7"H
This door has the same special molded side trim as CLA71040 Victorian door. Door comes with matching interior trim.

CLASSICS BY HANDLEY

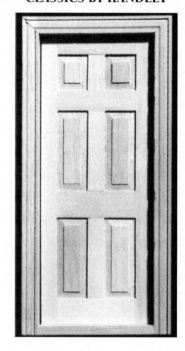

Standard Six-Panel Door

Stock No.: CLA76007
Price: $9.50
Dimensions: Fits opening 3"W x 7"H
This ever-popular, traditional door has grooved exterior trim. Door has interior molding to match exterior.

CLASSICS BY HANDLEY

Traditional Etched-Glass Door

Stock No.: CLA71311 (compote); CLA71312 (deer); CLA71313 (ship)
Price: $15.75
Dimensions: Fits opening 3-1/16"W x 7-9/16"H
Beautiful etched glass adds the finishing touch to this traditional door. Door has interior molding.

CLASSICS BY HANDLEY

Victorian Door

Stock No.: CLA76013
Price: $14.75
Dimensions: Fits opening 3-3/8"W x 8-5/16"H
Six-panel, highly-detailed door with transom molding.

CLASSICS BY HANDLEY

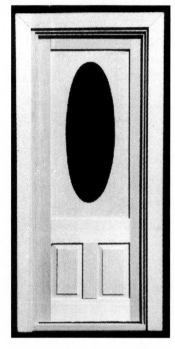

Victorian Oval-Glass Door

Stock No.: CLA70137
Price: $10.95
Dimensions: Fits opening 3-1/8"W x 7-9/16"H
Graceful Victorian door has a removable pane for easy painting or staining. Door comes with interior trim.

CLASSICS BY HANDLEY

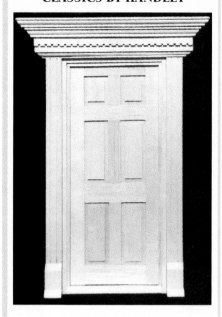

Yorktown Door

Stock No.: CLA76014
Price: $14.75
Dimensions: Fits opening 3-3/8"W x 7-7/16"H
Six-panel door with detailed door cap and dentil molding.

CLASSICS BY HANDLEY

Yorktown Exterior Door

Stock No.: CLA70117
Price: $14.49
Dimensions: Fits opening 3-15/16"W x 7-3/16"H
This lovely door, with interior trim, has 1/2 light windows and is highly detailed in the Yorktown tradition.

CLASSICS BY HANDLEY

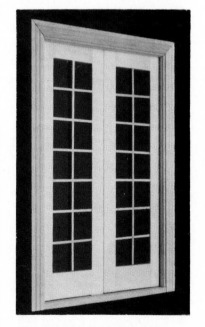

Classic French Doors

Stock No.: CLA76011
Price: $14.50
Dimensions: Fits opening 5-1/16"W x 7-9/16"H
Classic French door with removable mullions.

CLASSICS BY HANDLEY

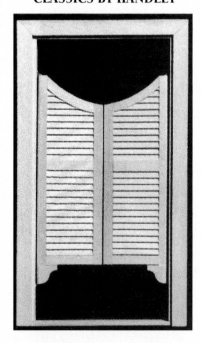

Double Swinging Door

Stock No.: CLA70134
Price: $8.95
Dimensions: Fits opening 3-1/2"W x 6-3/4"H
Classic swinging door, perfect for kitchen, bathroom, saloon or use your imagination.

Prices are approximate and subject to change

CLASSICS BY HANDLEY

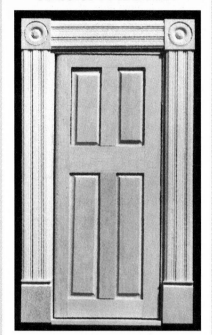

Fancy Inside Door

Stock No.: CLA70120
Price: $12.49
Dimensions: Fits opening 3-1/16"W x 6-15/16"H
This attractive door has assembled interior trim to match exterior trim. Corner blocks add a special touch.

CLASSICS BY HANDLEY

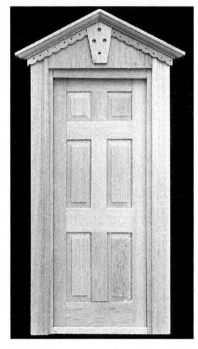

Fancy Victorian Outside Door

Stock No.: CLA71020
Price: $12.79
Dimensions: Fits opening 3"W x 7-3/16"H
This delightful door enhances the fancy Victorian series with the dainty, scalloped upper trim work. It also has interior molding.

CLASSICS BY HANDLEY

Fancy Victorian Outside Door

Stock No.: CLA71322 (rose); CLA71323 (urn)
Price: $15.75
Dimensions: Fits opening 3-1/2"W x 7-9/16"H
The dainty scalloped trim completes the Victorian look with the lovely etched glass pane. Door has interior molding.

CLASSICS BY HANDLEY

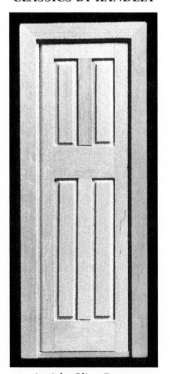

Inside Slim Door

Stock No.: CLA70133
Price: $7.50
Dimensions: Fits opening 2-5/16"W x 7"H
This four-panel door is ideal for those narrow walls between rooms. Door has interior trim.

HOUSEWORKS, LTD.

Victorian Glazed Exterior Door

Stock No.: 6033
Price: $9.50
This door features a removable acrylic pane that may be replaced with a LaserEtch insert. Stain the insert to make a beautiful Victorian statement. No interior trim. Size: 4-3/32"W x 7-9/16"H. Fits opening; 3"W x 7-3/8"H x 3/8"D; 1" scale.

HOUSEWORKS, LTD.

Victorian Oval Door

Stock No.: 6002
Price: $10.95
6002 - Detailed Victorian hood tops this exterior door with oval window. Removable acrylic pane. Interior trim not included. Size: 4-1/4"W x 8-1/2"H. Fits opening: 3-1/16"H x 7-7/16"H x 3/8"D.

HOUSEWORKS, LTD.

Assorted Panel Doors

Stock No.: 6025; 6026; 6023
Price: $12.95; $17.95; $10.95
6025 - Traditional Block and Trim Door - interior six-panel door with detailed corner blocks and trim. Interior trim. Size: 3-3/4"W x 7-5/16"H. Fits opening: 3"W x 7"H x 3/8"D. 6026 - Double Entry Doors - interior six-panel doors hinged to operate perfectly together. Interior trim. Size: 6-1/16"W x 7-1/8"H. Fits opening: 5-5/8"W x 6-15/16"H x 3/8"D. 6023 - Carolina Door - exterior six-panel door with lavish circlehead and removable acrylic pane. No interior trim. Size: 3-3/8"W x 7-3/4"H. Fits opening: 2-15/16"W x 7-1/2"H x 3/8"D.

HOUSEWORKS, LTD.
Assorted Exterior Doors

Stock No.: 6012; 6018; 6009
Price: $10.25; $9.50; $10.95
6012 - Crossbuck Door - exterior door with "crossbuck" panel, acrylic window, mullions and four section transom. No interior trim. Size 3-1/2"W x 7-3/4"H. Fits opening: 3-1/16"W x 7-9/16"H x 3/8"D. 6018 - Traditional Door - exterior door with two panel lower half, acrylic window upper half, mullions and four section transom. No interior trim. Size: 3-1/2"W x 7-3/4"H. Fits opening: 3-1/16"W x 7-9/16"H x 3/8"D. 6009 - Crossbuck Dutch Door - exterior door with lower "crossbuck" panel, upper acrylic window hinged to operate separately and four section transom. No interior trim. Size: 3-1/2"W x 7-3/4"H. Fits opening: 3-1/16"W x 7-9/16"H x 3/8"D.

HOUSEWORKS, LTD.

Federal Circle Pediment Exterior Door

Stock No.: 6032
Price: $10.95
This bold statement in exterior wood doors features a grooved frame and eight raised panels with a circle pediment. No interior trim. Size: 4-7/8"W x 8-7/8"H. Fits opening: 3-1/4"W x 7-1/2"H x 3/8"D; 1" scale

HOUSEWORKS, LTD.
Interior Panel Doors

Stock No.: 6007; 6021; 6008
Price: $9.95; $9.50; $9.50
6007 - Traditional Door - this interior six-panel door is effective for all of your interior door uses. Interior trim. Size: 3-7/16"W x 7-3/16"H. Fits opening: 3"W x 7"H x 3/8"D. 6021 - Traditional Door - interior five-panel door with detailed horizontal panels. Interior trim. Size: 3-7/16"W x 7-3/16"H. Fits opening: 3"W x 7"H x 3/8"D. 6008 - Classic Door - interior five-panel door is a stylish alternative for your interior door uses. Interior trim. Size 3-7/16"W x 7-3/16"H. Fits opening 3"W x 7"H x 3/8"D.

HOUSEWORKS, LTD.

Double Entry Deerfield Door

Stock No.: 6034
Price: $29.95
Exterior double six-panel wood doors hinged separately to operate perfectly together with intricate scroll pediment. No interior trim. Size: 7-3/16"W x 9-1/4"H. Fits opening: 5-9/16"W x 7-7/16"H x 3/8"D; 1" scale.

HOUSEWORKS, LTD.

Assorted Exterior Doors

Stock No.: 6013; 6004
Price: $14.75; $10.50
6013 - Victorian Door - exterior six-panel door with low pitch hooded doorcap, scalloped transom and fluted molding. Includes acrylic. No interior trim. Size: 5-1/8"W x 9-3/16"H. Fits opening: 3-3/8"W x 8-5/16"H x 3/8"D.
6004 - Traditional "Americana" Door - exterior door with eight raised door panels and four raised side panels. No acrylic. No interior trim. Size: 5-1/4"W x 8-3/8"H. Fits opening: 3-1/16"W x 7-9/16"H x 1/2"D.

HOUSEWORKS, LTD.

Split Six-Panel Interior Door

Stock No.: 6031
Price: $10.95
An innovative alternative to the traditional interior door. This door is hinged on both sides so that each side can operate separately. Includes interior trim. Wood. Size: 3-7/16"W x 7-3/16"H. Fits opening; 2-15/16"W x 6-15/16"H x 3/8"D; 1" scale.

HOUSEWORKS, LTD.

Sliding French Doors

Stock No.: 6030
Price: $17.95
This contemporary version of the classic French door has two separate door panels that slide side-to-side and the frame includes spring loaded tracks to allow easy removal of each door. No interior trim. Size: 5-3/8"W x 7-5/8"H. Fits opening: 5-3/16"W x 7-9/16"H x 3/8"D.

HOUSEWORKS, LTD.

Exterior Six-Panel Doors

Stock No.: 6010; 6014
Price: $22.50; $14.75
6010 - The Jamestown Door - exterior six-panel door with twin sidelights and detailed dentil molding. Includes acrylic. No interior trim. Size: 8-9/16"W x 8-1/16"H. Fits opening: 6-5/16"W x 7-7/16"H x 3/8"D.
6014 - Yorktown Door - exterior six-panel door with sculpted doorcap and complementing dentil molding. No interior trim. Size: 5-5/8"W x 8-1/8"H. Fits opening: 3-3/8"W x 7-7/16"H x 3/8"D.

Prices are approximate and subject to change

HOUSEWORKS, LTD.
Exterior Six-Panel Doors

Stock No.: 6028; 6027
Price: $23.95; $23.95
6028 - Deerfield Door - exterior six-panel door with sidelights and intricate scroll pediment. Includes acrylic, no interior trim. Size: 7-3/16"W x 9-3/16"H.
Fits opening 5-1/2"W x 7-3/8"H x 3/8"D.
6027 - Sunburst Door - exterior six-panel door with sidelights and detailed sunburst pediment. Includes acrylic, no interior trim. Size: 6-5/8"W x 8-5/8"H.
Fits opening: 5-1/2"W x 7-/8"H x 3/8"D.

HOUSEWORKS, LTD.

Saloon Door

Stock No.: 6029
Price: $8.95
Double louvered swinging doors in standard opening door frame. Wood. Includes interior trim. Size: 3-3/8"W x 7-1/4"H. Fits opening: 3"W x 7"H x 3/8"D.

HOUSEWORKS, LTD.
Traditional Panel Doors

Stock No.: 6001; 6000
Price: $8.75; $10.95
6001 - Traditional 4-Panel Door - exterior door with four raised door panels and four-section transom. No interior trim. No acrylic. Size: 3-1/2"W x 7-3/4"H. Fits opening: 3-1/4"W x 7-9/16"H x 3/8"D.
6000 - Traditional 6-Panel Door - exterior door with four-section transom. No interior trim. No acrylic. Size: 3-1/2"W x 7-3/4"H. Fits opening: 3-1/16"W x 7-9/16"H x 3/8"D.

HOUSEWORKS, LTD.
French Doors

Stock No.: 6011; 6022
Price: $14.50; $8.95
6011 - Classic French Doors - double entry French doors with preassembled grids and acrylic panes. Hinged to operate separately. For interior and exterior use. No interior trim. Size: 5-3/8"W x 7-11/16"H.
Fits opening: 5-1/16"W x 7-9/16"H x 3/8"D. No interior trim.
6022 - Single French Door - French door with preassembled grids and acrylic pane. For interior and exterior use. No interior trim. Size: 3-7/16"W x 7-11/16"H.
Fits opening: 3-1/16"W x 7-9/16"H x 3/8"D.

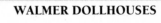

WALMER DOLLHOUSES

Victorian Interior Door

Stock No.: 1016
Price: See your local dealer.
Dimensions: Fits opening 7-1/16"H x 3-1/16"W; 1/12 scale
Elegant interior door has matching frame for opposite side, both featuring plinth blocks and rosettes. Designer Home component catalog available.

HOUSEWORKS, LTD.
Palladian Doors

Stock No.: 6015; 6016
Price: $23.50; $23.50
6015 - Palladian Door - two-panel lower half, acrylic window upper half and fan transom with acrylic pane. For exterior use. Mullions and interior trim. Size: 3-3/4"W x 8-7/8"H. Fits irregular opening: 3-5/16"W x 8-11/16"H x 3/8"D.
6016 - Palladian Double Entry Door - two narrow doors with panel lower half, acrylic windows upper half and fan transom with acrylic pane. Hinged to operate separately. For exterior use. Mullions and interior trim. Size: 3-11/16"W x 8-13/16"H. Fits irregular opening: 3-5/16"W x 8-11/16"H x 3/8"D.

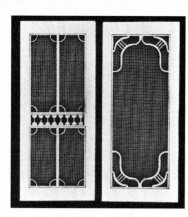

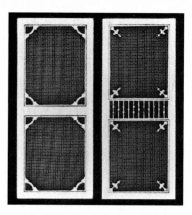

LASER TECH
Laser Cut Victorian Screen Doors
Stock No.: see below
Price: see below
All screen doors are made slightly oversized (2-7/8" by 6-11/16") to fit all doors and can be easily trimmed to fit your door openings perfectly. Left to right: SD-066-$11.50; SD-065-$11.40; SD-061-$11.40; SD-070-$11.50.

WALMER DOLLHOUSES

Lilliput Deck Door
Stock No.: 1002
Price: See your local dealer.
Dimensions: Fits opening 7-1/4"H x 4-1/4"W; 1/12 scale
Designed for Lilliput dollhouses with mansard roofs (12-1/2°). Features our #1010 Double French Door. Another of the Lilliput Custom components.

WALMER DOLLHOUSES

Hampton Oval Door
Stock No.: 1013
Price: See your local dealer.
Dimensions: Fits opening 7-1/2"H x 3-5/16"W; 1/12 scale
Oversize Victorian hooded pediment characterizes the Hampton Collection. Pane removes for finishing. Companion products: Hampton working and non-working windows with adjustable interior frames (#2070 & #2071). Designer Home catalog available.

WALMER DOLLHOUSES

Oval Door
Stock No.: 1119
Price: See your local dealer.
Dimensions: Fits opening 7-1/16"H x 3-1/16"W; 1/12 scale
A Lilliput dollhouse custom component. Removable pane.

WALMER DOLLHOUSES

Victorian Double Door
Stock No.: 1007
Price: See your local dealer.
Dimensions: Fits opening 7-7/16"H x 3-1/16"W; 1/12 scale
Part of Designer Home Victorian Collection.
Companion products: Non-working and working, standard and long slim windows and double working windows (#2066N, #2067W, #2068N, #2069W and #2074W respectively). Designer Home catalog available.

WALMER DOLLHOUSES
Ashton Door
Stock No.: 1020
Price: See your local dealer.
Dimensions: Fits opening 7-3/8"H x 5-7/16"W; 1/12 scale
Elegant six-panel entry door with scroll pediment. Companion product #2052 Ashton Window Pediment and #2029 and #2030 Working and Non-Working Windows.

WALMER DOLLHOUSES
Single French Door
Double French Door

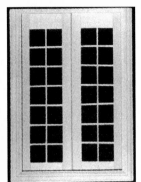

Stock No.: 1011; 1012
Price: See your local dealer.
Dimensions: 1/12 scale
Single fits opening 7-9/16"H x 3-1/16"H.
Double fits opening 7-9/16"H x 5-1/16"W.
Both doors have removable mullions. The
#1011 Double Door used in Sophistikit
Deck Door #1009. French Door #1010
without mullions is a Lilliput Custom
component.

WALMER DOLLHOUSES

Windsor Door

Stock No.: 1021
Price: See your local dealer.
Dimensions: Fits opening 7-9/16"H x 3-1/8"W;
1/12 scale
Architecturally detailed with reeding, dentil, plinth
and capital blocks. Mullions are removable.
Companion products: Windsor working and non-
working windows and casement windows (#2078,
#2079 & #2080, respectively). Designer Home
catalog available.

WALMER DOLLHOUSES
Victorian Door

Stock No.: 1008
Price: See your local dealer.
Dimensions: Fits opening 8-5/16"H x 3-7/16"W; 1/12 scale
Part of the Designer Home Victorian collection. Companion products:
working and non-working standard and long, slim windows. Designer
Home catalog available.

WALMER DOLLHOUSES
Hogarth Door

Stock No.: 1022
Price: See your local dealer.
Dimensions: Fits opening 8-3/4"H x 3-3/8"W; 1/12 scale
Hogarth Door is a Designer Home exclusive design. This
distinctive door includes a matching arched exterior frame.
Companion product: Hogarth Window with shutters (#2077N).
Designer Home catalog available.

WALMER DOLLHOUSES

Shop Door

Stock No.: 1014
Price: See your local dealer.
Dimensions: Fits opening 7-1/16"H x 3-1/16"W;
1/12 scale
Exclusive Designer Home product. Removable
pane. Designer Home catalog available.

WALMER DOLLHOUSES
Colonial Six-Panel Door
With Sidelights

Stock No.: 1004
Price: See your local dealer.
Dimensions: Fits opening 7-7/16"H x
6-5/16"W; 1/12 scale
One of the Designer Home Colonial
collection. Companion products: Colonial
working and non-working window and working
double window (#2064N, #2065W, #2073W).
Designer Home catalog available.

Hardware & Metal Parts

GREENLEAF PRODUCTS

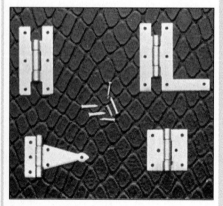

Miniature Brass Hinges

Stock No.: 9009H, 9009HL, 9009T, 9009B
Price: $4.50
The doors in your dollhouse can be hinged to open with these perfectly scaled hinges, four to a package complete with brass nails. Four styles: B, H, HL, and T.

HOUSEWORKS, LTD.

Brass Door Knobs

Stock No.: 1146; 1145
Price: $2.00; $2.25
1146 - Traditional Plain Brass Round Door Knob - with separate back plate for interior doors. 6 sets/pkg.
1145 - Etched Brass Victorian Door Knob - with separate back plate for interior doors. 4 sets/pkg.

HOUSEWORKS, LTD.

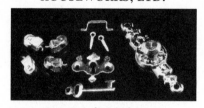

Assorted Hardware

Stock No.: 1103; 1104; 1105
1103: Gold-Plated Brass Chippendale Keyplate w/Key - six sets/pkg., $1.95.
1104 - Brass Furniture Casters - 12 pcs./pkg. $4.25.
1105 - Gold-Plated Brass Round Doorknob - 2 pcs./pkg., $1.95

HOUSEWORKS, LTD.

Crystal Hardware

1142 - Crystal Classic Knob with Key - $1.95.
1143 - Crystal Opryland Knob with Key - $1.95.
1140 - Crystal Provincial Knob - $1.95.
1144 - Crystal Door Knob - $3.50.
1141 - Crystal Medallion Knob - $1.95.
All come two to a package, except for 1144 which has six per package.

HOUSEWORKS, LTD.

Assorted Pulls

Stock No.: 1123; 1124; 1127
1123 - Gold-Plated Brass Window Handle Pull - 8 pcs./pkg., $2.50.
1124 - Gold-Plated Brass Chippendale Drawer Pull - 6 pcs./pkg., $1.95.
1127 - Gold-Plated Brass Round Cabinet Pull - 6pcs./pkg., $1.95.

HOUSEWORKS, LTD.

Assorted Knobs

Stock No.: 1115; 1114; 1116
1115 - White Enameled Brass Knob - 6pcs./pkg., $1.95.
1114 - Gold-Plated Brass Knob & Keyplate w/Key - 2 pcs./pkg., $1.95.
1116 - Gold-Plated Brass Knob - 6 pcs./pkg., $1.95.

HOUSEWORKS, LTD.

Gold-Plated Brass Hinges

Stock No.: 1130; 1131
1130 - Gold-Plated Brass "T" Hinge - 4pcs. w/24 nails, $2.25.
1131 - Gold-Plated Brass "H" Hinge - 4 pcs. w/24 nails, $2.25.

HOUSEWORKS, LTD.

Lock and Door Handle

Stock No.: 1134; 1139
1134 - Gold-Plated Brass "Americana" Lock w/Key - 1 set/pkg., $2.25. 1139 - Gold-Plated Brass "Opryland" Door Handle w/Key - 2 pcs./pkg., $1.75.

HOUSEWORKS, LTD.

Brass Pointed Nails

Stock No.: 1128; 1129
P1128 - Brass Pointed Pin-Nails - 6mm long, 100 pcs./pkg., $2.50. 1129 - Brass Pointed Nails - 4mm long, 100 pcs./pkg., $2.50.

HOUSEWORKS, LTD.

Door Knocker and Bell Pulls

Stock No.: 1107; 1108
1107 - Gold-Plated Door Knocker - 1pc./pkg., $1.95. 1108 - Gold-Plated Brass Bell Pull - 2 pcs./pkg., $1.50.

HOUSEWORKS, LTD.

Door Pull and Knobs

Stock No.: 1110; 1111
1110 - Gold-Plated Brass Door Pull - 2 pcs./pkg., $1.50. 1111- Gold-Plated Brass Medallion Knob - 2 pcs./pkg., $1.75

HOUSEWORKS, LTD.

Drawer Pull and Hinge

Stock No.: 1117; 1119; 1120
1117 - Gold-Plated Brass Double Flower Drawer Pull - 4 pcs./pkg., $1.50. 1119 - Gold-Plated Brass Square Drawer Pull - 4 pcs./pkg., $1.50. 1120 - Gold-Plated Brass Square Hinge - 4 pcs./pkg., $1.75.

HOUSEWORKS, LTD.

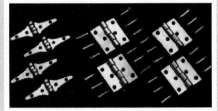

Gold-Plated Brass Hinges

Stock No.: 1121; 1122
1121 - Gold-Plated Brass Triangle Hinge - 4 pcs./pkg., $1.75. 1122 - Gold-Plated Brass Butt Hinge - 4 pcs. w/24 nails, $2.25.

MINIATURE HOUSE

HOUSEWORKS, LTD.

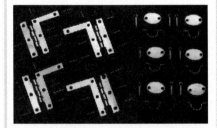

Hinge and Drawer Pull

Stock No.: 1132; 1133
1132 - Gold-Plated Brass "HL" Hinge - 4 pcs. w/28 nails, $2.50. 1133 - Gold-Plated Brass Hepplewhite Drawer Pull - 6 sets/pkg., $1.95.

Miniature Brass Door Knobs and Locks

MH5528 - Door knobs with key plates and keys. 2/pk., gold-plated brass, $1.95;
MH5578 - Victorian door knobs with keys, 2/pk., gold-plated brass, $1.75;
MH5612 - Ornate door knobs, 4/pk., polished brass, $3.20;
MH5568 - Box lock with key, 1/pk., gold-plated brass, $2.25;
MH5606 - Door knobs with plates, 4/pk., polished brass, $3.20;
MH5608 - Door knobs with keyholes, 4/pk., polished brass, $2.98.

HOUSEWORKS, LTD.

S-Hooks

Stock No.: 1101; 1102
1101 - Black-Enameled Brass - 4 pcs./pkg., $1.50.
1102 - Gold-Plated Brass - 4 pcs./pkg., $1.50.

MINIATURE HOUSE

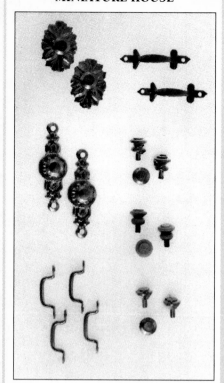

MINIATURE HOUSE

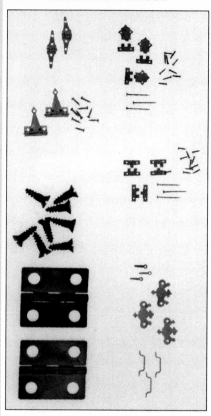

Miniature Brass Door Knobs and Pulls

MH5546 - Window pull handles, 6/pk., gold-plated brass, $2.50;
MH5510 - Colonial door knobs, 2/pk., gold-plated brass, $1.95;
MH5522 - Medallion door knobs, 2/pk., gold-plated brass, $1.75;
MH5554 - Round cabinet pulls, 6/pk., polished brass, $1.95;
MH5530 - White enameled round knobs, 6/pk., $1.95;
MH5532 - Round knobs, 6/pk., gold-plated brass, $1.95;
MH5520 - Door pulls, 2/pk., gold-plated brass, $1.50.

Miniature Brass Hinges and Pulls

MH5646 - Offset hinges with nails, 6/pk., polished brass, $3.50;
MH5644 - Flush hinges with nails, 4/pk., polished brass, $3.50;
MH5548 - Chippendale drawer pulls, 6/pk., gold-plated brass, $1.95;
MH5542 - Triangle hinges, 4/pk., gold-plated brass, $1.75;
MH5560 - Strap hinges with nails, 4/pk., polished brass, $2.25;
MH5672 - Dollhouse roof hinges with screws, 2/pk., satin-finished brass, $3.

JUST GETTING INTO

DOLLHOUSE

MINIATURES?

If you have a question

about dollhouse

miniatures, stop by

your local retail outlet

and ask the expert

behind the counter.

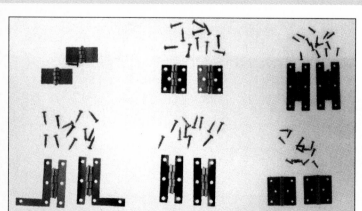

MINIATURE HOUSE
Miniature Brass Hinges.

MH5540 - Square hinges, 4/pk., gold-plated brass, $1.75;
MH5544 - "Butt" hinges with nails, 4/pk., polished brass, $2.25;
MH5666 - "H" hinges with nails, 4/pk., satin-finished brass, $3.50;
MH5562 - "H" hinges with nails, 4/pk., polished brass, $2.25;
MH5564 - "HL" hinges with nails, 4/pk., polished brass, $2.49;
MH5640 - "Butt" hinges with nails, 4/pk., satin-finished brass, $3.50.

Prices are approximate and subject to change

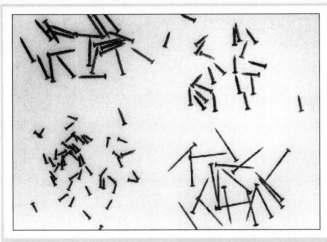

MINIATURE HOUSE
Miniature Brass Nails

MH5680 - Mini nails, 3/8" long, 100/pk., $3;
MH5678 - Mini nails, 3/32" long, 100/pk., $3;
MH5558 - Mini nails, 1/8" long, 100/pk., $2.25;
MH5556 - Mini nails, 1/4" long, 100/pk., $2.25.

OLD MOUNTAIN MINIATURES
Harmony Forge Hardware

Price: See your local dealer.
Dimensions: 1/12 scale
We proudly present more than 100 items in
1/12 scale—collector-quality reproductions of
searly-American hardware, fireplace accessories and
lighting devices. "Forged" Britannia alloy pieces
duplicate the rough surface created by the blacksmith's
hammer. Finished in a burnished satin black that will not
chip or peel but may be painted over if desired. Dealer
inquiries welcome.

SCIENTIFIC MODELS, INC.
Realife Miniatures Hardware

Stock No.: 801-856
Price: $2.99 - $4.29
Dimensions: 1" scale
A wide range of brass
finishing hardware and
accessories authentically
reproduced in 1" scale.
These items will add that
special touch to your
dollhouses and furniture.

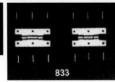
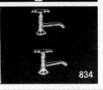

WALMER DOLLHOUSES

Sliding Door Bolt

Stock No.: 2323
Price: See your local dealer.
Dimensions: 1/12 scale
Exclusive Designer Home design, the bolt really
works!

WALMER DOLLHOUSES

Classic Brass Door Plate Set

Stock No.: 9305
Dimensions: 1/12 scale
This Designer Home exclusive is solid brass
featuring two door knobs, two back plates and
threaded rod. A beautiful feature for any home.

WALMER DOLLHOUSES

Victorian French Door Handles

Stock No.: 2324
Price: See your local dealer.
Dimensions: 1/12 scale
Designer Home exclusive hardware offers these
graceful brass-plated French door handles for
interior or exterior use.

WALMER DOLLHOUSES

WALMER DOLLHOUSES

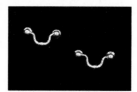

Drop Handle Drawer Pull

Stock No.: 105
Dimensions: 1/12 scale
A Designer Home exclusive, these perfectly scaled pulls are solid brass and the drop handles work. Add a touch of class to your furniture.

WALMER DOLLHOUSES

Cast Iron Faucets & Drain Pipe

Stock No.: 2321
Price: See your local dealer.
Dimensions: 1/12 scale
A Designer Home exclusive! Two faucets and drain pipe for the garden shed, workshop, garage or 19th century kitchen.

MINIATURE CORNER

Victorian Iron Fence

Stock No.: MG500/700
Dimensions: 1:12
All-metal Victorian fence and eave trim. Fence is 3-1/2" high, eave and balcony trim, 2" high. Sold in 4" and 6" sections. Posts separate. Working latch gate. See your local dealer.

Designer Home Decorative Hardware

All solid brass, Designer Home exclusives: 9401 - Georgian Door Knocker; 9402 - Victorian Door Plate Set (2 knobs, back plates and threaded rod); 9403 - Brass Door Kick Plate.

KIMBERLY HOUSE MINIATURES

Kimberly Grape Arbor Kit

Stock No.: KGA-101
Price: $42.52, plus shipping.
Dimensions:
8-3/4"W x 8"D x 8-1/2"H
Create realistic, attractive landscaping. Kit includes all materials for complete arbor as shown, including instructions. Easy-to-assemble precut wood frame and slat redwood flooring. All vine materials and ample grape supplies. Precut redwood with instructions for patio table and benches. Perfect accent for your dollhouse or alone in diorama or vignette. Shown in Dollhouses to Dream Houses, Book 2, in landscaping chapter. See your dealer or write Kimberly House.

Landscaping Materials

MODEL BUILDERS SUPPLY
Landscape and Garden Supplies

MBS developed its wide range of materials many years ago for professional model-makers, where quality and authenticity are paramount. Our bushes, hedges, ground cover, tree foliage and grasses are all permanently colored and nondrying, can be squeezed and handled without damage. Our tree frames from 2" to 8" are unique, fully three-dimensional molded plastic. Just push branches to the desired position and apply chosen color and texture of foliage from the 24 types. Numerous grades of gravel, pebbles and rocks also available. See full range in our catalog or at your dealer.

WHAT'S NEXT?

Roll Roofing - Asphalt

Price: $7.14 plus shipping
Dimensions: 6" x 24" sheet
Same material as our asphalt shingles. Use for widow's walks, mansard roofs, flat roofs, driveways and landscaping.

Lumber Supplies

Golf Bag

WORKSHOP WISDOM

A tubular Life Savers container, minus its cap, is a good basis on which to construct a golf bag. The outside of Nancy's was covered with glued-on leather from an old glove, the side pouches being the tips of the glove fingers. The carrying strap is a strip cut from the same glove. The band around the top and bottom are a contrasting color of 1/8" (3mm) wide ribbon. Buckles and loops can be readily bent from paper staples. Make the clubs from shiny paper clip wire with Fimo heads, that stand the bag by the front door or in the corner of the office. Glove fingers can also be used to make purses, chair covers, etc., too.

NANCY BECKER
NORTH BRANCH, MN

Workshop Wisdom *Courtesy of Nutshell News—7/94*

MODEL BUILDERS SUPPLY

Top Quality Basswood Sticks, Strips, Sheets, Dowels, Clapboard & Angles

1/16" sq. to 3/8" sq.; 1/32", 1/16", 3/32" & 1/8" x 3" and 4" widths, 1/8" to 1/2" diameter; all 24" long. Plywood too!

NORTHEASTERN SCALE MODELS, INC.
Laser Cut Trim

The laser allows us to manufacture intricate wood trims for dollhouse and miniature projects. All items are in 1" =1' scale, except as noted. One piece per package except as noted. Basswood.

GBC-1 1250 Gingerbread Trim - $6
GBD-1 1251 Gingerbread Trim - $6
APX-4 1233 Apex Trim - $5.18
APX-3 1232 Apex Trim - $6
APX-5 1235 Apex Trim - $5.18
RFB-1 1261 Roof Finial - $1.85
AGC-1 1270 Gingerbread/Apex
Combination (2 per pkg.) - $14.50

Also available in 1/2" scale as follows:
GBC-1A 1252 Gingerbread Trim - $3.25
APX-4A 1234 Apex Trim - $3.30
APX-5A 1236 Apex Trim - $3.30
RFA-1A 1262 Roof Finial - $1.30
RFB-1 1263 Roof Finial - $1.30
AGC-1A 1271 Gingerbread/Apex
Combination (2 per pkg.) - $9.20

NORTHEASTERN SCALE MODELS, INC.
Laser Cut Trim

PBL-1 1201 Porch Baluster - Assembled with top and bottom rails - $21.75
PBL-2 1202 Porch Baluster - Assembled with top and bottom rails - $21.75
PBL-3 1203 Porch Baluster - Assembled with top and bottom rails - $21.75
GBA-1 1210 Gingerbread Trim - $4 (1)
GBB-1 1211 Gingerbread Trim - $3.40 (1)

BRA-1 1220 Bracket - $2.35 (4)
BRB-1 1221 Bracket - $2.35 (4)
BRC-1 1222 Bracket - $2.35 (4)
BRD-1 1223 Bracket - $2.35 (4)
BRE-1 1223 Bracket - $2.35(4)
APX-1 1230 Apex Trim - $3.80
APX-2 1231 Apex Trim - $3.80

MM	►	.75	1.0		1.5	2.0		3.0	4.0		5.0	6.0	8.0		10.0	12.5		25.0	50.0		
▼	IN.	1/32	.040	3/64	1/16	5/64	3/32	1/8	5/32	3/16	.200	1/4	5/16	3/8	.400	1/2	3/4	1	2	3	4
	.012	.16																			
.5	.020	.16	.16	.16	.16	.20	.20	.20	.22												
.75	1/32	.16	.16	.16	.16	.20	.20	.20	.23	.23	.23	.28	.31	.45	.51	.51	.51	.58	1.08	1.45	1.90
1.0	.040		.21	.21	.21	.21	.21	.21	.25	.25	.25	.28	.31	.45	.51	.51	.51	.58	1.14	1.45	1.90
	3/64			.23	.23	.23	.23	.23	.28	.28	.28	.36	.40	.45	.51	.51	.51	.63	1.39	1.70	2.21
1.5	1/16				.23	.23	.23	.28	.28	.31	.31	.40	.40	.51	.58	.58	.69	.83	1.39	1.70	2.21
2.0	5/64					.23	.28	.28	.28	.31	.31	.40	.40	.51	.58	.58	.69	.83	1.45	1.84	2.59
	3/32						.28	.28	.28	.31	.31	.40	.45	.58	.58	.63	.69	.83	1.45	1.84	2.59
3.0	1/8							.28	.36	.38	.38	.45	.45	.58	.58	.76	.89	.94	1.59	2.02	2.91
4.0	5/32								.36	.38	.38	.45	.51	.58	.58	.76	.89	.94	1.77	2.09	2.91
	3/16									.45	.45	.51	.58	.74	.76	.83	.93	1.01	1.77	2.28	3.22
5.0	.200										.45	.51	.58	.74	.76	.83	.93	1.08	2.02	2.59	3.80
6.0	1/4											.58	.58	.81	.81	.94	1.01	1.27	2.02	2.59	3.80
8.0	5/16												.83	.94	.94	1.01	1.10	1.27	2.21	3.04	4.23
	3/8													.94	.94	1.01	1.10	1.27	2.21	3.04	4.23
10.0	400														.94	1.01	1.10	1.27	2.35	3.36	4.74
12.5	1/2															1.01	1.10	1.32	2.53	3.47	4.88
	3/4																1.27	1.38	2.53	3.85	5.06
25.	1																	1.59	3.16	4.37	5.50
50.	2																		6.33	8.60	10.63

NORTHEASTERN SCALE MODELS, INC.
Wood Strips and Sheets

Stock No.: see below
Price: see below
Dimensions: 1" scale
Tolerances: Wood strips up to 1" wide are cut to precise dimensions. Sheets 2" wide or more are cut to a close tolerance of 1/8" (3mm) plus or minus. All strips, sheets and structural shapes are 22" long or more. Finish: Because of the inherent character of wood and the tooling employed in cutting, most strips and sheets have one surface smoother than the other. Modelers are advised to inspect stock to take advantage of this. Shaded spaces indicate sizes that are available in basswood or mahogany.

CLASSICS BY HANDLEY

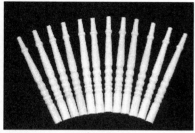

Balusters

Stock No.: CLA70201
Price: $2.25
Dimensions: 1/4"W x 2-5/8"L
These detailed spindles create a very distinctive front porch or staircase. Total of 12 per package.

Millwork

CLASSICS BY HANDLEY

Balusters

Stock No.: CLA70202
Price: $3.98
Dimensions: 1/4"W x 3-1/8"L
Highly-detailed balusters with dowel stub to stabilize installation. Rounded cap makes spindles work well as newel posts. Total of 12 per package.

CLASSICS BY HANDLEY

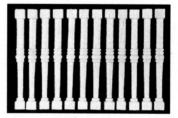

Balusters

Stock No.: CLA77025
Price: $3.50
Dimensions: 3/16"W x 2-5/8"L
Fine detailing and square bases on these spindles finish a staircase or railing. Total of 12 unfinished wood spindles per package.

CLASSICS BY HANDLEY

Balusters

Stock No.: CLA70207
Price: $3.79
Dimensions: 3/16"W x 2-7/16"L
Unusual rounded cap and high detail make these balusters a good choice. Could be used as a small newel post. Total of 12 unfinished wood balusters per package.

CLASSICS BY HANDLEY

Balusters

Stock No.: CLA70209
Price: $3.98
Dimensions: 3/16"W x 2-9/16"L
Detailing and symmetrical style add charm to these balusters. Total of 12 per package.

CLASSICS BY HANDLEY

Balusters

Stock No.: CLA70229
Price: $3.89
Dimensions: 3/16"W x 2-1/2"L
Fine detailing and square bases on these spindles finish a staircase or railing. Total of 12 unfinished wood balusters per package.

CLASSICS BY HANDLEY

Balusters

Stock No.: CLA70235
Price: $4.29
Dimensions: 3/16"W x 2-1/2"L
These spindles have dainty, finely-turned detailing. Total of 12 per package.

Prices are approximate and subject to change

CLASSICS BY HANDLEY

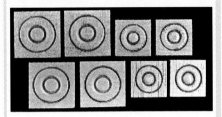

Corner Blocks

Stock No.: CLA70236 (3/4"); CLA70265 (5/8")
Price: $1.75, 3/4" sq.; $1.75, 5/8" sq.
A distinctive addition to trim work on many projects. Four unfinished blocks per package.

CLASSICS BY HANDLEY

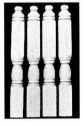

Newel Posts

Stock No.: CLA70200
Price: $3.25
Dimensions: 7/16"W x 3-11/16"L
Distinctive styling. Posts match the newel posts on CLA70252 Stair Kit. Four posts per package.

CLASSICS BY HANDLEY

Porch Fence

Stock No.: CLA70241
Price: $7.25
Dimensions: 2-1/2"H x 11-3/8"L
Porch fence is assembled and ready to use. Made of unfinished wood. Three per package.

CLASSICS BY HANDLEY

Porch Posts

Stock No.: CLA70210
Price: $5.95
Dimensions: 7/16"W x 9"L
These wood posts are great to use with a lower porch roof. Four posts per package.

CLASSICS BY HANDLEY

Porch Posts

Stock No.: CLA70269
Price: $5.95
Dimensions: 1/2"W x 11"L
These wood posts have finely-turned detail work. Four posts per package.

CLASSICS BY HANDLEY

Porch Posts

Stock No.: CLA77010
Price: $4.25
Dimensions: 7/16"W x 12"L
These wood porch posts are designed in a casual style. Four posts per package.

CLASSICS BY HANDLEY

Spindles

Stock No.: CLA70226; CLA70227; CLA70228
Price: $4.10
Dimensions: 14"W x 1-1/8"H
A perfect touch of Victorian detailing to finish your dollhouse or miniature construction. Total of 12 unfinished wood spindles per package.

CLASSICS BY HANDLEY

Staircase Spindles

Stock No.: CLA70246
Price: $3.50
Dimensions: 3/16"W x 2-5/8"L
Lovely spindles enhance a formal staircase or can create an outstanding porch. Total of 12 unfinished spindles per package.

CLASSICS BY HANDLEY

Traditional Newel Posts

Stock No.: CLA77012
Price: $2.35
Dimensions: 7/16"W x 3-7/16L
These traditional wood newel posts are finely turned and highly detailed. Four per package.

CLASSICS BY HANDLEY

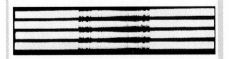

Veranda Corner Posts

Stock No.: CLA77010
Price: $4.25
Dimensions: 1/2"W x 12"L
The perfect way to beautifully finish your porch. Four posts per package.

HOUSEWORKS, LTD.

Classic Stair Rail

Stock No.: 7220
Price: $3.95
Elegant, classic rail to match #7205 and #7204 Centurion newel posts. Grooved to accept #7202 Centurion baluster. 1" scale. Set includes square bottom rail. Two sets per package. Top rail size: 1/4"H x 1/4"W x 18"L; bottom rail size: 5/32"H x 5/16"W x 18"L.

HOUSEWORKS, LTD.

Porch Spindles

Stock No.: 7009
Price: $3.50
Dimensions: 7/32"W x 2-5/8"L
These multi-purpose spindles can be used on the interior or exterior of the house and even in the yard or walkway as fence spindles. 12 per package.

HOUSEWORKS, LTD.

Veranda Spindle

Stock No.: 7029
Price: $4.95
Dimensions: 2"L x 3/8"W
Completes your front porch or stairway. 12 per package.

HOUSEWORKS, LTD.

Porch Railing Set

Stock No.: 7011
Price: $5.50
Includes curved top rail and squared bottom rail. Top: 7/16"W x 7/16"H x 18"L. Bottom: 7/16"W x 3/8"H x 18"L. Both grooved to accept 7025 and 7009 spindles easily. 2 sets per pkg.

HOUSEWORKS, LTD.

Assorted Posts

Stock No.: 7030; 7010
Price: $5.50; $5.95
Dimensions: 12"L x 7/16"W; 12"L x 7/16"W
7030 - Porch Post - 4 per pkg.
7010 - Veranda Corner Post - though the decorative posts are excellent for your veranda, they are most commonly used on the porch from floor to ceiling. 4 per pkg.

HOUSEWORKS, LTD.

Balusters and Newel Posts

A. 7202 - Centurion Baluster - 12 per pkg. Finely detailed thin stair spindle with square base and pointed top. Size 2-5/8"H x 5/32"W x 5/32"D. $4.25.
B. 7203 - Traditional Baluster - 12 per pkg. Double urn design, thin stair spindle with square base and top. Size: 2-5/8"H x 3/16"W x 3/16"D. $4.95.
C. 7204 - Narrow Centurion Newel Post - 6 per pkg. Thin, finely detailed newel post with finial top to match #7202 spindles. Size: 3-1/2"H x 5/16"W x 5/16"D. $3.75.
D. 7205 - Centurion Newel Post - 6 per pkg. Heavier version of #7204 newel post. Size: 3-1/2"H x 3/8"W x 3/8"D. $4.25.
E. 7206 - Thin Classic Newel Post - 6 per pkg. Simple design narrow newel post with flat finial top. Size: 3-1/2"H x 1/4"W x 1/4"D. $4.95.

HOUSEWORKS, LTD.

Wood Head Blocks

Stock No.: 7064
Price: $2.95
Dimensions: 9/16" square
Decorative square trim used most commonly on the corners of door frames. Matches 7044 trim and 6025 door. 12 per pkg.

HOUSEWORKS, LTD.

Balusters

Stock No.: 7025
Price: $3.95
Dimensions: 3/16"W x 2-1/2"L
Square base turned baluster for porch or stairs. 12 per package.

HOUSEWORKS, LTD.

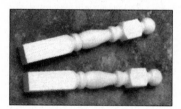

Newel Post

Stock No.: 7012
Price: $3.95
Dimensions: 3-1/2"L x 7/16"W
Handcrafted, turned posts for stairs or porch. 6 per package.

HOUSEWORKS, LTD.

Classic Porch Rail

Stock No.: 7211
Price: $3.95
Simple, classic porch rail with square bottom rail. Both pieces grooved to accept all Houseworks spindles except #7029 veranda spindle. Two sets per pkg. Top rail size: 1/4"H x 3/8"W x 18"L; bottom rail size: 3/16"H x 3/8"W x 18"L.

QUAD COMPANY
tiny turnings

Stock No.: 2000, 4000, 1000, and 3000 (top to bottom)
Price: $6 per package
Dimensions: 1/8" to 1/4" in diameter, 6-1/4" to 6-3/4" long. Finely detailed hardwood turnings with a unique interlocking design. Use for 1/4", 1/2" or 1" scale. Full line of 1" scale furniture kits available priced $3.00 to $18.00. Send LSASE for brochure.

WALMER DOLLHOUSES
Gingerbread Trims

Price: See your local dealer.
Dimensions: All 24"L; 1/12 scale
5245 - Interior or Door & Window Frame;
5249 - Sophistikit Gingerbread; 5250 -
Scroll Trim; 5257 - Large Scallop; 5259 -
Ocean Spray; 5260 - Hole & Slit; 5261 -
Dentil Fascia; 5262 - Dentil.

WALMER DOLLHOUSES

Assembled Rails

Price: See your local dealer.
Dimensions: All 12"L; 1/12 scale
Assembled Rails #3032, #3032A (for Widow's Walk,
decks, etc.) and #3033. Use with Designer Home
newel posts #3006 and #3007 or between Porch
Posts #3001, #3002 or #3003.

START A NEW HOBBY AND MEET NEW FRIENDS: JOIN A MINIATURES CLUB!

WISCONSIN CRAFTS

Quality Craftwoods

Lengths of wood, measuring 24" long, come in
basswood, maple, walnut, cherry, red oak and
butternut. The pieces are available in 2", and 4"
widths and come in various thicknesses for
building to scale. Both sides of each board are
pre-sanded.

Modeling Compounds

DEE'S DELIGHTS, INC.

FIMO

Price: See your local dealer.
Dimensions: 45 colors and three sizes available.
Fimo is a fine-grained modeling compound that
hardens easily in a home oven. We import Fimo
and sell through dealers only. Offering three sizes
of blocks, kits and lacquer. The miniaturist's first
choice. See your local dealer.

EBERHARD FABER GMBH
FIMO Modeling Material

Stock No.: 8000
Price: see your dealer
Dimensions: see below
55 by 55 by 15 mm/65 g small block, 165 by
55 by 30 mm/350 g large block. FIMO, the
fantastic and most popular modeling material,
is the leading product of its kind in Europe. It's
versatile and easy to handle and hardens in the
oven at 265° (20 to 30 minutes). Available in
42 brilliant colors, it's ideal to create the finest
decorative accessories for your dollhouse and
to make exciting and imaginative objects
(miniatures, figures, fashion jewelry,
decorations, pictures, nameplates
and a lot more).

MODEL BUILDERS SUPPLY
Modeling, Mold and Casting Compounds

Modeling Compounds: Cernit - the premier modeling material with the porcelain effect, hardens in hot water or oven. Miliput - the famous two-part mix epoxy modeling compound allows about five hours working time. Klean Klay - non-drying, sulfur-free modeling clay will not contaminate mold compounds. Mold Compounds: Vinamold, Plasticast R.T.V. - two-part, cold set silicone rubber compounds, fast cure and thixotropic for "skin molds." Casting Materials: Alumilite and Plasticast - plastic casting plastic, liquid to solid in three and four minutes. MBS Casting Resin - superior, clear casting resin for embedments, dyes. MBS Casting Plasters - professional quality, slow and fast sets. Durina - instant powdered papier mache, microwave to set. Saws, sands and paints easily. Microballoons - lightweight filler for castings. Brochure/catalog, $2.

T'NEE PRODUCTS
Polymer Clay

Price: $10 sample box, ppd.
Introducing the new Polymer Clays!
Friendly Clay - 24 colors,
featuring the new China Doll Flesh;
24 pre-made design "Millefiori Canes";
Granitex Clay - eight colors, looks like stone;
Shaped Sticks - many designs available.
Wholesale and retail.

Friendly Clay™

Millefiori Cane
SLICE & BAKE

"CHOP-M-STIX"

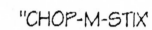

GRANITEX

ALESSIO MINIATURES

Cove Dentil Molding

Stock No.: 23A
Price: $2
Dimensions: 3/32" x 1/4"; 22"L
This molding provides the perfect finishing touch for the top of your room, porch or roof line.

Moldings

ALESSIO MINIATURES

Dentil Molding

Stock No.: 23
Price: $1.10
Dimensions: 3/32" x 1/4"; 22"L
This dentil molding is to be used on roof eaves and around the tops of rooms.

ALESSIO MINIATURES

Dentil Moldings

Stock No.: 19
Price: $1.10 per length
Dimensions: 24" lengths; 1/8" x 3/8"
Dentil moldings to be used on roof eaves, around tops of rooms, etc. Pine. American-made.

ALESSIO MINIATURES

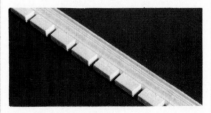

Large Crown Dentil Molding

Price: $2 per length
Dimensions: 1/8" x 3/8"; 22"L
Dentil moldings to be used on roof eaves, around tops of rooms, etc. Pine. American-made.

CLASSICS BY HANDLEY

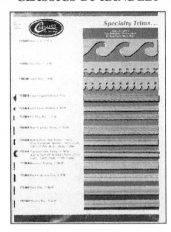

Decorative Wood Trim

Dimensions: 24"L
Variety of gingerbreads, cornices and other trims.
Uses are limited only by one's imagination.
70312 - $2.59; 70301 - $2.98; 70300 - $2.98;
70302 - $1.98; 70303 - $1.49; 70308 - $1.49;
70309 - $1.49; 70310 - $1.59; 70311 - $1.98;
70304 - $1.59; 70305 - $1.59; 70306 - $1.59;
70307 - $1.59.

CLASSICS BY HANDLEY

Decorative Wood Trim

Dimensions: 24"L
Variety of gingerbreads, cornices and other trims.
Uses are limited only by one's imagination.
77008 - $1.95; 77067 - $2.10; 77042 - $1.05;
77068 - $2.60; 77047 - $1; 77048 - $.95;
77056 - $.95; 77060 - $2.99; 77062 - $4.99;
77063 - $3.25; 77065 - $3.25; 77069 - $.95;
77055 - $1.35.

CLASSICS BY HANDLEY

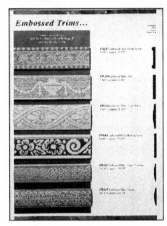

Embossed Trims

Dimensions: Approximately 23-1/2"L
Attractive variety of embossed trims. Uses are
limited only by one's imagination.
78137 - $2.98; 78139 - $2.98; 78141 - $2.98;
78143 - $2.98; 78145 - $2.49; 78147 - $2.49.

CLASSICS BY HANDLEY

Embossed Trims

Dimensions: Approximately 23-1/2"L
Attractive variety of embossed trims. Uses are
limited only by one's imagination. 78109 - $1.98;
78113 - $1.98; 78103 - $1.98; 78159 - $1.49;
78163 - $1.98; 78165 - $1.98; 78167 - $1.98;
78171 - $1.89; 78153 - 1.89; 78135 - $1.89;
78127 - $1.89.

CLASSICS BY HANDLEY

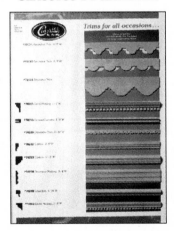

Decorative Wood Trim

Dimensions: 24"L
Variety of gingerbreads, cornices and other trims.
Uses are limited only by one's imagination.
72131 - $2.19; 72132 - $1.95; 72133 - $2.79;
70215 - $2.79; 70216 - $1.69; 70225 - $3.29;
70232 - $1.69; 70233 - $1.98; 70238 - $1.98;
70240 - $1.39; 70262 - $2.79.

CLASSICS BY HANDLEY

Decorative Wood Trim

Dimensions: 24"L
Variety of gingerbreads, cornices and other trims.
Uses are limited only by one's imagination.
70263 - $3.19; 70264 - $2.60; 70266 - $3.49;
70268 - $1.75; 70271 - $3.49; 70272 - $1.49;
70296 - $1.95; 70295 - $1.80; 70298 - $1.39;
70299 - $1.98; 71381 - $1.10; 71383 - $1.05

NORTHEASTERN SCALE MODELS, INC.
Moulding and Panels (All moulding are 24" long)

Description	Number	Size	Price
QUARTER ROUND	364QRD	3/64	.70
	116QRD	1/16	.75
	564QRD	5/64	.75
	332QRD	3/32	.75
	18QRD	1/8	.90
HALF ROUND	364HRD	3/64	.70
	116HRD	1/16	.75
	564HRD	5/64	.75
	332HRD	3/32	.75
	18HRD	1/8	.90
	532HRD	5/32	.95
	316HRD	3/16	.95
	14HRD	1/4	1.05
ROUNDS	364RND	3/64	.70
	116RND	1/16	.75
	564RND	5/64	.75
	332RND	3/32	.75
	18RND	1/8	.90
COVE	116COV	1/16	.75
	564COV	5/64	.75
	332COV	3/32	.75
	18COV	1/8	.90
	532COV	5/32	.95
	316COV	3/16	.95
	14COV	1/4	1.05
DOUBLE BEAD	364DBL	3/64	.70
	116DBL	1/16	.75
	564DBL	5/64	.75
	332DBL	3/32	.75
	18DBL	1/8	.90
PICTURE FRAMES	PFA-3	3/92	.75
	PFA-4	1/8	.90
	PFA-6	3/16	.95
	PFA-8	1/4	1.05
	PFB-4	1/8	.90
	PFB-6	3/16	.95
	PFB-8	1/4	1.05
	PFC-6	3/16	.95
	PFC-8	1/4	1.05
	PFD-4	1/8	.90
	PFD-6	3/16	.95
	PFE-5	5/32	.95
	PFE-6	3/16	.95
CROWN/ CORNICE	COA-10	5/16	1.05
	COA-16	1/2	1.40
	COB-8 (1/2" scale)	1/4	.90
CORNER ANGLE	TRA-12	3/8	2.05
	TRA-16	1/2	2.20
CORNER BLOCK	CBA-18	9/16	2.45
	CBB-18	9/16	2.45

Description	Number	Size	Price
BASEBOARD	BBA-8 (1/2" scale)	1/4	.95
	BBA-16	1/2	1.40
	BBB-16	1/2	1.40
	BBC-16	1/2	1.40
	BBD-16	1/2	1.40
CHAIR RAIL	CRA-6	3/16	.90
	CRA-8	1/4	.95
	CRB-8	1/4	.95
SUB-RAIL	HRC-10	5/16	1.05
HAND RAIL	HRA-8	1/4	1.10
	HRA-12	3/8	1.40
	HRA-16	1/2	1.75
HAND RAIL	HRB-10	5/16	1.50
PORCH RAIL TOP	PRA-9	9/32	1.40
PORCH RAIL BOTTOM	PRB-8	1/4	.95
DOOR & WINDOW CASING	DCA-8 (1/2" scale)	1/4	.95
	DCA-16	1/2	1.40
	DCB-8	1/4	.95
	DCB-12	3/8	1.25
	DCC-16	1/2	1.40
	DCD-16	1/2	1.40
	DCE-12	3/8	1.25
	DCF-12	3/8	1.25
	DCG-16	1/2	1.40
JAMB	DJA-16	1/2	1.40
	DJB-16	1/2	1.40
THRESHOLD	THA-24	3/4	2.00
DOOR FRAMES	DFA-14	7/16	1.60
	DFA-20	5/8	1.75
	DFA-24	3/4	1.90
	DFA-14G	7/16	1.60
	DFA-20G	5/8	1.75
	DFA-24G	3/4	1.90
DOOR PANELS Raised on both sides	DPA-32-3	2 3/16 x 3	1.25
	DPA-32-6	2 x 3	1.25
	DPA-48-2	2 3/16 x 3	1.25
	DPA-70-1	2 3/16 x 2 3/16	1.00
WINDOW HEADER	WHA-11	.335	1.20
	WHA-15	.460	1.60
	WHA-16	1/2	1.60
WINDOW JAMB	WJA-11	.335	1.15
	WJA-15	.460	1.45
	WJA-16	1/2	1.45
WINDOW SILL	WSA-16	1/2	1.45
	WSA-20	5/8	1.60

Description	Number	Size	Price
WINDOW SASH	SFA-4	1/8	.90
	SFA-5	5/32	.95
	SFA-5G	5/32G	.95
	SFA-6	3/16	.95
	SFA-8	1/4	1.05
WINDOW OUTSIDE CASING	WCA-12	.335	1.20
	WCA-16	1/2	1.60

HARDWARE pg. 6 in catalog

Description	Number	Size	Price
BUTT HINGES —doz.	HWA-10	5/16 x 3/8	5.75
PIANO HINGE —ea.	HWA-250		9.15
DOOR KNOB/ DUMMY BRASS	HWC-1		3.65
DOOR KNOB WORKING	HWC-2		9.75
DOOR KNOB TEMPLATE	HWC-3		2.90
FLATWIRE		.010 x 1/16	.45 per ft.

MISCELLANEOUS Available in 24" lengths
pg. 6 in catalog

Description	Number	Size	Price
SHUTTER FRAME	SFC-5	5/32	.95
	SFC-6	3/16	.95
SHUTTER STOCK	CLC-5	3 1/2 x 24	4.25
STAIR STRINGER	SRA-14	3/4 x 14	1.25
	SRA-22	3/4 x 22	1.60
STAIR RISER	SRB-20	5/8	.75
STAIR TREAD	SRC-28	7/8	.95
GUTTER	GA-12	3/8	1.60
WAINSCOT TRIM	MMA-6		1.05
	MMB-6		1.05
	MMC-6		1.05
WAINSCOT PANELS (Raised on one side only)	DPB-32-3	2 3/16 x 3	1.25
	DPB-32-6	2 x 3	1.25
	DPB-48-2	2 3/16 x 3	1.25
	DPB-70-1	2 3/16 x 2 3/16	1.00
FLOORING (RANDOM)	1/16 x 3	1/2 x 24	2.65

Prices are approximate and subject to change

CLASSICS BY HANDLEY

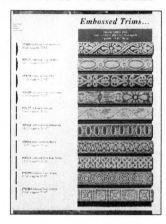

Embossed Trims

Dimensions: Approximately 23-1/2"L
Attractive variety of embossed trims. Uses are limited only by one's imagination.
78121 - $1.89; 78131 - $1.98; 78133 - $1.89;
78129 - $1.89; 78157 - $1.89; 78123 - $1.89;
78161 - $1.89; 78173 - $1.89; 78169 - $1.89;
78125 - $1.89.

HOUSEWORKS, LTD.

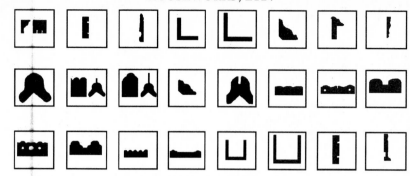

Wood Trims and Mouldings
See your local dealer for sizes and prices.

UNIQUE MINIATURES

Moldings

Dimensions: length, 18"; width varies from 3/8" to 1"
Cast in polyester resin. Can be painted or stained. Moldings can be used as cornices and in conjunction with ceiling applique's. Moldings are ideal for edge trim around a table or cabinet. Many styles to choose from. Send $3 for a complete catalog. Made in USA.

LASER TECH

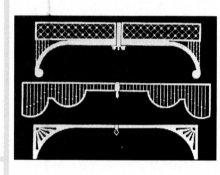

Laser Cut Grilles

Stock No.: see below
Price: see below
Elegant grilles that are made in three pieces to be easily trimmed to fit any porch or room opening.
Top to bottom:
G-031-$11.50;
G-030-$10.45;
SA-035-$8.53 (also available in 1/2" scale).

LASER TECH

Laser Cut Trims

Stock No.: see below
Price: see below
Made of 3/32 basswood. A variety of trims whose uses are limited only by one's imagination. They range in length from 5-3/4" to 12"L.
Top to bottom:
ET-120-$8.35;
RT-130-$3.85;
RT-121-$7.15;
RT-131- $3.85;
GEX-029-$6.05;
GEX-028-$3.40.

ALESSIO MINIATURES

Roofing Materials

Shingles

Price: $2.50 - $3.30 per sq.ft. (approximately)
Dimensions: 1" x 3/4"
American-made shingles in pine, redwood, cedar and hardwood. All shingles are processed by hand to ensure our high quality standards. Also available—our cedar fish-scale and cedar hexagon shingles, as shown in photo. No one makes a higher quality shingle!

CLARE-BELL BRASS WORKS

Rooster Weather Vane

Stock No.: 1910-100
Striking brass weather vanes. All have exquisite details and turn. Catalog, more than 200 items, $2. See your local independent miniatures dealer.

CLARE-BELL BRASS WORKS

Schooner Weather Vane

Stock No.: 1918-100
Catalog, more than 200 items, $2. See your local independent miniatures dealer.

CLARE-BELL BRASS WORKS

Train Weather Vane

Stock No.: 1912-100
Catalog, more than 200 items, $2. See your local independent miniatures dealer.

CLARE-BELL BRASS WORKS

Trotter Weather Vane

Stock No.: 1911-100
Catalog, more than 200 items, $2. See your local independent miniatures dealer.

CLARE-BELL BRASS WORKS

Whale Weather Vane

Stock No.: 1917-100
Catalog, more than 200 items, $2. See your local independent miniatures dealer.

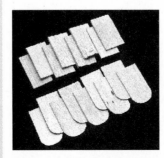

CLASSICS BY HANDLEY
Squarebutt Shingles/Fish Scale Shingles

Stock No.: CLA70276; CLA70277
Price: $2.50; $2.75
CLA70276 - Squarebutt Shingles styled like hand-split shakes. Each package contains 100 pieces and covers about 76 square inches.
CLA70277 - Fish Scale Shingles have a smooth finish. There are 100 pieces per package. Each pack covers about 76 square inches.

CLASSICS BY HANDLEY

Cedar Shingles

Stock No.: CLA70259
Price: $21.50
Dimensions: 3/4"W x 1-1/4"H
These square built shingles add the perfect finishing touch to a dollhouse roof. There are 1,000 pieces per bag. Covers approximately 760 square inches.

DURA-CRAFT, INC.

Plain Shingles

Stock No.: SH70
Price: See your local dealer.
Dimensions: Covers approx. 260 sq. in. per bag
Split redwood shingles with hand-cut look.
350/bag with header.

GREENLEAF PRODUCTS

Wood Shingles

Stock No.: see below
Price: $4.60
Dimensions: see below
Greenleaf's wood veneer shingles come in three shapes: rectangular, fishscale and octagonal. They paint and stain beautifully—choose the style that suits your taste. There are 300 shingles per package, covering 170 square inches; amounts required for Greenleaf houses are printed on the package headers.
9002 rectangular, 9005 fishscale, 9006 octagonal.

CORONA CONCEPTS
Birch Shingles

Stock No.: 4701; 4702; 4703
Dimensions: 1-1/2" x 3/4"; 1" scale
Birch veneer shingles can be painted or stained to add that special detail—to turn your dollhouse into a dream house. Each bag contains 400 shingles which covers 225 square inches. Easy-to-follow instructions are printed on the inside of each header. See your local dealer.

HOUSEWORKS, LTD.
Shingles

Stock No.: 7103; 7104; 7105; 7106
Price: $26.95; ($18.95 for 7106)
7103 - Octagon Butt Shingles - hand split cedar shakes. 1,000 pcs. per pkg. Covers 760 square inches. Can be reversed for use as square butts. Same as 7003. Shingle size; 3/4" x 1-1/4".
7104 - Square Butt Shingles - classic hand split cedar shakes. 1,000 pcs. per pkg. Covers 760 square inches. Same as 7004. Shingle size: 3/4" x 1-1/4"
7105 - Fishscale Shingles - half circle wooden butts. 1,000 pcs. per pkg. Covers 760 square inches. Same as 7005. Shingle size: 23/32" x 1-1/4"
7106 - Square Butt Shingles - Douglas fir shingles taken from the hearts of U.S. forests. 1,000 pcs. per pkg. Covers 760 square inches. Shingle size: 3/4" x 1-3/16".

HOUSEWORKS, LTD.
Shingles

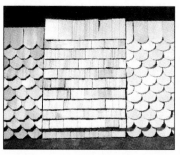

Stock No.: 7003; 7004; 7005
Price: $3.25; $3.25; $3.50
Pictured left to right.
7003 - Octagonal Butt Shingles - made of hand spilt cedar. 100 pcs per bag, covers approximately 76 sq. inches. Shingle size: 3/4"W x 1-1/4"L.
7004 - Wooden Shingles - can be used to create the traditional Early American Shaker roof. 100 pcs. per bag. Shingle size: 3/4"W x 1-1/4"L.
7005 - Fishscale Roofing Shingles - made of high quality wood and will add Victorian styling to your dollhouse. More than 100 pcs per bag, covers 76 sq. inches. Shingle size: 23/32"W x 1-1/4"L.

MINIATURE HOUSE
3-D Polystyrene Adobe Roof Panel

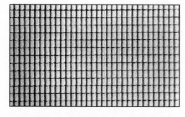

Stock No.: MH5330
Price: $6.50
Dimensions: 10-3/4"W x 16-3/4"L
This Spanish-type roof panel is a prepainted red adobe clay color. Easily cut with scissors or razor and amazingly realistic.

MINIATURE HOUSE

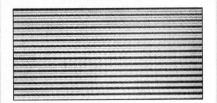

3-D Polystyrene Tin Roof Panel
Stock No.: MH5335
Price: $4.98
Dimensions: 4" x 8"
Prepainted to look like galvanized tin roofing, this realistic replica has many possible applications. Three panels per package.

PRECISION PRODUCTS

Plastic Veneer Styrene Sheets
Price: $7 per sheet
Dimensions: 15" square
Wood shakes, New England shingles, asphalt and fancy shingles, slate, old Spanish tile and corrugated roof. Made in USA.

MODEL BUILDERS SUPPLY

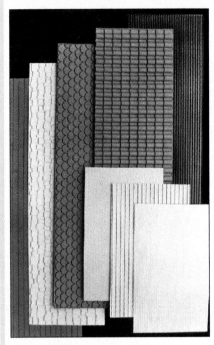

3-D Textured Roof Sheets
Price: $5.70; $3; $9.08
Dimensions: 7" x 24"; 7" x 12"; 14" x 24"
MBS sheets include round tiles, split shakes, Spanish tiles, regular shingles, stand-up rib and corrugated various colors available. Also in 1/2", 1/4" and 1/8" scales. Apply with MBS "Fast Fix," RTV silicone adhesive or double-sided tape.

WHAT'S NEXT?
Cedar Shakes

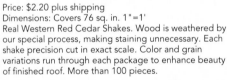

Price: $2.20 plus shipping
Dimensions: Covers 76 sq. in. 1"=1'
Real Western Red Cedar Shakes. Wood is weathered by our special process, making staining unnecessary. Each shake precision cut in exact scale. Color and grain variations run through each package to enhance beauty of finished roof. More than 100 pieces.

WHAT'S NEXT?

Roll Roofing - Asphalt
Price: $7.14 plus shipping
Dimensions: 6" x 24" sheet
Same material as our asphalt shingles. Use for flat roofs, mansard roofs, widow's walks, driveways, and landscaping.

WHAT'S NEXT?

Asphalt Roofing Shingles
Price: $8.18 plus shipping
Dimensions: Per Sq. Ft.
Museum quality asphalt shingles, continuous belt. Thirteen colors—Colonial Brown, Frost White, Gray, Black, Canyon Red, Spruce Green, Desert Tan, Black/White Blend, Federal Blend, Mahogany, Imitation Gray Slate, and Imitation Vermont Red Slate, and Plain.

WHAT'S NEXT?

Asphalt Roofing Shingles
Price: $8.18 plus shipping
Dimensions: Per Sq. Ft.
Museum quality asphalt shingles, continuous belt. Thirteen colors—Colonial Brown, Frost White, Gray, Black, Canyon Red, Spruce Green, Desert Tan, Black/White Blend, Federal Blend, Mahogany, Imitation Gray Slate, and Imitation Vermont Red Slate, and Plain.

VISIT A MINIATURES MUSEUM ON YOUR VACATION

Shutters

ALESSIO MINIATURES

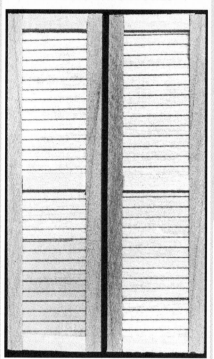

Custom-Made Shutters

Price: $3 per pair
Dimensions: made to order
These shutters are available in widths of 1",
1-1/4" and 1-1/2" and in custom-made lengths.

CLASSICS BY HANDLEY

Louvered Shutters

Stock No.: CLA75019
Price: $2.95
Dimensions: 1-3/8"W x 5-3/16"H
These louvered shutters fit standard working and
non-working windows. Two per package.

FOR FAST SERVICE, VISIT YOUR LOCAL MINIATURES SHOP

CLASSICS BY HANDLEY

Louvered Shutters

Stock No.: CLA75025
Price: $2.95
Dimensions: 1-5/16"W x 4-5/8"H
These louvered shutters are precisely detailed and
add an additional touch of realism to your
dollhouse. Two per package.

CLASSICS BY HANDLEY

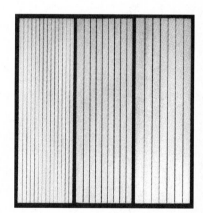

Clapboard Siding

Unfinished wood siding is available in 24" and 12"
lengths and comes 10 pieces per pack. 24" sidings
are: CLA75450 - 1/4" lap; CLA75455 - 3/8" lap;
CLA75460 - 1/2" lap.
12" sidings are: CLA75465 - 1/4" lap;
CLA75470 - 3/8" lap; CLA75475 - 1/2" lap.
CLA75450, CLA75460 - 3-1/2" x 24" - $27.96.
CLA75455 - 3-1/2" x 24" - $28.50.
CLA75465, CLA75470, CLA75475 - 3-1/2" x 12" -
$13.98.

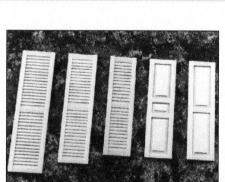

HOUSEWORKS, LTD.
Assorted Shutters

Stock No.: 5018; 5019; 5025; 5022; 5017
Price: 5017, 5018 and 5022 - $3.25
5019 and 5025 - $2.95
Dimensions:
5018 - Louvered Shutters - 2 pcs./pkg. Size
1-1/2"W x 5-11/16"H. Fits windows 5030, 5031.
5019 - Louvered Shutters - 2 pcs./pkg. Size:
1-3/8"W x 5-3/16"H. Fits windows 5024, 5023.
5025- Louvered Shutters - 2pcs./pkg. Size:
1-1/4"W x 4-5/8"H. Fits windows 5051, 5001,
5041, 5002, 5042, 5037, 5015, 5000, 5032, 5044.
5022 - 3-Panel "Americana" Shutter - 2
pcs./pkg. Size: 1-1/4"W x 4-11/16"H. Fits same
windows as 5025.
5017 - 2-Panel Jamestown Shutter - 2 pcs./pkg.
Size: 1-1/4"W x 4-11/16"H. Fits same windows
as 5025.

Siding Materials

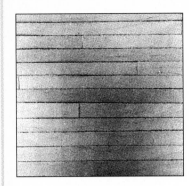

CORONA CONCEPTS
Birch Clapboard Siding

Stock No.: 4704
Dimensions: 12" x 3/4"; 1" scale
Birch veneer clapboard siding is the perfect finish for the exterior of any dollhouse. The natural wood can be painted or stained as you desire. Each bag contains 60 pieces which covers 360 square inches. Easy-to-follow instructions are printed on the inside of each header. See your local dealer.

ARE YOU INTERESTED IN BECOMING A RETAILER OR MAUFACTURER?

Contact: The Miniatures Manufacturers

Industry of America

1100-H Brandywine Blvd.,

PO Box 2188

Zanesville, OH 43702-2188

(614) 452-4541

HOUSEWORKS, LTD.
Clapboard Siding

7035 - 1/4" Lap Width Clapboard Siding - each sheet is 24"L x 3-1/2"W. $36.95.
7036 - 3/8" Lap Width Clapboard Siding - each sheet is 24"L x 3-1/2"W. $36.95.
7037 - 1/2" Lap Width Clapboard Siding - each sheet is 24"L x 3-1/2"W. $36.95.
7038 - 1/4" Lap Clapboard Siding - each sheet is 12"L x 3-1/2"W. $18.95.
7039 - 3/8" Lap Clapboard Siding - each sheet is 12"L x 3-1/2"W. $18.95.
7040 - 1/2" Lap Clapboard Siding - each sheet is 12"L x 3-1/2"W. $18.95.
7336 - MDF 3/8" Lap Clapboard Siding - each sheet is 24"L x 3-1/2"W. $19.95.
All standard packs include 10 sheets.
All clapboard made in USA except #7336

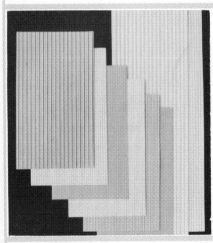

MODEL BUILDERS SUPPLY
3-D Siding Sheets

Price: $5.70; $3; $9.08
Dimensions: 7" x 24"; 7" x 12"; 14" x 24"
More MBS easy-to-use sheets. Three spacings of clapboard for 1:12 scale, 2.3 x 4 per inch. Board and batten 3 and 4 per inch. Our recently introduced stucco sheets are proving very popular for ceilings as well as walls. In three textures, white and adobe. Siding and corrugated now available in a metallic sheet 7" x 12", $3.99.

PRECISION PRODUCTS

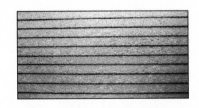

Plastic Veneer Styrene Sheets

Price: $7 per sheet
Dimensions: 15" square
3", 4", 6" and 12" lap siding, Board 'n Batten, 6" V-groove siding, 9" rough wood siding, corrugated. Made in USA.

Clapboard	Sheet size .080″ × 3½″ × 22″		
CLB-8			1/4
CLB-12			3/8
CLB-16			1/2
	Sheet size .080″ × 3½″ × 36″		
CLB-8-36			1/4
CLB-12-36			3/8
CLB-16-36			1/2
Beaded Clapboard			
CLE-12			3/8
CLE-16			1/2

NORTHEASTERN SCALE MODELS, INC.
Siding

Stock No.: see below
Price: see below
Dimensions: see below
Specifications: 1/16" thick, 3-1/2"W x 24"L (with the exception of 36" clapboard)
Clapboard CLB-8 36"L/1/4" lap - $4.55 ea.
Clapboard CLB-12, 36"L/3/8" lap - $4.55 ea.
Clapboard CLB-16, 36"L/1/2" lap - $4.55 ea.
Beaded Clapboard CLE-12, 3/8" lap - $2.65
Beaded Clapboard CLE-16, 1/2" lap - $2.65
Bead and Board SIG-8 - $2.65
Bead and Board Hollow SIH-4 - $2.65

Staircases

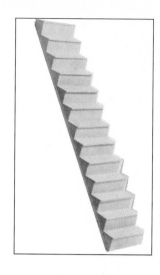

ALESSIO MINIATURES

Staircase

Stock No.: 88; 89; 90; 91
Dimensions: 2-1/2"W, 10" ceiling or custom-made
88 - Staircase with tread, stained, $10; 89 - Staircase with tread, unstained, $8.50; 91 - Staircase, custom-made to fit your house, $9. Affordable quality. American-made.

CLASSICS BY HANDLEY

Assembled Narrow Stairs

Stock No.: CLA70251
Price: $6.00
Dimensions: 2"W x 11-1/8"L
Wood stairs created to fit in that space too small or a full-sized staircase.

CLASSICS BY HANDLEY

Curved Staircase

Stock No.: CLA70221 (left curve); CLA70222 (right curve)
Price: $43.00
Dimensions: 3"W of riser/stringer x 9"H
This wood staircase has a highly-detailed, elegant Victorian look. Fully assembled. For use with 9" or 10" ceiling.

CLASSICS BY HANDLEY

Fancy Stair Kit

Stock No.: CLA70280
Price: $18.50
Dimensions: 3"W
This wood kit has a dainty, graceful Victorian look. Preassembled railing. For 10" ceiling.

CLASSICS BY HANDLEY

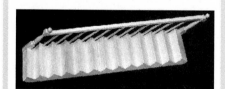

Preassembled Stair With Handrail

Stock No.: CLA70283
Price: $17.50
Dimensions: 3"W
Unfinished wood staircase, ready to stain or paint. Square balusters and handrail. Assembled railing separate.

HOUSEWORKS, LTD.

Simple Stair Kit

Stock No.: 7100
Price: $13.95
Dimensions: 11-5/16" x 2-1/4" riser/stringer
Narrow stair kit contains stair railings and flat decorative spindles to complete the stairway and landing rail. Designed to fit smaller dollhouses.

CLASSICS BY HANDLEY

Stairs With Landing Kit

Stock No.: CLA70252
Price: $20.00
Dimensions: 2-7/8"W
This unfinished wood kit has a number of possibilities for assembly. Includes all necessary spindles and newel posts.

CLASSICS BY HANDLEY

Straight Stair Kit

Stock No.: CLA70220
Price: $18.98
Dimensions: 3"W x 12-1/2"L
Stair kit with components can be adjusted for 9" or 10" ceilings. Kit includes riser/stringer assembly, two newel posts, 11 balusters and separate landing step.

HOUSEWORKS, LTD.

Straight Staircase Kit

Stock No.: 7000
Price: $19.95
Dimensions: 3-3/16"W x 14"L riser/stringer
All wood. Detailed kit contains riser/stringer assembly, 13 treads, 13 balusters, two newel posts and one handrail. Can be adjusted to varying floor to ceiling heights, 9" to 10".

HOUSEWORKS, LTD.

Stair Accessories

Stock No.: 7019; 7020
Price: $3.50; $1.75
7019 - Staircase Spindles - delicately sculptured spindles to rise between your stair treads and handrail. 12 per pkg. Size: 3/16"W x 2-5/8"L.
7020 - Stair and Landing Handrail - notched on underside to accommodate 7019 spindles. Size: 1/4"W x 1/4"H x 18"L. Both match 7000 stair kit.

MINIATURE CORNER

Spiral Staircase

Stock No.: M7002
Price: $45
Dimensions: 1:12
Spiral staircase kit. Wood parts reinforced with brass rod. Height is adjustable. All parts included. Imported from Germany. Sized for 10" ceilings.

KIMBERLY HOUSE MINIATURES

Kimberly Spiral Staircase Kit

Stock No.: SP-102
Price: $30.54
Dimensions: Fits up to 10" ceiling.

KIMBERLY HOUSE MINIATURES

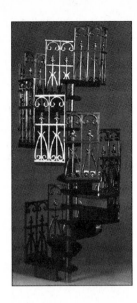

Kimberly Spiral Staircase Kit

Stock No.: SP-103
Price: $25.28
Dimensions: Fits up to 10" ceiling

VISIT A MINIATURES MUSEUM ON YOUR VACATION

WALMER DOLLHOUSES

Staircase Kit

Stock No.: 4001
Price: See your local dealer.
Dimensions: Fits 10" ceiling
May be assembled left or right.

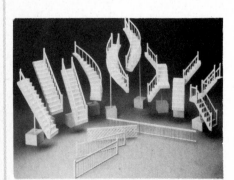

THE LAWBRE COMPANY
Staircases and Railings

All Lawbre staircases are completely assembled in clear pine stock and ready to finish. Stock staircases are 10"H and 2-7/8"W with smooth birch spindles. They can have rails on the left, right or both sides and curve or turn left or right. Decorative turned spindles are also available as well as any custom size or configuration to fit your needs. Rail sets complement the staircases in smooth birch spindles or decorative turned spindles. Lattice work and widow's walk are also available. All are fully assembled and ready to finish.

From left to right:
1147 - $29.95; 1101 - $23.95; 1106 - $28.95
1122 - $36.95; 1126 - $41.95; 1127 - $41.95
1117 - $34.95; 1111 - $29.95; 1136 - $52.95
In front: 1141- 10" x 2-1/2" railing with smooth birch spindles and two posts, $9.95; 1186 - 10" x 2-1/2" railing with decorative turned spindles and two posts, $18.95; 1191 - 10-3/4" x 2-1/2" fully assembled lattice work section, $10.95; 1192 - 20" x 2-1/8" widow's walk section, $9.95.

WALMER DOLLHOUSES

Curved Staircase
Stock No.: 4010
Price: See your local dealer.
Dimensions: Fits 10" ceiling
90° curved staircase (left only) available as a kit or assembled.

WALMER DOLLHOUSES

Straight Staircase
Stock No.: 4006/4007
Price: See your local dealer.
Dimensions: 10" ceiling; 1/12 scale
Sophisticated styling, shaped treads, graceful, turned balusters and posts. Available kit or assembled right or left.

WALMER DOLLHOUSES

Lilliput Custom Staircase
Stock No.: 4016
Price: See your local dealer.
Dimensions: Fits 8-1/2" ceiling; 1/12 scale
For those who want to customize their Lilliput kits, these staircases are made to fit. Available as kits, assembled right or left.

Non-Working Windows

ALESSIO MINIATURES

Victorian Non-Working Window
Stock No.: 404
Price: $7.70
Dimensions: Fits opening 2-1/2" x 4-29/32"
Elegant Victorian non-working window. Four over four. Removable glass. Affordable quality. American-made.

ALESSIO MINIATURES

Victorian Non-Working Window
Stock No.: 405
Price: $7.70
Dimensions: Fits opening 2-1/2" x 4-29/32"
Elegant Victorian non-working window. Six over six. Affordable quality. American-made.

ALESSIO MINIATURES

Bay, No Windows
Stock No.: 470
Price: $6.50
Dimensions: Fits opening 5-3/4" x 7-3/4"
Elegant bay. Interchangeable windows. Affordable quality. American-made.

ALESSIO MINIATURES

Bay, Non-Working Windows

Stock No.: 474 Price: $11.30
Dimensions: Fits opening 5-3/4" x 7-3/4"
Elegant bay. Non-working windows.
Interchangeable windows. Affordable quality.
American-made.

ALESSIO MINIATURES

Bay, Four Over Four Windows

Stock No.: 472
Price: $15.05
Dimensions: Fits opening 5-3/4" x 7-3/4"
Elegant bay. Four over four. Interchangeable
windows. Affordable quality. American-made.

ALESSIO MINIATURES

Bay, Six Over Six Windows

Stock No.: 471 Price: $15.05
Dimensions: Fits opening 5-3/4" x 7-3/4"
Elegant bay. Six over six. Interchangeable
windows. Affordable quality. American-made.

ALESSIO MINIATURES

Yorktown Non-Working Window

Stock No.: 427
Price: $5.50
Dimensions: Fits opening 2-1/2" x 5"
Non-working window. One over one. Affordable
quality. American made.

ALESSIO MINIATURES

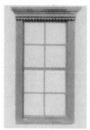

Yorktown Four Over Four Non-Working Window

Stock No.: 430 Price: $7.50
Dimensions: Fits opening 2-1/2" x 4-29/32"
Non-working window. Four over four. Affordable
quality. American-made.

ALESSIO MINIATURES

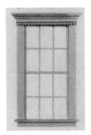

Yorktown Six Over Six Window

Stock No.: 429
Price: $7.50
Dimensions: Fits opening 2-1/2" x 5"
Non-working window. Six over six. Affordable
quality. American-made.

ALESSIO MINIATURES

Four Over Four Classical Window

Stock No.: 404C
Price: $7
Dimensions: Fits opening 2-1/2" x 4-29/32"
Elegant classical window. Four over four.
Affordable quality. American-made.

ALESSIO MINIATURES

Six Over Six Classical Window

Stock No.: 405C
Price: $7
Dimensions: Fits opening 2-1/2" x 5"
Elegant classical window. Six over six. Affordable
quality. American-made.

ALESSIO MINIATURES

Six Over Six Classical Double Window

Stock No.: 435 Price: $9
Dimensions: Fits opening 5" x 5"
Lovely double window. Six over six. Affordable
quality. American-made.

ALESSIO MINIATURES

Classical Double, Four Over Four Window

Stock No.: 436 Price: $9
Dimensions: Fits opening 5" x 5"
Lovely classical double window. Four over four.
Affordable quality. American-made.

ALESSIO MINIATURES

Triple Classical Four Over Four Window

Stock No.: 445C Price: $13.50
Dimensions: Fits opening 7-1/2" x 5"
Classical, triple four over four window. Affordable
quality. American-made.

ALESSIO MINIATURES

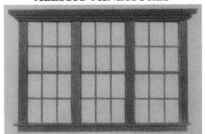

Triple Classical Six Over Six Window

Stock No.: 444C Price: $13.50
Dimensions: Fits opening 7-1/2" x 5"
Classical, triple six over six window. Affordable
quality. American-made.

Prices are approximate and subject to change

ALESSIO MINIATURES

Triple Victorian
Four Over Four Window

Stock No.: 445A Price: $17.50
Dimensions: Fits opening 7-1/2" x 5"
Lovely Victorian triple window. Four over four
(24-light). Affordable quality. American-made.

ALESSIO MINIATURES

Triple Victorian
Six Over Six Window

Stock No.: 444A Price: $17.50
Dimensions: Fits opening 7-1/2" x 5"
Lovely Victorian triple window. Six over six.
Affordable quality. American-made.

ALESSIO MINIATURES

Dentil Victorian Double Window

Stock No.: 443A
Price: $13.70
Dimensions: Fits opening 7-1/2" x 5"
Victorian dentil double window. Four over four.
Affordable quality. American-made.

ALESSIO MINIATURES

Triple Dentil Victorian Window

Stock No.: 445D
Price: $19
Dimensions: Fits opening 7-1/2" x 5"
Elegant Victorian triple dentil window. Four over
four. Affordable quality. American-made.

ALESSIO MINIATURES

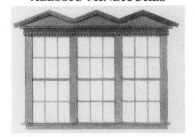

Triple Dentil Victorian Window

Stock No.: 444D
Price: $19
Dimensions: Fits opening 7-1/2" x 5"
Elegant Victorian triple dentil window. Six over six.
Affordable quality. American-made.

ALESSIO MINIATURES

Non-Working Window

Stock No.: 404A
Price: $5.70
Dimensions: Fits opening 2-1/2" x 4-29/32"
Non-working four over four window. Removable
glass. Affordable quality. American-made.

ALESSIO MINIATURES

Non-Working Window

Stock No.: 405A
Price: $5.70
Dimensions: Fits opening 2-1/2" x 4-29/32"
Non-working six over six window. Removable
glass. Affordable quality. American-made.

ALESSIO MINIATURES

Victorian Dentil
Non-Working Window

Stock No.: 403
Price: $8.20
Dimensions: Fits opening 2-1/2" x 4-29/32"
Elegant Victorian dentil non-working window. Four
over four. Removable glass. Affordable quality.
American-made.

ALESSIO MINIATURES

Non-Working Window
With Separate Victorian Top

Stock No.: 411 (Non-working window); 412
(Victorian Top)
Price: $3.20 (411); $2 (412)
Dimensions: Fits opening 2-1/2" x 5"
Non-working window. One over one. Separate
Victorian top. Removable glass. Affordable quality.
American-made.

ALESSIO MINIATURES

Victorian Dentil
Non-Working Window

Stock No.: 406
Price: $5.90
Dimensions: Fits opening 2-1/2" x 5"
Elegant Victorian dentil non-working window.
One over one. Removable glass. Affordable quality.

ALESSIO MINIATURES

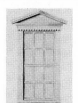

Victorian Dentil
Non-Working Window

Stock No.: 408
Price: $8.20
Dimensions: Fits opening 2-1/2" x 4-29/32"
Elegant Victorian dentil non-working window. Six
over six. Removable glass. Affordable quality.
American-made.

ARCHITECTURAL ETCETERA

Cast Windows

Stock No.: 340 - 349
Price: $14 - $32
Dimensions: Fits opening 7"H x 2-1/2"W
All windows are supplied complete. The interior frames and trims are as finely-detailed as the exteriors. Only real glass is used. Windows have an adjustable feature that allows them to fit any total wall thickness from 5/16" to 5/8". Our catalog gives all useful dimensions. Front doors in matching architectural style are available. The details really are worth looking at. Molded resin and glass.

ARCHITECTURAL ETCETERA

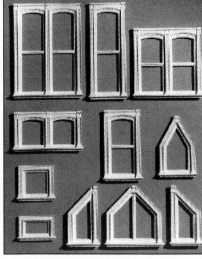

Cast Windows

Stock No.: 360 - 379
Price: $15 - $30
Dimensions: Fits opening 7"H x 2-1/2"W
All windows are supplied complete. The interior frames and trims are as finely-detailed as the exteriors. Only real glass is used. Windows have an adjustable feature that allows them to fit any total wall thickness from 5/16" to 5/8". Our catalog gives all useful dimensions. Front doors in matching architectural style are available. The details really are worth looking at. Molded resin and glass.

CLASSICS BY HANDLEY

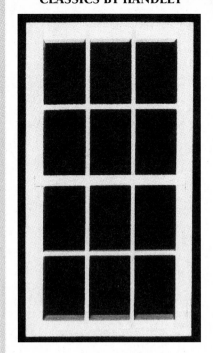

12-Light Window

Stock No.: CLA75024
Price: $4.98
Dimensions: Fits opening 2-9/16"W x 5-1/16"H
Classic, 12-light window without panes—class without expense. Fits standard window openings.

CLASSICS BY HANDLEY
24-Panel Picture Window

Stock No.: CLA75007
Price: $7.75
Dimensions: Fits opening 6-11/16"W x 5-1/16"H
This picture window is perfect for a roombox. Store fronts and libraries often have this window.

CLASSICS BY HANDLEY

Two-Light Window

Stock No.: CLA70105
Price: $4.10
Dimensions: Fits opening 2-9/16"W x 2-9/16"H
Two-light window, without panes, works well in attics or bathrooms. Two windows per card.

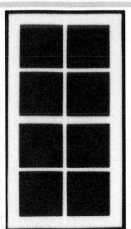

CLASSICS BY HANDLEY
Eight-Light Window

Stock No.: CLA75023
Price: $4.90
Dimensions: Fits opening 2-9/16"W x 5-1/16"H
This standard eight-light window is an inexpensive way to have attractive windows in your dollhouse. Fits standard window openings.

CLASSICS BY HANDLEY

Two-Light Window

Stock No.: CLA70107
Price: $3.98
Dimensions: Fits opening 2-9/16"W x 5-1/16"H
This window without panes matches CLA70105 and CLA70108.

Prices are approximate and subject to change

CLASSICS BY HANDLEY
Fancy Victorian
Non-Working Double Window

Stock No.: CLA71026
Price: $12.98
Dimensions: Fits opening 5-1/16"W x 5-1/16"H
This window with the dainty scalloped trim (CLA70225) has removable panes and interior trim. Separate mullions included.

CLASSICS BY HANDLEY

Four-Light Window

Stock No.: CLA75004
Price: $6.25
Dimensions: Fits opening 2-9/16"W x 2-9/16"H
Four-light window without panes is excellent for attics and dormers. Two per package.

CLASSICS BY HANDLEY

Deluxe Standard
Non-Working Window

Stock No.: CLA71043
Price: $7.26
Dimensions: Fits opening 2-9/16"W x 5-1/16"H
Top-of-the-line non-working deluxe standard window with removable panes has molded exterior and interior trim. Separate mullions included.

CLASSICS BY HANDLEY

Fancy Victorian
Non-Working Single Window

Stock No.: CLA71024
Price: $7.29
Dimensions: Fits opening 2-9/16"W x 5-1/16"H
This window adds dainty charm to a Victorian home. It has removable panes for easy painting and interior trim. Separate mullions included.

CLASSICS BY HANDLEY

Octagonal Window

Stock No.: CLA71110
Price: $4.95
Dimensions: Fits opening 2-1/16"diameter
Octagonal window with preassembled interior trim. Perfect for the attic.

CLASSICS BY HANDLEY

Octagonal Window
With Etched Glass

Stock No.: CLA71111
Price: $7.95
Dimensions: Fits opening 2-1/16"diameter
The etched glass in this window adds charm to the attic or wherever you choose to place it. Assembled interior trim included.

CLASSICS BY HANDLEY
Picture Window

Stock No.: CLA70108
Price: $6.75
Dimensions: Fits opening 6-7/8"W x 5-1/16"H
Picture window without panes has the same trim style as CLA70105 and CLA70107.

CLASSICS BY HANDLEY

Small Yorktown
Non-Working Window

Stock No.: CLA70116
Price: $5.95
Dimensions: Fits opening 2-1/16"W x 4-1/16"H
This window has the same elegant design as CLA70101, CLA70102 & CLA70104. It also has interior trim.

CLASSICS BY HANDLEY

Yorktown
Non-Working Double Window

Stock No.: CLA70102
Price: $11.25
Dimensions: Fits opening 4-9/16"W x 5-15/16"H
Perfect for that large space. Same appealing design of CLA70101 single window and CLA70117 door.

CLASSICS BY HANDLEY

Standard Non-Working
Double-Hung Window

Stock No.: CLA71130
Price: $6.00
Dimensions: Fits opening 2-9/16"W x 5-1/16"H
Non-working standard single window has removable panes and interior trim.

CLASSICS BY HANDLEY

Victorian
Non-Working Double Window

Stock No.: CLA71046
Price: $14.98
Dimensions: Fits opening 5-1/16"W x 5-1/16"H
Top-of-the-line non-working deluxe standard window with removable panes. Has molded exterior and interior trim. Separate mullions included.

CLASSICS BY HANDLEY

Victorian
Non-Working Single Window

Stock No.: CLA71042
Price: $7.49
Dimensions: Fits opening 2-9/16"W x 5-1/16"H
This elegant window has removable panes and molded exterior and interior trim. Separate mullions included.

CLASSICS BY HANDLEY

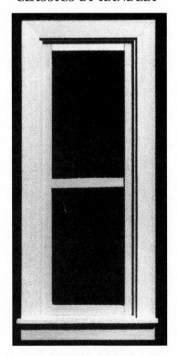

Narrow Non-Working
Double-Hung Window

Stock No.: CLA70118
Price: $4.98
Dimensions: Fits opening 2-5/16"W x 5-13/16"H
This narrow window has interior trim and is perfect for a tall, slim space.

CLASSICS BY HANDLEY

Victorian Window

Stock No.: CLA75042
Price: $7.95
Dimensions: Fits opening 2-9/16"W x 5-1/16"H
Elegant Victorian non-working window with removable panes.

Prices are approximate and subject to change

CLASSICS BY HANDLEY

Yorktown
Non-Working Single Window
Stock No.: CLA70101
Price: $6.98
Dimensions: Fits opening 2-5/16"W x 5-13/16"H
This attractive window has rounded upper sash and dentil molding to add special distinction. It also has interior trim.

CLASSICS BY HANDLEY

Yorktown
Non-Working Window
Stock No.: CLA75041
Price: $7.95
Dimensions: Fits opening 2-9/16"W x 5-1/16"H
Traditional Yorktown non-working window with removable panes.

DESIGN TECNICS MINIATURES

Architect's Choice Windows
Dimensions: 1"
Wide choice of sizes in Classic and Bracketed Styles fit openings for most shells and Architect's Choice Dollhouse Plans. 2-1/2" wide in heights of 3", 4", 5", 6". 5" wide double in heights of 4", 5", 6". Combines look of operating sash with convenience of removable polycarbonate "glass" for ease of painting. Matching paneled doors are 3" x 7".

HOUSEWORKS, LTD.
Non-Working Windows
Stock No.: 5042; 5032; 5041
Price: $5.95; $7.95; $8.95
5042 - Victorian Non-Working Window - includes removable acrylic pane. No interior trim.
Size; 3-7/8"W x 6"H.
Fits opening: 2-9/16"W x 5-1/16"H x 1/2"D.
5032 - Traditional Non-Working Window - includes removable acrylic pane. No interior trim.
Size: 2-31/32"W x 5-5/16"H.
Fits opening 2-9/16"W x 5-1/16"H x 1/2"D.
5041 - Yorktown Non-Working Window - includes removable acrylic pane. No interior trim.
Size 3-13/16"W x 5-7/8"H.
Fits opening: 2-9/16"W x 5-1/16"H x 1/2"D.

HOUSEWORKS, LTD.

Victorian
Bay Window
Stock No.: 5035
Price: $26.95
Highly detailed bay window includes trim, acrylic panes and mullions. No interior trim. Size: 4-5/8"W x 10-1/4"H.
Fits opening:
3-9/16"W x 5-3/8"H.

HOUSEWORKS, LTD
Single-Light Windows
Stock No.: 5040; 5038; 5039
Price: $5.95; $6.25; $6.95
5040 - Traditional Single-Light Window - complete with sill and acrylic pane. Does not include interior trim. Size: 3"W x 3-3/16"H.
Fits opening: 2-9/16"W x 2-15/16"H x 1/2"D.
5038 - Yorktown Single-Light Window - detailed dentil molding, sill and acrylic pane. Does not include interior trim. Size 3-5/8"W x 3-1/2"H.
Fits opening: 2-9/16"W x 2-15/16"H x 1/2"D.
5039 - Victorian Single-Light Window - detailed hooded cap, sculpted brackets and sill. Includes acrylic pane. Does not include interior trim.
Size: 3-5/8"W x 3-13/16"H.
Fits opening: 2-9/16W x 2-15/16"H x 1/2"D.

HOUSEWORKS, LTD.
Assorted Windows

Stock No.: 5003; 5051
Price: $6.50; $6.95
5003 - Standard 8-Light Window With Shutters - no acrylic, no interior trim. Size 4-1/16"W X 5-1/4"H. Fits opening: 2-9/16"W x 5-1/16"H x 3/8"D. 5051- Traditional Non-Working Window - traditional two-pane window with pediment. Includes removable acrylic pane. Does not include interior trim. Size: 3-1/2"W x 5-3/8"H. Fits opening: 2-9/16"W x 5-1/16"H x 1/2"D.

Puttin' On The Glitz

N eed to do a little gilding of picture frames or furniture? Save on brush clean-up by using alcohol-based, gold permanent markers. Just apply, wait a second or two, then quickly wipe off the excess with a soft rag, repeating the process as often as necessary.

HOUSEWORKS, LTD.
Assorted Windows

Stock No.: 5052; 5045; 5047
Price: $7.50; $4.95; $4.95
5052 - Round Window - with interior trim. Includes acrylic. Size: 2-9/16" diameter. Fits opening: 2-1/16" diameter x 3/8"D.
5045 - Octagon Non-Working Window - Complete with acrylic pane and interior trim. Size: 2-1/4" square. Fits opening: 2-1/16" diameter (round opening) x 3/8"D.
5047 - Octagon Louvered Attic Vent - finely detailed outer molding. Inside is louvered wood to give the illusion of a vent. Square interior trim. Will match #5045. Size: 2-1/4"W x 2-1/4"H octagon. 1" scale.
Fits opening 2"Wx2"H octagon.

HOUSEWORKS, LTD.
24-Light Windows

Stock No.: 5021; 5007
Price: $12.75; $7.95
5021 - Yorktown 24-Light Window - 24-light study window with detailed dentil molding and removable acrylic pane. Interior trim not included. Size: 8"W x 5-13/16"H. Fits opening 6-13/16"W x 5-1/16"H x 1/2"D.
5007 - Traditional 24-Light Window - 24-light storefront or study window. Interior trim not included. Size: 8"W x 5-5/16"H.
Fits opening: 6-3/4"W x 5-1/16"H x 3/8"D.

HOUSEWORKS, LTD.
Assorted Windows

Stock No.: 5048; 5004
Price: $10.95; $6.25
5048 - Circlehead Window - accessory to traditional windows or to be used alone as gable or attic window. Includes mullions and removable acrylic pane. Two per pkg. Includes interior trim. Size: 2-3/4"W x 1-9/16"H. Fits opening: 2-1/2"W x 1-7/16"H x 1/2"D.
5004 - Single Window - the four light single trimmed window is perfect as a dormer window. Two per pkg. No acrylic, no interior trim. Size: 2-11/16"W x 2-11/16"H. Fits opening: 2-9/16"W x 2-9/16"H x 3/8"D.

ANTHONY CALLAWAY
RENTON, WA

Workshop Wisdom

Courtesy of *Nutshell News*—*12/94*

HOUSEWORKS, LTD.
Standard Light Windows

Stock No.: 5024; 5023
Price: $4.95; $4.95
5024 - Standard 12-Light Window - no acrylic, no interior trim. Size: 2-3/4"W x 5-1/4"H.
Fits opening: 2-9/16W x 5-1/16"H x 3/8"D.
5023 - Standard 8-Light Window - no acrylic, no interior trim. Size 2-3/4"W x 5-1/4"H.
Fits opening: 2-9/16"W x 5-1/16"H x 3/8"D.

MINIATURE HOUSE

One Light Window
Without Trim/Pane

Stock No.: MH105A
Price: $3.10
These windows fit openings measuring 2-9/16"W x 2-9/16"H x 5/16"D in size.

MINIATURE LUMBER SHOPPE

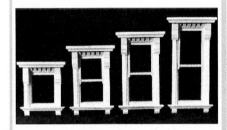

Victorian Windows

Price: See your local dealer.
Dimensions: 1" scale
Wide choice of sizes and styles (Victorian shown) fit openings for most shells and Architect's Choice Dollhouse Plans. 2-1/2" wide in heights of 3", 4", 5", 6". 5" wide double in heights of 4", 5", 6". Combines look of operating sash with convenience of removable poycarbonate "glass" for ease of painting. Matching paneled doors are 3" x 7".

WALMER DOLLHOUSES

Hampton
Non-Working Window

Stock No.: 2070N
Price: See your local dealer.
Dimensions: Fits opening 5-1/16"H x 2-9/16"W; 1/12 scale
Designer Home exclusive feature: assembled interior frame adjusts to wall thickness. Removable pane. Companion products: Hampton oval door (#1013); Single light window (#2093). Designer Home catalog available.

WALMER DOLLHOUSES

Victorian Slim Window

Stock No.: 2068N
Price: See your local dealer.
Dimensions: Fits opening 7-1/16"H x 2-3/4"W; 1/12 scale
Part of the Designer Home Victorian collection. See the Designer Home catalog for all varieties of long slim windows.

PRECISION PRODUCTS

Plastic Veneer
Styrene Sheets

Price: $7 per sheet (white);
$9 per sheet (crystal clear)
Dimensions: 15" square; 1/2" scale.
Detail sheets, station windows and doors, colonial windows and doors.
Made in USA.

WALMER DOLLHOUSES
Lilliput Custom Windows

Stock No.: 2060; 2062
Price: See your local dealer.
Dimensions: Fits opening 4-13/16"H x 2-1/2"W; 1/12 scale
These windows are specially designed for the customization of Lilliput kits without having to enlarge openings.

WALMER DOLLHOUSES
Hogarth Window With Shutters
Stock No.: 2077N
Price: See your local dealer.
Dimensions: Fits opening 6-5/8"H x 2-5/8"W;
1/12 scale
Exclusive Designer Home design and features. The arched shutters actually fit window's interior. Matching arched interior frame provided. Removable panes.

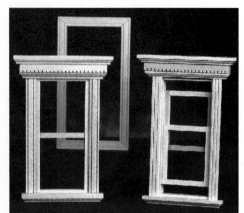

WALMER DOLLHOUSES
Colonial Windows
Stock No.: 2064N; 2065W
Price: See your local dealer.
Dimensions: Fits opening 5-1/16"H x 2-9/16"W; 1/12 scale
Part of the Designer Home Colonial Collection, these windows have exclusive and unique features. Both windows have assembled, interior frames which adjust to wall thickness. The working window has spring-loaded removable sashes.

WALMER DOLLHOUSES
Single-Light Windows
Stock No.: 2091; 2092; 2093
Price: See your local dealer.
Dimensions: All fit opening 2-15/16"H x 2-9/16"W; 1/12 scale
Windows may be used in any small space. All with removable panes. Companion product: Designer Home Single-Light Dormer #2094.

ALESSIO MINIATURES

Victorian Dentil Working Window
Stock No.: 407
Price: $7
Dimensions: Fits opening 2-1/2" x 5"
Elegant Victorian dentil working window. Spring loaded. One over one. Removable glass.

Windows, Working

Prices are approximate and subject to change

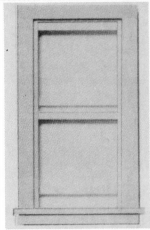

ALESSIO MINIATURES
Working Double-Hung Window

Stock No.: 410
Price: $5
Dimensions: Fits opening 2-1/2" x 5"
Double-hung, working window. Spring loaded. One over one. Removable glass. Affordable quality. American-made.

SHOW SANTA
WHAT YOU WANT
FROM
THE
MINIATURES
CATALOG

ALESSIO MINIATURES

Bay Working Windows

Stock No.: 473 Price: $14
Dimensions: Fits opening 5-3/4" x 7-3/4"
Bay with working windows. Interchangeable windows. Affordable quality. American-made.

ALESSIO MINIATURES

Working Classical Window

Stock No.: 428 Price: $6.50
Dimensions: Fits opening 2-1/2" x 5"
Elegant, working classical window. Affordable quality. American-made.

ALESSIO MINIATURES

Double Working
Dentil Victorian Window

Stock No.: 441A Price: $13.70
Dimensions: Fits opening 5" x 5"
Elegant double working dentil Victorian window. One over one. Affordable quality. American-made.

ALESSIO MINIATURES

Classical Double Window

Stock No.: 422
Price: $11.50
Dimensions: Fits opening 5" x 5"
Elegant classical double working window. One over one. Affordable quality. American-made.

ALESSIO MINIATURES

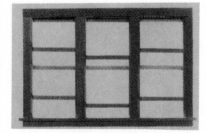

Triple Working
One Over One Window

Stock No.: 447 Price: $15.50
Dimensions: Fits opening 7-1/2" x 5"
Working triple window. One over one. Affordable quality. American-made.

ARCHITECTURAL ETCETERA

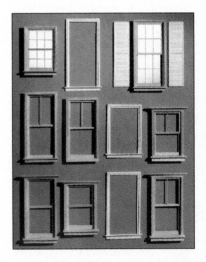

Wood Windows

Stock No.: 430 - 453
Price: $8 - $15
Available separately for the first time, these wood windows are the ones used on The Lawbre Company houses. Some are working, some non-working. some have micro glass panes, some plastic panes, but all panes are removable for easier decorating. All come with complete exterior trim for a 3/8" wall thickness only. Interior window trim, shutters and cast sills or over-window pediments are extra. Order our catalog for information on sizes, basic parts, optional parts, glass or plastic panes, etc.

ALESSIO MINIATURES

Triple Working Classical
One Over One Window

Stock No.: 447C Price: $17.50
Dimensions: Fits opening 7-1/2" x 5"
Working classical triple window. One over one. Affordable quality. American-made.

ALESSIO MINIATURES

Triple Working
Dentil Victorian Window

Stock No.: 447D Price: $22.50
Dimensions: Fits opening 7-1/2" x 5"
Elegant triple working dentil Victorian window. One over one. Affordable quality. American-made.

ARCHITECTURAL ETCETERA

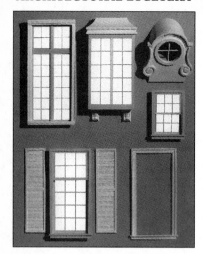

Wood Windows

Stock No.: 465 - 479
Price: $15 - $32
Our wood windows have been made to match those found in historical homes. Careful attention has been given to size and scale as well as reproduction of detail. We use clear pine for the wood parts and cast urethane resin for detail parts. The windows come fully assembled with assembled window muntin grids and fit a wall thickness of 3/8" plus the 3/32" thickness of sheet clapboard siding. All windows shown have micro glass panes.

ARCHITECTURAL ETCETERA

Wood Windows

Stock No.: 480 - 487
Price: $16 - $24
The casement windows measure 7-1/2" or 6-1/2" high, appropriate for apartment buildings or large country houses. They are non-working with removable micro glass panes. The single and double windows with cast exterior frames are working with plastic panes.

CLASSICS BY HANDLEY

Elegant Victorian Double-Hung Window

Stock No.: CLA75002
Price: $9.25
Dimensions: Fits opening 2-9/16"W x 5-1/16"H
Elegant Victorian working window with removable panes.

CLASSICS BY HANDLEY

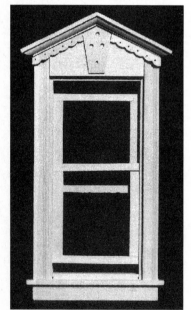

Fancy Victorian Single Working Window

Stock No.: CLA71022
Price: $8.49
Dimensions: Fits opening 2-9/16"W x 5-1/16"H
This working window adds dainty charm to a Victorian home. It has removable panes for easy painting and molded exterior and interior trim. Separate mullions included.

CLASSICS BY HANDLEY

Fancy Victorian Double Working Window

Stock No.: CLA71028
Price: $14.49
Dimensions: Fits opening 2-5/16"W x 5-1/16"H
This double window with the dainty scalloped trim has molded side trim and matching interior trim. The panes are removable for easy finishing. Separate mullions are included.

CLASSICS BY HANDLEY

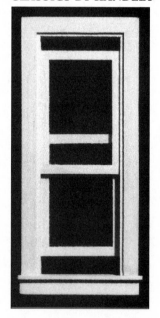

Narrow Double-Hung Working Window

Stock No.: CLA70109
Price: $6.49
Dimensions: Fits opening 2-5/16"W x 5-13/16"H
This working window has interior trim and is ideal for a narrow space.

CLASSICS BY HANDLEY

Standard Double-Hung Window
Stock No.: CLA71000
Price: $6.98
Dimensions: 2-9/16"W x 5-1/16"H
Working standard double-hung window with removable panes and interior trim and has separate mullions included.

CLASSICS BY HANDLEY

Slim Double Working Window
Stock No.: CLA70124
Price: $12.98
Dimensions: 4-1/2"W x 5-7/8"H
This working window has removable panes and interior trim.

CLASSICS BY HANDLEY

Standard Window
Dimensions:
Fits opening 2-9/16"W x 5-1/16"H
Versatile standard window with removable panes.
Interior trim included with CLA71010.
CLA71010 - Working - $6.79.
CLA71032 - Non-Working - $5.49.

CLASSICS BY HANDLEY

**Victorian
Single Working Window**
Stock No.: CLA71044
Price: $10.00
Dimensions: Fits opening 2-9/16"W x 5-1/16"H
This elegant window has removable panes and molded exterior trim. Interior trim matches. Separate mullions are included.

CLASSICS BY HANDLEY

**Victorian
Double-Working Window**
Stock No.: CLA71048
Price: $15.49
Dimensions: Fits opening 5-1/16"W x 5-1/16"H
A distinctive addition to the Victorian series, this window has removable panes and interior trim. Separate mullions included.

CLASSICS BY HANDLEY

Working Deluxe Standard Window
Stock No.: CLA71045
Price: $6.98
Dimensions: Fits opening 2-9/16"W x 5-1/16"H
Working deluxe standard window has removable panes and interior trim. This top-of-the-line window has molded exterior trim and complements the new Victorian series. Separate mullions are included.

CLASSICS BY HANDLEY

Attic Window

Stock No.: CLA70119
Price: $6.19
Dimensions: Fits opening 2-1/8"W x 2-1/4"H
The perfect attic window for the charming scallop-trimmed Victorian series.

CLASSICS BY HANDLEY

Double Swing-Out Window

Stock No.: CLA70112
Price: $7.49
Dimensions: Fits opening 3-7/16"W x 2-5/8"H
This unusual window swings out from the sides. It includes panes and interior trim.

CLASSICS BY HANDLEY

Small Working Window

Stock No.: CLA70110
Price: $4.98
Dimensions: Fits opening 2-1/16"W x 3-15/16"H
This operating double-hung window is ideal for small spaces such as attics or bathrooms. Window has interior trim.

Outdoors/Indoors

Mary prefers to see a window in a hatbox or closed-in room scene but is loathe to cut holes in the wall, so she offers this answer to her problem. She glues a suitable picture of an outdoor scene to the wall then constructs a window frame, complete with clear plastic glazing, which she glues over the picture. A set of drapes or sheers completes the assembly. Make the frame so that the glass stands about 1/8" (3mm) or more from the picture to give the illusion of depth.

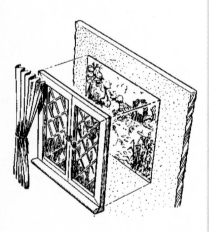

*MARY SIMONSON
SOMERSET, NJ*

Workshop Wisdom
Courtesy of *Nutshell News*—11/94

HOUSEWORKS, LTD.
Palladian Windows

Stock No.: 5049; 5014
Price: $21; $14.75
5049 - Circlehead Double Casement Window - Palladian-styled window complete with working inner vertical panes and outer removable acrylic panes. Includes acrylic fan and interior trim.
Size: 5-7/8"W x 7"H. Fits irregular opening: 5-5/8"W x 6-7/16"H x 1/2"D.
5014 - Palladian Working Window - double hung, fully functional formal French window. Includes removable acrylic pane for fan light, interior trim, acrylic and mullions.
Size: 4-1/8"W x 7-1/8"H. Fits irregular opening: 3-1/16"W x 6-13/16"H x 1/2"D.

HOUSEWORKS, LTD.
Side-by-Side Windows

Stock No.: 5037; 5015
Price: $18.25; $19.25
5037 - Yorktown Side-by-Side Window - double hung, fully functional windows with detailed cap and dentil molding. Includes acrylic and mullions, no interior trim. Size: 6-3/8"W x 5-13/16"H.
Fits opening: 5-1/16"W x 5-1/16"H x 1/2"D.
5015 - Victorian Side-by-Side Window - double hung and fully functional windows with low pitch hooded caps and sculpted brackets. Includes acrylic and mullions, no interior trim.
Size 6-5/16"W x 6-3/16"H.
Fits opening: 5-1/16"W x 5-1/16"H x 1/2"D.

HOUSEWORKS, LTD.
Slim Windows

Stock No.: 5030; 5031
Price: $10.95; $8.95
Dimensions:
5030 - Victorian Slim Window - double hung and fully functional window has rounded top sash and includes back frame moldings, acrylic and mullions. Size: 3-7/8"W x 7-11/16"H. Fits opening: 2-3/4"W x 7-1/16"H x 1/2"D.
5031 - Traditional Slim Window - double hung and fully functional. Includes back frame moldings, acrylic and mullions. Size: 3-1/4"W x 7-5/16"H. Fits opening: 2-3/4"W x 7-1/16"H x 1/2"D.

HOUSEWORKS, LTD.
Traditional Working Windows
Stock No.: 5000; 5044
Price: $7.25; $13.95
5000 - Traditional Working Window - double hung and fully functional. Mitered corners, self-framing exterior and six mullions. Includes acrylic and interior trim. Size 2-31/32"W x 5-5/16"H.
Fits opening: 2-9/16"W x 5-1/16"H x 1/2"D.
5044 - Traditional Side-by-Side Window - double hung and fully functional windows are self framing and include mullions. Includes acrylic and interior trim. Size: 5-7/16"W x 5-5/16"H. Fits opening: 5-1/16"W x 5-1/16"H x 1/2"D.

START A NEW HOBBY AND MEET NEW FRIENDS: JOIN A MINIATURES CLUB!

HOUSEWORKS, LTD.
Working Windows
Stock No.: 5001; 5002
Price: $8.95; $9.25
5001 - Yorktown Working Window - double hung and fully functional. Sculpted pediment accented by dentil molding. Includes acrylic, interior trim and six mullions. Size: 3-13/16"W x 5-13/16"H.
Fits opening: 2-9/16"W x 5-1/16"H x 1/2"D.
5002 - Victorian Working Window - features low pitch, hooded window cap with sculpted brackets and six mullions. Includes acrylic and interior trim. Size: 3-13/16"W x 6"H.
Fits opening: 2-9/16"W x 5-1/16"H x 1/2"D.

NUTSHELL NEWS MINIATURES TOURS ARE FUN! FOR INFORMATION CALL 1-800-677-9412

HOUSEWORKS, LTD.
Working Windows
Stock No.: 5046; 5050
Price: $7.50; $7.95
5046 - Traditional Working Attic Window - smaller double hung, fully functional window. Includes acrylic and interior trim. Size: 2-1/2"W x 4-5/16"H.
Fits opening: 2"W x 4"H x 3/8"D.
5050 - Working Casement Window - great for kitchens, bathrooms or attics. Includes acrylic panes and outer sill. Does not include interior trim. Size: 3-7/8"W x 2-7/8"H. Fits opening: 3-3/8"W x 2-5/8"H x 1/2"D.

HOUSEWORKS, LTD.
Assorted Bay Windows
Stock No.: 5008; 5020
Price: $16.50; $28.50
5008 - Nonworking Bay Window - features three 8-light windows. Acrylic and interior trim not included. Size: 9-5/8"W x 6-13/16"H.
Fits opening: 6-15/16"W x 5"H.
5020 - Working Bay Window - features three double hung, fully functional windows with mullions and acrylic panes. No interior trim.
Size: 9-1/2"W x 6-13/16"H.
Fits opening: 6-15/16"W x 5"H.

WALMER DOLLHOUSES

Hampton Working Window

Stock No.: 2071W
Price: See your local dealer.
Dimensions: Fits opening 5-1/16"H x 2-9/16"W;
1/12 scale
Exclusive design and feature from Designer Home!
The working window has spring-loaded removable
sashes.

WALMER DOLLHOUSES

Victorian Slim Working Window

Stock No.: 2069W
Price: See your local dealer.
Dimensions: Fits opening 7-1/16"H x 2-3/4"W;
1/12 scale
Part of the Designer Home Victorian collection,
this window has spring-loaded removable sashes!
See all working windows in our Designer Home
catalog.

WALMER DOLLHOUSES

Working Casement Window

Stock No.: 2075W
Price: See your local dealer.
Dimensions: Fits opening 2-5/8" x 3-5/16";
1/12 scale
The perfect window for bathrooms, kitchens
basements or attics. Double windows open out.

SHOW SANTA
WHAT YOU WANT
FROM
THE
MINIATURES
CATALOG

WALMER DOLLHOUSES
Traditional
Double Working Window

Stock No.: 2072W
Price: See your local dealer.
Dimensions: Fits opening 5-1/16"h x 5-1/16W;
1/12 scale
Exclusive Designer Home features and design.
Spring-loaded removable sashes within unitized
window. Plus assembled interior frame which
adjusts to wall thickness. Designer Home catalog
available.

Prices are approximate and subject to change

JUST GETTING INTO

DOLLHOUSE

MINIATURES?

If you have a question

about dollhouse

miniatures, stop by

your local retail outlet

and ask the expert

behind the counter.

WALMER DOLLHOUSES
Full Casement Window

Stock No.: 2076
Price: See your local dealer.
Dimensions: Fits opening 5-1/16"H x 3-5/16"W;
1/12 scale
This is a Designer Home exclusive. This unique window opens either in or out. Send for Designer Home catalog.

WALMER DOLLHOUSES
Windsor Casement Window

Stock No.: 2080W
Price: See your local dealer.
Dimensions: Fits opening 4-1/16"H x 2-9/16"W;
1/12 scale
Companion product to Windsor Windows (#2078N & #2079W) and Windsor Door (#1021). Window frames feature reeding to match door. Exclusive Designer Home product.

WALMER DOLLHOUSES
Windsor Working Window

Stock No.: 2079W
Price: See your local dealer.
Dimensions: Fits opening 5-1/16"H x 2-9/16"W;
1/12 scale
Exclusive Designer Home design and features: vertical reeding, spring-loaded removable sashes, removable mullions, assembled interior frame adjusts to wall thickness. Companion products are Windsor Door (#1021) and Windsor Casement (#2080W).

Waxing Poetic

WORKSHOP WISDOM

Melissa puts it very nicely – wax adhesive is to the dollhouse what Post-It-Notes are to the paper pushers of business. She uses little pieces of it to hang pictures, drapes, mirrors, etc., so they can be changed at a whim. She also applies it to the bottoms of lamps etc. so that they do not slide off the tables when the dollhouse is moved. To hang rodded drapes, for instance, she digs out dots of wax, applies them to the window frame, then presses the ends of the rod into it.

MELISSA BAILEY
NEWARK, NJ

Workshop Wisdom

Courtesy of *Nutshell News—12/94*

Window Stock Parts & Kits

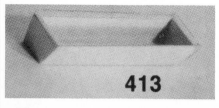

413

414

ALESSIO MINIATURES
Window Box
Stock No.: 413; 414
Price: $4
Add that special touch to your dollhouse windows with our window boxes. #413 (large); #414 (small). Also available, #309 - custom adjustable window box kit.

OCTOBER IS NATIONAL DOLLHOUSE AND MINIATURES MONTH! STOP BY YOUR LOCAL SHOP!

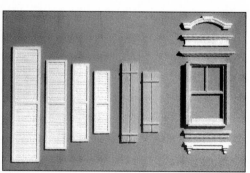

ARCHITECTURAL ETCETERA
Optional Window Parts
Stock No.: 490 - 495; 454 - 459
Price: $1.50 - $4
Shutters, over-window pediments, window sills in a variety of sizes and styles for use with any window. For size comparison, the large shutter at left in photo measures 7-5/8"H x 1-7/8"W.

HOUSEWORKS, LTD.

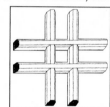

Mullions
Stock No.: 7043
Price: $1.50
Preassembled molded window grid mullions made of white ABS plastic. Easily trimmed to fit sash with knife or nail clippers. Four grids per package. Size: 1-11/16"W x 2-1/16"H. Fits windows #5000, 5032, 5044, 5037, 5015, 5001, 5041, 5002, 5042, 5051.

Mini Labels

WORKSHOP WISDOM

Ask your local grocery store, pharmacy or beautician for their junk mail, because in it you will find a priceless collection of mini labels in the planograms — the diagrams that show how to best display the products on the store shelves. Cut out, then glued around suitable dowels or blocks with silver-painted ends, they will provide you with a wonderful set of canned, bottled or boxed products for your pantry or mini store.

*ELLEN GALD
VIROQUA, WI*

Workshop Wisdom

Courtesy of *Nutshell News—7/94*

NOONMARK

Extra Thin Glass
Price: see below
Made of real 3/64" thick micro-glass. Imparts a brilliance and clarity to your window which is not obtainable with plastic. Custom cut to order or bulk sheets. Each piece is $.60, plus $.06 per square inch, plus shipping.

Prices are approximate and subject to change

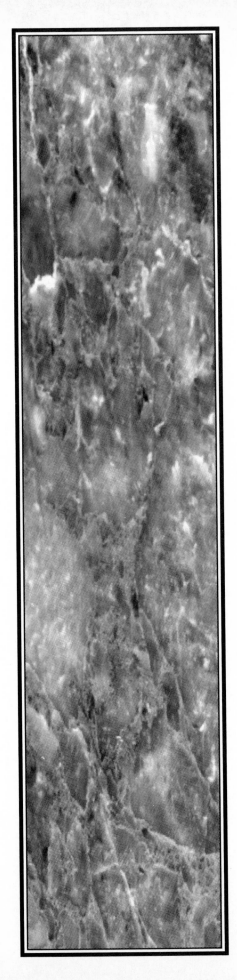

ELECTRICAL SYSTEMS & ACCESSORIES

Ceiling Fixtures

CIR-KIT CONCEPTS, INC.

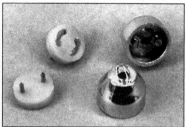

Ceiling Canopy

Stock No.: CK800
Price: $4.49
A dramatic new way of making any chandelier removable. Unique design allows quick "twist-on/twist-off" operation. Beautiful brass plating complements any hanging chandelier. Also available in gold-plated version (CK800-1, $5.49).

CIR-KIT CONCEPTS, INC.

Porcelain Type Ceiling Fixture

Stock No.: CK501
Price: $6.49
Dimensions: see below
This fixture may be taped directly into a tape run and brass bradded in place. Perfect for those hard-to-reach areas. Consists of 1-1/2" segment of tape with bulb and base plate attached.

CIR-KIT CONCEPTS, INC.

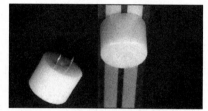

Large Pin-In Ceiling Globe

Stock No.: CK841
Price: $4.98
The easiest-to-install ceiling light yet! Simply place over tape run and pound in. Constructed of tough Lucite plastic. May also be used as tester.

CIR-KIT CONCEPTS, INC.

General Store Lamp

Stock No.: CK320
Price: $9.95
Dimensions: see below
This ceiling fixture may be used for lighting a general store or as a period setting. Incorporates a 12V bulb and hand-blown glass chimney. Dimensions are 3"H with 1-1/2" diameter shade. Bright brass plated.

CIR-KIT CONCEPTS, INC.

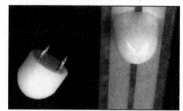

Small Pin-In Ceiling Globe

Stock No.: CK842
Price: $3.98
Dimensions: 3/8"
A smaller version of the CK841; measuring 3/8" in diameter, 12V bulb enclosed. Approximately 60 mA current drain.

CIR-KIT CONCEPTS, INC.

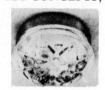

Patterned Glass Ceiling Shade Kit

Stock No.: CK509
Price: $9.49
Dimensions: see below
Completely transparent and embellished with distinctive cut glass pattern. Come with 12V bulb and instructions. Solid brass mounting rim. Diameter 1", 1/2"H.

CLARE-BELL BRASS WORKS

Hanging Shell Lamp

Stock No.: 2025-130
New product! Each glass shade unique. Includes ceiling plate and chain. Replaceable bulb. See your local miniatures dealer.

ELECT-A-LITE

Three-Light Chandelier

Three hand-blown globes with candle-flame, 12V bulbs and brass-looking base complete our lovely chandelier. 2-1/4" from ceiling. 9807 - amber globes, $26.30; 9808 - frosted globes, $26.30; 9809 - white globes, $26.30.

ELECT-A-LITE

Ceiling Globe

Stock No.: 9825
Price: $6.40
Ceiling globe on brass stem.
White translucent globe.

ELECT-A-LITE

Ceiling Connector

Stock No.: 109
Price: $3.95
A twist on/off Ceiling Connector. Connect the top part to your ceiling and the bottom to your ceiling fixture. Then you can take the fixture down any time you want and even replace it if you want—easily! Molded plastic pieces with brass pins.

ELECT-A-LITE

Ceiling Lamp

Stock No.: 9816 (clear globe);
9817 (frosted globe)
Price: $7.50
The starburst pattern on our ceiling globes gives the look of cut glass. 12V bulb. 1" in diameter.

ELECT-A-LITE

Ceiling Lamp
With Large Tulip Shade

Stock No.: 9818
Price: $7.20
A large, frosted tulip shade adorns our ceiling fixture with brass-look base. Complete with a 12V, candle flame, replaceable bulb. 1-1/16" long.

ELECT-A-LITE

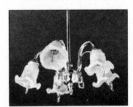

Ceiling Lamp
With Small Tulip Shade

Stock No.: 9819
Price: $7
Ceiling fixture with small, frosted tulip and brass-looking base comes complete with a 12V, replaceable, candle flame bulb. 1" length.

ELECT-A-LITE

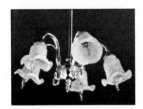

Frosted Five-Light Chandelier

Stock No.: 9812
Price: $43.80
An elegant Victorian chandelier with five frosted tulip shades. Candle flame, 12V, replaceable bulbs included. 2-5/8" from ceiling.

ELECT-A-LITE

Tulip Four-Light Chandelier

Stock No.: 9811
Price: $35.50
Our four-arm chandelier has clear glass shades and replaceable, 12V, candle flame bulbs.

ELECT-A-LITE

Tulip Five-Light Chandelier

Stock No.: 9810
Price: $38.50
This elegant five-arm chandelier has white tulip shades and replaceable, 12V, candle flame bulbs.

HOUSEWORKS, LTD.

Palace Five-Arm Chandelier

Stock No.: 2009
Price: $34.95
Palace chandelier. Five-arm brass colonial with replaceable candle flame bulbs. 325 mA For use with 12V systems. The perfect addition to any miniature house.

HOUSEWORKS, LTD.

Dome Ceiling Fixture

Stock No.: 2011 (gold); 2012 (silver)
Price: $7.95
Dimensions: 1" scale
Intricately detailed, loop design dome ceiling light. 65 mA bulb. For use with 12V systems. Bulb not replaceable.

HOUSEWORKS, LTD.

Tiffany Chandelier

Stock No.: 2008
Price: $5.95
Swag style with hand painted amber shade, 18" of swag chain and spare bulb. 65 mA for use with 12V systems.

HOUSEWORKS, LTD.

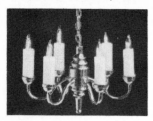

Six-Arm Colonial Chandelier
Stock No.: 2010
Price: $37.95
Six-arm brass masterpiece with replaceable candle flame bulbs. 390 mA For use with 12V systems.

HOUSEWORKS, LTD.

Americana Swag Lantern
Stock No.: 2002
Price: $5.75
Antique brass with white translucent plastic shade. Candleflame bulb 65 mA for use with 12V systems. Replaceable bulb.

MINIATURE HOUSE

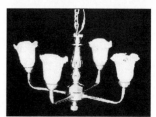

Four-Arm Chandelier With Tulip Shades
Stock No.: MH633
Price: $33.50
Solid brass construction with individual clear tulip shades. 12V screw-in candle flame bulbs for easy replacement.

MINIATURE HOUSE

Hanging Light
Stock No.: MH632
Price: $8
Dimensions: 1" in diameter
Unique hanging light has a half-globe chimney. An economical way to dress up any room. For use in 12V systems.

MINIATURE HOUSE

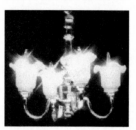

Four-Light Frosted Chandelier
Stock No.: MH756
Price: $37.50
This elegant chandelier has hand-blown, frosted glass tulip shades and replaceable 12V candle flame bulbs. Metal work is gold-tint plating.

MINIATURE HOUSE

Large Half-Globe Ceiling Fixture
Stock No.: MH684
Price: $7.50
Frosted half-globe shade has a hobnail look and fancy treatment in center. Use with 12V system. 1-1/2" in diameter.

MINIATURE HOUSE

Plastic Chandelier
Stock No.: MH612
Price: $6.76
This crystal-look chandelier has a 12V replaceable bulb in the center, surrounded by five candles. An economical fancy look.

MINIATURE HOUSE

Plastic Chandelier
Stock No.: MH758
Price: $8
Attractive, inexpensive chandelier has brass rod and a replaceable 12V screw-in bulb.

MINIATURE HOUSE

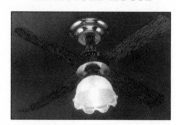

Single Tulip Ceiling Fan
Stock No.: MH719
Price: $15.50
Elegant ceiling fan. Detailed design enhanced by the tulip shade makes it a must for the miniatures enthusiast.

MINIATURE HOUSE

Six-Light Colonial Chandelier
Stock No.: MH789
Price: $36.00
Elegance in miniature is the phrase to describe this 12V brass chandelier. It has replaceable candle flame bulbs and two extra white glass tubes.

MINIATURE HOUSE

Small Brass Hanging Coach Lamp
Stock No.: MH764
Price: $16
Dainty brass hanging coach lamp has a 3" chain. Ideal for an entrance way. Lamp has a replaceable 12V bulb.

MINIATURE HOUSE

Small Half-Globe Ceiling Fixture
Stock No.: MH681
Price: $6
Dimensions: 1" diameter
Elaborately trimmed ceiling fixture with a white half globe. For use with 12V systems. Metal work is gold-tint plating.

MINIATURE HOUSE

Three-Light Frosted Chandelier

Stock No.: MH748
Price: $25
Dainty, frosted tulip shades set off this unique chandelier. The 12V bulbs are replaceable. Metal work is gold-tint plating.

MINIATURE HOUSE

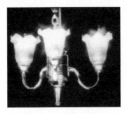

Three-Light Tulip Chandelier

Tulip shades add elegance to this chandelier. It has 12V replaceable bulbs. MH734 - Frosted Shades, $25; MH736 - Clear Shades, $24.

MINIATURE HOUSE

Three-Tulip Ceiling Fan

Stock No.: MH721
Price: $28
The same exquisite detail you've come to expect from Miniature House. Three elegant tulip shades with simple, gold-plated base.

MINIATURE HOUSE

Tiffany Hanging Lamp

Stock No.: MH600 (white); MH601 (colored)
Price: $7
This swag-type, hanging Tiffany chandelier is equipped with a replaceable 12V, screw-in bulb. Metal work is gold-tint plating.

MINIATURE HOUSE

Tiffany Hanging Lamp

Stock No.: MH617; MH617W (white)
Price: $3.50
This non-electric hanging swag-type lamp has a multicolored shade. An inexpensive way to dress up a dollhouse. Also available in white.

MINIATURE HOUSE

Tulip Hanging Lamp

Stock No.: MH635
Price: $6.50
Hanging light has white fluted tulip shade and 12V bulb. Metal work is gold-tint plating.

MINIATURE HOUSE

Two-Arm Chandelier

Stock No.: MH660
Price: $15
This authentic reproduction of a gasolier adds a unique touch to any room. The 12V screw-in bulbs are surrounded by frosted shades. Metal work is gold-tint plated.

MINIATURE HOUSE

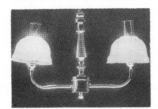

Two-Light Chandelier

Stock No.: MH722
Price: $15
This quaint, two-light chandelier has clear glass chimneys and frosted shades. The 12V candle flame bulbs are replaceable. The metal work is gold-tint plating.

MINIATURE HOUSE

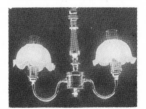

Two-Light Chandelier With Fluted Shades

Stock No.: MH726
Price: $13
Frosted shades enhance this chandelier which has clear chimneys. It has 12V screw-in bulbs and gold-tint plating.

MINIATURE HOUSE

White Hanging Globe Light

Stock No.: MH615
Price: $7.26
Ideal for a high ceiling in an entrance way, or shorten the chain and use it in a kitchen or bath. For use with 12V systems.

MINIATURE HOUSE

Americana Swag Lantern

Stock No.: MH704
Price: $5.50
This lantern, authentic in reproduction detail, has an antiqued-brass look and a white translucent shade. Use in a 12V system.

MINIATURE HOUSE

Ceiling Fan With Light

Stock No.: MH630 (for 12V system)
Price: $13
Perfect for any room in the house, this ceiling fan has a globe light mounted directly under the blades. It hangs 2" from the ceiling and is 4" across.

MINIATURE HOUSE

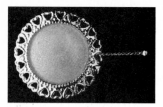

Ceiling Fixture
Stock No.: MH729
Price: $9.26
Dimensions: 1-1/4"
This fixture is gold and comes with a frosted, 3V or 12V bulb.

MINIATURE HOUSE

Ceiling Light Globe
Stock No.: MH652
Price: $6
Classic white globe ceiling fixture has many applications in your dollhouse (for use in a 12V system). Metal work is gold-tint plating.

MINIATURE HOUSE

Ceiling Light With Large Tulip Shade
Stock No.: MH650
Price: $6.50
This ceiling fixture has a large, frosted, tulip shade. The 12V bulb is replaceable. The metal work is gold-tint plating.

MINIATURE HOUSE

Ceiling Light With Small Tulip Shade
Stock No.: MH651
Price: $6.50
Ceiling fixture has small frosted tulip shade and replaceable 12V bulb. Metal work is gold-tint plating.

MINIATURE HOUSE

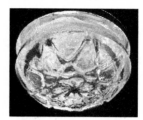

Clear Ceiling Light
Stock No.: MH669
Price: $6.50
This versatile ceiling fixture has a clear shade with a star pattern which causes the light to dance. The 12V bulb is replaceable.

MINIATURE HOUSE

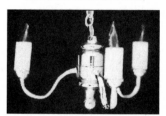

Colonial Three-Light Chandelier
Stock No.: MH624
Price: $24
This authentic solid brass 12V chandelier comes complete with three replaceable candle flame bulbs.

MINIATURE HOUSE

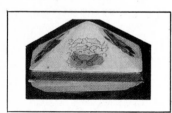

Contemporary Ceiling Fixture
Stock No.: MH682
Price: $8
Just the fixture for your contemporary setting. Nursery decals are separate in package. For use in a 12V system.

MINIATURE HOUSE

Deluxe Three-Tulip Ceiling Fan
Stock No.: MH720
Price: $32
Exquisitely detailed ceiling fan with simulated wood grain paddles and three elegant tulip shades. Even the detailed gold-plated base captures the elegance of the Victorian era.

MINIATURE HOUSE

Deluxe Tulip Ceiling Fan
Stock No.: MH719
Price: $15.50
Dimensions: 3-3/4"W x 1-1/2"H
This deluxe tulip ceiling fan is gold-plated with twisted blades. For use with a 12V power system only.

MINIATURE HOUSE

Desk/Ceiling Lamp
MH697 - (white glass with rose print), $8;
MH698 - (clear glass with rose print), $8.26.

MINIATURE HOUSE

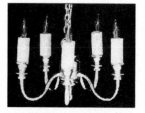

Five-Light Chandelier
Stock No.: MH623
Price: $36.50
This lovely, solid brass chandelier adds elegance to any room and has replaceable 12V candle flame bulbs that screw in for easy replacement.

MINIATURE HOUSE

Five-Light Palace Chandelier
Stock No.: MH788
Price: $32
This lovely, brass chandelier is perfect to formalize any miniature setting. The 12V candle flame bulbs are replaceable. Two extra white glass tubes are included.

MINIATURE HOUSE

Frosted Ceiling Light

Stock No.: MH671
Price: $7
Dimensions: 1" in diameter
For a more muted effect, this fixture with the cut glass look has a frosted shade. It has a 12V screw-in bulb.

MINIATURE HOUSE

Tiffany Hanging Lamp

Stock No.: MH800
Price: $6
Dimensions: 1"=1'
Tiffany hanging lamp features amber shade with silver trim and gold chain. Includes 12V replaceable bulb.

MINIATURE HOUSE

Hanging Lamp

Stock No.: MH831
Price: $10.25
Dimensions: 1" = 1'
Fancy, crystal hanging lamp with gold trim. 12V replaceable bulb included.

MINIATURE HOUSE

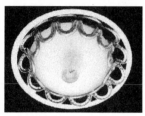

Ceiling Lamp

Stock No.: MH832
Price: $10.75
Dimensions: 1"=1'
This elegant ceiling lamp is frosted white with gold trim. 12V replaceable bulb included.

MINIATURE HOUSE

Ceiling Lamp

Stock No.: MH833
Price: $8.75
Dimensions: 1"=1'
Sparkling crystal ceiling lamp with gold trim. 12V replaceable bulb included.

MINIATURE HOUSE

Hanging Lamp

Stock No.: MH834
Price: $9.50
Dimensions: 1" = 1'
Gold hanging lamp with gold chain. Includes 12V replaceable bulb.

MINIATURE HOUSE

Ceiling Lamp

Stock No.: MH838
Price: $8.75
Dimensions: 1" = 1'
Ceiling lamp is frosted white. Includes 12V replaceable bulb.

JEFFREY W. VIGEANT

Krystle

Stock No.: 1001
Made of Swarovski Austrian crystals, five arms, loaded with prisms and ball crystals, three pea bulbs in center.

JEFFREY W. VIGEANT

Maura

Stock No.: 4001-R
Timeless beauty. Four delicate arms with candles set in gold roses. Replaceable bulbs.

JEFFREY W. VIGEANT

Evelyn

Stock No.: 4003
Five arms with clear glass tulip globes. Made of Swarovski Austrian crystals and unique custom prisms. One pea bulb in center.

JEFFREY W. VIGEANT

Anna

Stock No.: 5003
Made of diamond cut Swarovski Austrian crystals, eight delicate prisms encircle a ball crystal hung from the base. One pea bulb in center.

Electrical Parts & Accessories

AZTEC IMPORTS INC.

Transformers

Stock No.: T8769, T8770, T8772, T8773, T8775
Price: See your local dealer.
Circuit breaker protected 12V transformers for all your lighting needs. T8769 (3 Watt), T8770 (5 Watt), T8772 (10 Watt), T8773 (20 Watt), T8775 (40 Watt).

CIR-KIT CONCEPTS, INC .

12V Showcase Bulb (Super Bright)

Stock No.: CK1018-3
Price: $1.98
Provides up to 50 percent more light than ordinary fluorette bulb. Excellent for perimeter lighting or indirect roombox illumination. Draws 220 mA at 12 volts.

CIR-KIT CONCEPTS, INC .

Spotlight Bulb With 12" White Wires

Stock No.: CK1010-10
Price: $2.98
Bulb contains built-in lens and rotates 360 degrees, plus front to back for complete maneuverability. Consumes approximately 200 mA at 12 volts.

CIR-KIT CONCEPTS, INC.

Fluorette Socket

Stock No.: CK1019
Price: $2.49
Specially constructed holder for fluorette bulbs. Imbedded nails automatically make electrical contact when pounded into tape. Also available with tabs for soldering (CK1019-1, $1.98).

CIR-KIT CONCEPTS, INC.

12V "Flame Tip" GOR Bulb

Stock No.: CK1010-4
Price: $1.49
Use where a candle flame look is required. Consumes approximately 50 mA. GOR bulb, 1/8" diameter with 8" white wires.

CIR-KIT CONCEPTS, INC.

Two-Pole Terminal Block

Stock No.: CK1049
Price: $3.75
Dimensions: see below
Use for interconnecting wires of all sizes. One or more wires may be attached to each screw terminal. Measures 1-1/2" long. Also available in 4-pole (CK1049-1 $4.10) and 6-pole (CK1049-2 $4.39).

CIR-KIT CONCEPTS, INC.
Dimmer Extension Cord

Stock No.: CK802
Price: $24.95
Dimensions: 6' long
A truly simple way to dim dollhouse lights. Plug transformer into cord and adjust to desired level. May also be used for controlling speed of power tools up to 2.5 A.

CIR-KIT CONCEPTS, INC.

Brass Switch Plate Cover

Stock No.: CK1011A
Price: $1.98
The finishing touch for all CK1011 switches. Engraved brass. "Snap-on" fit. Protruding toggle for added feel of realism.

CIR-KIT CONCEPTS, INC.

Hollow Tube Plug

Stock No.: CK1004-2
Price: $2.98
An adaption of our regular CK1004 plug. Wires are fed into hollow tubes. Creates an extremely real and authentic looking plug.

CIR-KIT CONCEPTS, INC.

Brass Outlet Cover

Stock No.: CK1003A
Price: $1.98
The finishing touch for any CK1003 outlet. Engraved brass trim makes this the perfect complement to any room decor. Simply snap on.

CIR-KIT CONCEPTS, INC.

Lead-In Wire
(with on/off switch)

Stock No.: CK1008-1 Price: $5.50
This 6' long lead-in wire is great for connecting 12 volts from any screw-lug type transformer to a tape wired house. Allows for control of dollhouse power at the lead wire. Also available with fuse holder (CK1008-2, $6.75).

CIR-KIT CONCEPTS, INC.

Miniature Slide Switch

Stock No.: CK1011
Price: $3.69
Most remarkable switch yet invented. Entire outer body slides for ON/OFF operation. Only hammer required for installation. Molded-in nails, no loose parts.

CIR-KIT CONCEPTS, INC.

Test Probe

Stock No.: CK204
Price: $3.95
Use this handy tool for checking power along any tape run, even under wallpaper. Constructed with two sharp pins, a self-contained light bulb and safety cap. Overall length: 2" with .175" pin spacing.

CIR-KIT CONCEPTS, INC.

Large Hollow Eyelets

Stock No.: CK1023-2
Price: $1.29 (pkg. of 20)
Dimensions: 3/16"L, .054" I.D., .068" O.D.
These brass eyelets allow insertion of large lamp plugs at any point along tape run. Simply make starter holes and install with CK1044 awl.

CIR-KIT CONCEPTS, INC.

Small Hollow Eyelets

Stock No.: CK1023
Price: $.98 (pkg. of 20)
Dimensions: 1/8"L, .044" I.D., .062" O.D.
These brass eyelets are a substitution for 1/8" brads in making electrical connections. Their larger size simplifies electrical installation. Just use the CK1044 awl.
Also available in 110 paks (CK1023-1; $4.98).

CIR-KIT CONCEPTS, INC.

12V Transformers

Stock No.: see below
Price: see below
CK1009A, 10W, 1A, powers 16-23 GOW bulbs, $20.95.
CK1009B, 5W, 0.5A, powers up to 10 GOW bulbs, $14.95.
CK1009C, 20W, 2A, powers 32-46 GOW bulbs, $26.95.
CK1009D, 40W, 4A, powers 64-100 GOW bulbs, $31.95.
Each transformer from the inexpensive 5 watt unit to our 40 watt powerhouse is circuit-breaker protected. These built-in circuit breakers eliminate any possibility of transformer burn out. Screw lugs on back provide easy access to 12V output. Use for smallest roombox to largest dollhouse.

CIR-KIT CONCEPTS, INC.
Glowing Embers

Stock No.: CK865
Price: $11.95
Dimensions: 1/12 scale
Add a warm glow to any fireplace. Simply install, plug in, and enjoy the realism of a lighted log set. Comes equipped with special 12V orange bulb and universal plug. No separate transformer required. Will not cause dollhouse lights to flicker.

CIR-KIT CONCEPTS, INC.

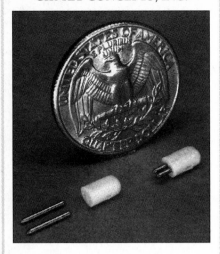

Plug

Stock No.: CK1004
Price: $1.98
The smallest electrical plug made! May be connected to any miniature lamp with household pliers and used over and over again. Mates with CK 1003 outlet. Instructions included.

CIR-KIT CONCEPTS, INC.

Outlet

Stock No.: CK1003
Price: $1.98
First "to scale" and operational outlet ever made. Built with offset nails to allow mounting on vertical or horizontal tape run. Mates with CK1004 and CK1004-2 plugs. Measures .25" by .42".

CIR-KIT CONCEPTS, INC.

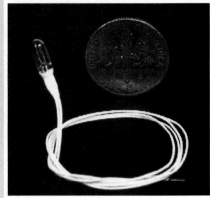

GOW Bulbs

Stock No.: see below
Price: see below
CK1010-1 12V (w/8" black wires) $1.15.
CK1010-1A 12V (w/8" white wires) $1.15.
CK1010-2 16V (w/8" white wires) $1.15.
CK1010-2A 16V (w/8" black wires) $1.15.
CK1010-18 3V (w/18" white wires) $1.15.
CK1010-21 12V (w/12" brown wires) $1.20.
CK1010-22 12V (w/18" brown wires) $1.25.
GOW bulbs measure approximately 1/8" in diameter and are guaranteed for 10,000 operational hours. 12V bulbs draw approximately 60 mA and 16V bulbs approximately 40 mA. Use 16V bulbs where soft, non-glaring light is preferred and 12V bulbs in locations where brighter illumination is necessary.

CIR-KIT CONCEPTS, INC.

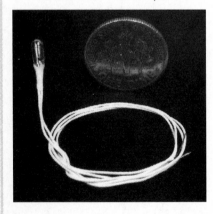

GOR Bulbs

Stock No.: see below
Price: see below
CK1010-6A 12V (w/8" black wires) $1.39.
CK1010-6B 12V (w/8" white wires) $1.39.
CK1010-6C 16V (w/8" black wires) $1.39.
CK1010-6D 16V (w/8" white wires) $1.39.
CK1010-20 12V (w/12" brown wires) $1.49.
CK1010-23 12V (w/8" brown wires) $1.20.
GOR bulbs measure approximately 3/32" in diameter. 12V bulbs draw approximately 55 mA and 16V bulbs approximately 35 mA. Other characteristics same as GOW bulbs.

CIR-KIT CONCEPTS, INC.

Vignette Light Set

Stock No.: CK1047
Price: $9.95
Use for 115V back lighting any vignette box or miniature room. Contains removable switch and plug for easy cord threading. No transformer necessary. Includes 4W bulb.

CIR-KIT CONCEPTS, INC.

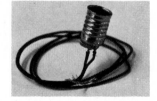

Screw-Base Bulb Socket

Stock No.: CK1010-8
Price: $1.39
Use with CK1010-7 series bulbs for making "screw-in bulb" type fixtures. Has 8" black leads. Also available with white wires (CK1010-8A).

CIR-KIT CONCEPTS, INC.
Tapewire, 5' Roll

Stock No.: CK1002
Price: $2.95, 5' roll
Dimensions: see below
Since 1976, the most popular method of wiring a dollhouse. Completely eliminates the "rats nest" of wiring involved in conventional wiring. Super adhesion allows installation on any surface, even metal. No possibility of overlap shorts with new "sandwich-type" construction. 5/8" wide adhesive tape has 3/16" wide copper foils imbedded between .001" layers of Mylar. Now with color coded copper strips. Also available in 15' (CK1001 $7.95) and 50' (CK1017 $23.95) rolls.

CIR-KIT CONCEPTS, INC.

Three-Watt Transformer

Stock No.: CK1009F
Price: $12.95
Perfect for any installation requiring five or less bulbs. Plugs into wall and provides 12 volts out across screw-lug terminals. Lowest price anywhere.

CIR-KIT CONCEPTS, INC.

Green Heat Shrink Tubes

Stock No.: CK1033
Price: $1.89 (pkg. of 12)
Use for interconnecting green bulb wires. Measure 1/2" long. Made of green polyethylene heat shrink plastic. Also available in clear tubes (CK1033-3).

CIR-KIT CONCEPTS, INC .

12V Screw-Base Bulb

Stock No.: CK1010-7
Price: $1.39
Use with CK1010-8 socket, to make lamps where easy bulb replacement is desirable. 60 mA at 12 volts. Also available in 16V (CK1010-7A) and 8V (CK1010-7C) versions.

CIR-KIT CONCEPTS, INC.

12V Fluorette Bulb (Clear Glass)

Stock No.: CK1018-1
Price: $1.59
Dimensions: 1/4" x 1-1/2"
Ideal for backlighting or indirect miniature illumination. Snaps into CK1019 holder for easy installation. Consumes 80 mA. Also available in frosted glass (CK1018-2).

ELECT-A-LITE

Ceiling Plug

Stock No.: 430
Price: $3.90
1" scale. The ceiling plug is used for attaching chandeliers directly into the copper tape run. Can be painted to match color scheme. 100% reliable and easily removed. Made in the USA.

ELECT-A-LITE

White Shrink Tube

Stock No.: 440
Price: $2.10
Used to join lamps and fixtures to plug wires by heat shrinking without solder or tools. Provides insulation against bare wires touching. Comes in 2-1/2" lengths, two per package. Made in the USA.

ELECT-A-LITE

12V Lighting Transformer

Stock No.: 119
Price: $19.90
American-made transformer with USFPC cord assembly. In-line fuse, switch and patented two-pronged end plug. All one unit, ready-to-use. 21-bulb capacity. 12V, 15 watts.

ELECT-A-LITE

12V Lighting Transformer

Stock No.: 140
Price: $29.95
American-made transformer with USFPC cord assembly. In-line fuse, switch and patented two-pronged end plug. All one unit, ready-to-use. 42-bulb capacity. 12V, 40 watts.

ELECT-A-LITE

Bi-Prong Test Tool

Stock No.: 450
Price: $3.90
Used during installation, for locating tape runs after decorating, finding a break or testing the transformer. Universal, 12V, two-pronged tester. Made in the USA.

ELECT-A-LITE
Copper Foil Double Tape Wire

Stock No.: 239; 259
Price: 30' for $14.30; 50' for $20.90
Wire your dollhouse with a single run of adhesive-backed mylar encasing two 3/16" copper foil tapes. The run is 5/8" wide, and the mylar protection eliminates shorts caused by tape-to-tape contact. Two-color tape makes continuity easy to follow.

ELECT-A-LITE

Candle Flame Replacement Bulbs

Stock No.: 530
Price: $5.50
These 12V, screw-base bulbs are for replacement in miniature lamps and lighting fixtures using candle flame bulbs. Four per package.

Electrical Systems & Accessories

ELECT-A-LITE

Copper Foil Tape

Stock No.: 219
Price: 675" for $5.70
Single copper foil tape 1mm thick and 3/16" wide has a long-aging, pressure-sensitive adhesive protected by easily-removable, peel-off interliner. Easily installed in two parallel runs. No nailing, drilling, grooving or cutting. No tools required.

ELECT-A-LITE

Electrified Christmas Wreath Kit

Stock No.: 610
Price: $27.50
This wreath is prewired with 10 light-emitting diodes (LEDs) in molded plastic. Ready to decorate with greenery, ribbon and beads, which are included. Our patented plug is also included to easily install on any double tape run. Made in the USA.

ELECT-A-LITE

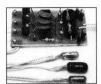

Flickering Fire Unit

Stock No.: 660
Price: $27.90
American-made, solid state electronic control unit with three bulbs contains three separate circuits to allow the bulbs to flicker at random or different rates, creating a most realistic illusion of a burning fire. This miniaturized unit will operate two sets of three bulbs or two different fireplaces. Will not flicker anything else in Your dollhouse—only what you connect to it.

ELECT-A-LITE

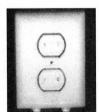

Rectangle Plug

Stock No.: 420
Price: $3.90
1" scale. This one-piece plug is for attaching table and floor lamps directly into the copper tape run. Can be used for two lamps at one time. 100% reliable and easily removed for redecorating. Made in the USA.

ELECT-A-LITE

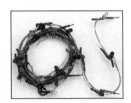

Multi-Purpose, 21-Light Christmas String

Stock No.: 620
Price: $37.90
String of mixed-color, light-emitting diodes (LEDs). Perfect for decorating miniature trees. American-designed and made, these lights can be used with any 12V system for thousands of hours without the inconvenience of bulbs burning out.

ELECT-A-LITE
Sconce Attachment

Stock No.: 400
Price: $2.90
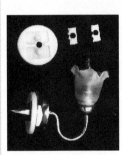
1" scale sconce attachment is used to attach wall sconces and fixtures directly to copper tape runs through wallpaper and paint. Sconce wires attach to prongs (lamp not included). Easily removed for redecorating or bulb changing. Made in the USA.

ELECT-A-LITE

Splicing/Insulating Tape

Stock No.: 480
Price: $2.70
Used to hold in-line splices and right angle splices tightly together and as an insulated separator between copper tape crossovers so they cannot touch. Pre-cut for easy handling and color coded. Two sheets of 32 pieces per packing. Made in the USA.

ELECT-A-LITE

Standard Replacement Bulbs

Stock No.: 531
Price: $5
Extend the life of your miniature electrical fixtures using our screw base 12V replacement bulbs. For lamps and lighting fixtures using standard bulbs. Four per package.

ELECT-A-LITE

Switching Bridge

Stock No.: 470
Price: $13.50
Used to attach a series of roomboxes using only one transformer. 18" bridge has USFPC with in-line fuse, switch and two patented end plugs. Completely assembled and ready to use. Made in USA.

ELECT-A-LITE

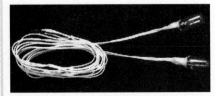

Test Bulb

Stock No.: 490
Price: $3.90
Used for testing electrical installations or electrifying new or existing lamps or fixtures. 12" pigtail leads may be cut to desired length. 80 mA. Two per package.

ELECT-A-LITE

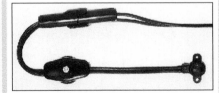

Lead-In Assembly

Stock No.: 460
Price: $8.50
Used with screw terminal transformer. Provides any transformer with a preassembled cord with in-line fuse, switch and patented end plug. Comes without fuse. Made in the USA.

ELECT-A-LITE

Wall Receptacles

Stock No.: 390
Price: $4.70
Plug-in, single wall receptacles. For use with tape wiring systems. Plugs into tape. Four per package.

ELECT-A-LITE

Wall Switch

Stock No.: 410
Price: $5.70
1" scale. Wall switch allows lights to be turned on and off just like your own home. One-piece unit plugs directly into the copper tape runs. Made in the USA.

HANDLEY HOUSE

Complete Doorbell Kit

Stock No.: HH304
Price: $10.95
The complete doorbell kit comes with solid state doorbell buzzer, wiring and push button doorbell switch. Complete instructions included. Easy to install in a finished house. 12V AC.

HOUSEWORKS, LTD.

Assorted Bulbs

Price: $4.95; $5.50
2103/Screw Base Candle Flame Bulbs with socket. 12V, 65 mA. Two sets. 2101/Screw Base Candle Flame Bulbs. 12V, 65 mA Four pieces.

HOUSEWORKS, LTD.

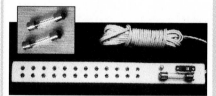

Power Strip & Fuses

Stock No.: 2203; 2216
Price: $7.25; $1.75
2203 - Power Strip - with on/off switch. One piece. Use with 12V transformer.
2216 - Fuses - 1500 mA fuse. Four pcs. per package.

HOUSEWORKS, LTD.

Brass Grommets & Insertion Tool

Stock No.: 2205; 2225
Price: $1.50; $5.95
2205 - Brass Grommets - for electric receptacle (plugs). 1/8" deep and fits Houseworks plugs. To be used with tape wire systems. 20 pieces per package.
2225 - Insertion Tool - makes it easier to insert grommets into your projects.

HOUSEWORKS, LTD.

Flicker Flame Unit

Stock No.: 2019
Price: $3.75
12V, 150 mA for fireplaces. Includes plug and two spare bulbs. Use with separate transformer.

HOUSEWORKS, LTD.

Electrical Wiring

Stock No.: 2217
Price: $4.50
For miniature wiring projects. 50 feet per package, two conductor wire, 32 gauge.

HOUSEWORKS, LTD.

12V Lighting Transformer

Stock No.: 2219
Price: $19.95
12V, U.L. approved. Features automatic circuit breaker. Output of 1333 mA Illuminates up to 21, 12V 65 mA bulbs.

HOUSEWORKS, LTD.

Battery Console

Stock No.: 2212
Price: $2.75
For use with 3V systems. Requires two "C" cell 1.5V batteries. Batteries not included.

HOUSEWORKS, LTD.

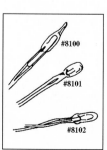

Assorted Bulbs

Stock No.: 8100; 8101; 8102
Price: $.89 each
8100 - Candle Flame Bulb - 16V, white 8" wire, 40 mA.
8101 - Grain of Wheat Bulb - 1.5V, green 8" wire. Good for making Christmas tree light strings, approximately 6 mA.
8102 - Grain of Wheat Bulb - 16V, white 8" wire, 40 mA.

HOUSEWORKS, LTD.

3-V Replacement Screw Base Bulbs

Stock No.: 2213
Price: $2.75
65 mA Four pieces.

HOUSEWORKS, LTD.

Bulbs

Stock No.: 2215; 2214
Price: $2.95; $2.95
2215 - 12V, 65 mA bulbs with sockets. 24" two conductor wire and male plugs. Two sets.
2214 - 12V, 65 mA replacement bulbs. 4 pcs.

HOUSEWORKS, LTD.

Lighting Control Panel

Stock No.: 2200
Price: $14.95
12V lighting control panel for tape and hardware systems. Controls up to eight separate circuits with on/off operation. Includes diode for dimming operation. Also includes fuse and test bulb. Use with 12V transformer.

HOUSEWORKS, LTD.

Single Wall Receptacles

Stock No.: 2218; 2204
Price: $3.95; $1.95
2204 - Male Plugs - six pieces.
2218 - Plug-In Single Wall Receptacles - for use with tape wiring systems. Plugs into tape. Accepts 2204 plug. Four pieces.

HOUSEWORKS, LTD.

Receptacle Extension Cords

Stock No.: 2202; 2201
Price: $2.75; $3.25
2202 - Single Receptacle Extension Cord With Plug - four pieces. 2201 - Triple Receptacle Extension Cord With Plug - two pieces.

MINIATURE HOUSE

Christmas Tree Lights

Stock No.: MH638; MH690 (replacement bulbs)
Price: $30; $7.50
Bright and beautiful Christmas tree lights have 14 replaceable 12V bulbs, with two extra. Replacement bulbs are available.

MINIATURE HOUSE

12V Christmas Tree Bulbs

Stock No.: MH690
Price: $7.50
The package contains four 12V colored bulbs, assorted colors, to replace bulbs in MH638 Christmas tree lights or to add color in a light fixture or lamp.

MINIATURE HOUSE

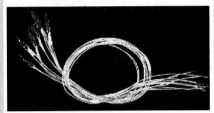

12V Flame Tip Bulbs

Stock No.: MH692
Price: $9
These 12V candle flame tip bulbs are on 8" white wires. There are six bulbs per package.

MINIATURE HOUSE

1500 Milliamp Fuses

Use these fuses to protect both transformer and lighting fixtures. MH778 - 1500 mA, $1.75; MH779 - 2000 mA, $2.50; MH780 - 4000 mA, $2.50; Each package contains 4 fuses.

MINIATURE HOUSE

3V Round Screw-Base Bulbs

Stock No.: MH687
Price: $2.25
These 3V, round, screw-base bulbs are for replacement in 3V lamps and light fixtures and come four per card.

MINIATURE HOUSE

Amber Glass Chimneys

Stock No.: MH688
Price: $7
Hand-blown amber glass chimneys to change the color emphasis of an existing light or create a new one. Four per card.

MINIATURE HOUSE

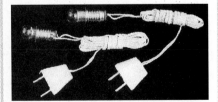

Bulbs With Sockets

Stock No.: MH622
Price: $2.75
Create your own lighting fixtures with these bulbs with sockets. There are two 12V sets per package.

MINIATURE HOUSE

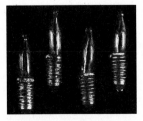

Candle Flame Screw Bulbs

Stock No.: MH611 (12V); MH639 (3V)
Price: $5.50; $7.50
Candle flame screw bulbs come four to a package.

MINIATURE HOUSE

Round Screw Base Bulbs

Stock No.: MH621
Price: $2.75
Each package has four round, screw-base, 12V bulbs to serve as replacements for lamps and lighting fixtures.

Prices are approximate and subject to change

MINIATURE HOUSE

Christmas Tree Lights

Stock No.: MH782 (colored); MH781 (clear)
Price: $36.50; $36.50
These multi-colored or clear lights cascade from a central point. The set has 15 12V bulbs.

MINIATURE HOUSE

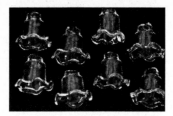

Clear Glass Tulip Shades

Stock No.: MH667
Price: $5.75
Dimensions: 1/2" high
Replacement shades for lamps and light fixtures, or create your own. There are four per card.

MINIATURE HOUSE

Flickering Light Unit

Stock No.: MH714
Price: $3.75
Flickering light unit for fireplaces has flame-colored bulbs and comes with a plug and two spare 12V bulbs.

MINIATURE HOUSE

Frosted Glass Tulip Shades

Stock No.: MH668
Price: $6.25
Dimensions: 1/2" high
Frosted glass tulip shades to create your own light fixtures or replace shades in existing ones. Four per card.

MINIATURE HOUSE

Glass Chimneys

Stock No.: MH665 (clear); MH666 (frosted)
Price: $5 (clear); $5.25 (frosted)
Glass replacement chimneys for lamps and light fixtures come four per card, 11/16" high.

MINIATURE HOUSE

Hand-Blown Glass Globes

Stock No.: MH685 (white); MH693 (clear); MH686 (frosted)
Price: $5.26; $5.26; $6 (frosted)
Four hand-blown replacement globes per card.

MINIATURE HOUSE

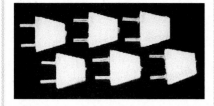

Male Plug

Stock No.: MH658
Price: $1.50
Package contains six male plugs.

MINIATURE HOUSE

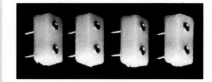

Plug-In Single Wall Outlet

Stock No.: MH776
Price: $6.25
No fuss, no bother. Just plug directly into tape wire for an "instant" outlet. Four per package.

MINIATURE HOUSE

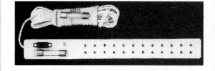

Power Strip With Switch and Fuse

Stock No.: MH653
Price: $7.25
This 12V power strip has a fuse and an off/on switch. Holds 12 male plugs.

MINIATURE HOUSE

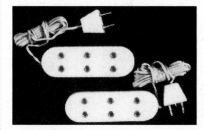

Triple Receptacles

Stock No.: MH656
Price: $2.75
Each triple receptacle has three female plugs and one male plug, as well as an extension cord. For use with 12V systems. Two per package.

MINIATURE HOUSE

Single Receptacles

Stock No.: MH655
Price: $3.25
These single receptacles have a male and female plug and extension cord included. Four per package. For use with 12V systems.

MINIATURE HOUSE

Strip Light

Stock No.: MH619
Price: $8.76
Each strip light comes with one spare bulb and is 2" long.

MINIATURE HOUSE

Superfine Single-Strand Wire
Stock No.: MH691
Price: $6.50
Superfine, single-strand, white wire is 50' long.

MINIATURE HOUSE

Three-Volt Battery Box
Stock No.: MH610
Price: $2.95
This economical dresser is actually a battery box which holds two size C batteries to power your 3V system. Holds up to three lights. 2-1/2"W x 2-1/4"H x 1-1/4"D.

MINIATURE HOUSE

Chandelier Modification Kits.
Stock No.: MH783 - MH786
Price: $6.25
Completely change the look and style of chandeliers with these unique chimneys and shades. Available in four colors: White (MH783); Clear (MH784); Amber (MH785); and blue (MH786).

MINIATURE HOUSE

Two-Strand Wire, 50 ft.
Stock No.: MH654
Price: $4
This two-strand wire is 50' long and is perfect for wiring a dollhouse.

MINIATURE HOUSE

White Replacement Tubes
Stock No.: MH694
Price: $6
White glass tubes for chandeliers and other lighting fixtures. Six per package.

MINIATURE HOUSE

Replaceable Bulbs
Stock No.: MH807
Price: $4.95
Dimensions: 1" = 1'
12V replaceable bulbs. Two per pack.

MINIATURE HOUSE

Battery Box
Stock No.: MH839
Price: $8.95
Dimensions: 1" = 1'
Brown battery box; 3V; two "C" batteries required.

WORKSHOP WISDOM

Scotch brand adhesive foam mounting squares have many uses. One cut into a rectangle and with a ball point pen spring glued across the top very closely resembles a spiral bound note pad. Don't throw away that plaid paper backing, either. It can be put to use to make place mats or folded to resemble table napkins.

*JANE FREEMAN
NEW YORK, NY*

Workshop Wisdom Courtesy of *Nutshell News*—1/94

WORKSHOP WISDOM

Simulated fluorescent ceiling lights can be made from a used up propane cigarette lighter and 16-volt grain of wheat bulbs operating on 12 volts. Make sure the lighter (a) is totally exhausted, then cut off the burner head. Insert a pair of the bulbs, then glue in place a wooden plug (b), taking the lead out through slots in the plug. To dress up the light unit, you can add a frosted light diffuser (c), made from folded drafting Mylar. Then cover the edges of the unit with a strip of stick-on wood grain shelf paper (d). Take the lead up through a small hole in the ceiling, then attach the unit to the ceiling with a small blob of tub sealer, so that it can be peeled free if repair is required.

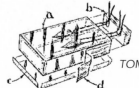

*TOM AND MARY KEMPTON
BALTIMORE, MD*

Workshop Wisdom Courtesy of *Nutshell News*—12/93

Prices are approximate and subject to change

| **MINI-MAGIC** | **MINI-MAGIC** | **MINI-MAGIC** |

Doll House Wiring Video

Stock No.: Video
Price: Retail cost $20
In this video you will see: How to install Cir-Kit Concepts, Inc. 2-conductor tape wire, a ceiling light, a wall switch, a wall outlet, and a fluorette socket. Send $3.50 for brochure. Patent pending. Made in the USA.

Ceiling Canopy Quick Tool

Stock No.: MM800-A
Price: $8, plus shipping
Specially designed to ease the installation of Cir-Kit Concepts, Inc.'s ceiling canopies CK800 and CK800-1. This tool does just that. Patent pending. Made in the USA. Send $3.50 for brochure.

Fluorette Socket Ease Tool

Stock No.: MM1019-A
Price: $10, plus shipping.
Installing Cir-Kit Concepts, Inc.'s fluorette socket CK1019 is made simple by using this specially designed tool. Patent pending. Made in the USA. Send $3.50 for brochure.

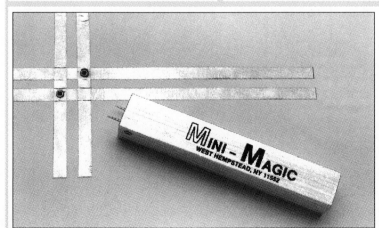

MINI-MAGIC "Connect-It"

Stock No.: MM1322
Price: Retail cost $11
"Connect-It" is designed to help with the installation of most any 2-conductor tape wire. Prior to this tool you made one connection at a time. This tool now allows you to make both electrical connections at one time. Send $3.50 for brochure. Patent pending. Made in the USA.

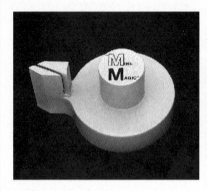

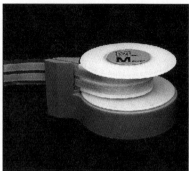

MINI-MAGIC
"Tape Ease"

Stock No.: MM1001
Price: Retail cost $16
Our newest tool has been designed to accept Cir-Kit Concepts, Inc. CK1001 2-connector tape wire and feed it off at the proper height of a little more than 1" from the floor. The reason for that is so that after you have installed your tape line, have papered your walls and applied your rug to the floor, the thickness of the rug now brings you to the proper height of 1" on center to accept Cir-Kit Concepts, Inc. wall plug. Patent pending. Made in the USA. Send $3.50 for brochure.

MINI-MAGIC

MINI-MAGIC

MINI-MAGIC

Easy On

Stock No.: MM1003-1011A
Price: $10, plus shipping.
This metal tool helps in the installation of Cir-Kit Concepts, Inc.'s miniature light switch CK1011 and wall outlet CK1003. It's two tools in one. Patent pending. Made in the USA. Sent $3.50 for brochure.

"Plug-It"

Stock No.: MM777
Price: Retail cost $11
This tool is designed to help with the installation of Houseworks and Miniature House plug and outlet. Send $3.50 for brochure. Patent pending. Made in the USA.

"Sconce-It"

Stock No.: MM007
Price: Reatil cost $10
Our tool "Sconce-It" is designed to help with the installation of Cir-Kit Concepts Inc., #CK801 sconce adapter. Send $3.50 for brochure. Patent pending. Made in the USA.

Prices are approximate and subject to change

Electrical Systems

CIR-KIT CONCEPTS, INC.

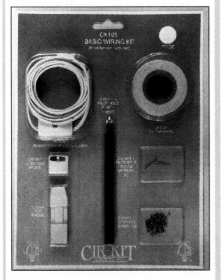

Basic Wiring Kit

Stock No.: CK105
Price: $24.95 plus shipping
Dimensions: all scales
Contains all starter kit electrical parts, except the transformer. You decide which transformer is most appropriate for your dollhouse. An excellent bargain!

CIR-KIT CONCEPTS, INC.

Battery Holders

Stock No.: see below
Price: see below
CK211, "AA" Size, 2 Cell, 3.0V $2.79.
CK211-1,"C" Size, 2 Cell, 3.0V $3.39.
CK211-2, "D" Size, 2 Cell, 3.0V $4.19.
CK211-3, "AAA" Size, 2 Cell, 3.0V $2.49.
CK211-4, "D" Size, 1 Cell, 1.5V $3.15.
CK211-5, "C" Size, 1 Cell 1.5V $2.39.
CK211-6, "AA" Size, 1 Cell, 1.5V $2.19.
CK211-7, "AA" Size, 8 Cell, 12V $3.75.
CK211-8, 9V Battery Clips (2 pak) $1.89. These battery holders accommodate a wide range of battery sizes and provide numerous output voltage and current options. Special design locks each battery in place. Has 18" lead wires.

CIR-KIT CONCEPTS, INC.

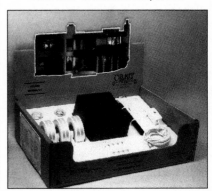

Deluxe Wiring Kit

Stock No.: CK100
Price: $109.98
The ultimate wiring kit. Enough tape and transformer power to wire a 10 or 11-room dollhouse. Includes eight each of our famous Cir-Kit outlets and plugs as well as two sparkling, cut-glass ceiling shades. No previous electrical experience necessary. Extremely thorough and well-illustrated instructions. Also now includes a 40-watt transformer. Ten percent savings over buying parts separately.

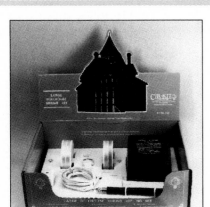

CIR-KIT CONCEPTS, INC.
Large House Wiring Kit

Stock No.: CK103
Price: $71.95
This kit has all the basic starter kit items plus a double quantity of brads and tape wire. Large enough to wire a 9 or 10-room dollhouse. Contains a high-power transformer with automatic circuit breaker capable of lighting 32 to 46 bulbs. Lead wire contains built-in on/off switch. No special tools necessary.

FOR FAST SERVICE, VISIT YOUR LOCAL MINIATURES SHOP

CIR-KIT CONCEPTS, INC .
Round Wire Kit

Stock No.: CK104
Price: $57.95
The ideal kit for round wiring enthusiasts. Contains the most comprehensive round wiring instructions ever written. Instructions cover groove wiring, surface wiring and proper installation procedures for all types of lighting fixtures. Contains powerful 20W transformer for lighting 32 to 46 bulbs and sufficient hookup wire for a six to eight-room dollhouse.

CIR-KIT CONCEPTS, INC.

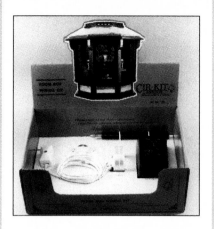

Room Box Wiring Kit

Stock No.: CK102
Price: $35.95
The perfect size kit for any small wiring project. Circuit breaker transformer will power up to 10 miniature bulbs. Features 5' of easy-to-use tape wire.

CIR-KIT CONCEPTS, INC.
Starter Wiring Kit

Stock No.: CK101
Price: $53.95
The most popular wiring kit in the industry today. Uses easy-to apply two-conductor tape wire with embedded copper foils. Wires a five or six-room dollhouse. The 10-watt circuit-breaker protected transformer has a capacity for 16 to 23 bulbs. Lead wire includes on/off switch. Complete instructions included. No previous electrical experience required.

ELECT-A-LITE
Single Copper or Double Tape Wire

American-made kits contain all materials needed to electrify any miniature dollhouse, train board or roombox. Easy to install. Thorough instructions that are easy to follow. Nationwide toll-free 800 service number if you need help or have questions. 100% reliable, with full warranty! Single copper tape kits: 110 - $43.90; 120 - $57.90; 142 - $91. Double tape wire kits: 115 - $47.90; 125 - $61.90; 145 - $95. Our 142 and 145 kits for big houses and 42 bulbs are best buys with ceiling plugs, a lamp and a lamp shade/fixture. Made in the USA. You buy with total confidence!

J. HERMES

Flora Lites

Price: $2.50 - $10
Battery operated, 2AA, various wire lengths and bulbs. Ideal for roomboxes. Also 10-light sets, clear or colored, steady-burn or twinkle.

MINIATURE HOUSE

Wiring Set

Stock No.: MH657
Price: $20
Everything needed to wire a dollhouse, except a transformer. Contains power strip with fuse and switch. The set includes 12 single receptacles, two triple receptacles and an extra fuse.

ARE YOU INTERESTED IN BECOMING A RETAILER OR MAUFACTURER?

Contact: The Miniatures Manufacturers
Industry of America
1100-H Brandywine Blvd.,
PO Box 2188
Zanesville, OH 43702-2188
(614) 452-4541

Outdoor Lighting

AZTEC IMPORTS INC.

Coach Lamps

Stock No.: D9236, M1754, M1719, T8760, T8764, T8717
Price: See your local dealer.
Dimensions: In order as above: 4-1/4"H, 5"H, 1-3/4"H, 1-1/4"H, 1-1/4"H, 1-1/2"H
(D9236) Battery-powered street light, (M1719) Large coach lamp, (T8760) Set/2 Coach Lights, (T8764) Hanging coach lamp, (T8717) Lantern, (M1754) 12V Street lamp.

CLARE-BELL BRASS WORKS

Brass Coach Lamps

Stock No.: 1790-130 (brass); 1790-330 (black finish)
Sold in pairs. Replaceable bulbs. Catalog, more than 200 items, $2. See your local independent miniatures dealer.

CLARE-BELL BRASS WORKS

Elegant Colonial Coach Lamps

Stock No.: 1791-130
Dimensions: 1"=1' scale
Solid brass, gold-plated. Sold in pairs. Replaceable bulbs. Catalog, more than 200 items, $2. See your local independent miniatures dealer.

CLARE-BELL BRASS WORKS

Hanging Coach Lamp

Stock No.: 1792-130
Dimensions: 1"=1' scale
Solid brass. Ceiling plate and 2" of chain included. Replaceable bulbs. Catalog, more than 200 items, $2. See your local independent miniatures dealer.

ELECT-A-LITE

Brass Carriage Lamp

Stock No.: 9801
Price: $14.80
Our authentic reproduction of a carriage lamp will enhance any entryway. Complete with a 12V, replaceable, candle flame bulb. 1-7/8" long.

MINIATURE HOUSE

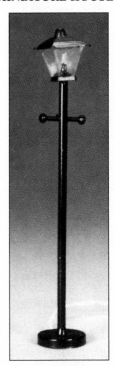

Black Plastic Post Lamp

Stock No.: MH706
Price: $8
This post lamp is an economical way to add authenticity to the exterior of your dollhouse. For use with a 12V system. It stands 5" high.

MINIATURE HOUSE

Black Coach Lamp

Stock No.: MH609 (3V); MH628 (12V)
Price: $4.76; $5
MH609 is especially made for 3V electrification systems. MH628 is a 12V lamp. Both are finished in black.

MINIATURE HOUSE

Brass Carriage Lamp

Stock No.: MH614
Price: $13
This lovely solid brass carriage lamp has a replaceable, 12V, candle flame bulb. An authentic reproduction with a hexagonal base.

MINIATURE HOUSE

Gold Coach Light

Stock No.: MH625
Price: $9
There are two economical coach lights per box.
For use in 12V systems.

MINIATURE HOUSE

Gold Coach Light

Stock No.: MH629
Price: $5.25
Inexpensive 12V coach lamp with gold-painted
plastic trim.

MINIATURE HOUSE

Small Brass Coach Lamps

Stock No.: MH760
Price: $30
Dimensions: 1-1/2"H x 5/8"D
Pair of solid brass coach lamps are smaller than
MH614. Have screw-in, 12V candle flame bulbs.
Sold by the pair.

THE LAWBRE COMPANY

Outdoor Lighting Fixtures

Stock No.: 0501 - 0505
Price: $25 - $70
Beautifully hand-finished lamp posts with screw-in
type replaceable bulbs. Bishop's Crook, 15"H;
Street Lamp, 7-3/4"H, Gallery Lamp Post, 4-1/2"H,
Gallery Lamp Post, 3-1/4"H, Sconce, 2-1/4"H.

Table & Floor Lamps

CIR-KIT CONCEPTS, INC.

Tiffany Shade Floor Lamp

Stock No.: CK808
Price: $12.95
Floor lamp with Tiffany-style lamp shade.
Equipped with replaceable 12V screw-in bulb.
Stands 4-3/4" high with shade diameter of 1-1/2".

CLARE-BELL BRASS WORKS

Elegant Candlestick

Stock No.: 1716-130
Dimensions:1"=1'
Electrified, elegant candlestick available in round
or hex base. Solid brass, gold-plated. Also
available in non-electric. See your local dealer.

CLARE-BELL BRASS WORKS

Candlesticks, Round Base

Stock No.: 1800-111
Solid brass, gold-plated. Catalog, more than 200
items, $2. See your local independent miniatures
dealer.

CLARE-BELL BRASS WORKS

Oil Lamp

Stock No.: 1776-130
Dimensions: 1" = 1'
Solid brass, gold-plated oil lamp. Electric or non-
electric. Shade may be ordered in tall, clear, short,
frosted or tole-painted. See your local dealer.

CLARE-BELL BRASS WORKS

Contemporary Bedroom Lamp

Stock No.: 2022-130
Solid brass and gold-plated base with contemporary floral or plain cloth shade. Replaceable 12V bulb. Catalog, more than 200 items, $2. See your local independent miniatures dealer.

CLARE-BELL BRASS WORKS

Contemporary Table Lamp

Stock No.: 2021-130
Solid brass and gold-plated base with contemporary floral or plain cloth shade. Replaceable 12V bulb. Catalog, more than 200 items, $2. See your local independent miniatures dealer.

CLARE-BELL BRASS WORKS

Hurricane Lamp

Stock No.: 1750-130
Solid brass. Replaceable bulbs. Hand blown glass chimney. Catalog, more than 200 items, $2. See your local independent miniatures dealer.

CLARE-BELL BRASS WORKS

Orient Express Lamp

Stock No.: 1986-130
Solid brass, gold-plated, hand blown glass and electrified. Replica of Orient Express gas lamp. Replaceable bulbs. Catalog, more than 200 items, $2. See your local independent miniatures dealer.

DOLL HOUSE SHOPPE

Table Lamps

Price: See your local dealer.
Dimensions: 1" scale
All of our lamps are handmade and original. Most are fully electrified, and most are available in a choice of colors.

ELECT-A-LITE

Brass Desk Lamp

Stock No.: 9814
Price: $6.90
Our brass lamp will enhance any desk or secretary. 12V bulb. 1-1/8" high.

ELECT-A-LITE

Hurricane Lamp With White Shade

Stock No.: 9822
Price: $6.80
Our table lamp is complete with white shade and globe and 12V bulb.

ELECT-A-LITE

Table Lamp With Scalloped Shade

Stock No.: 9823
Price: $6.80
This table lamp comes with a white scalloped shade, brass-color base and trim and 12V replaceable bulb. 2-3/8" high.

ELECT-A-LITE

Floor Lamp

Stock No.: 9824
Price: $7.90
Lovely brown and brass-toned floor lamp. White shade with gold braid trim.

ELECT-A-LITE

Table Tiffany With Multi Colors

Stock No.: 9821
Price: $7
Multi-colored Tiffany table lamp has an antiqued brass-looking base. Complete with a 12V standard replaceable bulb. 2" high.

ELECT-A-LITE

Electric Candles

Stock No.: 9826
Price: $13
Traditional brass candlesticks. Sold in pairs. Lovely in any setting. Replaceable bulbs 12V.

Electrical Systems & Accessories

ELECT-A-LITE

Floor Lamp

Stock No.: 9827
Price: $7.90
Elegant, brass-like finished floor lamp. White shade with gold braid trim. 12V.

HOUSEWORKS, LTD.

Antique Brass Webster with Crown Finial

Stock No.: 2006
Price: $4.95
Dimensions: 1" scale
Tiffany table lamp. Antique brass finish. Hand painted Webster shade with finial. Includes spare bulb. 65 mA For use with 12V systems.

MINIATURE HOUSE

Table Lamps

Stock No.: MH613
Price: $3.76
These cute, non-electric lamps come in assorted colors and styles. Two per package.

MINIATURE HOUSE

Three-Tulip Straight Floor Lamp

Stock No.: MH710
Price: $15.50
This eclectic mixture of the Victorian and Contemporary eras creates a unique floor lamp. The three 12V candle flame bulbs are replaceable. Gold-tint plating.

MINIATURE HOUSE

Table/Desk Lamp

Stock No.: MH703
Price: $12.50
Table/desk lamp with large frosted tulip shade.

MINIATURE HOUSE

Table/Desk Lamp

Stock No.: MH705
Price: $12.50
Fringed table/desk lamp with rose decal.

MINIATURE HOUSE

Tiffany Table Lamp

Stock No.: MH607
Price: $6.26
Lamp is multi-colored with an antiqued brass-looking base. It has a replaceable 12V screw-in bulb and stands 2" high. An extra bulb is included.

MINIATURE HOUSE

Three-Tulip Arched Floor Lamp

Stock No.: MH712
Price: $15.50
This elegant floor lamp creates an exquisite atmosphere. The unusual base and arched posts are gold-tint plating. Lamp stands 4-1/8" high.

MINIATURE HOUSE

Tiffany Table Lamp

Stock No.: MH608
Price: $5
This lamp has a multi-colored shade with an antiqued brass-looking base. It has a replaceable 12V screw-in bulb and stands 2" high. An extra bulb is included.

MINIATURE HOUSE

Tiffany Table Lamp

Stock No.: MH627
Price: $6.50
Lamp has a white removable shade trimmed in gold. Bulb is screw-in and an extra bulb is included. For use in a 12V system. Lamp stands 1-7/8" high.

Prices are approximate and subject to change

MINIATURE HOUSE

Tiffany Table Lamp

Stock No.: MH631
Price: $6.50
An attractive lamp with a white diamond-patterned shade. It has a 12V screw-in bulb and an extra bulb is included in package. Lamp stands 1-7/8" high.

MINIATURE HOUSE

Tiffany Table Lamps

Stock No.: MH620
Price: $11.50
Lamps with multi-colored shades come two per box. Replaceable 12V bulbs, 2 extra per box. Styles are assorted. Lamps stand 1-7/8" high.

MINIATURE HOUSE

Victorian Floor Lamp

Stock No.: MH762
Price: $11.50
This graceful Victorian floor lamp has a large fluted tulip shade and a gold-toned maple leaf on the arch of the post. It comes with a replaceable 12V screw-in bulb.

MINIATURE HOUSE

Wall/Desk Lamp

Stock No.: MH661
Price: $7
The curve-necked lamp is very versatile, useful both as a wall light or a desk lamp. The 12V bulb is replaceable. Metal work is gold-tint plating.

MINIATURE HOUSE

White Table Lamp Painted Design

Stock No.: MH663
Price: $8.76
Ceramic-looking base has a painted design. Shade is white, trimmed in gold braid. The lamp has a 12V, screw-in bulb and stands 2-1/2" high.

MINIATURE HOUSE

Victorian Floor Lamp

Stock No.: MH647
Price: $7.50
This lovely floor lamp has a white half-globe shade. Metal work is gold-tint plating. An economical way to dress up your Victorian home. For use in a 12V system, it stands 4-1/4" high.

MINIATURE HOUSE

Ballerina Table Lamp

Stock No.: MH670
Price: $8.26
Perfect for the little girl's room, this charming lamp has a white shade trimmed in gold paint. The metal work is gold-tint plating. For use in a 12V system. It stands 2-3/8" high.

MINIATURE HOUSE

Bedroom Table Lamp

Stock No.: MH664
Price: $8.76
Small table lamp has a ginger jar shaped base and a removable white cloth shade. The 12V bulb is replaceable. Metal work is gold-tint plating.

MINIATURE HOUSE

Bedroom Table Lamp

Stock No.: MH662
Price: $8.50
This mini boudoir lamp has a graceful base and a white cloth shade. The 12V screw-in bulb is replaceable. The metal work is gold-tint plating. It stands 1-1/4" high.

MINIATURE HOUSE

Brass Desk Lamp

Stock No.: MH708
Price: $6.26
The brass desk lamp is ideal for the office or teen's desk. Use with a 12V system.

MINIATURE HOUSE

Hurricane Table Lamp

Stock No.: MH805
Price: $18.25
Dimensions: 1"=1'
This beautiful hurricane table lamp features hand-blown, red tinted glass with gold trim. Includes 12V replaceable bulb.

MINIATURE HOUSE

Hurricane Table Lamp

Stock No.: MH806
Price: $18.25
Dimensions: 1"=1'
This beautiful green hurricane table lamp features hand-blown glass with gold trim. Includes 12V replaceable bulb.

MINIATURE HOUSE

Hanging Table Lantern

MH713 - Hanging table lantern (white), $11.
MH715 - Hanging table lantern (frosted), $11.
MH717 - Hanging table lantern (clear), $12.50.

MINIATURE HOUSE

Elegant Table Lamp

Stock No.: MH813
Price: $10.95
Dimensions: 1"=1'
Elegant table lamp with clear, hand-blown glass, rose print and gold base. Includes 12V replaceable bulb.

MINIATURE HOUSE

Elegant Table Lamp

Stock No.: MH814
Price: $10.95
Dimensions: 1"=1'
This lamp has white shade and gold base. Includes 12V replaceable bulb.

MINIATURE HOUSE

Table Lamp

Stock No.: MH815
Price: $10.95
Dimensions: 1"=1'
This lamp features a white, pleated shade and silver base. Includes a 12V replaceable bulb.

MINIATURE HOUSE

Table Lamp

Stock No.: MH816
Price: $10.95
Dimensions: 1"=1'
This unique table lamp features a white, pleated shade and silver base. Includes 12V replaceable bulb.

MINIATURE HOUSE

Table Lamp

Stock No.: MH817
Price: $10.95
Dimensions: 1"=1'
This lamp comes with a white, pleated shade, silver base and trim. 12V replaceable bulb included.

MINIATURE HOUSE

Elegant Table Lamp

Stock No.: MH818
Price: $10.95
Dimensions: 1"=1'
Elegant table lamp, hand-blown, white glass with rose print and silver base. 12V replaceable bulb included.

MINIATURE HOUSE

Table Lamp

Stock No.: MH819
Price: $10.95
Dimensions: 1"=1'
This table lamp comes with a white, pleated shade and silver base. 12V replaceable bulb included.

MINIATURE HOUSE

Table Lamp

Stock No.: MH820
Price: $11.50
Dimensions: 1"=1'
This table lamp comes with a white shade and silver base. 12V replaceable bulb included.

MINIATURE HOUSE

Elegant Table Lamp

Stock No.: MH802
Price: $11.50
Dimensions: 1"=1'
This lovely table lamp features hand-blown glass with flower design and gold base. Includes 12V replaceable bulbs.

Prices are approximate and subject to change

MINIATURE HOUSE

Floor Lamp

Stock No.: MH801
Price: $9.25
Dimensions: 1"=1'
This handsome floor lamp features white shade with gold trim, gold stand & base and clear shelf in the center of stand. Includes 12V replaceable bulbs.

MINIATURE HOUSE

Table Lamp

Stock No.: MH808
Price: $8.95
Dimensions: 1"=1'
This dainty table lamp features a white shade and gold base. Perfect for an office or bedroom. Includes 12V replaceable bulb.

MINIATURE HOUSE

Modern Table Lamp

Stock No.: MH810
Price: $10.95
Dimensions: 1"=1'
This modern table lamp features a white shade and black & teal base with gold trim. Includes 12V replaceable bulb.

MINIATURE HOUSE

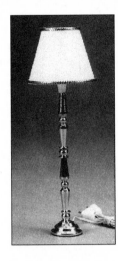

Floor Lamp

Stock No.: MH718
Price: $7.50
Lovely floor lamp has a gold-toned base and white plastic shade trimmed with gold braid. It is equipped with a replaceable 12V screw-in bulb and stands 4-1/2" high.

MINIATURE HOUSE

Table Lamp

Stock No.: MH811
Price: $9.95
Dimensions: 1"=1'
This unique table lamp can also be used as a ceiling lamp. Black & white base with gold trim. Includes 12V replaceable bulb.

MINIATURE HOUSE

Elegant Table Lamp

Stock No.: MH812
Price: $10.95
Dimensions: 1"=1'
Elegant table lamp has frosted, hand-blown glass with flower print and gold base. Includes 12V replaceable bulb.

MINIATURE HOUSE

Modern Table Lamp

Stock No.: MH824
Price: $12.50
Dimensions: 1" = 1'
This modern table lamp has white shade, red-swirl design base and gold trim. 12V replaceable bulb included.

MINIATURE HOUSE
Children's Lamps

MH793 - Angel, $11.26. MH798 - Kitty, $11.
MH799 - Large Teddy, $11. MH792 - Little Girl, $10.
MH795 - Small Teddy - $11. MH796 - Elephant, $9.25.
MH797 - Puppy, $10.26.

MINIATURE HOUSE

Floor Lamp

Stock No.: MH716
Price: $9.26
Floor lamp with white plastic shade trimmed with gold braid. It is equipped with a replaceable 12V screw-in bulb and stands 4-3/4" high.

MINIATURE HOUSE

Table Lamp

Stock No.: MH825
Price: $10.75
Dimensions: 1"=1'
This elegant table lamp comes with a white, scalloped shade, gold base and trim. 12V replaceable bulb included.

MINIATURE HOUSE

Table Lamp

Stock No.: MH826
Price: $10.75
Dimensions: 1"=1'
Table lamp with white shade and silver base. 12V replaceable bulb included.

MINIATURE HOUSE

Elegant Table Lamp

Stock No.: MH837
Price: $9.95
Dimensions: 1"=1'
Beautiful, crystal table lamp with gold base and trim. Includes 12V replaceable bulb.

MINIATURE HOUSE

Table Lamp

Stock No.: MH835
Price: $9.50
Dimensions: 1"=1'
Unique, crystal table lamp with gold base and trim. Includes 12V replaceable bulb.

MINIATURE HOUSE

Double Ceiling/Desk Lamp

Stock No.: MH672
Price: $14.26
The entwined necks of this double light enhance the beauty of the frosted, fluted shades. For use in a 12V system. It has screw-in replaceable bulbs. Metal work is gold-tint plating.

MINIATURE HOUSE

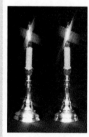

Electric Candles

Stock No.: MH768
Price: $14.50
Dainty solid-brass candle stands have 12V candles. Sold in pairs.

MINIATURE HOUSE

Hurricane Lamp

Stock No.: MH766
Price: $9
Solid-brass replica with hand-blown chimney is 12V and is a lovely addition to any miniature project.

MINIATURE HOUSE

Gold-Fringed Table Lamp

Stock No.: MH602
Price: $6.26
Removable white shade with gold braid and fringe accents this lamp. It has a replaceable screw-in bulb. The base is gold-tint plating. Use with 12V systems only. It stands 3" high.

MINIATURE HOUSE
Children's Lamps

Stock No.: MH791, MH794
Price: $11.26; $9.25
Dimensions: 2"H
MH791 - Gold and white shade with black and white horse, red and yellow saddle and reins.
MH794 - Gold and white shade with yellow duck. Both supplied with a 12V bulb.

MINIATURE HOUSE

Hurricane Lamps
Stock No.: MH695; MH696
Price: $18.25
MH695 - Hurricane Table Lamp - hand-blown white glass with rose print. MH696 - Hurricane Lamp - hand-blown clear glass with rose print.

MINIATURE HOUSE

Karo-Style Table Lamp
Stock No.: MH604
Price: $6
This lovely reproduction has a white chimney and antiqued brass-look finish on the base. For use in 12V systems, it's 2-1/8" high.

MINIATURE HOUSE

Karo Table Lamp With Shade
Stock No.: MH702
Price: $6
This karo table lamp has a white translucent shade and antiqued brass-look base. It is 2-1/8" high. For use in a 12V system.

MINIATURE HOUSE

Miniature House Lights
Stock No.: MH723; MH725; MH727
MH723 - Elegant Desk Lamp, $9.50.
MH725 - Table Lamp, White Pleated Shade, $8.26.
MH727 - Rhinestone Ceiling Chandelier - $21.

MINIATURE HOUSE

Shell Table Lamp
Stock No.: MH775
Price: $11
This gold-plated, bendable shell table lamp is supplied with a 3 or 12V bulb. It is 1-1/4" high.

MINIATURE HOUSE

Table Lamp
Stock No.: MH642
Price: $6
Lamp has scalloped plastic shade and dark base. The 12V bulb is replaceable and an extra bulb is included. Available in white or peach, it stands 2-3/8" high.

MINIATURE HOUSE

Table Lamp
Stock No.: MH643
Price: $6.26
Lamp has plastic removable shade and replaceable 12V bulb. Extra bulb included. Dark base. Available in white or peach, it stands 2-1/2" high.

MINIATURE HOUSE

Table Lamp
Stock No.: MH699
Price: $10.50
Elegant table lamp that is white blown glass with rose print.

MINIATURE HOUSE

Table Lamp
SPrice: $7.76
Lamp has a white shade trimmed in gold braid. It has a replaceable 12V screw-in bulb and stands 2-3/8" high.
MH618 - gold-toned base;
MH618A - dark-stained base.

MINIATURE HOUSE

Table Lamp
Price: $7.76
MH707 - Glazed Ceramic Table Lamp (pastel pink);
MH709 - Glazed Ceramic Table Lamp (ivory);
MH711 - Glazed Ceramic Table Lamp (pastel blue).

MINIATURE HOUSE

Table Lamp With Clear Globe
Stock No.: MH759
Price: $11.75
The ball globe with tulip design makes an attractive addition to your dollhouse. The simple gold-plated base will enhance any decor. It works with a 12V system.

MINIATURE HOUSE

Table Lamp With White Shade
Stock No.: MH757
Price: $9.75
Electric lamp with modern white shade and gold-plated base. Supplied with a 12V bulb.

NI-GLO® LAMPS

Hand China Painted Lamp

Stock No.: 7; 20; 30; 43
Graceful Victorian table lamp adds a unique touch to any room. Floral designs. Replaceable, 12V light. Made in USA.

NI-GLO® LAMPS

Hanging Victorian Chandeliers

Stock No.: 25; 48
Fancy chandeliers with solid brass filigree trim. Hand china painted dome decorated with roses. Replaceable 12V light. Made in USA.

NI-GLO® LAMPS

Victorian Table Lamps

Stock No.: 23; 31; 24; 34
Exquisitely handcrafted and decorated translucent porcelain shades with or without crystals. Replaceable, 12V light. Made in USA.

NI-GLO® LAMPS

Handcrafted Brass Floor Lamp

Stock No.: 64
Hand china painted. Solid brass floor lamp creates cozy living room. Shade decorated with pink multi-colored cabbage roses. Replaceable, 12V light. Made in USA.

NI-GLO® LAMPS

Handcrafted Brass Floor Lamp

Stock No.: 101
Handcrafted antique floor lamp, available in solid brass or bronze finish. Replaceable 12V light. Made in USA.

NI-GLO® LAMPS

Solid Bronze Lamp Base

Stock No.: 50; 57; 26
Hand china painted shade with solid antique bronze-finished base. All Ni-Glo® lamps have replaceable 12V light. Made in USA.

TITMOUSE COLLECTIBLES
Tiffany Lamps

Price: $42.99 floor lamp/
$24.99 table lamp. Plus shipping.
The artistry of "Tiffany" floor lamps. The beauty of pierced paper table lamps. Lamps that make a statement. Lamps that provide that perfect touch. Glorious variety of "Tiffany" designs— also available as chandeliers. Custom orders and dealer inquiries welcome.

JEFFREY W. VIGEANT

Halloween Boo! Lamp

Stock No.: 111H-R
This spooky little ghost is the perfect "Trick or Treat" item. Replaceable bulb.

JEFFREY W. VIGEANT

Elegant Table Lamp

Stock No.: 602-R
Dimensions: 2" tall
Antique, white shade set atop a body of gold-plated brass. Understated elegance.

JEFFREY W. VIGEANT

Egg Folk Nursery Lamps

Shown left to right. 106-R - Blue egg; 108-R - Lavender egg; 110-R - Pale green egg. Replaceable bulbs. Extraordinary detail. Heirloom quality.

JEFFREY W. VIGEANT

Nursery Novelties Lamps

100-R - Boy Bunny; 102-R - Girl Bunny. Lamps of unequaled detail. Replaceable bulbs.

JEFFREY W. VIGEANT

Oriental Table Lamp

Stock No.: 603-R
Dimensions: 2.5" tall
The dark teal body is beautifully detailed. Design is hand painted in gold, white and copper. Gold plated brass accents. Replaceable bulb.

JEFFREY W. VIGEANT

Fancy Table Lamp

Stock No.: 604-R
Dimensions: 2.5" tall
Orange and cream body set on a distinctive base of gold-plated brass. Replaceable bulb.

JEFFREY W. VIGEANT

Victorian Lamps

Dimensions: 1.5" tall
605-R - Victorian Globe Lamp; 606-R - Victorian Tulip Lamp. Base features etched design. Replaceable bulbs.

Wall Fixtures

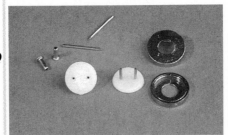

CIR-KIT CONCEPTS, INC.
Sconce Adapter

Stock No.: CK801
Price: $4.95
Dimensions: 1/2" diameter—1" scale
Using this adapter a sconce may be removed and installed in one simple push-pull operation. For the first time ever, a sconce may be easily mounted on the same side of the wall as the tapewire. The snap-on adapter ring is fully brass plated making it suitable for even the most ornate of wall fixtures.

"D" DESIGN AND REPAIR

Angel Wall Sconce

Stock No.: LA-1
Price: $33 (w/elect.); $14 (non-elect.)
Dimensions: 2-1/4"W x 1-1/2"H
Romantic angel lighting for table, floor and wall. Sconce comes with replaceable bulbs or non-electric (candles not included). Available in four finishes.

ELECT-A-LITE

Wall Sconce With Two Tulips

Stock No.: 9806
Price: $12.70
Two-arm wall sconce with dainty, frosted tulip shades and brass-looking base. Replaceable candle flame 12V bulb included. 1" long.

ELECT-A-LITE

Wall Lamp With Candle

Stock No.: 9803
Price: $6.90
One-arm candle sconce with brass-looking base comes with a replaceable12V candle flame bulb. 1" long.

ELECT-A-LITE

Wall Sconce
With Frosted Canted Tulip

Stock No.: 9804
Price: $7.50
One-arm canted wall sconce with frosted tulip shade. Comes with 12V replaceable candle flame bulb. 1" long.

ELECT-A-LITE

Wall Lamp With Two Candles

Stock No.: 9802
Price: $13.40
This wall sconce with two arms and brass-looking base comes with two replaceable 12V candle flame bulbs. 1" long.

HOUSEWORKS, LTD.

Colonial
Coach Lantern

Stock No.: 2014
Price: $14.75
Brass lantern with replaceable candle flame bulb. 65 mA For use with 12V systems.

HOUSEWORKS, LTD.

Colonial
Wall Sconce

Stock No.: 2013
Price: $14.25
Two-arm brass sconce with replaceable candle-flame bulbs. 130 mA For use with 12V system.

MINIATURE HOUSE

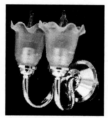

Double-Tulip Wall Sconce

Stock No.: MH673
Price: $11
The lovely, frosted tulip shades add elegance to your miniature creation. The 12V candle flame bulbs are replaceable. Metal work is gold-tint plating.

MINIATURE HOUSE

Bar Light

Stock No.: MH659
Price: $15
This bar light has many uses—make-up area, bar display boxes, contemporary settings. It has three 12V bulbs, Metal work is gold-tint plating.

MINIATURE HOUSE

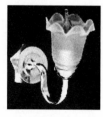

Canted Wall Sconce

Stock No.: MH640
Price: $6.50
This canted wall sconce has a frosted tulip shade. Metal work is gold-tint plating. For use in 12V systems.

MINIATURE HOUSE

Canted Wall Sconce With Globe

Stock No.: MH641
Price: $7.76
Lovely canted wall sconce has a white globe shade. Metal work is gold-tint plating. Bulb is 12V.

MINIATURE HOUSE

Wall Lamp With Candle

Stock No.: MH605
Price: $6
This brass-tone sconce has a hexagonal back and a 12V candle flame bulb.

MINIATURE HOUSE

Wall Lamp With Two Candles

Stock No.: MH606
Price: $14
This two-arm wall sconce works with any 12V electrification system. Metal work is gold-tint plating.

MINIATURE HOUSE

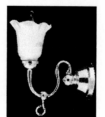

Wall Sconce

Stock No.: MH636
Price: $8
A lovely addition to any hallway, bedroom or bathroom. The sconce has a white fluted tulip shade and a 12V screw-in candle flame bulb. Metal work is gold-tint plating.

MINIATURE HOUSE

Wall Sconce

Stock No.: MH701
Price: $9.50
Wall sconce with back plate reflector.

Prices are approximate and subject to change

MINIATURE HOUSE

Wall Sconce
Stock No.: MH761
Price: $13.25
Medallion wall sconce with clear globe and gold-plated base and medallion. Comes with a 12V bulb.

MINIATURE HOUSE

Wall Sconce With White Globe
Stock No.: MH603
Price: $4.50
A classic sconce perfect for lighting stairs, hallways or porches. Metal work is gold-tint plating. 12V only.

MINIATURE HOUSE

Wall Sconce
Stock No.: MH803
Price: $9
Dimensions: 1" = 1'
This attractive wall sconce features hand-blown glass with gold trim. 12V replaceable bulb included.

JEFFREY W. VIGEANT

Wall Sconces
Stock No.: 601-R
Made of fine, gold-plated brass. Candles set in gold roses feature replaceable bulbs. Sold as a pair.

WORKSHOP WISDOM

I n the January '90 issue of NN, Ingrid found one solution to the problem of effectively displaying a German stove. Here is another, that has the benefit of not occupying valuable wall space. Sandie had someone use a table saw to cut a piece of wood to the shape shown, so that it would fit in the corner of the kitchen to create a floor-to-ceiling chimney breast. Be sure to wallpaper the kitchen first, cover the chimney breast next with either wallpaper or brick, *then* glue it into place. Although I have not illustrated it, I seem to recall that stoves stood on a stone or cement hearth that had a raised curb, which retained spilled hot ashes.

*SANDY KNOWLES
RIVER, VA*

Workshop Wisdom *Courtesy of* Nutshell News—11/93

Misc. Electrification

Subscribe to *Nutshell News* and learn how you can make miniatures yourself! Call toll free: (800) 446-5489

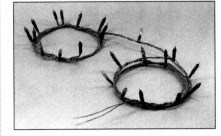

CIR-KIT CONCEPTS, INC
24-Bulb Colored Flame-Tip Christmas String
Stock No.: CK1020-7
Price: $35.95
This string is constructed with the smallest "flame-shape" bulbs made (.079" in dia.), making them a perfect "to scale" light source for any Christmas tree. Same length as CK1020-5. Also available with clear bulbs (CK1020-8, $33.95).

CIR-KIT CONCEPTS, INC.

Cir-Kit Tape Wiring Video

Stock No.: CK1015-4
Price: $29.95
Dimensions: VHS Format
This instructional video describes in detail all the steps involved in tape wiring a dollhouse. Filmed by a professional studio it not only shows the application of tapewire in a full-size dollhouse, but the installation of outlets, switches, sconce adapters, and ceiling canopies as well. Running time, 27 minutes.

CIR-KIT CONCEPTS, INC.

24-Bulb Colored Christmas String

Stock No.: CK1020-5
Price: $31.95
The first of its kind. String wound around tree in concentric circles from top to bottom. 1" between bulbs. 24" lighted length. 12" green lead wire. Also available with clear bulbs (CK1020-6, $29.95).

ELECT-A-LITE

Electrified Christmas Wreath Kit

Stock No.: 610
Price: $27.50
This wreath is prewired with 10 light-emitting diodes (LEDs) in molded plastic. Ready to decorate with greenery, ribbon and beads, which are included. Our patented plug is also included to easily install on any double tape run. Made in the USA.

ELECT-A-LITE

Multi-Purpose, 21-Light Christmas String

Stock No.: 620
Price: $37.90
String of mixed-color, light-emitting diodes (LEDs). Perfect for decorating miniature trees. American-designed and made, these lights can be used with any 12V system for thousands of hours without the inconvenience of bulbs burning out.

MINIATURE HOUSE

Tie Pin

Stock No.: MH616
Price: $7.26
Dimensions: 3/4"H x 1/2"W
This lovely, Miniature House, non-working light pin looks great on any tie or blouse. It comes in gold with a clear bulb.

MINIATURE HOUSE

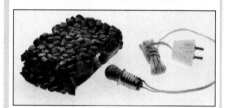

Glowing Embers

Stock No.: MH804
Price: $9.95
Dimensions: 1" = 1'
These glowing embers give a realistic look to any fireplace. Includes 12V replaceable bulbs.
Size: 1" x 1-1/2".

WORKSHOP WISDOM

A jar of colored lollipops on your mini store counter would be the finishing touch. Elmer's colored glue is now available, so put drops of the glue (a) on waxed paper, cut plastic sticks (b) from clothing tags, nylon bristle or nylon monofilament, and insert them into the glue drops. Once they are dry, peel them from the paper. I am told that food coloring mixes well with regular white glue; if that is the case, the color range is endless.

*DIANE NALEFSKI
BLOOMINGTON, IL*

Workshop Wisdom
Courtesy of *Nutshell News—2/94*

WORKSHOP WISDOM

Ever heard of Pasta Alphabets? They are about 3/16" (5mm) tall, and when painted they can be glued to store front signs, Christmas stockings, and elsewhere. The samples supplied by Lois were eye-catching in gold.

*LOIS WITTNER
SAN DIEGO, CA*

Workshop Wisdom Courtesy of *Nutshell News—2/94*

Prices are approximate and subject to change

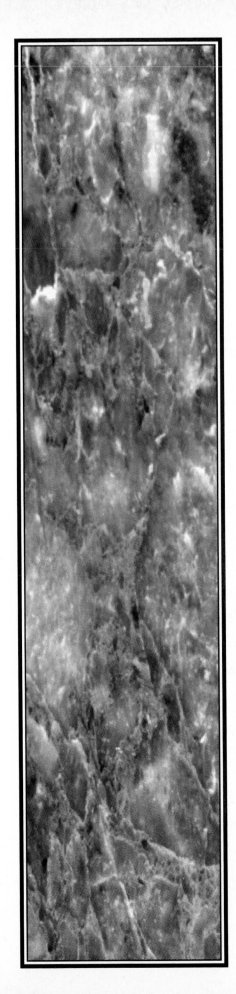

INTERIOR DECORATING

MATERIALS

Fabric & Trim

Miniature Designer Fabrics

Price: $6 - $8.50 per panel
Dimensions: 9" x 16" approximately; 1", 1/2", some 1/4" scale
Designer fabrics suitable for upholstery and interior decor in silks and cotton. Can be printed in many different colors. Send $5 for prices and samples.

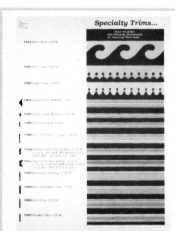

CLASSICS BY HANDLEY
Specialty Trim

Stock No.: CLA70300 - CLA70312
CLA70300 - Picket Trim - 5/8" x 24", $2.98;
CLA70301 - Fleur Trim - 5/8" x 24", $2.98;
CLA70302 - Large Cornice Molding - 5/8" x 24", $1.98;
CLA70303 - Small Crown Molding - 7/16" x 24", $1.49;
CLA70304 - Baseboard Molding - 7/16" x 24", $1.59;
CLA70305 - Door & Window Trim - 3/8" x 24", $1.59;
CLA70306 - Interior Door Trim - 7/16" x 24", $1.59;
CLA70307 - Interior Window Trim - 3/8" x 24", $1.59;
CLA70308 - Chair Rail, flat - 1/4" x 24", $1.49;
CLA70309 - Door & Window Casing - 7/16" x 24", $1.49;
CLA70310 - Bottom Porch/Stair Rail - 5/16" x 24", $1.59;
CLA70311 - Top Porch/Stair Rail - 5/16" x 24", $1.98;
CLA70312 - Wave Trim - 7/8" x 24", $2.59.

VICTORIAN TRIMS & LACES/DOLL FAIRE MINIATURES

Ribbons and Lace

Our large selection of trims includes six sizes of silk ribbon, 1/16" - 1-1/4", bunka dyed to match the silk ribbon, small braids, cotton laces, 20 colors of tiny picot and 32 colors of soutache. We also carry fabric glue. Miscellaneous findings catalog, $4.

Fireplaces

ARCHITECTURAL ETCETERA

Firebox and Grate with Coals

Stock No.: 240 - 246
Price: $14 - $15
Two sizes of fireboxes are available with soot and ash, interior dimensions are 2-7/8"W x 2-7/8"H x 11/16"D and 2-5/8"W x 2-5/8"H x 3/4"D. The glowing coals have a 12V bulb and finished grate.

ARCHITECTURAL ETCETERA

Louis XVI Fireplace

Stock No.: 200 -209
Price: $35 - $95
Dimensions: Mantle height 3-3/4"
Model shown finished white with details highlighted in gold.

ARCHITECTURAL ETCETERA

Louis XVI Fireplace

Stock No.: 200 - 209
Price: $35 - $95
Dimensions: Mantle height 3-3/4"
Shown wood grained in warm walnut with built-in mirror.

ARCHITECTURAL ETCETERA

French Empire Fireplace

Stock No.: 210 - 219
Price: $35 - $95
Dimensions: Mantle height 4-1/4"

The Architectural Etcetera fireplaces are supplied superbly woodgrained in warm walnut or white paint, with or without gold highlighting. Fireplaces are also available unfinished with a white or walnut primer coat. All standard models come complete with a firebox and hearth and simulated marble surround. Mantles only are also available without the wood frame. They come with a firebox plus a hearth and/or marble surround (where appropriate) either finished or primed. We offer 10 different marble surround colors. Our catalog gives full details.

ARCHITECTURAL ETCETERA

French Empire Fireplace

Stock No.: 210 - 219
Price: $35 - $95
Dimensions: Mantle height 4-1/4"
This model is also available without panels.

ARCHITECTURAL ETCETERA

Victorian Carved Mantle

Stock No.: 230 - 234
Price: $35 - $50
Dimensions: Mantle height 4"
This model does not require the wood frame behind mantle.

ARCHITECTURAL ETCETERA

Renaissance Revival Fireplace

Stock No.: 220 - 229
Price: $28 - $75
Dimensions: Mantle height 4-3/4"
Model shown wood grained in warm walnut.

AZTEC IMPORTS INC.

Fireplaces

Stock No.: T6893-Stone, D3119-Brick,
D5200-Williamsburg
Price: See your local dealer.
Dimensions: 1"=1'
A variety of fireplaces including stone (T6893) Brick (D3119) and Williamsburg (D5200). Also available are walnut, mahogany, marble, white, and oak.

CIR-KIT CONCEPTS, INC.

Fireplace With Flickering Lights

Stock No.: CK866
Price: $24.95
Dimensions: 3-3/4"H x 4-15/16"W x 1-5/16"D
All-wood construction with brass fire box. Includes a two-bulb flickering unit, wood logs and decorative brass trim. Use with separate CK1009F 12V transformer.

CLARE-BELL BRASS WORKS

Fan Fire Screen

Stock No.: 1783-100Solid brass, gold-plated. Line of fireplace accessories available includes fireplace tools, fender, andirons, logs and log carrier. See your local dealer.

CLARE-BELL BRASS WORKS

Andirons

Stock No.: 1781-100
Dimensions: 1" = 1' scale
Solid brass, gold-plated andirons. Catalog, more than 200 items, $2. See your local independent miniatures dealer.

CLARE-BELL BRASS WORKS

Fireplace Tool Set

Stock No.: 1985-100
Dimensions: 1" = 1'
Solid brass, gold-plated tool set. The finest quality found. Catalog, more than 200 items, $2. See your local independent miniatures dealer.

CLASSICS BY HANDLEY

Fireplace Set

Stock No.: CLA72400
Price: $8.98
Dimensions: 4-3/4"W x 3"H x 1-1/2"D
Economical, stained wood fireplace with black base. Set also has mantel clock, bellows, tool set, wood logs and andirons. Painted wood and metal.

ELECT-A-LITE

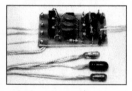

Flickering Fire Unit

Stock No.: 660 Price: $27.90
American-made, solid state electronic control unit with three bulbs contains three separate circuits to allow the bulbs to flicker at random or different rates, creating a most realistic illusion of a burning fire. This miniaturized unit will operate two sets of three bulbs or two different fireplaces. Will not flicker anything else in Your dollhouse—only what you connect to it.

HANDLEY HOUSE Mini Collectibles Fireplace Set

Stock No.: CLA91329
Price: $17.50
Dimensions: 1" = 1'
Eight-piece, walnut fireplace set includes fireplace, brass tools w/stand, clock and andirons.

HANDCRAFT DESIGNS INC. Assorted Fireplaces

Stock No.: see below
Price: See your local dealer.
Dimensions: 1/12 scale
Products shown, left to right: 3928W, 3512M and 3927S. Wood with carved, simulated brick or printed brick.
3928 is available in white paint or walnut stain finish (3928S).
3512 is available in antique white paint (3512W) or walnut stain (3512S).
3927 (4-1/4"H by 5"W by 2"D at base) is available in antique white paint (3927W) or mahogany stain (3927M).
Other fireplaces available as well as a complete line of accessories and tools.

HOUSEWORKS, LTD.

Double Mantle Fireplace

Stock No.: 2405
Price: $19.95
Elegant Victorian style wooden fireplace with fine detailing and grooved wood columns. No hearth. Size: 5"H x 6"W x 1-11/16"D; 1" scale.

HOUSEWORKS, LTD.
Assorted Fireplaces

Stock No.: 2403; 2401
Price: $13.75; $15.50
2403 - Jamestown Fireplace. This fireplace boasts handcrafted molding and refined beveled edges. Hearth attached. Size: 4-3/16"H x 5-15/16"W x 1-13/16"D.
2401- Monticello Fireplace. Traditional colonial style with detailed moldings and turned, sculpted posts. Hearth not attached. Size: 5-1/8"H x 6-1/8"W x 1-5/8"D.

HOUSEWORKS, LTD.

Assorted Fireplaces

Stock No.: 2022; 2402
Price: $24.50; $19.95
2022 - "Americana" Fireplace - electric fireplace includes brass fire box, two bulb flickering unit, natural logs and two spare bulbs. Use with separate 12V transformer. Size:3-5/8"H x 5"W x 1-5/16"D.
2402 - Orleans Fireplace - features gracefully sculpted front rising to a beautiful beveled mantle. Hearth not attached. Size: 3-21/32"H x 4-3/8"W x 1-3/8"D.

JEFFREY W. VIGEANT

Smoldering Ashes!

Stock No.: SP-875-R
Create a realistic look for your miniature fireplace. Replaceable screw bulb won't flicker dollhouse lights!

THE LAWBRE COMPANY

Victorian Mirrored Fireplace

Stock No.: 1085
Price: $18.95
Dimensions: 6"H x 5"W x 1"D
Cast in Hydrocal cement. Available in white only. Shown painted with acrylic paints and stains.

MODEL BUILDERS SUPPLY

Brick and Stone Fireplaces

These are new, solidly cast designs with subtle authentic detailing that sets them apart from any other. Three styles. All brick with tile hearth, all stone, stone with tile hearth. Available fully finished and grouted except wood mantle (you finish to choice), or ready for you to color and grout, or use as is. Interlocking chimney breast extensions available for extra high or cathedral ceilings. Unfinished sets, $28. Finished sets, $45.

THE LAWBRE COMPANY

Period Fireplaces

Cast in Hydrocal cement, available in white, black marbled, rose marbled or finished.
Early American Kitchen - 1061/white (crane included) $23.95, 1062/finished, brick red (shelf and crane included), $39.95;
French Console - 1066/white, $14.95, 1067/black marbled, $19.95, 1068/rose marbled $19.95.

THE LAWBRE COMPANY

Eastlake Fireplace

Stock No.: 1091
Price: $18.95 plus shipping
Dimensions: 1" = 1' scale
Cast in Hydrocal cement. Available in white only.
Shown finished.

UNIQUE MINIATURES

Period Fireplaces

Dimensions: Victorian mantle - 4-1/2"H x 6-1/2"W
x 7/8"D
These finely-decorated ornate fireplaces can easily
be stained or painted. With a choice of seven
fireplaces, there is a style to fit any room.
Send $3 for a complete catalog.
Made in the USA.

THE LAWBRE COMPANY

Period Fireplaces

Cast in Hydrocal cement, available in natural
white, black marbled, rose marbled or finished.
Federal - 1050/white, $14.95; 1051/black marbled,
$19.95; Victorian - 1056/white, $14.95; 1057/black
marbled, $19.95.

THE LAWBRE COMPANY

Period Fireplaces

Victorian Columned - 1071/white, $14.95;
1072/black marbled, $19.95; Salem Corner -
1076/white only (beveled wall section included),
$18.95.

Flooring

CORONA CONCEPTS

Birch Floor Tiles

Stock No.: 4705
Dimensions: 1" x 1"; 1" scale
1" floor tiles can be stained and glued to create a
beautiful parquet or regular wood floor pattern.
Each bag contains 400 pieces which covers 400
square inches. See your local dealer.

GREENLEAF PRODUCTS

Dollhouse Floor Tiles

Stock No.: 9003
Price: $4.60
These 1" square wood floor tiles come 250 to a
package and can be stained or glued to create a
variety of wood floor patterns. A beautiful
"finishing touch."

HANDLEY HOUSE

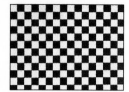

True Elegance Vinyl Floor

Stock No.: HH162 - HH166
Price: $7.25
Dimensions: 6" x 8"
These panels are handcrafted of 1/2" colored and white vinyl squares. Excellent choice for kitchens, baths, foyers or halls. Available in blue/white, green/white, red/white, yellow/white or white/white. Glossy vinyl.

HANDLEY HOUSE

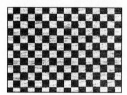

True Elegance Checkerboard Specialty Floor

Stock No.: HH151
Price: $8.95
Dimensions: 6" x 8"
US hardwood veneers. Hand-laid 1/2" dark and light squares enhance this unique floor. Ideal for foyers, baths, kitchens or use your imagination.

HANDLEY HOUSE

True Elegance Basket-Weave Specialty Floor

Stock No.: HH152
Price: $8.95
Dimensions: 6" x 8"
US hardwood veneer. Comprised of all light, hardwood 1" squares, this hand-laid floor can be stained or simply finished with a varnish or wax. Trim to size and install.

HANDLEY HOUSE

True Elegance Four-Finger Parquet Floor

Stock No.: HH141
Price: $8.95
Dimensions: 6" x 8"; 1/4"W x 1"L strips
US hardwood veneers. This classic parquet floor, hand-laid on a flexible backing, is made of light and dark US hardwoods. Floor can be inlaid with other True Elegance Flooring or can be used as is.

HANDLEY HOUSE

True Elegance Four-Finger Parquet Floor

Stock No.: HH142
Price: $8.95
Dimensions: 6" x 8"; 1/4"W x 1"L strips
All light US hardwood veneer comprises this distinctive floor. Can be stained, varnished or waxed. Simply cut to size.

HANDLEY HOUSE

True Elegance Four-Finger Parquet Floor

Stock No.: HH144
Price: $8.95
Dimensions: 6" x 8"; 1/4"W x 1"L strips
US walnut veneer. Hand-laid walnut strips make up this lovely parquet floor. Ready to cut to size, install and stain or varnish to suit your taste.

HANDLEY HOUSE True Elegance Finished Hardwood Floor

Stock No.: HH101-110
Price: $10.50
Dimensions: 11" x 17"
US hardwood veneers. These beautiful floors are handcrafted in the USA and come to you on flexible backing, ready to cut to size, install and stain or varnish to suit your taste. All floors are made of fine native US hardwood veneers, bound to a flexible backing. Available in 10 distinctive patterns, three different woods.

HANDLEY HOUSE

True Elegance Herringbone Floor

Stock No.: HH131
Price: $8.95
Dimensions: 8" x 11"; 1/4"W strips
US hardwood veneers. Distinctive hand-laid hardwood floor has 1/4" wide light and dark strips. Many unusual applications possible—contemporary wall and ceiling treatments, as well as flooring uses.

HANDLEY HOUSE Playscale Flooring

Stock No.: HH8001; HH8002
Price: $14.95
Dimensions: 18"H x 22"W; Playscale
HH8001 - Dark and light wood, 1/2" strips;
HH8002 - Light wood, 1/2" strips;
HH8003 - Dark wood, 1/2" strips.

HANDLEY HOUSE

True Elegance
Herringbone Floor

Stock No.: HH133
Price: $8.95
Dimensions: 8" x 10-1/2"
US hardwood veneers. Unusual specialty floor is hand-laid with 1/2" wide light and dark hardwood strips. Pattern is 1/2" repeat. Applications are limited only by one's imagination.

HANDLEY HOUSE

True Elegance
Pinwheel Floor

Stock No.: HH145; HH517; HH518
Price: $8.95
US hardwood veneers. Unique pinwheel designed floor is available in three sizes: HH145 - 6" x 8", 1/2" strips; HH517 - 5" x 6" , 1/4" strips; and HH518 - 5" x 6", 1/4" strips. 1/2scale.

HANDLEY HOUSE

True Elegance
Sawtooth Specialty Floor

Stock No.: HH154
Price: $8.95
Dimensions: 6" x 8"
US hardwood veneers. An unusual distinctive sawtooth pattern of alternating light and dark woods sets this floor apart. Hand-laid on a flexible backing, ready to install and finish to your specifications.

HANDLEY HOUSE

True Elegance Picture Frame
Parquet Floor, 3/4" Squares

Stock No.: HH111
Price: $11.98
Dimensions: 11" x 17"
US hardwood veneers. Lovely specialty flooring with picture frame accent is handmade of US hardwood veneers and is on a flexible backing. Simple to cut to size and wax or varnish to suit your taste.

HOUSEWORKS, LTD.

Parquet Flooring

Stock No.: 7007
Price: $15.25
Dimensions: 2"W x 6"L
Genuine wood parquet pattern. Six sheets per package. Covers 72 sq. in.

HOUSEWORKS, LTD.

Southern Pine
Random Plank Flooring

Stock No.: 7123
Price: $11.25
Dimensions: 11" x 17". Covers 187 sq.in.
Made of genuine wood veneers laminated to a special paper to ensure easy staining, varnishing and installation. One sheet per package.

HOUSEWORKS, LTD.

Black Walnut Flooring

Stock No.: 7021
Price: $14.25
Dimensions: 11" x 17". Covers 187 sq.in.
Made of genuine wood veneers laminated to a special paper to ensure easy staining, varnishing and installation. One sheet per package.

HOUSEWORKS, LTD.

Random Plank Flooring

Stock No.: 7024
Price: $11.95
Dimensions: 11" x 17. Covers 187 sq.in."
Made of genuine wood veneers laminated to a special paper to ensure easy staining, varnishing and installation. One sheet per package.

HOUSEWORKS, LTD.

Red Oak Flooring

Stock No.: 7022
Price: $11.95
Dimensions: 11" x 17". Covers 187 sq.in.
Made of genuine wood veneers laminated to a special paper to ensure easy staining, varnishing and installation. One sheet per package.

HOUSEWORKS, LTD.

Red Oak Random Plank Flooring

Stock No.: 7122
Price: $11.25
Dimensions: 11" x 17". Covers 187 sq.in.
Made of genuine wood veneers laminated to a special paper to ensure easy staining, varnishing and installation. One sheet per package.

HOUSEWORKS, LTD.

Southern Pine Flooring

Stock No.: 7123
Price: $11.95
Dimensions: 11" x 17". Covers 187 sq.in.
Made of genuine wood veneers laminated to a special paper to ensure easy staining, varnishing and installation. One sheet per package.

Prices are approximate and subject to change

J. HERMES

Paper Flooring

Stock No.: 413
Price: $1.25/sheet
Dimensions: 11" x 17"
Paper wood flooring, easy to lay, inexpensive, finishes beautifully with varnish or lacquer. Can even be stained. Many other flooring patterns available.

MINIATURE HOUSE

No Wax Marble Floors

Price: $5.76
Dimensions: 8-3/4" x 11-1/2"
No wax marble floors can be the perfect finish to a miniatures room. They are available in:
MH5958 (white);
MH5955 (pink);
MH5957 (Nile green);
MH5956 (black).

MINIATURE HOUSE

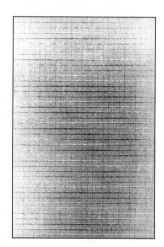

Three-Dimensional Polystyrene Tile Panels

Price: see below
Dimensions: 10-3/4"W x 16-3/4"L
This economical tile is perfect for kitchens, bathrooms, ice cream parlors…or use your imagination.
MH5930 (black/white), $6.50;
MH5302 (red/white);
MH5303 (blue/white), $5.50
and new MH5315 (pastel pink), $5.50.

MINIATURE HOUSE

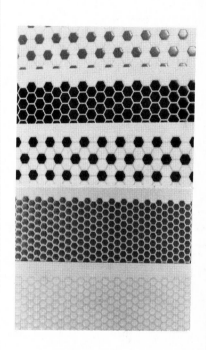

"No Wax" Flooring

Made of Kromecoat No Wax.
Large Hexagon - $6.40, 10-1/2" x 16-1/2":
MH5910 (solid white),
MH5911 (solid pink),
MH5912 (solid blue),
MH5913 (red & white),
MH5914 (black & white),
MH5915 (solid black).
Small Checkerboard - $5.26, 7-3/4" x 10-3/8":
MH5920 (solid white),
MH5921 (black & white),
MH5922 (red & white),
MH5923 (solid pink),
MH5924 (solid blue),
MH5925 (blue & white).
Large Checkerboard - $6.50, 10-1/2" x 16-1/2":
MH5930 (black & white),
MH5931 (red & white),
MH5932 (blue & white),
MH5933 (pink & white).
Tiny Hexagon - $5.26, 7-3/4" x 10-3/8":
MH5950 (solid white),
MH5951 (solid pink),
MH5952 (solid blue),
MH5953 (solid rust),
MH5954 (solid mauve).

MINIATURE HOUSE

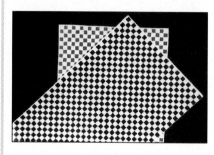

Hardwood Flooring

Price: $10.50
Dimensions: 11"W x 17"L
MH511 - Tan Oak Flooring - 1/4" strips with random joints;
MH512 - Very Light Pine/Ash Flooring - 1/4" strips with random joints;
MH513 - American Walnut Flooring - 1/4" strips with random joints;
M516 - Tan Oak Flooring, mixed widths with random joints;
MH518 - Mixed Dark & Light Flooring - 1-1/4" strips with random joints;
MH519 - American Walnut Flooring - mixed widths with random joints.

MINIATURE HOUSE

Three-Dimensional Polystyrene Tile Panels

Price: $5.50
Dimensions: 10-3/4"W x 16-3/4"L
These polystyrene tile panels are accurately scaled 1" to 1'. Easily cut with scissors or razor. Applies quickly, cleanly with double-faced tape.
MH5300 (white),
MH5305 (pastel yellow),
MH5310 (pastel blue),
MH5315 (pastel pink).

MODEL BUILDERS SUPPLY

3-D Floor, Patio Surfaces

Price: $5.70; $3

Dimensions: 7" x 24"; 7" x 12"

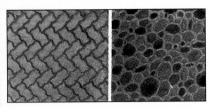

MBS floor sheets offer a wide variety of interesting, easy-to-use designs; dressed stone, pebble stone, interlocking brick, quarry tiles. 1", 1/2", 1/4"; 5, 10, 13, and 16 squares per inch. Same sizes in grey, white and clear that look like ceramic tile when painted from behind in texture colors and patterns.

MODEL BUILDERS SUPPLY

Hardwood Floor Strips

Fifty pieces 12"L x 1/4" or 3/8"W, .025" thick. Makes beautiful, real wood floors. Apply with contact cement, sand lightly, varnish, sand lightly, varnish 2nd coat. Looks gorgeous! Check this value. Package of 1/4" strips, covers over 1 sq.ft., $4.52. Package of 3/8" strips, covers over 1-1/2 sq.ft., $5.28.

MODEL BUILDERS SUPPLY

Printed Paper Flooring

Price: $2.85, 2 pcs.

Dimensions: 8" x 10"

Heavy paper printed sheets in many colors of tile, marble, parquet, strip wood, stone, herringbone paving. Apply with MBS "Fast Fix" or double-sided tape.

OMNIARTS OF COLORADO

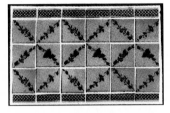

Mural Tile Kits

Price: $6 - $18

One-half inch square, photographically reproduced tiles using Brooke Tucker method. Many designs available including Victorian, Mexican and contemporary. Easy to use.

PRECISION PRODUCTS

Plastic Veneer Styrene Sheets

Price: $7 per sheet

Dimensions: 15" square

5" and 10" rough planking, 3" pegged board, patio brick (two styles). Made in USA.

THE LAWBRE COMPANY

Flooring Tiles

Price: $9.95

These flooring tiles, cast in Hydrocal cement, are extremely versatile. Each package covers 36 sq. inches. Can be painted with acrylic paints or stains. 64 pcs./pkg. 1022/black-veined marble, 1023/quarry tile, 1021/white.

THE LAWBRE COMPANY
Slate Flooring Kit

Stock No.: 1026

Price: $9.95

Dimensions: 1" = 1' scale

Slate flooring tiles are cast in Hydrocal cement. Each package covers 36 square inches and comes with 16 pieces each of 3 different sizes. Instructions, mortar and spacing stick included.

Prices are approximate and subject to change

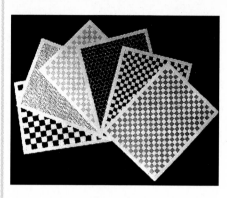

WHAT'S NEXT?
Tile Flooring

Price: $3.25 plus shipping
Dimensions: 9" x 12" sheet 1"-1' scale
Smooth, polished look, printed on varnished card stock. Available in green and white, yellow and black, black and white, 1/2" squares, white hexagon, terra cotta quarry tile, black and white 3/4" square tiles and beautiful new 4-color Seixas.

for Paneling & Trim Walls-Ceilings

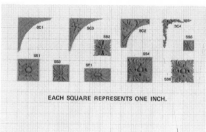

EACH SQUARE REPRESENTS ONE INCH.

ARCHITECTURAL ETCETERA
Cast Ornamentation

Price: $1.50 - $3.50
Dimensions: 1" = 1'; various sizes
These architectural pieces can be used as ceiling ornaments, borders, spandrels, etc. Our castings are very high quality reproduced in primed resin. They may be drilled, sawed or routed just like wood. Treat your imagination to our incredible collection of details.

ARCHITECTURAL ETCETERA

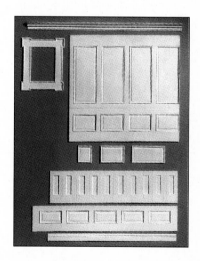

Wall Panels, Wainscot, Cornice and Baseboard

Stock No.: 255 - 271
Price: $2.50 - $18
Cast polyurethane resin wall panels and wainscot are adjustable both in height and width with the addition of 3/32" basswood strips. Available in both white primer for painting or warm walnut for staining. Instructions are included. These beautifully crafted components make it possible to realize a classic room in a fraction of the usual time.

EACH SQUARE REPRESENTS ONE INCH.   MINI TRIMS

ARCHITECTURAL ETCETERA
Interior or Exterior
Cast Ornamentation

Price: $1.50 - $5
Dimensions: 1" = 1"; various sizes
Beautifully detailed castings. May be stained or painted and applied with any type of glue. Primed resin.

ARCHITECTURAL ETCETERA

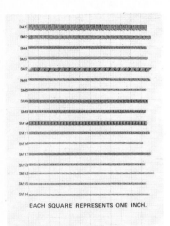

EACH SQUARE REPRESENTS ONE INCH.

Moldings

Price: $2.50 - $3
Dimensions: 1 " = 1'; various sizes
Adding a touch of elegance is easy with these delicately-detailed moldings and trims. Primed for your finishing, filling voids and holes isn't necessary with these quality architectural details. May be used for chair rail, wainscot, door trim, panel trims, etc. Easily cut with a razor saw. Any type of paint may be used. Primed resin. Many more designs are available than are shown here.

WORKSHOP WISDOM

As we have many times discovered, jewelry findings have a number of uses, so here is a new one. This type, bent to shape and glued to a drawer, is a very nice decorative drawer pull.

CAROLYN LAUKKONEN
RICHMOND, B.C., CANADA

Workshop Wisdom
Courtesy of *Nutshell News*—6/94

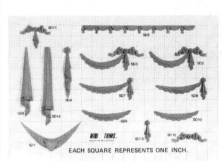

EACH SQUARE REPRESENTS ONE INCH.

ARCHITECTURAL ETCETERA
Medallions & Ceiling Ornamentation

Price: $2 - $7
Dimensions: 1 " = 1'; various sizes
Highly-detailed medallions can be used as ceiling decoration. Exceptional quality. May be sawed or drilled like wood. Any type of paint may be used. Primed resin.

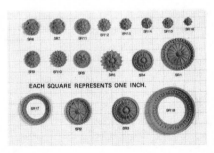

EACH SQUARE REPRESENTS ONE INCH.

ARCHITECTURAL ETCETERA
Resin Cast Drapery, Swags and Jabots

Price: $2 - $4
Dimensions: 1 " = 1'; various sizes
Useful as interior detail or to decorate the exterior of a roombox. Pre-primed and easily finished with any paint or can be finished to look like wood. Primed resin.

EACH SQUARE REPRESENTS ONE INCH.

ARCHITECTURAL ETCETERA
Rosettes, Floral and Classical Details & Ceiling Ornamentation

Price: $2 - $6
Dimensions: 1 " = 1'; various sizes
Our rosettes, floral and classical details are all meticulously reproduced in pre-primed resin. Many more architectural details and trims and moldings are represented in our catalog. Primed resin.

EBERHARD FABER GMBH
FIMO Modeling Material

Stock No.: 8000
Price: see your dealer
Dimensions: see below
55 by 55 by 15 mm/65 g small block, 165 by 55 by 30 mm/350 g large block. FIMO, the fantastic and most popular modeling material, is the leading product of its kind in Europe. It's versatile and easy to handle and hardens in the oven at 265° (20 to 30 minutes). Available in 42 brilliant colors, it's ideal to create the finest decorative accessories for your dollhouse and to make exciting and imaginative objects (miniatures, figures, fashion jewelry, decorations, pictures, nameplates and a lot more).

Rugs&Carpeting

VISIT A MINIATURES MUSEUM ON YOUR VACATION

HANDCRAFT DESIGNS INC.

J. HERMES

Stair Runner Kits

Stock No.: 618
Price: $14.95 - $15.95; plus shipping
Beautiful imported tapestry stair/hall runners add a touch of elegance to any 1" (or 1/2") vignette or dollhouse. Brass rods (solid), fringe. Made of the finest materials. Assorted colors.

Rugs

Price: See your local dealer.
Pictured is a selection of transfer printed rugs for the nursery and every other room in the dollhouse. This unique transfer process affords exact reproductions of real carpets at a fraction of the cost of all other miniature rugs. Simply, the best selection of color and sizes at the best prices.

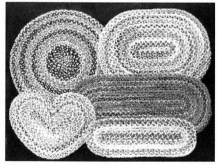

LITTLE THINGS BY JODY
Braided Rugs

Dimensions: 1" scale
Handmade braided rugs produced in several shapes and hundreds of color combinations from assorted yarns. They will complement "Country", "Victorian", "Modern", "Nursery", "Christmas", etc. or they can be custom-crafted for your unique decor and/or room size. See your local dealer.

d. ANNE RUFF MINIATURES
Prettipoint Rug Kits

Price: $11.95 each plus shipping
Dimensions: 1" scale
Color these beautiful carpets to coordinate with your decor. Silk-screened designs on napped cotton fabric. Color with fine tip felt pens. 1207 - Chinese Key, 8" x 9-3/4";1209 - Garden Path, 6-3/4" x 9-3/4"; 1208 - Garden Trellis, 6-3/4" x 8-3/4"; 1211 - Country Gardens (two rugs), 5" x 7". Shown are four of the 11 different styles.

MACDOC DESIGNS
Oriental Rugs
MacDoc Designs is a complete source for the finest Oriental rugs in miniature. Hundreds of contemporary and traditional colors and patterns are available. Styles range from informal to sophisticated, country to contemporary, floral patterns to animal prints. Extra large (7" x 10"), large (6" x 8"), medium (4" x 6"), runners (3" x 8") and small (3" x 5") are approximate sizes available. See your local miniature retailer for selection.

Navajo Indian Rugs
Navajo Indian rugs by various weavers from the Southwest. Handspun natural wool and dyes.

MINIATURE RUGS BY JOAN ADAMS

Sheared Punchneedle Rugs
Price: $2.75
1/12th sheared punchneedle rug catalog of over 40 designs. Graphs, transparency graphs, completed rugs, canvas, punchneedles and embroidery scissors available. Kits for needlepoint.

MINISCULES

Carpet
Dimensions: 1:12 scale
Finely-textured and patterned carpeting now available for your dollhouse or roombox. A wide variety of colors and patterns available to match any decor. Wholesale only—see your local dealer.

MODEL BUILDERS SUPPLY

Broadloom
Price: $3
Dimensions: 18" x 27"
Compare this value! Solid color carpet/broadloom. Fine acrylic pile in white, beige, forest green, burgundy, pink, medium grey. Also in AstroTurf green. Apply with MBS "Fast Fix" or double-sided tape. New colors: light grey and dusty rose.

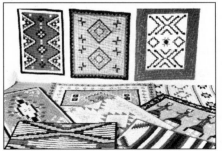

OLD MOUNTAIN MINIATURES
Navajo-Style Rugs
Price: $8.50 to $45, kits; $17.50 to $132, finished.
These are some of our needlepoint rugs taken from actual Navajo rug designs. We have Two Gray Hills, Burntwater, Hubbell Revival, Chinle, Yei'i, Crystal Trading Post, Ganado and other styles. Colors vary considerably. Ask your local miniatures dealer for our kits and finished pieces.

THE KESHISHIAN COLLECTION
Heriz, Mohtashem and Savonnerie
Stock No.: 020; 018; 028
Price: $45
Dimensions: 8" x 10"; 6-1/2" x 10"; 8" x 10"
Charm, elegance, sophistication. All of these plus the magic of the Keshishian rug. At better shops everywhere. Brochure, $5, refundable with first purchase.

THE KESHISHIAN COLLECTION
Jardin Des Fleurs

Stock No.: 031
Price: $47
Dimensions: 8-1/2" x 11"
A bouquet of flowers for your floor. No imagination needed with a Keshishian. Seen at better shops. Brochure, $5, refundable with first purchase.

Tapestries

MACDOC DESIGNS

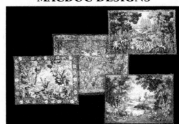

Tapestries

MacDoc Designs is a complete source for beautiful miniature tapestries. A variety of sizes and themes are currently available. Scenes ranging from mythology to rural and epic backgrounds add richness and style to miniature settings. See your local miniature retailer for selection.

THE KESHISHIAN COLLECTION
Marie Antoinette

Stock No.: 016
Price: $49
Dimensions: 9" x 12"
Recognized miniaturists who know specify carpets from the Keshishian Collection. At better shops worldwide. Brochure, $5, refundable with first purchase.

THE KESHISHIAN COLLECTION
Tapestries

Price: See below
No imagination needed. Bring the magic of a Keshishian tapestry into your home. Left, clockwise: March to the Castle, $43; Lady With the Unicorn, $43; The Boar Hunt, $43; English Tapestry, $25. Brochure, $5, refundable with first purchase.

Wall Coverings

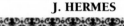

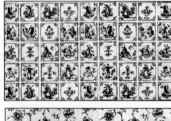

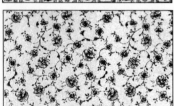

J. HERMES
Wallpaper

Price: $1.25 - $1.50/sheet
Dimensions: 11" x 17"
Wallpapers are both original and researched designs. Patterns for every room in the house: living room, bed and bath, kitchen and nursery. Papers available for wood, floors and ceilings. Exterior papers in brick, clapboard, stone and roofing shingle and shake patterns. Printed paper.

J. HERMES

Flocked Wallpaper

Stock No.: 1100
Price: $.75 - $3/sheet
Dimensions: 5" x 8" and 11" x 17"
This wallpaper is available in many designs and color combinations. You can add a touch of elegance to a boudoir, living room, parlor or saloon. Paper with flocking.

J. HERMES

Tile Papers

Stock No.: 481; 482
Price: $2/sheet Dimensions: 11" x 17"
Authentic style, multi-color printed tile papers. With the Southwestern influence so popular, this paper will be a beautiful addition to your Spanish adobe or casa. Printed heavy stock paper.

MODEL BUILDERS SUPPLY

Wall Coverings

MBS has dozens of non-wallpaper surfaces. See our listings under Brick & Stone, Siding Materials, Flooring for marble, stucco, tile, paneling.

MINISCULES

Wallpaper

Dimensions: 1:12 scale
Fine quality prepasted wallpapers. More than 150 patterns to choose from. Durable, vinyl-coated papers are easy to work with and resist fading. Wholesale only—see your local dealer.

WORKSHOP WISDOM

Zebra paper clips, already painted in stripes, can be cut and used in many miniature projects. June has used them as candy canes, legs for toys, and coat hangers. Use is only limited to your imagination.

*JUNE FUERSTENHAEFER
DARIEN, IL*

Workshop Wisdom Courtesy of *Nutshell News—1/94*

Prices are approximate and subject to change

Window Treatments

d. ANNE RUFF MINIATURES

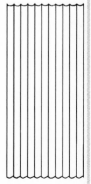

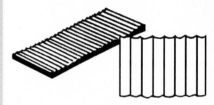

Pretty Pleater Tiny and Mini

Stock No.: PP1/4; PP1/2
Price: $14.95 plus shipping
Dimensions: 4-1/2" x 10-1/2"; 1/4" and 1/2" scale
These smaller scale pleaters are perfect for 1/4" and 1/2" scale curtains, dust ruffles, etc. They also work well for doll clothes and where tiny pleats are needed for 1" scale projects. Pretty Pleat Tiny has 11 pleats per inch and Pretty Pleat Mini has 7-1/2 pleats per inch.

WORKSHOP WISDOM

Small thread spools can easily be converted into flower pots. Paint them any desired color, decorate with a band or two of narrow chart tape, then add a display of miniature dried flowers.

JOHN TERPIN
E. AMHERST, NY

Workshop Wisdom
Courtesy of *Nutshell News—6/94*

d. ANNE RUFF MINIATURES

Pretty Pleater I

Stock No.: PP-1
Price: $23.95 plus shipping
Dimensions: 6-1/2" x 10-1/2"; 1" scale
This pleater is an easy-to-use pleating device especially designed to create pleats for 1" scale draperies and curtains. It can also be used for doll dresses. Each pleat is 1/4"W x 10-1/2"L, creating 5-1/2 pleats per inch.

d. ANNE RUFF MINIATURES

Window Collection

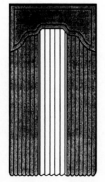

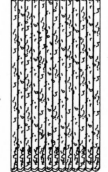

Dimensions: 1" scale
Coordinated collection of cornices, draperies and curtains packaged individually. Cornices and curtains available in 4", 5", 6" and 8" widths. Curtains and draperies are 8-1/2"high but can be shortened. Wide choice of fabrics or customer-supplied fabric.
WTB-1 - Tie-Back Drapery, $20; WST-1 - Straight Draperies, $15; WSH-1 - Sheer Curtain (ecru or white), $10; WLC-1 - Lace Curtain (ecru or white), $10; WC-1 - 4" Cornice, $8.

LASER TECH

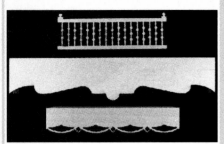

Cornices and Planter Boxes

Stock No.: see below
Price: see below
Made of 3/32 basswood in 1" scale.
Top to bottom:
C-052/Cornice (3" by 1/16"), $6.00;
C-153/Double Cornice (6-3/16" by 1-1/16"). $4.95;
WPB-050/Window Planter Box (3-7/8" by 3/4"),
$5.10.

MODEL BUILDERS SUPPLY

Skylights

MBS skylights are reflected in our silver mirror panels. Two per package. $7.50. Skylights $2.25 to $3.95.

NEW ENGLAND HOBBY SUPPLY, INC.

Barbara O'Brien Curtains

Available in more than 40 colors and styles. Fit all standard windows. SASE for brochure. See your local dealer for prices.

MODEL BUILDERS SUPPLY
Stained Glass Windows

Price: $1.71 each
MBS favorite designs for years. Easy to color yourself with transparent acrylics or permanent marker pens, then fill in the lead grooves with black marker point. Series 2 fits standard Houseworks and Carlson windows. Original series is adjustable to fit various apertures. The clear plastic is easily cut with craft knife or scissors.

JUST GETTING INTO DOLLHOUSE MINIATURES?

If you have a question about dollhouse miniatures, stop by your local retail outlet and ask the expert behind the counter.

WORKSHOP WISDOM

If you wish to use real lead as separators in your stained glass windows, obtain a roll of adhesive-backed lead Balancing Tape, as used on tennis racquets and usually obtainable from your local sporting goods store. Lay a piece of tape on a cutting mat or a sheet of glass and, using a new blade and a metal straightedge, cut strips to the width desired, then press in place on your window. It is best to paint your panes on the window first, using transparent glass paints, then apply the tape.

AGNETA DOMASZEWICZ

Workshop Wisdom Courtesy of *Nutshell News—12/93*

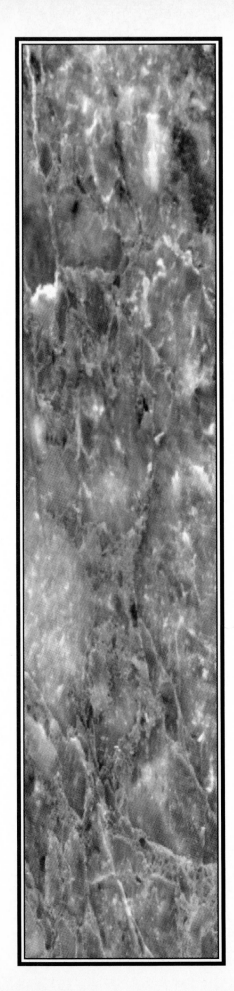

FURNITURE

Colonial & Federal

AZTEC IMPORTS INC.

Four-Piece Bedroom Set
Stock No.: T3209
Price: See your local dealer.
Dimensions: 1"=1' scale
Mahogany four-piece bedroom set includes double bed, mirrored dresser, nightstand and blanket chest. Also available in oak (T4209), white (T5209) and walnut (T6209).

GINSBURG COMPANY

3 Pc. Walnut Bedroom Set
Stock No.: 2914.00
Price: See your local dealer.
Dimensions: 1"=1'
Walnut 3 pc. bedroom set in beautiful wood with brass hardwood packaged in our new "Keepsakes" clamshell see-through package. Also available in oak and white finish.

CLARE-BELL BRASS WORKS

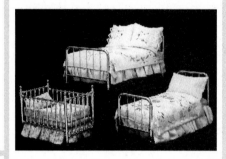

Dressed Brass Beds
Stock No.: See below
1701-D00 - Brass Crib
1703-D00 - Plain Brass Bed
1704-D00 - Plain Twin Brass Bed
All beds are solid brass with a gold-plated finish.Catalog, more than 200 items, $2. See your local independent miniatures dealer.

MINIATURE HOUSE

Double Bed
Stock No.: MH411
Price: $10.79
A lovely, inexpensive way to furnish a bedroom. All-wood, fabric-covered mattress. Early American oak.

MINIATURE HOUSE

Single Bed
Stock No.: MH410
Price: $7.98
All-wood, fabric-covered mattress. This oak-finished single bed is perfect for a child's room in your dollhouse.

NELLIE ORIGINALS
Handcrafted Furniture
Price: $25 - $110
Designed and made by Nelson Lewis. Signed, choose your finish. Some pieces available unfinished. Distinctive, affordable furnishings. Beds dressed, towels and pillows by Louise. Custom designs in linens and furniture.

SONIA MESSER CO., INC.

Period Furniture
Dimensions: 1" Scale
Exquisite collection of period furniture. Some bathroom and kitchen pieces. Price list and information, $1.

Colonial & Federal Kits

HOUSEWORKS, LTD.

EXECUTIVE DESK

Stock No.: 4008
Price: $22.95
Dimensions: 5-3/8"W x 2-19/32"D x 2-1/2"H; 1" scale
An elegant Sheraton knee-hole gentlemen's desk with solid back and nine working drawers. Kit contains all parts necessary to complete this unfinished wood piece, including hardware.

HOUSEWORKS, LTD.

Bow-Front Chest

Stock No.: 4003
Price: $14.95
Dimensions: 3-13/32"W x 1-11/16"D x 3-1/8"H; 1" scale
A classic chest of drawers with four working, bow-front drawers. Kit contains all parts necessary to complete this unfinished wood piece, including hardware.

HOUSEWORKS, LTD.

Chairside Chest

Stock No.: 4013
Price: $6.95
Dimensions: 2-5/16"W x 1-5/16"D x 1-11/16"H; 1" scale
Sheraton style chest with two working drawers. Same as base on gun cabinet. Kit contains all parts necessary to complete this unfinished wood piece, including hardware.

HOUSEWORKS, LTD.

Duncan Phyfe Dining Table

Stock No.: 4010
Price: $16.95
A traditional banquet-size dining table, designed with beautiful intricate Duncan Phyfe style legs. Kit includes all parts necessary to complete this unfinished wood piece. Size: 8"L x 4"W x 2-5/8"H. A regular-size table with leaf removed. Size: 6"L x 4"W x 2-5/8"H.

HOUSEWORKS, LTD.

Federal Bed

Stock No.: 4000
Price: $12.95
Dimensions: 4-5/8"W x 7"L x 3-1/2"H; 1" scale
Traditional double bed with solid curved design headboard and footboard. Kit contains all parts to complete this unfinished wood piece, including foam mattress.

HOUSEWORKS, LTD

Bow-Front Night Stand

Stock No.: 4001
Price: $7.95
Dimensions: 2-5/32"W x 1-3/8"D x 2-5/32"H; 1" scale
Commode style night stand with bow front and two working drawers. Kit contains all parts to complete this unfinished wood piece, including hardware.

HOUSEWORKS, LTD.

Executive Chair

Stock No.: 4009
Price: $8.95
Dimensions: 2"W x 1-3/4"D x 3-7/8"H; 1" scale
A Martha Washington style upholstered chair. Kit includes all parts necessary to complete this unfinished wood piece, including cotton fabric.

HOUSEWORKS, LTD.

Bow-Front Lingerie Chest

Stock No.: 4002
Price: $15.95
Dimensions: 2-3/16"W x 1-3/8"D x 4-9/16"H; 1" scale
The tall, narrow chest has seven working drawers with bow fronts. Kits contain all parts to complete this unfinished wood piece, including hardware.

HOUSEWORKS, LTD.

Bow-Front Wardrobe

Stock No.: 4004 Price: $15.95
Dimensions: 3-13/32"W x 1-23/32"D x 6"H; 1" scale
The bow-front wardrobe has two working doors and one working drawer. Interior has two shelves on one side and dowel rod for hanging clothes on opposite side. Kit contains all parts to complete this unfinished wood piece, including hardware.

HOUSEWORKS, LTD.

Gun Cabinet

Stock No.: 4005
Price: $12.95
Dimensions: 2-15/16"W x 1-5/16"D x 6-7/16"H; 1" scale
The classic design gun cabinet with divider piece for guns includes Plexiglas for the door. The base contains two working drawers. Kit contains all parts necessary to complete this unfinished wood piece, including hardware.

HOUSEWORKS, LTD.

Hepplewhite Buffet

Stock No.: 4012
Price: $18.95
Dimensions: 6-1/16"W x 2-5/32"D x 3-7/32"H;
1"scale
This beautifully designed buffet with tapered legs has unusual rounded doors and drawers. Kit contains all parts necessary to complete this unfinished wood piece, including hardware.

HOUSEWORKS, LTD.

Hepplewhite Shield-Back Arm Chair

Stock No.: 4006
Price: $7.95
Dimensions: 1-13/16"W x 1-1/2"D x 3-1/4"H;
1" scale
Shield-back 18th century style chair has short curved arms allowing chair to go under the table, and upholstered seat. Kit contains all parts necessary to complete this unfinished wood piece, including cotton fabric.

SHENANDOAH DESIGNS, INC.

The Chippendale Collection

Price: $8.49-$32.99 (kit)
The Chippendale Collection contains some of the finest miniature wood furniture kits available. All parts are pre-cut and some are even pre-carved to enable you to construct 1/12 scale versions of some of Chippendale's finest designs. The pieces pictured are only a few of the many designs available. Mahogany.

SHENANDOAH DESIGNS, INC.
The Colonial Collection

Price: see below
Dimensions: 1/12 scale
The furniture will add a touch of country to any collection. The designs were adapted from the finest of the country craftsmen who made this style so popular. The 10 designs of this collection are now available in 1/12 scale assembled and ready to finish. $8.49-$16.49 (kit), $11.49-$24.99 (assembled/sanded), and $16.99-$34.99 (finished).

OLD MOUNTAIN MINIATURES
Colonial Furniture Kits

Build with the best and most unique line of 14th to 18th-century colonial furniture kits on the market. All precision cut, including hardware and full instructions. Also available custom-finished in your choice of stain or paint.* Ask your local miniatures dealer for our kits or finished pieces.
*New—many kits now available in hardwoods.

Country

AZTEC IMPORTS INC.

Iron Scroll Beds

Stock No.: T6052 (double); T6321(single)
Price: See your local dealer.
Dimensions: 1"-1' scale
Sturdy yet ornate grey iron beds feature scroll hearts on head and footboards. Perfect for that cabin or farmhouse.

d. ANNE RUFF MINIATURES
Country Bedroom Furniture
Stock No.: CB-1
Dimensions: 1" scale
Handcrafted all-brass bed dressed in coordinated linens. Covers invitingly pulled back. Fringed throw hangs over foot of bed, $160. Skirted slipper chair with pillow, $40; draped table, $12.50; non-electric decorator lamp, $15; oval floral rug, $25.

FOX HOLLOW MINIATURES

Antique Collector's Cupboard
Price: $200
Dimensions: 7" x 4" x 1-1/2"
Genuine antique miniatures found at flea markets from Covent Gardens to the Marche des Puces fill this country blue cupboard. Each signed piece is unique.

RENÉE BOWEN - MINIATURIST
Shaker and American Country
Offering the simplicity of Shaker and the charm of country. Extensive line of furniture, decorative accessories, toys, games and quilts available through the mail or through my retail shop in Maine. Always adding new items and will consider custom work. See index for details.

SCIENTIFIC MODELS, INC.

Realife Miniatures
Country Bedroom
Stock No.: 207
Price: $35.95
Made of basswood and brass. Re-create the country's most popular home decor with these authentic reproductions. Add that warm country atmosphere to your dollhouse or miniature collection with our easy-to-assemble kits at 1/5 the cost of assembled pieces. Complete instructions included. No special tools are required. Country bedroom kit includes a four poster bed with mattress, blanket chest, pre-decorated dower chest, washstand and hooded cradle. Approximately 12 cotton balls required for pillow stuffing, not included. Bed 5"W x 6-1/8"H. American-made.

SCIENTIFIC MODELS, INC.

Realife Miniatures
Country Kitchen
Stock No.: 194
Price: $37.95
Kit includes all materials necessary to make four pieces shown (stove, sink, ice box and hoosier cabinet). Materials include pre-cut basswood parts, brass hardware, metal castings, stain, gloss coat, brush, sandpaper, glue and instructions. American-made.

SCIENTIFIC MODELS, INC.

Realife Miniatures
Country Living Room
Stock No.: 206
Price: $35.95
Made of basswood, brass and cotton fabric. Re-create the country's most popular home decor with these authentic reproductions. Add that warm country atmosphere to your dollhouse or miniature collection with our easy-to-assemble kits at 1/5 the cost of assembled pieces. Complete instructions included. No special tools are required. Country living room kit includes settle bench, sofa, tavern table, sea chest and Shaker candle stand. (Approximately 24 cotton balls required for pillow stuffing, not included.) Settle bench 4-1/2" W x 4"H.

SIR THOMAS THUMB

Painted Country Furniture

Beautifully antiqued pine and painted country furniture. Authentic, realistic, excellent finishes. Cupboard, quilt rack with homespun quilts. Benches, table, settle, bucket bench, etc. Pine. Blue or red. Catalog available.

THE MINI MERCHANT

Country Furniture

Price: $18 to $54
Dimensions: 1" scale
For your cabin or man's den. Main colors are navy and tan.

THE MINI MERCHANT

Overstuffed Furniture

Price: $18 to $54
Dimensions: 1" scale
Great for the library or hunting cabin. Main colors are green, red and tan with touches of gold. Armchair available.

Country Kits

DURA-CRAFT, INC.

Bedroom Furniture Kit

Stock No.: BR40
Price: See your dealer
This beautifully crafted country furniture is something to really please the collector or young ladies. The kits are die-cut 1/8" plywood that is easily assembled. Can be painted or stained to the color scheme of your home. Twelve pieces: bed, linen chest, dresser, baby cradle, wall mirror, two nightstands, chest of drawers, vanity and stool, full length mirror and picture frame. Foil mirrors included. Mattresses, chair pad and doilies not included.

DURA-CRAFT, INC.

Dining Room Furniture Kit

Stock No.: DR10
Price: See your dealer
This beautifully crafted country furniture is something to really please the collector or young ladies. The kits are die-cut 1/8" plywood that is easily assembled. Can be painted or stained to the color scheme of your home. Thirteen pieces: table with four chairs, china cupboard, serving cart, desk and chair, four picture frames.

DURA-CRAFT, INC.

Kitchen Furniture Kit

Stock No.: KR30
Price: See your dealer
This beautifully crafted country furniture is something to really please the collector or young ladies. The kits are die-cut 1/8" plywood that is easily assembled. Can be painted or stained to the color scheme of your home. Nine pieces: kitchen cabinet, stove, table and four chairs, refrigerator and picture frame.

DURA-CRAFT, INC.

Living Room Furniture Kit

Stock No.: LR20
Price: See your dealer
This beautifully crafted country furniture is something to really please the collector or young ladies. The kits are die-cut 1/8" plywood that is easily assembled. Can be painted or stained to the color scheme of your home.
Twelve pieces: sofa, three end tables, piano and bench, two armchairs, coffee table, entry table, two picture frames. Cushions and doilies not included.

WALMER DOLLHOUSES

Miss Muffet Living Room

Stock No.: 822
Price: $7.50 (See your local dealer.)
Dimensions: 1/12 scale
Eight-piece living room set for children. These are die-cut kits made from fine-grained white wood. At this price, a child may be given freedom to paint and color to her heart's content.

WALMER DOLLHOUSES

Miss Muffet Bathroom

Stock No.: ,827
Price: ,$7.50; (See your local dealer.)
Dimensions:1/12 scale
Miss Muffet bathroom five-piece set. Precision die-cut, easy to assemble, fun to decorate. Collect all seven rooms for your special young collector.

WALMER DOLLHOUSES

Miss Muffet Nursery

Stock No.: 825
Price: $7.50 (See your local dealer.)
Dimensions: 1/12 scale
Seven-piece nursery set make a wonderful child's room. Other Miss Muffet room kits are Living Room (#822); Dining Room (#823); Study (#824); Kitchen (#826); Bathroom (#827); Master Bedroom (#821).

WALMER DOLLHOUSES

Miss Muffet Master Bedroom

Stock No.: 821
Price: $7.50 (See your local dealer.)
Dimensions: 1/12 scale
Five-piece bedroom set. All Miss Muffet furniture room kits feature pieces with working drawers and doors. These kits are simply perfect for kids.

European

OMNIARTS OF COLORADO
Gilt Furniture

Price: $100 - 300 finished
This 16th-century furniture is cast by lost wax process and gold plated. Some with marble tops. By John Hodgson of England. Tables, chairs, mirrors and torchieres.

OMNIARTS OF COLORADO

English Period Chairs

Price: $45 (assembled); $23 (kits)
Dimensions: 1" = 1'
Highly detailed pewter chairs from English history for you to paint as desired. Handcrafted in England. Several styles available.

Southwestern

Southwestern Kits

MAISON DES MAISONS

Furniture

Equipales furniture, leather and reed. Various colors of leather available. Navajo sterling coffee set and oak trastero. 1/2" and 1" available.

FANTASY CRAFT

Beehive Hearth Kit

Stock No.: SWBH
Price: Kit $19.95; Finished $29.95
Authentic corner "Beehive" cooking hearth is available in an easy-to-assemble kit with stucco and electric fire unit or already finished and ready to install.

FANTASY CRAFT

Southwest Furniture Kits

Stock No.: SWF
Price: $4.95 - $$18.95
Dimensions: 1" scale
Create your own Southwest furniture from kits! Easy instructions! Sofa, love seat and arm chair include cushion fabric and stuffing. Beds have matresses and bedspread fabric. Bench $9.95; chair $6.95; sofa $14.95; love seat $12.95; armchair $10.95; single bed $16.95; double bed $18.95; end table $5.95; coffee table $9.95; dining table $4.95; dining chair $6.95.

Victorian

ALICE LACY, LTD.
Wire Wicker Furniture

Alice Lacy, Ltd. Wire Wicker and Software. Wicker is the generic name for woven furniture which lends itself to the scrolly ornateness that is Victorian. The sofa and coffee table pictured are appropriate in any setting. Skilled craftsmen braid, coil, bend, and solder wire to make the wicker furniture according to Alice Lacy's specifications. Sold at fine shops almost everywhere.

AZTEC IMPORTS INC.

Victorian Parlor Set

Stock No.: T3218
Price: See your local dealer.
Dimensions: 1"=1' scale
Perfectly sized for the smaller living room or roombox, this parlor set includes lady's and gent's chairs, loveseat and marble-topped table in mahogany.

CLARE-BELL BRASS WORKS

Dressed Brass Beds

Stock No.: See below
1702-D00 - Canopy Bed; 1700-D00 - Fancy Dressed Bed; 1706-D00 - Wagon Wheel Bed with footboard; 1707-D00 - Wagon Wheel Bed without footboard; 1699-D00 - Fancy Twin Bed. A "D" indicates dressed bed. Available dressed or undressed. All beds are solid brass with a gold-plated finish.Catalog, more than 200 items, $2. See your local independent miniatures dealer.

d. ANNE RUFF MINIATURES

Classic Bedroom Furniture

Stock No.: LB-1
Price: See your local dealer.
Dimensions: 1" scale
Handcrafted all-brass bed dressed in white or ecru lace with luxurious lace-trimmed pillows. Matching lace-skirted dressing table and stool. Boudoir lamps (non-electric) and mirror. Queen Anne slipper chair. Matching cornice and draperies with lace curtain.

EMME'S MINIATURES

Working Grandfather Clock

Price: $56.95 plus $2.95 shipping & handling
Dimensions: 1" scale
Quartz accuracy, Victorian styling, walnut finish, ornate carvings, opening front door, pendulum and replaceable battery makes this a must for the collector.

WORKSHOP WISDOM

Paints often come in large containers and the miniaturist only uses a little per project, so the paint dries in the can well before it has been used up. Janice saves small screw-top or snap-top containers, such as 35mm film canisters, make-up bottles, and empty 1/4 fl. oz. (7.5ml) Testors enamel bottles (clean out with mineral spirits). Fill your small jars and seal the large can tightly. Janice put Saran Wrap over the top of the jar before screwing on the lid to prevent the paint drying. The secret to storing paint is to keep the air out of the can; as the paint level drops, add ball bearings, old screws, etc. to bring the level up to the top of the can before attaching the lid; then with the top hammered tightly in place, store the can inverted.

JANICE HALE
BEDFORD, MA

Workshop Wisdom
Courtesy of *Nutshell News*—2/94

HANDCRAFT DESIGNS INC..
Hyde Park Bedroom

Stock No.: see below
This late Victorian bedroom grouping was inspired by furnishings in the Blue Room at Hyde Park. All four case pieces are based on the originals in FDR's boyhood room. There are common architectural motifs indicating a "set" of furniture. Wood in walnut stain, white marble, brass. From left to right:
3502-Hyde Park dresser;
3503-Hyde Park nightstand;
3504-Hyde Park bed (dressings not included);
3508-Hyde Park wardrobe;
3526-brass clothes pole.

HANDLEY HOUSE
Classics by Handley Bedroom Set/4
Classics by Handley Bedroom Set/4

Stock No.: CLA06209/CLA03209
Price: $54/$54
Dimensions: 1" to 1'
Color: multi-color flora, walnut/ivory, mahogany
Classics by Handley sets feature gold-plated hardware (where applicable), extra hand finishing steps and the Classics logo burn brand. Includes a quality control packaging system with open-front boxes for easy viewing, durable box sides and easily-removable vinyl inner pack.

HANDLEY HOUSE
Classics by Handley Dining Room Set/6
Classics by Handley Dining Room Set/6

Stock No.: CLA90603/CLA03145
Price: $60.50/$54
Dimensions: 1" to 1'
Color: mauve cushions, mahogany/ivory cushions, mahogany
Classics by Handley sets feature gold-plated hardware (where applicable), extra hand finishing steps and the Classics logo burn brand. Includes a quality control packaging system with open-front boxes for easy viewing, durable box sides and easily-removable vinyl inner pack.

START A NEW HOBBY AND MEET NEW FRIENDS: JOIN A MINIATURES CLUB!

HANDLEY HOUSE
Mini Collectibles
Victorian Living Room

Stock No.: CLA91309
Price: $47.50
Dimensions: 1" = 1'
Five-piece walnut Victorian living room set with mauve fabric. Includes sofa, two chairs, coffee table and end table.

HANDLEY HOUSE
Classics by Handley Living Room Set/7
Classics by Handley Living Room Set/7

Stock No.: CLA90003/CLA90001
Price: $28.50/$31.50
Dimensions: 1" to 1'
Color: multi-color floral, walnut/multi-color floral, walnut
Classics by Handley sets feature gold-plated hardware (where applicable), extra hand finishing steps and the Classics logo burn brand. Includes a quality control packaging system with open-front boxes for easy viewing, durable box sides and easily-removable vinyl inner pack.

Prices are approximate and subject to change

HANDLEY HOUSE
Classics by Handley Victorian Living Room Set/5
Classics by Handley Victorian Living Room Set/5
Stock No.: CLA90251/CLA90255
Price: $48/$51.50
Dimensions: 1" to 1'
Color: mauve and walnut/ivory, pink and mahogany
Classics by Handley sets feature gold-plated hardware (where applicable), extra hand finishing steps and the Classics logo burn brand. Includes a quality control packaging system with open-front boxes for easy viewing, durable box sides and easily-removable vinyl inner pack.

GREENLEAF PRODUCTS
Dollhouse Furniture Kits
Stock No.: 9010, 9030
Price: $45.90, $25.90
There's terrific value in these kits—Greenleaf's best selling items. Available in 56-piece or 30-piece version. In addition to the die-cut wooden pieces (1" to 1' scale), we've added plastic mirrors and "glass" for frames, along with foam batting for upholstering. Paint or stain the pieces to the color scheme of your choice, and let your decorating abilities come to the fore! Die-cut plywood.

Victorian Kits

SCIENTIFIC MODELS, INC.

Realife Miniatures
Victorian Bedroom Kit
Stock No.: 200
Price: $32.95
Museum quality detailing makes this furniture comparable to replicas that cost up to $75 assembled. Kit includes bed, nightstand and dresser. Bed is 7" high. No sewing or special tools required to build kit. Kit also includes pre-cut and numbered basswood parts, foam upholstery materials, metal hardware, simulated marble table tops, sandpaper, craft glue, brush, wood stain, gloss coat and complete instructions. American-made.

SCIENTIFIC MODELS, INC.
Realife Miniatures
Bathroom
Stock No.: 197
Price: $32.95
Authentic reproductions in basswood. Kit includes all materials to make five pieces shown plus two rugs and three towels. Materials include pre-cut basswood parts, brass hardware, tub, sink, bowl, stain gloss coat, brush, sandpaper, glue and instructions.

20th Century

Make a bunch of grapes by first rolling a small cone of Fimo, inserting a small twig for a stem, then baking it hard. Next, coat the cone with glue and roll it in coriander seeds until completely covered. Allow to dry thoroughly. When the cone is dry, you can paint the seeds with pale green artist's acrylic. Bear in mind that a bunch of grapes will take a definite form if laid in a fruit bowl, for instance, so curve the Fimo form accordingly.

INGRID KNIGHT
YUCCA VALLEY, CA

Workshop Wisdom
Courtesy of *Nutshell News—11/93*

DEE'S DELIGHTS, INC.

Chrysnbon Kits

Stock No. ; see below
Price: See your local dealer.
Chrysnbon kits are easy to assemble, easy to customize, authentically detailed. More than 40 different kits of home furniture and accessories – all accurately scaled in wood-grained polystyrene for a realistic look. Available at your local dealer, send $3 for a complete Chrysnbon product brochure and a list of dealers in your area. CHR2112/Cook Stove Kit—authentic replica of a cook stove, complete with lid lifter, two trivets, match safe, two sad irons, grate shaker, large and small cast iron skillets and stove board with decal. No painting necessary.

DEE'S DELIGHTS, INC.

Chrysnbon Kits

Stock No.: see below
Price: See your local dealer.
CHR2111 - Victorian Bathroom Kit. With a claw-footed bathtub, tank-top commode with pull chain, radiator, mirrored medicine cabinet, stool and swan decals. CHR2114 - Round Table Kit. Features a beautiful replica of a claw-foot round oak table, expandable with two leaves and accented with two cane seat chairs.

SCIENTIFIC MODELS, INC.

Realife Miniatures Kitchen

Stock No.: 191
Price: $37.95
Original design. Kit includes all materials to make five furniture pieces shown (shelf, refrigerator, upper cabinet, lower cabinet, stove—sink and stove hood also included). Materials include pre-cut basswood parts, brass hardware, stain, gloss coat, brush, sandpaper, glue and instructions. American-made.

Early 20th Century

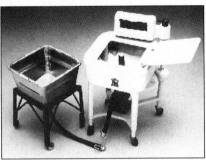

DEE'S DELIGHTS, INC.
Appliances

Stock No.: see below
Price: see below
Authentic, die-cast metal reproductions of "old faithful" appliances. Designed in miniature by Jacqueline Kerr Deiber, these high-quality metal replicas recreate the memories of your childhood. DDL7516/wringer washer, $42; TIN50-20/metal tub, $16; DDL7510/Roper range, $42; DDL7512/monitor top refrigerator, $42; DDL7514/porcelain kitchen sink, $21. All are quality-made with movable parts and are 1" scale. See your local dealer.

MAISON DES MAISONS
Horn Furniture

Price: $35 - $125, plus shipping.
Kit $17.50 - $75, plus shipping.
Dimensions: 1" and 1/2" scale
Horn furniture, finished and kits, with a variety of prices. Sofa, chair, lamps, baskets and fireplace tools.

1930-Contemporary

AZTEC IMPORTS INC.

Spindle Bunkbed

Stock No.: D0624 (oak)
Price: See your local dealer.
Dimensions: 1"=1' scale
Delicate spindles grace the head and foot of this oak bunkbed. Will separate to make twin beds. Also available in white with blue floral covers (T5038).

BY BARB

Contemporary Lucite Furniture
Assorted styles and colors. Handcrafted in the USA by Barb.

DOLL HOUSE SHOPPE
Electronic Equipment
Price: See your dealer.
Dimensions: 1" scale
Shown here are our corduroy recliner, video game TV with controls, stereo with speakers, boom box, white or walnut clock radio, Walkman, computer, two portable TV sets, our starshoot game and our console TV.

CLASSICS BY HANDLEY

Bookcase Units
Stock No.: CLA75010; CLA71074
Price: $7.95; $11.98
All wood. These bookcase units are ideal for your dollhouse or miniature store.
CLA75010 (single) is 3-3/8"W x 7-3/8"H x 1-1/4"D.
CLA71074 (double) is 6-3/8"W x 7-3/8"H x 1-1/4"D.

DONNA'S MINI EMPORIUM
Living Room Set
Price: Completely finished, $12 plus shipping
Dimensions: 1" scale
This colorful three-piece mini print living room set is one of the many features we have to offer. Handmade.

HANDLEY HOUSE
Mini Collectibles Bedroom Set
Stock No.: CLA91305
Price: $42.50
Dimensions: 1" = 1'
Five-piece walnut bedroom set includes Cannonball bed, four-drawer chest, dresser w/mirror and night stand.

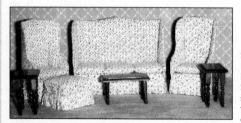

HANDLEY HOUSE
Mini Collectibles Living Room Set
Stock No.: CLA91311
Price: $22.50
Dimensions: 1" = 1'
Seven-piece walnut living room set includes sofa, two chairs, ottoman, coffee table and two end tables. Fabric is white with floral design.

Do you want to list your items in *The Miniatures Catalog?* Call (800) 446-5489 for listing information.

HANDLEY HOUSE
Mini Collectibles
Youth Bedroom Set

Stock No.: CLA91300
Price: $30
Dimensions: 1" = 1'
Three-piece white youth bedroom set includes bed w/pillow, and dresser & night table with gold-plated hardware.

MAISON DES MAISONS

Contemporary Furniture

Beautiful whitewashed Southwest furniture by Joe Turner. Many designs and artists available.

ROYAL MINIATURES

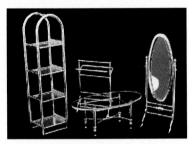

Brass Furniture

Price: $8.50 - $20
Shown is a small selection from our large line of brassware. Many pieces are 14K gold-plated. Other styles available.

THE MINI MERCHANT

Upholstered Furniture

Price: $48 to $54
Contemporary look with traditional flair. Many other fabrics and colors available.

THE MINI MERCHANT

Upholstered Furniture

Price: $42 - $48
Dimensions: 1" scale
Upholstered in ultrasuede. Other fabrics available.

Bathroom

DURA-CRAFT, INC.

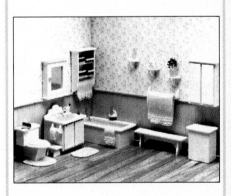

Bathroom Furniture Kit

Stock No.: BT60
No house is complete without this beautifully crafted country bathroom furniture set. The kit is die-cut from 1/8" plywood that is easily assembled. Can be painted or stained to the color scheme of your home. Fifteen pieces: bathtub, commode, sink with cabinet, toilet paper holder, step stool, medicine cabinet with mirror, towel shelf, towel rack, bench, hanging cabinet, clothes hamper, soap dish, three knickknack shelves (rugs, etc., not included).

AZTEC IMPORTS INC.

Outhouse

Stock No.: D2502
Price: See your local dealer.
Dimensions: 6-1/4"H x 3-5/8"W x 3-1/2"D.
1"=1' scale
Pine "necessary" features seating for two, paper roll, shingled roof, half-moon windows and brass-hinged door.

AZTEC IMPORTS INC.

White Bath Set with Flowers

Stock No.: T6296
Price: See your local dealer.
Dimensions: 1"=1' scale
Porcelain four-piece bath set features gold trim and delicate floral decal. Commode has two-piece walnut seat.

DONNA'S MINI EMPORIUM
Ceramic Bathroom Set

Completely finished three-piece bathroom set includes tub, toilet and sink. Comes in white with contrasting seat or in pastel colors. Accessories available include toothbrush/toothpaste, toilet brush and bath tissue. Ceramic. American-made.

HANDLEY HOUSE
Mini Collectibles
Playstuf Bathroom Set

Stock No.: CLA91105
Price: $26.50
Dimensions: 1" = 1'
Three-piece Playstuf Bathroom Set . 100% real hardwood construction with smooth, rounded edges and non-toxic finish. Rugged dollhouse furniture created for kids.

HANDLEY HOUSE
Mini Collectibles
Bathroom Set

Stock No.: CLA91025
Price: $17.50
Dimensions: 1" = 1'
Victorian, three-piece white ceramic bathroom set with flower decal. Includes tub, toilet, sink.

HANDLEY HOUSE
Mini Collectibles
Bathroom Set

Stock No.: CLA91206
Price: $26
Dimensions: 1" = 1'
Victorian, four-piece white ceramic bathroom set with flower decal and gold trim. Includes tub, toilet, sink and mirror.

WORKSHOP WISDOM

Pat needed to form a lace-edged doily to drape over a 3-1/2" (89mm) round table. Not having a cardboard tube that size, she rolled her own from card, then taped and stapled it together. Pulling the doily over the tube form, she pinned it into the desired pattern of folds, then generously sprayed it with starch. After the doily had dried, it was removed from the tube and placed over the table, where it fit and "draped" perfectly. The last craft store I was in stocked a number of usefully-sized, rigid foam cylinders that would make handy molds, since the foam readily accepts pins.

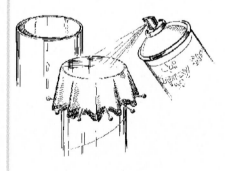

PAT BALAZS
RAVENNA, OH

Workshop Wisdom
Courtesy of *Nutshell News*—4/94

HANDLEY HOUSE
Mini Collectibles
Top Flush Bathroom Set
Stock No.: CLA91303
Price: $24
Dimensions: 1" = 1'
Three-piece white top flush bathroom set includes toilet, bathtub and sink. With floral decal.

HUDSON RIVER DOLL HOUSES

Towel Cupboard
Dimensions: 2-3/4" x 1-1/4" x 6-1/2"; 1"=1' scale
Towel cupboard containing towels, perfume tray, kleenex, bubble bath and two rolls of Scott tissue. Large choice of colors. Wholesale only. See your local dealer.

MINIATURE CORNER
Victorian Bathroom
Metal-baked enamel with rose garland trim bathroom. High German quality. Coal-fired, turn-of-the-century water heater/shower. Matching wallpaper available. Bath pieces also without decoration sold individually. Faucets turn, flusher works, wood toilet seat. A Bodo Hennig product. See your local dealer.

Kitchen

AZTEC IMPORTS INC.

White and Oak Kitchen Set
Stock No.: T5136, T5334
Price: See your local dealer.
Dimensions: 1"=1'
Oak and white lower kitchen set of seven features oak counter tops and knobs (T5334). Kitchen is complete when you add upper cabinet set of four in white.

DOLL HOUSE SHOPPE
Kitchen Furnishings
Price: See your dealer.
Dimensions: 1" scale
Shown are our washboard, food processor, knife block with knives, microwave and cart, country basket, pie and basket, message center, heart base paper towel holder, toaster oven, salt-and-pepper/napkin holder, paper towel and magazine rack and wall note pad. All are original and handmade.

GINSBURG COMPANY

6 Pc White Kitchen Set
Stock No.: 2920.03
Price: See your local dealer.
Keepsakes by Ginsburg Company's Carriage House is packaged in our see-through clam shell package. Furniture is easy to display with damage control. Also available in oak and walnut. 1" = 1"

HANDLEY HOUSE
Mini Collectibles
Kitchen Set

Stock No.: CLA91249
Price: $32
Dimensions: 1" = 1'
Five-piece kitchen set, white. Includes
table, two chairs, hutch and icebox.

HANDLEY HOUSE
Mini Collectibles
Kitchen Set

Stock No.: CLA91245
Price: $23
Dimensions: 1" = 1'
Four-piece, oak kitchen set. Includes
refrigerator, sink, stove and hanging
cabinet.

START A NEW
HOBBY AND
MEET NEW FRIENDS:
JOIN A
MINIATURES CLUB!

WORKSHOP WISDOM

Bobbie had little success with painting round dots with a brush, especially dots that should be of identical size, such as doll's eyes. She eventually found a dental stimulator, a rubber-tipped instrument made by Butler Gum, who also makes toothbrushes with a similar rubber tip at the end of the brush handle. Putting a smear of paint on a palette, she used the tip to successfully "rubber stamp" identical round dots in a very clean, crisp manner.

BOBBI FISCHER
MT. VERNON, WA

Workshop Wisdom
Courtesy of *Nutshell News*—4/94

HANDLEY HOUSE
Mini Collectibles
Kitchen Set

Stock No.: CLA91006
Price: $29
Dimensions: 1" = 1'
Six-piece, oak kitchen set. Includes table, two
chairs, sink, stove and refrigerator.

HANDLEY HOUSE
Mini Collectibles
Kitchen Set

Stock No.: CLA91247
Price: $32
Dimensions: 1" = 1'
Five-piece, oak kitchen set. Includes
table, two chairs, stove and refrigerator.

Prices are approximate and subject to change

HANDLEY HOUSE
Mini Collectibles
Kitchen Set

Stock No.: CLA91005
Price: $29
Dimensions: 1" = 1'
Six-piece, white kitchen set. Includes table, two chairs, stove, sink and refrigerator.

HANDLEY HOUSE

HANDLEY HOUSE
Mini Collectibles
Playstuf Kitchen

Stock No.: CLA91120
Price: $29
Dimensions: 1" = 1'
Three-piece Playstuf Kitchen Set. 100% real hardwood construction with smooth, rounded edges and non-toxic finish. Rugged dollhouse furniture created for kids.

Mini Collectibles
Kitchen Set

Stock No.: CLA91319
Price: $25
Dimensions: 1" = 1'
Forty-five piece kitchen work center includes white butcher's rack, butcher block w/knives, tea service, cookbook, four bowls w/plates, 16 pieces silverware, five cooking utensils and four measuring cups.

SHOW SANTA
WHAT YOU WANT
FROM
THE
MINIATURES
CATALOG

HANDLEY HOUSE
Mini Collectibles
Kitchen Table Set

Stock No.: CLA91335
Price: $25
Dimensions: 1" = 1'
32-piece oak kitchen table set includes table, four chairs, hanging lamp, four plates & bowls, 16 pieces silverware, box of cookies and milk.

Here is a unique method of creating bushes. Purchase a few rigid foam eggs from the craft store, cutting and gluing them as desired, two methods being shown here. Glue a dowel or twig into the bottom, long enough for the final "planting" in your mini garden. Paint the eggs with dark green acrylic and when dry, spread a thick layer of carpenter's glue or similar all over, followed immediately by a generous sprinkling of green landscaping material from the model railroad store. Sandpaper strips wrapped around various sizes of dowel are useful for shaping topiary bushes.

*PENNY SMITH
KENT, WA*

Workshop Wisdom
Courtesy of *Nutshell News*—5/94

HANDLEY HOUSE
Classics by Handley Kitchen Set/6
Classics by Handley Kitchen Set/6

Stock No.: CLA05002/CLA05802
Price: $40/$40
Dimensions: 1" to 1'
Color: white/blue
Classics by Handley sets feature gold-plated hardware (where applicable), extra hand finishing steps and the Classics logo burn brand. Includes a quality control packaging system with open-front boxes for easy viewing, durable box sides and easily-removable vinyl inner pack.

SHENANDOAH DESIGNS, INC.

The Kitchen Collection

Stock No.: 3400 and 4400
Price: see below
Dimensions: 1" to 1' scale
The Kitchen Collection consists of 1" to 1' modular cabinets that allow the builder to construct a custom kitchen to fit any dollhouse. Countertop and trim kits provide the materials needed to add the final touches. The cabinets are made of mahogany and feature raised panel doors and drawers, set off with rich brass hardware. Kits for the stove, sink and oven front add details lacking in many kitchens, 3400 series kits; 4400 series assembled/unfinished. Kits $2.49 to $19.49; assembled/unfinished $8.49 to $21.99.

Nursery

AZTEC IMPORTS INC.

Nursery Set

Stock No.: T5153A
Price: See your local dealer.
Dimensions: 1"=1' scale
White baby's room includes crib with patchwork mattress, dressing table with patchwork pad, toy box, coat rack and child's rocker. Also available in oak (T4153A).

CLASSICS BY HANDLEY

Baby Cradle

Stock No.: CLA00893
Price: $5.15
Wood. Painted white and yellow. White baby crib with yellow trim and checkered material on mattress.

CLASSICS BY HANDLEY

Baby Crib

Stock No.: CLA03909
Price: $6.25
Wood. Painted white and yellow. White baby crib with yellow trim and checkered material on mattress.

Prices are approximate and subject to change

HANDCRAFT DESIGNS INC.

DURA-CRAFT, INC.
Nursery Furniture Kit

Stock No.: NR70

A home is not a home without a nursery. This beautifully crafted country nursery is die-cut 1/8" plywood that is easily assembled. Can be painted or stained to the color scheme of your home. Twelve pieces: crib, changing table, dresser, rocking chair, pram, child's swing chair, rocking horse chair, scooter, toy box and three picture frames.

HANDLEY HOUSE
Mini Collectibles
Nursery Set

Stock No.: CLA91000
Price: $22.50
Dimensions: 1" = 1'
Four-piece, white and pink nursery set includes crib w/mattress, dresser, walker and potty seat.

A, B, C Nursery Grouping

Stock No.: see below
Price: See your local dealer.
Dimensions: 1/12 scale
A nursery room full of complementing items: From "A, B, C" decorated furniture to a "1, 2, 3" decorated rug, complete with matching wallpaper of letters and numbers created in 4-color process. Together they represent a contemporary, colorful nursery. Shown:
Wallpaper #1000,
Rug #1078,
Crib #3720,
Toy box #3722,
Dresser #3721,
Lamp #3723,
Changing table #3724,
Rocking horse chair #4007,
Mini dollhouse #4005.

HANDLEY HOUSE
Mini Collectibles
Nursery Set

Stock No.: CLA91030
Price: $23
Dimensions: 1" = 1'
Four-piece, oak nursery set includes crib with mattress, dresser, walker and potty seat.

HANDLEY HOUSE
Mini Collectibles
Nursery Set

Stock No.: CLA91213
Price: $23
Dimensions: 1" = 1'
Four-piece, pink and white nursery set with teddy bear decal. Includes play pen with mattress, changing table, toy chest and coat rack.

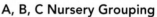

HANDLEY HOUSE
Mini Collectibles
Nursery Set

Stock No.: CLA91215
Price: $28.50
Dimensions: 1" = 1'
Four-piece, oak nursery set includes play pen with mattress, changing table, toy chest and rocking horse.

Mini Collectibles
Canopy Crib Set

Stock No.: CLA91327
Price: $27.50
Dimensions: 1" = 1'
Two-piece white canopy crib set includes canopy crib with mattress and Gloucester rocker.

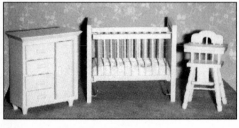

HANDLEY HOUSE
Mini Collectibles
Playstuf Nursery Set

Stock No.: CLA91125
Price: $27
Dimensions: 1" = 1'
Four-piece Playstuf Nursery Set includes crib, highchair, mattress and changing table. 100% real hardwood construction with smooth, rounded edges and non-toxic finish. Rugged dollhouse furniture created for kids.

HANDLEY HOUSE
Mini Collectibles
Nursery Set

Stock No.: CLA91307
Price: $17.50
Dimensions: 1" = 1'
Three-piece white nursery set includes dresser, crib w/mattress and high chair.

MINIATURE HOUSE

Baby Dresser

Stock No.: MH898
Price: $5.98
Wood. Painted white and yellow. This in expensive baby dresser is painted white with yellow trim. Drawers and doors open.

MINIATURE HOUSE

Baby High Chair

Stock No.: MH897
Price: $5
Wood. White and yellow paint. White baby high chair with yellow trim. Tray is removable.

MINIATURE HOUSE

Baby Playpen

Stock No.: MH896
Price: $6
Wood and fabric. White and yellow paint. This attractive playpen has a white and yellow checkered pad.

MINIATURE HOUSE

Baby Rocking Chair

Stock No.: MH894
Price: $2.79
Wood. White and yellow paint. Baby rocking chair is white with yellow trim.

Prices are approximate and subject to change

MINIATURE HOUSE

Chair for Baby's Room
Stock No.: MH892
Price: $2.79, completely finished
Wood. Painted white and yellow. White chair with yellow trim and checkered material on seat. Also ideal for kitchens.

MINIATURE HOUSE

Oak Potty Chair With Pot
Stock No.: MH887
Price: $8.98
Wood with metal pot. Stained and varnished. Cute potty chair has door in front. Chair is oak-stained.

OMNIARTS OF COLORADO

Baby Carriages
Price: $100 - $200 finished
Baby carriages and prams handcrafted in England of metal, fabric and leather by the Robersons. Several styles available.

Outdoor

CLASSICS BY HANDLEY
Porch Swing
Dimensions: 4-1/2"W x 1-3/4"H
Swing is all wood, chain is metal. Traditional porch swing to be suspended from the ceiling with chains. Available stained, varnished or painted. CLA74081 (walnut) $9.98; CLA74082 (oak) $10.49; CLA74083 (white) $12.50.

DURA-CRAFT, INC.

Outdoor Furniture Kit
Stock No.: OD80
Complete your home with a set of outdoor furniture. This beautifully crafted kit is die-cut from 1/8" plywood and easy to assemble. Can be painted or stained. Five pieces: working love seat swing, table with umbrella, two lounge chairs with pull-out leg rests and food cart.

DOLL HOUSE SHOPPE

Birdhouses
Price: see your dealer
Shown are our barn birdhouse, two-story birdhouse, peaked birdhouse, our mini birdhouse, and our bird feeder. Stands are included. All are handmade by us in the USA.

HANDLEY HOUSE

Picket Fence and Gate
Price: $2.79 assembled, unfinished
Handmade in the USA of native hardwood. Pickets are .02" thick by 1/8" wide and have pointed tops. Fence panel (HH315) is 7"W x 3-1/4"H. Gate panel (HH316) is 2-3/8" W x 3-3/4"H. Walnut.

KIMBERLY HOUSE MINIATURES

Kimberly Lawn Swing Kit

Stock No.: LS-100
Price: $32.95
Your swing will glide back and forth, to bring back memories of times gone by. All pieces are precut and drilled. Step by step instructions.

SHENANDOAH DESIGNS, INC

The Porch and Patio Collection

Stock No.: 3600 and 4600
Price: see below
1/12 scale versions of the ever popular "Adirondack" or "Country Craftsman" style. 3600 series kits; 4600 series assemble unfinished. Mahogany. $5.99 to $12.99 kits; $6.49 to $18.99 assembled, unfinished.

FOR FAST SERVICE, VISIT YOUR LOCAL MINIATURES SHOP

AZTEC IMPORTS INC

Office Furniture

Stock No.: T6140, T6066, T6561A, T6562A
Price: See your local dealer.
Dimensions: 1"=1' scale
Walnut roll top desk (T6140) also available in oak (T4140) and mahogany (M0671), desk chair (T6066). Four-drawer file cabinet in walnut (T6561A) and two-drawer file cabinet (T6562A).

HANDLEY HOUSE
Mini Collectibles
Office Set

Stock No.: CLA91274
Price: $28.50
Dimensions: 1" = 1'
Three-piece oak office set includes desk, coat rack and swivel chair.

Do you want to list your items in *The Miniatures Catalog?* Call (800) 446-5489 for listing information.

HANDLEY HOUSE
Mini Collectibles
Office Set

Stock No.: CLA91272
Price: $28.50
Dimensions: 1" = 1'
Three-piece wanlut office set includes desk, coat rack and swivel chair.

Prices are approximate and subject to change

KIMBERLY HOUSE MINIATURES
Kimberly Showcase Kits

Stock No.: LD-1K (is shown)
This kit is easy to assemble and finish. The shelf and Plexiglas removes for easy cleaning. The style fits any era. All sizes are 3-1/2" high. Sizes available:
LD-1K 6"W x 2"D - $8.64
LS-1K 6"W x 1-1/2"D - $7.98
MD-1K 4"W x 2"D - $7.98
MS-1K 4"W x 1-1/2"D - $7.54
SD-1K 2"W x 2"D - $7.54
SS-1K 2"W x 1-1/2"D - $6.99

KIMBERLY HOUSE MINIATURES
Kimberly Bakery and Candy Case Kits

Materials and finish: Plexiglas with wood base. Kit easy to assemble and finish. Shelf and Plexiglas remove for easy cleaning. Style fits any era.
BK-1 5"W x 2"D x 3-1/4"H - $11.94
BK-2 5"W x 3"D x 6-1/2"H - $15.90
See your dealer or write Kimberly House.

TERI'S MINI WORKSHOP

Beauty Parlor

Furniture and accessories for a miniature beauty parlor. Many color choices available.

Wicker

THREE BLIND MICE

1" Scale Office Furniture and Supplies

Same price for finished or unfinished (we supply hardware for unfinished). $30, desk w/typing stand; $25, desk without stand; $12, two-drawer file; $14, four-drawer file; $17, drafting table; $35, Xerox machine; $20, water cooler; $20, storage cabinet; $12, desk chair. Made of wood.

ALICE LACY, LTD.
Wire Wicker Furniture

Alice Lacy, Ltd. Wire Wicker and Software Designed by Alice Lacy. Wicker is the generic name for woven furniture. Skilled craftsmen solder iron wire to make the wicker furniture according to Alice Lacy's specifications. In the real world of wicker the Loyd Loom woven styles followed the highly popular Bar Harbor patterns. Alice Lacy's 1995 designs, are inspired by the 1920's loomed work of Marshal Loyd. Today, loomed furniture is to be found in elegant houses both large and small in Britain and the Continent as well as in the US. Sold at fine shops almost everywhere.

MOONLIGHT MINIATURES
Wicker Furniture

Dimensions: 1" scale
A complete line of delicately, handwoven wicker furniture. Available in white or natural. Items shown: rocking chair, sewing basket and child's rocking horse at $45 each plus shipping. Retail only. For price list send $2 (deductible from first order).

OMNIARTS OF COLORADO
Wicker Furniture Kits

Price: $3 - $19
Material: Cotton cord, covered wire, wood. Designer series kits use waxed linen cord. Pieces available include beds, vanities, stools, wall and pier mirrors, étageres, chairs, sofas, tables, plant stands, chaises, baby carriages, high chairs, potty chairs, conversation chairs, cribs, cradles, lamps, bird cages, swings, coat racks and more. New items available regularly.

WARLING MINIATURES
Warling Wicker Furniture

Price: $3-$135
Signed, sealed and dated pieces range from reproductions of a bygone era to pure fantasy pieces. They encompass a broad time frame from Victorian to modern styles. Completed pieces or kits available. Kits contain natural waxed linen cord, wood, sealed covered wires, fabrics and/or hardware.

Miscellaneous

AZTEC IMPORTS INC.

English Telephone Booth

Stock No.: T5299
Price: See your local dealer.
Dimensions: 8-1/2"H x 4-1/2"W x 4-1/2"D. 1"=1' scale
English style phone booth in red includes crank style phone. Also available in oak (T4299) and hunter green (T5999).

ANN WEINER MINIATURES
Aged Furniture with the Worn Look

Dimensions: 1" Scale
Handcrafted furniture that looks old for a special setting. Over 60 items. Retail or sold to shops. Request on business letterhead with TAX ID form. Send $1.00 or four 32¢ stamps for list. Hutches, bookcases, Adirondack furniture, tables, cupboards, potties, mirrors, baskets, etc. WE DO CUSTOMIZED MARBELIZING ON RAW WOOD THAT YOU SUPPLY AND GOLD LEAFING - Rooms or Furniture.

BRENDA VAN ORSOUW ADAMS MINIATURES

Tilt Top Table and Screen

Fine hand painted miniatures available in 1" and 1/2" scale. Furniture, paintings and accessories. Custom orders, individual and dealer inquiries welcomed. Retail prices: Tilt-top $39; Screen $28; plus shipping.

BY GRACE
Customized Furniture

Let us help you create a memorable moment from the past or the desires of your dreams. We specialize in customized beds of walnut, oak, mahogany, brass or wire, with designer or period linens. A variety of styles from Colonial to Contemporary. Room suites are a specialty. Also nursery, juvenile, novelty are available. Scale: 1" = 1'. Priced according to selection (see catalog). Free shipping in USA on prepaid orders only. Price list with color photos, $2.50 plus LSASE.

CLASSICS BY HANDLEY

Wrought Iron Table With Four Chairs

Stock No.: CLA03750
Price: $10
Metal with fabric cover. This set is comprised of a table and four chairs, painted white with checkered tablecloth and seat covers. Also perfect for a soda or ice cream shop.

EBERHARD FABER GMBH
FIMO Modeling Material

Stock No.: 8000
Price: see your dealer
Dimensions: see below
55 by 55 by 15 mm/65 g small block, 165 by 55 by 30 mm/350 g large block. FIMO, the fantastic and most popular modeling material, is the leading product of its kind in Europe. It's versatile and easy to handle and hardens in the oven at 265° (20 to 30 minutes). Available in 42 brilliant colors, it's ideal to create the finest decorative accessories for your dollhouse and to make exciting and imaginative objects (miniatures, figures, fashion jewelry, decorations, pictures, nameplates and a lot more).

START A NEW HOBBY AND MEET NEW FRIENDS: JOIN A MINIATURES CLUB!

FANTASY FABRICATIONS

Original-design furniture, lamps, fireplaces, topiary trees, and much more. We have designs in contemporary, Victorian, art deco, and oriental. Choose from our stock, or we will match your colors. We specialize in special orders with a money-back guarantee. We will work from your picture or drawing and make a special miniature just for you. We can also create a special scene in a breakaway box or roombox. Color brochures $2.50.

HANDCRAFT DESIGNS INC.
Young Collectors Series

Stock No.: see below
Price: See your local dealer.
Dimensions: 1/12 scale
Shown is a loft bunk bed on leg extenders over a dresser and desk with chair. These lacquered, hardwood pieces with painted red accent colors are representative of our house full of children's playable furniture in our Young Collectors Series.
Shown are item numbers 4760B, 4762, 4763, 4764.

FOX HOLLOW MINIATURES

Antique Collector's Cupboard

Price: $200
Dimensions: 7" x 4" x 1-1/2"
Genuine antique miniatures found at flea markets from Covent Gardens to the Marche des Puces fill this country blue cupboard. Each signed piece is unique.

HANDLEY HOUSE
Mini Collectibles
Dining Room Set

Stock No.: CLA91265
Price: $34
Dimensions: 1" = 1'
Four-piece, mahogany dining room set. Includes table, two chairs and hutch.

HANDLEY HOUSE
Mini Collectibles
Dining Room Set

Stock No.: CLA91267
Price: $34
Dimensions: 1" = 1'
Four-piece, oak dining room set. Includes table, two chairs and hutch.

WORKSHOP WISDOM

Tudor, Victorian, and similar houses usually call for multi-pane windows. Stella found that if she cut and trimmed the sides from a plastic strawberry basket, she could glue these on the outside of the window glass, probably using a smear of rubber cement. She recommends painting the glazing bars before adding them to the windows.

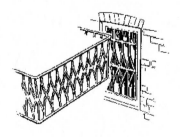

*STALLA HEXTER
KENSINGTON, CA*

HANDLEY HOUSE
Mini Collectibles
Bunk Bedroom Set

Stock No.: CLA91235
Price: $35
Dimensions: 1" = 1'
Four-piece, walnut bunk bedroom set. Includes bunk bed w/mattress & pillow, dresser, coat rack and magazine rack.

Workshop Wisdom
Courtesy of *Nutshell News—12/93*

Subscribe to

Nutshell News

and learn how you

can make miniatures

yourself!

Call toll free:

(800) 446-5489

HANDLEY HOUSE
Mini Collectibles
Playstuf Bedroom Set
Stock No.: CLA91100
Price: $28
Dimensions: 1" = 1'
Five-piece Playstuf Bedroom Set. Includes bed w/mattress, side table, vanity and seat. 100% real hardwood construction with smooth, round edges and non-toxic finish. Rugged dollhouse furniture created for kids.

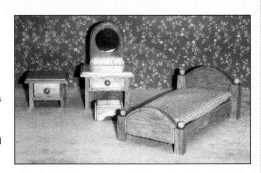

HANDLEY HOUSE
Mini Collectibles
BedroomSet
Stock No.: CLA91292
Price: $33
Dimensions: 1" = 1'
Three-piece, oak bedroom set. Includes bed w/mattress & pillow, side table w/drawers and dresser. Fabric is cream with flowers.

HANDLEY HOUSE
Mini Collectibles
Modern Living Room Set
Stock No.: CLA91225
Price: $33
Dimensions: 1" = 1'
Five-piece, modern living room set. Includes sofa, chair, ottoman, coffee table and side table. Fabric is cream w/floral design. Tables are walnut.

WORKSHOP WISDOM

Glass domes and the matching bases in which to place vignettes are quite expensive, and so are custom-made Plexiglas covers. Watch your local K-Mart or Target store flyers for sales – often you will find terrariums advertised very inexpensively. Remove the plant; the glass cover and base will house your vignettes very nicely, as they come in a multitude of styles. Also, Eleanor Rector shows how to make domes from 2-litre bottles in Workshop Wisdom (NN Sept. '85; and in *Workshop Wisdom Dollhouse Crafting Tips*, available from Kalmbach Publishing.)

HANDLEY HOUSE
Mini Collectibles
Playstuf Living Room Set
Stock No.: CLA91115
Price: $28
Dimensions: 1" = 1'
Six-piece Playstuf Living Room Set. Includes sofa with cushion, chair with cushion, side table and lamp. 100% real hardwood construction with smooth, rounded edges and non-toxic finish. Rugged dollhouse furniture created for kids.

PATRICIA TOWNSEND
REDWOOD CITY, CA

Workshop Wisdom
Courtesy of *Nutshell News*—4/94

HANDLEY HOUSE
Mini Collectibles
Playstuf Dining Room Set

Stock No.: CLA91113
Price: $22.50
Dimensions: 1" = 1'
Five-piece Playstuf Dining Room Set. Includes table and four chairs. 100% real hardwood construction with smooth, rounded edges and non-toxic finish. Rugged dollhouse furniture created for kids.

HANDLEY HOUSE

Mini Collectibles
Bedroom Set

Stock No.: CLA91035
Price: $32
Dimensions: 1" = 1'
Four-piece oak bedroom set. Includes bed with mattress and pillow, dresser, side table and coat rack. Fabric is cream with floral pattern.

HANDLEY HOUSE
Mini Collectibles
Dining Room Set

Stock No.: CLA91020
Price: $26
Dimensions: 1" = 1'
Six-piece walnut dining room set. Includes hutch, table and four chairs.

HANDLEY HOUSE
Mini Collectibles
Dining Room Set

Stock No.: CLA91045
Price: $26
Dimensions: 1" = 1'
Six-piece oak dining room set. Includes hutch, table and four chairs.

JOIN A MINIATURES CLUB ... OR START ONE!

WORKSHOP WISDOM

Every lobby should have a coat rack, and this one was put together from craft sticks and thorns from a rose bush. Pauline's was tastefully decorated with little flowers, then varnished before being glued to the wall. Add a coat or two, a hat, and even scarves for effect.

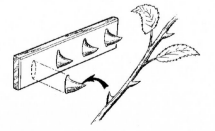

*PAULINE BRIGNANO
WEST HARTFORD, CT*

Workshop Wisdom
Courtesy of *Nutshell News*—5/94

Prices are approximate and subject to change

HANDLEY HOUSE

HANDLEY HOUSE
Mini Collectibles
Bedroom Set

Stock No.: CLA91010
Price: $32
Dimensions: 1" = 1'
Four-piece, walnut bedroom set. Includes bed with mattress and pillow, dresser, side table and coat rack. Fabric is cream with taupe stripes and flowers.

Mini Collectibles
Piano Set

Stock No.: CLA91282
Price: $12.50
Dimensions: 1" = 1'
Two-piece oak piano set includes piano, sheet music and seat.

HANDLEY HOUSE
Mini Collectibles
Living Room Set

Stock No.: CLA91015
Price: $22.50
Dimensions: 1" = 1'
Seven-piece living room set, brown floral fabric. Includes couch, two chairs, one ottoman, coffee table and two side tables. Walnut.

HANDLEY HOUSE
Mini Collectibles
Living Room Set

Stock No.: CLA91040
Price: $22.50
Dimensions: 1" = 1'
Seven-piece living room set, pink floral fabric. Includes couch, two chairs, one ottoman, coffee table and two side tables. Walnut.

WORKSHOP WISDOM

A quickly-detachable curtain rod enables drapes to be changed at a whim. This lady glues eyelets (Cir-Kit #1023-1) to the walls with Quick-Grab (5 Minute epoxy or thick CA glue will work, too), then bends a 3/32" (2.5mm) inside diameter brass tube (Sig #2099) to the shape shown. Thread the drapes on the tube, then plug the ends of the tube into the eyelets. If you know a friendly electrician, thick copper wire will work well, instead of tubing. Try 12 or 14 gauge wire.

*TALMADGE PHELPS
PALMYRA, NY*

HANDLEY HOUSE
Mini Collectibles
Sewing Room Set

Stock No.: CLA91207
Price: $20
Dimensions: 1" = 1'
Five-piece sewing room includes sewing machine, chair, vacuum, body form, scissors, yarn, patterns, fabric and tape measure.

Workshop Wisdom
Courtesy of *Nutshell News*—5/94

HANDLEY HOUSE
Mini Collectibles
Pool Table Set
Stock No.: ,CLA91323
Price: $25
Dimensions: 1 " = 1'
Twenty-four piece, mahogany pool table set includes pool table, stool, three pool sticks w/rack, balls, ball rack and hanging lamp.

WORKSHOP WISDOM

When she peeled the net backing from those sheets of clay bricks, Jane discovered that the mesh, when colored with permanent markers, made perfect miniature afghans. As a plus, she also found that if you place the mesh on a sheet of stiff pastel paper and use it as a stencil, stippling the markers through the mesh, the resulting repeat patterns on the paper created excellent mini gift wrap paper.

*JANE FREEMAN
NEW YORK, NY*

Workshop Wisdom
Courtesy of *Nutshell News—3/94*

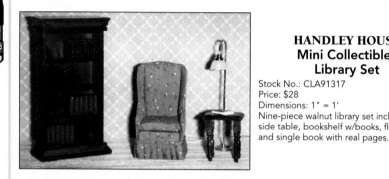

HANDLEY HOUSE
Mini Collectibles
Library Set
Stock No.: CLA91317
Price: $28
Dimensions: 1 " = 1'
Nine-piece walnut library set includes chair, side table, bookshelf w/books, floor lamp and single book with real pages.

HANDLEY HOUSE
Mini Collectibles
Ice Cream Parlor
Stock No.: CLA91331
Price: $25
Dimensions: 1 " = 1'
32-piece ice cream parlor set includes four chairs, table, four plates & bowls, silverware, cake ice cream and bubble gum machine.

WALMER DOLLHOUSES
Bookcases
Price: See your local dealer.
Dimensions: All 7-3/8"H x 1-3/8"D; 1/12 scale
5500 - Corner Bookcase (7-1/8"H);
5501 - Single Bookcase;
5502 - Double Bookcase;
5503 - Triple Bookcase. Stain, paint or varnish to fit into every room, shop and decor.

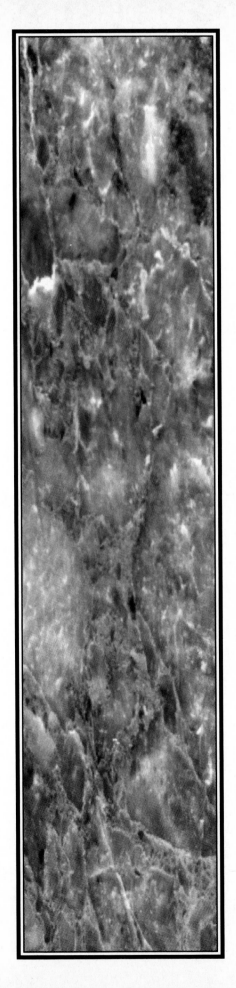

DOLLHOUSE DOLLS

&

DOLL ACCESSORIES

Character Dolls

ALICE ZINN
Dolls - Character & Dollhouse
Price: $40 - $125
New this year! Alice Zinn has created a line of individually hand-sculpted, mostly posable dolls with exceptional detail and personality. Holiday dolls, fantasy figures, tourists, families, kids, clowns in every conceivable kind of outfit. Custom challenges welcomed. Shown are sorcerer, $110; "Barbra…in concert," $110; boy in baseball outfit, $85; Santa Claus with pack of toys, $85; girl with Easter bonnet and basket, $85; "Colleen" in green dress, $75; and toddler in bunny outfit, $45.

AZTEC IMPORTS INC.

Modern Dolls by Town Square
Stock No.: 00002-00030
Price: See your local dealer.
Dimensions: Men-6", Women-5-1/2", Girl-3", Boy-3-1/2", Baby-2". 1"-1' scale
Modern dolls available in family sets or individually. Poseable with removable clothing. Also available (00068) Grandfather, and (00066) Grandmother.

AZTEC IMPORTS INC.

Victorian Dolls by Town Square
Stock No.: 00040, 00060, 00050
Price: See your local dealer.
Dimensions: Men-6", Women-5-1/2", Girl-3", Baby-2". 1"=1' scale
Victorian family sets of four in blonde (00040), brunette (00050) and black (00060) are poseable and have removable clothing.

CAROL'S CREATIONS IN MINIATURE

Dollhouse Dolls
Price: $45-$220, plus shipping
Dimensions: 1" and 1/2" scale
Original dolls sculpted out of Fimo. Authentically dressed in the finest fabrics. All eras. Poseable. Special orders welcome. $3 for list and photos. Specify era.

DONNA'S MINI EMPORIUM

Dollhouse Dolls
Price: Assortment
Dimensions: 1" scale
Ceramic dolls are hand painted. Bisqued or glazed, they are completed with muslin cloth, then stuffed with polyfiber and pipe cleaner to make them bendable. Only babies are jointed.

DONNA'S MINI EMPORIUM

Jointed Baby
Price: $20
Ceramic dollhouse doll.

GARCIA & VELEZ CO.

Porcelain Babies
Price: Wholesale only
Dimensions: 1"=1'
Porcelain babies, three months to six months. Handmade crochet dresses can be sold separately.

HDW

Porcelain Dolls

Stacy Hofman dolls dressed by Nancy Crossno: Naval Officer, $330 complete, $130 as kit. Lady, $395. Many periods available as well as custom colors and elaborate costuming.

HDW

Bitsy

Bitsy, all porcelain 1-1/2" doll, $165 ppd, in elaborate period dress. Teensy, all porcelain 1-1/4" doll, $155 ppd.

HDW

Genuine Pewter Cats

Mama cat and kittens - $35 painted, $7 unpainted; Seated cat - $22 painted, $5 unpainted; Lying cat - $22 painted, $5 unpainted. All priced ppd.

KITTY MACKEY'S RELATIVE DIMENSIONS
Hand-Sculpted Figures

Price: $275 and up
Dimensions: 1/12 scale
Hand-sculpted figures by I.G.M.A. Artisan Kitty Mackey. No molds or pre-formed parts are used for these fine collectibles, which are sculpted from your photo or description. Any time period; historical characters meticulously researched for accuracy. Satisfaction guaranteed. Thank you for your interest in miniatures!

J. HERMES

Mini Babies

Stock No.: 201 - 204
Price: $1.75; $2.55
German imports. Full color "anatomically correct" 1" scale boy and girl babies in four positions: sitting, standing, crawling and prone. Dressed or undressed. Plastic.

LULIE'S ZOO

Animal Head Figures

Stylin' Cats and Lion Kings and Fairies are my passions; Pups and Pigs and Creeping Things all wearing unique fashions! It's a jungle in here! Scale 1" - 1' and 1/2" and 1/4". Price: $200-$450.

MINIATURE HOUSE

Dollhouse Babies

Stock No.: MH3530
Price: $6.25
Bendable plastic with removable clothing. An infant and a toddler to add to your dollhouse family are 1" scale and fully bendable.

MINIATURE HOUSE

Dollhouse Children

Stock No.: MH3520
Price: $8.25
Bendable plastic with removable clothing. These boy and girl dolls are fully bendable, life-like and very affordable. Dolls are 1" scale.

MINIATURE HOUSE
Dollhouse Family

Stock No.: MH3500
Price: $17.50
Bendable plastic with removable clothing. These 1" scale dollhouse dolls are more realistic and life-like than most and are priced to fit any budget.

MINIATURE HOUSE

Dollhouse Adults

Stock No.: MH3510
Price: $11.30
Bendable plastic with removable clothing. These all-plastic, bendable dolls in contemporary clothing are 1" scale.

ROSALIE WHYEL
MUSEUM OF DOLL ART

Dolls—Character & Dollhouse

Price: prices vary
Our museum store carries a wide variety of dolls to inhabit your miniature homes. Our artists include Dorothy Hoskins, Galia Bazylko, Joanne Callander, and Sylvia Lyons.

TERI'S MINI WORKSHOP

Child in Bubble Bath

"Honey, I'm washing the kid."

PETITE PEOPLE PLUS
Fine Porcelain Dollhouse Dolls

Price: See below.
Dimensions: 1" and 1/2" scale.
Fine porcelain dollhouse dolls and fantasy figures dressed in silk and cotton fabric. Many popular 1" and 1/2" scale dolls, individually china painted that look like real people. Dressed men, ladies, teens, toddlers and babies are available in the proper ethnic color porcelain. Cats, rabbits, frogs in other colors. Wigs, doll kits and many accessories available. Unassembled, painted kits $16.75; assembled, unfinished (no hair, not dressed) $24; basic dressed $36.50; custom orders more.

THE SMALL DOLL COMPANY
Dollhouse Dolls

Stock No.: 3017
Price: $75 - $200; plus shipping
Dimensions: 1" and 1/2" scales.
Exquisite, handcrafted, porcelain dollhouse people. All dolls feature leather shoes, fine imported fabric, lace and hair. Some dolls are from our original molds.

Doll Clothing

FOX HOLLOW MINIATURES

Muddy Old Boots

Price: $25
Dimensions: 1-3/4"
The famous Muddy Old Boots from Merrie Old England by the talented Dorothy Kitching. A "must" for every back door!

GREAT FABRICATIONS

Miniature Designer Fabrics
Price: $6 - $8.50 per panel
Designer doll fabrics in silk habotai or taffeta, cotton batiste or lawn. Can be printed in many different colors. Send $5 for samples and prices.

MARY AGNES MURPHY

Clothing Accents
Price: $4-$20
Beautiful, handmade clothing. 1" scale. Layette to adult. Perfect accent for any miniature setting. Many more items available. Send SASE for complete price list.

MINIATURE HOUSE

Dress Form
Stock No.:MH2319
Price: $2.49
This black dress form for the sewing room is made of solid metal, perfectly proportioned.

MINIATURE HOUSE

Hat Stands
Stock No.: MH2067; MH2068
Price: $1.89
These lovely hat stands are made of wood with turned bases.

MINIATURE HOUSE

Ladies' Hats
Stock No.: MH2070
Price: $4.49Fine, felt ladies' feathered hats with three rosebuds. Available in burgundy, red, blue and green. These quality hats fit hat stands MH2067 and MH2068.

PRESTIGE LEATHER

Belts, Purses & Shoes
Assorted belts, purses & shoes in a variety of colors. Belts $2 to $3. Purses $10 to $16. Shoes $8 to $22.

R & N MINIATURES
Miss Muffy's Mannequins
Dressed in the finest materials and lace, these look magnificent in a dress shop or sewing room. From left -
RMPB - Debutante;
RMPE - Nanny;
RMPA - Widow;
RMPC - Southern Belle;
RMPD - Flapper;
RMPF - Society; $47.50 each.
RMPH - Matching hat , $22.50;
RMPP - Matching purse, $15.50;
APLI price list, $2.

THE DOLLS' COBBLER

Slicker Sets
Price: $33
Three-piece set in girl's, boy's and men's rainwear available in a variety of colors.

ROSALIE WHYEL
MUSEUM OF DOLL ART
Dollhouse Accessories
Price: prices vary
Always a delightful selection of sought-after dollhouse accessories and the dolls to use them. Unique and unusual items by artists Susan Harmon, Carl Bronsdon, Galia Bazylko, Dorothy Hoskins and Sylvia Lyons. Call, FAX, or write for current stock.

Dollmaking Supplies & Molds

Clothing Patterns

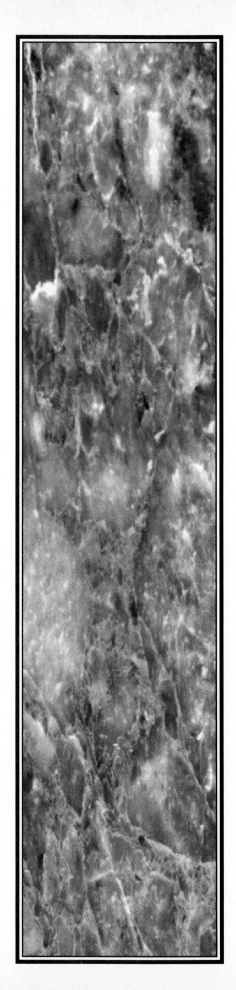

1" SCALE

ACCESSORIES

Animals

ALICE ZINN
Dogs, Cats, Birds & Other Pets

Custom made to your order, available in all breeds and scales. Also available are monkeys, rabbits, guinea pigs, turtles, fish, mice, parrots, hamsters, lizards, ant farms, ferrets and snakes. Accessories available include dog collars, leashes, beds, cat litter box, scratching post, pet food, toys and more. American-made.

ALICE ZINN
Wild Birds and Animals

Barnyard birds and animals, wild birds, raccoons, skunks, fox, etc. Forest and jungle animals, circus animals, open- and closed-tail peacocks. Custom work welcomed.

B.J. ENTERPRISE

Pussy Willow Persians

Price: $10 and up
Dimensions: 1/12 scale
Persian cats are made of pussy willows. Each one is unique as to style and color. They are in sacks, hat boxes, baskets & on chairs. Families also.

BERRY-PATCH DESIGNS

Miniature Bears

Miniature bears and bunnies scaled to be toys or occupants of a setting. Available finished or in kits. Bear making supplies also available! Catalog $2.

START A NEW HOBBY AND MEET NEW FRIENDS: JOIN A MINIATURES CLUB!

Prices are approximate and subject to change

WORKSHOP WISDOM

Mini Books

Realistic mini books for the book case. Cut photos of books from book catalogs as in (a). Then, using plenty of white glue, attach the picture to a piece of stiff card. While the glue is wet use the edge of a ruler or a blunt dinner knife to score between the books as shown in (b) so that it raises the back of the books and gives them curvature. Fold the ends of the card strip back (c), then push the stack of "books" into the book case.

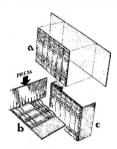

JOAN COOMBS
BANNING, CA

Workshop Wisdom
Courtesy of *Nutshell News—8/94*

CUSTOM CREATIONS BY RIKA

Animal Figures (Dogs)

Price: $39.95-$49.95
Collectible animal figures sculpted by IGMA Artisan Leslie Frick. Custom painting available. (Golden Retriever, Collie, Chihuahua, Boston Terrier, Springer, Cocker, Bernese, Fox Terrier, and more).

CUSTOM CREATIONS BY RIKA

Animal Figures (Cats)

Price: $39.95
Collectible animal figures sculpted by IGMA Artisan Leslie Frick. Beautifully hand painted by the artist. Kittens available and are suitable for 1/2" scale.

CUSTOM CREATIONS BY RIKA

Woodland Animals

Price: $12.95-$49.95
Woodland animals sculpted by IGMA Artisan Leslie Frick. (Also available: opossum, mother fox with three kits, snake and skunk).

D-LEPRECHAUN

Horses

Dimensions: 1" & 1/2" Scale
Realistically painted with hair manes and tails. For information/order form—send LSASE. Retailer and wholesaler. Also foods and hats at shows and CIMTA. Quality handwork by an IGMA Artisan.

DOLL HOUSE SHOPPE

Dollhouse Dogs
Dimensions: 1"=1'
Dollhouse dogs—34 large breed pets. See your local dealer. Wholesale only.

MAISON DES MAISONS

"Little Creatures"
Price: $100 to $290, plus shipping.
Beautiful hand sculpted animals limited editions exclusive to Maison des Maisons by Dave Ritch.

THE DUCK POND

Duck Decoys and Animals
Price:$6 and up
Dimensions:1" scale
Painted and unpainted miniature woodcarvings of duck decoys and wildlife. Assembled unfinished $3 and up. Completely finished $6 and up. Retail and wholesale. For more information send LSASE.

MARY HOOT MINIATURES
Peaceable Kingdom
Original Hand-Painted Miniature Animals

Price: $20 and up
Dimensions: 1", 1/2" and larger scales
A world of animals—dogs, cats, barnyard, wild animals, endangered animals, and more. All original, all handcrafted. These are the finest quality you can find. Skillfully hand painted on cloth forms in amazing detail. Each one a tiny work of art and highly collectible. Limited quantities. Send $1 plus SASE for color brochure.

THE WORLD'S SMALLEST CO.

Dimensions: Apprx. 1-1/4" tall. Scale 1"=1'
Every wise little Owl collects our wild and pet birds. Our birds are cast in pewter and meticulously hand painted. Great birdhouses too!

Bathroom Accessories

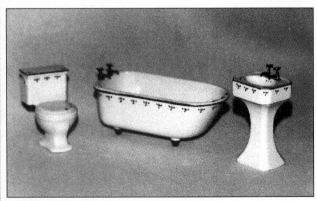

DOLLHOUSE MINIATURES
Hand Painted Ceramic Bath Set

Price: $24/set
Three-piece hand painted bathroom set with brass faucets. Available in white with pink, rose, yellow, light blue or dark blue flowers. Also available in solid colors. Ceramic. American-made.

HOUSEWORKS, LTD.

Bath Set

Stock No.: 8500
Price: $35
Includes bathtub, sink and toilet. Each piece is genuine porcelain. Bathtub and sink feature gold-plated brass fixtures and drains. Toilet features gold-plated brass handle and wooden seat.

Ceiling Fan

WORKSHOP WISDOM

Need a ceiling fan? Cut and glue two Popsicle sticks in the shape of a cross (a) then sand, stain and varnish them. Glue large beads or jewelry findings above and below the center as shown, then decorate with more jewelry findings if desired. Glue a piece of brass tube (b) to the center, then attach it to the ceiling of your mini room.

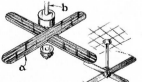

ALICE SCHULER
FLORAL PARK, NY

Workshop Wisdom Courtesy of *Nutshell News—10/94*

THE ANGEL OF KITS

Judy Berman opened the door to our dreams

By Jeanne Delgado

PHOTOGRAPHY BY CHRIS BECKER, DARLA EVANS, JIM FORBES

"LET ME LIVE IN MY HOUSE BY THE SIDE OF THE ROAD — AND BE A FRIEND TO MAN..."

They're easy, authentic, and affordable. They are also charming, versatile, and enormously popular. They are Chrysnbon kits, and for a great many of us they were the door into miniatures. But did you know that Judy Berman, the founder of Chrysnbon, entered our hobby through a real door?

Judy, who worked in a piano/organ store, was seeking the perfect place to display the 1½" scale theater organ her son John had made for her Christmas present. "There was this old five-panel door in my house," she said, "standing there all day doing absolutely nothing but opening and closing. I thought it was high time to put it to more practical use — such as a display case for

my sentimental possessions." John replaced four of the door panels with glass and built a lighted display box behind them. Judy's treasures were duly installed. The tiny organ looked lovely there, but it needed some accessories, Judy decided. Maybe a rug and a lamp — and some wallpaper? It wasn't long before the baby shoes and Judy's other memorabilia were moved out and the door display became a four room dollhouse.

John taught Judy how to use some of his tools — and more important — decided a scale of one inch to the foot would be easier for her to master. Miniatures in 1967 were hard to find and expensive. Judy began making "lampshades from toothpaste caps and candlesticks from toothpicks," in the lulls between customers at the organ store. When Marshall Field & Co. in Chicago asked to sell them, Judy supplied 1500 accessories, all handmade! The Miles Kimball catalog also became an early customer after seeing

what Judy did with the six dozen clock face buttons she'd ordered from them.

By the early 1970s, Judy had become a cottage industry. She recruited two friends to help and managed to involve her whole family in her new company. (Chrysnbon is named for Judy's daughter-in-law Chrystine and daughter Bonnie.)

"From the beginning enough people believed in me to give me the courage to go on," Judy often said. She began with an extensive line of accessories but, "I always knew I wanted to develop a line of affordable furniture, because of the difficulty I had finding things I liked for my dollhouse."

For Chrysnbon furniture Judy made two choices. She chose to replicate the nostalgic Victorian styles in her grandmother's home because she wanted to recapture a part of the past for her children and grandchildren. And she decided to make her furniture in plastic.

"At shows I kept hearing, 'My husband would kill me if I paid that much for a teacart!' There was no way the average family could afford to indulge in this hobby that had brought me so much happiness," she realized. "It was a desperate feeling that somebody had to do something to keep perpetuating the hobby. I thought if we made the furniture in plastic — and put in the detail — and scaled it so it looked real instead of clunky, we could develop a nice line of plastic furniture. But," she admitted, "I had no idea of the cost involved! I thought it was a very inexpensive process. I was very fortunate to have a friend with great faith in me who financed the cost of tooling."

Fortunately too, Judy had son John, an engineer and model maker who could translate her ideas onto paper and shepherd them through the

modeling, engraving, and molding stages.

The reasoning behind the decision to make the furniture in kit form was two-fold. First, kits reduced the shipping costs and the risk of damage, which enables lower pricing, and second, they're fun. Assembling a kit gives a real sense of accomplishment (and it's virtually impossible to put a Chrysnbon kit together any way but the way it's supposed to go). Their appeal is universal and as Judy said, "If you are going to do what's supposed to be fun, don't make a chore of it!" The perfect scale and detailing of her kits won immediate acceptance with hobbyists. Many believe they are largely responsible for the popularity of roomboxes and vignettes as seasonal decorations and for personalized gifts.

Each of Judy's designs was meticulously researched, faithfully copied from actual full size pieces. It wasn't long, however, before hobbyists — and Judy — discovered the fun of "kitbashing" them. Judy's book *Chrysnbon Cut-Ups, Vol. I,* published in 1982, offered 16 new furniture pieces made by combining parts from different kits. Many of Judy's own roomboxes shown here contain these imaginative crafted pieces as well as the standard Chrysnbon kit furniture and accessories. Unfortunately, Judy's declining health prevented a second edition of the book from being published as she had planned. That long-awaited *Volume II,* is now scheduled for publication in late 1995 by Dee's Delights, a major miniatures distributor. Dee's Delights purchased Chrysnbon in 1988 and has continued the Chrysnbon tradition of excellence.

Judy received many honors in her lifetime including the Mel Prescott Award, the Academy of Honor of the National Association of Miniature Enthusiasts; a stairway named for her at the new NAME headquarters, and shortly before her death in November, 1994, the International Guild of Miniature Artisans' Crystal Award for Lifetime Achievement.

"I'm a realist," Judy once said, "but in six square inches I can build a dream." More than any other single person, Judy Berman opened the door to the world of miniatures to everyone. Judy built her dream, and she made it possible for all of us to build our own.

> *"I'm a realist, but in six square inches I can build a dream."*

The window in the "Blue and White sitting Area" is almost identical to one in Judy's own home where she also displayed favorite glass pieces. She copied many of them for Chrysnbon. All roomboxes by Judy Berman.

The Eagle Living Room was the favorite of Judy's younger son, Rob. It contains many of Judy's favorite things, especially eagles! The most striking accent in the room is the portrait of Judy by miniature painter Marjorie Adams. The pencil sketches of eagles on the side wall are by Judy's son John and are miniatures of full size sketches in her home. On the opposite wall, a hutch (the Chrysnbon kitchen cabinet minus the doors) holds part of Judy's miniature eagle collection. Above the fireplace is one of Judy's favorite sayings, "Let Me Live in My House by the Side of the Road and Be a Friend to Man." Another replica, this motto also hung in Judy's own studio workshop.

The room itself is enchanting but even more so is the patio outside the window. Patio furniture was devised from Chrysnbon sewing machine parts by Shirley Dressler, a sister of Linda McMahon, one of Judy's workers. Notice the side table — also a kitbash using the sewing machine legs. Many items in the room, including the eagle mirror and the tall clock are Chrysnbon accessories. Notice too, the clever dining area using just half a table top against the wall.

Judy included clever accessories (that didn't need to be painted) in most of her kits. The cook stove in the "Ole Oak Kitchen," for instance, comes with the trivets and the match safe on the wall, the cast iron skillets, sad irons, and a grate shaker on the stove, and a decal-decorated stove board under it. The hat rack hanging in the hall and the spice cabinet came in other kits. The sink kit includes the pump, a wash basin, water pail with a dipper, soap dish and soap, the towel bar, and on the wall, the shelf with coffee mill and a comb dish with comb. And yes, we know the horseshoe is upside down!

This little room, shown in one of the "Treasure View" boxes she designed, was the prototype of Judy's kitcrafting — making new furniture pieces from existing Chrysnbon kits. The Eastlake style settee and chair were made from components of the hall stand. The fireplace used parts from the organ, the table is built from curved china cabinet elements, and the shelf is from the legs of the Victorian table!

"Blue Gingham Country" is a favorite of John Berman's "for all the memories of the effort involved in creating many of the items in it!" John says it was probably the most technically challenging of all the rooms. Don't you love the attached pantry idea?

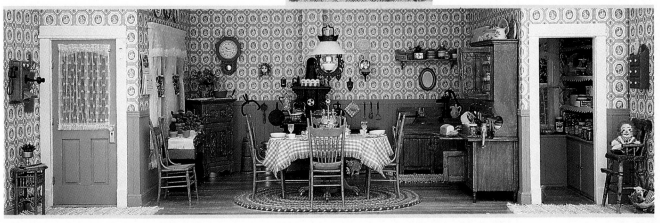

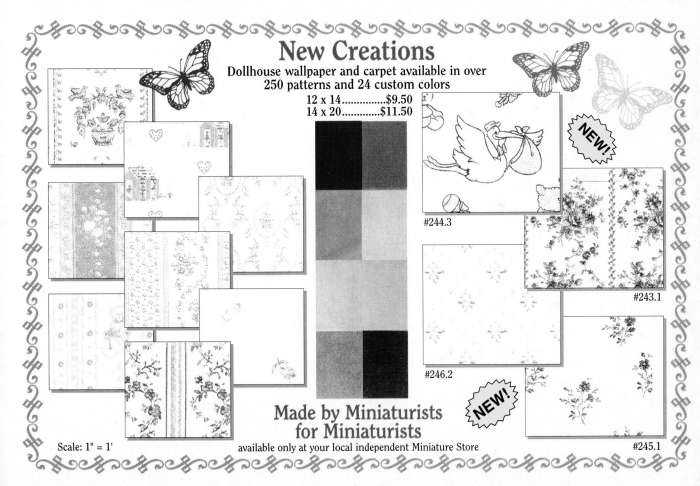

New Creations

Dollhouse wallpaper and carpet available in over 250 patterns and 24 custom colors

12 x 14..............$9.50
14 x 20............$11.50

NEW!

#244.3

#243.1

#246.2

#245.1

NEW!

Made by Miniaturists for Miniaturists

Scale: 1" = 1'

available only at your local independent Miniature Store

CUSTOMIZING A CHRYSNBON KIT
Make Yours Country

By Christine Paul
PHOTOS BY THE AUTHOR

Materials

✔ **Chrysnbon Kitchen Hutch #F-280**
✔ **Liquitex tube acrylics - red oxide, prussian blue**
✔ **Liquitex concentrated colors (2 oz. bottle) - French gray/blue**
✔ **Small, flat, smooth bristle paint brush**
✔ **Detail brush**
✔ **Palette (I recycle microwave frozen dinner trays)**
✔ **Paper towels**
✔ **Tweezers**
✔ **Water container**
✔ **Spray sealer**
✔ **Plastic adhesive**

I started my love affair with miniatures when I was just out of high school. While going to college I worked two part-time jobs to cover expenses, which unfortunately didn't include purchases for my dollhouse. The owner of the miniatures shop that I frequented introduced me to Chrysnbon kits and mentioned that they were not only affordable, but easily painted to fit into any decorating scheme. That was all I needed to hear! Those first kits, a kitchen table and chairs, a hutch and a bathroom set were the starting points of my miniatures collection.

All right. You've got your kit and now you stare at it trying to decide how to paint it. This invariably happens to everyone at one point or another so don't panic. To get inspiration, I keep a two-drawer file cabinet filled with nothing but clippings from decorating magazines, newspaper articles, etc. This collection did not happen overnight, but it is never too late for you to start your own. I divide my subject matter into categories: Houses, Rooms, Furniture, Sculpture, etc. (This is also a good way to avoid clutter. Cut out only the parts you want to save and throw the rest of the magazine into the recycling pile.) When I want to start a new project, out comes the appropriate file and off I go. Whenever I see a good all around style book on decorating I'll pick that up to add to my reference library.

I chose the color scheme of the hutch by flipping through my copy of Country Living's *Country Decorating* by Bo Niles, published by Hearst Books. In one of the rooms pictured there was an open shelf cupboard filled with white dishes that just jumped out at me. The rustic look of the red bottom layer of paint peeking out from under the layer of slate blue looked like just the ticket. Of course this type of layering can be done with any colors, it's only a question of what you like, and how old you want your piece to look.

Before starting the painting process, read through your assembly instructions. Separate the main parts of the hutch from the sprue trees, but leave the small bits such as the handles and knobs attached so they don't get lost. (They are also easier to paint if left attached.) Note areas where glue is to be applied to avoid scraping paint off later.

Right now peeling, faded paint is very "in," and with just a couple simple steps you will have an old country classic in 1" scale. I chose colors that can be used without too much mixing. The back of the hutch will not show, so it can be used as a paint test area. You will want to practice your brush strokes to get just the right touch. Squeeze a dime-sized blob of red oxide onto your palette. Keep your water container close by. This first layer of paint is going to be more of a "wash" than a layer. Moisten your flat brush and dab into the paint picking up a bit, not a lot. Test your paint on a paper towel. You want it to be a bit wet, not thick and gloppy. Working on only one piece at a time, apply your paint, wait a bit, then dab off excess. You should still be able to see some of the color of the plastic through the haze of paint. If paint pulls away from the plastic, it is too wet. Apply again if necessary, then dab. When one piece is covered to your satisfaction move on to the next. When in doubt about what areas to paint, paint just the front. You can always touch up missed areas.

After all pieces are dry, the blue layer

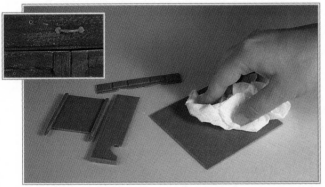

of paint can be applied. To achieve the slate color used, you will need to mix a bit of the prussian blue with the French gray/blue. I place small blobs of each next to each other and touch my brush into each as I work. This helps to create a mottled effect when the paint is applied. Again, use the back of the hutch to test your strokes. This layer should be applied with a dry brush. You want to cover the areas gradually, allowing the red to show through here and there. I tend to paint one stroke at a time, barely touching the surface and sweeping across in one swift motion. When you are satisfied with your technique, finish painting the rest of the pieces.

Once the fronts of the hutch pieces are painted, apply a single coat of clear spray sealer to protect the finish while you assemble the hutch. (Follow

manufacturer's instructions on using spray sealer.) Follow the assembly instructions for the bottom half of the hutch. Save the handles and knobs for later. Some areas may stand out that will need touching up, but don't worry too much. Once glue has dried then you can tackle those areas. At this point you should be able to see your country hutch really coming together.

Think about what you would like to do for the top portion in the way of painting. Are you going to be storing dishes on the shelves, canned goods, etc.? You may want to add a third layer of the French gray/blue on the inside shelf area to show off those items better. An acetate window set is included in this kit. Do you want to use those in the upper doors, or make a leaded glass set yourself? You want to ask those questions before you glue the upper half together as painting or inserting "glass" is much easier beforehand.

My dishes are white, so I chose to paint the inside to match the outside. After assembly of the top portion, check for needed touch-ups. After everything is put together, the knobs and handles can be added. I wanted them to stand out so I used the red oxide. The detail brush is good for this job, and you don't even need to squeeze any paint from the tube. Just touch the tip of the brush to the paint at the top of the tube and you have plenty. When dry, apply a quick spray of sealer. Using your fingernail, snap the knobs from their tree. I then pick up the knob with tweezers and apply

a tiny smidgen of adhesive and set it in place. The same goes for the handles. A bit of paint may chip off but it is easier to touch a spot of paint than to try to paint the whole knob or handle without getting paint where you don't want it.

For the final step in creating your masterpiece, place the top of the hutch on the bottom portion to see the full effect of your handiwork. You may want to use a bit of the French gray/blue to swipe a few highlights here and there on your hutch. Remember, less is more.

It's amazing what a little paint can do. For very little money, and a bit of your time you can create a miniature masterpiece that is uniquely yours. Don't forget to work on your reference library, and the next time you need just the right piece of furniture for that empty spot in your roombox or setting, check out the Chrysnbon furniture kits and get to work.

Other Good Resource Books

Painted Furniture
By Diane M. Weaver
1995 Sterling Publishing Co., Inc.

Paint Magic
(or anything by Jocasta Innes)

IT'S IN THE BAG!

Make this easy Rock-a-bye Baby roombox for a new arrival

By June Fuerstenhaefer

Paper gift bags make wonderful roomboxes. They come plastic coated, in many different sizes and designs. When fitted with matboard inside they can be turned into an economical gift or a scaled-down holiday decoration. Card shops and gift wrap departments are the best sources. Some bags have such delightful scenes on the front they can inspire the actual scene that you do inside.

A few simple ingredients can add up to a unique gift to welcome a new baby. The side wall even has a calendar with the baby's birth date circled. (In the case of a shower gift the calendar can be added after the blessed event.) This is a good project for someone who wants to experiment with wallpaper and moldings in a small quantity. Cutting and fitting is easy to correct without investing in a lot of materials. I hope you have just as much fun making and giving this gift bag as I did.

Contents of the Baby's Room

- ✓ Rocking Chair – Chrysnbon kit #2403WH Arrowback Rocker
- ✓ Bassinet – Wilton cake decoration
- ✓ Night Stand – from ready made chest, instructions given
- ✓ Picture Frame – painted molding
- ✓ Picture – Gift wrap or print
- ✓ Shelf with pegs – instructions given
- ✓ Calendar – mini size
- ✓ Toys & stuffed animals
- ✓ Baby care products – metal miniatures & reproductions

Materials & Tools

- ✓ Gift Bag approx. 7 1/2"W x 10"H x 3"D
- ✓ Matboard cut to fit 4 sides and top & bottom (approx. 20" sq.)
- ✓ Base – 2 layers of foamcore board, 3" x 8"
- ✓ Wallpaper, back and sides – 16" x 10"
- ✓ Acetate sheet for openings – approx. 12" x 12"

- ✓ Wood baseboard and crown molding, 14" of each
- ✓ Carpet – white adhesive back felt or white carpet
- ✓ Lace around front opening – 1/2" wide
- ✓ Gathered lace for bassinet – 1 1/2" wide
- ✓ 1/2" wide pleated lace
- ✓ Cotton or batiste fabric, approx – 8" sq.
- ✓ Satin Ribbon for handle, 3/16" – 3-4 yds
- ✓ White silk ribbon – 1/8" wide for bows
- ✓ White Bunka
- ✓ Braided trim 1/8" wide
- ✓ Heart shape sewing notion for pillow
- ✓ Ruler
- ✓ X-Acto knife with #11 blade
- ✓ Scissors
- ✓ Glues: Tacky, Quick Grab, YES, 527
- ✓ Paint: white, pink, pale green
- ✓ Brushes
- ✓ Tapes: 3M Magic Mending, Cellophane tape, Double stick tape

INSTRUCTIONS FOR MAKING THE BAG!

START HERE ▼

To cut matboard, use a new sharp blade in your X-Acto knife and a metal (not plastic) ruler or T-square. First, score the matboard with the knife, then cut deeper, and the third time cut all the way through. Cut foamcore in the same three-step manner. Replace your blade with a new sharp blade the minute it seems dull.

Liner: Remove bag handles, if possible, so they will be out of the way. Replace them later with satin ribbon for a softer look. Cut matboard front and back pieces by measuring the inside width of the bag and subtracting 1/16". For height, measure up from the bottom to just below handle; subtract 1/16" from measurement to allow for matboard top.

Measure side of the bag, subtract 1/16" from width and cut same height as front and back. Make second side the same way. Test-fit all four pieces inside the bag and adjust size if necessary. You will be moving matboard lining in and out several times, so while lining should fit snugly, you don't want it to strain or tear the paper bag. Be sure the liner fits easily before you cut out front opening from the bag. Do not cut the opening at this time.

Measure top opening of the bag and cut a lid this size from matboard. The lid sits on top of the other four matboard pieces. For lid, use a matboard color to complement the bag or plan to cover the lid in gift paper or flat lace later. Cut a window in the lid to let in more light, leaving 1/2" to 3/4" border on all four sides.

Use 3M Magic Mending tape to

Our bag has a teddy bear design on the "back" side. If your gift bag has a picture on one side only, be sure to cut the opening in the plain side.

hinge the two sides and back matboard pieces together. Lay all three pieces flat on table side by side, white side or back of matboard facing up, then tape. The tape will be covered with wallpaper. Note, tape is not on the back, but rather on the side facing you as you look into the bag. Insert the hinged liner in the bag to make sure it fits. Make any needed adjustments.

Wallpaper

Lay hinged sides and back matboard flat. Use an oversize piece of paper taking care to match the top edge of the paper to the matboard. Leave the excess at sides and bottom. Glue wallpaper with a waterless glue like YES glue or a spray adhesive. Spread a thin coat of glue with a credit card. Position the paper, smooth into place, cover with wax paper and weight with books. When dry, turn over and trim excess paper.

Front Opening

Fit a heavy piece of cardboard inside

the bag and support it with books or a box so you have something to cut against. Measure carefully allowing at least 2" all around to frame the opening. Use an X-Acto knife rather than a scissors to get a nice straight cut. After cutting the opening, reinforce bag corners on the inside with two layers of clear tape. Lace trim will be added around the opening edge as a finishing touch.

Slide the front matboard inside the bag. Trace the bag opening, remove, and cut opening in matboard. Cut an acetate sheet (available at art stores), sized to cover front window opening and opening in lid. When the bag is complete, use a waterless glue like 517 or Quick Grab to attach the acetate windows on the inside, being careful no glue shows on front or top. Slide front window in place.

Base

Make a base of at least two layers of foamcore to bring the scene up to a better viewing height. Be sure the base sits about 1/2" below the window opening. Base is cut 1/8" smaller on both dimensions to allow room for matboard liner to slide around it. Glue foamcore pieces together but not to the bag. Dry-fit foamcore base in bag to check fit. Remove and cover with white carpet or white felt.

Assembly

Dry-fit side and back assembly, front with opening cut and the carpeted base. Place the lid on top. Trim or sand any edges that may be too tight. Remove everything and place a small amount of double stick tape on the sides and back of bag near the top. Fold the wallpapered assembly sides inward and carefully slide into bag. Make contact with the tape and press in place. Next, position the front opening matboard in place but don't

glue or tape. Use double stick tape on the carpeted foamcore base and press in place. Make sure you can slide the front opening in and out.

Moldings

Measure for baseboard molding. Cut and fit left side first, then the back and finally the right side. Trim each piece of molding with the X-Acto knife as you go. Cut at a 45° angle and fit each piece before you go on to the next. Paint and allow to dry before gluing with Tacky glue. After gluing, brace with a scrap of foamcore to apply pressure until dry. Attach a painted ceiling molding in the same manner or you can substitute a wallpaper border. These finishing touches make the room seem complete and lived in.

Furniture Placement

Position rocker, chest, and bassinet at angles to each other. Check height of the shelf and picture. Use Blue Tak temporarily to help in this "arranging stage." Notice shelf toys are high and low and are placed in front of the picture at corners. Pencil mark the picture and shelf positions, remove all contents and lay the bag on its back in order to glue the picture and shelf in place. Use a square cut card to line up the picture frame with the sides and top of the bag. Attach with Quick Grab glue. Position the shelf and glue it. Allow to dry. All furniture and toys are glued in in the same manner.

Finally glue the ruffle to the front opening on the inside or outside, your choice. Be neat at the corners!

Tape-hinge the covered top panel at the back by sliding two small pieces of cellophane tape at top rear portion of back panel. Fold tape forward. Place lid on top and press tape to underside of lid. Lift lid and slip the acetate lined front panel in place.

Furnishings

I used three rows of lace on the bottom of a Wilton plastic cake

The foundation of our beautiful bassinet is this Wilton plastic cake decoration, shown here just as it comes from the package.

decoration and two rows to cover the hood. (White ribbon added at the sides with a white rose gives a white-on-white look which is very pleasing to look at and appropriate for either boy or girl.)

Using Tacky glue, start at the back of the bassinet with the bottom row of 1½" pre-gathered lace. Place glue on the top edge of lace only. Lace should just touch the floor. Add the next layer in the same way at a mid point. Glue the top layer just under the rim or edge of bassinet. Add a small braided cord or ribbon to finish off the outside edge. I covered the top edge with white Bunka cord, unraveled.

The hood is covered inside with ½" pleated lace. However any gathered lace will work. Cover the outside of the hood with two overlapping pieces of the same lace used on the bottom. Cut an oval piece of cardboard to fit about ½" down inside the bassinet. Pad this "mattress" with cotton and cover with a thin piece of white flannel. (My favorite source for flannel is the little shoe polish cloths that some hotels give.) Before gluing the flannel "blanket," add a sheet turndown made of a piece of cotton lace with decorative stitching on the edge. Make a small pillow from white batiste. I filled mine with fine kitty litter to allow for "plumping and shaping." Add white Bunka for trim just inside the edges and glue a tiny bow in the center. A pink rose bud is also a nice touch.

The rocker is one of my favorite Chrysnbon pieces. Follow the instructions in the kit and then paint it with white acrylic paint. You can add decorative painting simply by using the end of a toothpick to make "dot flowers". (See

Bassinet

Rocker

These items are shown larger than actual size in order to show detail

fig. 1) Repeat the colors on the rungs of the rocker. (You can also check the nail care department for flower decals in soft colors. They are the right size and easy to apply.)

Make the seat cushion from white batiste, lightly padded and add Bunka to the edges. The heart-shaped back cushion is a decorative piece found in a fabric store. Just add flat padding cut from a cosmetic wipe to the back and glue a bow on the front. Glue in place in the rocker. The bear is made from white pompons (see fig. 2) using a permanent marker to make the eyes and nose.

Shelf

Night Stand

The night stand is made from a purchased chest with a drawer in it. I added the legs and curved pieces of wood to the sides and back on the top surface. A brass drawer pull and decorative painting brought a simple piece of furniture up to something with "personality." This is an optional piece for this space because the shelf has pegs and looks great with baby clothes hanging from it (see fig 3) with perhaps a diaper bag added on the floor.

The picture should be large enough to give height to the room and be at least two-thirds the width of the shelf. The frame is made from frame molding that has a profile with two ridges, painted pink and pale green to repeat the shelf decoration. The molding has a ridge in back to receive the picture. Cut molding at 45° using a miter box and corresponding saw. Glue the picture to an index card using YES glue (waterless) before inserting in the frame. Mount to the wall with Tacky glue.

The shelf alone can be a nice project for a group. For this reason we have listed the tools and materials for it separately. The milled wood strips can be purchased in 2' lengths and divided among the group members. The shelf is an easy project because it uses stock decorative wood trims. It has a carved look but only involves straight cuts. A lace trim could be substituted for the scalloped front edge. (See diagrams.)

SUPPLIES: Tacky glue, X-Acto knife or miter box & saw, 3/32" drill, paint and brush, sandpaper.

WOOD: Basswood 7"L x 1/2"W x 3/32" thick; Scallop trim (type A) 6" long; Large scallop trim (type B) 3" long. Carved wood toothpicks (Pier 1 Imports) or dowels or metal mini hooks.

Cut shelf and backboard from 1/2" wide basswood. On backboard, measure in 5/8" from each side and just below center line (see Fig. 1) and drill two 3/32" holes. Center backboard to shelf (1/2" in from each side) and glue. Allow to dry against a right angle surface. Cut 1/2" off each carved end of toothpick (or use dowels or metal mini hooks). Sand to fit if needed and glue into holes.

Cut two 7/16" pieces "A" trim and glue to sides of shelf. Cut 3 3/4" piece "A" trim and glue to front of shelf.

Cut 4 pieces from "B" trim as shown. Glue 2 of each back-to-back to create 3/32" thick shelf supports. Sand the corners where indicated. Glue the supports on each side of backboard and under the shelf.

Lightly sand any uneven edges and then apply two coats of paint or stain. Decorate if desired. Try a contrasting color on front edges of supports, peg tips and Type "A" trim. A second color looks nice painted just up from the first color on the "A" trim and on carved part of pegs.

Color copy a Birth Certificate to hang in the nursery or use as a gift tag.
(Just glue on index card and tuck in bag, or punch a hole in a corner and tie around handle with a ribbon.)

Fig. 1
**Easy flowers or heart designs for back of rocker or shelf
(Paint with a toothpick!)**

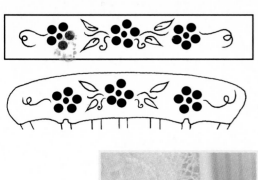

All patterns shown actual size

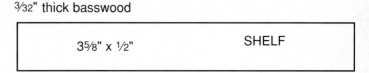

³/₃₂" thick basswood

3⁵/₈" x ½"	SHELF

³/₃₂" thick basswood

2⁵/₈" x ½"	BACKBOARD

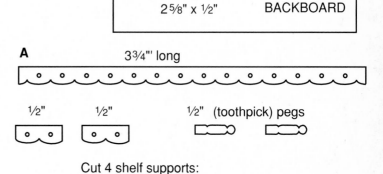

A   3¾"' long

½"   ½"   ½" (toothpick) pegs

Cut 4 shelf supports:
(will become 2 supports when glued totether)

cut   cut   cut   cut

B

Glue 2 together for each support

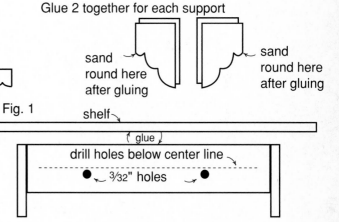

sand round here after gluing   sand round here after gluing

Fig. 2
**Actul size pattern for
making bear from pompons**

Fig. 3
**Alternate idea for shelf
(in place of using night stand)**

Fig. 1   shelf

glue

drill holes below center line

³/₃₂" holes

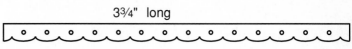

3¾" long

**Pattern ideas
for decorating**

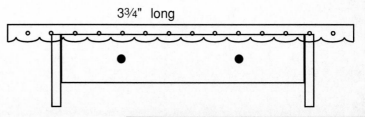

3¾" long

LENHAM POTTERY
Bathroom Furnishings

These slip-cast, white-glazed porcelain baths, wash basins and toilet kits are handmade. Also available are metal plumbing castings and gold or nickel-plated taps. Write for brochure. Made in England.

MODEL BUILDERS SUPPLY

Bathtub Kit With Enclosure

Price: $14.44
Dimensions: 5-1/2" x 2-5/8"
White bathtub with chrome showerhead, taps and faucets, tile surround supplied clear for reverse coloring to your choice. Easy instruction. Assembly about 15 minutes.

MODEL BUILDERS SUPPLY

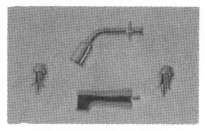

Shower & Bath Taps

Stock No.: FSH-12S; FSH-12G
Price: $7.30
Dimensions: 1:12 scale
Beautifully crafted, chrome or gold shower head, taps and spout.

MODEL BUILDERS SUPPLY

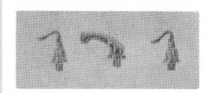

Sink Set, Fancy

Stock No.: FVS-12G
Price: $5.70
Beautifully crafted, fancy taps and spout in gold for pedestal or vanity bathroom sinks.

MODEL BUILDERS SUPPLY

Sink Set, Regular

Stock No.: FVS-12S
Price: $5.32
Beautifully crafted taps and spout in chrome for pedestal or vanity bathroom sinks.

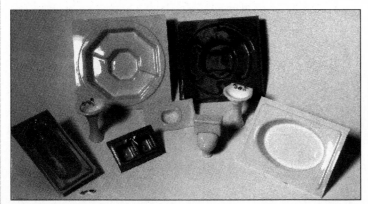

MODEL BUILDERS SUPPLY
Bathroom Items

Octagonal hot tub, $7.56; Round hot tub, $6.80; Oval tub, $4.52; Regular tub, $3.76; Pedestal sink, $4.75; Vanity sink, $2.24; Toilet, $4.75. Available in white and clear, (to be painted from reverse); hot tub also in red and black. Regular chrome or gold tub taps and showerhead, $7.30 per set. Regular chrome sink set, $5.32. Fancy gold sink set, $5.70. Ask your favorite dealer for MBS products.

TERI'S MINI WORKSHOP

Bath Accessories

Enhance your bathroom with matching accessories. Available in many colors and patterns to complement your decor. Guest towel, $4; towel, $5; wall shelf, $15; floor unit, $18; accessory set, $14.

Bedroom Accessories

KASEY'S

Quilt Kits

Price: $4.95 and up
Create beautiful Amish and traditional dollhouse quilts using foundation piecing. Quilt kits, instruction booklets and fabric packs are available.

LENHAM POTTERY

Blue Bedroom Toilet Set

This set includes water carrier, jug, basin, potty, jardiniere and hip bath. English-made. Porcelain, white glazed, ceramic transfers. Write for brochure.

SHOW SANTA WHAT YOU WANT FROM *THE MINIATURES CATALOG*

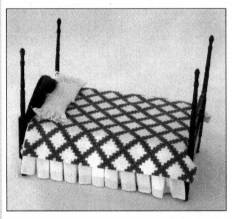

LITTLE COMFORTS
Double Irish Chain Quilt Kit

Price: $15 plus $3 shipping
Dimensions: approx. 7x7, 1" scale
Actual quilt patterns adapted for cross stitch. Kits include everything needed to complete a 1" scale quilt. More than 10 designs available. Beginners' instructions also included in kit. Wholesale prices available. Quilts fit on any 1" scale bed. Now you can have a custom bed at a fraction of the cost.

MINI QUILTS BY ALICE HANSON

Quilts and Linens

Pieced quilts, coordinating dust ruffles and pillows. Pieced and applique-type wall hangings.

THE MINI MERCHANT
Quilts

Price: $85 and up
Dimensions: 1" scale
Charm, log cabin, houses, baby blocks. Any color combination. Double or single bed size. Matching pillows available. Great for wallhangings, too.

Prices are approximate and subject to change

Books, Magazines & Calendars

HOUSEWORKS, LTD.

Miniature Books
Stock No.: 5013; 5012
Price:$1.95; $1.75
These handcrafted books are actually bound with loose pages. Packaged in assorted colors: red, blue, green, maroon. All have gold trim on spine. 5013 - Size: 7/8"H x 9/16"W x 3/16"thick, 12 pcs./pkg. 5012 - Size: 3/4"H x 1/2"W x 1/8"thick, 12 pcs./pkg.

HOUSEWORKS, LTD.
Bookcases
Stock No.:5011; 5010; 5029; 5009
Price:$17.95; $8.50; $10.95; $18.50
5011- Three-Unit Bookcase - with full shelves.
Size: 9-5/16"W x 7-3/8"H x 1-5/16"D.
5010 - One-Unit Bookcase - with non-functional cabinet.
Size: 3-3/8"W x 7-3/8"H x 1-3/8"D.
5029 -Three-Shelf Corner Cabinet - with fluted and paneled front.
Size: 3-1/2"W x 7-1/4"H x 1-1/2"D.
5009 - Three-Unit Bookcase - with non-functional cabinets.
Size: 9-5/16"W x 7-3/8"H x 1-3/8"D.

MINIATURE CORNER

Library Book Kits
Price: $18
Leather-look library book kits. Each kit makes more than 50 realistic books. English, European and reference libraries available. Easy directions. Use only glue and scissors.

Ceramic & Porcelain

BUTT HINGE POTTERY
Stoneware
Wheel-thrown stoneware miniatures capturing the spirit of traditional New England pottery for use in many dollhouse settings from the kitchen and bedroom to the garden or general store. Wholesale only. Custom orders available. See your local dealer for further information.

BY BARB

Ceramic Dishes
Ceramic dishes and accessory sets in an assortment of colors and designs. Aprons, place mats, napkins, flatware and glassware to match. Can be made to order. Available in 1" and 1/2" scale. Made in the USA.

DOLLHOUSE MINIATURES

Ceramic Kitchenware
Price: $1-$12
Dinnerware, pots, pans, canister sets, bowls. Each piece is carefully poured, hand painted and fired with a floral design. Available in white with pin, rose, yellow, light blue or orange flowers. American-made.

DONNA'S MINI EMPORIUM
Ceramic and Porcelain

Our exclusive 38-piece ceramic dinnerware set can beautify any table. Other handmade items include flower basket, kitchen block, various vases, and more. American-made.

Quimper Fish Platter

Dimensions: 1" scale
Incomparable china in miniature in the historic patterns of Quimper, Pink Lustre, Thistleware, Dedham Pottery, Chinese Export, Rose Medallion and others. Please send SASE for price list.

KATE'S CATS

Price: $30
Dimensions: 1" scale
Assorted porcelain items with a cat motif in 1/12 scale. Teapot, cream and sugar, cat boxes, etc. Catalog $2.

"KRAFTS" BY BETTY JEAN

Ceramic Crockery

Stock No.: 1
Price: $3 - $5 plus shipping
A large assortment of styles and sizes with gray "salt-glaze" finish. Decorated with hand painted blue designs. Assorted blue and white spongeware also.

RON BENSON MINIATURES

Ceramics

Porcelain 17th, 18th, and 19th century reproductions, period sculptures, bowls and candlesticks. Bennington pitcher c. 1850. Staffordshire items. American-made.

RON BENSON MINIATURES

MINIATURE CORNER
Reuiter Porcelain

Price: $6 up
Dimensions: 1:12
Fine German porcelain in Victorian rose pattern. Available in many patterns and styles. Full coffee, tea and dinner sets, gift boxed. Numerous accessories at affordable prices.
See your local dealer.

PRECISION PRODUCTS

Porcelain Powder

Also mold making rubbers, casting materials, dyes and fillers, etc. $PINcaster and accessories. Made in USA.

RON BENSON MINIATURES

Wonderful Sevres Urns, c. 1790

Price: $65 / pair
Dimensions: Just over 1-1/4" tall
Produced shortly after the revolution in the classic style. They retain the grace of the neoclassical era but foreshadow the Empire style of Napoleon. Trimmed in pure gold. Available in cobalt blue or black.

Ceramics

Dimensions: 1" = 1'; 1-1/4" tall
Sculptures, cachepots, umbrella stands, French urns, angels, cottages, castles and swan vase American-made. Porcelain.

Prices are approximate and subject to change

RON BENSON MINIATURES

Ceramics
Sculptures, candlesticks, dogs, cats, animals, Staffordshire and Worchester figurines. 18th and 19th century. American-made.

RON BENSON MINIATURES

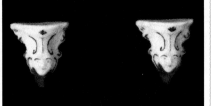

Staffordshire Brackets
Price: $55 / pair
Dimensions: 3/4"H—shelf just under 1/2"D
Unusual baroque male head with chin whiskers. Multi-colored details—very rare, c.1740.

ROYAL MINIATURES

High-Quality Porcelain
Price: $3 - $2.60
Dimensions: 1" scale
Shown is just a sampling of the best-quality collectible pieces. Wholesale only. Imported.

ROYAL MINIATURES

Quality Porcelain Accessories
Price: $2 - $8
Shown is a small sampling of our large line of bone china and porcelain miniatures. Wholesale only. Quantity discounts for manufacturers and distributors available.

Country

FOX HOLLOW MINIATURES

Muddy Old Boots
Price: $25
Dimensions: 1-3/4"
The famous Muddy Old Boots from Merrie Old England by the talented Dorothy Kitching. A "must" for every back door!

ROYAL MINIATURES

Handcrafted Baskets
Price: $2 - $3
Shown is a small sampling from our large line of baskets. All are quality-crafted and inexpensively priced. Quantity discounts available. Imported.

CLASSICS BY HANDLEY

Fireplace Tools
Stock No.: CLA00449
Price: $6.95
Tools are painted with a gold-tint color. Set has stand, brush, shovel and poker.

Fireplaces

Food

BY BARB

Judaic Foods

We specialize in ethnic Judaic foods: bagels and lox, matzoh, chicken soup, Seder plates, gefilte fish, hamantashen and more. Available in 1" and 1/2" scale. Handcrafted in the USA by Barb.

CATHY'S HANDCRAFTED MINIATURE ACCESSORIES
Assorted Foods

Crates, baskets and trays of handcrafted apples, bananas, grapes, oranges, carrots, eggplants, gourds, mushrooms, potatoes and pumpkins. Also pizza, candies, cookies, cakes and popcorn.

DONNA SMOLIK'S DESIGNS

Candy, Cookie & Food Designs

Price: $1.75 - $4.25 each
Dimensions: 1", 1/2", 1/4" scales
Candies, fruits, vegetables, meats—slice your own with a single-edged razor blade. Can be used in 1", 1/2" or 1/4" scales.

FOX HOLLOW MINIATURES

Pumpkin Soup Board

Price: $25
All the ingredients for hearty harvest soup—diced pumpkin and potatoes, sliced onions, carrots, squash, celery, mushrooms—arranged around a scallop-edged pumpkin shell.

FOX HOLLOW MINIATURES

Gingerbread House Board

Price: $25
A gingerbread house under construction: a bowl of icing with an egg beater, measuring spoons, spatula, recipe and lots of Christmas candies sprinkled about.

VISIT A MINIATURES SHOP WHILE TRAVELING

FRAMBOISIER, INC.
Japanese Noodle

Dimensions: 1/12 scale
Handcrafted Japanese foods 1" scale. Popular lunch menu in Japan. Noodle with Tempura, $15; Noodle with Sushi, $15. All products made in Japan. The utmost attention paid to detail and quality. Catalogs and price lists available at $5, Visa or Amex.

Prices are approximate and subject to change

FRAMBOISIER, INC.
Sushi

Dimensions: 1/12 scale
Handcrafted Japanese foods 1" scale. Sushi from $14. Lunch box from $13. All products made in Japan. The utmost attention paid to detail and quality. Catalog available at $5, Visa or Amex.

GRAMARYE KEEP

Scale Food, Kitchen and Fireplace Accessories

Price: $.50 to $35
American-made. Custom banquets a specialty.
Catalogs: Period $5, Modern $5.

FRAMBOISIER, INC.
Sukiyaki

Dimensions: 1/12 scale
Handcrafted Japanese foods 1" scale. Japanese traditional foods. Sukiyaki, $28; Kiseki, $40; Oden, $19. All products made in Japan. The utmost attention paid to detail and quality. Catalogs and price lists available at $5, Visa or Amex.

HANKY PANKY CRAFTS

Cakes and Flowers

Make flowers, plants and trees with Pretty Petal Punches using tape, preserved leaves, colored or painted paper. Punches and mini cake catalog, $1.

HUDSON RIVER DOLL HOUSES

Cake Tin

Dimensions: 1" diam., 1/4" high; 1"=1' scale
Cheese, cookie or cake tins with lots of different holiday and brand name labels. Wholesale only. See your local dealer.

LITTLEFOOT MINIATURES

Breakfast

Price: $4.50 - $8 ppd.
Dimensions: 1" scale
Grapefruit halves, boiled eggs, bacon, eggs and toast, waffles, pancakes with syrup, bacon and eggs in skillet or fry pan. Pitchers of milk, OJ and syrup.

LITTLEFOOT MINIATURES

Drinks

Price: Pitcher, $4 - $6; Glass, $1.50 ppd.
Dimensions: 1" and 1/2" scale
Many kinds available. OJ, milk, chocolate milk, beer, grape, red drink, ice tea, water, pop, orange drink, lemonade and many more. Punch and alcoholic drinks also available.

LITTLEFOOT MINIATURES

Salads

Price: $10 - $20 ppd.
Dimensions: 1" and 1/2" scale
Handcrafted in Canada by David Slater. Tossed and Caesar salads available in a variety of wooden, plastic and glass bowls.

LITTLEFOOT MINIATURES

Sliceable Candy Sticks

Price: $2 ppd.
Dimensions: 1" and 1/2"
2" long sticks to slice your own candy for dishes, gingerbread houses or projects. Assortment of five 1" sticks for $5.

LITTLEFOOT MINIATURES

Sliceable Fruit and Vegetable Sticks

Price: $4 ppd.
Dimensions: 1" and 1/2" scale
2" long sticks to slice your own kiwi, onion, tomato, cucumbers, strawberry, citrus fruit, pineapple, etc. with single edged razor. Assortment of slices, $10.

LITTLEFOOT MINIATURES

Pizza

Price: $6 ppd.
Dimensions: 1-1/4" diameter
Handmade in Canada by Jen McCarty. Specify toppings like pepperoni, onion, pineapple, ham, bacon, olives, tomato, peppers and mushrooms.

LITTLEFOOT MINIATURES

Baked Goods

Price: $8 - $15 ppd.
A variety of unique items available, including two-tiered trays of cookies, etc. and glass plates of candies and cookies. Fruit flan on cake plate. Our specialty is a mouse in a box of doughnuts.

"PANNIKINS" BY M.E

Foods and Beverages

Price: $.25 to $25
Handcrafted foods and beverages in both 1" and 1/2" scale. Fruits and vegetables, seasonal, international, regional, ethnic and period favorites, plus all supplies and "empties" for the do-it-yourselfer. Price list - $2.50.

WORKSHOP WISDOM

Ice Cream Cones

A 1/4" (6mm) diameter dowel sharpened in a pencil sharpener, then cut off as shown, can be painted with flat acrylics to resemble an ice cream cone. Add a blob of latex caulking to the top with, perhaps, a few pieces of glitter to give that cold look, and you have a sparkling, giant-size ice cream cone – in miniature of course.

SHIELA BENSON
GALLIPOLIS FERRY, WV

Workshop Wisdom
Courtesy of *Nutshell News*—9/94

PRECIOUS LITTLE THINGS
Food

Outfit your home, roadside stand or store with our exceptional, handcrafted foods in 1", 1/2" and 1/4" scales. Our oh-so-real fruits and vegetables are available loose or in containers, as well as in table, door and mantel decorations. We also offer sweet shop and bakery products.

R & N MINIATURES
Party Fare

Price: $4.50 - $24.95
Entertain with elegance with these scrumptious buffet dishes.
N161A - Dinner Rolls, $4.50 each;
N700 - Finger Sandwiches, $15.95;
N707C - Ceasar Salad or
N708 - Garden Salad, $10.95 each;
N706 - Deli Meat & Cheese Tray, $19.95;
N200 - Vegetable Tray w/Dip, $22.95;
N709 - Petit Fours & Chocolates, $24.95.
APLI price list, $2.

R & N MINIATURES
Platters and Plates

Price: $12.95 - $14.95
For Sunday dinner or any special occasion, serve these savory platters and plates:
N04 - Turkey Platter, $14.95;
N804 - Turkey Plate, $12.95;
N802 - Roast Beef Platter, $13.95;
N803 - Roast Beef Plate, $12.95;
N06 - Ham Platter, $12.95;
N805 - Ham Plate, $12.95;
N07 - Country Ham Platter, $12.95;
N806 - Country Ham Plate, $12.95.
APLI price list, $2.

R & N MINIATURES
Produce

Price: $1.65 - $23.95
Fresh farm produce in natural or aged containers, packages of loose fruits and vegetables. Our Virginia products include bagged country ham, slab bacon peanuts, potatoes, apples, peaches, sweet potatoes, cream cans, pumpkins, Virginia crocks and churns from Vernon Pottery. Price list, $2.

ROYAL MINIATURES

Food

Price: $1.60 - $6.90
Dimensions: 1" scale
Shown are only a few of our many tasty miniatures. Wholesale only. Imported.

THE KITCHEN CAPTIVE

Various Foods

Dimensions: 1" and 1/2" scale
Ranges from simple to elegant presentation of baked goods, main course items, fancy desserts and food and beverage trays. Retail only. Fimo, Sculpey, resin. LSASE for price sheet.

WENZEL MINIATURES

Assorted Foods

Price: $10 (one pumpkin per vine);
$18 (two per vine); $23 (three per vine)
We offer a variety of fruits, vegetables and food in preparation. Shown are handcrafted pumpkins on the vine. Great for your garden or fall decorating.

WENZEL MINIATURES

Assorted Foods

Price: $5, plus shipping
We offer quality food and settings. Shown are herbed oils and vinegars.

Garden & Landscaping

ALESSIO MINIATURES
Picket Fence and Gate

Stock No.: 310 (Picket Fence); 311 (Gate)
Price: $3.30 (310); $1.60 (311)
Dimensions: Fence: 3-1/2"H x 8"L
Gate: 3-1/2"H x 2-13/16"W
Wood picket fence and gate. Meet your outside needs with affordable quality. American-made.

ALESSIO MINIATURES

Sandbox

Stock No.: 303; 304; 305; 306
Dimensions:n Approximately 4" x 4
A charming addition to your backyard.
303 - unpainted, $3.30.
304 - red with sand, $4.50.
305 - stained with sand, $4.50.
306 - replacement sand, $.60.

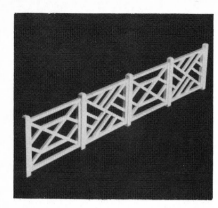

ARCHITECTURAL ETCETERA
18th Century Chinese Chippendale Fence

Price: $12
Two patterns form an intriguing design. Use in garden as a fence or as sides of a bridge. Also can be used as roof trim. Package has four fence sections (two each style) and five posts. Can be cut to fit. Each section: 2-1/8"H x 3/16"D x 3-1/16"W. Each post: 2-1/2"H x 1/4"D x 1/4"W. Total width 13-1/4".1" = 1' scale.

FOX HOLLOW MINIATURES

Muddy Old Boots

Price:$25
Dimensions:1-3/4"
The famous Muddy Old Boots from Merrie Old England by the talented Dorothy Kitching. A "must" for every back door!

GREENLEAF PRODUCTS
The Greenhouse

Stock No.:9069
Price:$25.90
Dimensions:10-1/2"H x 14"W x 15"D, 1" to 1' scale
Easy-to-read and follow instructions. Can be used as part of a miniature dollhouse project, or by planting seedlings it makes for an excellent classroom observational project. All pre-cut Luan plywood comes complete.

HOUSEWORKS, LTD.

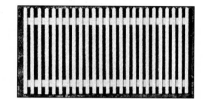

Picket Fence

Stock No. 7503
Price: $10.95
Wood picket fence sections constructed with evenly spaced 1/4" pickets. 4 pcs. per pkg. Size: 6"W x 3-1/8"H x 3/16"D; 1" scale.

HOUSEWORKS, LTD.

Picket Fence Gate

Stock No.: 7504
Price: $4.25
Gate consisting of evenly spaced 1/4" wooden pickets. 4 pcs. per pkg. Matches #7503 picket fence. Size: 2"W x 3-1/8"H x 3/16"D; 1" scale.

HOUSEWORKS, LTD.

Fence Posts

Stock No.:7015
Price:$2.95
Wooded square posts with pointed top for picket and crossbuck fences. 6 per pkg. Size: 1/2"sq. x 3-9/16"H; 1" scale.

HOUSEWORKS, LTD.

Crossbuck Fence

Stock No.:7501
Price:$9.95
Wooden three section design crossbuck fence. 6 pcs. per pkg. Size: 7-11/16"W x 2-13/16"H x 3/16"D; 1" scale.

HOUSEWORKS, LTD.

Crossbuck Fence Gate

Stock No.: 7502
Price: $1.95
One section wooden crossbuck design gate to match #7501 Crossbuck Fence. 2 pcs. per pkg. Size: 2-11/16"W x 2-19/32H x 3/16"D; 1" scale.

"KRAFTS" BY BETTY JEAN

Terra Cotta Pots

Stock No.: 2
Price: $.50 to $5 plus shipping
Large assortment of terra cotta flower pots, urns, cactus dishes, strawberry jars, bonsai pots and other items in several sizes.

MARLENE GILBERT
HOUSEPLANTS IN MINIATURE

Patio Pot of Flowers

Price: $23-$40 each
Color bowl of flowers for patios, each containing a variety of colors. Other patio plants available, including bird of paradise. Limited mail order. Footed Patio Pot: $28 each, approx. 1-5/8" across, 1-1/8" high.Sizes vary, 1" scale.

R & N MINIATURES
Garden Accessories

Price: $14.50 - $15.50
Merely a sample of our Garden Accessories and Kits. More to choose from. Order our GPLI price list, $2.
RNG36 - Scarecrow, $15.50,
RNG36K (kit), $12.50; RNG560 - Haystack, $14.50,
RNG560K (kit), $12;
RPP1 - Pile of Pumpkins, $14.50,
RPP1K (kit), $11.50; RNG47W - Wagon w/Watermelons, $15.50;
RNN47 - Wagon w/Pumpkins, $15.50.

R & N MINIATURES

"Flowers by the Inch"

Price: $4.50 per inch, plus $4.50 shipping
1-1/2" sections of handcrafted flowers sold by the inch @ $4.50 per inch. F1 - Iris; F2 - Red Tulips; F3 - Pink Tulips; F4 - Yellow Daffodills; F5 - White Daffodills; F6 - Purple Hyacinth; F7 - Pink Hyacinth; GPLI price list, $2.

ROYAL MINIATURES

Garden Accessories

Price: $1 - $3
Shown is a selection from our line of outdoor and garden accessories. All pieces authentically reproduced in 1" scale.

SIR THOMAS THUMB

The Finest Garden Tools

Dimensions:1" = 1' scale
Hedge clippers, leaf rakes, nursery forks, shovels, hoes, wheelbarrows, beehives with bees and lots more. Realism in wood and metal.
Catalog available.

THE LAWBRE COMPANY

Garden Vases and Urns

Stock No.: 0200 - 0206
Price: $6 - $16
These cast planters and vases are a terra cotta color (except for 0205 and 0206 which are black with verdigris finish). American-made.

THE LAWBRE COMPANY
Garden Accessories

Stock No.: 0300-0319
Price: $6 - $24
Each of these items is hand-finished and ready for adding to your landscape. Included are finely-detailed garden statues and ornaments. American-made.

THE LAWBRE COMPANY
"Iron and Brick" Gates and Fencing

Stock No.: 0450 - 0465
Price: $12 - $120
For the complete landscape. These components can be used in many ways and combinations. Available finished or in kit form. Resin and metal castings.

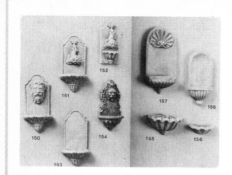

THE LAWBRE COMPANY
Wall Fountains, Niches and Bowls
Stock No.: 0150 - 0158
Price: $5 - $14
These cast fountains and bowls are finished in a terra cotta color (except 0154, which is finished in black and verdigris). American-made.

THE LAWBRE COMPANY

Free Standing Fountain
Stock No.: 0100, 0101, 0102
Price: $89; $99
Beautifully finished and complete with "water lily leaves" and "water," these are the finest in garden fountains. Non-working. American-made.

WORKSHOP WISDOM

Chrome Steel Racks

You might find one of these chromed steel racks in the corner of the kitchen with stainless steel cookware stacked or hung on it. Get a pack of molded plastic factory windows from the model railroad store, clip the tabs (gates) along one side of each window, then bend it upwards through 90 degrees. Corner notch two basswood strips, rub two or three coats of white glue into each stick and allow to dry before lightly sanding. The glue will nicely seal the grain before you paint the whole rack bright silver.

JANE FREEMAN
NEW YORK, NY

Workshop Wisdom
Courtesy of *Nutshell News*—8/94

Crystal & Glassware

LINDEN SWISS MINIATURES

Finished Gift Set
Stock No.: 202
Dimensions: 1" scale
One wine bottle with two wine glasses. Displayed with gift box. American-made. See your local dealer.

LINDEN SWISS MINIATURES

Fluted Champagne Glasses
Dimensions: 1" scale
Set of four 1" scale elegant champagne glasses. Instructions included for making glasses look crystal clear. See your local dealer. American-made. Acrylic.

ROYAL MINIATURES

Hand-Blown Crystal
Price: $1.50 - $9
Hundreds of styles available—many are Royal exclusives! Shown is a small sampling of our large line of glassware. Customer designs welcome. Imported.

ROYAL MINIATURES

Glass Crystal
Price: $6.20 - $12.90
Dimensions: 1" scale
For high-quality, collectible, handblown glassware, we have the best pieces at inexpensive prices.

Prices are approximate and subject to change

Holiday & Seasonal

BY BARB

Jewish Holidays

We have been offering a complete line of Judaic miniature accessories ever since 1978. Hanukkah, Passover, Bat and Bar Mitzvah, Sabbath, Purim, etc. We also offer a complete line of ethnic Judaic food. Handcrafted in the USA by Barb.

CATHY'S HANDCRAFTED MINIATURE ACCESSORIES
For the Holidays

Handcrafted Easter baskets, trick-or-treat bags, Indian corn, pumpkins, wreaths, stocking sets, shopping bags, packages and much more.

CIR-KIT CONCEPTS, INC.

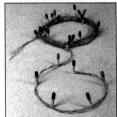

24-Bulb Colored Xmas String

Stock No.: CK1020-5
Price: $31.95
The first of its kind. String wound around tree in concentric circles from top to bottom. 1" between bulbs. 24" lighted length. 12" green lead wire. Also available with clear bulbs (CK1020-6 $29.95).

DONNA SMOLIK'S DESIGNS

Candy, Cookie & Food Designs

Price: $1.75 - $4.25
Dimensions: 1", 1/2", 1/4" scales
Candies, fruits, vegetables, meats—slice your own with a single-edged razor blade. Can be used in 1", 1/2" or 1/4" scales.

DOLL HOUSE SHOPPE

Decorated Ultimate Tree

Stock No.: 4598 (kit) 4597 (finished)
Available finished or in kit form. Kit includes ribbon, roses and baby's breath. Available in several color combinations. Wholesale only.

ELECT-A-LITE

Electrified Christmas Wreath Kit

Stock No.: 610
Price: $27.50
This wreath is prewired with 10 light-emitting diodes (LEDs) in molded plastic. Ready to decorate with greenery, ribbon and beads, which are included. Our patented plug is also included to easily install on any double tape run. Made in the USA.

ELECT-A-LITE

Multi-Purpose, 21-Light Christmas String

Stock No.: 620
Price: $37.90
String of mixed-color, light-emitting diodes (LEDs). Perfect for decorating miniature trees. American-designed and made, these lights can be used with any 12V system for thousands of hours without the inconvenience of bulbs burning out.

FOX HOLLOW MINIATURES

Christmas Collector's Cupboard

Price: $125
Dimensions: 8-1/2" x 3-1/2"
This corner cupboard is filled with everything a collector's heart desires, down to a tiny "snowbaby" and a readable copy of the antique Night Before Christmas.

FOX HOLLOW MINIATURES

Pumpkin Carving

Price: $22
The ultimate pumpkin carving scene: jack-o'-lantern, knife and spoon, candy apple, sugared doughnut, cookies, candy corn—it's all here, down to the last pumpkin seed.

FOX HOLLOW MINIATURES

Pumpkin Soup Board

Price: $25
All the ingredients for hearty harvest soup—diced pumpkin and potatoes, sliced onions, carrots, squash, celery, mushrooms—arranged around a scallop-edged pumpkin shell.

FOX HOLLOW MINIATURES

Gingerbread House Board

Price: $25
A gingerbread house under construction: a bowl of icing with an egg beater, measuring spoons, spatula, recipe and lots of Christmas candies sprinkled about.

J. HERMES

Miniature Gift Wraps

Price: $.35 each
Easy-folding, full-color gift wraps for all occasions. Christmas, Hanukkah, birthday, new baby, Easter, Valentine's Day, St. Patrick's Day and Halloween. More than 100 designs available.

"KRAFTS" BY BETTY JEAN

Holiday Items

Stock No.: 3
Price: $2.50 - $10 plus shipping
Holiday plates for Valentine's Day, Halloween, Fall and Christmas are available. Three lighted jack-o'-lanterns in 1" scale and two in 1/2" scale. Also much more.

LITTLEFOOT MINIATURES

Punch Sets

Stock No.: LFM126; LFM127
Price: $15 ppd.
Filled punch bowl, eight cups and ladle. Choose before, during or after party. Specify season, occasion or theme and/or color. Extra cups available. 1" scale.

LITTLEFOOT MINIATURES

Gingerbread Houses

Stock No.: LFM131
Price: $20 ppd.
Dimensions: 1" and 1/2" scale
Unique decorated gingerbread houses, $20; undecorated shells, $4; unassembled kits, $3; complete kit $10.

R & N MINIATURES

Gingerbread

Dimensions: 1" = 1' scale
Spicy gingerbread dough with rolling pin and cutter, gingerbread men on sheet and on plate, pkg. of three gingerbread men, gingerbread house. Price list, $2.

R & N MINIATURES

Valentine's Day

Dimensions: 1" = 1' scale
Valentine's Day accessories include red cookie dough with rolling pin and cutter, iced cookies on plate, heart candy box with chocolates and Valentine lollipops. Price list $2.

ROSALIE WHYEL MUSEUM OF DOLL ART

Holiday Miniatures

Festive accessories created by artist Carl Bronsdon to transform your miniature settings. Choose from gingerbread houses to a Halloween tree with cats and ghosts.

TREASURE WORKS

Worn Sandals

Stock No.: TS010
Price: $22 Sterling—$20 Bronze; ppd.
Dimensions: approx. 7/8" x 3/8"; 1"=1'
These charming sterling silver or bronze sandals have the look of leather. They appear to be "worn" with toe and heel imprints.

WENZEL MINIATURES

Gingerbread Houses

Price: $12 and $25 (Limited editions-$150 and up)
Dimensions: 1/4" or 1/2" scale and 1" scale
Handcrafted gingerbread houses. No two exactly alike. We also offer many varieties of quality food and settings.

Jewelry

OMNIARTS OF COLORADO
Crown Jewels of England

Souvenir of collector quality coronation sets—St. Edward's, Imperial State, Prince of Wales', Queen Victoria's, Queen Mother's and British Imperial Crown of India crowns, Spencer tiara, Charles II scepter, orb, ring and bracelets. George IV diadem, Honors of Scotland, ampulla and spoon, scepter with dove. Others available.

OMNIARTS OF COLORADO

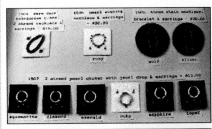

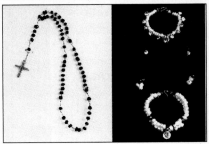

Jewelry

Price: $12 - $35 finished
Necklaces (with earrings) that unclasp to fit on a doll. Made of tiny beads and pearls with rhinestones or genuine precious stones. Rosaries and genuine pearls also available. Many colors.

Kitchen

BODEGA
"I Hate Housework"

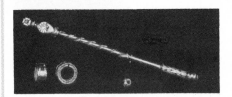

Stock No.: 859
Price: $4 plus shipping
Dimensions: 2"; 1" scale
Exclusive design of Bodega. Add the finishing touches with our handcrafted accessories for inside and outside of the dollhouse, printer's tray or collector box. Wholesale only.

BUTT HINGE POTTERY

Stoneware

Wheel-thrown stoneware miniatures capturing the spirit of traditional New England pottery for use in many dollhouse settings from the kitchen and bedroom to the garden or general store. Wholesale only. Custom orders available. See your local dealer for further information.

DONNA SMOLIK'S DESIGNS

Candy, Cookie & Food Designs

Price: $1.75 - $4.25 each.
Dimensions: 1", 1/2", 1/4" scales
Candies, fruits, vegetables, meats—slice your own with a single-edged razor blade. Can be used in 1", 1/2" or 1/4" scales.

GARCIA & VELEZ CO.

Kitchen Items

Dimensions: 1" scale
Lovely kitchen items in copper or German silver. Assorted baskets, plates, pitchers, pans, trays, much more!

LENHAM POTTERY

Porcelain and Stoneware

Dimensions: 1" scale
This is a selection of household items in slip-cast ceramic (porcelain). Also available are stoneware and white glazed kitchen sinks with fittings. Write for brochure.

LINDEN SWISS MINIATURES

Beer Mug

Stock No.: 639
Dimensions: 1" scale
One mug per package. Has a frosted look. Instruction included for making mug look crystal clear. See your local dealer. American-made.

LINDEN SWISS MINIATURES

Creamer and Sauces

Stock No.: 1209
Dimensions: 1" scale
Stock your shelves with realistic cans with details such as rims and circular indentations on top. Jars are hollow. American-made. Easy instructions for assembly. See your local dealer.

LINDEN SWISS MINIATURES

Egg Cup

Stock No.: 661
Dimensions: 1" scale
Just the thing for your Bed and Breakfast, dining room or kitchen. Made from acrylic, clear. Made in the USA.

LINDEN SWISS MINIATURES

Finished Canned Goods

Stock No.: 201
Dimensions: 1" scale
For the modern kitchen. An assortment of seven finished cans and one jar. Ready to be placed in the pantry. American-made. See your local dealer.

LINDEN SWISS MINIATURES

Oysters and Shrimp

Stock No.: 1202
Dimensions: 1" scale
Food from the sea! We have 12 kits with modern canned goods to choose from. Easy instructions for assembly. All products are American-made. See your local dealer.

LINDEN SWISS MINIATURES

Cork Screw

Stock No.: 803
Handmade cork screw for your bar or table. Has a brass handle. Made in the USA.

LINDEN SWISS MINIATURES

Dinner Plate

Stock No.: LSM-401
Dimensions: 1" scale
Set of four clear dinner plates. Also have salad bowls and platters available. American-made. See your local dealer.

MODEL BUILDERS SUPPLY

Double Kitchen Sink

Stock No.: DKS-12; SKS-12
Price: $3; $2.66
Double kitchen sink and single kitchen sink come in a stainless steel color and clear for custom coloring from reverse, looks just like colored ceramic. Chrome swing faucet set, $7.30 (not incl.) Sinks also in 1/2" scale.

MODEL BUILDERS SUPPLY

Microwave Kit

Price: $6.80
This simple kit takes about 15 minutes to assemble with only a craft knife and a sparing amount of glue. Tinted glass window and molded inner compartment. Illustrated instructions.

MODEL BUILDERS SUPPLY

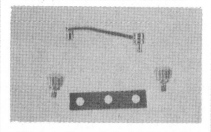

Kitchen Taps & Swing Faucet

Stock No.: FKS-12S
Price: $7.30
Dimensions: 1:12 scale
Beautifully crafted, chrome-plated set.

Prices are approximate and subject to change

MODEL BUILDERS SUPPLY
Appliances

Acrylic and molded styrene, enameled finishes. Fridge and stove are white with black acrylic doors. Washer and dryer are white with decal on top. Non-opening. Fridge $13.30, stove $14.40, washer $10.83, dryer $10.83. 1:24 scale: fridge $9.08, stove $10.60. 1:12 kits: fridge $9.31, stove $9.69, washer $7.56, dryer $7.56, microwave $6.80. Kits come in white only.

MODEL BUILDERS SUPPLY

Collector Series Appliances

Not crude or clumsy. These appliances are excellent, accurate reproductions for the discriminating collector. Acrylic and molded styrene. Fridge doors open to reveal full interior detail with two crisper trays. Stove has opening oven and storage drawer below. White. Frost-free fridge $74.48, Self-cleaning oven $72.73. Interior light option, add $10.

ROYAL MINIATURES

Kitchen Accessories

Price: $1.50 - $6.60
Dimensions: 1" scale
Shown is just a sampling of our huge line of kitchenware accessories. Wholesale only.

SIR THOMAS THUMB

Country Kitchenware

Many beautiful handcrafted pieces including wooden bucket, slaw cutter, pie board, rolling pin, carved wooden bowls, grain scoop, apple butter paddle, etc. Catalog.

TERI'S MINI WORKSHOP

Kitchen Shelf and Kitchen Towel

Price: Towel $4; Shelf $18
Flowers, vegetables, animals and lots of other patterns decorate the self-printed towels. Each unit is just a little different.

THE DUCK POND

Kitchen and Workshop Accessories

Price: $1 and up, plus shipping
Dimensions: 1" scale
Unpainted wooden spoons, rolling pins, scoops. Retail and wholesale. For more information send LSASE.

Kits

ALL THROUGH THE HOUSE

Assorted Kits

Price: $2 - $8, plus shipping & handling
Kits available for all accessories shown and more not shown. There are 150 more handcrafted accessories for your mini home. Send LSASE for mailer.

JEAN'S WEE THINGS

Leather Kits

Stock No.:1993
Many different kits available in 1/2" or 1" scale trunks, suitcases, tapestry bags, New England style—Sou'westers, Southwestern style vests, Santa suits, footwear and more. Prices vary from $12 and up. Send $1 plus LSASE. Request leather kits c/o Jean's Wee Things. Shipping additional.

KASEY'S

Quilt Kits

Price: $4.95 and up
Create beautiful Amish and traditional dollhouse quilts using foundation piecing. Quilt kits, instruction booklets and fabric packs are available.

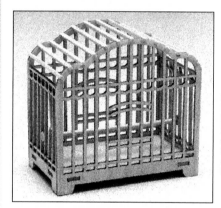

NORTHEASTERN SCALE MODELS, INC.
Miniature Bird Cages

Stock No.: B100-B105
Price: $9.95 - $23.95, plus shipping
Dimensions: 1"=1' scale
Introducing six miniature bird cage kits that capture the elegance and spirit of a bygone era. Each bird cage is precision scaled, painstakingly detailed and laser cut from select basswood. Step by step instructions make assembly easy.

ALICE ZINN

Shoes and Boots

Price:$3.50 - $18
Dancing shoes, ballet, toe, exercise, child and women's tap shoes, sandals, slippers, boots and saddle shoes. All sports shoes. Genuine leather. American-made.

Leather

ALL THROUGH THE HOUSE

Leather Accessories

Price: see below
Hunting boots/$12; log carrier/$3.75; men's shoes/$12; brief case/$6.50; belt/$3; gloves/$3; wallet/$3.50; dirty boots on paper/$14 and more. Send LSASE for mailer.

GARCIA & VELEZ CO.

Saddles

Price: Wholesale: $5.50-$9.50, plus shipping
Dimensions: 1"=1'
Handmade fine leather saddles—Western, English or pony. Good for Breyer horses, too. Beautifully finished.

MAISON DES MAISONS

Equipales Furniture

Equipales furniture, leather and reed. Various colors of leather available. Navajo sterling coffee set and oak trastero. 1/2" and 1" available.

MAISON DES MAISONS

Indian Artifacts

Native American Indian dresses, cradleboards, baskets and other artifacts by Tu Moonwalker, Rainbow Hand, Kay and Joe Franek and many Native American artists.

MAISON DES MAISONS

Leather Furniture

Price: $300 to $400, plus shipping.
Dimensions: 1" scale
Beautiful leather sofas, chairs and benches by Gail Steffey. Various colors and styles available.

PRESTIGE LEATHER

Footwear

Shoes available in assorted styles and colors. Prices range from $8 to $22.

PRESTIGE LEATHER
Western Wear

Cowboy boots in snakeskin or leather with matching holsters and hats to dress up your cowboy or put in a western scene. Chaps in various colors Vests are made of suede or deerskin, with or without fringe. We also have vests made of calf hair with beautiful markings—each one unique.

PRESTIGE LEATHER
Silver Show Saddles & Bridles

Beautiful carved saddles trimmed with sterling silver and silver bridles to match. Saddle $160. Bridle $70. Available in brown or black. Other colors on request.

PRESTIGE LEATHER
Mini Tack

Western saddles $40 to $50. Bridles $20. Matching saddlebags $10 to $11.

PRESTIGE LEATHER

English Saddle & Riding Boots

English saddle $40
English boots $22

THE DOLLS' COBBLER

Shoes and Boots

Price: $10-$25
Colonial to contemporary—all leather, authentic and realistic by Sylvia Rountree. IGMA Fellow. Shoemaker since 1970. Some available in 1/2" scale.

TREASURE WORKS

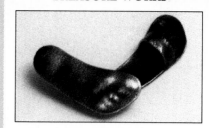

Worn Sandals

Stock No.: TS010
Price: $22 Sterling—$20 Bronze; ppd.
Dimensions: approx. 7/8" x 3/8"; 1"=1'
These charming sterling silver or bronze sandals have the look of leather. They appear to be "worn" with toe and heel imprints.

THE DOLLS' COBBLER

Leather Luggage

Price: see below
All are real working pieces with choice silk or liberty cotton linings coordinated with rich leather finishes. Six pieces now available include a new man's top hat box, round lady's hat box, suitcase and trunk, all $48 retail; plus a leather satchel or a "Mary Poppins" carpet bag at $28.

Lighting Fixtures & Lamps

AZTEC IMPORTS INC.

LAMPS

Price: See your local dealer.
Dimensions: 1"=1' scale
A variety of lamps for every room in the house and out. Shown Seaman's Lantern (M1777), Rocking Horse Lamp (D8420) and Tiffany Table Lamp (D5400). All 12 volts.

CLARE-BELL BRASS WORKS

Elegant Candlestick

Stock No.: 1716-111
Solid brass, gold-plated. Elegant candlestick available in round or hex base. Also available electric. See your local miniatures dealer.

CLARE-BELL BRASS WORKS

Colonial Wall Sconce

Stock No.: 1853-130
Solid brass. Sold singly. 1" to 1' scale, gold-plated. Matches the six-arm chandelier. Replaceable bulbs. Catalog, more than 200 items, $2. See your local independent miniatures dealer.

CLARE-BELL BRASS WORKS

Electric Candles, Round Base

Stock No.: 1800-131
Solid brass electric candles. Sold in pairs. Gold-plated. Replaceable bulbs. Also available in non-electric, and hex or square base. Catalog, more than 200 items, $2. See your local independent miniatures dealer.

Prices are approximate and subject to change

CLARE-BELL BRASS WORKS

Hurricane Wall Sconce

Stock No.: 1771-130
Solid brass, gold-plated, electric or non-electric, round base. Sold singly. Catalog, more than 200 items, $2. See your local independent miniatures dealer.

CLARE-BELL BRASS WORKS

Wall Sconces, Round

Stock No.: 1770-131
Dimensions: 1" to 1' scale
Replaceable bulbs. Round or hex back. Catalog, more than 200 items, $2. See your local independent miniatures dealer.

CLARE-BELL BRASS WORKS

Three-Arm Hurricane Chandelier

Stock No.: 1852-130
Comes with clear glass or tole-painted glass chimneys. Replaceable bulbs. Includes ceiling plate and 2" of chain. Also available: Four-Arm Hurricane Chandelier. See your local independent miniatures dealer.

CLARE-BELL BRASS WORKS

Six-Arm Chandelier

Stock No.:1850-130
Solid brass, gold-plated. Includes ceiling plate and 2" of chain. Replaceable bulbs. Available in Four-Arm and Five-Arm styles. Also available in non-electric.

THE LIGHTING BUG, LTD
Five-Light Chandelier

Stock No.: 311
Price: $81
Dimensions: 1-5/8"W x 1-1/8"H; 1" scale
Almond with floral designs or matte black finish. Flame bulbs. Handcrafted. Replaceable flame bulbs available at extra cost. 2-1/2" chain with ceiling plate. We also have a full line of 1/2" scale items. 12V.

WORKSHOP WISDOM

Family Pictures

Some of the major stores give a "special" on family portraits, and included with the mass of low price pictures are several tiny photos suitable for mounting in charm bracelets or necklaces. Kathy frames these and hangs them in her dollhouse so that it has current family pictures on the walls.

KATHY KOONS
OVIEDO, FL

Workshop Wisdom
Courtesy of *Nutshell News*—10/94

THE LIGHTING BUG, LTD.
Four Arm, Six Bulb Chandelier

Stock No.: 623
Price: $129
Dimensions: 1-5/8"H x 2-1/2"W; 1" scale
Glass & brass with much Victorian class. Handcrafted. Replaceable bi-pin bulbs available at extra cost. 2-1/2" chain with ceiling plate. We also have a full line of 1/2" scale items. 12V.

THE LIGHTING BUG, LTD
Four-Light Brass Chandelier

Stock No.: B
Price: $101
Dimensions: 2-3/4"W x 1-1/2"H; 1" scale
All brass, elegant. Frosted shades with raised design. Handcrafted. Replaceable bi-pin bulbs available at extra cost. 2-1/2" chain plus ceiling plate. We also have a full line of 1/2" scale items. 12V.

THE LIGHTING BUG, LTD.

Brass Bridge Lamp With Silked Shade

Stock No.: MMM
Price: $60.50
Dimensions: 4-1/2"H; 1" scale
Handcrafted in the US. Brass with silked shade. We also have a full line of 1/2" scale items. Replaceable bi-pin bulb available at extra cost. 12V.

THE LIGHTING BUG, LTD.

Brass Floor Lamp With Silked Shade

Stock No.: YYY
Price: $54.50
Dimensions: 4-9/16"H; 1" scale
Handcrafted. Brass with silked shade. Also available in replaceable bi-pin bulb at extra cost. A full line of 1/2" scale items available. 12V.

THE LIGHTING BUG, LTD.

Oil Lamp With Ornate Legs & Glass Chimney

Stock No.: 201
Price: $65
Dimensions: 4-7/16" chimney; 1" scale
Handcrafted. Brass. Glass globe with decal plus chimney. Also available in replaceable bi-pin bulb at extra cost. Full line of electrified 1/2" scale available. 12V.

Medical Office

JUST GETTING INTO DOLLHOUSE MINIATURES?

If you have a question about dollhouse miniatures, stop by your local retail outlet and ask the expert behind the counter.

PRECIOUS LITTLE THINGS

Medical and Dental Office Accessories

Authentically labeled medicines for doctor, dentist, home, store, contemporary/old time. Surgical gloves, movable hypodermic, plaster cast, enema bag, folding screen and more. Color catalog $3.50 or ask your local dealer.

TERI'S MINI WORKSHOP

Doctor's Office

Doctor's office supplies including doctor's bag and modern dental supplies. American-made.

Prices are approximate and subject to change

MODEL BUILDERS SUPPLY

Mirrors

MBS manufactures 1mm-thick plastic mirror in blue, bronze, brass, copper, green, gold, grey, pink and violet as well as regular silver. Dimensions: 3-3/8" x 12", two per pack, $7.22. Mirrorcraft pack, 10 pcs., one of each, 3-3/8" x 6", $9.08. Larger sheets available. Breaks exactly after one easy cut on face side with sharp craft knife. Many decorative uses. MBS skylights shown.

Mirrors&Screens

UNIQUE MINIATURES

Gilded Ornate Mirrors and Picture FramesThis wide selection provides ornate mirrors and picture frames to suit any taste. The ornate mirrors come with distortion-free mirrors of unbreakable Plexiglas. The picture frames are also available with mirrors. Many styles from which to choose. Send $3 for complete catalog. Made in USA.

Musical

AZTEC IMPORTS INC.

Juke Box Radio

Stock No.: S8087
Price: See your local dealer.
Dimensions: 5-1/2"H x 3-1/4"W x 1-7/8"D.
1"=1' scale.
AM/FM radio really works. Flashing lights highlight front. Uses three "C" batteries. Perfect size for your soda shop or rec room.

LIGIA'S MINIATURES

Adjustable Music Stand

Stock No.: 501
Price: $31 ppd.
Totally collapsible, exact replica. Perfect for study or music room. We also make a brass equatorial telescope on wood tripod, excellent for your study.

PRESTIGE LEATHER

Guitar with Leather Case

Price: $65
This guitar fits perfectly in its beautifully handcrafted leather case which is lined with red or tan suede.

THE KEN MANNING COLLECTION

Miniature Musical Stringed Instruments

Price: Various
Dimensions: 1" scale
Beautiful top quality one inch scale stringed musical instruments handcrafted from many different types of hardwoods and exotic woods.

Needlework & Linens

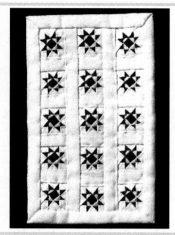

ALICE LACY, LTD.
Needlework and Linens

Alice Lacy, Ltd. Wire Wicker and Software Designed by Alice Lacy. Pastel prints for star quilts and pillows are hand pieced. There are bolts of fabric from which to make matching dust ruffles and curtains. A new bed has spaces in the woven headboard to hold fabric valances, and the decorator's screen is designed for cloth panels. Moreover, there are pillows and seat cushions—plain, tufted, or embroidered to fit wicker chairs and couches. The 15-star quilt shown has approximately 300 separate bits of cloth. Sold at fine shops almost everywhere.

AZTEC IMPORTS INC.

Sewing Machines

Price: See your local dealer.
Dimensions: 1"=1' scale
For all your sewing room needs. Treadle machine in walnut and black (T8000), sewing basket (MA2212), dressmakers set (D4252), and walnut sewing machine (D7780).

OCTOBER IS NATIONAL DOLLHOUSE AND MINIATURES MONTH! STOP BY YOUR LOCAL SHOP!

GINSBURG COMPANY

5 Pc. Walnut Sewing Room

Stock No.: 2929.00
Price: See your local dealer.
Dimensions: 1" = 1' scale
5 pc. walnut sewing room packed in our "Keepsakes" clam shell see-through package. This packaging allows for easy display and is completely visible.

KASEY'S

Quilt Kits

Price:$4.95 and up
Create beautiful Amish and traditional dollhouse quilts using foundation piecing. Quilt kits, instruction booklets and fabric packs are available.

LITTLEFOOT MINIATURES

Sampler Kit

Price: $30 ppd.
Dimensions: 2" x 2-1/2"; 8000 stitches
Handcrafted in Canada by Caraline Stanley. Kit includes 40 mesh canvas, tapestry needle, DMC floss, frame, graph and detailed instructions. A history of samplers is included. 1" scale.

MINIATURE CORNER
Collector Sewing Machine

Stock No.: BH6710
Collector-quality, working sewing machine. Even pressure foot holds fabric! Floor and table models. Victorian wood dress form with tape. Fine German quality by Bodo Hennig. Doll by Erna Meyer. See your local dealer.

RENÉE BOWEN - MINIATURIST

Hooked on Knots

Price: $15, plus shipping.
Dimensions: 1"=1' scale
Kits for 12 authentic New England hooked rugs. All material included plus easy-to-follow instructions. Fun to make, beautiful when finished. SASE for flyer.

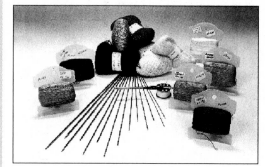

WEE THREE
Needlework Supplies

Dimensions: 1" to 1' scale
Needlework supplies for 1" to 1' scale. To create your needlework projects, here are size 2/0 to 7/0 knitting needles, small sewing and beading needles, fine yarns and threads for knitting, crocheting, sewing and tatting. Send $2 for catalog of supplies.

THE MINI MERCHANT

Knitted Afghans

Price: $25 to $35
Dimensions: 1" scale
These drape beautifully and will stay in position. Hundreds of colors available.

Nursery

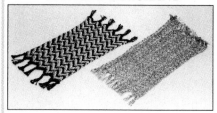

EMPRESS ARTS AND CRAFTS
Nursery Room Furniture

Price: $9 - $14
Dimensions: 1" scale
Windsor Collection iron wire furniture. Ornate hand-soldered iron wire furnishing resembling turn-of-the-century wicker. More than 200 designs to choose from. Potted flowers and arrangements available to fill the room settings. Wholesale only.

ROYAL MINIATURES

Baby Supplies

Price: $1.50 - $4
Shown is a small sampling from our wide selection of baby needs. Wholesale only. Imported.

WORKSHOP WISDOM

Butterflies on your flowers, butterflies basking on your window ledge! These butterflies were cut from catalog ads. This one, apparently from an ad for a fashion watch, is about 3/16" (5mm) from tip to tip. Coat the ad first with Mod Podge, then use a #11 blade to carefully cut around it. Add antenna cut from the fine bristles of a brush, then fold the butterfly in a V before gluing to your flowers.

LOIS WITTNER
SAN DIEGO, CA

Workshop Wisdom
Courtesy of *Nutshell News*—3/94

Paintings, Prints
Watercolors, Etchings

BARBARA STANTON

Miniature Oil Paintings

Award-winning artist will custom paint portraits, landscapes, etc., from your photo or mine. No catalog, just price list and examples of work. Original one-of-a-kind pieces also available.

ALESSIO MINIATURES
Paintings

Price: See your local dealer.
Beautiful paintings for your dollhouse. Many themes to choose from. Hundreds available. Custom prints also available.

INNOVATIVE PHOTOGRAPHY

Miniature Artwork

Price: $3-$7.50
Color maps: United States, World, North American territories and three antique maps; George Washington, color; Abraham Lincoln, black/white, two sizes framed or unframed. American-made.

MARLENE GILBERT
HOUSEPLANTS IN MINIATURE

Watercolor Paintings

Price: $10-$20 each
Dimensions: Vary. Average 2" x 3"
Original contemporary one-of-a-kind watercolor paintings, unframed. Floral, landscape, abstract and Southwest.

PRESTIGE LEATHER

Carved Leather Pictures

Price: $30
Each leather picture is unique, handcarved and detailed. Each is numbered and signed by the leather artist. Done in a wide variety of subjects.

PERRAULT MINIATURES
Wood Frames

Unfinished miniature wood frames to show off your prized miniature artwork. There are more than 50 styles from which to choose.

Prices are approximate and subject to change

CLARE-BELL BRASS WORKS

Inkwell With Quill

Stock No.: 1728-100
Brass inkwell holds genuine quill. Catalog, more than 200 items, $2. See your local independent miniatures dealer. 1" = 1' scale.

Paper Accessories

Period Accessories

ALICE ZINN

Accessories

Contemporary shoes, hats, clothing, leather goods, toys, nursery items, stationery, bath shop, audio-visual, garden, sporting goods, outdoor birds, pets, Oriental accessories and Chinese food. American made.

BUTT HINGE POTTERY

Stoneware

Wheel-thrown stoneware miniatures capturing the spirit of traditional New England pottery for use in many dollhouse settings from the kitchen and bedroom to the garden or general store. Wholesale only. Custom orders available. See your local dealer for further information.

ELLIOTT'S

Price: from $15, plus shipping
Ornate mantel clocks, mirrors and decorative items. Gilded clocks and mirrors to decorate the finest miniature rooms. Urns and figural decorations, all handmade.

JEFFREY W. VIGEANT

Classic Candelabrums

704-NE - 19th Century, six candles;
705-NE - Rosemount, four candles;
706-NE - Fretwork bowl with four candles.

JEFFREY W. VIGEANT

Fretwork Bowl Filled with Fruit

Stock No.: 706-FF
Makes a spectacular addition to any table. Four accent candles.

JEFFREY W. VIGEANT

Rosemount Bowl With Dried Flowers

Stock No.: 707-DF
This exquisite fretwork-style bowl filled with a dried flower arrangement adds a timeless touch of elegance to any room setting.

JEFFREY W. VIGEANT

Christmas Centerpieces

708-AT - Red Apple Tree
708-GB - Golden Ball Centerpiece.

LINDEN SWISS MINIATURES

Apothecary Jars

Stock No.: 600
Dimensions: 1" scale
Set of five apothecary jars, each jar a different size. American-made. See your local dealer.

LINDEN SWISS MINIATURES

Canning Jars

Stock No.: 530
Dimensions: 1" scale
Old-fashioned canning jars. Three per package. Three-quart, one-quart and pint size. Each jar has simulated zinc lid. American-made. See your local dealer.

LINDEN SWISS MINIATURES

Finished Canned Goods

Stock No.:200
Dimensions: 1" scale
An assortment of seven finished vintage canned goods and one jar. Ready to put on your shelf. American-made. See your local dealer.

LINDEN SWISS MINIATURES

Fish and Vegetables

Stock No.: 1107
Dimensions: 1" scale
Just one of nine kits of vintage canned goods. Instructions for easy assembly. All products are American-made. See your local dealer.

LINDEN SWISS MINIATURES

Stokely's Finest Fruits

Stock No.: 1102
Dimensions: 1" scale
We have vintage canned goods from 1933 to 1938—Stokely brand. Comes in kit form with instructions for easy assembly. All products are American-made. See your local dealer.

NANTASY FANTASY CREATIONS

Cash Register

Stock No.: 834-1
Dimensions: 1-1/2"H x 1-1/2"D x 1"W
Turn of the century, cherry wood construction. Cash drawer opens. A fine example of more than 90 handcrafted items included in our full color catalog.

OMNIARTS OF COLORADO

Arms and Armor

Price: $5 - $300 finished
These arms and armor are handcrafted and made of cast metal. Included in the selection are shields, weapons, cannon and suits of armor. Also available are plastic model armor kits in six styles. American-made and imported.

OMNIARTS OF COLORADO

Shields and Crests

Price: Under $3
Wall and furniture trims, shields, crests, objects d'art, cast candlesticks, etc. American-made.

OMNIARTS OF COLORADO

Medieval Accessories

Price: Varies, plus shipping
Handmade accessories including bearskin rugs, wall torches, clocks, hunting birds, boots, headdresses, magic books and ingredients, armored horses, mastiffs, chain mail, musical instruments, etc.

OMNIARTS OF COLORADO

Tapestries

Price: $6 - $10
Woven Gobelin tapestries from France, $6 each. Tapestry mounted on a decorative rod, $10 each. Imported.

Prices are approximate and subject to change

Photographs

Plants&Flowers

HANKY PANKY CRAFT

Cakes and Flowers

Make flowers, plants and trees with Pretty Petal Punches using tape, preserved leaves, colored or painted paper. Punches and mini cake catalog, $1.

HDW

Plants and Flowers

Beautiful wire-edged, enamel-type flowers. To be used in landscaping gardens, as single plants in pots or as bouquets. Send SASE for pricing.

HOUSEWORKS, LTD.

Terra Cotta Pots

Price: $.95
Petite terra cotta pots. Imported. 8001/Small flower pot. Size: 9/16"H x 5/8" top diameter. 8002/Large flower pot. Size: 9/16"H x 3/4" top diameter. 8004/Fluted pot. Size:11/16"H x 3/4" top diameter. 8003/Urn: Size: 13/16"H x 11/16"W. 8005/Strawberry pot. Size: 1-1/16"H x 3/4"W.

J. HERMES

Treated Greenery

Price: $.50 (small bag); $3 (large bag)
Large bag of forest green lycopodium is enough for one 6" or 8" Christmas tree (using a bottle brush or sisal tree form). Any extra can be used for a small garland or wreath. Small bag is enough for a wreath, garland or other "mini" decoration.

HELEN M. DAVID, IGMA ARTISAN
Artistic Floral Arrangements

My flowers are made from high quality papers, with each petal and/or leaf either punched or hand cut to proper size and shape. Added realism is achieved by hand painting selected flower petals, leaves and the detailing of calyxes and flower centers as required. Completely finished arrangements only.

MARLENE GILBERT
HOUSEPLANTS IN MINIATURE

Houseplants

Price: $8-$45
Dimensions: sizes vary from 1/2" to 6" high.
Scale 1". (Poinsettia approx. 1".)
More than 600 handcrafted houseplants, including poinsettias in five colors, quilled flowers, anthuriums, palms, ferns, dracaenas and African violets. Limited availability by mail order.

School & Office Accessories

Plant Stand

WORKSHOP WISDOM

This plant stand was assembled from the pusher parts of two different sizes of solid stick deodorant. The transparent sketch shows the parts needed from inside the container. Painted flat black to resemble wrought iron then set with potted plants, the unit would grace any home. The plant pots, by the way, are toothpaste tube caps! The base might need some clay inside, for stability.

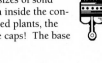

*MARY STIEBER
BRIGHTON, CO*

Workshop Wisdom Courtesy of *Nutshell News—9/94*

PRESTIGE LEATHER

Briefcase

Price: $14
Fine leather briefcase available in black or brown. Can be opened.

Prices are approximate and subject to change

Sculptures & Statues

CLARE-BELL BRASS WORKS

Deer Weather Vane
Stock No.: 1913-100
Catalog, more than 200 items, $2. See your local independent miniatures dealer.

CLARE-BELL BRASS WORKS

Eagle Weather Vane
Stock No.: 1916-100
Catalog, more than 200 items, $2. See your local independent miniatures dealer.

CLARE-BELL BRASS WORKS

Gabriel Weather Vane
Stock No.: 1915-100
Catalog, more than 200 items, $2. See your local independent miniatures dealer.

SPECIAL SELLERS

Designer Gingerbread House
Stock No.: GB 822
Price: $9 to $50, plus shipping.
Dimensions: Approx. 1" high; 1" scale
Collector-quality gingerbread houses in more than 30 styles. Featured is Santa gingerbread workshop with elf. Wholesale invited.

Southwestern & Indian

MAISON DES MAISONS

Indian Artifacts
Native American Indian dresses, cradleboards, baskets and other artifacts by Tu Moonwalker, Rainbow Hand, Kay and Joe Franek and many Native American artists.

MAISON DES MAISONS

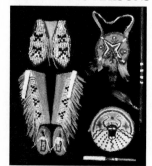

Rainbow Hand
Authentic miniature reproductions of Indian artifacts by Rainbow Hand.

MAISON DES MAISONS

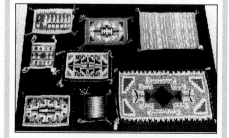

Navajo Indian Rugs
Navajo Indian rugs by various weavers from the Southwest. Handspun natural wool and dyes.

MAISON DES MAISONS

Indian Pottery
Pottery by various Southwest artists—Joseph Lonewolf, Geri Naranjo, Mae Tapia, Dolores Curran, Teresa Wildflower and others.

MAISON DES MAISONS

Indian Arts and Crafts

Native arts and crafts by Southwest Indian artists. Kachinas (figures of native dancers), storytellers and naciementos (nativities). American-made.

OMNIARTS OF COLORADO

American Indian Arts

Price:$15 and up
Offered here are superbly crafted American Indian arts including baskets, headdresses, pottery, garments, weapons, ceremonial items by Rainbow Hand and others. American-made.

PRESTIGE LEATHER

Shields and Drums

Shields have southwest or wildlife designs and are trimmed with one or more realistic leather eagle feathers. Drums are plain or painted with southwest designs.

THE LAWBRE COMPANY

Sculptures

Stock No.: 0651 - 0655
Price: $18
Dimensions: 7/8" to 1-3/4"
These western sculptures are made from metal castings with antique bronze finish. Five different styles for a western look in decor.

Sports Equipment

ALICE ZINN

Sports Equipment

Tennis, baseball, hockey, basketball, golf, soccer, skiing, backpacking, roller skating, fishing, surfing, water skiing, etc. American-made.

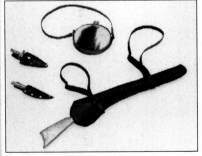

PRESTIGE LEATHER
Sporting Goods

Ice skates and roller skates available in white, black and natural-$27. Snow shoes-$29. We also have canteens made of leather, suede or calf hair-$10. Leather knife sheaths with hunt knife or dagger-$5, and leather scabbard with Winchester rifle-$12.

DOLL HOUSE SHOPPE

Sports Equipment

For the wall, our tennis rack or baseball rack with equipment. Others shown: two golf bags, clubs, Walkman, aerobics gift basket, two tennis bags, backpacks. All handmade.

ROYAL MINIATURES

Sporting Goods

Price:
$1 - $2.50
Shown are just a few of the many sporting goods and other miniature accessories available. Customer designs are welcome.

TERI'S MINI WORKSHOP

Sports Equipment

Sports equipment from tiny golf balls to a fully equipped pool table.

THE DOLLS' COBBLER

English and Western Saddlery

Price: see below
Accurate to the last detail. Saddles, bridles, whips and horse collars. $2 (riding crop), $50 (Victorian side saddle).

THE DOLLS' COBBLER

Hip Boots and Waders

Price: $25-boots; $30-waders
Catch of the day—hip boots and overall waders for the miniature fishing enthusiast.

THE LAWBRE COMPANY

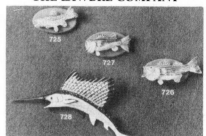

Fish Trophies

Stock No.: 0725; 0726; 0727; 0728
Price: $40; $40; $40; $60
Hand painted and mounted on walnut plaques (except sailfish). Realistic coloring and finish. American-made.

PRESTIGE LEATHER

Golf Bag

Price: $25
Just what you need for your mini golfer. Various colors.

THE LAWBRE COMPANY

Sporting Trophies

Stock No.: 0700 - 0707
Price: $45 - $75
These hand painted trophy heads have exquisite detail and are mounted on walnut plaques. American-made.

THE LAWBRE COMPANY

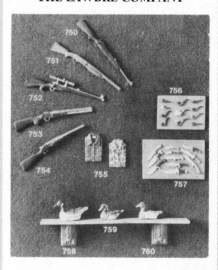

Sporting Trophies

Stock No.: 0750 - 0760
Price: $9 - $30
These rifles, shotguns, pipe and knife collections, shirts and game birds are all hand painted in exquisite detail for your game room. American-made.

THE WORLD'S SMALLEST CO.

Rifles/Fishing Rods

Standing gun cabinet, complete line of rifles and fishing rods. Handcarved hardwood stocks and metal barrels add authenticity to these accurately and beautifully detailed pieces. Catalog available.

THREE BLIND MICE

1" Scale Gym Equipment

Price: see below
$30, five-door locker; $14, single locker; $20, weight set; $15, slant board; $10, sweat suit.

VICKI'S MINIATURES

Gym Equipment

Price: $1.50 - $39.95
Dimensions: 1" scale
Handcrafted, detailed gym equipment including weight bench, barbell holder with barbells, weight belt and dumbbells (in white, blue and brown). Send for free brochure.

DONNA'S MINI EMPORIUM

Store and Shop Accessories

A complete line of assorted handmade kitchen accessories including flyswatter, mop, paper towel, bags, rolling pin, bug spray, etc. American-made.

Specialty Shop

CLASSICS BY HANDLEY

Standing Gum Ball Machine

Stock No.: CLA03624
Price: $1.50
A must for the general store, this gum ball machine is 3" tall and has a red painted metal base and realistic multi-colored gum balls.

CLASSICS BY HANDLEY

Gum Ball Machine

Stock No.: CLA03490
Price: $1.20
Approximately 1" tall, this gum ball machine has a painted red metal base and multi-colored gum balls.

INNOVATIVE PHOTOGRAPHY

Postcard Racks

Price: see below
Handcrafted postcard and hanging display racks—postcards, black/white and sepia: French, Victorian and Cowboys and Indians. Color: Holidays, kewpies, scenics, foreign and assorted. Suggested retail price: $11.95/24 color cards; $9.95/24 black/white; $35 postcard rack; $25 hanging display rack. American-made.

MINIATURE HOUSE

Bushel Baskets

Natural colored bushel baskets. MH2011 - small, $2.79; MH2012 - medium, $2.89; MH2013 - large, $2.89.

MINIATURE HOUSE

Produce Boxes

MH2009 - four slats, $1; MH2010 - eight slats, $1.20. Perfect for the general store. All wood.

Prices are approximate and subject to change

Toys & Games

SIR THOMAS THUMB

Barrels Galore!

Rain barrels, whiskey barrels with spigots and stands, and wooden kegs are just a few of the many items we have for your general store. Catalog available.

THREE BLIND MICE

1" Scale Kiln

Price: $25

ALICE ZINN

Games

Mah Jongg with leather case, pinball, foosball, knock hockey, Slinky, Rummy Tile and 3-D Tic-Tac-Toe. American made.

ALL THROUGH THE HOUSE

Games

Price: see below
Darts/$7.50; baseball bat, ball and glove/$7.50; tennis racket/$8; kite/$7.50; cribbage game with cards/$8; painter's palette/$4; checkers/$8; jump rope/$1.50; backgammon/$8. Send LSASE for mailer.

DONNA'S MINI EMPORIUM

Toys and Games

Our handmade toys are made of wood and paper. The assortment consists of crayons, peg sets, blocks, records, xylophone and other items. American-made.

JEAN'S WEE THINGS

Kits 'n Caboodle

Stock No.: 1993
Unusual kits available: 1-1/2" dressed rag dolls, $15; jointed teddy bears, $5; trunks for dolls or teddy, $10; Easter cake, $10; Easter basket, $2; ribbon candy, $2.50; poinsettias, $3; shell tulips, $5; Christmas wreaths, $3-$5; daffodils, $3; and more! Shipping additional. Brochure, $1 and SASE to Kits 'n Caboodle, c/o Jean's Wee Things.

OMNIARTS OF COLORADO

Handcrafted Toys

Price: $5 and up
Dimensions: 1" = 1'
Omni bears of chenille in their own box, Fimo character bears by Martie Blackmon, Noah's Ark of hand painted pewter from England, others.

ROYAL MINIATURES

Toys and Games

Price: $1 - $2
Shown are just a few of the many toys and games available. Many other styles available. Customer designs are welcome.

Weddings

Workshop Accessories

DOLL HOUSE SHOPPE

Wedding Accessories

Price: See your local dealer.
Dimensions: 1" scale
All miniatures shown are lovingly handmade. We have 165 pieces of wedding furniture and accessories in all. Completely finished.

ALESSIO MINIATURES

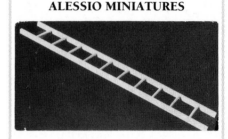

Wooden Ladder

Stock No.: 15
Price: $1.50
Dimensions: 10"L x 1"W
Wooden ladder can be cut to any length for convenience. American-made.

PRESTIGE LEATHER

Tool pouch with tools

Price: $13
Leather tool pouch with belt can be buckled on your mini craftsman or placed in the workshop. Includes 4 tools.

SIR THOMAS THUMB

Woodworker's Tools

Collector-quality carpenter/handyman tools, both historic and modern. Workbench, shaving horse, wood planes, saws, augers, chisels, hammers, blacksmith tools, etc. Realism in wood and metal. Catalog available.

TERI'S MINI WORKSHOP

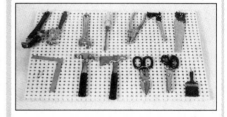

Tool Rack

Price: $12
Dimensions: 1" = 1'
Fourteen tools on a tidy peg board.

Miscellaneous

BODEGA

Beer Cooler With Lid

Stock No.: 705
Price: $6.50 plus shipping
Dimensions: 1" x 2"; 1" scale
Lid is removable on this very popular beer or pop cooler. Exclusive design of Bodega. We sell quality handcrafted accessories for dollhouses and collector boxes. Wholesale only.

CATHY'S HANDCRAFTED MINIATURE ACCESSORIES
Assorted Accessories
Handcrafted accessories for inside and outside the house. Bath mat and towel sets, laundry baskets, grocery bags, glasses, knitting, garden hoses, trimmed mailboxes, garbage cans and much more.

START A NEW HOBBY AND MEET NEW FRIENDS: JOIN A MINIATURES CLUB!

DONNA SMOLIK'S DESIGNS

Candy, Cookie & Food Designs
Price: $1.75 - $4.25 each.
Dimensions: 1", 1/2", 1/4" scales
Candies, fruits, vegetables, meats—slice your own with a single-edged razor blade. Can be used in 1", 1/2" or 1/4" scales.

FOX HOLLOW MINIATURES

Muddy Old Boots
Price: $25
Dimensions: 1-3/4"
The famous Muddy Old Boots from Merrie Old England by the talented Dorothy Kitching. A "must" for every back door!

HANDCRAFT DESIGNS INC..
Accessories Sampling
Pictured is a sampling of accessories showing a wide variety of items both proprietary and "open market," Busts of musical masters, thinkers and statesmen (others not shown). The finest hand painted china. Foods and flowers in ceramic. Pewter pieces for every room in the house and every period. Special emphasis on table top items and fireplace accessories.

JUDITH SOKOLOW

Rosemaled Oval Wooden Box (Tina)
Price: $25
Dimensions: 1-1/8" x 1-1/2" x 1/2"high
Painted wooden oval "tina." Rosemaled in Norwegian style in blue or rust background. Furniture painted in Norwegian styles, upon request.

"KRAFTS" BY BETTY JEAN

Rubber Stamps
Stock No.: 4
Price: $1.50 - $2.50 plus shipping
Stamps to personalize towels, pillowcases, curtains, greeting cards, welcome signs, shopping bags and more. Great for personal or group projects. Stamp brochure only, LSASE.

LIGIA'S MINIATURES

Working Kaleidoscopes
Stock No.: 701-03
Price: $32 plus shipping
World's smallest working kaleidoscopes, in three different styles. All brass with wonderful colors inside. Walnut stand, $19.50.
Also see our ad under Musical.

LITTLEFOOT MINIATURES

Snow Globes

Price: $16 ppd.
Dimensions: 5/8"H x 1/2"; 1" scale
Handcrafted in Canada by Judi McLeod. They really do shake "snow" with no leaks. Many figures available. Special orders considered.

MULTI-MINIS, INC.

Manufacturers of over 2500 miniature accessories. 1" scale. Wholesale only. Made in America.

ROYAL MINIATURES

Grandfather and Mantle Clocks

Dimensions: 1" scale
Shown is a small selection of our 1" scale real, working grandfather, mantle and carriage clocks. Available in a variety of styles and finishes.

SPECIAL SELLERS

Victorian Gift Basket

Stock No.: MS 171
Price: $14, plus shipping.
Dimensions: 1-3/8" x 1/2"; 1" scale
Elegant gift baskets in more than 20 varieties including all seasons. Featured is Victorian gift basket with fan, nosegay, and soaps. Wholesale invited.

THE DUCK POND

Workshop Accessories

Price: $1 and up, plus shipping
Dimensions: 1" scale
Unpainted mallets, pitchforks, shovels, bucksaws, ox yokes, tool boxes. Retail and wholesale. For more information send LSASE.

THE LAWBRE COMPANY

Decorative Architectural Details

Stock No.: 0401 - 0420
Price: $4 - $14
These items can add the finishing touch to your decor. All are cast products with various finishes.

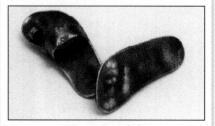

THE LAWBRE COMPANY
Decor Items

Stock No.: 0600 - 0611
Price: $7 - $55
These items are carefully hand painted to accent inside or outside settings. Some pieces are wired and all have exquisite detail. American-made.

THE MINI MONEY MINT, HENRY & CHERI ACKLES

Miniature Money

Price: $2 for 84 1/12 scale bills or 49 1/8 scale bills
Give your dolls the cash they need for all their mini-needs! Six denominations. The money is accurate, precise, double-sided and the only money copyrighted by the Copyright Office for miniaturists.

TREASURE WORKS

Worn Sandals

Stock No.: TS010
Price: $22 Sterling—$20 Bronze; ppd.
Dimensions: approx. 7/8" x 3/8"; 1"=1'
These charming sterling silver or bronze sandals have the look of leather. They appear to be "worn" with toe and heel imprints.

Prices are approximate and subject to change

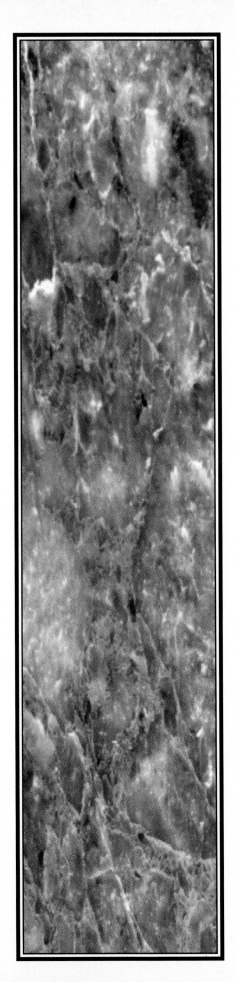

COLLECTIBLE

MINIATURES

BUTT HINGE POTTERY

Stoneware
Wheel-thrown stoneware miniatures capturing the spirit of traditional New England pottery for use in many dollhouse settings from the kitchen and bedroom to the garden or general store. Wholesale only. Custom orders available. See your local dealer for further information.

FINE CHINA IN MINIATURE

Quimper Fish Platter
Dimensions: 1" scale
Incomparable china in miniature in the historic patterns of Quimper, Pink Lustre, Thistleware, Dedham Pottery, Chinese Export, Rose Medallion and others. Please send SASE for price list.

FOX HOLLOW MINIATURES

Christmas Collector's Cupboard
Price: $125
Dimensions: 8-1/2" x 3-1/2"
This corner cupboard is filled with everything a collector's heart desires, down to a tiny "snowbaby" and a readable copy of the antique Night Before Christmas.

GAIL'S TINY TREASURES

Teddy Bears
Dimensions: Just under 1/2" Scale
Gail's Tiny Treasures is proud to introduce our new line "A Bear to Remember Collectibles." The miniature settings come in Nostalgic, Prehistoric, Futuristic, Fairy Tale, and Holiday themes which are irresistible to all ages. Each scene is signed and numbered. Custom orders are welcome. Please send $2 and a LSASE for brochure.

"J" DESIGNS

Collectible Miniatures
Price: $25 to $150, plus shipping
Dimensions: 1" & 1/2" scale
One-of-a-kind collectibles. All-media paintings and animals. Portraits from your photo. LSASE plus $1.50 for brochure and prices, etc.

REIS MINIATURE ART

Miniature Original Oil Paintings
Price: $35 to $100 ppd.
Dimensions: 1" x 1" to 3" x 5"
Miniature oil paintings by Albert J. Reis. Perfect for collectors with a passion for miniatures. Framed or unframed, landscapes, seascapes, natural themes. A wise investment.

Decorated Walls

WORKSHOP WISDOM

The homes magazines often show walls decorated by using a sponge to apply multiple colors. Kristin imitated the technique in her dollhouse but found it much more convenient to use an old toothbrush. Paint the wall as normal, then use the toothbrush to stipple on the second color, experimenting with different pressures until the result pleases.

KRISTIN OMRENG
SCARSDALE, NY

ROSALIE WHYEL MUSEUM OF DOLL ART

Collectible Miniatures
Price: prices vary
We have a continuously changing stock of collectible miniatures—dolls, furniture and accessories; antique and new. Please phone or FAX for our current list.

Workshop Wisdom Courtesy of *Nutshell News*—10/94

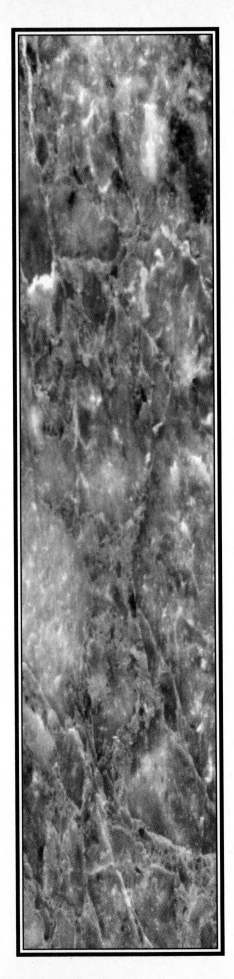

FASHION
SCALE

Accessories

Metal Roof

Make this Key West metal roof by marking and folding file folder card stock as shown. Glue the folded card to a stiff paper backing, then cover the whole roof with aluminum foil. Some old church roofs had the same appearance but were covered with copper sheet, in which case the roof should be painted a light verdigris green ... the same color as the Statue of Liberty. This particular roof was made for a Victorian style porch.

JOHN MOORE
LEHIGH ACRES, FL

Workshop Wisdom *Courtesy of* Nutshell News—8/94

ROYAL MINIATURES

Playscale Accessories
Price: $1.80 - $4.10
Shown are a few of the fashion scale pieces in our line. Wholesale only. Imported.

HOUSEWORKS, LTD.

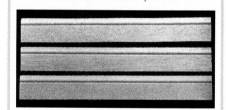

Baseboard Molding
Stock No.: 97042
Price: $4.25
Baseboard molding with groove on the back to accept hardwire for electrification. Wood. 3 pcs./pkg. Size: Playscale; 3/4"W x 1/8"D x 24"L.

Building Supplies

HOUSEWORKS, LTD.

Window Pediments
Stock No.: 97070
Price: $4.95
Each triangle shaped pediment unit has three sections unassembled. Wood. 5 units/pkg. Size: Playscale; 6"W x 1-1/2"H x 7/8"D.

HOUSEWORKS, LTD.

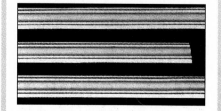

Crown Molding
Stock No.: 97047
Price: $6.95
Finely detailed crown molding. Wood. 3 pcs./pkg. Size: Playscale; 3/4"W x 1/2"D x 24"L.

HOUSEWORKS, LTD.

Crossbuck Exterior Door
Stock No.: 96012
Price: $18.50
Crossbuck exterior pre-hung door with nine-light window. Plexiglas and trim not included. Wood. Size: Playscale; 5-11/16"W x 12-5/16"H x 9/16"D. Fits opening: 5"W x 12"H x 3/8"D.

HOUSEWORKS, LTD.

Circlehead Double Casement Window

Stock No.: 95049
Price: $23.50
Circlehead double casement non-working window with interior trim. Wood. Plexiglas not included. Size: Playscale; 8"W x 10-1/8"H x 7/8"D. Fits irregular opening; 7-7/16"W x 9-7/8"H x 3/8"D.

HOUSEWORKS, LTD.

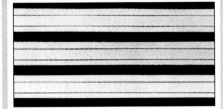

Door and Window Casing

Stock No.: 97041
Price: $3.55
Grooved wood trim for door and window casing. 3 pcs./pkg.
Size: Playscale; 1/2"W x 3/16"D x 24"L.

HOUSEWORKS, LTD.

Octagon Shingles

Stock No.: 97007
Price: $8.95
Shingle with corners cut off on one end for octagonal design. Can be reversed to use as square butt shingles. Wood. 300 pcs./pkg. Covers approximately 465 sq.in. with 1/4" in. overlap.
Size: Playscale; 1"W x 2"H x 1/16"D.

HOUSEWORKS, LTD.

Porch Post

Stock No.: 97030
Price: $9.25
Wood turned veranda type porch post. 4 pcs./pkg. Size: Playscale; 3/4"sq. x 13"H.

HOUSEWORKS, LTD.

Jamestown Exterior Door

Stock No.:96010
Price: $38.95
Jamestown style exterior door with pre-hung classic six-panel door. Sidelight windows have removable Plexiglas. Wood. Size: Playscale; 12-9/16"W x 13-3/16"H x 1-5/8"D. Fits opening 10"W x 12-7/16"H x 3/8"D. Trim not included.

HOUSEWORKS, LTD.

Palladian Exterior Door

Stock No.: 96015
Price: $20.95
Palladian exterior door with pre-hung 12-light door. Interior trim included. Plexiglas not included. Wood. Size: Playscale; 5-7/16"W x 13-1/4"H x 5/8"D. Fits irregular opening: 5"W x 13"H x 3/8"D.

HOUSEWORKS, LTD.

Palladian Window

Stock No.: 95014
Price: $15.50
Palladian style, 12-light, non-working window with interior trim. Wood. Plexiglas not included.
Size: Playscale; 4-1/2"W x 10-3/8"H x 7/8"D. Fits irregular opening: 4"W x 9-7/8"H x 3/8"D.

HOUSEWORKS, LTD.

Twelve-Light Window

Stock No.: 95024
Price: $9.50
Twelve-light, non-working window. Wood. Plexiglas and trim not included. Size: Playscale; 4-5/16"W x 8-5/16"H x 1/2"D. Fits opening: 4"W x 8"H x 3/8"D.

HOUSEWORKS, LTD.

Traditional Double-Hung Window

Stock No.: 95032
Price: $9.50
Traditional double-hung, non-working window with removable Plexiglas. Wood. Size: Playscale; 5-1/16"W x 8-9/16"H x 3/4"D. Fits opening: 4"W x 8"H x 3/8"D. Trim not included.

HOUSEWORKS, LTD.

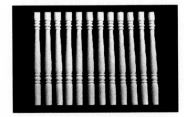

Porch Spindle

Stock No.: 97009
Price: $5.50
Wood turned spindle to fit 97011 pre-drilled railings. 12 pcs./pkg. Size: 5/16"W x 4-1/4"L; Playscale.

HOUSEWORKS, LTD.

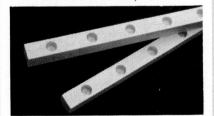

Pre-Drilled Railing

Stock No.: 97011
Price: $5.95
Top and bottom railings pre-drilled to accept 97009 porch spindles. Wood. 2 sets/pkg.
Size: 1/2"W x 1/2"H x 14"L; Playscale.

HOUSEWORKS, LTD.

Diamond Embellishments

Stock No.: 97001
Price: $2.59
Diamond-shaped wooden pieces for trim on shutters, etc. 50 pcs./pkg. Size: 9/16"H x 9/16"W; Playscale.

Dollhouse Plan Books

HOUSEWORKS, LTD.

**Playscale
Victorian
Townhouse
Planbook**

Stock No.: 93101
Price: $6.95
28 pages; fashion scale.
Author: Don
Saddlemire. Instructional
plans for fashion doll
Victorian Townhouse.
Includes four to seven
spacious rooms, a
closet, divided storage
drawer. Finished size:
26"W x 22"D x 58"H.

HOUSEWORKS, LTD.

Playscale Country House Planbook

Stock No.: 91201
Price: $6.95
24 pages; fashion scale. Author, Don Saddlemire.
Instructional plans for fashion doll Country
Farmhouse. Includes three to five spacious rooms,
gingerbread porch, full length closet, divided
storage drawer. Finished size: 26"W x 23"D x 46"H.

HOUSEWORKS, LTD.

**Playscale
Estate
Planbook**

Stock No.: 91401
Price: $6.95
32 pages; fashion
scale. Author, Don
Saddlemire.
Instructional plans for
fashion doll Estate
House. Includes five
huge rooms, two
closets and two
divided storage
drawers. Finished size:
48"W x 45"H x 24"D.

Kitchen Sinks

WORKSHOP WISDOM

Save those little jelly containers the next time you eat out. Trimmed around and painted gloss white, they can be set into your mini counter top for neat no-cost kitchen sinks. Completed with stylish mini chromed faucet, the unit will make the lady of the (doll) house proud.

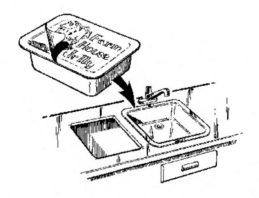

*MARYANN DOMINGUEZ
ALBUQUERQUE, NM*

Workshop Wisdom Courtesy of *Nutshell News—9/94*

Prices are approximate and subject to change

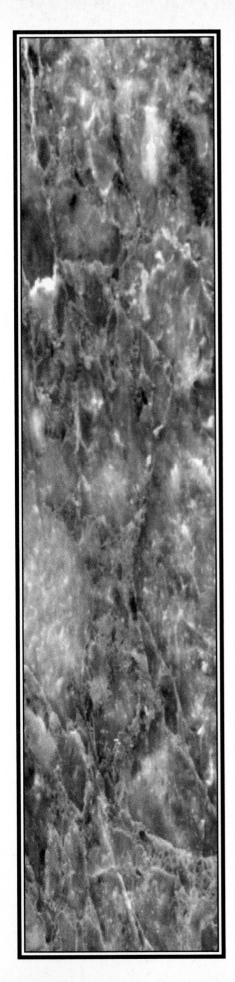

SMALLER
SCALE

½" Scale Accessories

CLARE-BELL BRASS WORKS

Candlesticks
Stock No.: 1270-110
Dimensions: 1/2" = 1' scale
Solid brass, gold-plated. Catalog, more than 200 items, $2. See your local independent miniatures dealer.

DONNA SMOLIK'S DESIGNS

Candy, Cookie & Food Designs
Price: $1.75 - $4.25 each.
Dimensions: 1", 1/2", 1/4" scales
Candies, fruits, vegetables, meats—slice your own with a single-edged razor blade. Can be used in 1", 1/2" or 1/4" scales.

LINDEN SWISS MINIATURES

Canning Jars
Stock No.: 730
Dimensions: 1/2" scale
One-quart size old-fashioned canning jars in 1/2" scale with simulated zinc lid. Three per package. American-made. See your local dealer.

LINDEN SWISS MINIATURES

Margarita Glasses
Stock No.: 752
Dimensions: 1/2" scale
Set of four glasses. Nice addition to your bar. Glasses have a frosted look. Instructions included to make glasses look crystal clear. American-made.

MÄRKLIN TRAINS

Märklin Z Trains
Stock No.: 15610 (full line includes other gauges)
Price: $14.95 (See your local dealer.)
Dimensions: Z scale 1:220
The smallest operating electric railway in the world. Märklin "Z" offers you the most complete line of Z gauge starter sets. locomotives, rolling stock, track and accessories.

ROYAL MINIATURES

1/2" Scale Accessories
Price: $1.50 - $3
Shown is a selection from our line of 1/2" scale porcelain, glassware and spatterware. Many other pieces and styles available. Customer designs are welcome!

LINDEN SWISS MINIATURES

"Evening for Two"
Stock No.: 726
Dimensions: 1/2" scale
Includes two each: dinner and salad plates, soup bowls, water and wine goblets, one bottle of wine and candles with holders in 1/2" scale. See your local dealer. All products are American-made.

JOIN A MINIATURES CLUB
...
OR START ONE!

½" Scale Building Supplies

GRANDT LINE PRODUCTS, INC.

1/2" Scale Chimney

Stock No.: 3926
Price: $3, plus shipping
Dimensions: 3"H x 11/16"W; 1/2" scale.
This is only one item in our 1/2" scale line of products. Molded in easy-to-work-with polystyrene plastic, they can be modified to suit any roof contour. Polystyrene plastic (red-brown).

GRANDT LINE PRODUCTS, INC.
1/2" Scale Windows and Doors

Price: $3-$4.75, plus shipping
Dimensions: 1/2" scale
These are nicely detailed in easy-to-work with grey polystyrene plastic. Working doors are cast separately from frames. All sets include window "glass." Use with 5/16" plywood walls.

GRANDT LINE PRODUCTS, INC.

1/2" Scale Diamond Window

Stock No.: 3919
Price: $4.25, plus shipping
This window is made of easily adaptable styrene plastic (grey). Window has both inside and outside frames and window "glass." Use with 5/16" plywood walls.

GRANDT LINE PRODUCTS, INC

1/2" Scale Architectural Details

Price: $1.95-$2.20, plus shipping
Dimensions: 1/2" scale
This trim is beautifully detailed grey polystyrene plastic for the discriminating miniaturist. Parts are easily adaptable with a hobby knife and liquid cement. Accepts paint easily.

HANDLEY HOUSE

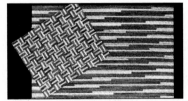

1/2 Scale
Pre-laid Hardwood Floors

Dimensions: 8" x 11"; 5" x 6"; 1/2" scale
US hardwood veneer, vinyl. These are carefully handcrafted floors on a flexible backing. Easily installed by trimming to size. Varnish or wax, etc., to suit. HH501-HH505 random length floors, $8.95; HH511-HH518 specialty and parquets, $8.95; HH522-HH525 vinyl checkerboard flooring, $6.95.

GRANDT LINE PRODUCTS, INC.

Wheels

Stock No.: 3909, 3910
Price: Four/$2
Plastic "wood spoke" wheels…baby buggy wheels in grey polystyrene plastic. 1/16" bore for axles. Use for buggies, wagons, caissons, etc. American-made.

HOUSEWORKS, LTD.

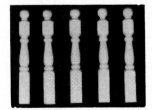

Newel Post

Stock No.: H7012
Price: $2.75
Dimensions: 1-3/4"H x 1/4" square
Six per polybag.

HOUSEWORKS, LTD.

Traditional "Americana" Door

Stock No.: H6004
Price: $7.25
Exterior door with eight raised door panels and four raised side panels. No acrylic, no interior trim. Size: 2-11/16"W x 4-3/16"H x 3/4"D. Fits opening: 1-17/32"W x 3-13/16"H x 5/16"D.

HOUSEWORKS, LTD.

Staircase Kit

Stock No.: H7000
Price: $16
Riser/stringer assembly. 13 treads, 13 balusters, two newel posts, one handrail. Adjustable to varying ceiling heights. Size: 5" ceiling height.

HOUSEWORKS, LTD.

Traditional Interior Door

Stock No.: H6007
Price: $6.95
Six-panel door for all interior door uses. Interior trim included. Size: 1-11/16"W x 3-9/16"H.
Fits opening: 1-1/2"W x 3-1/2"H x 5/16"D.

HOUSEWORKS, LTD.

24-Light Bay Window

Stock No.: H5008
Price: $14.95
Non-working bay features three 8-light windows with angled hood. No acrylic, no trim.
Size: 4-7/8"W x 3-7/16"H x 1"D.
Fits opening: 3-3/8"W x 2-1/2"H.

HOUSEWORKS, LTD.

Assorted Windows

Stock No.: H5043; H5032
Price: $14.50; $5.95
H5043 - Palladian Window - non-working French window with fan light pediment and sill. Includes acrylic and interior trim. Size: 1-15/16"W x 3-5/8"H x 3/8"D. Fits opening: 1-9/16"W x 3-7/16"H x 5/16"D.
H5032 - Traditional Non-Working Window - self-framing with six mullions and sill. Trim, acrylic. Size: 1-5/8"W x 3"H x 3/8"D.
Fits opening: 1-9/32"W x 2-25/32"H x 5/16"D.

HOUSEWORKS, LTD.

Louvered Shutters

Stock No.: H5025
Price: $3.50
Dimensions: 2-1/2"H x 1/2"W
Two per package.

HOUSEWORKS, LTD.

Classic French Doors

Stock No.: H6011
Price: $12.50
Classic double entry French doors with grids and acrylic panes. Hinged to operate separately. Size: 2-11/16"W x 3-7/8"H. Fits opening: 2-9/16"W x 3-13/16"H x 5/16"D.

HOUSEWORKS, LTD.

Dormer

Stock No.: H7002
Price: $8.95
Dimensions: 2-5/8"W x 3"H x 3-3/16"D
Unit includes dormer and one four-light shutter window. Designed for 45 degree pitch roof. No acrylic, no trim.

HOUSEWORKS, LTD.

Gold-Plated Brass Doorknob and Doorknob with Keyplate

Stock No.: H1114; H1116
Price: $3 each
H1114 - Doorknob with Keyplate - six pieces per package. H1116 - Doorknob - 12 pieces per package.

HOUSEWORKS, LTD.

Yorktown Door

Stock No.: H6014
Price: $9.75
Exterior six-panel door with sculpted doorcap and dentil molding. Interior trim included.
Size: 2-13/16"W x 4"H x 3/4"D.
Fits opening: 1-11/16"W x 3-3/4"H x 5/16"D.

HOUSEWORKS, LTD.

Victorian Door

Stock No.: H6013
Price: $14.50
Exterior six-panel door with low pitch hooded doorcap and scalloped transom. Includes acrylic and interior trim. Size: 2-5/8"W x 4-5/8"H x 3/4"D. Fits opening: 1-11/16"W x 4-5/32"H x 5/16"D.

HOUSEWORKS, LTD.

Victorian Non-Working Window

Stock No.: H5042
Price: $10.50
Features low pitch hooded cap with sculpted brackets. Includes acrylic, mullions and interior trim. Size: 1-15/16"W x 3-1/4"H x 3/4"D. Fits opening: 1-9/32"W x 2-25/32"H x 5/16"D.

HOUSEWORKS, LTD.

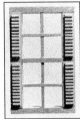

Standard 8-Light Window With Shutters

Stock No.: H5003
Price: $3.75
Standard 8-light window with shutters. No acrylic, no interior trim. Size: 1-13/16"W x 2-15/16"H.
Fits opening: 1-9/32"W x 2-25/32"H x 5/16"D.

HOUSEWORKS, LTD.

Veranda Corner Post

Stock No.: H7030
Price: $3.75
Dimensions: 6"L x 1/4"sq.
Four pieces per polybag.

HOUSEWORKS, LTD.

Shingles

Stock No.: H7004; H7005
Price: $5.25
H7004 - Square Butt Shingles - Cedar shingles, 400 per package. Covers approximately 76 square inches. Polybagged. Shingle size: 3/8"W x 5/8"H x 1/32"D.
H7005 - Fishscale Shingles - wooden half-circle butts. Shingle size: 3/8"W x 5/8"H x 1/32"D.

HOUSEWORKS, LTD

Traditional 4-Panel Door

Stock No.: H6001
Price: $4.95
Exterior door with four raised door panels and four section transom. No interior trim.
Size: 1-11/16"W x 3-7/8"H.
Fits opening: 1-9/16"W x 3-13/16"H x 5/16"D.

HOUSEWORKS, LTD.
"H" Scale Millwork

H7020 - Stair and Landing Handrail - Size: 1/8"W x 3/16"H x 12"L, $1.
H7041 - Door and Window Casing - 6 pcs./pkg. Size: 1/4"W x 1/16"D x 12"L, $2.75.
H7011 - Porch Railing Set - two sets per pkg. Size: 7/32"W x 3/16"H x 12"L, $3.75.
H7019 - Staircase Spindle - 12 pcs. per polybag. Size: 1-5/16"H x 3/32"W, $2.75.
H7009 - Porch Spindle - 12 pcs. per polybag. Size: 1-5/16"H x 3/32"W, $3.25.

HOUSEWORKS, LTD.

Standard Light Windows

Stock No.: H5024; H5023   Price: $4.75; $5.25
H5024 - Standard 12-Light Window - includes acrylic, no interior trim. Size: 1-7/16"W x 2-15/16"H x 3/8"D. Fits opening: 1-9/32"W x 2-25/32"H x 5/16"D. H5023 - Standard 8-Light Window - includes acrylic, no interior trim. Size: 1-3/8"W x 2-15/16"H x 3/8"D. Fits opening: 1-9/32"W x 2-25/32"H x 5/16"D.

HOUSEWORKS, LTD.
1/24th Scale "Brickmaster" Brick

Stock No.: H8207; H8206
Price: $5.25; $7.50
H8207 - "Brickmaster" Brick Corners - styrene plastic, common joint brick corner. Size: 3/4"H x 3/4"D x 11-1/2"L.
H8206 - "Brickmaster" Brick Sheet - styrene plastic, common brick sheet. Sheet size: 10-7/8"L x 5-5/16"W. Covers approximately 60 sq.in. Brick size: 3/32"W x 3/32"D x 5/16"L

HOUSEWORKS, LTD.

Victorian Bay Window

Stock No.: H5035
Price: $19.95
Detailed bay window with acrylic and mullions. No interior trim. Size: 2-5/16"W x 5-3/32"H x 1"D. Fits opening: 1-7/8"W x 2-13/16"H.

HOUSEWORKS, LTD.

Yorktown Non-Working Window

Stock No.: H5041
Price: $8.95
Sculpted pediment accented by dentil molding. Includes acrylic, interior trim and mullions.
Size: 2-1/16"W x 3-3/16"H x 5/8"D.
Fits opening: 1-9/32"W x 2-25/32"H x 5/16"D.

FOR FAST SERVICE, VISIT YOUR LOCAL MINIATURES SHOP

MODEL BUILDERS SUPPLY

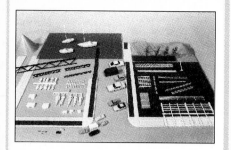

MBS Scratchbuilding Supplies

MBS has everything for 1/2" and 1/4" architectural scale modeling. Brick, stone, tile, siding, clapboard, interlock paving, stucco, wood shake, pantile, Spanish tile and shingle roofing. Skylights, windows, doors, window glass in bronze, grey, green, blue, pink. Very wide range of furniture and appliances. Extensive range of top quality permanent trees, foliage, grasses. many fences, railings, balustrades, Georgian columns, lattices, structural sections, trusses, plastic strips and sheets, paints, adhesives and many more specialized items and accessories.

PRECISION PRODUCTS

Plastic Veneer Styrene Sheets

Price: $7 per sheet
Dimensions: 15" square
30 styles in 1/2" scale. Brick, stone, siding, planking, roofing, etc. Made in USA.

1/2" Scale & Electrical Interior Decorating

BRODNAX PRINTS
1/2" Scale Wallpaper

Designed and printed just for smaller scales, this wonderful new collection offers a houseful of decorating choices. With patterns ranging from country casual to formal Regency to French provincial, you'll find the perfect setting for your fine 1/2" scale furnishings. Each pattern has companion prints in similar colors for a coordinated look that's especially important in smaller scales. Papers are shown in full color on the actual stock for easy ordering. Color catalog $1.

CIR-KIT CONCEPTS, INC .

12V Micro-Flame Bulb

Stock No.: CK1010-11
Price: $2.49
Smallest flame-tip bulb made. Only 0.079" in diameter. Comes with small gauge 12" wire. Works on 12 volts. Current 40 mA. Guaranteed 10,000 hours.

CIR-KIT CONCEPTS, INC.

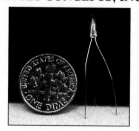

12V Micro-Flame Bulb

Stock No.: CK1010-12
Price: $1.79Same size and characteristics as CK1010-11. Constructed with solid wires. Use as replacement bulbs for light fixtures equipped with plug-in bulbs and receptacles.

CIR-KIT CONCEPTS, INC .

1.5V GOR Bulb
With 8" GreenWires

Stock No.: CK1020
Price: $1.20
Use 12 of these in series to make your own Christmas light string or use individually across a 1.5V source such as our CK1009G transformer. Small size makes them ideal for any scale. Each bulb consumes only 35 mA at 1.5 volts. Approximately 3/16" long by 3/32" diameter. Also available in colors.

J. HERMES

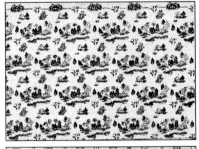

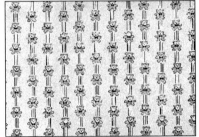

1/2" & 1/4" Scale Wallpaper

Price: $.35/sheet
Dimensions: 5-1/2" x 8-1/2"
Papers for the smaller scale interior and exterior.
Linoleums, flooring and wallpaper prints, bricks,
siding and roofing prints. More than 300 designs
and color combinations available. Printed paper.

1/2" Scale Furniture

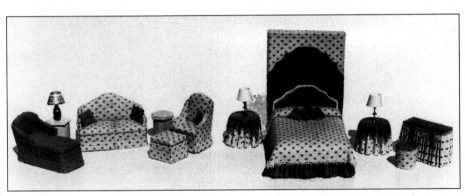

d. ANNE RUFF MINIATURES
1/2" Upholstered Furniture

Stock No.: Kit #6
Price: $16.95 plus shipping
Dimensions: 1/2" scale
Upholstered 1/2" furniture available as
finished pieces (priced from $10 to $30) in
wide choice of fabrics or customer-supplied
fabric; or as a kit (12 pieces as shown),
$16.95.

GREENLEAF PRODUCTS
19-Piece Furniture Kit

Stock No.: 9067
Price: $15.90
This 19-piece furniture kit is ideal for small
houses such as the Tiffani and Santa's
Cottage. Includes a living room, kitchen and
two bedrooms. All pieces are pre-cut with
easy-to-follow instructions. Create the
perfect decor for your house by staining,
painting or stenciling these all-wood items.

MOONLIGHT MINIATURES

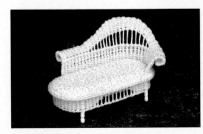

Wicker Furniture

Dimensions: 1/2" scale
Complete line of delicately handwoven wicker
furniture. Shown: Victorian Fainting Couch; $35 plus
shipping. Retail only. For price list send $2
(deductible from first order).

OMNIARTS OF COLORADO
Wicker Furniture Kits

Price: $2.50 - $9.25 kit
Wicker furniture kits of cotton cord (white or ecru), covered wire and wood. Pieces available include beds, vanities, stools, wall and pier mirrors, chairs, sofas, tables, decorative screens, fernery, planters, dog beds, baby carriages, high chairs, cribs, cradles, porch swings and more. Complete line for the entire hose will be available soon.

THE MINI MERCHANT

1/2" Upholstered Furniture

Price: $16 to $49
Dimensions: 1/2" scale
Overstuffed and cozy. Your fabric or mine. More styles available.

THREE BLIND MICE

1/2" Scale
Office Furniture and Supplies

Price: see below
Same price for finished or unfinished. $30, desk w/typing stand $25, desk without stand; $12, two-drawer file; $14, four-drawer file; $17, drafting table; $20, water cooler; $12, desk chair. Made of wood. Also available are 1/2" scale accessories shown on desk.

1/2" Scale & Houses Plans Displays

VISIT A MINIATURES MUSEUM ON YOUR VACATION

d. ANNE RUFF MINIATURES
1/2" Hat Box
Christmas Vignette

Dimensions: 6-1/2" x 4-1/2" x 5"; 1/2" scale
This delightful Christmas setting inside a 1/2" hat box is created from three separate 1/2" kits.
#11 - Hat Box Kit ($15.95) contains pre-cut foam core components;
#6 - Furniture Kit ($16.95) contains materials for 12 pieces of furniture;
#12CH- Fabric and Trim Kit ($32.95) contains all the fabric, trim and accessories to complete box as shown.

GREENLEAF PRODUCTS
The Fairfield

Stock No.: 8015
Price: $69.90 (Kit)
Dimensions: 20"H x 15"W x 16"D; 1/2" scale
Picture this table center—a beautifully detailed 1/2" scale dollhouse no bigger than a placemat. Make it perfectly Victorian in every aspect, even including a tower chamber, four fireplaces and a wrap-around porch. Six rooms, attic, secret tower room, shingles included. Pre-cut plywood.

Paint Brushes

For applying small amounts of paint or stain, pick up a packet of those inexpensive, throw-away, foam eye make-up brushes. They are ideal for dealing with miniature projects when a regular brush is really too large. At 49¢ for 12, they are a good investment.

JOANNE CLERES
ARVADA, CO

Workshop Wisdom
Courtesy of *Nutshell News—9/94*

HOUSEWORKS, LTD.
1/24th Scale Porch Shell Kit

Stock No.: H9004
Price: $25
1/2" scale. Porch Shell Kit by Houseworks, inspired by the best-selling book Porches Across America by Nancy Van Horn. Kit includes everything that you need to complete a 1/24th scale, free-standing porch shell. The pre-cut 3/8" and 1/4" cabinet-grade plywood ensures that your porch will be sturdy and last a lifetime. The complete instructions show in detail the easy assembly. The pre-cut openings for the windows and doors allow you to choose from a wide range of Houseworks components as well as accessories for the rest of the porch. Wood. These kits are great for club projects and workshops. Accessories and components not included. Finished size: 7-7/8"H x 6-7/8"W x 5"D.

HOUSEWORKS, LTD.
1/24th Scale Colonial Shell

Stock No.: H1003H
Price: $107
Dimensions: 16-1/2"H x 16-5/8"L x 8"D
Kit includes 3/8" cabinet-grade plywood, front opening designs, step-by-step instructions and a 3-in-1 Dollhouse Planbook for your reference. Write to Houseworks for information on the Houseworks Component Sets.

HOUSEWORKS, LTD.
1/24th Scale Georgian Shell

Stock No.: H1002H
Price: $120
Dimensions: 16-1/2"H x 16-5/8"L x 11-1/4""D
Kit includes 3/8" cabinet-grade plywood, front opening designs, step-by-step instructions and a 3-in-1 Dollhouse Planbook for your reference. Write to Houseworks for information on the Houseworks Component Sets.

Touching Up Plants

Finding that her old stock of potted plants and miniature paper flowers, which had been hidden away for years, had generally deteriorated and faded, this lady freshened things up with colored markers and got exceptional results. After touching up she "set" the color with a light coating of hair spray.

JANE STEINMETZ
MARINE CITY, MI

Workshop Wisdom
Courtesy of *Nutshell News—8/94*

HOUSEWORKS, LTD.
1/24th Scale Victorian Shell

Stock No.: H1001H
Price: $135
Dimensions: 16-1/2"H x 16-5/8"L x 11-1/4""D
Kit includes 3/8" cabinet-grade plywood, front opening designs, step-by-step instructions and a 3-in-1 Dollhouse Planbook for your reference. Write to Houseworks for information on the Houseworks Component Sets.

HOUSEWORKS, LTD.
1/24th Scale
Thornhill Shell

Stock No.: H9001
Price: $200
A classic dollhouse with the most prestigious and spacious interior on the market. Kit includes all plywood parts pre-cut to fit, 14 spacious rooms, quoins (pre-cut mitered corner blocks), dentil trim on front gable, chimneys, front steps, hinges and magnets.

d. ANNE RUFF MINIATURES

1/4" Scale Hat Box Vignette

This tiny box measures only 3-1/2" x 5" x 3-1/2", but it will hold a complete room setting. Three separate kits make up the complete box.
#21 - Hat Box Kit, $15.95;
#23 - Furniture Kit (includes both living room and bedroom furniture), $19.95;
Fabric and Trim Kits - #22P (pink), #22B (blue), #22G (green) (each includes pleated curtain), $24.95.

¼" & Smaller Scale Miniatures

DONNA SMOLIK'S DESIGNS

Candy, Cookie & Food Designs

Price: $1.75 - $4.25 each.
Dimensions: 1", 1/2", 1/4" scales
Candies, fruits, vegetables, meats—slice your own with a single-edged razor blade. Can be used in 1", 1/2" or 1/4" scales.

BRODNAX PRINTS
1/4" Scale Wallpaper

Designed and printed just for smaller scales, the 1/4" collection includes tile prints, borders and flooring for a houseful of coordinated wallpapers. Patterns range from delicate pastels in the Country Cottage Collection to cute nursery prints to dramatic jewel-tone Victorian motifs. Each pattern has matching companion papers in similar colors. Papers are shown in full color on the actual stock, so it's easy to tell exactly what you're ordering. Color catalog, $1.

Prices are approximate and subject to change

THE DUCK POND

Noah's Ark

Price: $30 plus shipping
Dimensions: 1/4" and up
Painted or unpainted miniature woodcarvings of Noah's Ark with large selection of birds and animals. Retail and wholesale. For more information send LSASE. Assembled, unfinished, $15. Completely finished price $30.

DURA-CRAFT, INC.
Old West Village

Stock No.: OW955
Price: See your dealer
Dimensions: HO scale (approx 1/8"=1')
These kits are perfect for miniatures and railroad enthusiasts. Include pre-cut wooden structures, fancy silk-screened windows and gingerbread trim, precut window trim and shakes. Ten pieces include: mansion, hotel, blacksmith shop, sheriff office, train depot, engine house, water tower, train trestle, wood shed and outhouse. Easy-to-follow instructions.

DURA-CRAFT, INC.
Old Towne Village

Stock No.: OT950
Dimensions: HO scale (approx. 1/8"=1')
Perfect for the miniature and railroad enthusiasts of all ages. Delightful village setting. Eight pieces including barn, church, two houses, school, store, water wheel and covered bridge. Windows, trim, shakes and fencing included. All wood structures, pre-cut pieces for easy assembly. Easy-to-follow instructions.

GRANDT LINE PRODUCTS, INC.
1/4" scale Architectural Details

Price: $1.25-$4, plus shipping
Dimensions: 1/4" scale
Super detailed structural parts and accessories for the discriminating smaller scale miniaturist. Most castings are in grey styrene plastic…easy to adapt with a hobby knife and liquid cement. Accepts paint easily. Polystyrene plastic.

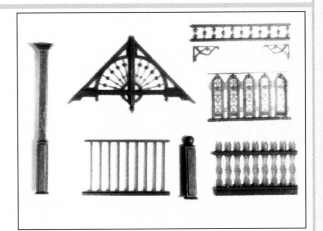

GRANDT LINE PRODUCTS, INC.
1/4" Scale Windows and Doors

Price: $1.25-$4, plus shipping
Dimensions: 1/4" scale
Super detailed structural parts and accessories for the discriminating smaller scale miniaturist. Most castings are in grey styrene plastic…easy to adapt with a hobby knife and liquid cement. Accepts paint easily. Polystyrene plastic.

GRANDT LINE PRODUCTS, INC.
HO Scale Structure Details

Price: $1.25-$4, plus shipping
Dimensions: 1:87 scale (HO)
Architectural and detail parts for the miniaturist in smaller scales. Items show super detail, down to wood grain on "wood" parts. Cast in adaptable polystyrene plastic.

GREENLEAF PRODUCTS

The Greenleaf Town

Stock No.: 8018
Price: $33.90
Dimensions: 1/4" scale
Greenleaf has taken their ever popular village additions and created a scenic "Town" that will make any 1/4" scale train layout more authentic. Pre-cut Luan plywood kit comes complete with all the detail needed to achieve this effect. Our "Town" features a General Store, Train Depot, Firehouse, Bandstand (gazebo) and our newest additions, a Library and Sweet Shop. Complete with easy-to-read instructions and our Greenleaf warranty. Approximately 1/4" scale.

OCTOBER IS NATIONAL DOLLHOUSE AND MINIATURES MONTH! STOP BY YOUR LOCAL SHOP!

GREENLEAF PRODUCTS

The Greenleaf Sweetshop & Library

Stock No.: 8027
Price: $17.90
Dimensions: 1/4" scale
The Sweetshop and Library are new additions to expand the Greenleaf Village or to use individually. They are ideal for use in train layouts or for Christmas decor. The stately Library with columns and the cute sweetshop bring added dimensions to the Greenleaf Village setting.

ITTY BITTY BITS

1/4" Victorian Living Room Set

Dimensions: 1/4" scale
The elegance of days gone by in 1/4" scale. Handcrafted wood construction with fabric upholstery. A variety of finishes and fabrics available. Set includes sofa, chair and coffee table. $40 for all three pieces.

GREENLEAF PRODUCTS

Greenleaf Village

Stock No.: 8016
Price: $33.90
Dimensions: see below
The Greenleaf Village is as cute as can be in Christmas settings, works great as individual gift boxes or display boxes and also has applicability for use with O trains. All six buildings are beautifully designed and include a church, school, carriage house, store, Tudor and scaled down Arthur dollhouse replica, charming and quaint! Approximately 1/4" scale, however, not true to scale. 1/8" die-cut plywood.

ITTY BITTY BITS

1/4" Four Poster Bedroom Set

Dimensions: 1/4" scale
Classic design in 1/4" scale. Handcrafted wood construction. Comes undressed to be customized to match your setting. A variety of finishes available. Set includes bed, armoire and chest. Non-working drawers. $45 for all three pieces.

GREENLEAF PRODUCTS

Greenleaf Village Station And Store

Stock No.: 8025
Price: $17.90
Dimensions: see below
These two little charmers are perfect for Christmas decorating and in train layouts. The Village Station and Country Emporium are very easy to build and were designed to accompany our popular Greenleaf Village kit. Use individually or to expand the village. Approximately 1/4" scale, however, not true to scale. 1/8" die-cut plywood.

GREENLEAF PRODUCTS

The Greenleaf Village Firehouse and Bandstand

Stock No.: 8026
Price: $17.90
Dimensions: see below
The Firehouse and Bandstand can be used to expand our popular Greenleaf Village set or displayed individually. Use them in a winter setting for Christmas decor or as part of your train layout. Typical of firehouses and bandstands in small towns across the country, this firehouse was immortalized in a Norman Rockwell painting. Approximately 1/4" scale. 1/8" die-cut plywood, cardboard shingles and trim.

ITTY BITTY BITS

1/4" Sleigh Bedroom Set

Dimensions: 1/4" scale
Perfect for your country or colonial home. Handcrafted wood construction. Comes undressed to be customized to match your setting. A variety of finishes available. Set includes bed, armoire and chest. Non-working drawers. $45 for all three pieces.

ITTY BITTY BITS

1/4" Baby Grand Piano

Dimensions: 1/4" scale
You can almost hear the music coming from this wonderfully detailed piano. Handcrafted wood construction. White or Black finish. $25 for piano and stool.

ITTY BITTY BITS

1/4" Dining Room Set

Dimensions: 1/4" scale
The perfect finishing touch for your 1/4" house. Handcrafted wood construction with fabric upholstery. A variety of finishes and fabrics available. Set includes table, four chairs, buffet and hutch. Non-working drawers. $55 for all seven pieces.

ITTY BITTY BITS

1/4" Southwest Set

Dimensions: 1/4" scale
Rustic Southwestern cut-out design is perfect for your tiny adobe dwelling. Handcrafted wood construction. A variety of finishes available. Set includes bench, chair and table. $30 for all three pieces.

ITTY BITTY BITS

1/4" Contemporary Living Room Set

Dimensions: 1/4" scale
This classic design can work in most any setting. Handcrafted wood construction with fabric upholstery. A variety of finishes and fabrics available. Set includes sofa, chair and coffee table. $40 for all three pieces.

ITTY BITTY BITS

1/4" Nursery Set

Dimensions: 1/4" scale
Brighten up the nursery with bunnies and teddy bears. Handcrafted wood construction. A variety of finishes available. Set includes crib, dresser and changing table. $35 for all three pieces.

ITTY BITTY BITS

1/4" Chaise

Dimensions: 1/4" scale
The perfect spot to curl up with a good book. Handcrafted wood construction with carved legs and fabric upholstery. A variety of finishes and fabrics available. $15.

J. HERMES
1/4" Scale Plastic Furniture Sets

Stock No.: PF-1
Price: $1.99 per set
Dimensions: 1/4" to 1" scale
Five different sets, "wood tone" den, bedroom, dining room, kitchen and "white" bathroom. Included is a sheet on "kit bashing" to make different pieces.

LINDEN SWISS MINIATURES

Tumbler

Stock No.: LSM-323
Dimensions: 1/4" scale
Set of four glasses for iced tea, milk, or bar drinks. American-made. See your local dealer.

LINDEN SWISS MINIATURES

Wine Glasses

Stock No.: LSM-333
Dimensions: 1/4" Scale
Set of four wine glasses. American-made. See your local dealer.

LINDEN SWISS MINIATURES

Wine Bottle

Stock No.: LSM-336
Dimensions: 1/4" scale
One taper-shaped wine bottle. Clear. American-made. See your local dealer.

LINDEN SWISS MINIATURES

Wine Bottle

Stock No.: LSM-337
Dimensions: 1/4" scale
One clear blunt-shaped wine bottle. American-made. See your local dealer.

MODEL BUILDERS SUPPLY

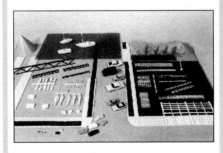

MBS Scratchbuilding Supplies

MBS has everything for 1/2" and 1/4" architectural scale modeling, down to 1:1000. Brick, stone, tile, siding, clapboard, interlock paving, stucco, wood shake, pantile, Spanish tile and shingle roofing. Skylights, windows, doors, window glass in bronze, grey, green, blue, pink. Very wide range of furniture and appliances. Extensive range of top quality permanent trees, foliage, grasses. Many fences, railings, balustrades, Georgian columns, lattices, structural sections, trusses, plastic strips and sheets, paints, adhesives and many more specialized items and accessories.

PARKER HOUSE MINIATURES

1/4" Scale Victorian Houses

Stock No.: 55
"Aunt Julia's House," finished outside. All houses are center-split and electrified. Windows, doors and finishing materials for inside and outside are available. Made of 1/8" birch plywood throughout. Available as shells or finished houses. Other houses available: "Shannon House," "Tracy House," "Court St. House," "Hale House" and two and three-story display houses.

Prices are approximate and subject to change

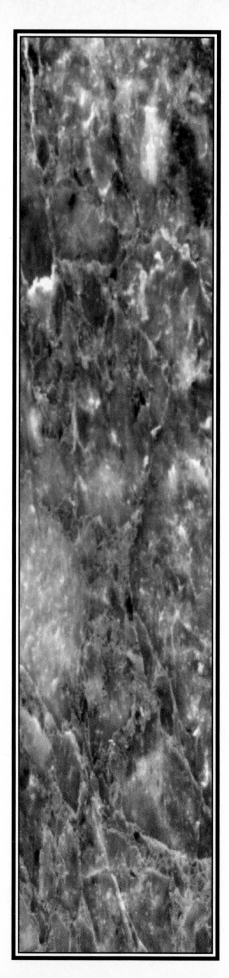

PUBLICATIONS & PLANS

Books for Collectors

DOUGLESS, LTD.

Dougless Guide to Appraisal and Record-Keeping

Price: $4 plus 75¢ postage
Dimensions: 8" x 16"
Author: Dougless Strickland Bitler. Details for keeping records, protecting your heirs, how-to for appraisals, donations, insurance, resale and more. 8" by 16" cardstock folded into eight panels, worksheet enclosed. Ask your dealer or order from Dougless, Ltd. Also distributed by Dee's Delights.

DOUGLESS, LTD.

Dougless Guides

Price: see below
Dimensions: see below
Author: Dougless Strickland Bitler, Nutshell News review: "For a miniaturist planning an authentic setting, guides for the period are indispensable (and) proof there's nothing frivolous about your hobby." Only source for all details of North American home: 10,000 terms, 28,000 sold since 1980. First decision: kitchen, which and when? (open hearth/iron stove/white range/wood tubs/dry sink/pump/faucets) Thirty more categories. Guides are 8-1/2" by 16" cardstock folded in eight panels. Full set (nine guides/one digest/one tartan case), $39 ($2 postage). Mention this ad and get a full set for $35 ppd. $4 each (60¢ postage), any three $12 ppd. Ask your dealer or order from Dougless, Ltd. Also distributed by Dee's Delights.
Guides available:
I. Oriental - Part One, Ten Centuries (Home and Background)
I. Oriental - Part Two, Ten Centuries (Art and Symbolism)
II. Tudor and the Twenties (16C and 20C)
III. Early Colonial, 1607-1699
    Stuart
    Puritans
    Pilgrims
IV. Late Colonial, 1700-1776
    Williamsburg
    Georgian
V. Federal 1783-1829
VI. Empire, 1830-1860
    Greek Revival
    Antebellum
    Early Victorian
VII. Mid-Victorian, 1850-1880
VIII. Late Victorian, 1880-WWI
    Edwardian

DOUGLESS, LTD.

Ask Dougless
Volumes I, II, III, IV, V

Price: $9.95 plus $2.55 Postage. ($12.50) Two for $22; three for $33; four for $44; five for $55.
Dimensions: 8-1/2" x 11"; 100-plus pages
Publisher: Dee's Delights. Author: Dougless Strickland Bitler. Nutshell News review: "Done in the same breezy style as her popular workshops and columns, entertaining as well as edifying, designed specifically for the miniaturist."
Volume I: Kitchen, bathrooms, wallpaper, windows, doors, styles and more.
Volume II: Lighting (candle, kerosene, gas, electric), china patterns, fireplace/furnace, designs and more.
Volume III: Illustrated charts: kitchens and baths (1609-1920s); cabinetmakers: Chippendale, Hepplewhite, etc.; architecture examples 1500-1918; much more.
Volume III reviews: Nutshell News: "Hurrah! It's more of the same—invaluable reference—indexed wealth of information." Miniature Collector: "Facts in a social as well as historical context—leavened with Dougless' considerable good humor." Ask your dealer or order from Dougless, Ltd. Also distributed by Dee's Delights.
Volume IV: More of the same plus "The 20th Century & How It Grew."
Volume V: Hot off the press!

DOUGLESS, LTD.

Dougless Weed Society
Join
DOUGLESS WEED SOCIETY
(No dues, no meetings, no obligations)
Cloisonne pin, membership card
NEWSLETTER, $5.75 (2000 word text plus historical trivia, puzzles, etc.)
NEWSLETTER ONLY, $2.50 ppd.
(published by Dougless Ltd.)

ROSALIE WHYEL
MUSEUM OF DOLL ART

Books For Collectors

Price: prices vary
Basic volumes and how-to's (new and occasional out of print) on miniatures of all types. Write, phone, or FAX for list of titles in stock.

EMF PUBLISHING

Dolls House Handbook

An annual reference guide to dolls house shops and museums containing dolls houses and miniatures around the world. Listed in each description are the name, address, telephone number, contact, parking facilities and much, much more. A must for the miniatures enthusiast.

CIR-KIT CONCEPTS, INC.

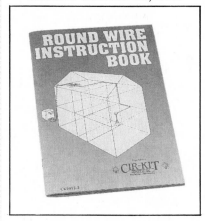

Cir-Kit Concepts Installation Instructions

Stock No.: see below
Price: see below
These books provide detailed and concise instructions for both tape and round wiring methods. Contain master layout drawings and instructions on the installation of all electrical components. Provide many shortcuts and money-saving ideas. Published by Cir-Kit Concepts, Inc.
Tape Wiring, CK1015, $3.95;
Round Wiring, CK1015-2, shown $4.65.
Shipped first class.

How-To

ALICE ZINN

How-To Booklets

Price: $5 ea. plus 55¢ postage ea.
Dimensions: 1/12 scale
Oriental Ornaments - 27 pp. Patterns and instructions for kimono, Chinese pin cushion, chopsticks and more.
No Sew Clothes - 24 pp. Patterns and instructions for folded shirt, leather jacket, vest, tie set and more.
Shoe It Yourself - Patterns and instructions for men's and women's slippers, children's bunny slippers, canvas Chinese shoes, saddle shoes, and penny loafers; Shoe It Yourself, Volume 2 - 19 pp. Leather boots, sandals, high-heeled clogs, tennis shoes, baby shoes and two different shoe boxes.
Open Sesamini - 24 pp. Patterns and instructions for purse, checkbook, key, keycase, wallet, attache case, luggage set and sofa bed, all of which open and close.
Petite Pampered Pets - 16 pp. Accessories for your mini furry friends include patterns and instructions for carrying case, leash, collars, toys and more.
Shoot It Yourself - Professional photographer offers 16 pp. of text and photos to assist you in taking better photos of your miniatures.

BETTY LAMPEN KNITTING BOOKS

Knitting Pattern Books.

A collection of 3 books consisting of "Sweaters for Teddy Bears," "Miniature Sweaters Book I," and "Miniature Pullovers." Patterns, diagrams and photos help you through each project.

DEE'S DELIGHTS, INC.

Basic Landscaping in Miniature

Stock No.: BOY138
Price: $6.49
Dimensions: 16 pages
Author: Dot & Candi Moore. Learn landscaping techniques — how to make shrubs, trees, ground covers, elevations, ponds, vines and much more. See your local dealer.

DEE'S DELIGHTS, INC.

Millie's FIMO Notebook

Stock No.: BOY137
Price: $5.49
Dimensions: 16 pages
Author: Millie Beacham. Contains basic, step-by-step illustrations for working with Fimo modeling compound. A must-have! See your local dealer.

DORSETT PUBLICATIONS, INC.

A Cabinetmaker's Guide For Dollhouse Furniture

Price: $8 each volume (except Vol. 8, $10)
A 10-volume edition of miniatures designs by the late Helen Dorsett. Each volume contains numerous detailed scale drawings, photographs and instructions by James Dorsett, prepared in a handy 8-1/2" x 11" loose-leaf format.

DESIGN TECNICS MINIATURES

The Dollhouse Builder's Handbook

Price: $7.95
Dimensions: 52 pages
Written and illustrated by Fred Stephenson, author of "The Architect's Angle" for Nutshell News, this thorough reference book covers dollhouse construction, exterior treatments, interior finishing, electrification, and much more.

GREENBERG BOOKS,
A DIVISION OF KALMBACH PUBLISHING CO.

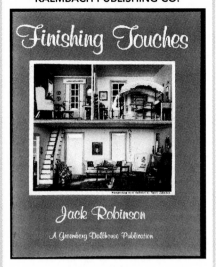

Finishing Touches

Stock No.: 10-6600
Price: $7.95 plus shipping
Dimensions: 8-1/2" x 11"; 64 pages
Learn how to create lightweight, realistic bricks and concrete blocks, wooden floors and simple but realistic trim to beautify and individualize any dollhouse. 15 b&w photos and 40 illustrations. By Jack Robinson. Softbound. $3 shipping for 4th class (or $4.50 UPS, continental US only); add $5 for Canada; other foreign, add $10.

GREENBERG BOOKS,
A DIVISION OF KALMBACH PUBLISHING CO.

How to Build Miniature Furniture and Room Settings

Stock No.: 10-7780
Price: $9.95 plus shipping
Dimensions: 8-1/2" x 11"; 72 pages
Standard miniature kits become finely-crafted furniture with the step-by-step instructions in this favorite guide. Learn to create life-like period rooms from kit materials or from scratch. 132 b&w photos. By Judy Beals. Softbound. $3 shipping for 4th class (or $4.50 UPS, continental US only); add $5 for Canada; other foreign, add $10.

GREENBERG BOOKS,
A DIVISION OF KALMBACH PUBLISHING CO.

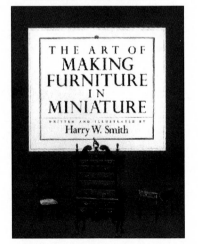

The Art of Making Furniture in Miniature

Stock No.: 10-7825
Price: $29.95 plus shipping
Dimensions: 8-1/2" x 11"; 320 pages
A comprehensive guide to making miniature furniture. Provides step-by-step instructions. Written in clear language and accompanied by detailed photographs and line drawings. 450 b&w and 16 color photos. 100-plus diagrams. By Harry Smith. Perfect-bound. $3 shipping for 4th class (or $4.50 UPS, continental US only); add $5 for Canada; other foreign, add $10.

GREENBERG BOOKS,
A DIVISION OF KALMBACH PUBLISHING CO.

Workshop Wisdom Dollhouse Crafting Tips from Nutshell News

Stock No.:, 10-7745
Price: $9.95 plus shipping
Dimensions: 8-1/2" x 11"; 64 pages
Favorite tips and techniques from readers explain how to construct furniture, roofs, knickknacks, people, tools, curtains, eating utensils and more. Each idea is simply and clearly illustrated. 218 illustrations. Compiled by Kathleen Zimmer Raymond. Illustrated by Jim Newman. Softbound. $3 shipping for 4th class (or $4.50 UPS, continental US only); add $5 for Canada; other foreign, add $10.

Prices are approximate and subject to change

HOUSEWORKS, LTD.

Everything You Wanted to Know About Dollhouses but Didn't Know Who to Ask

Stock No.: 1008
Price: $9.95

56 pages. Author: Nancy Van Horn. An instructional guide to finishing a dollhouse or miniature project. Includes a sequence of steps to finishing a dollhouse and a section by section format of instructions for shingling, applying clapboard, etc. Written for the novice or the more accomplished miniaturist.

HOUSEWORKS, LTD.

Craft Designs

Stock No.: 1006
Price: $4.95

16 pages; 1" scale. Author Rebecca Zimpher. Instructional book showing holiday and year-round craft designs using popular Houseworks Miniature Components.

KALMBACH PUBLISHING CO.

ABC's of Dollhouse Finishing

Stock No.: 12134
Price: $19.95 plus shipping
Dimensions: 8-1/4" x 10-3/4"; 150 photos
Dollhouse expert Barbara Warner uses five popular dollhouse kits to illustrate construction and finishing techniques. From roofing to wallpapering, step-by-step instructions guide you to success. In specific sections such as finishing formulas, gluing procedures, landscaping and tools, Warner provides insider tips to help you enhance your finishing techniques.$3 shipping for 4th Class (or $4.50 UPS, continental US. only); add $5 for Canada; other foreign, add $10.

KALMBACH PUBLISHING CO.

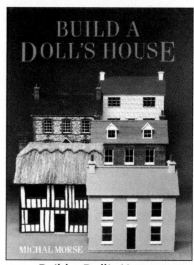

Build a Doll's House

Stock No.: 12130
Price: $19.95 plus shipping
Dimensions: 8-1/2" x 11"; 112 pages
Creating your ideal doll's house is easy with "Build a Doll's House." Clear woodworking instructions and step-by-step sketches show every stage of construction from planning through wiring and decorating. 52 color photos and hundreds of illustrations capture the exterior's and interior's close-up details. Available in the US only. $3 shipping for 4th Class (or $4.50 UPS, continental US only).

KALMBACH PUBLISHING CO.

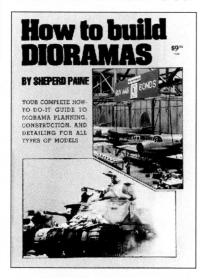

How to Build Dioramas

Stock No.: 12047
Price: $14.95 plus shipping
Dimensions: 8-1/4" x 11-1/4"; 104 pages
Weathering techniques, painting figures and shadow box construction are some of the topics master modeler Sheperd Paine covers in his book. He explains in 104 pages how he designs, plans and builds his dioramas from the ground up. The book includes four projects that illustrate techniques which you can use in your next miniatures project. Softbound. $3 shipping for 4th class (or $4.50 UPS, continental US only); add $5 for Canada; other foreign, add $10.

KIMBERLY HOUSE MINIATURES

Dollhouses to Dream Houses— Book 3

Price: $6.95
Featuring the Beaumont, the Willowcrest, and the Emerson Row House. All enhanced beyond the manufacturer's dreams. Full of photos and diagrams.

KIMBERLY HOUSE MINIATURES

Dream on with Kimberly House

Price: $6.25
Full of photos and diagrams to guide you. Several projects that you can copy or redesign for your dollhouse setting. Instructions for making water, trees, patios, streams, rockery, plants, flowers, lawn, and contour landscaping. Exciting concepts to enhance entryways to dollhouses.

KIMBERLY HOUSE MINIATURES
Kimberly Corner
Dimensions: 24 pages
A bi-monthly paper for the miniature crafter. 24 pages of fun and miniature projects. The ever popular K.C. Project Insert. Write for a free trial copy.

KITTY MACKEY'S
RELATIVE DIMENSIONS

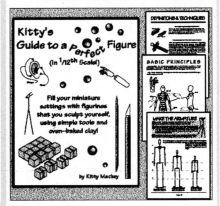

QUAD COMPANY

The Complete Guide to tiny turnings
Stock No.: 5000
Price: $5.50
Dimensions: 20 pages
An instruction manual describing the complete line of "tiny turnings" components in 1/4", 1/2" and 1" scale. Highlights kits available and provides ideas for original projects.

Figure Sculpting Book
Price: $22.50; plus $2.50 shipping (US), $4 (Canadian), $7 (Foreign)
Dimensions: 8-1/2" x 11" - 50 pages
In Kitty's Guide to a Perfect Figure (in 1/12th Scale!) I.G.M.A. Artisan Kitty Mackey shares her techniques for sculpting realistic FIMO figures. Step-by-step instructions, abundantly illustrated with 62 b/w photos and dozens of drawings. Please see ad in Dollhouse Dolls & Doll Accessories for photos of figures.

N.A.M.E.

Join a club and share!

The National Association

of Miniature Enthusiasts.

130 N. Rangeline Rd.

Carmel, IN 46032

(317) 571-8094

Catalogs

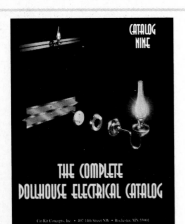

CIR-KIT CONCEPTS, INC.
Cir-Kit Concepts Miniatures
Electrical Catalog #9
Price: $4 (shipped first class)
The most expansive and detailed miniature electrical catalog ever published. Provides photos and in-depth descriptions of all Cir-Kit electrical items. Includes wide variety of hard-to-find light bulbs, miniature tools, lighting fixtures and electrical accessories. The complete reference guide for all things electric.

ELECT-A-LITE

Information Sheets
Our color sheets showing all our kits, components and lamps are free. Just call 1-800-EAL-KITS and leave us your name and address. Elect-A-Lite offers everything you need to wire a miniature's project in either Single Foil Tape or Double Tapewire in Myular. You'll find all our products are Guaranteed and most are molded by us.

KALMBACH PUBLISHING CO.

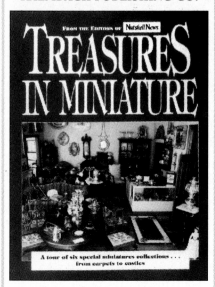

Treasures in Miniature

Stock No.: 12113
Price: $16.95 plus shipping
Dimensions: 8-1/2" x 11-1/2"; 104 pages
A tour of six outstanding private miniature collections provides a fascinating, detailed look at some of the finest work by contemporary miniatures artists. Each chapter focuses on a different collection, providing extensive information about the items shown in each photo. 120-plus color photos. From the editors of Nutshell News. Perfect-bound. $3 shipping for 4th class (or $4.50 UPS, continental US only); add $5 for Canada; other foreign, add $10.

KIMBERLY HOUSE MINIATURES

"Not Just a Catalog"

Price: $4
This catalog contains ideas, tips, and projects. Many photos and diagrams to entice you. (You will also find Kimberly products in this catalog).

SANDY'S LACE AND TRIMS

Lace and Trims Catalog

Large selection of antique and new lace and trims. Six sizes silk ribbon, silk pleating, cottons, silks, wools, batiste and wide variety of mini-prints. Also bunka, crystals, dolls, patterns, hair, watch cases, straw, bear fur, knitting and crochet needles, brasses, trunk kits. And much more. Catalog $2.

THE DOLLHOUSE FACTORY

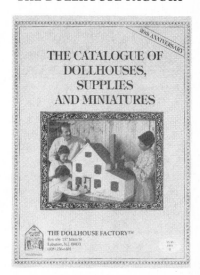

The Catalogue of Dollhouses, Supplies and Miniatures

Price: $5.50
Dimensions: 120 pages
This 120 page publication by Robert V. Dankanics features more than 4,300 items plus helpful hints on how the professionals do it. Not only is there a vast array of products featured but also very useful information on how to use them. Softcover.

PRECISION PRODUCTS

Catalog/Handbook

Price: $2 post paid Catalog/handbook of mold making rubbers, casting materials, dyes and fillers, etc., $PINcaster and accessories. Where small quantities have very small prices.
Made in USA.

PRECISION PRODUCTS

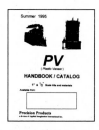

Catalog/Handbook

Price: $3 post paid
Catalog/handbook of plastic veneer construction and materials. Includes pack of either 1" or 1/2" samples. Made in USA.

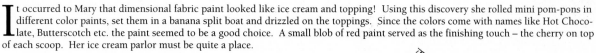

I Scream Ice Cream!

It occurred to Mary that dimensional fabric paint looked like ice cream and topping! Using this discovery she rolled mini pom-pons in different color paints, set them in a banana split boat and drizzled on the toppings. Since the colors come with names like Hot Chocolate, Butterscotch etc. the paint seemed to be a good choice. A small blob of red paint served as the finishing touch – the cherry on top of each scoop. Her ice cream parlor must be quite a place.

MARY KINLOCH
CLEARWATER, FL

 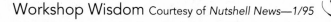

Dollhouse Plan Books

GREENLEAF PRODUCTS
Dollhouses To Dream Houses, Book 1

Price: $7.40
Thirty-six pages containing 103 detailed photos and 35 step-by-step diagrams. Also included are interior decorating ideas, exterior decorating techniques, creative customizing and remodeling, easy instructions for lighting and wiring, and product sources. All photographs were from our customers' dollhouses at different stages of completing their Dream Houses. All this and more...See your dealer or write Kimberly House.

Subscribe to *Nutshell News* and learn how you can make miniatures yourself!
Call toll free:
(800) 446-5489

GREENLEAF PRODUCTS
Dollhouses to Dream Houses, Book 2

Price: $8.00
Seventy-two page, softcover catalog containing 118 detailed photos and 75 step-by-step diagrams. Also includes information on platforms and their value, gluing chapter and chart, and landscaping techniques. Different houses than Book 1. See your dealer or write Kimberly House. Also available: Book I-$7.40 and Book III-$7.10.

HANDLEY HOUSE
Handley House Dollhouse Plan Book

Stock No.: HH5900
Price: $9.95
Dimensions: 105 pp.
Three completely different house plans are included in this 105-page book. Packed with helpful new hints and professional building tips, these books guide you step-by-step, using 172 photographs, illustrations and complete easy-to-follow instructions for both the novice and master builder.

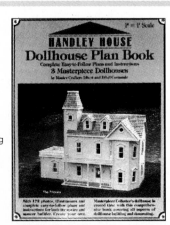

HOUSEWORKS, LTD.

Birdhouses Across America

Stock No.: 1009
Price: $5.95
13 pages. Author: Bill Laffler. The step-by-step planbook includes three uniquely styled houses: the Cottage, the Victorian or the Gothic Revival. Included are instructions to convert the birdhouses to 1/2" scale dollhouses.

HOUSEWORKS, LTD.

Porches Across America

Stock No.: 1007 Price: $5.95
12 pages; 1" scale. Author: Nancy Van Horn. Instructional book that shows you how to create a free-standing porch scene. The book includes a revolutionary full size iron-on cutting pattern that allows you to iron your cutting pattern directly onto your wood.

HOUSEWORKS, LTD.

Houseworks Dollhouse Plan Book

Stock No.: 1001 Price: $5.95
36 pages; 1" scale. Author: Garth Close. Builds three complete houses (Georgian, Victorian and Colonial). Has over 100 step-by-step photos, diagrams, patterns and decorating tips to build three quality dollhouses. #1 Bestseller in Plan Books.

DESIGN TECNICS MINIATURES

Architect's Choice Dollhouse Plans

Seven open-back designs for 3/8" wood construction in 1" scale are designed by Fred Stephenson, author of "The Architect's Angle" in Nutshell News. Each set of shell plans includes suggestions for exterior treatment. Designs #3 (shown) and #7 are $7.95, and the other five are $5.95.

Dollhouse Plans [plans only]

FOR FAST SERVICE, VISIT YOUR LOCAL MINIATURES SHOP

Dolls & Doll-making

WEE THREE

SCALE
KNITTING & CROCHETING
FOR THE
CONNOISSEUR IN MINIATURE

BY JEANNE BELL

WITH 1" to 1' SCALE PATTERNS
USING
SCALE YARNS and TOOLS

Scale Knitting and Crocheting for the Connoisseur in Miniature

Price: $7.50
Dimensions: 1" to 1' scale
Expert status is certainly not required, but you should be familiar with knitting and crocheting terms to complete the patterns in this book. Included are designs for three afghans, two bedspreads, a pillow, a toy, a pullover sweater and an infant shell sacque—all in accurate 1" to 1' scale. 23 pages. Supplies catalog included upon request. Postage $2.00.

DORSETT PUBLICATIONS, INC.

The Scale Cabinetmaker

Stock No.: L-150
Price: $27; one year, four issues
Since 1976, the mini scale modeler's quarterly. From beginners to advanced. Tool use and workbench techniques. Furniture, roombox and house plans. The hobby how-to magazine.

Magazines & Calendars

KALMBACH PUBLISHING CO.

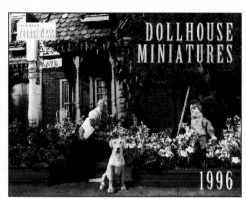

Dollhouse Miniatures
1996 Calendar

Stock No.: 68087
Price: $10.95 plus shipping
Dimensions: 14" x 11"; 13 color photos
12 full-color photos capture imaginatively creative scenes like the stormy night in "Thunder City," the dusty old "Western Town," the quaint grocery of the "Victorian Village" and the European Art Nouveau style of "The Round House." Descriptive text accompanies each photo, plus plenty of room to note appointments. $3 shipping for 4th Class (or $4.50 UPS, continental US only); add $5 for Canada; other foreign; add $10.

KALMBACH PUBLISHING CO.

Nutshell News

Price: $34.95 per year (US); outside the US add $10 for postage/handling
Nutshell News is a colorful, monthly magazine covering every aspect of the miniatures hobby. Coverage of major miniatures shows, work by readers, tours of collections, artisan profiles and do-it-yourself projects are included in every issue. Nutshell News is the one source you need to keep abreast of everything happening in the world of miniatures. 12 issues per year.

Videos

ELECT-A-LITE

Instructional Video

Price: $9.50 (Video); $6.50 (Student Kit)
Instructional Video which coordinates with Elect-A-Lite's Student Kits. Available for Single Foil Tape (#521) or Double Tapewire in Mylar (#526). These are excellent videos and for the novice in miniature electrification the combination of these videos and the Student Kits is all you'll need. When you finish you'll feel competent to tackle any miniature wiring project. The Student Kit for Single Foil (#520) and the Student Kit for Double Tapewire in Mylar (#525) are sold separately.

STEELE MINIATURES

Jeffrey R. Steele
Video/How-To-Do

Stock No.: 161/L
Price: Chair $29.95, with kit $50; Table $24.95, with kit $40; plus shipping $3 each.
New from Steele Miniatures—the video classroom and "The Basic Upholstered Chair" by Diamond Productions. New! "The Faux Marble Table" using Steele's popular wet-into-wet watercolor/salt resist technique. Kit owners and scratch builders complete with Steele from start to finish.

Prices are approximate and subject to change

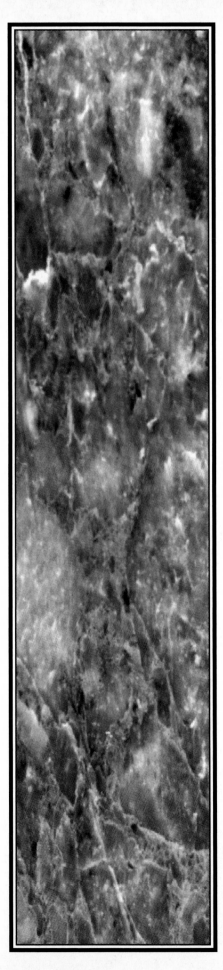

TOOLS & FINISHING SUPPLIES

Adhesives & Glues

AZTEC IMPORTS INC.

Glues

Price: See your local dealer.
Full line of glues includes Super Wood Glue (C4005), Quick Tack Glue (C4004), Zap-a-Gap (C4006) and Alteco (C4000). Also glue sticks (C4002).

EBERHARD FABER GMBH

FIMO Modeling Material

Stock No.: 8000
Price: see your dealer
Dimensions: see below
55 by 55 by 15 mm/65 g small block, 165 by 55 by 30 mm/350 g large block. FIMO, the fantastic and most popular modeling material, is the leading product of its kind in Europe. It's versatile and easy to handle and hardens in the oven at 265° (20 to 30 minutes). Available in 42 brilliant colors, it's ideal to create the finest decorative accessories for your dollhouse and to make exciting and imaginative objects (miniatures, figures, fashion jewelry, decorations, pictures, nameplates and a lot more).

HANDCRAFT DESIGNS INC.
Mini-Hold #1300 & E-Z Hold #1400 Price:

See your dealer.
#1300-The original, superior and most widely-known temporary adhesive used in the miniature world. Keeps furniture from sliding in settings, holds accessories on furniture without damage to surface. Also, the best and easiest product used by doll artisans everywhere to hold eyes in position for final cementing.
#1400-Our specially-formulated adhesive for dollhouse wallpaper. Designed for easy surface coverage and excellent compatibility with all types of wallpaper, glossy, flat or textured.

HANDLEY HOUSE

Handley Hot Melt

Stock No.: HH321, HH321A (clear)
Price: $2.40
Handley Hot Melt is our own special adhesive for dollhouse construction and possesses superior bonding characteristics. Six 4" sticks per package. Also available in bulk, 72 sticks per pack.

J. HERMES

Adhesives and Glues

Price: $.50 - $2
Powdered paste and "Yes" glue for wallpaper. "Super Sealer" is used for semi-gloss finish on paper flooring, wood and tile. Also used to make decals, oil cloth and tiles. "Tacky" is used for wood and crafts.

NUTSHELL NEWS MINIATURES TOURS ARE FUN! FOR INFORMATION CALL 1-800-677-9412

Prices are approximate and subject to change

KIMBERLY HOUSE MINIATURES
Kimberly Wallpaper Paste

Stock No.: WP-8
Price: $4.39 (8 oz. Jar)
Without a doubt, Kimberly Wallpaper Paste gives the best results for your dollhouse decorating needs. Easy to work with, will allow moving paper into position. Cleans off face of paper with damp cloth, does not stain. May be used for applying decorator cloth to walls as well.

PRECISION PRODUCTS

Quick*Grab

America's #1 all-purpose adhesive. Crystal clear Quick*Grab bonds everything quickly. Waterproof, weatherproof and paintable. Made in USA.

Hand Tools

CIR-KIT CONCEPTS, INC

Awl

Stock No.: CK1044
Price: $4.49
This awl is designed specifically for installation of the CK1023 series of eyelets. Use for creating starter holes and placement of eyelets. Wood handle formed to fit hand. Chrome-plated. Overall length: 4-5/8".

CIR-KIT CONCEPTS, INC.

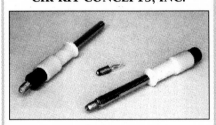

Bulb Extractor

Stock No.: CK1051
Price: $3.95
Use this handy tool to end the frustration of removing screw-base bulbs from lighting fixtures. Simply push down over bulb and turn to remove.

CIR-KIT CONCEPTS, INC.

5" Locking Forceps, Curved Tip

Stock No.: CK1046
Price: $7.98
Useful tool for holding and inserting 1/8" brass brads into tape run connection points. Stainless steel. Locking handle grips.
Specifications: 5" long.

CIR-KIT CONCEPTS, INC .

Four-Foot Solder Spool

Stock No.: CK1033-1
Price: $2.69
Use this high-quality solder in conjunction with the CK1053 soldering iron for all your soldering needs. Composed of 60 percent tin, 40 percent lead.

CIR-KIT CONCEPTS, INC.

Brass Head Hammer

Stock No.: CK1041
Price: $9.95
A small, 5-1/2" long hammer with brass head and serrated steel handle. Well balanced. Ideal for pounding any small nail of brad. Useful in those areas with limited access.

CIR-KIT CONCEPTS, INC.

Jewelers Screwdriver Set

Stock No.: CK1050
Price: $3.98
These nickel-plated screwdrivers are a must when working with any small gauge screw. Each has swivel head with blades ranging from .049" to .079" in width. Lengths, 3" to 3-3/8".

CIR-KIT CONCEPTS, INC..

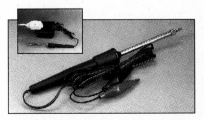

Low-Voltage Soldering Iron

Stock No.: CK1053
Price: $9.95
This low-voltage soldering iron works on 12V instead of 115V AC. Melts solder in three or four minutes. Use with 12V transformer or car battery.

CIR-KIT CONCEPTS, INC .

Mini Drill

Stock No.: CK201
Price: $5.95
This tool is a must for any miniature builder. Ideal for those areas where a power drill just won't reach. Only 4-1/2" long. High gear ratio provides a surprisingly fast turning speed. Accepts all bits in No. 60-80 range. Hollow handle for bit storage.

CIR-KIT CONCEPTS, INC.

Short-Nose Pliers

Stock No.: CK1042
Price: $12.95
High-quality pliers with serrated jaws and plastic-coated, spring-loaded handles. Excellent for a multitude of miniature projects. A "must" for handling small nails and brads.

HOOKED ON MINIATURES

Paper Punches

Price: starting at $4.25 to $70, plus shipping. Paper punches for making flowers. 2,000 designs. Catalog $1 plus LSASE. We do ship outside the USA.

J. HERMES

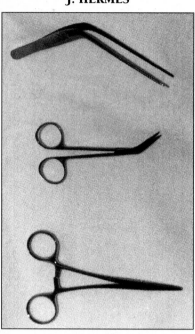

Surgical Instruments

Price: $2.95 - $25
Complete line of highest-quality surgical instruments. Line includes forceps, scissors, scalpel blades and handles, tweezers in various shapes and sizes. J. Hermes is able to offer these instruments at very affordable prices. All tools are made of stainless steel and are ideal for home or shop workbench.

MINIATURE CORNER

Miter Cutter

Cut perfect miters, trim shingles and strips with ease using this superb German tool. Replaceable blade and five-year warranty. See your dealer for prices.

SHOW SANTA WHAT YOU WANT FROM *THE MINIATURES CATALOG*

Paints &Finishes

GREENLEAF PRODUCTS

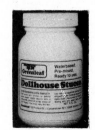

Stucco

Stock No.: 9020
Price: $7.90
The dollhouse stucco is waterbased. It is great for foundations, chimneys or for an authentic Tudor look. Just add water and you will have mortar, stucco or textured paint depending on the amount of water that you use. It also can be tinted.

KIMBERLY HOUSE MINIATURES
Kimberly Premixed Stucco

Price: $8.64 (pint)
Latex-based material in white, ivory, sand or gray (concrete). Ideal for ceilings, bays, interior walls or exterior. Concrete is ideal for sidewalks, patios or porches. Stucco covers tape wiring, woodgrain, and a multitude of sins. One pint will cover an average 7-room house. Clean up with soapy water. May be painted over. A beautiful complement to Kimberly Masonry. See your dealer or write Kimberly House.

Prices are approximate and subject to change

Power Tools

DREMEL
16" Variable Speed Scroll Saw

Stock No.: 1695
Price: $408.00
The Model 1695 16" variable speed scroll saw is a precision bench or stand mounted tool designed to complement any home workshop. Precision scroll cuts are easy with the variable speed control. With 200 to 2,000 blade strokes per minute, you can easily and accurately cut soft and hard woods, plastics and metals. The saw uses either pin or plain end blades and features convenient blade storage. The 12" round table made of die cast aluminum provides workers with a large workbase to complete a variety of projects. A dust bloser and clear plastic guard keep the blade free of dust and obstruction. This versatile, heavy duty scroll saw is great for making toys, puzzles, names, fretwork and jewelry because of its 2" thick cutting capacity.

DREMEL

Two-Speed Scroll Saw

Stock No.: 1672
Price: $301.50
Versatile and heavy-duty, the 1672 two-speed Scroll Saw makes scroll and interior cuts accurately and easily. It features the Quick Change Blade System for fast, simple blade changes. The 1672 features quick release tension lever to quickly tension and detention the blade. Quick Change Blade Adapter for fast plain-end blade changes. Easy access door for quick and convenient access to lower blade assembly. Two speed motor, low speed-890 SPM, and high speed-1790 SPM for cutting all kinds of materials. Accepts both pin and plain-end blades for cutting wood, plastic and metal. Dust port for vacuum hose to keep work environment clean. Blade length gauge for setting proper distance between blades. Smooth 12-inch round die cast aluminum table evenly supports workpiece around the blade. Adjustable table tilts 0 degrees to 45 degrees for accurate bevel cuts. Sturdy cast iron base for increased stability while cutting. Dual lamp bosses to install optional 1304 Magnifier lamp on either side of saw.

DREMEL

Dremel Disc/Belt Sander

Stock No.: 1731
Price: $189
Dremel Model 1731 Disc/Belt Sander is the perfect addition to workshops that require the versatility of a disc/belt sander. Sharpens, sands, deburrs, polishes and finishes most woods, plastics, metals and ceramics. Smooth 7" diameter die cast aluminum table pivots 60 degrees and locks into position for angle sanding. Includes miter gauge for angle and compound angle sanding. Removable rear platen for light finishing of curved work. Inside sanding capability for large curved surfaces. Includes one medium-grit sanding disc, one medium-grit sanding belt and miter gauge.

DREMEL

Drill Press

Stock No.: 212
Price: $58.70 (See your local dealer.)
The Model 212 Drill Press Stand accepts Dremel Moto-Tool Models 395, 285 and 275. It is designed for precision drilling, routing and grooving. The Model 212 features a 36 sq. in. work surface and a 3" throat depth. The table is slotted for both guides and hold downs. Tool carriage is adjustable from 0 to 3 inches. Moto-Tool not included.

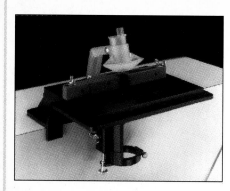

DREMEL
Shaper/Router Table

Stock No.: 231
Price: $43.40 (See your local dealer.)
Dremel's Shaper/Router Table converts the Moto-Tool into a bench-mounted wood shaper. Clamp it to a workbench and easily and accurately perform professional slotting, edge trimming, grooving and sanding of irregular shapes. The work table measures 8" x 6".

JOIN A MINIATURES CLUB ... OR START ONE!

DREMEL

Dremel MultiPro™ Tool Kit

Stock No.: 3955
Price: $139.95 plus shipping.
The Dremel MultiPro™ Tool is a compact, lightweight rotary tool with speeds up to 30,000 rpm. A tapered housing shape provides for comfortable finger tip control and a quick change collect nut is available for use with bits up to 1/8". A thrust bearing provides greater drilling capacity. Other features include easy motor brush replacement, conveniently positioned shaft lock switch and a 6-ft., two-wire flexible cord. Three models available are variable speed, two-speed and single-speed kits with various accessory/bit assortments.

DREMEL

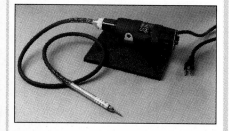

Variable Speed Moto-Flex

Stock No.: 332
Price: $156.60 (See your local dealer.)
The 332 V.S. Moto-Flex Tool features solid state variable speed control (7,500-25,000 rpm) and a three-position selector switch with variable speed override. The 34" thermoplastic rubber-covered flex-shaft has spring-type strain reliefs on both ends. Lightweight, aluminum, ball bearing, 1/2" diameter hand piece. Detachable 360 degree swivel base and wall hanger device adds versatility. Also includes one open end wrench and one No. 480 collet in tool. Motor .95 amp., 120V, 50-60 Hz. AC only. Bronze bearing motor.

DREMEL

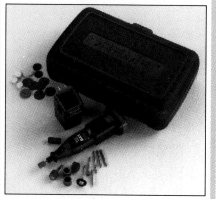

Two-Speed Cordless MultiPro™ Kit

Stock No.: 7700
Price: $81.95
The Dremel Two-speed Cordless MultiPro™ is a compact cordless rotary tool designed for precision projects. Use it anywhere precision drilling, sanding, shaping or grinding is required. The 7.2V tool can be used with all 1/8" and smaller shank Dremel tool bits. It comes equipped with a rechargeable, removable battery pack and its own unique plug-in battery charger. The 7.2V tool is compact, lightweight and designed to provide pinpoint accuracy and control when working on intricate or finely-detailed projects.

MICRO • MARK

MicroLux Tilting Arbor Table Saw

Stock No.: 80463
Price: $299, plus shipping
The new MicroLux is more powerful, more accurate and smoother running than any other saw its size. And because it's the world's first variable speed table saw, it will cut metal and plastic, as well as wood. Includes a self-aligning rip fence, calibrated miter gauge, blade guard and an 80-tooth fine cut blade for balsa and basswood up to 1" thick, hardwood up to 1/4" thick (hardwood up to 1" with optional carbide blade). Blade dia. 3-3/8" with 10mm hole. Made in Japan exclusively for Micro•Mark. Perfect if you care about precision and are serious about producing quality work.

Prices are approximate and subject to change

INDEX *to* MINIATURES SHOPS

Betsy's on Ross

A Complete Doll & Miniatures Shop, Bears too!

106 N. Ross • Auburn AL 36830
Betsy Judkins Ph. 334-821-1816

the ELF SHELF

2212-A Whitesburg Dr.
Huntsville, Alabama 35801
(205)536-2894

TOYS FOR ALL REASONS
Miniature Doll Houses & Accessories
Collector Dolls...Playmobile
Brio...Unusual Toys

Mon.-Fri. 10-5:30
Saturday 10-5:00   BETH & BRYAN TATUM
Special Holiday Hours   Owners

ALABAMA

BETSY'S ON ROSS

106 N. Ross St., Auburn, AL 36830. (334) 821-1816. Mon.-Sat., 10 a.m.-5 p.m. A complete miniatures shop. Dollhouses from kits to finished. Large selection of furniture and accessories in 1" and 1/2" scales. Special handcrafted items. Collector dolls and bears, too.

THE ELF SHELF

2212-A Whitesburg Dr., Huntsville, AL 35801. (205) 536-2894. Mon.-Fri., 10 a.m.-5:30 p.m.; Sat., 10 a.m.-5 p.m. Special Holiday hours. Two blocks south of Huntsville Hospital. Full line miniatures shop. We ship anywhere.

ARIZONA

ABBY'S ATTIC

242 S. Wall St., Chandler, AZ 85224. (602) 899-6257 - (800) 420-6257. Mon.-Sat., 9 a.m.-5 p.m. Everything in miniature. We feature local artisans and also carry a full line of manufactured items.

MinELAINE MINIATURES

PO Box 2062, at the "Y" - Hwy. 179 & 89A, Sedona, AZ 86339. (520) 282-2653. Every day 10 a.m.-5 p.m. Miniatures by Gerald Crawford, Gary Larsen, Leonetta, Pete Acquisto, and many more artists. A wide range of accessories available. Unusual, handcrafted selection of Indian and Southwest miniatures.

OLD PUEBLO MINIATURES

2907 E. Grant Rd., Tucson, AZ 85716. (520) 322-9390. Tues.- Sat., 10 a.m.-5 p.m. Tucson's finest full-service dollhouse store. We build, paint, shingle, electrify, wallpaper and floor. Custom orders welcome. Local artisans featured. Books, kits, tools, components, furnishings. Southwest specialists.

THE DOLL HOUSE

Hilton Village, 6107 N. Scottsdale Rd., Scottsdale, AZ 85250. (602) 948-4630. Orders only—(800) 398-3981. Crossroads Festival, 4811 E. Grant Rd., Suite #125, Tuscon, AZ 85712. (520) 323-8387. Open seven days a week. Mon.-Sat. 10 a.m.-5:30 p.m.; Sun. 10 a.m.-4 p.m. Arizona's largest and most complete miniatures shops, carrying the work of national artists, local handcrafters and manufactured items, dollhouses and accessories.

CALIFORNIA

ACCENT ON MINIATURES

23011 Moulton Pkwy., C-2, Laguna Hills, CA 92653. (714) 855-8800. 10 a.m.-5 p.m. weekdays; noon-4 p.m. Sun. Dollhouses, building supplies, furniture, handmade items, custom design, building, remodeling, and wiring. No job too small or too large.

ANGELA'S MINIATURE WORLD

2237 Ventura Blvd., Camarillo, CA 93010. (805) 482-2219, FAX (805) 987-1091. Mon.-Fri. 10 a.m.-5:30 p.m.; Sat. 9 a.m.-5 p.m.; The complete miniatures shop — dollhouses, unique miniatures, collectibles and building supplies for the dedicated miniaturist. We're between Los Angeles and Santa Barbara, one block off U.S. 101 (Ventura Freeway).

Abby's Attic

242 S. Wall Street
Chandler, AZ 85224

Dolls
Dollhouses
Miniatures
Victorian Greeting Cards

(602) 899-6257
(800) 420-6257

OLD PUEBLO Miniatures
2907 E. Grant Rd.
Tucson, AZ 85716

YOUR DOLLHOUSE DEPARTMENT STORE
(520) 322-9390

Featuring work by Joe & Kay Franek,
Gloria Bogulas, Gale Manning,
Judy Michelet, Charlotte Blackmore,
Phyllis Miller, Marian Sweet,
Mary Onwiler, Bill Lankford & our own workshop.

MinElaine in Sedona
Northern Arizona's
Complete Miniatures Shop

• A wide range of accessories available
• Home of Astolat Castle

At the Y-Hwy.179 & 89A
PO Box 2062 • Sedona, AZ 86339 • 520-282-2653
Hours: Every day 10 a.m.-5 p.m.

For the small beginnings of
wonderful dreams...
Open 7 Days

DOLLHOUSES • MINIATURES
EXCEPTIONAL DOLLS &
STUFFED ANIMALS

The Doll House

Scottsdale: Hilton Village (602) 948-4630
6107 N. Scottsdale Rd., Scottsdale, AZ 85250
Orders only—1-800-398-3981
Tucson: Crossroads Festival (520) 323-8387
4811 E. Grant, Suite #125, Tucson, AZ 85712

---

dollhouses, building materials,
furniture, custom service

1/2" scale * 1" scale

ACCENT on MINIATURES
23011 Moulton Pkw. C-2
Laguna Hills, CA 92653
LAKE FOREST EXIT I - 5 FWY

(714)855-8800

BARB GREGORY

Angela's Miniature World

The Los Angeles Area
The Quality House for
The Miniatures Enthusiast

2237 Ventura Blvd.
Camarillo, CA 93010

805-482-2219
FAX-805-987-1091

Mon.-Fri., 10 AM-5:30 PM
Sat., 9 AM-5:00 PM

316

BEARLY BIG ENOUGH

2314 Pacific Ave., Stockton, CA 95204.
(209) 948-2088. Tues.-Sat., 10 a.m.-5:00
p.m.; Sun./evenings, by appointment.
We've got what it takes to make your mini
house a mini home, with miniatures,
dollhouses, building supplies, teddy bears,
workshops and classes.

CLEO'S ATTIC MINIATURES

1888 S. Chester Ave., Bakersfield, CA
93304. (805) 831-9405. Tues.-Sat., 10 a.m.-5
p.m. We have a complete line of everything
you need for building your dollhouse from
start to finish. Mail order. We're service-
oriented.

COOPER'S DOLL HOUSE STUDIO

129 First St., Tannery Bldg., Benicia, CA
94510. (707) 745-9411; (800) 801-9411.
Mon.-Sat., 10 a.m.-5 p.m.; Sun., 11 a.m.-4
p.m., Thurs., 10 a.m.-8 p.m. Complete
miniatures shop on the waterfront in
historical downtown Benicia. Ongoing
dollhouse workshop with a professional
builder. Mini making classes available.

D AND J HOBBY & CRAFTS

96 San Tomas Aquino Rd., Campbell, CA
95008-1620. (408) 379-1696. Open seven
days a week. Largest miniatures store in the
South Bay area. We have it all! Although we
have no catalog, we do sell mail order. Send
SASE for your specific inquiries.

DOLL FAIRE MINIATURES/
VICTORIAN TIMES

2310 Monument Blvd., Pleasant Hill, CA
94523. (510) 680-1993, FAX (510) 932-8711.
Mon.-Sat., 10 a.m.-5 p.m. Closed Sunday.
Complete line of miniatures including
landscaping supplies. Many custom and
one-of-a-kind items from national artisans.

DOLL HOUSE LADY

8964 Huntington Dr., San Gabriel, CA
91775. (818) 793-7433. Full line store.
Largest selection. Everything for the
collector. Catalog $25 plus shipping and
handling.

ENCHANTED MINIATURES

2033 W. La Habra Blvd., La Habra, CA
90631. (310) 697-1460. FAX (310) 694-6021.
Tues.-Sat., 10:30 a.m.-5 p.m. Unusual one-
of-a-kind accessories and furniture. Custom
handcrafted wicker, house kits, shells and
custom finishing. Extensive inventory
including Bespaq Corp., Zack Fox, Ron
Benson, Nicole and Blauer.

FOXFIRE MINIATURES

724 Main St., Half Moon Bay, CA 94019.
(415) 726-6915. "Best kept secret in
miniatures." A full service shop specializing
in unique, one-of-a-kind items.

GALLERY OF MINIATURES

580-B Grand Ave., Carlsbad, CA 92008. (619) 729-3231. Tues.-Sat., 10 a.m.-5 p.m., Mon. by appointment only. Full miniatures shop. Many handcrafted items.

KAREN'S MINIATURE SHOP

3824-1/2 Ocean View Blvd., Montrose, CA 91020. Tues.-Sat., 11 a.m.-5:30 p.m., Dollhouses, dolls, furniture, carpets, wallpaper and all accessories. Silk ribbons and small laces. Low prices!

KINDER TOYS

1974 Union St., San Francisco, CA 94123. (415) 673-1780. Open seven days a week, 10 a.m.-6 p.m. Selected collectible miniatures by artisans as well as moderately-priced and playable furniture. Come in and play!

LARIANNE'S SMALL WONDERS

1910 E. Main St., Ventura, CA 93001. (805) 643-4042. A quality well-stocked miniatures shop featuring local and national artists: Acquisto, Oldham, Partelow, Leonetta, Rainbow Hand, Jo Parker, David Edwards of Scotland and many more. Building supplies, houses—everything. Friendly, helpful service, easy to find off 101.

MINIATURE COTTAGE SHOP

1260 Main St., Morro Bay, CA 93442. (805) 772-7858. Tues.-Fri., 10 a.m.-5 p.m.; Sat. & Sun., 10 a.m.-4 p.m. Specializing in handcrafted items made locally. Miniatures shop shelving and accessories.

MINIATURE ESTATES

1451 S. Robertson Blvd., Los Angeles, CA 90035. (310) 552-2200. FAX (310) 552-2829. Tues.-Sat., 10 a.m.-5 p.m.; Sun., 1-5 p.m. Closed Monday. Southern California's largest source for dollhouses, supplies, furniture and accessories for children and adult collectors.

MINIATURE SHOP AT HOBBY CITY

1238 S. Beach Blvd., Anaheim, CA 92804. (714) 826-4420. Two miles south of Knott's Berry Farm on Hwy. 39. Open seven days a week, 10 a.m.-6 p.m. In business for 40 years and a member of N.A.M.E. Three stories tall. All miniatures.

MOTT'S MINIATURE DOLLHOUSE SHOP™

7700 Orangethorpe Ave., #8, Buena Park, CA 90621-3457. (714) 994-5979, FAX (714) 521-1437. Open daily at 10 a.m., seven days. Call to place your order right now at (800) 874-6222*. 800+ pages, half in color. Refundable deposit plus shipping, $25 ppd. to all US, $30 to Canada, $35 other. Plus, you get money-saving coupons good for Hundreds of Dollars in free and discounted merchandise. Or, order from your own "From Our House to Your House" catalog. *Our toll free number is for Credit Card orders only. $25 minimum. No wholesale.

Ms. McPhyzz

1486 Solano Ave., Albany, CA 94706. (510) 524-1226. Mon.-Sat., 10:30 a.m.-5:30 p.m. A full service miniatures shop, Ms. McPhyzz attracts discriminating collectors as well as beginning enthusiasts from all over the San Francisco Bay area.

Ms. Peggie's Place

5063 Cass St., San Diego, CA 92109. (619) 483-2621. Tues.-Sat., 10 a.m.-5 p.m.; Sun. or Mon., by appointment only. Full miniatures shop. A world of miniatures in one tiny shop. No catalog available. Many top artisans—Trompe l'oeil dollhouses by commission.

My Doll's House

1218 El Prado, Suite #136, Torrance, CA 90501. (310) 320-4828. 10 a.m.-6 p.m. daily, 7 days; evenings by appointment. South Bay's friendliest and best place to fill your dollhouse, miniatures and collectible needs. Variety of kits, custom work available, free advice and electrical wiring classes. We feature classes by local artisans. Full service miniatures shop with senior discounts.

Peg's Dollhouse

4019 Sebastopol Rd., Santa Rosa, CA 95407. (707) 546-6137. Tues.-Sat., noon-5 p.m. Located in an old Victorian house. Each room is full of miniatures — something for every age at affordable prices.

Petite Designs

10523 Santa Monica Blvd., Los Angeles, CA 90025-4907. (310) 477-9388. Open Tues.-Sat., 10:30 a.m.-5:30 p.m. A complete miniatures and dollhouse emporium. Supplies, classes. All-service shop.

Petite Elite Shop

(In the Carole & Barry Kaye Museum of Miniatures) 5900 Wilshire Blvd., Los Angeles, CA 90036. (213) 937-MINI, FAX (213) 937-2126. Tues.-Sat. 10 a.m.-5 p.m., Sun. 11 a.m.-5 p.m. More than 14,000 sq. ft. of incredible miniature works of art. The most comprehensive collection of artisans' miniature items for sale. Truly a collector's paradise.

Pleasant Dreams
Dollhouses & Miniatures

615 Merchant St., Suite E, Vacaville, CA 95688. (707) 448-MINI (488-6464). Mon.-Fri., 10 a.m.-6 p.m.; Sat. 8 a.m.-5 p.m. Necessities to accessories. Dollhouse kits, shells, furniture, miniatures, electrical, landscaping, unique handcrafted items, books, plans and more. Friendly service, knowledgeable staff, quality products, convenient location.

Salmagundi

109 S. Brown St., Hanford, CA 93230. (209) 584-3603. Tues.-Thur., 10 a.m.-6 p.m.; Fri., 10 a.m.-5 p.m.; Sat., 10 a.m.-4 p.m. "Salmagundi" means a "little of this and a little of that." Dollhouses, kits, dolls, furniture, miniature accessories. Electrical and building supplies. We will special order. Classes and seminars given. Personal attention with your projects.

THE DENVER DOLLHOUSE

1300 E. Evans Ave., Denver, CO 80210.
(303) 744-9262. Tues.-Sat., 10 a.m.-5 p.m.,
Sun., 12-4 p.m. or by appointment. Full line
miniatures shop. Local artisans featured.
Friendly service with expert advice.

CONNECTICUT

DOLLHOUSES PLUS

211 Coram Ave., Shelton, CT 06484. (203)
924-6966. Mon.-Fri., 10 a.m.-7 p.m.; Sat.-
Sun., 10 a.m.-3 p.m. Complete lines of all
your miniatures needs. Build it, electrify it,
decorate and furnish it, or have us do it.
Something for everyone.

HOBBY HOUSE

405 E. Putnam Ave., Cos Cob, CT 06807.
(203) 869-0969. Mon.-Sat., 10 a.m.-5:30
p.m. Complete hobby shop, R/C, trains,
model kits, supplies, dollhouses and
dollhouse accessories.

MOLLY BRODY MINIATURES

135 Washington St., S. Norwalk, CT 06854.
(203) 838-4337. Tues.-Sat., 10:30 a.m.- 5:30
p.m.; Sun., noon-5 p.m.; closed Mon. New
England's largest selection of miniatures,
dollhouses, construction materials, and
accessories.

RUSSELL CRAFTS

481 Danbury Rd., Rt. 7, New Milford, CT
06776. (203) 354-5287. Mon.-Sat., 9:30 a.m.-
5:30 p.m.; Sun., 10 a.m.-5 p.m. More than
150,000 miniature items. More than 100
dollhouses to select from. Specializing in
handcrafted pieces at affordable prices.
Worth a trip from anywhere!

THE SMALL COLLECTOR

199 Ethan Allen Hwy., Ridgefield, CT 06877.
(203) 438-1956. Tues.-Sat. 10 a.m.-5 p.m.;
closed Sun. and Mon., unless by
appointment. Summer Hours, June, July
and August - Tues.-Fri. 4 p.m.-8 p.m.; Sat.
10 a.m.-5 p.m. Dollhouses assembled and in
kits, supplies and original handcrafted items
from local artisans.

WHIMSIES

18 Lewis St., Greenwich, CT 06830. (203)
629-8024. More than 200 miniature rooms
on display, dollhouses, furniture,
accessories, kits, supplies, many imported
and handmade items. All price ranges. We
assemble, electrify, paper, paint, repair, and
custom build.

DELAWARE

TINY TOWN/COUNTRY CRAFTS

1145 Savannah Road, Lewes, DE 19958.
(302) 644-1557. Mon., Tue., Thur., Fri. and
Sat., 10 a.m. -5 p.m.; Sun., noon -5 p.m.
Closed Wed. Dollhouses, kits, miniatures,
crafts, custom woodworking.

CONNIE'S CRAFTS, GIFTS, & MINIATURES

Osceola Flea & Farmers' Market, Booth A42-48, Hwy. 192, Kissimmee, FL 34744. (407) 846-9088, FAX (407) 333-0592. Fri.-Sun., 9 a.m.-5 p.m. Located 21 miles from Disneyworld, 1800 sq. ft. of minis, dollhouses, furniture, components, roomboxes, electrical kits and more!

DOLLIE'S DOLLHOUSE

1670 Wells Rd., Suite 108, Orange Park, FL 32073. (904) 269-9701. Mon.-Sat., 10 a.m.-5 p.m. Located southwest of Jacksonville, exit U.S. 21 South, off I-295 South. Quality collector dolls, bears, dollhouses and miniatures for the child or the discerning collector. Retail only. You won't be disappointed.

HASLAM'S DOLL HOUSES

7208 S. Tamiami Trail, Sarasota, FL 34231. (941) 922-8337. Mon.-Fri., 10 a.m.-5 p.m.; Sat. 10 a.m.-4 p.m. The finest in miniatures, dollhouses, furniture, accessories and building supplies.

HOBBY MART

11433 US 19 S., Clearwater, FL 34624. (Just south of Ulmerton.) (813) 573-7890. Mon.-Fri., 10 a.m.-7 p.m.; Sat., 10 a.m.-6 p.m.; Sun., 11 a.m.-6 p.m. Miniatures, trains, r/c cars, planes and boats and plastics. We have 8,000 square feet of fun!

INCH HIGH MINIATURES, INC.

1609 Biltmore St., Port St. Lucie, FL 34984. Tues.-Sat., 10 a.m.-5 p.m.; other hours by appointment. Full-service shop with many unique lines, one-of-a-kinds and quality handmade accessories.

KAREL'S KORNER

In Chelsea Square, 3243 E. Silver Springs Blvd. (Hwy 40), Ocala, FL 34470. (904) 732-2250. Mon.-Fri., 10 a.m.-5 p.m.; Sat., 10 a.m.-4 p.m. Convenient to dining, lodging and RV resorts. Two miles west of Silver Springs/Wild Waters attractions. Miniatures, dolls' houses, dolls, supplies, furniture and accessories for the miniatures enthusiast. Specializing in "Tomorrow's Heirlooms."

MINIATURES IN MIAMI

13056 South West 133rd Ct., Miami, FL 33186. (305) 251-4055. Open seven days. A full-line miniatures shop including a large selection of building supplies. Call for class information. Many famous artisans scheduled. Call for directions and hours.

SORENSEN'S

NW Promenade, 6745 Manatee Ave. W, Bradenton, FL 34209. (813) 795-1490; FAX (813) 794-5354. Mon.-Sat., 10 a.m.-5 p.m. A complete miniatures shop. We will ship anywhere.

THE DOLL HOUSE CORNER

8 S.E. Fourth Ave., Delray Beach, FL 33483. (Just one mile east of 95 - Atlantic Ave., Exit 42.) (407) 272-7598. Mon.-Sat., 10 a.m.-5 p.m. Shortened hours May 1-Oct. 1. Please call for information. Family-owned since 1978. Complete line of miniatures for the beginner and collector.

THE TOY BOX

in Peddler's Village, 4657 S. US 1, Suite Q, Rockledge, FL 32955. (407) 632-2411. Tues.-Sat., 10 a.m.-5 p.m.; Sun., noon-5 p.m.; closed Mon. A full miniatures shop in business 14 years, same location.

TINY WORLD MINIATURES

34211 Blanton Rd., Dade City, FL 33525. (904) 567-3820. Tues.-Sat. 10 a.m.-5 p.m. (closed July and August). Since 1977, the biggest little shop in West Central Florida. Everything you need to build and furnish your miniature home.

GEORGIA

MINIATURE DESIGNS

2399 Lawrenceville Hwy., Suite 10, Lawrenceville, GA 30244. (404) 339-6849. Mon.-Sat., 10 a.m.-6 p.m.; Thurs., 10 a.m.-7:30 p.m.; Sun., 12-5 p.m. 2,400 square feet, one-stop shop for all your miniature needs. Labor services at reasonable prices! All dollhouse kits 15-20% off every day! We gladly ship and fill special orders. Catalog available.

HAWAII

MY FAVORITE THINGS

1050 Ala Moana Blvd., Honolulu, HI 96814. (808) 596-8048. Open seven days a week. We specialize in handcrafted local miniatures including foods, plants, Hawaiian and Oriental specialties.

ILLINOIS

ALL SMALL MINIATURES

12 Smith, The Black Smith Shoppes, Frankfort, IL 60423. (815) 469-4111. Mon.-Sat., 10 a.m.-5 p.m.; Sun., noon-5 p.m. Our selection is a fantasyland for any miniaturist, beginner or collector. Please come and see us.

BLACKBERRY HARVEST

18120 Dixie Highway, Homewood, Il 60430. (708) 957-4332, FAX (708) 957-4409. Wed., 10 a.m.-5 p.m.; Thurs., noon-9 p.m.; Fri., 10 a.m.-5 p.m.; Sat., 10 a.m.-5 p.m. Twenty-five miles from downtown Chicago. Full line dollhouse shop, featuring Noel & Pat Thomas dollhouses. Very unusual line of miniatures. More than 3000 handmade accessories. Allow yourself 2-1/2 hours to see everything.

DONNA'S DOLLHOUSE CENTER

1029-A Burlington, Downers Grove, IL 60515. (708) 969-6150. Tues.-Sat., 10 a.m.-5:00 p.m.; Sun., noon-4 p.m.; closed Mon. Complete shop—dollhouses, miniature building supplies and collector's box items.

LOLLY'S

1054 Dundee Ave., Elgin, IL 60120. (708) 697-4040. Tues.-Sat., 10 a.m.-5 p.m. A large complete miniatures shop. 20 miles west of O'Hare Airport; six blocks south of I-90 on Rt.25.

THINK SMALL BY ROSEBUD

3209 N. Clark, Chicago, IL 60657. (312) 477-1920. Wed.-Thurs., 10 a.m.-8 p.m.; Fri., 10 a.m.-3 p.m.; Sat., Tues., 10 a.m.-5 p.m.; Sun., noon-5 p.m. No Sun. summer hours. Closed Mon. A full service shop for builders and collectors. Workshop available for customers to build and finish houses and small projects. Located near Wrigley Field.

INDIANA

P & D POTPOURRI

100 S. Main St., Crown Point, IN 46307-4052. (219) 663-8969. Mon.-Sat., 10 a.m.-5 p.m.; Fri., 10 a.m.-7 p.m.; closed Sunday. "The Dollhouse Shoppe." Largest dollhouse and miniatures shop in northwest Indiana. A full line shop with everything needed to begin and finish your dollhouse or roombox. We specialize in service and are happy to special order for you. Sorry, no catalog.

IOWA

DESIGNS BY DANN

6408 Sunset Terrace, Des Moines, IA 50311-1834. (515) 255-5392. Tues., Wed. & Fri., noon-6 p.m.; Sat. 10 a.m.-2 p.m.; or call for an appointment. Specializing in tools, lumber and wood trims, glues, wallpaper, books, electrical, flooring, furniture and flower kits, domes and room boxes. Will special order. Mail orders welcome. Workshops available.

GRAMMA HONEY'S DOLLHOUSES & MINIATURE FURNISHINGS

(Cottage Inn Restaurant), 302 S. Jefferson, Indianola, IA 50125. (515) 961-4546. Mon.-Fri., 10 a.m.-4:30 p.m.; Sat., 10 a.m.-3 p.m. Fifteen minutes south of Des Moines. Full-line miniatures shop.

HOBBY CRAFT SHOP

21 West Main St., Marshalltown, IA 50158. (515) 752-9788. Tues.-Fri., 11 a.m.-5:30 p.m.; Sat. 9 a.m.-3 p.m.; closed Sun. & Mon. Full-line shop for dollhouses, food, furniture, electrical supplies, lumberyard, wallpaper, carpet, flooring, paint and tools. Also model trains, airplanes, kites, beads and jewelry supplies.

LITTLE HOUSE OF MINIATURES ON CHELSEA LANE

615 Sycamore St., Waterloo, IA 50703. (319) 233-6585. Mon.-Sat., 10 a.m.-5 p.m. Expanded showroom. Dollhouses, electric and building supplies. Wallpaper, carpeting, furniture, dolls and accessories. Gift certificates available.

MINIATURE WORLD & GIFTS

130 - 5th St., West Des Moines, IA 50265. (515) 255-5655. Mon.-Sat., 10 a.m.-5 p.m.; Sun., 12-4 p.m. Complete miniatures shop with miniatures for collectors—dollhouses, handmade dolls, foods, furniture, building supplies, wallpaper, fabrics and electrical components.

MOSTLY MINIATURES

450 Bluff St., Dubuque, IA 52001. (319) 588-2357. Mon.-Sat., 9 a.m.-5 p.m.; Sun., noon-5 p.m. A complete miniatures store for beginners and collectors. Quality dollhouses and kits, furniture, accessories, building supplies, handcrafted items. Custom assembly. Will ship.

OUR HAPPY LITTLE HOMES MINIATURE SHOPPE

3806 Douglas Ave., Des Moines, IA 50310. (515) 255-4377. Tues.-Fri., 10 a.m.-6 p.m., 10-5 Memorial Day thru Labor Day; Sat., 10 a.m.-5 p.m.; or by appointment. Extended holiday hours. Full line of kits, materials, components, electrical supplies, wallpaper, flooring, accessories. Also handmade & specialty items, mail order, workshops, custom work, electrification, exterior/interior finishing. 800 page catalog. Cost $19 & $4 shipping, refundable with $100 purchase.

V & G MINIATURES AND COLLECTIBLES

Willowbrook Plaza, 1631 4th SW, Mason City, IA 50401. (515) 423-9379. Mon.-Fri., 10 a.m.-6 p.m., Thur. 10 a.m.-8 p.m., Sat. 10 a.m.-5 p.m. Everything you need to finish and furnish your dollhouse! We custom build, repair and model on site. Friendly service and advice given freely. Visa and MasterCard.

KANSAS

MEMORIES IN MINIATURE DOLLHOUSE MUSEUM & SHOPPE

618 E. Broadway, Newton, KS 67114. (316) 283-1747. Call for seasonal hours. The Shoppe is on display in a c. 1886 Victorian Cottage. Incorporated with a dollhouse museum (see museum listings), featuring selected handcrafted miniature items. Workshops and collector's club offered. New home of "by Grace" customized miniatures.

KENTUCKY

MINI SPLENDID THINGS

626 Main St., Covington, KY 41011. (606) 261-5500. Daily, 10 a.m.-5 p.m.; Sun., 12-5 p.m. (April - Dec.). Catalog available. Full line miniatures shop. Many handcrafted items.

WOODFORD LANDING MINIATURES

2632 Frankfort Ave., Louisville, KY 40206. (502) 893-7442. Mon.-Sat., 11 a.m.-5 p.m., closed Tues. Dollhouse kits, furniture kits, accessories, building supplies, lighting, furniture, exclusive handmade items. Lessons, kit assembly and custom houses on request.

MAINE

THE DOLLHOUSE SHOP

Bangor, ME. (See ad for further address details.) (207) 764-5443. Miniatures, dollhouses, building supplies, classes. Specializing in handcrafted bedroom and kitchen accessories.

MARYLAND

A LITTLE SOMETHING, LTD.

Harbor Place #98, 210 E. Pratt St., Baltimore, MD 21202. (401) 332-0711. Open daily, evenings. Hundreds of miniatures, dolls and paper dolls. Annette Peterson, Wee Folk, Mary McCann and Royal Vienna Dolls. Collectibles and gifts.

DEBBIE'S DOLLHOUSE
150 Airport Dr., Unit 1, Westminster, MD 21157. (410) 876-9235 FAX (410) 848-6005. Mon.-Fri., 9 a.m.-5 p.m., Sat. 10 a.m.-4 p.m. a full-service miniatures shop. We also offer electrificiation and building services. We mail out a newsletter with monthly sales specials.

FAVORITE THINGS
York & Monkton Rds., Hereford, MD 21111. 10 min. N of Hunt Valley off I-83. (410) 343-0400. Mon.-Sat., 11 a.m.-5 p.m.; Sun. noon-5 p.m. Five rooms of dollhouses. Building and decorating supplies. Furnishings, accessories, collectibles and gifts. Bradford Exchange and Ashton-Drake Dolls. Custom work and special orders.

JUST STUFF INC.
4505 Queensbury Rd., Riverdale, MD 20737. (301) 277-0666 or (800) 794-9510 (MD only). Tues.-Fri.., 10 a.m.-7 p.m.; Sat. 10 a.m.-5 p.m.; Closed Sun. and Mon. Complete dollhouse accessories, supplies and miniatures. Also custom work.

STRAWBERRY PATCH
12100 Belair Rd., Kingsville, MD 21087. 1/2 mile N. of Sunshine Ave. (410) 817-4117 or 679-4662. Tues.-Sat., 11:00-5; Sun. & Mon. by appointment. Call for holiday hours. Dollhouses, furniture, accessories, building and electrical supplies, handcrafted items, wallpaper and dolls.

THE HOUSE OF TINY TREASURES
7301 Belair Rd., Baltimore, MD 21206. Tues.-Fri., 12-6 p.m.; Sat., 12-5 p.m.; Sun., 12-3 p.m. Closed Mondays. (410) 661-2131. (800) 754-2131 in Maryland. Baltimore's fastest growing miniatures shop. Complete line of dollhouses, miniatures and handcrafted items. Just 20 minutes from downtown—and one mile off of Interstate 95 & 695.

MASSACHUSETTS

CRYSTAL BROOK MINIATURE SHOP
Rt. 20, PO Box 354, Brimfield, MA 01010-0354. (413) 245-7647. 10 a.m.-5 p.m., six days a week, closed Tues.; closed mid-May to mid-June. Complete selection of miniature furniture, accessories, kits, building supplies and books.

DEN OF ANTIQUITY
67 High St., Danvers, MA 01923. (508) 774-7220. Tues., 10 a.m.-2 p.m.; Wed.-Fri., 10 a.m.-2:30 p.m.; Sat., 10 a.m.-3 p.m.; Sun., noon-4 p.m.; or by appointment (take exit 23N off Rt. 128). Dollhouses, dolls, kits, miniatures, furniture, lighting, building materials and supplies.

DENNISPORT DOLLHOUSE
497 Upper County Rd. (off Route 134), Dennisport, MA 02639. (508) 398-9356. Cape Cod's full-time, full-service mini store catering to beginners and collectors with furniture, accessories, quality components and books. Off Rt. 6 at Exit 9, turn south on Rt. 134, turn left at third set of lights. We are approximately 1 mile straight ahead, on the right.

DEPOT DOLLHOUSE

215 Worcester Rd., Framingham, MA 01701. (508) 872-5444, FAX (508) 872-7480, or (800) 882-1162. Open daily, 10 a.m.-5 p.m. Competitive pricing.

DIVIDED HOUSE OF GIFTS

255 Elm St., Rt. 110, Salisbury, MA 01952. (508) 462-8423 - FAX (508) 462-2688. Daily, 10 a.m.-5 p.m. Custom dollhouses made on premises, clapboards machined into wood, our designs or yours. Full line of miniatures, accessories and building supplies. We're worth the visit!

DOLLS & DWELLINGS

1840 N. Main St., Sheffield, MA 01257. Open daily, 9 a.m.-5:30 p.m. Area's largest dollhouse and miniatures supplier—from basics to finish, furnishings to restoration, kits or assembled, expertise and advice.

FLIGHT OF FANCY

45 Main St., Westboro, MA 01581. (508) 366-0775. Tues. - Sat., 10 a.m.-5p.m.; Sun., 1p.m.-5p.m. Full service miniatures shop, dollhouses (models on display), electrical supplies, lumber, hardware, furniture, wallpaper, rugs, landscaping, handcrafted miniature by top artisans. Just 5 miles from Mass. Pike, exit 11A.

HOMETOWN MINIATURES

36 Pittsfield Rd., Lenox, MA 01240. (413) 637-4778. Open daily 10 a.m.-6 p.m. Offering a full line of dollhouses, scale furniture and miniature accessories. Located in the heart of the Berkshire Mountains, just three miles from Tanglewood.

LINDA'S "WEE MANOR"

779 Chief Justice Hwy., Rt. 3A, Cohasset, MA 02025. (617) 383-6635. Tues.-Fri. 10:30 a.m.-5 p.m.; Sat. 10 a.m.-4 p.m.; Sun. noon-4 p.m. No time to work on your dollhouse? Let us do it for you. "Wee" are a full service shop. Call about our year-'round classes.

OLDE TIME
CRAFTS & COLLECTIBLES

RR2 Box 179, Holland, MA 01521. (413) 245-3002. Mon.-Thur., 10 a.m.-6 p.m.; Fri., 10 a.m.-7 p.m.; Sat., 9 a.m.-5 p.m.; closed Sun. Handcrafted exclusives include one-room/multi-room houses, kits, accessories… Available at Hog Heaven Hobbies in Sturbridge, MA and at shows. Call for directions and/or show dates.

THE DOLLHOUSE TREASURE SHOPPE

832 Washington St., Braintree, MA 02184. (617) 380-7532. Sun. - Mon. noon-4 p.m.; Tues.-Fri. 10 a.m.-5 p.m., Sat., 10 a.m.-4 p.m. Closed Sundays April through Labor Day. A travelers delight, specializing in unique handcrafted items from all over the US. Large selections in all departments. Visa and MasterCard.

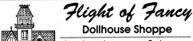

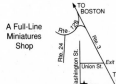

THE WOODHOUSE SHOP

312 Elm St., S. Dartmouth, MA 02748. (508) 993-5014. Mon.-Sat., 9:30 a.m.-5 p.m. Closed in Feb. In the miniatures business 26 years with the largest selection in the area: Dollhouses, building components, electrical components, furniture and accessories. Visa and Mastercard accepted.

MICHIGAN

DOLLHOUSE & MINIATURE STUDIO

12554 Dix/Toledo Rd., Southgate MI 48195. (313) 284-1355, (800) 381-1355. Mon.-Sat., 10 a.m.-6 p.m.; Sun 11 a.m.-4 p.m. Mail orders accepted (including Canadian). We refurbish Greenleaf, Duro-Craft and all kit houses. Wonderful selection of kits including Wallmer, Real Good Toys and Celerity. We have most anything needed for your dollhouse. Attention RR and plane enthusiasts, visit our lumber yard. It's one of the most complete around.

HARVEY'S
MINIATURES & DOLLHOUSES

416 Thornapple Village Plaza, PO Box 340, Ada, MI 49301. (616) 676-3071. Tues.-Sat., 10 a.m.-5:30 p.m. Miniatures, dollhouses, handcrafted miniatures. More than 50 percent handcrafted. Everything for the collector or dollhouse owner. If we don't have it, we can get it. Something for all ages. Gift register. Service with a smile.

JEANIE'S TEENIES

17910 E. Ten Mile Road., Eastpointe, MI 48021. (810) 776-0400. Tue.-Fri. 11 a.m.-7 p.m.; Sat., 10 a.m.-6 p.m. We have a complete miniatures selection. More than 6000 different items from which to choose including dollhouses, lighting, furniture, accessories and local artisan handcrafts. Classes offered. We specialize in service!

MINIATURE MAKERS' WORKSHOP

4515 N. Woodward Ave., Royal Oak, MI 48073-6211. (810) 549-0633. Mon.-Sat., 10 a.m.-5 p.m. Retail only. Supply catalog, $25 plus postage. One-of-a-kind furniture, accessories, dolls and dollhouses. Custom tools, display boxes and large turntables. Seminars and classes.

MURIEL'S DOLL HOUSE

824 Penniman Ave., Plymouth, MI 48170. (313) 455-8110. A complete miniatures shop! Large selection of handcrafted miniatures from around the world as well as a full line of furniture, lighting, wallpaper, carpeting, paints, dollhouse kits and assembled models.

PAT'S VILLAGE
MINIATURES & GIFTS

18518 W. Outer Dr., Dearborn, MI 48128. (313) 359-0400. Mon.-Fri., 10 a.m.-6 p.m.; Sat. 10 a.m.-4 p.m. New miniature store in Dearborn, Michigan, not far from Greenfield Village. We carry 1/4″, 1/2″, and 1″ scale merchandise and also offer classes in all three scales. We specialize in new and unique miniatures.

PINOCCHIOS

465 S. Main St., Frankenmuth, MI 48734. (517) 652-2751. FAX (517) 652-3630. Open 7 days a week from 10 a.m.-6 p.m. Miniature mail order catalog (FROM OUR HOUSE FOR YOUR HOUSE) $15 + $4.50 Ship U.S., $8.50 Canada. Handcrafted Miniatures by over 200 artisans. We also carry Wee Forest Folk. Open 362 days a year.

Seedlings
Miniatures & Gifts
Fine Miniatures ❧ Dollhouses
Gifts ❧ Floral

128 S. River Avenue
Holland, MI
(616)392-4321

The
**Cake &
Miniature
Place**

- Dollhouses & Miniatures
- Fully Assembled or Kits
- Electrical & Building Supplies

Mon. 10-9
Tues. Wed. Thurs. Fri. 10-5:30
Sat. 10-3 **(616) 457-1850**
135 Chicago Dr., Jenison, MI 49428

Mini Temptations

A full line miniatures shop the beginners friend and the collectors choice.

3633 W. 95th
Overland Park, KS 66206
913-648-2050

Orders 1-800-878-8469

Kimberly
House

HOME OF THE
KIMBERLY CORNER

**WHEN IN LAS VEGAS VISIT
KIMBERLY WORLD of MINIATURES**

1775 E. TROPICANA #10
(IN THE LIBERACE MUSEUM PLAZA)
(702)253-9790
OPEN 10-6 EVERY DAY
SEND FOR FREE COPY KIMBERLY CORNER

SEEDLINGS

128 S. River Ave., Holland, MI 49423. (616) 392-4321. Mon.-Thurs., 9:30 a.m.-5:30 p.m.; Fri., 9:30 a.m.-8 p.m.; Sat., 10 a.m.-3 p.m.; closed Sun. Full-line miniatures shop. Unique one-of-a-kind items. Many handcrafted items.

SHADOW BOX

3026 Glade St., Muskegon, MI 49444. (616) 737-0320. Mon.-Fri., 10 a.m.-6 p.m.; Sat., 10 a.m.-5 p.m. Dollhouses—assembled or kits, building and decorating supplies, furniture and accessories, collector boxes and miniatures, handcrafted gifts.

THE CAKE & MINIATURE PLACE

135 Chicago Dr., Jenison, MI 49428. (616) 457-1850. Located in Fables Center. Mon., 10 a.m.-9 p.m.; Tues, Wed., Thurs., Fri., 10a.m.-5:30 p.m.; Sat. 10 a.m.-3 p.m. Dollhouses and miniatures. Fully assembled or kits. Electrical and building supplies. We will special order.

MINNESOTA

MINIATURE MERCHANT

Miniature Merchant, Bandana Square, St. Paul, MN 55108. (612) 645-7079. Mon.-Fri., 10 a.m.-9 p.m.; Sat., 10 a.m.-6 p.m.; Sun., noon-5 p.m. Dollhouse kits and miniatures, railroad, die-cast autos, military miniatures.

MISSOURI

MINI TEMPTATIONS

3633 W 95th, Overland Park, KS 66206. (913) 648-2050. Mon.-Fri., 10 a.m.-6 p.m.; Sat. 10 a.m.-5 p.m. A full-line dollhouse shop. A large selection of furniture, building supplies, handmade miniatures, Madam Alexander dolls and Dept. 56 houses. Catalogs available. 1-800-878-8469.

MONTANA

ON A SMALLER SCALE

1405 Central Ave., Billings, MT 59102. (406) 259-0692. Tues.-Sat., 10 a.m.-6 p.m. Specializing in dollhouses and scale miniatures. Whether you need supplies, help or just a friendly smile, we're here for you.

NEVADA

KIMBERLY HOUSE

1775 E. Tropicana #10, Las Vegas, NV 89119. (702) 253-9790. Open seven days a week, 10 a.m.-6 p.m. Full-line shop. Home of the KIMBERLY CORNER. Send for your free trial copy of KIMBERLY CORNER.

NEW JERSEY

CAMERA-CRAFT & HOBBY-"DOLLHOUSE COUNTRY"

599 Pompton Ave. (Rte. 23), Cedar Grove, NJ 07009. (201) 857-1585, FAX (201) 857-0033. Mon.-Fri., 9:30 a.m.-6 p.m.; Sat., 9 a.m.-1 p.m. More than 9,199 different dollhouse miniatures on display. More than 80 different dollhouses in stock. Many one-of-a-kind originals by "Marilyn." No catalog.

SHADOW BOX
3026 Glade St.
Muskegon, MI
(616) 737-0320

miniatures & gifts

Open Mon. - Fri. 10 am - 6 pm, Sat. 10 am - 5 pm
New Location, next to Business 31 at Summit

**MINIATURE
MERCHANT**

Matt & Pat Lindgren

(612) 645-7079

Bandana Square
St. Paul, MN 55108

"On A Smaller Scale"
Specializing in Dollhouses and Miniatures
Tina Williams
(Owner)

1405 Central Avenue
Billings, MT 59102
(406) 259-0692
Open Tues. - Sat. • 10 a.m. - 6 p.m.

DOLLHOUSE COUNTRY
LARGEST SELECTION OF DOLLHOUSES AND ACCESSORIES IN THE TRI-STATE AREA.
OVER 9,199 DIFFERENT DOLLHOUSE ITEMS ON DISPLAY!
MANY EXCLUSIVES!

OVER 35 DOLLHOUSES ON DISPLAY

OVER 100 DIFFERENT MODELS AVAILABLE
HOURS: WEEKDAYS 9:30 - 6   SATURDAYS 9 - 1   CLOSED SUNDAY

CAMERA - CRAFT & HOBBY
599 POMPTON AVENUE (RT. 23)
CEDAR GROVE, NEW JERSEY 07009
(201) 857-1585

CAPE MAY MINIATURES

208 Ocean St., Cape May, NJ 08204. Orders (800) 544-8777. Phone/Fax (609) 884-7999. Open year 'round. IGMA artisans. Truly a full service miniatures shop.

FRAN'S MINIATURES

104 Main St., Hightstown, NJ 08520. (800) 307-0054. The only full-line shop in central New Jersey catering to creators and collectors of fine miniatures. Featuring over 100 room settings.

JEAN JOHNSON MINIATURES

421 Higgins Ave., Brielle, NJ 08730. (908) 528-7478. Mon.-Sat. 11:00 a.m.-5:00 p.m.; Closed Sun. A very large stock of dollhouses, furniture, accessories and building supplies. Specializing in handcrafted miniatures. This is the largest selection of stock in this area.

LET'S PLAY HOUSE

334 Atlantic City Blvd., Rt.166 - S. Tom's River, N.J. 08757 (908) 240-3222. Tues.-Thurs. & Sat., 10 a.m.-5 p.m.; Fri., 10 a.m.-7 p.m.; Sun., noon-4 p.m.; closed Mon. Complete miniatures and dollhouse shop with largest selection of dollhouses, accessories, building supplies, wallpaper, lamps, etc. Largest line of dolls, bears and doll supplies. No catalog available.

LIN'S CORNER AT ROHSLER'S ALLENDALE NURSERY & FLOWER SHOPPE

100 Franklin Tpke., Allendale, NJ 07401. (201) 327-7788. Mon.-Sat., 11 a.m.-4 p.m.; holidays—extended hours. A shop devoted to handcrafted and unusual miniature accessories and fine furniture. We specialize in dollhouse exteriors, interiors and electrification.

MINIATURES & MORE

1723 Springfield, Pennsauken, NJ 08110. (609) 662-3331. Wed., Fri., 10 a.m.-4:30 p.m.; Thur., 10:30 a.m.-6:00 p.m.; Sat., 10:00 a.m.-4:00 p.m. Closed Sun., Mon. and Tues. Miniatures of all kinds, kits and everything else in between. Handcrafted items also. Prices for all budgets. We offer personalized shopping—give us your wish list...we'll fill it.

MINIATURES & MORE

39 Main St. (Rt.124), Madison, NJ 07940. (201) 822-0240. Tues.-Sat., 10 a.m.-5 p.m. Quality kits, custom dollhouses, roomboxes. Furniture, accessories, many handcrafted and unique pieces. Sturdy, handcrafted furniture for children. Building and electrical supplies. Assembly and wiring.

NANA'S DOLLHOUSE & MINIATURE SHOP

#54 English Plaza (off White St.), Red Bank, NJ 07701. (908) 842-4411. Tues.-Sat., 10 a.m.-5 p.m. Complete line of dollhouses, furnishings, wiring, building supplies and accessories.

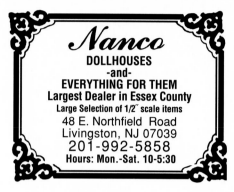

Nanco
DOLLHOUSES
-and-
EVERYTHING FOR THEM
Largest Dealer in Essex County
Large Selection of 1/2" scale items
48 E. Northfield Road
Livingston, NJ 07039
201-992-5858
Hours: Mon.-Sat. 10-5:30

Rose's Dollhouse Goodies
Complete Miniatures Store
ROSE McDONOUGH - PROPRIETOR

123 E. Main St.
Moorestown, NJ 08057

Customized Dollhouses • Collectibles • Domes &
Display Cases • Classes • Goebel Miniatures
609-778-1484

WHERE THE PROFESSIONALS SHOP!
- Vast Selection
- Extensive Catalogue ($5.50)
- Knowledgeable Information
SHOWROOM HOURS
Tues. - Sat. 11-6; Thurs. 11-9

THE DOLLHOUSE FACTORY™

157 Main St. Box 456-CM
Lebanon, NJ 08833
(908) 236-6404 • FAX (908) 236-7899

DOLLHOUSE ANTICS
Enter the World of Fine Miniatures
1343 Madison Avenue
(at 94th Street)
New York, NY 10128
(212) 876-2288
No Catalog

NANCO DOLLHOUSES
48 E. Northfield Rd., Livingston, NJ 07039. (201) 992-5858. Mon.-Sat., 10:00 a.m.-5:30 p.m. Complete line of building supplies, furniture, tools, plans, lumberyard and accessories. Large selection of 1/2" scale items. Catalog for mail orders available.

PETITE INNOVATIONS
243 High St., Burlington, NJ 08016. (609) 386-7476. Mon.-Sat., 10 a.m.-6 p.m.; plus 7-9 p.m. on Fri. We are a full service retail miniatures shop, dedicated to quality merchandise, building and electrical services, handcrafted accessories and mail order catalogs.

ROSE'S DOLLHOUSE GOODIES
123 E. Main St., Moorestown, NJ 08057. (609) 778-1484. Daily, 10 a.m.-4 p.m.; call for additional hours. South Jersey's newest full line miniatures store, specializing in handcrafted miniatures, custom construction, wiring, collectibles, Goebel Miniatures, classes, all scales. Miniaturists' supplies available. Twenty minutes from Philadelphia.

THE DOLLHOUSE BARN
154 Rt. 15, Lafayette, NJ 07848. (201) 383-4214. Mon.-Sat., 10 a.m.-5 p.m.; Sun., 11 a.m.-5 p.m.; closed Wed. Collectors and professionals are joined by the novice naming us "the source" for seemingly unlimited supplies in the world of miniatures.

THE DOLLHOUSE FACTORY
157 Main St., Box 456-CM, Lebanon, NJ 08833. (908) 236-6404, FAX (908) 236-7899. Tues.-Sat., 11 a.m.-6 p.m.; Thurs., 11 a.m.-9 p.m. The source for serious miniaturists with a vast selection of miniatures, dollhouses and accessories, plus supplies, tools, books, plans and knowledgeable information. Catalog, 120 pages, $5.50. See our display ad on page

NEW YORK

AURELIA'S WORLD OF DOLLS, INC.
2025 Merrick Rd., Merrick, NY 11566. (516) 378-3556. Mon.-Sat., 10 a.m.-6 p.m. Unique miniatures, fine china, complete line of linens, dollhouse dolls.

DOLLHOUSE ANTICS
1343 Madison Ave., New York, NY 10128. (212) 876-2288. Mon.-Fri., 11 a.m.-5:30 p.m.; Sat., 11 a.m.-5 p.m. Wide range of quality kits, finished houses, furniture and accessories. Expert staff will help decorate and advise the do-it-yourselfer.

EILEEN GODFREY MINIATURES
Pine View Studio, P.O. Box 472, 78 Westchester Ave., Pound Ridge, NY 10576. (914) 764-1950. Tues.-Sat., 11 a.m.-5 p.m. Call for special appointment. Handcrafted miniatures for the beginner and serious collector.

X Dollhouse Kits   X Handcrafted Linens
X Room Boxes   X Wiring
X Miniature Furnishings   X Building Supplies
Catalog set - $15 refundable
Petite Innovations
243 High St. • Burlington, NJ 08016
609-386-7476 • 1-800-775-7733
Mon. thru Sat. 10-6,
plus Fri. eve. 7-9

The Dollhouse Barn
Dollhouses
Miniatures
Supplies
We treat your house as if it were our house,
using the utmost quality and craftmanship.
Mon.-Sat., 10-5 • Sun., 11-5 • Closed Wed.
154 Rt 15   Henry & Joan Corona
Lafayette, NJ 07848   **(201) 383-4214**

Dolls of Distinction
Aurelia's World of Dolls, Inc.
2025 Merrick Rd.
Merrick, N.Y. 11566
(516) 378-3556
Aurelia Santangelo

Eileen Godfrey   Miniatures
Pine View Studio
**Handcrafted miniatures for
the beginner and serious collector**
P.O. Box 472
78 Westchester Avenue
Pound Ridge, NY 10576
(Scotts Corners)
Hours: Tues.-Sat. 11 a.m. - 5 p.m.
Or call for special appointment
914-764-1950

FANTASTICAL DOLL HOUSE

661 Rte. 28, Kingston, NY 12401. (914) 338-9100. Open every day 10:30 a.m.-5:30 p.m. A complete selection of miniatures, dollhouses (kits and custom built), furniture (assembled or kits), electrical accessories. Top manufacturers and work of local artisans. Mini lumberyard and greenhouse. Also carry large selection of collector's dolls

FREDA'S FANCY

295 Fairview Ave., Bayport, NY 11705. (800) 451-0078. 51 Bunker Hill Rd. Killingworth, CT 06417. (800) 451-0058. Primarily handcrafted museum-quality miniatures. Send $5 for new color catalog of distinguished artisans. Check for summer 1995 opening of Connecticut Museum Shop.

HELENA'S MINIATURE SHOP

363 Merrick Rd., Lynbrook, NY 11563. (516) 596-0931. Tues.-Sat., 11 a.m.-6 p.m. Everything you need to completely furnish your dollhouse. Free expert advice.

LADY MELISSA'S MINIATURES

7 King Arthur Court, Saratoga Springs, NY 12866. (518) 581-7677. Open seven days a week, 10 a.m.-5 p.m., evenings by appointment. A complete miniatures shop offering a variety of dollhouses, furniture and accessories for everyone.

LASTING TREASURES

Lasting Treasures, Box 6, 757 Rte. 25A, Rocky Point, NY 11778. (516) 821-0808. Tues.-Thurs., Sat., 9:45 a.m.-5:00 p.m.; Fri., 9:45 a.m.-6:00 p.m.; Sun., noon-4:00 p.m.; closed first week of June and Sundays in June and July. Celebrating our 13th year. Specializing in handcrafted miniatures, quality homes and shops. Fully-stocked mini lumber yard, electrical supplies, wallpaper. Newsletter $2 per year.

LITTLE THINGS

129 Main St., Irvington, NY 10533. (914) 591-9150. Tues.-Sat., 10 a.m.-5 p.m. Specializing in handcrafted accessories from all around the world. Also good, general and helpful advice.

MANHATTAN DOLL HOUSE

176 - 9th Ave., New York, NY 10011. (212) 989-5220. Mon.-Fri., 11 a.m.-5:45 p.m.; Sat., 11 a.m.-5 p.m.; Sun., noon - 5 p.m. One of the largest selections of dollhouses and accessories, new and antique dolls and building components. Doll repair also available. We build dreams, and sometimes fantasies.

MINIATURE MANOR

283 Willis Ave., Mineola, NY 11501. (516) 294-3960. Daily 11 a.m.-5 p.m. A complete shop with decorating services and smiles available. Twenty years of dollhouse experience.

MINIMAE

212-22 - 48th Ave., Bayside, NY 11364. (718) 225-4144. FAX (718) 631-5197. Tues.-Sat.; 10 a.m.-5:30 p.m. Dollhouse kits, ready built and custom built. Dollhouse repair, electric installation and general renovation. Complete line of supplies, accessories and furniture. Hands-on workshops.

MY DOLLHOUSE

7 S. Broadway, Nyack, NY 10960. (914) 358-4185. Tues.-Sun., 11 a.m.-5 p.m.; closed Mon. Stop in or call with your questions. We teach wiring, wallpapering and flooring. No job too small. Let us help you with your problems.

NEVER GROW UP

4 West Market St., Corning, NY 14830. (607) 937-3157. Mon.-Sat., 10 a.m.-6 p.m. Everything for the miniatures enthusiast. Located in the heart of the finger lakes of New York, on Historic Market St. in Corning, New York.

NIAGARA HOBBY & CRAFT MART

3366 Union Rd., (1/2 mile from Walden Galleria Mall), Buffalo, NY 14225. (716) 681-1666. FAX (716) 681-6061. Mon.-Fri., 10 a.m.-9 p.m.; Sat., 10 a.m.-8 p.m.; Sun., 10 a.m.-5 p.m. Large selection of name brand dollhouse furniture, dollhouses and miniatures. Many built-up houses on display.

OLD POST MINIATURES

81 Primrose Hill Road, Rhinebeck, NY 12572. (914) 876-4800. Tues.-Sat., 10 a.m.-4 p.m.; Sun. in Dec. Full line dollhouse shop. Dollhouses—kits or built, building and electrical supplies; wall and floor covering; landscaping, handcrafted miniatures. Custom work available.

SLEPPIN'S

47-38 - 199th St., Flushing, NY 11358. (718) 229-5152 - FAX (718) 229-0223. By appointment only. Building, electrification, renovations and repairing. Huge inventory. All brands and types of miniatures in stock at all times. Treat yourself to a new experience in miniatures shopping.

THE DOLL & DOLLHOUSE SHOP

8455 Main St., Williamsville, NY 14221. (716) 632-8240. Mon.-Sat., 10 a.m.-5 p.m.; special Christmas hours. We specialize in building supplies for dollhouses, miniatures, furniture kits, teddy bears, dolls, supplies and repairs.

TINY DOLL HOUSE

1146 Lexington Ave., New York, NY 10021. (212) 744-3719. Mon.-Fri., 11 a.m.-5:30 p.m.; Sat., 11 a.m.-5 p.m. A full service shop that caters to the beginner and advanced miniatures hobbyists and collectors.

TREASURES BY PAULA K., INC.

Village Plaza, Rt. 202 & Lovell St.,
Lincolndale, NY 10540. (914) 248-7262;
(800) 899-7285. Located in Somers, NY. A
full-line miniatures and dollhouse shop.
1,200 square feet of inventory including
many handcrafted items. We will build,
electrify and wallpaper your dollhouse.

NORTH CAROLINA

GINGERBREAD HOUSE OF MINIATURES

2170 Lawndale Dr., Greensboro, NC 27408.
(910) 273-2831. Mon.-Sat., 10 a.m.-5 p.m.
Full line miniatures shop. We carry all major
lines of components, the work of many local
handcrafters and 1/2" and smaller scale
specialties. Complete custom finishing and
in-house workshops.

MINIATURES OF WILMINGTON

4410 Wrightsville Ave., Wilmington, NC
28403. (910) 799-7897. Tues. thru Sat., 10
a.m.-6 p.m. Convenient location, minutes
from I-40. A full service shop with a wide
variety of dollhouses and accessories for
the beginner or collector.
Visa/MC/Discover. Mail orders happily
filled.

MISS MUFFET'S MINIATURES

A Division of The Mini Maker®, 1622 S.
Hawthorne Rd., Winston-Salem, NC 27103.
(910) 765-7972. Tues.-Sat., 10 a.m.-5:30
p.m. A complete miniatures shop —
continuing to grow for you. Buy in kits or
assembled with custom finishing available.
Accepting Visa, MasterCard and American
Express.

PJ's MINIATURES

5818 Hwy. 74 West, Monroe, NC 28110.
(704) 821-9144. Orders call (800) 791-7336,
FAX (704) 821-7336. Mon.-Sat., 10 a.m.-5
p.m. Located just outside Charlotte with
more than 2.400 sq. ft. We offer the largest
selection of miniatures in the Carolinas.
Something for the beginner or collector.

WEE CREATIONS

748 D East Chatham St., Cary, NC 27511.
(919) 469-9618. Mon.-Sat. 10 a.m.-6 p.m.
Full service shop devoted to dollhouses and
miniatures.

NORTH DAKOTA

JUDY'S COLLECTABLES

616 - 3rd. St. N., Fargo, ND 58102. (701)
234-0358. Mon.-Sat., 10 a.m.-4 p.m. Call for
summer hours. Full service miniatures shop.
Everything you need from start to finish
plus all the extras that make your dollhouse
a home! Located one block east of St.
Luke's ramp

LORI'S DOLL CLOSET

15 S. Third St., Grand Forks, ND 58201.
(701) 795-0234. Mon.-Fri., 10 a.m.-6 p.m.;
Sat., 10 a.m.-5:30 p.m. Complete miniature
home builder store, furniture and
accessories. Collectible Barbies, Ginnys,
bears, paper dolls and more.

OHIO

CALICO CORNER GENERAL STORE

Crystal Plaza, 4652 E. Liberty Ave., Vermilion, OH 44089. (216) 967-4830. Mon.-Sat., 10 a.m.-5 p.m.; Thur. 10 a.m.-8 p.m.; Sun. noon-4 p.m. A full service dollhouse and miniatures shop here to serve you year 'round. Boasting a unique toy and furniture store. Full scale dolls, puppets and plush animals for the collector or just for fun. All this just E. of the Vermillion River.

GREENHOUSE MINIATURE SHOP

6616 Monroe St., Sylvania, OH 43560. (419) 882-8259. Mon.-Fri., 10 a.m.-5 p.m.; Sat., 10 a.m.-4 p.m. Evening hours by appointment. Visit our full service miniatures shop, established 17 years. Classes and handcrafted items.

GUBBY'S LI'L HUT

170 N. Park Ave., Warren, OH 44481-1177. (216) 394-6464. Mon. 10 a.m.-8 p.m.; Tues.-Sat., 10 a.m.-5 p.m.; Sun. by appointment only. Custom home builders. Everything for your mini needs. Friendliest service in the Tri-County area.

LI'L HOUSE

Forest Fair Mall, I-275, Exit 39, Cincinnati, OH 45240. (513) 671-4901. Mon.-Sat. 10 a.m.-9 p.m.; Sun., noon-5 p.m. Large selection of dollhouses, furniture and miniatures of all types. Convenient hours.

PRISCILLA'S DOLLHOUSE AND BED & BREAKFAST

5 S. West St., Westerville, OH 43081. (614) 882-3910. Call for hours. Near Columbus, Ohio, in historic Westerville. A full line miniatures shop established 20 years ago. Classes and handcrafted items. No catalog.

REMEMBER WHEN

9328 Chillicothe Rd., Rt. 306, Kirtland, OH 44094. (216) 256-3721. Tues.-Sat., 10 a.m.-5 p.m.; Sun., noon-4 p.m. A full service, complete line miniatures shop with a strong focus on miniatures from quality national and local artisans. Classes and custom work available.

THE LITTLE VILLAGE

21 S. Main St., PO Box 1052, Waynesville, OH. (513) 897-0333. Wed.-Fri., 11:30 a.m.-5:30 p.m.; Sat., 11 a.m.-6 p.m.; Sun., 12-5 p.m. Extended hours, Nov.-Dec. Full service miniatures shop. Dollhouses, furniture, landscaping, building and electrical supplies. Many handcrafted items.

THE MINIATURE SHOPPE AT TOWNE SQUARE

23 Public Square, Suite L-2, Medina, OH 44287. (216) 725-2133; FAX (216) 722-8455. Mon.-Sat., 10 a.m.-6 p.m.; Sun., 12-5 p.m. Dollhouses, miniatures, kits, complete line of building supplies, collectibles, Walt Disney Classic Collection.

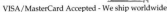

OKLAHOMA

ALL THINGS SMALL

6444 NW Expressway, #420D, Oklahoma City, OK 73132 (405) 721-8336. Tues.-Fri., 10 a.m.-6 p.m.; Sat., 10 a.m.-4 p.m. The finest selection of quality kits, accessories, building, landscaping and electrical supplies in central Oklahoma. Handcrafted items by national and local artisans. We build, wire and repair on site. Customer service is our specialty.

SUSIE'S MINIATURE MANSION

623 E. Don Tyler, Dewey, OK 74029. (918) 534-2003. Daily, 10 a.m.-5 p.m. Over 4,500 sq. ft. Oklahoma's largest and greatest selection of dollhouses. Impressive line of furniture, accessories and building supplies. Full service, mail order available. Well worth the drive.

OREGON

COASTAL HOUSE OF MINIATURES

425 SW Hwy. 101, P.O. Box 394, Depoe Bay, OR 97341. (503) 765-2468. Open seven days a week, 10 a.m.-5 p.m. Located on the central Oregon coast. Everything in miniatures: dollhouses, building supplies, lumber, kits, furniture and accessories, including special handcrafted items by local artisans.

DAISY'S ESSENTIALS, INC.

1517 SW Sunset Blvd., Portland, OR 97201. (503) 452-8216. Tues.-Sat., 10 a.m.-6 p.m. Specializing in dolls by Dollykins, Angel Children, Judy Orr and London Supply Co. I also carry Bespaq, Aztec, Enrique Quintanar, Olszewski, Mama Bear Creations, Miniature Rose, plus many others. I also have a large assortment of gifts.

LOOKINGGLASS MINIATURES

Lookingglass Miniatures, 635 NE Chestnut Ave., Roseburg, OR 97470. (503) 673-5445. Mon.-Fri., 10:30 a.m.-5 p.m.; Sat., 10:30 a.m.-4 p.m. Closed Sun. Everything to finish your dollhouse or roomboxes. Dollhouses, furniture, lumber, kits, landscaping, dolls and doll kits. We welcome all to visit our shop.

MARY PAUL MINIATURES

11511 S.W. Pacific Hwy., Portland, OR 97223. (503) 244-4490 Mon.-Sat., 10 a.m.-5 p.m. The total miniatures store. Full line of furniture, accessories, books, dolls, quilts, rugs, building components, electrical, house shells, and kits, Northwest Handcrafters' work and authentic "Heritage Colors" paint. Wholesale paint dealership information: LSASE.

THE STAIRWELL

1790 Center St. NE, Salem, OR 97301-4356. Mon., 1-4 p.m.; Tues.-Sat., 10 a.m.-4 p.m. Full line for dollhouse decorators and builders as well as dollhouse people.

PENNSYLVANIA

A-C'S EMPORIUM

100 E. McMurray Rd., Rte. 19, McMurray, PA 15317. (412) 942-4120. Mon.-Sat., 10 a.m.-5 p.m.; open Thurs. until 7 p.m. Dollhouses, kits, complete building center and mini lumber department. Large selection of wallpaper and carpets. Electrical kits/food items. Specializing in handcrafted miniatures. A complete miniatures shop.

The Builder's & Collector's Choice in Dollhouse Supplies

3311 Liberty Street, Liberty Village
Erie, PA 16508, (814) 864-5959

Tue, Thu, Fri 10-5. Wed 10-8; Sat 10-4

CAROLYN'S
Dollhouses & Miniatures

Hours:

Monday to
Saturday 10-5
Oct-Mar./Sun. 10-4
Closed Tuesday

1684 DeKalb Pike
Blue Bell, PA 19422
(610) 279-5099

The Area's *Largest* Miniatures Shop!
Charlene & Chris

From the Past

Dollhouses & Miniatures
• Furniture • Accessories
• Building Supplies

Open 7 Days
Mon.-Fri. 11-5, Sat. 10-5
Sun. 12-5

Box 382 • Route 73 • Skippack, PA 19474

(610) 584-5842

NEW HOPE, PENNSYLVANIA
in Beautiful Bucks County

New Hope Miniatures
127C South Main Street
New Hope, PA 18938
215-862-5833

🌿 Doll Houses   🌿 Miniatures
🌿 Furniture   🌿 Accessories

OPEN 7 DAYS A WEEK, YEAR 'ROUND! • 1-800-296-4133

ACD MINIATURES

3311 Liberty St., Erie, PA 16508. (814) 864-5959. Tues., Thurs., Fri., 10 a.m.-5 p.m.; Wed., 10 a.m.-8 p.m.; Sat., 10 a.m.-4 p.m.; closed Sun. and Mon. Full line shop, with quality houses, roomboxes, building and wiring supplies and the work of local artisans.

BARB'S MINIATURE COTTAGE

Trexler Mall, Trexlertown, PA 18087. (610) 366-0546. Mon.-Sat. 10 a.m.-9 p.m.; Sun., 12-5 p.m. Nationally-known artisans for the true collector. Quality houses. Assembly on premises available. Classes. Experienced staff. Displays.

CAROLYN'S

1684 DeKalb Pike, Blue Bell, PA 19422. (610) 279-5099. Mon.-Sat., 10 a.m.-5 p.m.; Open Sun., Oct.-March, 10 a.m.-4 p.m.; closed Tuesday. Full service for beginner to advanced. Dollhouses, furnishings and accessories.

DOLL HOUSE DECOR

Rt. 100, PO Box 223, Village of Eagle, PA 19480. (610) 458-5669. Tues.-Sat., 10 a.m.-5 p.m.; Sun., during Nov. and Dec., 1-4 p.m. Full line miniatures shop, specializing in high-quality dollhouses and accessories, many handcrafted. Large variety of unusual room displays.

FROM THE PAST

Box 382, Rt. 73, Skippack, PA 19474. (610) 584-5842. Mon.-Fri., 11 a.m.-5 p.m.; Sat., 10 a.m.-5 p.m.; Sun., noon-5 p.m. One-stop shop for all your dollhouse needs. Handmades and limited edition items available.

JUST MINIATURE SCALE

100 S. Pennsylvania Ave., Greensburg, PA 15601. (412) 838-0505. Mon.-Sat., 10 a.m.-5 p.m. Established in 1981. Selection is enormous. Service and knowledge set us apart. Come to browse or buy—you'll enjoy! Fifteen minutes from either Irwin or New Stanton exit from PA turnpike.

NEW HOPE MINIATURES

127C South Main St., New Hope, PA 18938. (215) 862-5833, (800) 296-4133, FAX (215) 862-3984. Open seven days year 'round. Handcrafted items by leading artisans are our specialty. Large selection of houses. Full-service friendly, knowledgeable help. A must shop for collectors as well as the beginner.

THE DOLL & MINI NOOK

336 W. Broad St., Quakertown, PA 18951. (215) 536-4242 - 1 (800) 591-6886. Tues.-Thurs., 10 a.m.-4 p.m.; Fri., 10 a.m.-6 p.m.; Sat., 10 a.m.-4 p.m.; closed Sun. and Mon. Call for summer hours. Dollhouse kits, large selection of furniture and accessories, electrical components and building supplies. Full line of collectible dolls.

BARB'S
MINIATURE COTTAGE

Barb's Miniature Cottage
Trexler Mall • Trexlertown, PA
(610) 366-0546

Approx. 5 mi. west of Allentown on Rt. 222
Call for directions.
Mon.-Sat. 10-9; Sun. 12-5

You've Got A Friend In Pennsylvania

DOLL HOUSE DECOR, INC.

Dollhouses and Fine Accessories
Tues.-Sat. 10-5

Rt. 100 - P.O. Box 223
Village of Eagle, PA 19480

1-1/2 miles north of PA Turnpike, exit 23

(610) 458-5669

DOLLHOUSES

VISIT
Western Pennsylvania

just miniature scale

40 minutes East of Pittsburgh
15 minutes from PA Turnpike
Downtown Greensburg, Pennsylvania
Mon. - Sat. 10-5

jms   100 S. Pennsylvania Ave.
Greensburg, PA 15601
412/838-0505

MINIATURES

PEG SZEKELY   336 W. BROAD STREET
(215) 536-4242   QUAKERTOWN, PA 18951
(800) 591-6886

The Doll & Mini Nook

COLLECTIBLE DOLLS
DOLL-RELATED ITEMS, DOLLHOUSES
AND MINIATURES

HOURS
TUES.-THURS. 10-4
FRI.   10-6
SAT.   10-4
CLOSED SUN.-MON.
(Call for summer hours)

THE DOLLHOUSE

223 York Rd., Warminster, PA 18974. (215) 443-7781. Mon.-Sat., 10 a.m.-5p.m.; Sun., noon-4 p.m.; closed Sundays from April through September. Complete selection of dollhouses, furniture, kits, accessories, dolls, handcrafted items, tools, building and electrical supplies. Custom services available.

VILLAGE MINIATURES

2012 Marietta Ave., Lancaster, PA 17607. (717) 397-2650. Mon.-Fri., 10 a.m.-5 p.m., Sat., 10 a.m.-4 p.m., closed Wed. We will build from a plan or kit. We also do house repairs and will restore old homes. All building supplies in stock.

WEE HOME SHOPPE

279 Mill St., Danville, PA 17821. (717) 275-6538. Tues.-Sat., 10 a.m.-4:30 p.m. Friendly, full line shop featuring custom houses, quality house and furniture kits, building, decorating and wiring supplies, accessories "in all scales!"- many by area artisans. Classes. Creative customer assistance. Parking in the rear.

RHODE ISLAND

MINIATURE OCCASIONS & DOLLS

57 Bellevue Ave., Newport, RI 02840. (401) 849-5440 or (800) 358-4285. Mon.-Sat., 10 a.m.-5 p.m. Summer hours later. In the Newport historic shopping district, our store/workshop features a range of dollhouses and furnishings. We will even do an exact copy of your real home. We ship anywhere. Our desire is to meet your miniatures desires. Don't forget we are a full service doll hospital to meet all the restoration needs of our customers. Good things come in small packages.

THE TINY TOUCH

223 County Rd., (behind Getty Gas), Rt. 114, Barrington, RI 02806. (401) 245-8820. Tues.-Fri., 10 a.m.-5:30 p.m.; Thur., 10 a.m.-7 p.m.; Sat., 10 a.m.-4 p.m. Special Christmas hours. Friendly, full-line shop. Quality houses and furniture, building and wiring supplies, carpeting and wallpaper and many accessories. Helpful service.

SOUTH CAROLINA

CHERISHABLES

104 Trinity St., Uptown Exchange, Abbeville, SC 29620. (803) 459-5662. FAX (803) 459-5463. Mon.-Thur., 10 a.m.-5 p.m.; Fri.-Sat. 10 a.m.-8 p.m.; Sun. 1 p.m.-5 p.m. Cherishables is located in historical Abbeville, SC. Dollhouses, titles and transfers, furniture, lighting, kits, Ron Benson's porcelain sculptures and other fine accessories. Will ship.

CRAFTY ANN'S DOLLHOUSE SHOPPE

2005 Beltline Blvd., Columbia, SC 29204. (803) 782-0440. Mon.-Fri., 11 a.m.-5 p.m.; Sat., 11 a.m.-3 p.m. Dollhouse shop with everything for the miniatures enthusiast. Dollhouses, furniture kits, building supplies, books and accessories for beginners and collectors. Personnel to assist you.

JACKIE & PAT'S DOLLHOUSES

3050 Wade Hampton Blvd., Taylor, SC 29687. (803) 292-2877. Mon.-Fri., 10 a.m.-6 p.m.; Sat., 10 a.m.-5 p.m.; closed Sun. Dollhouses, building materials, furniture and accessories. Electrification and assembly available.

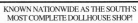

TENNESSEE

INNOVATIVE MINIATURES & CRAFTS

7616 Lee Hwy., Chattanooga, TN, 37421. Just off I-75. (615) 899-1903. One of the South's largest shops. Everything for the miniaturist and collector. Handcrafted items from national artisans. Stables, horses and accessories, Fashion dollhouses, forts, castles, military miniatures, flower punches.

MINIATURE COTTAGE INC.

410 E. Iris Dr., Nashville, TN 37204. (615) 298-2872. Mon.-Sat., 10 a.m.-5 p.m. Most complete miniatures specialty shop in the Southeast. Ideas and service abound! Hard-to-find tools, building supplies, accessories and collectibles. All services available.

MINIATURE GALLERY

(901) 398-MINI. 1-800-274-ELFS. By appointment. All services—custom and stock work.

MY SMALL WORLD

(c/o The Salt House), 127 Fox St., Jonesborough, TN 37659. (615) 753-5113. Mon.-Sat., 10 a.m.-5 p.m.; Sun., 1 p.m.-5 p.m. Complete line of building materials and accessories. Dolls and dollhouses. Many handcrafted and locally crafted items.

RED BARN DOLLHOUSES & MINIATURES

1747 Murfreesboro Rd., Manchester, TN 37355. (615) 728-2968. Tues.-Sat., 10 a.m.-5:30 p.m. Finished houses, kits, house plans, Victorian and Contemporary furniture, accessories, lighting and building components.

SUZANNE ANDREW'S MINIATURE SHOPPE

3915 Nolensville Rd., Nashville, TN 37211. (615) 833-5555. Mon.-Sat., 10 a.m.-5:30 p.m.; open Sun. Nov.-Dec., 1-5 p.m. till Christmas. Handcrafted miniatures by national artisans, dollhouses custom built or kit, electrification, painting, wallpapering, furniture and accessories.

TEXAS

COLIBRI'S, INC.

5600 W. Lovers Lane, Suite 139, Woodlane Plaza Shopping Center, Dallas, TX 75209. (214) 352-3394. Mon.-Sat., 10 a.m.-6 p.m. A complete dollhouse and miniatures shop. Custom work available. Will ship anywhere in the world.

KAREN'S MINIATURES

6020 Doniphan, Suite B1, El Paso, TX 79932. (915) 584-9889. Tues.-Sun., 9 a.m.-5 p.m. Full line miniature store. Building supplies, Bespaq furniture, etched brass kits, garden furniture kits in 1/4″, 1/2″ and 1″ scale. Now with Cat's Meow Village.

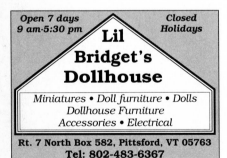

MINIATURE MAGIC

8650 Spicewood Springs Rd., #112, Austin, TX 78759. (512) 918-1800, FAX (512) 918-1800. Mon.-Sat. 10 a.m.-7 p.m. Dollhouses, dollhouse accessories, furniture, lighting, building supplies, dollhouse kits, dolls, animals, Barbies and teddy bears. Discover, Visa and MasterCard. Layaway and mail order.

THROUGH THE KEYHOLE

12215 Coit Rd., 102 Olla Podrida, Dallas, TX 75251. (214) 387-2923. Mon.-Sat., 10 a.m.-6 p.m.; Thurs., 10 a.m.-9 p.m.; Sun., noon-6:00 p.m. The complete dollhouse shop with the largest selection in Dallas. A dollhouse department store for all your miniatures needs.

UTAH

SHUTT'S MINIATURES

4152 So. 1785 West, Carriage Square, Salt Lake City, UT 84119. (801) 965-9636. Weekdays, 10 a.m.-6 p.m.; Sat., 10:30 a.m.-3 p.m. Largest complete miniature store in Salt Lake City. Classes available. Everything you need for your dollhouse.

VERMONT

FRED'S DOLLHOUSE & MINIATURE CENTER

RR #2, Box 2134, Route 7, Pittsford Village, VT 05763. (802) 483-6362. Mon.-Sat., 9 a.m.-5 p.m.; Sun., noon-5 p.m. Vermont's most unique dollhouse and miniatures showcase, with more than 1,000 miniatures on display. We specialize in Vermont-made dollhouses and custom building. 92-page catalog, $5.

LIL BRIDGET'S DOLLHOUSE

Rt. 7 N., Box 582, Pittsford, VT 05763. (802) 483-6367. Open seven days a week, 9 a.m.-5:30 p.m.; Closed holidays. Doll hospital, dollhouses, dolls, paper dolls and plush dolls. Doll furniture, doll books, dollhouse furniture, miniatures and electrical.

VIRGINIA

BELL'S EXCLUSIVES

4 E. Nine Mile Rd., Highland Springs, VA 23075. (804) 328-0121. Tues., Wed., Fri., Sat., 10 a.m.-3 p.m.; Thurs., 10 a.m.-8 p.m.; closed Sun. and Mon. Also by appointment. Miniatures, dolls, houses, kits and accessories. Everything needed to complete a dollhouse. A true miniature heaven. Plan to spend the day, but it will take longer to see all the wonderful little things.

CASTLEMILL MINIATURES

Located in Blue Ridge Creations—A Crafters Gallery, 22 East Main St., Berryville, VA 22611. (703) 955-0053. Mon.-Sat., 9:30 a.m.-5:30 p.m.; Sun. noon-5 p.m. Dollhouses - kits and custom assembling, Miniature - furniture, accessories, dolls, building supplies. Handcrafted pieces including Amish buggies, unique garden accessories with real rose topiaries in Chippendale planters and matching arbors, benches, chairs and tables.

MINIATURES FROM THE ATTIC

111 Park Ave., Falls Church, VA 22046. (703) 237-0066. FAX (703) 237-0070, call first. Friendly, knowledgeable service. Large selection of quality dollhouses and kits. Building, wiring, decorating services and supplies. Handcrafted items, many by local artisans. We build, wire, repair and remodel on site. Classes.

Once upon a time

**120 Church Street NE
Vienna, Virginia 22180
(703) 255-3285**

Full service miniatures shop within a unique toy store. Dollhouse kits, building supplies, furniture, dolls, landscaping, wiring.

Mon. - Sat. 10-5 • Sun. 12 - 5 (Oct. thru May)

The Tiny Dwelling

**1510 King Street
Alexandria, VA 22314
(703) 548-1223**

Dollhouses, furniture, accessories
**Something for the beginner
and the advanced collector**
3 Blocks East of KING ST. METRO
Hours: Tues.-Sat. 10-5:30 • Sun. 12-5
Closed Mondays
NO CATALOG AVAILABLE

The Dollhouse Cottage

Over 21 years in miniatures.
Plus, a huge selection of Madame Alexander Dolls.

13821 100th NE
Kirkland, WA 98034
(206) 821-1579

Hart Miniatures

Dollhouse Kits • Furniture • Wiring
Building Supplies • Wallpaper
Handcrafted Items • Dolls
"How-To" Books

Greenleaf • Tobe Tailored
Dollhouse Shoppe • Smidgens • Jacquelines
• Itty Bitty Critters • Monkey Business

10917 149th St. E. • Puyallup, WA 98374
(206)840-0424

ONCE UPON A TIME

120 Church St., N.E., Vienna, VA 22180. (703) 255-3285. Mon.-Sat., 10 a.m.-5 p.m.; Sun., noon-5 p.m. Oct. through May. A full service miniatures shop within a unique toy store. Dollhouses, kits, building supplies, furniture, dolls, landscaping and wiring.

R & N MINIATURES

458-C Wythe Creek Rd., Poquoson, VA 23662. (804) 868-7103. Tues.-Fri., 10 a.m.-6 p.m.; Sat., 10 a.m.-4 p.m. Everything to finish and furnish your dollhouse. The most complete selection of quality kits, accessories and building supplies in Southern Virginia. Handcrafted items are our specialty. Price list, $2.

THE TINY DWELLING

1510 King St., Alexandria, VA 22314. (703) 548-1223. Tues.-Sat., 10 a.m.-5:30 p.m., Sun., 12-5 p.m., closed Mondays. A complete shop, accessories, kits, components, electric items, building supplies (wood, tools & glue). Friendly service!

WASHINGTON

CHRYSALIS

16 E. Main St., Auburn, WA 98002. (206) 804-0705; FAX (206) 804-6875. Mon.-Fri., 10 a.m.-6 p.m.; Sat., 10 a.m.-5 p.m.; Sun., 11 a.m.-4 p.m. Complete line of miniatures for the builder and collector. Monthly newsletter. Classes available. Mail order.

DOLLHOUSE COTTAGE

13821 100th NE, Kirkland, WA 98034. (206) 821-1579. Open Tues.-Sat. Full-line dollhouse miniatures shop. Just north of Kirkland.

FRITZ'S DOLLHOUSE

730 NW Gilman Blvd., PO Box 1121, Issaquah, WA 98027. (206) 392-6134. Mon.-Sat., 10 a.m.-6 p.m.; Sun., 11 a.m.-5 p.m. Unique handmade miniatures and accessories, dollhouses, classes and special orders.

HART MINIATURES

10917 - 149th St. E., Puyallup, WA 98374-3730. (206) 840-0424. Open seven days a week, 10 a.m.-5 p.m. We specialize in keeping prices reasonable for all budgets— beginners to collectors! Quarterly sales. Seasonal displays.

JODY'S SHOPPE/A WEE CO.

1314 E. 72nd., Tacoma, WA 98404. (206) 531-4220. Open 7 days a week, 11 a.m.-6 p.m. July and Aug., 11 a.m.-4 p.m. Store front, miniature houses and kits, all furnishings and accessories. Handcrafted items. We finish houses and do wiring. Classes available.

R & N Miniatures

Dollhouses & Accessories
Only 20 Minutes east of Williamsburg via
Interstate 64 (exit 256 B) Route 171 (Victory Blvd.)
**458-C Wythe Creek Rd.
Poquoson, VA 23662
(804) 868-7103**
Tues. - Fri. 10-6, Sat. 10-4 • Price List - $2.00

CHRYSALIS MINIATURES

16 EAST MAIN STREET
AUBURN, WASHINGTON 98002
(206) 804-0705 • FAX (206) 804-6875

BUILD A DREAM

Fritz's Dollhouse

Welcome!

Cindi Vee   206-392-6134

 We have classes & monthly specials

**Jody's Shoppe/
A Wee Company**

**1314 East 72nd
Tacoma, WA 98404** (Near K-Mart Store)
206-531-4220

The Pacific Northwest's complete miniatures shop, featuring local artists. Custom bldg. plans, kits, houses, wiring, furniture, dolls, lumber yard, accessories, supplies, handcrafted items.

**Open Tue-Sat 11 am-6 pm
Jul & Aug 11 am-4 pm**

LITTLE HABITATS

3238 Locker Rd. SE, Port Orchard, WA 98366. (206) 871-1100, (800) 856-6561. Mon.-Fri., 10 a.m.-5 p.m.; Sat., 10 a.m.-4 p.m. More than 2,600 sq. ft. of dollhouses and miniatures. Exclusive dollhouses by Stan Ohman. Shop is near Seattle. We are worth the visit.

MR. PEEPERS

6200 Sand Point Way N.E., Seattle, WA 98115. (206) 524-6464. Call for hours. Complete building and decorating supplies, Noel Thomas shells, kits, fashion dollhouses, handcrafted miniatures from local and national artisans, construction, repair and decorating services available.

MRS. GULLIVER'S

1362 Jadwin Ave., Richland, WA 99352. (509) 943-3803. Mon.-Fri., 10 a.m.-6 p.m.; Sat., 10 a.m.-5 p.m. Newest miniatures shop in eastern Washington. Full service. Classes and expert advice.

ROSALIE WHYEL MUSEUM OF DOLL ART

1116 108th Ave. NE, Bellevue, WA 98004. (206) 455-1116; FAX (206) 455-4793. While at the Museum, visit the Museum Store. It is always stocked with rare, hard to find miniature collectibles created by renowned artists; also, a large assortment of contemporary artist dolls.

ROSE'S FASCINATION SHOP

624 Edmonds Way, Edmonds, WA 98020. (206) 775-2017. Mon.-Sat., 9:30 a.m.-6 p.m.; Sun., noon-4 p.m. Full-service dollhouse and miniatures store with 1,700 sq. ft. of dollhouse shells and kits. We carry a complete line of furniture and accessories. The largest selection in the state of Washington.

SMALL WONDERS

3527 E. Sprague Ave., Spokane, WA 99202. (509) 535-5011. Mon., Tues., Thur.-Sat., 10 a.m.-5:30 p.m.; Sun., 11 a.m.-4:30 p.m. Closed Wed. 4,000 sq. ft. devoted to 1" scale miniatures. Complete supply of dollhouse kits, building materials, wallpaper, carpets, lighting and accessories. Beginner to collector.

SMALL WORLD USA

16401 Hwy. 99, Lynnwood, WA 98037. (206) 355-6007. Mon.-Sat., 10 a.m.-7 p.m.; Sun., 12-4 p.m. Come see us at our new location, historic Keelers Korner Gas Station. A full line miniatures store with a helpful staff. Shells, kits, electrical and building supplies and more.

TINY TREASURES

16421 Cleveland St., #F, Redmond, WA 98052. (800) 883-8261. Mon.-Fri., 12-7 p.m.; Sat., 10 a.m.-5 p.m. Complete line of mini-building materials and supplies! Friendly and knowledgeable service! Great variety of furnishings and accessories.

WOOD WORLD INC.

12459 Ambaum Blvd. SW, Suite A, Seattle, WA 98146-2660. (206) 246-1483, FAX (206) 246-1483. Open Tues.-Sat., 10 a.m. to 5:30 p.m. Open daily Dec 1-24, Closed Dec. 25 to Jan. 1. A full service miniatures shop with art wood and wood work. Custom designed miniature furniture available upon request. Specialize in exotic hardwoods.

WASHINGTON, D.C.

WASHINGTON DOLLS' HOUSE & TOY MUSEUM

5236 44th. St., NW, Washington, DC 20015. (202) 244-0024. Tues.-Sat., 10 a.m.-5 p.m.; Sun., noon-5 p.m.; closed Mon. Our museum shop contains a wide assortment of dollhouse furnishings for both beginners and collectors. Building and wiring supplies and publications. Antique dolls and toys on consignment.

WEST VIRGINIA

SUE'S PLACE

Rt. 1, PO Box 320-E, Philippi, WV 26416. (304) 457-5529. Tues.-Thurs., 10 a.m.-6 p.m.; Fri., 10 a.m.-8 p.m.; Sat., 10 a.m.-3 p.m. Located just minutes from the historical covered bridge on Route 250 and 119 South. A complete hobby shop and much more.

WISCONSIN

HOBBY CRAFT OF MADISON

6632 Odana Rd., Madison, WI 53719-1012. (608) 833-0489. FAX (608) 833-1118. Mon.-Fri., 9 a.m.-9 p.m.; Sat. & Sun., 9 a.m.-6 p.m. We've doubled our size and can offer more of everything you need to build, finish, and furnish your dollhouse! 10% discount to N.A.M.E. members. We ship free on all orders over $100. Check out our model trains, RC cars, planes and boats. Plastic models, art & unique craft supplies, wide range of construction hobby supplies.

LILLIPUT STUDIO

149 W. Main St., PO Box 235, Cambridge, WI 53523. (608) 423-9700. Mon.-Sat., 9 a.m.-5 p.m.; Sun., noon-5 p.m. Summer and holiday hours extended—call first. Specializing in accessories for the beginner or advanced miniaturist. Dollhouses and kits, furniture, supplies. Competent staff.

MINI-TIQUES

140 S. Main St., Thiensville, WI 53092. (414) 242-8053. Tues.-Sat. 10 a.m. - 5 p.m.; Dec., Sun. 11 a.m.-2 p.m. Specializing in dollhouses, dollhouse furniture and roomboxes. Unique handcrafted accessories and supplies including laces, trims, silk ribbon, wallpaper, flower punches and much more. Ask about our classes and our buyer's incentive program. Expert advice given freely! Catalog $3.

SMALL WORLD

416 E. Main St., Waukesha, WI 53186. (414) 544-6240. Tues., Wed., Fri., Sat., 10 a.m.-6 p.m.; Thurs., 10 a.m.-7 p.m.; April thru August, Sun., noon-4 p.m. A full service dollhouse shop. Building supplies, paints, wallpaper, wiring, furniture and accessories. Handcrafted items. Assembly, wiring and decorating available. Hometown, friendly service.

TINY TREASURES

Rt. 6, Box 1 Hwy 16E., Sparta, WI 54656. (608) 269-2533. FAX (608) 269-3684. Mon.-Sat., 10 a.m.-5 p.m.; Sun. by appointment. Unique and handmade miniatures. Everything you need to complete your mini house or roombox. Consignment , country crafts, and giftware.

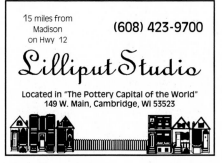

REFRACTIONS, THE HIGHLAND HOUSE GIFTS & COLLECTIBLES

115 Hwy. 20 East, Fonthill, Ontario, Canada L0S 1E0. (905) 892-4340, FAX (905) 735-2040. Selection of dollhouses and miniatures, including Concord, MacDoc rugs, Alice Lacey "wicker", B. Elster's Min. Corner. Good collection of fruits, vegetables and flowers for dollhouses. The shop also has collectible dolls, plates and hand-blown glass.

THE TOY FACTORY

10007-80 Ave., Edmonton, Alberta, Canada T6E 1T4. (403) 433-5482. Mon.-Fri., 9 a.m.-5 p.m.; Sat., 9 a.m.-3 p.m. Closed Sunday. We carry the largest selection of miniatures and fashion dollhouse supplies in Western Canada at the best prices possible.

UPSTAIRS DOWNSTAIRS DOLLHOUSES & MINIATURES

#105, 2250 Oak Bay Ave., Victoria, BC, Canada V8R 1G5. (604) 598-0887, FAX (604) 598-0897. Tues.-Sat., 10 a.m.-5 p.m. Complete miniatures retail store offering supplies, kits and handcrafted accessories for the Canadian miniaturist. 200+ page catalog available, $5. We specialize in mail order.

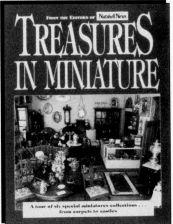
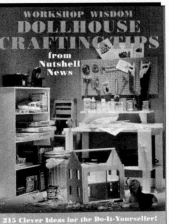

MINIATURES SHOW & SALES

Retail shows are held year around in hotels and civic centers throughout the country. Show dealers offer hard-to-find handcrafted items.

Dates and times are subject to change. Please check for complete and updated information before traveling long distances to a show. These consumer show listings are printed free of charge. Show dates for 1994 and 1995 should be sent in writing to: Editor, *The Miniatures Catalog*, 21027 Crossroads Circle, PO Box 1612, Waukesha, WI 53187.

1 9 9 5

OCTOBER 13-14
Williamsburg VA 7pm-9:30, 10-4. Williamsburg Dollhouse Miniatures Show & Sale. Ramada-Inn Historic Area. Fri. preview $10, incl. 2 day adm.; no children. Adm: $5; child 12 & under $2.50. No strollers. Info: Tom Bishop, PO Box 8571, Coral Springs FL 33075; 305-755-0373.

OCTOBER 13-14
Livonia MI 6:30pm-9:30, 9:30 to 3:30. Getzan Fall Miniature Show & Sale. Holiday Inn-Livonia West. Friday preview, $10, incl. Sat. Adm. Adm: $5. Info: J. Getzan, 1935 S. Plum Grove Rd. #350, Palatine IL 60067; 708-394-4654.

OCTOBER 13-15
Cherry Valley CA A Weekend Get-Away of Miniatures, Highland Springs Resort. First 100 - Reserve today. Minis-N-Mountains. Call or write to Minis-N-Mountains, 10626 Flaxton St., Culver City CA 90230-5443; 310-204-4114.

OCTOBER 14
Rochester NY Doll & Miniature Show & Sale. Monroe County Fairgrounds-Dome Center, Henrietta NY. Adm: $3.25 (12/older); child $1.75. Info: Kohlman-Finnerty Promotions, 311 Bramhall Dr., Rochester NY 14626; 716-723-1535.

OCTOBER 14-15
St. Louis MO 10-5, 11-4. Gateway Miniature Show & Sale. Harley Hotel, 3400 Rider Trail South, Earth City. Adm: $4.50; child $2. Info: Miniature Museum of Greater St. Louis, 208 Fawn Meadows, Ballwin MO 63011; 314-394-9576.

OCTOBER 14-15
Rockford IL 10-5, 11-4. Dreams Come True Dollhouse & Miniature Show & Sale. Ramada Inn. Adm: $3, 2-day pass $4; child $2. Info: Karin Skupien, 10337 Ellsworth Dr., Roscoe IL 61073; 815-623-2011.

OCTOBER 14-15
Renton WA 10-5, 11-4. 12th Annual Miniature Show & Sale. Renton Community Center. Adm: $3.50; child $1.50. Info: Tess Jones, 13233 168th Ave. NE, Redmond WA 98052; 206-556-0804; or Jean Sprague, 1530 38th E, Seattle WA 98112; 206-322-4765.

OCTOBER 14-15
Saratoga Springs NY 11-4. 3rd Annual Children's Museum at Saratoga Dollhouse & Miniature Show. New York State Armory, 61 Lake Ave. Sat. preview 10-11, $6. Adm: $4; child under 12 $2. Info: Mary Lou Hall, 26 Underwood Dr., Saratoga Springs NY 12866; 518-587-1579.

OCTOBER 14-15
Columbus OH 10-4, 10-4. Columbus Miniature Society Show & Sale. Aladdin Temple, 3850 Stelzer Rd. Adm: $3; child under 12 $1. No strollers. Info: Mary Lauer, 614-882-8354; or Susan Rensch, 614-272-7169.

OCTOBER 14-15
Olmsted Falls OH 10-5, 11-4. 2nd Annual Dollhouse Show & Sale. Grand Pacific Hotel, Corner of Columbia & Mill. Adm: $3. Info: Small Houses, 8064 Columbia Rd., Olmsted Falls OH 44138; 216-235-5051.

OCTOBER 14-15
Amarilla TX 12-5, 12-5. Magic Moments in Miniature. Amarillo Garden Center, 1400 Streit. Adm: $2; child 12 & under $1. Info: 806-352-3451.

OCTOBER 20-21
Plainville LI NY 7pm-9:30, 10-4. Long Island, NY Dollhouse Miniatures Show & Sale. Plaza Hotel-Plainview, LI. Fri. preview $10, incl. 2 day adm.; no children. Adm: $5; child 12 & under $2.50. No strollers. Info: Tom Bishop, PO Box 8571, Coral Springs FL 33075; 305-755-0373.

OCTOBER 20-21
Grand Rapids MI 1-9, 10-4. 15th Grand Affair in Miniatures. Mayflower Congregational Church, 2345 Robinson Rd. SE. Adm: $3.50. Info: Mayflower Women, 2345 Robinson Rd., SE, Grand Rapids MI 49506; 616-459-6255.

OCTOBER 21
Lakeville MA 9-3:30. Doll & Miniature Show & Sale. Lakeville United Church of Christ, Rte. 18 & 105. Adm: $2; child under 12 $1. Info: Florence Cornell; 508-947-0283.

OCTOBER 21
Crystal River FL 10-4:30. 7th Annual Dollhouse & Miniature Show & Sale. Crystal River National Guard Amory. Adm: $3; child under 12 $1.50. Info: Mary Hughes, 11 Fig Ct. W. SMW, Homosassa FL 34446; 904-382-2814.

OCTOBER 21-22
King of Prussia PA 11-5, 11-4. Greenberg's Great Train, Dollhouse & Toy Show. Valley Forge Convention Center. Adm: $5; child 6-12 $2; under 6 free. Info: Greenberg Shows, Inc.; 410-795-7447.

OCTOBER 21-22
Norcross GA 11-5, 11-4. Greenberg's Great Train, Dollhouse & Toy Show. North Atlanta Trade Center.. Adm: $5; child 6-12 $2; under 6 free. Info: Greenberg Shows, Inc.; 410-795-7447.

OCTOBER 21-22
Greensburg PA 10-5, 11-5. 17th Annual Dollhouse & Miniature Show & Sale. Mountain View Inn, Rte. 30 East. Adm: $3; child $1. Info: Anita Owen, 107 Evergreen Rd., Jeannette PA 15644; 412-837-8199.

OCTOBER 21-22
Medford OR 10-5, 10-4. Fun-A-Fair Doll, Bear & Miniature Show. Medford Armory, 1701 S. Pacific Hwy. Adm: $3.50; & child $2.00. Info: SASE Muriel Butler, 11340 Michael Rd., Central Point OR 97502; 503-855-7302.

OCTOBER 22
McLean VA 11-5. Tysons Corner Fall Show. Holiday Inn, McLean. Adm: $4; child $2. Info SASE Molly Cromwell, 4701 Duncan Dr., Annandale VA 22003.

OCTOBER 28
Melbourne FL 10-5. Brevard Assoc. of Miniaturists "Fantasies in Miniatures." Azan Shrine Temple, 1591 W. Eau Gallie Blvd. Adm: $3; under 6 free. Info: Dorothy Cotter, 407-777-2385; or Linda Boyd, 407-773-6759.

OCTOBER 28-29
Upper Marlboro MD 11-5, 11-4. Greenberg's Great Train, Dollhouse & Toy Show. The Show Place Arena, P. G. Equestrian Center. Adm: $5; child 6-12 $2; under 6 free. Info: Greenberg Shows, Inc.; 410-795-7447.

OCTOBER 28-29
Novi MI 11-5, 11-4. Greenberg's Great Train, Dollhouse & Toy Show. Novi Expo Center. Adm: $6; child 6-12 $2; under 6 free. Info: Greenberg Shows, Inc.; 410-795-7447.

OCTOBER 29

Batavia NY 9:30-4. 24th Doll, Miniature & Teddy Bear Show & Sale. Batavia Downs. Adm: $4; child free. Info: 716-343-6279; 716-343-3750; or SASE Saturday's Child, 2 Woodcrest Dr., Batavia NY 14020.

OCTOBER 29

Mt. Arlington NJ 10-4. New Jersey's Best Miniatures & Dollhouse Sale. Mt. Arlington Sheraton Hotel. Adm: $4; child under 12 $1. Info: American Show Mgmt., 8 Kingston Ln., Succasunna NJ 07876; 201-584-1566.

OCTOBER 29

Beaumont TX 10-6. 16th Annual Doll Show & Sale. Beaumont Hilton Hotel. Adm: $2; child under 12 $2. Info: Jan Ramirez, 409-727-0567; or 409-727-8597.

OCTOBER 29

Honolulu HI 9-5. Wai Kiki & Mini. Sheraton Waikiki. Adm: $2. Info: Teri's Mini Workshop, Box 387, Goldenrod FL 32733.

NOVEMBER 3-5

Elk Grove Village IL 7pm-9, 10-5, 11-4. 21st Annual WEE "c" Club Miniature & Dollhouse Show & Sale . Holiday Inn, 1000 Busse Rd. Fri. Preview , $7, incl. 3-day admit. Adm: $4. Info: Pat Marnell, 312-759-4210.

NOVEMBER 3-5

Toronto Ontario Canada 12-9, 10-8, 10-6. The Hobby Show. International Centre, Mississauga. Adm: $7.50; srs. & child 6-12 $4.25; under 6 free. Info: Ted Curl, 7 Avon Ct., Whitby Ont L1N 3H2, Canada; 905-428-6466.

NOVEMBER 4

Largo FL 10-4. Doll, Bear & Miniature Show & Sale. Honeywell Minnreg. Bldg. Adm: $3; child 10 & under $1. Info: Diana Gemmiti, 14690 54th Way N. Clearwater FL 34620; 813-536-8857.

NOVEMBER 4

Glendale CA 10-4. Happy Dolling Combined Doll & Miniatures Show & Sale. Glendale Civic Audit., 1401 N. Verdugo Rd, Adm: $4; srs. $3; child under 12 $2. Info: Barbara Korui, PO Box 6806, Burbank CA 91510-6806.

NOVEMBER 4-5

St. Charles MO 11-5, 11-4. Greenberg's Great Train, Dollhouse & Toy Show. St. Charles Exhibition Hall. Adm: $5; child 6-12 $2; under 6 free. Info: Greenberg Shows, Inc.; 410-795-7447.

NOVEMBER 4-5

Edison NJ 11-5, 11-4. Greenberg's Great Train, Dollhouse & Toy Show. Raritan Center Expo Hall. Adm: $5; child 6-12 $2; under 6 free. Info: Greenberg Shows, Inc.; 410-795-7447.

NOVEMBER 5

Burnaby British Columbia Canada 11-5. 4th Annual West Coast Dollhouse & Miniature Show & Sale (formerly New Westminster Show). Clarion Hotel, 4331 Dominion St. Adm: $4; srs. & child $2. No strollers. Info: John & Peggy Howard, 1537 Coquitlam Ave., Port Coquitlam BC V3B 1H6 Canada; 604-464-8536.

NOVEMBER 5

Hamilton, Ontario Canada 10-4. 13th Annual Dollhouse & Miniature Show & Sale. Mohawk College Students Centre, Fennell Campus.. Adm: $3; srs & child under 12 $2. Info: Paty Marotti, 27 E. 44th St., Hamilton Ont. L8T 3G6 Canada.

NOVEMBER 5

Danbury CT 10-4. Miniatures & Dollhouse Accessories Show & Sale. Ethan Allen Inn. Adm: $4.50; child under 10 $2. Info: Kitty Osker, 904-428-1718.

NOVEMBER 5

Frederick MD 11-5. 31st Annual Frederick Dollhouse & Miniatures Sale. Holiday Inn, I-270 at MD Rt. 85, exit 31A. Preview 9am-11, $10. Adm: $4, child under 12 $1. No strollers. No smoking. Info: Sally R. Hofelt, 17524 Longstreet Cir., Sharpsburg MD 21782; 301-432-5628.

NOVEMBER 11

Port St. Lucie FL 10-4. Doll, Teddy Bears & Miniatures Show & Sale. Polish American Social Club, 343 Prima Vista Ave. Adm: $3; child under 12 $1. Info: Olivia Hagerman; 407-489-6102.

NOVEMBER 10-12

King of Prussia PA 6pm-9, 10-5, 11-5. 27th Annual Philadelphia Miniaturia Show & Sale. Valley Forge Convention Center. Fri. preview $14, limited to 400, incl. 3-day admit. Adm: $6; child under 10 $3. Info: LSASE, Phila. Miniaturia, PO Box 518, Langhorne PA 19047; 215-355-2033.

NOVEMBER 11-12

Pennsauken NJ 11-5, 11-4. Greenberg's Great Train, Dollhouse & Toy Show. South Jersey Expo Center. Adm: $5; child 6-12 $2; under 6 free. Info: Greenberg Shows, Inc.; 410-795-7447.

NOVEMBER 12

Atlanta GA 10-4 13th Annual Christmastime in Dixie Miniatures Show & Sale. Ramada Dunwoody Convention Center. Adm: $4. Info: Valerie Rogers, Bright Star Promotions, 3428 Hillvale Rd., Louisville KY 40241; 502-423-STAR.

NOVEMBER 12

Elkhart IN 12th Annual Elkhart Dollhouse & Miniatures Show & Sale. United Labor Agency Hall, 3322 Middlebury St., Adm: $2; child $1. Info: Marcia Hicks, 610 S. Cavin St., Ligonier IN 46767; 219-894-3051.

NOVEMBER 17-18

Anaheim CA 5:30pm-9:30, 9-4. Southern California's Top Artisans' Miniature Show & Sale. Inn at the Park Hotel. Adm: $5; child 7-12 $3. Info: TAMS, 1241 Deer Trail Ln., Solvang CA 93463; 805-688-0638.

NOVEMBER 17-19

Ft. Lauderdale FL 7pm-9:30, 10-5, 11-5. 14th Annual Christmas Festival of Dolls, Bears and Dollhouse Miniatures Show & Sale. War Memorial Auditorium, 800 NE 8 St. Fri. preview admit $8 inc. 3 days. Adm: $5; child under 12 free. Info: Collectors Treasures; 305-722-3111.

NOVEMBER 18

St. Catharines Ontario Canada 10-4. G.N.O.M.E. Dollhouse Miniatures Show & Sale. Russell Avenue Community Center. Adm: $3; srs $2. Info: G.N.O.M.E. Club, 905-682-5832.

NOVEMBER 18

Ann Arbor MI 10-4. 6th Annual Ann Arbor Area Miniatures Show & Sale. Weber's Inn. Adm: $4. Info: Valerie Rogers, Bright Star Promotions, 3428 Hillvale Rd., Louisville KY 40241; 502-423-STAR.

NOVEMBER 18-19

Monroeville PA 11-5, 11-4. Greenberg's Great Train, Dollhouse & Toy Show. Pittsburgh Expo Mart. Adm: $5; child 6-12 $2; under 6 free. Info: Greenberg Shows, Inc.; 410-795-7447.

NOVEMBER 18-19

Houston TX 11-5, 11-4. Greenberg's Great Train, Dollhouse & Toy Show. George R. Brown Convention Center. Adm: $5; child 6-12 $2; under 6 free. Info: Greenberg Shows, Inc.; 410-795-7447.

NOVEMBER 18-19

Largo FL 10-5, 11-4. 17th Annual Dollhouse & Miniature Show & Sale. Honeywell Minn-Reg Bldg., 6340-126 Ave. South. Adm: $4; srs. $3.50; child 12 & under w/adult $1. Info: SEMTA, Charlene Blue, 5211 Casilla Way South, St. Petersburg FL 33712; 813-864-4160.

NOVEMBER 23 TO DECEMBER 3

Fort Wayne IN 12-7 daily. Dollhouse Festival. Chamber of Commerce, 826 Ewing St. Adm: $2.50; child $1.50. Info: Ft. Wayne Civic Theatre Guild, 219-493-4918.

NOVEMBER 24-26

Kenosha WI 10-5, 10-5, 11-4. Room Box Show. Miniature Village, 1725 50th St. Adm: free. Lillian & Harvey Knapp, 1725 50th St., Kenosha WI 53140; 1-800-383-0188.

NOVEMBER 25

St. George Ontario Canada 10-4. 2nd Annual St. George Miniature Dollhouse Show & Sale. St. George United Church Hall. Info: D. W. Miniatures, PO Box 234, St. George Ontario N0E 1N0 Canada; 519-448-3549.

NOVEMBER 25-26

Dallas TX 11-5, 11-4. Greenberg's Great Train, Dollhouse & Toy Show. Dallas Convention Center. Adm: $5; child 6-12 $2; under 6 free. Info: Greenberg Shows, Inc.; 410-795-7447.

NOVEMBER 25-26

Wilmington MA 11-5, 11-4. Greenberg's Great Train, Dollhouse & Toy Show. Shriners Auditorium. Adm: $5; child 6-12 $2; under 6 free. Info: Greenberg Shows, Inc.; 410-795-7447.

DECEMBER 2-3

Timonium MD 11-5, 11-4. Greenberg's Great Train, Dollhouse & Toy Show. Timonium Fairgrounds. Adm: $5; child 6-12 $2; under 6 free. Info: Greenberg Shows, Inc.; 410-795-7447.

DECEMBER 3

W. Springfield MA 10-4. 5th Annual Holiday in Miniatures. H.C.I.L. Bldg-Eastern States Expo Grounds. Info: Claire's Corner, 413-783-1520; or Crystal Brook, 413-245-7647.

DECEMBER 9-10

Fort Washington PA 11-5, 11-4. Greenberg's Great Train, Dollhouse & Toy Show. Fort Washington Expo Center. Adm: $5; child 6-12 $2; under 6 free. Info: Greenberg Shows, Inc.; 410-795-7447.

DECEMBER 30-31

West Palm Beach FL 11-5, 11-4. Greenberg's Great Train, Dollhouse & Toy Show. South Florida Fairgrounds. Adm: $5; child 6-12 $2; under 6 free. Info: Greenberg Shows, Inc.; 410-795-7447.

1 9 9 6

JANUARY 6-7

Virginia Beach VA 11-5, 11-4. Greenberg's Great Train, Dollhouse & Toy Show. Virginia Beach Convention Center. Adm: $4; child 6-12 $2; under 6 free. Info: Greenberg Shows, Inc., 7566 Main St., Sykesville MD 21784; 410-795-7447.

JANUARY 6-7

Jacksonville FL 11-5, 11-4. Greenberg's Great Train, Dollhouse & Toy Show. Greater Jacksonville Fairgrounds. Adm: $4; child 6-12 $2; under 6 free. Info: Greenberg Shows, Inc., 7566 Main St., Sykesville MD 21784; 410-795-7447.

JANUARY 13-14

Atlanta GA 11-5, 11-4. Greenberg's Great Train, Dollhouse & Toy Show. North Atlanta Trade Center. Adm: $4; child 6-12 $2; under 6 free. Info: Greenberg Shows, Inc., 7566 Main St., Sykesville MD 21784; 410-795-7447.

JANUARY 14

Sarasota FL 11-5. Sarasota Festival of Dollhouse Miniatures. Adm: $4; child $2. Info: Molly Cromwell, 4701 Duncan Dr., Annandale VA 22003; 703-978-5353.

JANUARY 20-21

Tampa FL 11-5, 11-4. Greenberg's Great Train, Dollhouse & Toy Show. Florida State Fairgrounds. Adm: $4; child 6-12 $2; under 6 free. Info: Greenberg Shows, Inc., 7566 Main St., Sykesville MD 21784; 410-795-7447.

JANUARY 20-21

Portland OR 10-5. 19th Annual Miniature Show & Sale, OMSI's Education Resource Center. Adm: $5; child $3. Info: D & K Enterprises, PO Box 5916, Vancouver WA 98668; 360-693-7629.

JANUARY 20-21

Gainesvile FL 10-5, 12-4. 6th Annual SEMTA Miniature Show & Sale. Gainesville Women's Club, 2809 W. University Ave. Adm: $4; srs. $3.50; child 12 & under w/adult $1. Info: Charlene Blue, 5211 Casilla Way S., St. Petersburg FL 33712; 813-864-4160.

JANUARY 21

Newark NJ 10-4:30. World of Mini Mania Miniature & Miniature Doll Show Holiday Inn North - Newark Airport. Adm: $5; srs.

w/ID $4.50; child $2.50. Info: SASE Victorian Vintage, PO Box 761, Clark NJ 07066; FAX 908-382-1910.

JANUARY 26-28

Fullerton CA 7pm-9:30, 10-5, 12-4. Southern California "Masters of the Miniature Arts" Show & Sale. Holiday Inn-Fullerton. Fri. preview $10 incl. 3-day admit, no children. Adm: $5, child 12 & under $2.50. No strollers. Info: Tom Bishop, PO Box 8571, Coral Springs FL 33075; 305-755-0373.

JANUARY 27-28

Upper Marlboro MD 11-5, 11-4. Greenberg's Great Train, Dollhouse & Toy Show. The Show Place Arena, P. G. Equestrian Center. Adm: $4; child 6-12 $2; under 6 free. Info: Greenberg Shows, Inc., 7566 Main St., Sykesville MD 21784; 410-795-7447.

FEBRUARY 2-3

Atlanta GA 7pm-9:30, 10-4. "Heart of Dixie" Dollhouse Miniature Show & Sale. Ramada Hotel & Conference Center Perimeter-Dunwoody. Fri. preview $10, incl. 2-day admit, no children. Adm: $5, child 12 & under $2.50. No strollers. Info: Tom Bishop, PO Box 8571, Coral Springs FL 33075; 305-755-0373.

FEBRUARY 3-4

Edison NJ 11-5, 11-4. Greenberg's Great Train, Dollhouse & Toy Show. Raritan Center Expo Hall. Adm: $4; child 6-12 $2; under 6 free. Info: Greenberg Shows, Inc., 7566 Main St., Sykesville MD 21784; 410-795-7447.

FEBRUARY 3-4

Janesville WI 10-9, 12-5. Fantasy Faire Miniatures Show & Sale. Janesville Mall, 2500 Milton Ave. Adm: free. Info: Janesville 1/12 Mini Club, 402 Lincoln St. Janesville WI 53545; 608-754-7219.

FEBRUARY 4

Charlotte NC 11-5. Charlotte Festival of Dollhouse Miniatures. Hyatt-Charlotte. Adm: $4; child $2. Info: Molly Cromwell, 4701 Duncan Dr., Annandale VA 22003; 703-978-5353.

FEBRUARY 9-11

Ft. Lauderdale FL 7pm-9:30, 10-5, 11-4. South Florida Dollhouse Miniatures Show & Sale. The Quest Quarters Suites Hotel. Fri. preview $10, incl. 3-day admit, no children. Adm: $5, child 6-12 $2.50. No strollers. Info: Rita DeMarco, 2026 Helton Creek Rd., Blairsville GA 30512; 706-745-3989; or Tom Bishop, 305-755-0373.

FEBRUARY 10-11

Columbus OH 11-5, 11-4. Greenberg's Great Train, Dollhouse & Toy Show. Franklin County Veterans Memorial. Adm: $4; child 6-12 $2; under 6 free. Info: Greenberg Shows, Inc., 7566 Main St., Sykesville MD 21784; 410-795-7447.

FEBRUARY 10-11

Sacramento CA 10-5, 10-4. Valentine's Miniature Show & Sale. Ben Ali Temple, 3262 Marysville Blvd. Info: Carol Blake, 707-374-2282.

FEBRUARY 15-25

Nutshell News Mini Tour of the Southwest US, including Arizona and southern California. Museums, provate collections, artisans. Info: A1 Tours and Travel, 2701 Sunset Point Rd., Clearwater, FL 34619; 800-677-9412; or outside US, 813-797-1477.

FEBRUARY 17

Punta Gorda FL 9-4. Doll, Toy, Bear & Miniature Show & Sale. Charlotte County Memorial Auditorium, 74 Taylor St. Adm: $2. Port Charlotte Doll Club of Florida, 18544 Ebb Ave., Port Charlotte FL 33948; 813-743-2180.

FEBRUARY 17

Palm Beach Gardens FL 10-4:30. Wonderful Miniatures Show & Sale. MacArthur's Holiday Inn. Adm: $4. Info: Bright Star Promotions, Inc. 3428 Hillvale Rd., Louisville KY 40241; 502-423-STAR.

FEBRUARY 17-18

Monroeville PA 11-5, 11-4. Greenberg's Great Train, Dollhouse & Toy Show. Pittsburgh Expo Mart. Adm: $4; child 6-12 $2; under 6 free. Info: Greenberg Shows, Inc., 7566 Main St., Sykesville MD 21784; 410-795-7447.

FEBRUARY 17-18

Morro Bay CA 10-4, 11-3. Central Coast Miniatures & Dollhouse Show & Sale. Masonic Temple, 13238 Atascadero Rd. Adm: $4; srs. $3; child $2.50. Info: Miniature Cottage Shop, 1260 Main St., Morro Bay CA 93442; 805-772-7858.

FEBRUARY 24

Enfield CT 9:30=4. Enfield Lions Club Dollhouse & Miniatures Show & Sale. Enfield Street School. Adm: $2.50; srs. & child $1. Info: Enfield Lions Club, PO Box 241, Enfield CT 06082; 203-745-2835.

MARCH 2-3

Pennsauken NJ 11-5, 11-4. Greenberg's Great Train, Dollhouse & Toy Show. South Jersey Expo Center. Adm: $4; child 6-12 $2; under 6 free. Info: Greenberg Shows, Inc., 7566 Main St., Sykesville MD 21784; 410-795-7447.

MARCH 2-3

Lincolnwood IL 10-5, 11-4. The North Shore Dollhouse & Miniature Show. Radisson Hotel. Info: Women's Council of Sacred Heart Church, 1077 Tower Rd., Winnetka IL 60093.

MARCH 3

Rockville MD 11-5. Mid-Atlantic Dollhouse Miniatures Show & Sale. Doubletree Hotel. Adm: $4, child $2. Info: Molly Cromwell, 4701 Duncan Dr., Annandale VA 22003; 703-978-5353.

MARCH 9

Boca Raton FL 9:30-5. Les Petits Collecteurs of South Florida. Boca Raton Community Center. Adm: $4; child under 12 $2. Info: Brenda Levenson; 305-782-3943.

MARCH 9

St. George Ontario Canada 10-4. 4th Annual St. George Spring Miniature Show &

Sale. St. George United Church Hall. Info: D. W. Miniatures, PO Box 234, St. George Ontario N0E 1N0 Canada; 519-448-3549.

MARCH 9-10

Indianapolis IN 10-5, 11-4. Hoosier Dollhouse Miniatures Show & Sale. Farm Bureau Bldg., Indiana State Fairgrounds. Adm: $. Info: Sandy Cox, 9411 E. 141 St., Fishers IN 46038; 317-773-1131.

MARCH 11-12

Seattle WA 10-5, 11-4. Seattle Dollhouse Miniatures Show. Seattle Center Flag Pavilion. Adm: $5; srs. $4; child $2. No strollers. Info: Pat Williams, 1376 SW Station Cir., Port Orchard WA 98366; 360-876-6644.

MARCH 16-17

Timonium MD 11-5, 11-4. Greenberg's Great Train, Dollhouse & Toy Show. Timonium Fairgrounds. Adm: $5; child 6-12 $2, under 6 free. Info: Greenberg Shows, Inc., 7566 Main Street, Sykesville MD 21784; 410-795-7447.

MARCH 16-17

St. Charles MO 11-5, 11-4. Greenberg's Great Train, Dollhouse & Toy Show. St. Charles Exhibition Hall. Adm: $5; child 6-12 $2, under 6 free. Info: Greenberg Shows, Inc., 7566 Main Street, Sykesville MD 21784; 410-795-7447.

MARCH 17

Calgary Alberta Canada 10-4. Public Day - Gathering - Calgary Miniatures Club. Marlborough Inn. Info: Sherrill Bedu, 264 Sunmills Pl. SE, Calgary Alberta Canada T2X 2P1; 403-256-4052.

MARCH 17

South Bend IN 10-4. Showcase of Miniatures, Dollhouse & Miniatures Show & Sale. Century Center, 120 S. St. Joseph St. Adm: $4; child $2. Info: Timeless Images, 8863 E. Black Point Rd., Syracuse IN 46567; 219-856-4356.

MARCH 17

Frederick MD 11-5. Frederick Dollhouse & Miniature Sale. Holiday Inn. Adm: $4. Info: Sally Hofelt, 17524 Longstreet Cir., Sharpsburg MD 21782; 301-432-5628.

MARCH 23-24

Hackensack NJ 11-5, 11-4. Greenberg's Great Train, Dollhouse & Toy Show. Fairleigh Dickinson University. Adm: $5; child 6-12 $2, under 6 free. Info: Greenberg Shows, Inc., 7566 Main Street, Sykesville MD 21784; 410-795-7447.

MARCH 23-24

Kansas City MO 10-5, 11-4. Miniature Fantasies Show & Sale. Plaza Inn, 45th & Main. Adm: $5; child 12 & under $2. Info: Sharon O'Neill, 9508 Walmer, Overland Park KS 66212; 913-341-5509.

MARCH 24

Rochester NY 10-5. Spring Into Miniatures. Holiday Inn. Adm: $4; child 10 & under $2. Info: Linda Moynihan, RR1 Box 435; Oneida NY 13421; 315-363-2890.

MARCH 24

Jamaica NY 10-4:30. World of Mini Mania Miniature & Miniature Doll Show-Fall Frolic. Holiday Inn North-JFK Airport, Belt Parkway Exit 150th St.. Adm: $5; srs. w/I.D. $4.50; child $2.50; tickets at door. No strollers. Info: Victorian Vintage, PO Box 761, Clark NJ 07066; 908-382-2133.

MARCH 29-31

Arlington Heights IL 7pm-9:30, 10-5, 11-4. Chicago "Masters of the Miniature Arts" Show & Sale. Radisson Hotel. Fri. preview $10, incl. 3-day admit, no children. Adm: $5; child 12 & under $2.50. No strollers. Info: Tom Bishop, PO Box 8571, Coral Springs FL 33075; 305-755-0373.

MARCH 30

Rochester NY 10-4. Doll & Miniature Show & Sale. Monroe County Fairgrounds-The Dome Center. Adm: $3.25 12 & older; child $1.75. Info: Kohlman Finnerty Promotions, 311 Bramhall Dr., Rochester NY 14626; 716-723-1535.

MARCH 30-31

Novi MI 11-5, 11-4. Greenberg's Great Train, Dollhouse & Toy Show. Novi Expo Center. Adm: $5; child 6-12 $2, under 6 free. Info: Greenberg Shows, Inc., 7566 Main Street, Sykesville MD 21784; 410-795-7447.

MARCH 30-31

Wilmington MA 11-5, 11-4. Greenberg's Great Train, Dollhouse & Toy Show. Shriners Auditorium. Adm: $5; child 6-12 $2, under 6 free. Info: Greenberg Shows, Inc., 7566 Main Street, Sykesville MD 21784; 410-795-7447.

MARCH 31

Mystic CT 10-4. Spring Festival of Miniatures & Dollhouses. Best Western. Adm: $3.50; srs. & child 5-12 $2.50; under 5 free. Info: Gerry & Harold Musselwhite, PO Box 1187, Westerley RI 02891; 401-596-9218.

APRIL 6

Largo FL 10-4. Doll, Bear & Miniature Show & Sale. Honeywell Minnreg Bldg. Adm: $3; 10 & under $1. Info: Diana Gemmiti, 14690 54th Way N., Clearwater FL 34620; 813-536-8857.

APRIL 12-13

Livonia MI 6:30-9:30, 9:30-3:30. Getzan Spring Miniature Show & Sale. Holiday Inn-Livonia West. Fri. preview $10, incl. 2-day admit. Adm: $5. Info: J. Getzan, 1935 S. Plum Grove Rd. #350; Palatine IL 60067; 708-394-4654.

APRIL 13-14

San Rafael CA 10-5, 11-4. Marin Miniature Show & Sale. Marin Center Exhibit Hall. Adm: $5; 62+ $4; child 6-12 $2. Info: Marin Miniature Shows, 20 Truman Dr., Novato CA 94947; 800-303-7349.

APRIL 14

Reading (Wyomissing) PA 10-4. 5th Spring Reading Area Dollhouse Miniatures Show & Sale. Sheraton Berkshire Hotel. Adm: $3.50; child 10 & under $1. Info: Diana Fogel, 322 Longview Rd., Boyertown PA 19512; 610-689-4825.

APRIL 14

Richmond VA 11-5. Old Dominion Show & Sale. Hyatt. Adm: $4; child $2. Info: Molly Cromwell, 4701 Duncan Dr., Annandale VA 22003; 703-978-5353.

APRIL 20-21

St. Louis MO 10-5, 11-4. Gateway Miniature Show & Sale. Harley Hotel, 3400 Rider Trail South, Earth City. Adm: 4.50; child $2. Info: 314-394-9576.

APRIL 20-21

Earth City MO 10-5, 11-4. Gateway Miniature Show & Sale. Harley Hotel, I-270 & I-70. Adm: $4.50; child $2. Info: Miniature Museum of Greater St. Louis, 208 Fawn Meadows, Ballwin MO 63011; 314-394-9576.

APRIL 26-28

Omaha NE 7pm-9, 11-5, 11-4. Children's Literature Show & Sale. Holiday Inn Central. Adm: $4, child 12 & under $1.50. Info: Edna H. Perkins. 806, Hogan Dr., Papillion NE 68046; 402-339-5071.

APRIL 27-28

New York NY 11-4:30, 11-4:30. International Guild of Miniature Artisans Show & Sale. Crown Plaza Hotel, Broadway & 49th. Adm: $8. Info: Roberta Partridge, 539 Randall Rd., Ballston Spa NY 12020; 518-885-5231.

APRIL 28

Wilmington DE 10-4. First State Mini Club Show & Sale. The Brandywine Terrace, 3416 Philadelphia Pike. Adm: $4.50; srs. $4; child under 12 $2.50. Info: First State Mini Club of Delaware, 118 Hunter Ct., Wilmington DE 19808; 302-239-2608.

MAY 1-15

Tour for Miniaturists in England, incl. London Dollshouse Festival. Info: Glenda Cavanaugh, 8117 Cowichan Rd., Blaine WA 98230-9566; 360-371-7497.

MAY 3-5

Dallas TX 5:45pm-11, 12-5,12-5. Miniature Mayfest. Clarion Hotel. Fri. preview $25. Adm: $4. Info: Dollhouse Museum of the Southwest, 2208 Routh St., Dallas TX 45201; 214-969-5502.

MAY 5

Sacramento CA 9-3. 17th Annual Springtime Parking Lot Faire & Flea Market. Elegant Dollhouse. Adm: free. Info: Elegant Dollhouse, 1120 Fulton Ave., Sacramento CA 94825; 916-484-0411.

MAY 5

Batavia NY 9:30-4. 24th Annual Doll, Miniature, Teddy Bear Show & Sale. Batavia Down. Adm: $4; child free. Info: Saturday's Child, 2 Woodcrest Dr., Batavia NY 14020; 716-343-3750, or 716-343-6279.

MAY 12

Bangor ME 10-4. Annual Mother's Day Sale Show. 10-4. Bangor Civic Center, 100 Dutton St. Adm: $2; 12 & under free. Info: Mainely Dolls Club, RFD 2 Box 3010; Dexter ME 04930; 207-924-6431.

MAY 18

Fresno CA 10-4. San Joaquin Valley Doll Club Show & Sale. Fresno Fairgrounds. Adm: $4. Info: Martha Allen, 1355 Garland Ave., Clovis CA 93612.

MAY 19

McLean VA 11-5. Tysons Corner Spring Show. Holiday Inn. Adm: $4; child $2. Info: Molly Cromwell, 4701 Duncan Dr., Annandale VA 22003; 703-978-5353.

MAY 25-26

New Orleans LA 12-5, 12-5. 12th Annual Gulf South Miniature & Dollhouse Event. Landmark Hotel-Metairie. Adm: $5. Info: National Kidney Foundation of LA, 8200 Hampson St., New Orleans LA 70118; 504-861-4500.

JUNE 2

Sturbridge MA 11-5. Sturbridge Festival of Dollhouse Miniatures. Host Hotel on Cedar Lake. Adm: $4; child $2. Info: Molly Cromwell, 4701 Duncan Dr., Annandale VA 22003; 703-978-5353.

JUNE 8

Largo FL 10-4. Doll, Bear & Miniature Show & Sale. Honeywell Minnreg Bldg. Adm: $3; 10 & under $1. Info: Diana Gemmiti, 14690 54th Way N., Clearwater FL 34620; 813-536-8857.

JUNE 15-16

King of Prussia PA 11-5, 11-4. Greenberg's Great Train, Dollhouse & Toy Show. Valley Forge Convention Center. Adm: $5; child 6-12 $2, under 6 free. Info: Greenberg Shows, Inc., 7566 Main Street, Sykesville MD 21784; 410-795-7447.

JULY 7

Boothbay Harbor ME 10-4. Downeast Miniatures. Boothbay Region Grammar School, Rte. 27. Adm: $3. Info: Sandy Shumway; 516-287-8407.

JULY 13-14

Belleville IL 10-4, 11-4. 12th Annual Belleville Dollhouse & Miniature Show. Belle-Clair Expo Center. Adm: $3. Info: Kay Kleber, 300 Ross Ln. Belleville IL 62220; 618-233-0940.

JULY 27-28

Lakeland FL 10-5, 11-4. Lakeland Miniature Guild Dollhouse & Miniatures Show & Sale. Lakeland Civic Center, 700 W. Lemon St. Adm: $4; child under 12 $1. Info: Lynn Johnson, PO Box 1486, Lakeland FL 33802-1486; 813-644-2819.

JULY 28

South Portland ME 10-4. Tiny Treasures Miniature Summer Spectacular. Sheraton Tara Hotel. Adm: $4, child $2. Info: Tiny Treasures, RR 1 Box 1133, Litchfield ME 04350; 207-268-4771.

AUGUST 10-11

Peoria IL 10-5, 11-4. 14th Annual PAMS Dollhouse Miniatures Show & Sale. Holiday Inn, Brandywine. Adm: $3, $5-two days. Info: Sandy Haddad, 449 E. Highpoint Dr., Peoria IL 61614; 309-691-7985.

AUGUST 11

Bemidji MN 10-4. 8th Annual Dolls, Toys, Teddy Bears & Miniature Show. Northern Inn. Adm: $2. Info: Sharon Geisen, 5827 Balsam Rd. NW, Bemidji MN 56601; 218-751-8277.

AUGUST 17-18

Cleveland OH 1-5, 10-4. 25th Annual Cleveland Miniature Society Fair. Holiday Inn, Strongsville. Sat. preview $8. Adm: $4; child $2. Info: Cleveland Miniature Society, PO Box 1043, Cleveland OH 44120; 216-468-0174.

SEPTEMBER

Final date to be announced. Nutshell News European Miniatures Tour including Denm,ark, Germany, and France, with an extension to Miniatura in England. For information contact A1 Tours and Travel, 2701 Sunset Point Rd., Clearwater FL 34621. 800-677-9412; from outside US 813-572-9071.

SEPTEMBER 6-7

Milwaukee WI 7pm-9:30, 10-4. Milwaukee Marketplace.

SEPTEMBER 7-8

Indianapolis IN 10-5, 11-4. Hoosier Dollhouse Miniatures Show. Farm Bureau Bldg., Indiana State Fairgrounds. Adm: $4. Info: Sandy Cox, 9411 E. 141 St., Fishers IN 46038; 317-773-1131.

SEPTEMBER 7-8

Seattle WA 10-5, 11-4. Seattle Dollhouse Miniature Show. Seattle Center Flag Pavilion. Info: Pat Williams, 1376 SW Station Circle, Port Orchard WA 98366; 360-876-6644.

SEPTEMBER 8

Timonium MD 11-5. Baltimore Festival of Dollhouse Miniatures. Holiday Inn. Adm: $4; child $2. Info: Molly Cromwell, 4701 Duncan Dr., Annandale VA 22003; 703-978-5353.

SEPTEMBER 8

Reading (Wyomissing) PA 10-4:30. 12th Annual Fall Reading Dollhouse Miniatures Show & Sale. Sheraton Berkshire Hotel. Info: Diana Fogel, 322 Longview Rd., Boyertown PA 19512; 610-689-4825.

SEPTEMBER 15

Fairfield CT 10-4. 9th Annual Doll, Dollhouse & Miniature Show. Stratfield School, 1407 Melville Ave. Adm: $2.50; srs $2; child under 12 $1. Info: Gail Pecora; 203-333-6525.

SEPTEMBER 14-15

Des Moines IA 10-5, 11-4. Tiny Treasures. Howard Johnson's Hotel & Convention Center. Adm: $4; child $2. Info: LSASE Noreen Christians, 7696 Alpine Dr., Des Moines IA 50322.

SEPTEMBER 21-22

Denver CO 10-5, 11-5. 16th Annual Miniatures Show & Sale. Holiday Inn, I-70 & Chambers. Adm: $4; srs. & child $4. Info: Denver Museum of Miniatures, Dolls & Toys, 1880 Gaylord St., Denver CO 80206; 303-322-1053.

SEPTEMBER 28

Largo FL 10-4. Doll, Bear & Miniature Show & Sale. Honeywell Minnreg Bldg. Adm: $3; 10 & under $1. Info: Diana Gemmiti, 14690 54th Way N., Clearwater FL 34620; 813-536-8857.

OCTOBER 5-6

Portland OR 10-5. 18th Annual Portland Miniature Show. OMSI's Education Resource Center. Adm: $4; child $3. Info: D & K Enterprises, PO Box 5916, Vancouver WA 98668; 360-693-7629.

OCTOBER 6

Maquoketa IA 10-4. KCHS Dollhouse, Miniature & Hobby Show & Sale. Jackson County Historical Museum, 1212 E. Quarry. Adm: $1.50; child under 10 free. Info: Jackson County Historical Museum, PO Box 1245, Maquoketa IA 52060; 319-652-5020.

OCTOBER 12

Rochester NY 10-4. Doll & Miniature Show & Sale. Monroe County Fairgrounds-The Dome Center. Adm: $3.25 12 & older; child $1.75. Info: Kohlman Finnerty Promotions, 311 Bramhall Dr., Rochester NY 14626; 716-723-1535.

OCTOBER 12-13

Amarilla TX 12-5, 12-5. Magic Moments in Miniatures. Amarillo Garden Center, 1400 Streit. Adm: $2; child 12 & under $1. Info: 806-352-3451.

OCTOBER 13

Bangor ME 10-4. Miniatures, Bears, Dolls & Toys Christmas in October Sale & Show. Bangor Civic Center, 100 Dutton St. Adm: $2; 12 & under free. Info: Mainely Dolls Club, RFD 2 Box 3010, Dexter ME 04930; 207-924-6431.

OCTOBER 13-22

Kenner LA County Fair & Wild West Show. The Esplanade. Info: 504-468-6116; or 407-876-3631.

OCTOBER 20

McLean VA 11-5. Tysons Corner Fall Show. Holiday Inn. Adm: $4; child $2. Info: Molly Cromwell, 4701 Duncan Dr., Annandale VA 22003; 703-978-5353.

OCTOBER 27-NOVEMBER 5

Dallas TX County Fair & Wild West Show. Collin Creek Mall. Info: 214-422-1070; or 407-876-3631.

NOVEMBER 1-3

Elk Grove Village IL 7pm-9:30, 10-5, 11-4. Wee "c"s Whimsical Wonderland. Holiday Inn. Info: Wee "c" Club Linda Ibbs, 1706, W. Sable Ln #302, Mt. Prospect IL 60056; 708-437-6218.

NOVEMBER 3

Frederick MD 11-5. Frederick Dollhouse & Miniature Sale. Holiday Inn. Adm: $4. Info: Sally Hofelt, 17524 Longstreet Cir., Sharpsburg MD 21782; 301-432-5628.

NOVEMBER 3

Burnaby British Columbia Canada 11-5, 11-5. 5th Annual West Coast Dollhouse & Miniature Show & Sale. The Clarion Hotel. Adm: $4; srs $2; child 6-12 $2. Info: John &

Peggy Howard, 1537 Coquitlam Ave., Port Coquitlam, BC Canada V3B 1H6; 604-464-8536.

NOVEMBER 10

Elkhart IN 10-4. 17th Annual Elkhart Dollhouse & Miniatures Show & Sale. United Labor Agency Hall, 3322 Middlebury St. Adm: $2; child $1. Info: Marcia Hicks, 610 S. Cavin St., Ligonier IN 46767; 219-894-3051.

NOVEMBER 23

St. George Ontario Canada 10-4. 3rd Annual St. George Christmas Miniature Show & Sale. St. George United Church Hall. Info: D. W. Miniatures, PO Box 234, St. George Ontario N0E 1N0 Canada; 519-448-3549.

DECEMBER 7

Largo FL 10-4. Doll, Bear & Miniature Show & Sale. Honeywell Minnreg Bldg. Adm: $3; 10 & under $1. Info: Diana Gemmiti, 14690 54th Way N., Clearwater FL 34620; 813-536-8857.

1 9 9 7

MARCH 8

St. George Ontario Canada 10-4. 5th Annual St. George Spring Miniature Show & Sale. St. George United Church Hall. Info: D. W. Miniatures, PO Box 234, St. George Ontario N0E 1N0 Canada; 519-448-3549.

MARCH 8-9

Seattle WA 10-5, 11-4. Seattle Dollhouse Miniature Show. Seattle Center Flag Pavilion. Info: Pat Williams, 1376 SW Station Circle, Port Orchard WA 98366; 360-876-6644.

MARCH 8-9

Indianapolis IN 10-5, 11-4. Hoosier Dollhouse Miniatures Show & Sale. Farm Bureau Bldg., Indiana State Fairgrounds. Adm: $. Info: Sandy Cox, 9411 E. 141 St., Fishers IN 46038; 317-773-1131.

APRIL 12

Rochester NY 10-4. Doll & Miniature Show & Sale. Monroe County Fairgrounds-The Dome Center. Adm: $3.25 12 & older; child $1.75. Info: Kohlman Finnerty Promotions, 311 Bramhall Dr., Rochester NY 14626; 716-723-1535.

MAY 1-15

Tour for Miniaturists in England, incl. London Dollhouse Festival. Info: Glenda Cavanaugh, 8117 Cowichan Rd., Blaine WA 98230-9566; 360-371-7497.

MAY 11

Bangor ME 10-4. Annual Mother's Day Sale Show. 10-4. Bangor Civic Center, 100 Dutton St. Adm: $2; 12 & under free. Info: Mainely Dolls Club, RFD 2 Box 3010; Dexter ME 04930; 207-924-6431.

MAY 18

Fresno CA 10-4. San Joaquin Valley Doll Club Show & Sale. Fresno Fairgrounds. Adm: $4. Info: Martha Allen, 1355 Garland Ave., Clovis CA 93612.

MAY 24-25

New Orleans LA 12-5, 12-5. 12th Annual Gulf South Miniature & Dollhouse Event. Landmark Hotel-Metairie. Adm: $5. Info:

National Kidney Foundation of LA, 8200 Hampson St., New Orleans LA 70118; 504-861-4500.

SEPTEMBER 6-7

Seattle WA 10-5, 11-4. Seattle Dollhouse Miniature Show. Seattle Center Flag Pavilion. Info: Pat Williams, 1376 SW Station Circle, Port Orchard WA 98366; 360-876-6644.

OCTOBER 11

Rochester NY 10-4. Doll & Miniature Show & Sale. Monroe County Fairgrounds-The Dome Center. Adm: $3.25 12 & older; child $1.75. Info: Kohlman Finnerty Promotions, 311 Bramhall Dr., Rochester NY 14626; 716-723-1535.

OCTOBER 12

Bangor ME 10-4. Miniatures, Bears, Dolls & Toys Christmas in October Sale & Show. Bangor Civic Center, 100 Dutton St. Adm: $2; 12 & under free. Info: Mainely Dolls Club, RFD 2 Box 3010, Dexter ME 04930; 207-924-6431.

NOVEMBER 22

St. George Ontario Canada 10-4. 3rd Annual St. George Christmas Miniature Show & Sale. St. George United Church Hall. Info: D. W. Miniatures, PO Box 234, St. George Ontario N0E 1N0 Canada; 519-448-3549.

MUSEUM DIRECTORY

On your next excursion, plan a stop at one of these museums and enjoy the wonderful world of miniatures!

ANGEL'S ATTIC

516 Colorado Ave.
Santa Monica CA 90401
213-394-8331

Hours: Thurs.-Sun. 12:30-4:30.
Adm: Adults $4; srs. $3; child under 12 $2.
A museum of antique dollhouses, miniatures, toys and dolls. Tours are available.

MAYNARD MANOR AT MINIATURE MART

1807 Octavia St.
San Francisco CA 94109
415-563-8745

Hours: By appointment only, Mon.-Fri. 10-3.
Adm: $6/person. No children under 12.
Maynard Manor is a 42-room dollhouse with more than 8,000 individual 1" scale miniature furniture and accessories designed by Ellen & John M. Blauer.

MOTT MINIATURES

7700 Orangethorpe Ave. Suite 8
Buena Park CA 90620
714-994-5979

Hours: Call for current hours.
Adm: Call for current information and group reservations.
Over 50 exhibits comprise the Mott Family Collection, including exhibits listed in the Guinness Book of Records. Established in 1949, the collection is the largest exhibit of antique miniatures in the world.

THE PALM SPRINGS DESERT MUSEUM

101 Museum Dr.
Palm Springs CA 92262
619-325-7186

Hours: Weekdays 10 a.m.-4 p.m.; Fri. 1-8; Sat. & Sun. 10 a.m.-4 p.m.; closed Mondays.
Adm: Adults $5; srs. $4; students/military & child 6-17 $2.
Museum is home to the Thomas Jefferson Diplomatic Reception Room and the Leo S. Singer Miniature Room Collection.

THE CAROLE & BARRY KAYE MUSEUM OF MINIATURES

5900 Wilshire Blvd.
Los Angeles CA 90036
213-937-6464

Hours: Tues.-Sat. 10 a.m.-5 p.m.; Sun. 11 a.m.-5 p.m.
Adm: Adults $7.50; srs. 60+ $6.50; students 13-21 $5; child 3-12 $3. Yearly membership $25/individual; $45/family.

This fabulous and exciting new museum is filled with outstanding exhibits from exclusively contemporary artists. There is a wonderful miniatures shop filled with artisans work. Entrance to shop is free.

THE DENVER MUSEUM OF MINIATURES, DOLLS & TOYS

880 Gaylord St.
Denver CO 80206
303-332-3704 (Recording),
303-322-3704 (Offices)

Hours: Tues.-Sat. 10 a.m.-4 p.m.; Sun. 1-4.
Adm: Adults $3; srs. 62+ $2; child 12 & under $2.
The museum displays miniatures, dolls and toys.

THE INTERNATIONAL MUSEUM OF MINIATURES

9 Capitol Hill Ave.
Manitou Springs CO 80829
719-685-1011

Hours: Winter 11 a.m.-4 p.m.; Summer: 10 a.m.-5 p.m.; Tea Room open 11 a.m.-4 p.m. Open 365 days a year.
Adm: Adults $3; srs. 60+ $2.50; child 6-12 $1, child under 6 free. Four collections are housed on the first floor of a National Historic Landmark first occupied in 1895, a project of the Manitou Springs Historical Society. There is a collection of international dolls and international buildings with dolls from each country represented. The Historical Society's collection of antique toys, furniture, and dolls is displayed, as well as "Little London-1888," an historical reconstruction of 17 of the buildings in Colorado Springs and Manitou Springs.

BARNUM MUSEUM

820 Main St.
Bridgeport CT 06604
203-331-9881

Hours: Tues.-Sat. 10 a.m.-4:30 p.m.; Sun. 12-4:30.
Adm: Adults $5; srs. & college students $4; child 4-18 $3.
The world's only museum dedicated to the life and times of P. T. Barnum and Bridgeport's industrial heritage. Built in 1893, highlights include a miniature circus, clown costumes, and personal mementos of Barnum, Tom Thumb and Jenny Lind. The Museum features temporary exhibits in a new wing designed by renowned architect Richard Meier.

DELAWARE TOY & MINIATURE MUSEUM

PO Box 4053, Rte. 141
Wilmington DE 19807
302-427-8697

Hours: Tues.-Sat. 10 a.m.-4 p.m.; Sun. 12-4.
Adm: Call for information on fees and tours.
The Museum is a historical reference of antique and contemporary dollhouses and miniatures; sample furniture; dolls, toys, trains, boats and planes from the 18 to the 20 centuries.

OLD TOWN HALL MUSEUM OF THE HISTORICAL SOCIETY OF DELAWARE

512 Marker St.
Wilmington DE 19801
302-655-7161

Hours: Tues.-Fri. 12-4; Sat. 10 a.m.-4 p.m.
Adm: Call for information.
Museum includes Model House which was made for the U.S. Sanitary Commission Fair in 1864. The house consists of 15 rooms, furnished with items by some of the finest craftsmen of the day.

SMITHSONIAN INSTITUTION'S NATIONAL MUSEUM OF AMERICAN HISTORY

14th St. & Constitution Ave. NW
Washington DC DC 20560
202-357-2700

Hours: Summer hours are June 5 to Labor Day 10 a.m.-6:30 p.m. Call for additional information.
Adm: None.
Museum has one dollhouse on display on the third floor.

WASHINGTON DOLL'S HOUSE & TOY MUSEUM

5236 - 44th St., NW
Washington DC DC 20015
202-244-0024

Hours: Tues.-Sat. 10 a.m.-5 p.m., Sun. 12-5.
Adm: Adults $3; srs. 65+ $2; child under 14 $1.
This pioneer museum features a carefully researched collection of antique dollhouses, dolls, toys and games. Two museum shops: one with doll house-related publications; one with fine handcrafted furnishings.

THE MARY MILLER DOLL MUSEUM

1523 Glynn Ave.
Brunswick GA 31520
912-267-7569

Hours: Mon.-Sat. 11 a.m.-5 p.m.
Adm: Adults $2; child 5-15 $1.50. Call ahead for group tours & rates.

On display is a panorama of more than 3,000 dolls collected world wide as well as a display of antique and modern dolls, miniature shops, dollhouses, doll furniture and toys.

UNION COUNTRY HISTORICAL SOCIETY MUSEUM

PO Box 35
Blairsville GA 30512
706-745-5493

Hours: June-Oct. Wed. - Sat. 10 a.m.-4 p.m.; or by appointment.
Adm: Donation.
Featured are the Enchanted Palace, a 30-room dollhouse based on Queluz, the President's Palace, Lisbon, Portugal; Velmamer, an antebellum model based on a house in Washington, Georgia and the Glen Morgan House, a copy of Jay Gould's home, Lyndhurst, on the Hudson River in New York. The houses were constructed by Margarita Morgan in the 1940s.

ART INSTITUTE OF CHICAGO

Michigan Avenue at Adams St.
Chicago IL 60603

Hours: Mon.-Fri. 10:30 a.m.-4 p.m.; open until 7:30 p.m. on Thurs.; Sat. 10 a.m.-4:30 p.m.; Sun. 12-4:30. Closed Christmas Day and Thanksgiving Day.
Adm: Free with general museum admission (suggested Adults $6; srs., students & child under 12 $3.)
On display are 68 Thorne Rooms.

BLACKBERRY HARVEST DOLLHOUSE MUSEUM

18120 Dixie Hwy.
Homewood IL 60430
708-957-4332

Hours: Wed. 10 a.m.-5 p.m.; Thurs. 12-9; Fri. & Sat. 10 a.m.-5 p.m.
Adm: Call for information.
Exclusively features over 3,000 handmade items & midwest. Exclusive on Noel & Pat Thomas dollhouses.

MIDWAY VILLAGE MUSEUM

6799 Guilford Rd.
Rockford IL 61107
815-397-9112

Hours: Thurs. & Fri. 12-4; Sat. & Sun. 12-5; or call ahead for information.
Adm: Adults $3; srs. 65+ $2; child 6-12 $1.
The Old Dolls' House Gallery of Miniature Homes houses a collection of antique and handcrafted doll houses created by Mrs. George W. Taylor.

MUSEUM OF SCIENCE & INDUSTRY

57th Street & Lake Shore Dr.
Chicago IL 60637
312-684-1414

Hours: Mon.-Fri. 9:30 a.m.-4 p.m.; Sat., Sun. & holidays 9:30 a.m.-5:30 p.m. (closed Christmas). Summers: 7 days 9:30 a.m.-5:30 p.m.
Adm: Adults $6; srs. 65+ $5; child 5-12 $2.50.
The museum features the 13-room castle donated by silent screen star Colleen Moore, offering visitors a trip into the land of fantasy.

MUSEUM OF MINIATURE HOUSES AND OTHER COLLECTIONS

111 E. Main St.
Carmel IN 46032
317-575-9466

Hours: Wed.-Sat. 11-4; Sun. 1-4.
Adm: Adults $2; child $1. Call for group tours & rates.
The Museum has approximately 50 roomboxes and vignettes and 120 houses in the permanent collection as well as two rooms of rotating exhibits, one of which is always miniatures.

CHILDREN'S MUSEUM OF INDIANAPOLIS

3000 N. Meridan
Indianapolis IN 46206
317-924-5431

Hours: 7 days Sun.-Sat. 10 a.m.-5 p.m.
Adm: Adults $6; srs. $5; youth $3.
Exhibits include: Ball, Chambers and Virginia Dugan Federal dollhouses as well as 18 miniature rooms "Mini Masterpieces."

SOUTH AMANA BARN MUSEUM

Box 124
South Amana IA 52334
319-622-3058

Hours: Daily Apr. 1-Oct. 31 (weather permitting) 9 a.m.-5 p.m.
Adm: Adults $3; 60+ $2.75; child grades 1-6 75¢; child grades 7-12 $1.50.
Housed in Amana horse barn, miniature replicas created by Henry Moore to preserve rural American architecture in miniature.

MEMORIES IN MINIATURE DOLLHOUSE MUSEUM & SHOPPE

618 E. Broadway
Newton KS 67114
316-283-1747

Hours: Sat. 10 a.m.-5 p.m.; Thurs. 6 p.m.-8 p.m. Tours and workshops by appointment-call ahead.
Adm: Call for information.
The museum is on display in an c.1886 Victorian Cottage. The museum is incorporated with a dollhouse Shoppe (see Shoppe listings). The exhibit consists of 10 assorted houses and buildings and an assortment of miniature scenes for you to experience a part of life from a bygone era. Although the collection is placed in a Victorian setting, each of the houses and buildings have been decorated and furnished to maintain style continuity, with much detail given to the furnishings.

THE BALTIMORE MUSEUM OF ART

Charles and 31st Sts.
Baltimore MD 21218
410-396-7100

Hours: Wed.-Fri. 10 a.m.-4 p.m.; Sat. & Sun. 11 a.m.-p.m.
Adm: Adults 19+ $5.50; srs. & fulltime students w/ID $3.50; child 7-18 $1.50. Museum members & 6 & under free. Free Museum admission to all visitors on Thursdays.
Museum features Cheney Rooms by Eugene Kupjack.

THE CHILDREN'S MUSEUM

300 Congress St. Museum Wharf
Boston MA 02210
617-426-6500

Hours: Tues. - Sun., 10 a.m. to 5 p.m.
Adm: Adults $7; srs. & child 1-15 $6; 1 year $2; free: members & child under one; Fridays 5 p.m. to 9 p.m. everyone $1.
On display are a variety of dollhouses and dolls from many different periods, including the Sayles, Nantucket, Colonial, 1897 Victorian, Kreger and Monks dollhouses.

PEABODY ESSEX MUSEUM

132 Essex St.
Salem MA 01970
508-745-9500

Hours: Nov. 1-Memorial Day Tues.-Sat. 10 a.m.-5 p.m.; Sun. Noon-5; Thurs. 10 a.m.-8 p.m.; Memorial Day Weekend-Oct. 31 Mon.-Sat 10 a.m.-6 p.m.; Sun. Noon-6; Thurs. 10 a.m.-9 p.m.
Adm: Adults $7; srs. & students w/ID $6; child 6-16 $4.
The toy and doll collection are children's playthings, not reproduction scale miniatures. Two featured dollhouses, dating to 1852 and 1876, are decorated with period furnishings.

WENHAM MUSEUM

132 Main St.
Wenham MA 01984
508-468-2377

Hours: Mon.-Fri. 11 a.m.-4 p.m.; Sat. 1-4.; Sun. 1-5.
Adults $3; srs. $2.50; child 6+ $1.
The seven large dollhouses on display are all made in Massachusetts. The most famous is the 1884 Chamberlain House, and the most popular is a four-foot replica of the Addam's House from the "New Yorker" magazine, TV and the movies.

YESTERYEARS MUSEUM

143 Main St.
Sandwich MA 02563
508-888-1722

May 15-Oct. 31 Mon.-Sat. 10 a.m.-4 p.m.
Adults $3; srs. $2.50; child under 13 $1.50. Special rates apply at beginning and end of season. Fifty cents a person less than full season rate.
This is primarily an antique museum featuring Nuremburg kitchens from 1730 to the 1920s, a 19th-century confectioner's shop, milliner's shop and pharmacy.

CHILDREN'S MUSEUM

67 E. Kirby
Detroit MI 48202
313-494-1210

Hours: Mon.-Fri. 1-4; Sat. 9 a.m.-4 p.m.
Adm: Call for information.
A variety of miniatures from various collections are on display. One of the more notable is the Jeremiah Hudson Dollhouse.

MINNESOTA HISTORICAL SOCIETY MUSEUM COLLECTIONS

345 Kellogg Blvd. W.
St. Paul MN 55102
12-296-8071

Hours: Call for information.
Adm: Call for information.
The collection contains eight dollhouses, five are furnished. Collections available by appointment.

HISTORIC HERMANN MUSEUM

PO Box 88
Hermann MO 65041
314-486-2017

Hours: Sun.-Sat. incl. holidays 10 a.m.-4 p.m. Closed Nov. 1-Apr. 1.
Adm: Adults $1; child 12-18 50¢; child under 12 free.
Two dollhouses furnished with miniatures are on display.

TOY & MINIATURE MUSEUM OF KANSAS CITY

5235 Oak St.
Kansas City MO 64112
816-333-2055

Hours: Wed.-Sat. 10 a.m.-4 p.m.; Sun. 1-4 .
Closed Mon., Tues. & major holidays & two weeks following Labor Day.
Adm: Adults $3; srs. & students $2.50; child 3-12 $1.50; child under three free. Call for tour and discount rate information.
The museum is located on the southwest corner of the University of Missouri-Kansas City campus, near the Country Club Plaza. It houses a unique collection of scale miniatures and antique toys, dolls, dolls' houses and trains. A gift shop offers a variety of miniatures and gift and toy items related to the exhibits, along with a Museum book with photographs and information about the collection.

THE GILA FAERIELAND MUSEUM

Hwy. 15, 4 Miles from
Gila Cliff Dwellings
Gila NM 88038
505-536-9495

Hours: Call ahead.
Adm: Call for information.
The dolls, toys, miniatures and dollhouses are the lifelong collection of Jane Horst. The houses were built by Jane Horst and Jack Morris, with the furnishings created by a variety of miniature artisans.

THE MUSEUMS AT STONY BROOK

1208 Rt. 25A
Stony Brook NY 11790
516-751-0066

Hours: Wed.-Sat. 10 a.m.-5 p.m.; Sun. 12-5.
Adm: Adults $6; srs. & students $4; child 6-12 $3.
The museum exhibit "illusion of Reality Period Miniature Rooms" depicts 15 rooms from the late 1600s to the 1930s.

FORBES MAGAZINE GALLERY MUSEUM

62-5th Ave.
New York City NY 10011
212-206-5548

Hours: Tues., Wed., Fri. & Sat. 10 a.m.-4 p.m.
Adm: Call for information.

Featured are a number of Eugene Kupjack Rooms including three Presidential rooms: Thomas Jefferson's bedroom & study at Monticello; George Washington's Surrender Room at Yorktown, and John Adams' Law Office. Also on view is one Faberge Room: Czarina Alexandra's Sitting Room at Alexandrovsky Palace.

MUSEUM OF THE CITY OF NEW YORK

5th Ave. at 103 St.
New York NY 10029
212-534-1672

Hours: Wed.-Sat. 10 a.m.-5 p.m.; Sun. 1-5.
Closed Mondays and legal holidays. Tues. pre-registered groups only.
Adm: Free, contributions are suggested: Adults $5; srs., students & child $3; $8 family.
There are nine dollhouses on permanent exhibition. The Stettheimer House of the 1920s, includes miniature original paintings and sculptures of the day.

THE NEW YORK HISTORICAL SOCIETY

170 Central Park West
New York NY 10024
212-873-3400

Hours: Call ahead.
Adm: Call for information.
Six display cases exhibit a rotating collection of miniatures, transportation toys, dolls, furniture, pull toys and banks.

THE STRONG MUSEUM

One Manhattan Square
Rochester NY 14607
716-263-2700

Hours: Mon.-Sat. 10 a.m.-5 p.m.; Sun. 1-5.
Adm: Adults $5; srs. & students w/ID $4; child 3-12 $3.
Collection contains: 20,000 miniatures from America, Asia and Europe during the 19th and 20th centuries; 243 dollhouses; 77 Steele rooms, and 52 additional miniature rooms.

TOWN OF YORKTOWN MUSEUM

1974 Commerce St.
Yorktown Heights NY 10598
914-962-2970

Hours: Tues.-Fri. 9:30 a.m.-4:30 p.m.; Sat. & Sun. 1-4; Mon. by appointment.
Adm: Donations.
One room in this museum is devoted to dollhouses and miniatures, including the 8' by 7' Marjorie Johnson Dollhouse set in the room's center. Miniatures Gift Shop.

QUEENS MUSEUM OF ART

Flushing Meadows Corona Park
Queens NY 11368
718-592-9700

Hours: Wed.-Fri. 10-5; Sat. & Sun. 12-5.
Tues. groups only: call in advance for group tour appointment.
Adm: Call for information.
The Panorama of the City of New York is a permanent attraction at the Queens Museum of Art.

ANGELA PETERSON DOLL & MINIATURES MUSEUM

101 W. Green Dr.
High Point NC 27260
919-885-3655

Hours: Tues.-Sat. 10 a.m.-5 p.m.; Sun. 1-5.
Adm: Adults $3; srs. & groups of 15 or more & students 15+ $2.50; child 6-14 $1.50.
More than 1,700 dolls, 800 miniatures, 15 fully furnished dollhouses on display. Also on exhibit is a six-foot miniature mobile home that is furnished.

ALLEN COUNTY HISTORICAL SOCIETY

620 W. Market St.
Lima OH 45801
419-222-9426

Hours: Sept.-May Tues.-Sun. 1-5; Jun.-Aug. Tues.-Sat. 10 a.m.-5 p.m.; Sun 1-5.
Adm: Call for information.
The Mount Vernon Room has as its centerpiece a model based on George Washington's home, Mount Vernon. It is surrounded by exhibits dating from or typical of the Washington era.

CLAGUE HOUSE MUSEUM OF WESTLAKE

1371 Clague Rd.
Westlake OH 44145
216-871-4964

Hours: Sun. 2-4:30; or by appointment.
Adm: Call for information.
Museum has a duplicate of the 1876 Clague House. In 1980, the Cleveland Miniature Society furnished the dollhouse, built in 1976.

SHAKER HISTORICAL SOCIETY

16740 S. Park Blvd.
Shaker Heights OH 44120
216-921-1201

Hours: Tues.-Fri. 2-5; Sun. 2-5.
Adm: Call for information.
On display are three authentic Shaker rooms furnished with the handcrafted work of Gus Schwerdtfeger.

WANDA'S MINIATURE MUSEUM

1611 N. Hwy. 75
Dewey OK 74029
918-534-3543

Hours: By appointment.
Adm: Adults & child $3; group tours welcome.
Exhibits include 1", 1/2" and 1/4" scale miniatures, house and specialty displays, toys, dolls, one-of-a-kind items and roomboxes.

THE IDA DENNIE WILLIS MUSEUM OF MINIATURES, DOLLS AND TOYS

628 N. Country Club Dr.
Tulsa OK 74127
918-584-6654

Hours: Wed.-Sat. 10:30 a.m.-4:30 p.m.
Adm: Adults $3; child under 17 $2. Call for information on group rates. Closed on some major holidays.
The Museum is housed in a 13-room, 1910 Tudor-style home adjacent to the Tulsa Country Club. You will find a variety of miniatures, 2,000 dolls, dollhouses, roomboxes, toys, Franklin Mint coins,

plates, angels, trains, control-line airplanes, lighted working carnival rides, stamps, coins. Seasonal holiday displays are also featured.

CHILDREN'S MUSEUM

3037 SW 2nd Ave.
Portland OR 97201
503-823-2227

Hours: Mon.-Sat. 9 a.m.-5 p.m.; Sun. 11 a.m.-5 p.m.
Adm: Adults $3.50; child $3.
Featured is the nine-room Dahlstrom Farmhouse built by Oregon textile artist Betty Ann Dahlstrom.

MARY MERRITT DOLL MUSEUM

843 Ben Franklin Hwy.
Douglassville PA 19518
610-385-3809

Hours: Mon.-Sat. 10 a.m.-5 p.m.; Sun. 1-5.
Adm: Adults $3; child 5-12 $1.
The collection includes 1,500 dolls dating from 1725 to 1900 and 35 dollhouses ranging from a three-story Queen Anne to a Towne House.

THE DOLL MUSEUM

520 Thames St.
Newport RI 02840
401-849-0405

Hours: Mon.-Sat. 10 a.m.-5 p.m.; Sun. 12-5.
Adm: Adults $2; srs. 65+ $1.50; child 5-11 $1.
On display are a Tynie Toy Townhouse, Thorne Dollhouse, Le Clerc Room, German red roof series dollhouse and Bliss lithograph dollhouse.

GIBBES MUSEUM OF ART

135 Meeting St.
Charleston SC 29401
803-722-2706

Hours: Tues.-Sat. 10 a.m.-5 p.m., Sun. & Mon. 1-5.
Adm: Adults $5; srs. & students $4; child $3.
Ten artisan quality miniature rooms are on display in the Elizabeth Wallace Gallery.

ENCHANTED WORLD DOLL MUSEUM

615 N. Main
Mitchell SD 57301
605-996-9896

Hours: Mar.-May, Oct. & Nov. Mon.-Sat. 9 a.m.-5 p.m.; Sun. 1-5; June-Sept., 8-8 daily. Winter months call ahead for appointment.
Adm: Adults 19-61 $3; adults 62+ $2.50 ; students 6-18 $1; under five free.
Visitors can see more than 4,000 antique and modern collectible dolls dating as far back as the 1400s.

CHILDREN'S MUSEUM OF OAK RIDGE

461 W. Outer Dr.
Oak Ridge TN 37830
615-482-1074

Hours: Mon.-Fri. 9 a.m.-5 p.m.; Sat. 11 a.m.-3 p.m. Tour groups welcome by appointment.

Adm: Call for information.
Nine Throne Miniature Rooms are on loan from the Knoxville Museum of Art.

DOLLHOUSE MUSEUM OF THE SOUTHWEST

2208 Routh St.
Dallas TX 75201
214-969-5502

Hours: Tues.-Sat. 10 a.m.-4:30 p.m.; Sun. 1-4.
Adm: Adults $4; srs. & child $2 ; group rates available.
Collection includes: Brooke Tucker roomboxes, 13 Biehl and Anderson Georgian miniature rooms and a unique collection of English made houses and much more. Also dolls and toys.

FRANKS ANTIQUE DOLL MUSEUM

211 W. Grand Ave. (US 80 West)
Marshall TX 75670
903-935-3065

Hours: By appointment.
Adm: Adults $2.50; child $1.50.
Displays include 2,000 dolls of all types and 2,000 toys & related items.

FANTASY ACRES MINIATURE MUSEUM

89 E. Benson Way
Sandy UT 84070
801561-5560

Hours: Mon.-Sat. 12-6; or by appointment.
Adm: $1/person; no child under 5. Groups by appointment.
Some of the attractions on exhibit are 14 dollhouses (Lucy, the Margate Elephant, 1/2-scale castle & 50s metal house; doll room & Enesco room; LGB trains on elevated tracks; z-scale trains in displays for dollhouse people to enjoy plus over 10 funning layouts.

SHELBURNE MUSEUM

US Rt. 7
Shelburne VT 05482
802-985-3344

Hours: Call for information.
Adm: Adults $15; students $9; child 6-14 $5; under 6 free.
Discover the diversity and delights of this national treasure, nestled on 45 acres in the heart of Vermont's scenic Champlain Valley. Described as New England's Smithsonian, Shelburne Museum is one of the world's great collections of American folk art, artifacts and architecture. Browse among 37 exhibition buildings housing 80,000 artifacts including dolls, dollhouses, folk sculpture, quilts and other textiles, toys, carousel figures, a miniature circus parade and the hand-carved Kirk Brothers Circus.

MUSEUM OF PLAYTIMES PAST AND PRESENT

3238 Locker Rd. SE
Port Orchard WA 98366
206-871-1100

Hours: Mon.-Fri. 10 a.m.-5 p.m.; Sat. 10 a.m.-4 p.m.; closed Sundays & major

holidays.
Adm: $1/person.
Visit Stan & Ursula Ohman's huge collection of old and new dollhouses, toys and dolls. Their charming miniature shop, Little Habitats is connected to the museum and features many collector quality miniatures.

HOUSE ON THE ROCK

5754 Hwy. 23
Spring GreenWI53588
608-935-3639

Hours: Call ahead for hours.
Adm: Regular: guests 13+ $13.50; child 7-12 $8.50; child 4-6 $3.50. Holiday: guests 13+ $8; child 7-12 $4; child 4-6 $3.50.
Two main areas of miniatures are the Dollhouse Maze, featuring 250 completely furnished dollhouses and the Miniature Circus Maze, a 1 million piece circus featuring every aspect of a circus extravaganza. The House on the Rock also displays collectibles of all kinds. Allow all day for tour.

ZWEIFEL'S MUSEUMS AND EXHIBITS

904-394-2836 or 407-876-3631

Call for locations of exhibits.
The White House Replica

MINIATURE WORLD - "THE GREATEST LITTLE SHOW ON EARTH"

649 Humboldt St.
Victoria BC Canada V8W 1A7
604-385-9731

Hours: Summer 8:30 a.m.-10 p.m. daily. Winter 10 a.m.-5 p.m. daily.
Adm: Call for information.
Museum features world's smallest working sawmill and two of the world's largest dollhouses, circa 1880; model railway; circus and much more.

POLLIWOG CASTLE

Division St. North,
Kingston Township, RR 1
Glenburnie Ontario
Canada K0H 1SO
613-548-4702

Hours: Tues.-Sun. 10:30 a.m.-5 p.m. Closed Mondays.
Adm: Call for information.
The Polliwog Museum is housed in a turn-of-the-century Ontario mansion and features several hundred antique dolls, toys, carriages, teddy bears and dollhouses.

Editor's Note: Museum listings are printed free of charge. Additions, deletions and corrections should be sent in writing to: Museum Listings, Nutshell News, 21027 Crossroads Cir., Waukesha WI 53187.

INDEX

MANUFACTURERS, ARTISANS & SUPPLIERS

A

ALESSIO MINIATURES

13 Everest Ct., Huntington Station, NY 11746. Wholesale only. Catalog and information sheets, free. pp. 57, 58, 70, 81, 82, 83, 84, 102, 106, 109, 110, 112-115, 122, 123, 130, 249, 266, 276

ALICE LACY, LTD.

One Front St., Bath, ME 04530. Wholesaler/designer, manufacturer. Line includes 80 designs of handcrafted iron wire furniture, designed by Alice Lacy for strength and beauty. In addition, embroidered cushions and hand-pieced quilts, bolts of small print fabrics and laces, hand-loomed rugs, poodles, a rag doll named "Maggie" with hand-smocked dresses, or patterns for the dress and pantaloons are available. Brochure, SASE. Price list available to dealers. Sold at fine shops almost everywhere. pp. 190, 207, 264

ALL THROUGH THE HOUSE

Amy Robinson — 5 Paquatanee Pl., Biddeford, ME 04005. Mail order and artisan. LSASE (55¢) for brochure. Handcrafted 1" and 1/2" accessories and kits. Always adding new items to make your mini house more "homey." There are 200-plus handcrafted items from which to choose. 60-plus kits. Great for clubs and in-store workshops. Reasonably priced. pp. 257, 258, 275, 286

ANN WEINER MINIATURES

64 Mae Belle Dr., Clark, NJ 07066. Handcrafted furniture that looks old for a special setting. Over 60 items. Retail or sold to shops. Request on business letterhead with TAX ID form. Send $1.00 or four 32¢ stamps for list. Hutches, bookcases, Adirondack furniture, tables, cupboards, potties, mirrors, baskets, etc. WE DO CUSTOMIZED MARBELIZING ON RAW WOOD THAT YOU SUPPLY AND GOLD LEAFING - Rooms or Furniture. p. 209

ARCHITECTURAL DETAILS J.M. OGREENC

PO Box 132, Lake Mills, WI 53551. Wholesaler, manufacturer, retailer, mail order. Brochure, free with LSASE. Cast resin windows, doors, decorative moldings and more. We specialize in roombox accessories. Custom designs and dealer inquiries welcome. p. 64

ARCHITECTURAL ETCETERA

888 Tower Road, Unit J, Mundelein, IL 60060. Wholesaler, manufacturer and mail order. Color catalog picturing more than 400 exclusive items, $6. A recently formed division of the Lawbre Company, Architectural Etcetera manufactures the finely-crafted architectural components, fireplaces and room settings designed by Daniel L. McNeil, co-founder of The Lawbre Company, and Derek Perkins, noted miniaturist. The details are worth looking at. pp. 62, 64, 65, 70, 71, 84, 85, 116, 123, 124, 130, 166-167, 175-176, 250

ARCHITECTURALLY DESIGNED DOLLHOUSES

PO Box 129, 40 Lakeview Dr., North Salem, NY 10560. Artisan of finished buildings, retail only. We construct collector-quality custom houses and shops in 1" scale. Ten models available. We are also a fully stocked miniatures shop. Price list available, LSASE. pp. 31, 38

AZTEC IMPORTS INC.

6345 Norwalk Rd., Medina, OH 44256. Wholesaler, distributor, for many product lines including: Town Square, Carriage House, Cir-Kit, Dragonfly, Chrysenbon, Falcon, Farrow, Greenleaf, Real Good Toys, Houseworks, Minicraft, Mini Graphics, Walmer, X-Acto and more. See your local hobby dealer. pp. 59, 62, 138, 151, 168, 184, 186, 191, 195, 197, 199, 202, 206, 208, 216, 260, 263, 264, 310. Please see display on the back cover.

B

B.J. ENTERPRISE

13301 60th Dr. NE., Marysville, WA 98271. Retailer. Brochure, LSASE and $2. Price List, LSASE. Pussy willow Persians. Mail orders and special orders. p. 222

RON BENSON MINIATURES

PO Box 5231, Richmond, VA 23220. Retail and wholesale. Catalog, $2. Porcelain miniatures of 18th and 19th century antiques including sculptures, bowls, cachepots and vases. All limited editions of 250. pp. 244-245

BERRY-PATCH DESIGNS

317 Somerset Dr., Ft. Walton Beach, FL 32547. Retailer, Mail order. Catalog $2. Miniature bears and bunnies, finished or kits. Bear-making supplies available. p 222

BODEGA

807 N. Creek, Dewey, OK 74029. Wholesaler, manufacturer. Catalog, $5. Manufacturers of quality handcrafted miniatures and shadow boxes, most items are of original design. Accessories include holiday, country and southwest items. Retail customers send LSASE for a store in your area. pp. 64, 255, 276

RENEE BOWEN - MINIATURIST

28 York St. (Rt. 1, South), Kennebunk, ME 04043. Wholesaler, artisan, retailer. Retail shop, open 10 a.m.-4 p.m. (closed Wed.) or send $2 for brochure of furniture, accessories, toys, games, quilts, etc. For rug flyer, send LSASE. pp. 187, 265

BRENDA VAN ORSOUW ADAMS MINIATURES

4112 Lazy River Lane, Durham, NC 27712. Wholesaler, retailer and mail order. Fine handpainted miniatures available in 1" and 1/2" scale. Furniture, paintings and accessories. Custom orders, individual and dealer inquiries welcomed. Price list available. See your local dealer. p. 209

BRODNAX PRINTS

3870 West Beverly Dr., Dallas TX 75209-5914. Wholesaler and mail order. Catalog, $1. More than 200 strictly smaller scale printed wallpapers, with new items frequently available. pp. 290, 294

BUTT HINGE POTTERY

One Butt Hinge Rd., Chelmsford, MA 01824. Wholesaler only, artisan. See your local miniatures dealer. We offer a large variety of wheel-thrown stoneware miniatures capturing the spirit of traditional New England pottery. The pieces lend themselves to use in many dollhouse settings from the kitchen and bedroom to the garden or general store. Well-fitted lids, finely-thrown spouts and unusual handles enhance many of the pieces. Custom orders available. pp. 243, 255, 267, 280

BY BARB

7 Aron Court, Bethpage, NY 11714. Artisan and manufacturer. Catalog, $3.75. See your local hobby dealer. Barb has designed and handcrafted contemporary miniature accessories since 1978. She is best known for her Judaic miniatures. Some of her other creations are scuba sets, bean bag chairs, scouting items, nursery accessories and a yellow slicker set. Barb also hand crafts an extensive line of ceramic dishes and accessory pieces. Now available are the Lucite tables, sideboards and chairs Barb designed to display her dishes. Recent additions include nursery and other newly designed Lucite furniture. pp. 196, 209, 243, 246, 253

BY GRACE

618 E. Broadway, Newton, KS 67114. Wholesaler, manufacturer, retailer, mail order, designer. Catalog, $2.50 plus LSASE. Unique "one-of-a-kind" customized beds (Country, Victorian, Contemporary, Traditional, Oriental, Colonial and European styles). Wood or brass finish with designer or period linens. Matching or coordinated upholstered love seats, chairs, chaise lounges, slipper chairs, round tables for the bedroom or other living spaces. Priced according to selection. Free shipping in USA on prepaid orders only. p. 209

C

CAROL'S CREATIONS IN MINIATURE

2327 Cleveland St., NE, Minneapolis, MN 55418. Doll artist. Price list with photos available, $3. Original dolls sculpted out of Fimo. Authentically dressed. All eras. p. 216

CATHY'S HANDCRAFTED MINIATURE ACCESSORIES

57-08—157 St., Flushing, NY 11355. Artisan, manufacturer, wholesaler, retailer. LSASE for price list. Handcrafted plants, flower boxes, floral arrangements, fruits, vegetables, foods, candies, holiday items and assorted accessories for inside and outside the house. Dealer inquiries welcome. Member CIMTA, MIAA. pp. 246, 253, 269, 277

CELERITY MINIATURE HOMES

PO Box 3882, Bartlesville, OK 74006. Wholesaler, manufacturer. Catalog, $5. Collector-quality dollhouses sold in kits, assembled shells or assembled with beautiful, unique, hand-finished exteriors. Houses handcrafted from 3/8" Aspen plywood. We are known for our fine

collection of Victorian homes, log cabins and children's dollhouses. See your local miniatures dealer or send LSASE for a dealer nearest you. pp. 18, 21, 22, 25, 35, 38, 39, 40, 50, 54, 62

CIR-KIT CONCEPTS, INC.

32 Woodlake Drive S.E., Rochester, MN 55904. Manufacturer. Manufacturer of tape wiring systems for dollhouses, including "to scale" outlets, plugs and switches. Our tape wire is now color coded to allow foolproof corner connections. We also produce ceiling and sconce adapters to allow easy removal and replacement of these fixtures. Price list available, or see your local hobby dealer. Catalog $4. pp. 132, 138-141, 149-150, 152, 161, 163-164, 168, 253, 290, 301, 304, 311-312. Please see display ad on the inside back cover.

CLARE-BELL BRASS WORKS

PO Box 218, Lovell, ME 04051. Manufacturer. 200 item catalog, $2. Made in the USA. Solid brass miniatures—1" to scale. All parts threaded for screw assembly. Brass beds, electric lamps and lighting fixtures, weather vanes, household items, accessories, etc. pp. 80, 81, 106, 132, 151, 152, 153, 168, 184, 191, 260-261, 267, 271, 286

CLASSICS BY HANDLEY

c/o Handley House, 5521 E. Rosedale, PO Box 8658, Ft. Worth, TX 76124 and 2 Fourth Street, Wheeling, WV 26003. Quality furniture sets and accessories, dollhouse building supplies and components. pp. 71, 72, 85, 86, 87, 98, 99, 103, 105, 106, 107, 109, 111, 116-119, 124-126, 166, 168, 192-193, 196, 202, 205, 209, 245, 274

COLLECTOR'S DISPLAY CASE CO.

Rt. 2 Box 73, Fremont, NE 68025. Wholesaler, retailer, mail order. Strong, clear, lightweight plastic cases allow perfect viewing from all sides. Each collectible is suspended in its own compartment, protected from dust, damage and theft. Can be wall mounted, or locked together when stacked. Dealer inquiries welcome. p. 62

CORONA CONCEPTS

RD4 Box 700A, Cooperstown, NY 13326. Manufacturer. Catalog, free. See your local hobby dealer. All wood dollhouse kits. pp. 18, 22, 25, 40, 107, 110, 170

CUSTOM CREATIONS BY RIKA

25996 Balsam, Franklin, MI 48025. Mail order and retailer. Brochure, $1 and LSASE with two stamps. Beautifully sculpted and hand painted animals. Custom painting from photographs on available breeds. p. 223

D

d. ANNE RUFF MINIATURES

1100 Vagabond Ln., Plymouth, MN 55447. Wholesaler, manufacturer, retailer and artisan. Brochure, photos and fabric swatches, $4 (refundable with order). Price list, LSASE. Upholstered furniture, window treatments, rugs and accessories—all scales. Prettipoint rug kits, Pretty Pleat Pleaters, Hat Box Vignette kits and many other accessory kits in all scales. pp. 177, 181, 187, 191, 291, 292, 294

"D" DESIGN AND REPAIR

341 Pennsylvania Ave., Buffalo, NY 14201. Wholesaler and retailer. Custom finishing, building and designing of dollhouses. Signed lighting fixtures. Custom wood floors. Send SASE and $2 for a brochure of lighting fixtures. Also includeed is one color photo. p. 161

D-LEPRECHAUN

3108 Superior La., MC-8, Bowie, MD 20715-1914. Artisan: retail, wholesale. For price list of painted and haired horses, send LSASE. Foods and hats at shows and CIMTA only. 1" and 1/2" scale. p. 223

HELEN M. DAVID, IGMA ARTISAN

8602 Rivercross, Houston, TX 77064. Artisan, mail order and miniature shows. Brochure, $3.75 LSASE. p. 270

DEE'S DELIGHTS, INC.

3150 State Line Rd, North Bend, OH 45052. Wholesaler and manufacturer. Catalog, 800 pages and more than 27,000 different items, $25 (refundable with $200 order). Information sheets available. Complete line of miniature furniture, furniture kits, accessories, building components, flooring, lighting, dolls, paints, glues, dollhouses, roomboxes, hobby books and Fimo modeling compound. pp. 18, 26, 29, 40, 77, 101, 194, 195, 301, 302

DESIGN TECNICS MINIATURES

6420 West 95th St., Suite 201, Overland Park, KS 66212. Manufacturer. Various publications and products in 1" scale and 1/4" scale are designed and produced by Fred Stephenson. The Dollhouse Builder's Handbook and Architect's Choice Dollhouse Plans are distributed by Miniature Lumber Shoppe, Dee's Delights, and New England Hobby Supply. Other products are available only through Miniature Lumber Shoppe. See your local dealer. pp. 72, 119, 302, 307

DOLL FAIRE'S VICTORIAN TIMES

2310 Monument Blvd., Pleasant Hill, CA 94523. Manufacturer. Catalog, $3. We build Victorian house shells which are unique in style and design. pp. 26, 40, 41

DOLL HOUSE SHOPPE

7313 Duvan Dr., Tinley Park, IL 60477. Manufacturer. Catalog, $10 (Wholesale-Dealers only). Extensive line of handcrafted miniatures. See your local hobby dealer. pp. 153, 196, 199, 205, 223, 253, 273, 276

THE DOLLHOUSE FACTORY

157 Main St., Lebanon, NJ 08833. Retailer, wholesaler, manufacturer, artisan and mail order. Catalog, $5.50. One of the oldest and most experienced companies specializing in dollhouses, miniatures, supplies, tools and professional information. "The Complete Dollhouse Center" in 1", 1/2" and 1/4" scales. p. 305. Please see display ad page 2.

THE DOLLS' COBBLER

Sylvia Rountree, PO Box 906, Berlin, MD 21811. Manufacturer. Catalog, $3.75. Maker of fine leather shoes, boots, saddlery and luggage for over 20 years. All are authentic in design and historically correct by IGMA Fellow since 1981. Shoemaker since 1970. pp. 219, 260, 273

DOLLHOUSE MINIATURES

PO Box 865013, Plano, TX 75086. Wholesaler, manufacturer, retailer and artisan. Catalog, $3. Price list available. Hand painted bathroom sets, dishes, mixing bowls, canister sets, and many other ceramic miniatures for every room in your dollhouse! pp. 224, 243

DONNA SMOLIK'S DESIGNS

424 Timberlake Dr., Azle, TX 76020. Artisan. Brochure, $1, refundable with order. Candy, cookie and food designs, intricately detailed. Slice your own with a single-edged razor blade. Can be used to create foods or Christmas decorations, fantasy creations, garnishes etc. pp. 246, 253, 255, 277, 286, 294

DONNA'S MINI EMPORIUM

c/o Donna Marie Barczak, PO Box 421, Medford, NY 11763-0421. Mail Order. Catalog, $1.25. More than 200 handmade accessories from which to choose. Available in an assortment of colors and designs upon request, including our exclusive 38-pc. ceramic dinnerware set, household items, toys, and miscellaneous accessories. pp. 196, 198, 216, 244, 274, 275

DORSETT PUBLICATIONS, INC.

630 Depot St., PO Box 2038, Christiansburg, VA 24073. Publisher. Brochure available. See your local miniatures dealer. Quarterly how-to magazine, The Scale Cabinetmaker. Period furniture scale modeling pattern books. pp. 302, 308

DOUGLESS, LTD.

150 North Ave., #303, Dept. K, Tallmadge, OH 44278. Retail, wholesale, and mail order. See your local dealer or order from Dougless Ltd. Send SASE for complete details. 1. Dougless Guides (30 categories for each American period). 2. (Book) Ask Dougless Vol. I (a must for miniaturists). 3. (Book) Ask Dougless Vol. II (more information for miniaturists). 4. (Book) Ask Dougless Vol. III (illustrated charts: kitchen, bath, architecture, cabinetmakers; more). 5. Ask Dougless Vol. IV (more of the same). 6. Lecture-Workshops; Programs; Symposiums. 7. Guide to Appraisal and Record-Keeping. Also distributed by Dee's Delights. p. 300

DREMEL

4915 21st Street, Racine, WI 53406. Manufacturer. Moto-Tools; Cordless MiniMite; Two-Speed & Variable Speed Scroll Saws; Disc-Belt Sander; Flex-Shaft Tools; Router Attachment; Shaper/Router Table; Flex-Shaft Attachment; Bits & Accessories. Free Brochure, price list available. pp. 313-314

DURA-CRAFT, INC.

PO Box 438, Newberg, OR 97132. Manufacturer. See your local miniatures dealer. Free catalog, price list, brochure and line drawings. Manufacturer of quality dollhouse kits, furniture kits and shakes. Product warranty. pp. 19, 22, 26, 31, 36, 41, 42, 43, 59, 107, 188-189, 197, 203, 205, 295

THE DUCK POND

Millcreek Shores, Box 419, Lampe, MO 65681-0419. Manufacturer. Miniature wood carvings. Price list available. All products offered are handmade and hand painted (if painted) by us at The Duck Pond—we offer all items retail and wholesale. pp. 223, 257, 278, 295

E

EBERHARD FABER GMBH

EFA Strasse 1, D-92318 Neumarkt/Opf., Germany. Manufacturer. See your local dealer. Modeling compounds to create miniatures and fashon jewelry. pp. 101, 176, 209, 220, 310

ELECT-A-LITE

15G Grant Road, PO Box 865, West End, NC 27376. Retailer, manufacturer and wholesaler. Original manufacturer of made-in-USA single or double copper tapewire and wiring kits for dollhouses. Service and full warranty. Line of 23 of the most popular imported miniature lighting fixtures. pp. 133, 141-143, 150, 151, 153-154, 161-162, 164, 168, 253, 304, 308. Please see display ad on inside front cover.

ELLIOTT'S

2707 Beaver Ave., Simi Valley, CA 93065. Wholesaler, retailer. Price list available - SASE. Handmade ornate and figural clocks and mantel ornaments. Custom creations considered. We are also continuing our quality gourmet foods. p. 267

EMF PUBLISHING

7 Ferringham Ln., Ferring, West Sussex, BN12 5ND England. Publisher of "The Dolls House Handbook." An annual reference guide to dollhouse shops and museums containing dollhouses and miniatures around the world. p. 301

EMME'S MINIATURES

440 Wilson St., Elkins, WV 26241. Retailer, mail order. Send SASE for free brochure. We offer a full line of dollhouse furnishings and accessories. Specializing in Victorian and Queen Anne. Custom orders available. p. 191

EMPRESS ARTS AND CRAFTS

971 Commonwealth Ave., #32, Boston, MA 02215. Wholesaler. See your local hobby dealer. Miniature wire furniture (Windsor collection), resin cage birds and hand-crafted clay flowers and arrangements. pp. 60, 265

F

FANTASY CRAFT

933 Carson Lane, Pomona, CA 91766. Manufacturer and mail order. Catalog, $5 (refundable with first order over $50). Heirloom, collector-quality, unique, original designs. Contemporary and Southwest dollhouse, roombox and furniture kits. Optional finishing and wiring kits available. Easily assembled, beautiful, top-quality 3/8" plywood, tongue-and-groove construction. Easy-to-follow instructions. Check, Visa, Mastercard or see your local retailer. We offer personal service and are happy to answer all your kit-building questions. pp. 20, 23, 34, 35, 43, 58, 65, 66, 190

FANTASY FABRICATIONS

PO Box 164, Turner, OR 97392. Manufacturer, retailer, mail order. Color brochure includes price list, $2.50. Original-design furniture, fireplaces, accessories and much more. Specializing in special orders with a money-back guarantee. p. 209

FINE CHINA IN MINIATURE

PO Box 352, Bristol, NH 03222. Mail Order. Catalog, brochure and price list available. Please send SASE for price list. Incomparable china in miniature in the historic patterns of Quimper, Pink Lustre, Thistleware, Dedham Pottery, Chinese Export, Tobacco Leaf, Rose Medallion and others. pp. 244, 280

R. B. FOLTZ & CO.

6401 Westhaven Dr., Suite E, Indianapolis, IN 46254. Please see display ad page 231.

FOX HOLLOW MINIATURES

12816 Cross Creek Ln., Herndon, VA 22071. Wholesaler, artisan, retailer, mail order. Catalog, $2. Intricately, minutely and exquisitely detailed, handcrafted, seasonal accessories, food and furniture. pp. 187, 210, 218, 245, 246, 250, 254, 277, 280

FRAMBOISIER, INC.

134 Shimo, Fussa, Tokyo 197 Japan. Wholesaler. Japanese exporter in Tokyo. Quality handcrafted sushi, sukiyaki, tempura, kaiseki and soba. Catalog available. Price list available.
pp. 246-247

THE FRETWORKER, KIRK RATAJESAK

PO Box 36, 405 W. 6th, Kimball, NE 69145. Artisan, retailer and wholesaler. Send LSASE for price list. Scrollwork, wall accessories and furniture pieces. All items are cut out personally by Kirk. Available in 1" and 1/2" scale. Some kits available. p. 74

G

G.E.L. PRODUCTS

19 Grove St., Vernon, CT 06066. Wholesaler only. Catalog free to dealers. Price list, dealers only. Manufacturer of quality solid wood dove-tailed dollhouse kits featuring exclusive, trouble-free machined clapboarding. 3/8" floors and outer walls. Sample and brochure on request. Dealers only. p. 43

GAIL'S TINY TREASURES

22451 Collins St., Woodland Hills, CA 91367. Introducing our new line "A Bear to Remember Collectibles." These are Teddy Bears in a variety of creative miniature settings. For brochure please send $2 and a LSASE. p. 280

GARCIA & VELEZ CO.

37 Cypress Boulevard East, Homosassa, FL 32646. Wholesaler, manufacturer, importer. Catalog, $2. Price list available. Dollhouse accessories—dolls, baskets, clothing. Natural materials used. All miniatures 1"=1' scale and some for 1/2". pp. 216, 256, 258

MARLENE GILBERT-HOUSEPLANTS IN MINIATURE

43 Deer Creek, Irvine, CA 92714. Mail Order (paintings and limited selection of plants), Artisan. More than 600 handcrafted houseplants (not all available by mail order). Many plants available at shows and by appointment only. Many one-of-a-kind. Original contemporary paintings, unframed. Price list available for $1. pp. 250, 266, 270

GINSBURG COMPANY

112 N. May St., Chicago, IL 60607. Wholesaler, importer. Catalog, $10 (refunded with first order). See your local miniatures dealer. Importer of fine miniatures. A complete line of miniature furniture and accessories. pp. 184, 199, 264

GRAMARYE KEEP

2131 Baxter St., Los Angeles, CA 90039. Retailer, wholesaler, manufacturer, mail order and artisan. Two types of catalogs Medieval-Period and Contemporary, $5 each. I make scale foods. I do custom orders and carry some food related accessories. Scale 1/3" thru 1", some Barbie. p. 247

GRANDT LINE PRODUCTS, INC.

1040 B Shary Ct., Concord, CA 94518. Manufacturer. Catalog, $4.75, ask for miniatures. Price list available. Detailed structural components and accessories in 1/2" scale and smaller. Extensive line of 1/4" parts. Most pieces cast in grey polystyrene: windows, doors, railings, chimneys, hardware, figures, wheels, stairs and more. pp. 287, 295, 296

GREAT FABRICATIONS

PO Box 6394, Eureka, CA 95502-6394. Manufacturer, mail order. Brochure, $5. Price list available. Miniature designer fabrics suitable for doll clothes or interior decor and upholstery. Printed in various colors on silk or cotton. pp. 166, 219

GREENBERG BOOKS, A Division of Kalmbach Publishing

A division of Kalmbach Publishing, 21027 Crossroads Circle, Waukesha, WI 53187. Free catalog. Leading specialty publisher on Railroading, Model Railroading, Miniatures, toys & collectibles and toy trains. p 302. Please see display ad page 1.

GREENBERG SHOWS, INC.

7566 Main St., Sykesville, MD 21784. See our display ad page 351.

GREENLEAF PRODUCTS

58 N. Main St., Honeoye Falls, NY 14472-0388. Manufacturer. Include $4 when requesting catalog. 1"-1' scale model wooden die-cut dollhouses, furniture kits, and building accessories. Easy tab slot assembly. Reinforce with glue. Clear and well illustrated instructions. There is a "Satisfaction Guaranteed" warranty in every box. Fast personal service. pp. 19, 23, 31, 35, 36, 37, 44, 45, 54, 60, 92, 107, 170, 193, 250, 291, 292, 296, 297, 306, 312

H

HANDCRAFT DESIGNS INC.,

63 E. Broad St., Hatfield, PA 19440. Wholesaler. Full line of authentic reproduction furniture, die-cast accessories as well as hand painted china line. We offer a wide selection of rugs at the best price points, along with the most realistic food and flowers in hand painted ceramic. Call for a complete full color catalog and ask for Cernit Modeling Compound and Air Dry Clay information too! Price list available or see your local hobby dealer. pp. 168, 177, 191, 203, 210, 277, 310

HANDLEY HOUSE

(two locations) 5521 E. Rosedale, PO Box 8658, Ft. Worth, TX 76124 and 2 Fourth St., Wheeling, WV 26003. Wholesaler. Catalog $17.50. Price list free. More than 18,000 miniature items. Every type of item available is represented in our selection, from dollhouse kits to every type of building supply and accessory used by hobbyists. pp. 72, 78, 85, 86, 87, 98, 99, 103, 105, 106, 107, 109, 111, 116-119, 124-126, 143, 166, 168, 171-172, 192-193, 196, 197, 198-199, 200-201, 202, 203-204, 205, 206, 209, 210-214, 245, 274, 286, 306

HANDLEY HOUSE

MINI COLLECTIBLES, c/o Handley House, 5521 E. Rosedale, P.O. Box 8658, Ft. Worth, TX 76124 and 2 Fourth Street, Wheeling, WV 26003. Manufacturer. Price list free. Over 48 unique Dollhouse Furniture Sets. Handcrafted of real wood and carefully chosen fabrics for authenticity and durability. pp. 168, 192, 196, 197, 198-199, 200-201, 203-204, 206, 210-214, 310

HANKY PANKY CRAFTS

(formerly Hanke's Crafts), 215 N. Galbraith, Blue Earth, MN 56013. Mail order. Catalog, $1. Supplies for miniature cake decorating and flowers. pp. 247, 270

HDW

PO Box 83, Colville, WA 99114. Wholesaler and retailer. Catalog, $5. Handmade 1" and 1/2" scale porcelain dolls, museum quality. Enamel plants and flowers. Pewter animal figures, painted and unpainted.
pp. 217, 270

J. HERMES

PO Box 4023, El Monte, CA 91734. Wholesaler and retailer. Catalog, $3. Manufacturers of 1", 1/2" and 1/4" scale wallpapers, gift wraps and linoleums. Distributor of unique accessories, tools adhesives, kits and more. pp. 150, 173, 177, 180, 217, 254, 270, 291, 298, 310, 312

HILL'S DOLLHOUSE WORKSHOP

9 Mayhew Dr., Fairfield, NJ 07006. Wholesale only. Catalog and information sheets, SASE. Wood sample on request. Manufacturers of birch type, 3/8" clear plywood dollhouse kits. Roomboxes, special order, your size. House parts dadoed for easy assembly. Openings fit Houseworks components. Custom openings to your order. All porch railings and interior stair and stairwell hole railings are Timberbrook's. All houses now have 1-1/2" foundations. p. 46

HOOKED ON MINIATURES

43805 N. Division St. Suite A, Lancaster, CA 93535. Retailer. Paper punches for making miniature paper flowers. Catalog $1. p. 312

MARY HOOT MINIATURES

8396 Winding Trail, Mason, OH 45040. Artisan. Send $2 and SASE for product list. Original handmade and hand painted animals. p. 224

HOUSEWORKS, LTD.

2388 Pleasantdale Rd., Atlanta, GA 30340. Wholesaler, manufacturer. Catalog, $5. Price list available to dealers. We provide the highest quality miniature dollhouse components. We specialize in windows, doors, hardware, bricks, fireplaces, siding, shingles, electrical items, lighting, LaserEtch Plexiglas inserts for windows and doors, and many other accessories. We also provide high-end dollhouse shell kits and component sets and publish instructional and plan books. pp. 19, 20, 32, 46, 73, 78, 87-89, 92, 93, 99, 100, 105, 107, 109, 110, 111, 112, 119, 120, 121, 126, 127, 130, 133, 134, 143, 144, 154, 162, 169, 172, 185-186, 224, 243, 250, 270, 282-284, 287-289, 293-294, 303, 307

HUDSON RIVER DOLL HOUSES

23 Ludlow Lane, Palisades, NY 10964. Manufacturer, wholesaler. Price list available. Accessories to the trade only. pp. 199, 247

I

INNOVATIVE PHOTOGRAPHY

1724 N.W. 36th, Lincoln City, OR 97367. Mail order. Catalog, $2.50. Specialize in miniature photographs, artistically framed in folders or sheets. Victorians, old masters, modern art, antique maps, babies, children, animals, wedding and birth certificates, photo albums. Postcards, postcard racks and hanging display racks. Custom reduction of your photos. pp. 266, 269, 274

ITTY BITTY BITS

6040 Milton #1107, Dallas, TX 75206. 1/4" scale handcrafted furniture for most any room of your tiny house. Wood construction with fabric upholstery. Good selection of styles and periods with more added every day. Catalog with color swatches $3. See your local hobby dealer. pp. 296-297

J

"J" DESIGNS

8636 Colbath Ave., Panorama City, CA 91402-3303. Mail order, retailer and artisan. One-of-a-kind miniatures. Paintings, steamer trunks, chests—leather and carved. Hand painted animals. Pond, fountains (landscaped). English cottages. LSASE and $1.50 for catalog. Price list available. p. 280

JANNA'S AND KAREN'S MOLDS

PO Box 3013, Walnut Creek, CA 94598. Manufacturer. Catalog, $3. Price list available. More than 200, 1" and 1/2" miniature doll molds. How-to booklets for painting, wigging and costuming miniature dolls. p. 220

JEAN'S WEE THINGS

157 Glen St., Rowley, MA 01969. Retail artisan, mail order. Brochures, $2. Personal miniature photography from your own photos! Kits 'n Caboodle, leather kits and other unusual kits available including trunks, suitcases, 1-1/2" rag dolls, teddies and more. pp. 258, 269, 275

K

K & J MINIATURE METAL WORKS

329 Los Cabos Lane, Ventura, CA 93001. Please see display ad page 10.

KALMBACH PUBLISHING CO.

21027 Crossroads Cir., PO Box 1612, Waukesha, WI 53187. Publisher of Nutshell News, The Miniatures Catalog and other quality hobby books and calendars. Free catalog. pp. 303, 305, 308. Please see display ad pages 1, 345.

KASEY'S

31 Shepherd St., Raleigh, NC 27607. Manufacturer. Brochure, LSASE. Quilt kits using foundation piecing, instruction booklets and fabric packages. pp. 242, 258, 264

KATE'S CATSS

Rt. 1, Box 51A, Eddy, TX 76524. Manufacturer. Catalog, $2. Porcelain pieces with a cat motif. Teapot, cream and sugar and cat boxes. p. 244

THE KESHISHIAN COLLECTION

PO Box 3002, San Clemente, CA 92674. Brochure, $5, refundable with first purchase. Oriental rugs and classic tapestries replicated in detail in miniature. Custom modifications. pp. 178-179

KIMBERLY HOUSE MINIATURES

1775 E. Tropicana #10, Las Vegas, NV 89119. Wholesaler, manufacturer, retailer, mail order and publisher. Catalog, $4, plus $2 shipping. See your local hobby dealer. Kimberly Bricks and Masonry Products; Premixed Stucco; Spiral and Deluxe Staircase Kits; Kimberly Tree, Shrubbery and Landscaping kits; Outdoor Furniture and Store Fixture Kits; Kimberly Wallpaper Paste; "Dollhouses To Dreamhouses" informative Books 1, 2, & 3; "Dream On With Kimberly House" Landscaping Book; KIMBERLY CORNER, 24 pages of projects and fun with Project Insert. pp. 96, 112, 206, 207, 303, 304, 305, 311, 312

THE KITCHEN CAPTIVE

414 E. Chapel Ave., Cherry Hill, NJ 08034. Handcrafter/mail order and shows. American handcrafted foods and beverages in 1" and 1/2" scale for kitchen and dining settings. Very simple to very fancy styles. Fine detail and large selection. Send LSASE for price list. p. 249

KITTY MACKEY'S RELATIVE DIMENSIONS

2401 Van Buren St., Ogden, UT 84401. Artisan. Brochure available. Home-based artisan. There are many talented people making colorful Victorian structures, but we take delight in reproducing historically accurate structures that may not be as pretty, but have more of a story to tell, such as the Sod House featured in Oct. 93-Jan. 94 issues of Nutshell News. We also accept commissions for hand-sculpted realistic figures (see section Dollhouse Dolls & Doll Accessories) and are available to teach figure-sculpting classes. We appreciate the interest and enthusiasm of fellow miniaturists, and promptly return phone calls and letters. pp. 217, 304

"KRAFTS" BY BETTY JEAN

215 West 11th St., Cherokee, OK 73728. Manufacturer—(retail only), mail order, retailer. Catalog, $2 & LSASE (55¢ stamps). Ceramic crockery, spongeware, vases, assorted flower pots, holiday items (some lighted), miniature rubber stamps and other accessories. All handcrafted. pp. 244, 250, 254, 277

L

BETTY LAMPEN KNITTING BOOKS

DEPT. NNC, 2930 Jackson St., San Francisco, CA 94115-1007. Knitting Pattern books—"Miniature Sweaters Book I", "Miniature Pullovers Book II" and "Sweaters for Teddy Bears" Books I and II. $6 each plus $1 postage for all 4. CA residents include sales tax. US funds only. pp. 220, 301

LASER TECH

6669-J Peachtree Industrial Blvd., Norcross, GA 30092. Manufacturer. Catalog price, $2. Manufacturer of laser dollhouse components ranging from trims and grilles to Victorian screen doors and engraved door inserts with the finest laser detail that is available. Send for our catalog showing our complete line of components. pp. 73, 74, 90, 105, 182

THE LAWBRE COMPANY

888 Tower Rd., Unit J, Mundelein, IL 60060. Manufacturer and mail order. Catalog, $4, refundable. Period designed miniature houses, custom designs or reproductions of existing homes, staircases, fireplaces and

architectural castings. Also, trophy items, garden statues, fountains and decorative pieces. pp. 28, 30, 32, 36, 47, 48, 49, 56, 60, 67, 80, 112, 152, 169, 170, 174, 251-252, 272-273, 278

LENHAM POTTERY

Miradouro, Bungay Road, Poringland, Norwich, NR14 7NB, England. Manufacturer, mail order. Specialists in own design of 1" scale slip-cast ceramic porcelain bathroom fittings and taps, kitchen sinks, bathroom suites, bedroom sets—plain or patterned. Plumbing fixtures. Architectural and garden stoneware. Scale horses and harness. Horses at 1/8", 1/10", 1/12", 1/16" scales. Brochures: $3 (dollar bills). pp. 241, 242, 256

THE LIGHTING BUG, LTD.

17 Kang, Willowbrook, IL 60514. Manufacturer. Brochure, $5. Electrified lighting fixtures for miniature rooms and dollhouses. Handcrafted in the US. Extensive product line in 1" and 1/2" scales. pp. 261-262

LIGIA'S MINIATURES

2315 Caracus St., La Crescenta. CA 91214. Manufacturer, mail order. Catalog, $2, refundable with first order. We manufacture unique accessories, specializing in enamels on silver and copper. Dealer discounts available. pp. 263, 277

LINDEN SWISS MINIATURES

PO Box 390571, Dept. MC, 41400 Terwilliger Rd., Anza, CA 92539-0571. Retailer, wholesaler, manufacturer, and mail order. Brochure, LSASE w/$.64 stamp; price list available. See your local miniatures dealer. Glass-like items: glasses, bottles and jars. Wine bottles with labels. Metal cans with labels. Our product comes in kit form. We do have a few finished items. All items are made in America. pp. 252, 256, 268, 286, 298

LITTLE COMFORTS

A division of Debbie's Dollhouses, 150 Airport Drive, Unit 1, Westminster, MD 21157. Wholesaler, retailer, mail order. Brochure of all our quilt designs, $1 plus LSASE. Our Kits are simplified for beginners. Over 10 designs available with new ones being added. Wholesale inquiries invited. Price list available. p. 242

LITTLE THINGS BY JODY

PO Box 639, Midvale, UT 84047-0639. Wholesaler. Handmade braided rugs. Assorted colors and sizes. Custom rugs made to complement special color or room size. Price list available to retail stores. See your local hobby dealer. p. 177

LITTLEFOOT MINIATURES

91 Fincham Ave., Markham, Ontario, Canada, L3P 4E2. Wholesaler, manufacturer, retailer, artisan. Brochure, $3, price list available. See your local hobby

dealer. Quality food products and work of other Canadian artisans. 1" scale and 1/2" scale. CIMTA and MIAA member. Dealer inquiries welcome. pp. 247-248, 254, 264, 277

LULIE'S ZOO

406-A, East 1st. Street, #1341, Long Beach, CA 90802. Manufacturer. Price list available. 1", 1/2", 1/4" dolls with animal heads, humans, fairies and angels, fully poseable and dressed. Porcelain. p. 217

M

MacDOC DESIGNS

405 Tarrytown Rd. #130, White Plains, NY 10607. Our beautiful, finely-detailed Oriental rugs enhance any miniature setting at affordable prices. We have hundreds of designs and many popular sizes. Special welcome mats and runners available, too. Intricate tapestries in new designs add a touch of class to any decor. Also available— a selection of Oriental-style pillows, hatboxes, perfume trays and other accessories. All rugs are available individually or in special groupings at attractive prices. pp. 178, 179

MAISON DES MAISONS

460 S. Marion Parkway, #1851B, Denver, CO 80209. Retail only. Mail order. Catalog, $5. By appointment only. Finest in Native American art. Native American artifacts including roomboxes, furniture, pottery, baskets, paintings, kachinas, dolls, kivas, plaza scenes and related items. China, paintings, bronze. Also fine art in miniature including silver by Smith, Palmer, Blacklock, Quintanar and Fisher. pp. 178, 190, 195, 197, 223, 258-259, 271-272

THE KEN MANNING COLLECTION

15486 85th Ave., Surrey, B.C. Canada, V3S 6V9. Mail order. Brochure $2. Price list available. 1" scale miniature stringed musical instruments. p. 263

MÄRKLIN TRAINS

PO Box 51319, New Berlin WI 53151-0319. Wholesaler. Märklin Z Trains. Distributor of the smallest operating electric railway in the world. Märklin "Z" offers you the most complete line of Z gauge starter sets, locomotives, rolling stock, track and accessories. Catalog #15610, $14.95. Price list available. See your local hobby dealer. p. 286

SONIA MESSER CO., INC.

4811 Glencairn Rd., Los Angeles, CA 90027. Wholesaler, manufacturer, importer, retailer, mail order. Very fine quality period furniture, exquisitely carved of walnut and mahogany. Some kitchen and bathroom items. Price list available, $1. p. 184

MICRO • MARK

340-MC Snyder Ave., Berkeley Heights, NJ 07922. Mail order. Catalog $1. We have an 80-page catalog with more than 2,000 hard-to-find tools and supplies for the miniaturist. p. 314

MINI COLLECTIBLES

c/o Handley House, 5521 E. Rosedale, PO Box 8658, Ft. Worth, TX 76124 and 2 Fourth Street, Wheeling, WV 26003. More than 48 unique Dollhouse Furniture Sets. Handcrafted of real wood and carefully chosen fabrics for authenticity and durability. pp. 168, 192, 196, 197, 198-199, 200-201, 203-204, 206, 210-214, 310

MINI GRAPHICS

2975 Exon Ave., Cincinnati, OH 45241. Please see display ad page 11.

THE MINI MERCHANT

16370 Canon Lane, Chino Hills, CA 91709. Wholesaler, manufacturer, retailer and mail order. Overstuffed upholstered furniture reminiscent of the '30s to contemporary. Custom quilts and afghans. Custom work available on furniture. pp. 188, 197, 242, 265, 292

THE MINI MONEY MINT, HENRY & CHERI ACKLES

89 E. Benson Way, Sandy, UT 84070-2662. Wholesaler and retailer. Send letter of request for wholesale terms. Manufacturer of miniature money for dollhouse dwellers. A division of Henry's House of Trains & Miniatures. p. 278

MINI QUILTS BY ALICE HANSON

3303 Garner St., Eau Claire, WI 54701. Artisan. Brochure $2. Price list available. Pieced quilts, coordinating dust ruffles and pillow. Pieced and applique-type wall hangings. p. 242

MINI-MAGIC

777 Donlon Ave, West Hempstead, NY 11552. Manufacturer, retailer. See your local dealer. Brochure, $3.50. Manufacturer of miniature electrical lighting tools. Retailer of a complete line of dollhouses, electrical supplies, furnishings and handcrafted miniatures. Dealer inquires invited. pp. 147-148

MINIATURE CORNER

1001 Lowry Ave., Jeannette, PA 15644. Wholesaler. See your local miniatures dealer. Unique, high-quality dollhouse products for collectors and children. Made by world famous German toy and doll makers. pp. 96, 112, 199, 243, 244, 264, 312

MINIATURE HOUSE

c/o Handley House, 5521 E. Rosedale, PO Box 8658, Ft. Worth, TX 76124 and 2 Fourth Street, Wheeling, WV 26003. The largest selection of 1" scale gold-plated lighting fixtures. The highest-quality miniature hardware, brick and flooring. pp. 78, 93-95, 107, 108, 121, 134-137, 144-146, 150, 151, 152, 154-159, 162-163, 164, 173, 184, 204-205, 217-218, 219, 274

MINIATURE LUMBER SHOPPE

812 Main St., Grandview, MO 64030. Wholesaler, Manufacturer, retailer, and mail order. We operate a full-line miniature store plus a wood products factory. We make our own sheetwood, stripwood, moldings, and other products in basswood and hardwoods. Our own 1" scale windows and doors are available in several styles and many sizes. We are also known for our broad 1/4" scale product line. Catalog prices: wood products, $2; 1/4", $2.50; 1/2", $1. p. 121

MINIATURE ROSE

13116 Concord St., Sterling Heights, MI 48313. Wholesaler and retail mail order. Victorian dressed mannequins handcrafted. Member CIMTA. Retail mail order and wholesale inquiries welcome. Please see display ad page 227.

MINIATURE RUGS
BY JOAN ADAMS

2706 Sheridan Dr., Sarasota, FL 34239. Catalog $2.75. Make checks payable to Joan Adams. 1/12th sheared punchneedle rug catalog of over 40 designs. Graphs, transparency graphs, completed rugs, canvas, punchneedles and embroidery scissors available. p. 178

MINIATURES BY CHONG HWA

PO Box 128, Kensington, CT 06037. Mail order. Specializing in 1" scale oriental items, oriental dollhouses and furniture. For video, send $9.50 check and resale tax number. Other inquiries please specify and include phone number and resale tax number. p. 58

MINISCULES

N2059 Pine Beach Road, Oostburg, WI 53070. Manufacturer. See your local hobby dealer. Prepasted wallpaper, patterned and textured carpeting. pp. 178, 180. Please see display ad page 6.

MODEL BUILDERS SUPPLY

40 Engelhard Drive #11, Aurora, Ontario, Canada L4G. Manufacturer, wholesaler, mail order. Catalog, $6. MBS produces some 148 patterns, textures and colors of 3-D plastic sheets for brick, block, stone, tile, paving, sidings, roofs, glass block, stucco and water. Also many skylights, tinted mirror plastic, grasses, trees, hedges, shrubs. Modern kitchen and bathroom items. Fireplaces, chimneys. Basswood strips, sheets, thin plywoods, dowels, hardwood veneer floor strips, clapboard sidings, corner angles, Aurora dollhouse kits, carpets. Casting, molding and modeling compounds. Supplies for all scales. Canadian distributors for numerous major miniaturist manufacturers. pp. 19, 23, 26, 46, 79, 96, 97, 102, 108, 110, 169, 174,

178, 180, 182, 241, 256-257, 263, 290, 298

MOONLIGHT MINIATURES

PO Box 235, West Bridgewater, MA 02379-0235. Retailer and mail order. Price list, $2. A complete line of handwoven wicker furniture in 1" and 1/2" scale. pp. 208, 291

MOTT MINIATURES

7700 Orangethorpe Ave., Suite 8, Buena Park, CA 90621-3457 Please see display ad page 240.

MULTI-MINIS, INC.

882 Washington St., P.O. Box 3054, So. Attleboro, MA 02703-0913. Manufacturer. p. 278

MARY AGNES MURPHY

527 Cherry St., Fall River, MA 02720. Wholesaler, manufacturer, retailer, mail order, artisan. Fine handknits, miniature clothing, handcrafted birch and twig furniture. Also unique wooden furniture and toys. Free brochure with SASE. pp. 214, 219

N

NANTASY FANTASY CREATIONS

35843 Matoma Blvd., Eastlake, OH 44095. Retail, wholesale, mail order. I.G.M.A. Artisan. Catalog, $4. Victorian reproductions and more. Over 90 handcrafted items shown in our full color catalog. Cameras, telescopes, golf set, telephones, saddles, gramophones, luggage, stereoscopes, cash register, microscopes, character dolls. p. 268

NELLIE ORIGINALS

6001 Edgewater Dr., Corpus Christi, TX 78412. Retail or wholesale. Information sheets LSASE. Fine, 1" scale, handcrafted furniture modeled from historical sites and other originals, all signed and numbered. Bedspreads, mattresses, pillows, towels. p. 184

NEW ENGLAND
HOBBY SUPPLY, INC.

71 Hilliard St., Manchester, CT 06040. Wholesaler, manufacturer. Price list and brochure with SASE. The Builder's Choice paints and landscaping. Barbara O'Brien curtains and accessories. Memory frames. See your local dealer. pp. 182, 313

NI-GLO® LAMPS

by Nicole, 5684 Sterling Rd., Hamburg, NY 14075-5813. Wholesaler and manufacturer. Color photo/catalog, $5. Free brochure. Price list available. See your local miniatures dealer. Original, intricately handcrafted lamps. Meticulously free-hand china painted designs. Fired in electric kiln several times to insure permanent color. Decals are not used on our fine line of porcelain pieces. All

lamps have replaceable 12V lights. Tiffany-style lamp is cast in solid bronze with antique finish. Porcelain lamps have brass component parts. State when ordering choice of floral or bird design you would like on your Contemporary, Victorian or Colonial lamp. Bone china dinner sets with matching floral arrangements, vases and umbrella stands also available. p. 160

NOONMARK

% Architectural Etcetera, 888 Tower Rd., Unit J, Mundelein, IL 60060. Manufacturer, retail and wholesale. Brochure, $1 and LSASE. Fine quality etched glass, mirrors and related products. pp. 81, 130

NORTHEASTERN
SCALE MODELS, INC.

99 Cross St., PO Box 727, Methuen, MA 01844. Manufacturer. Catalog, $1; price list available. See your local miniatures dealer. Fine quality wood moldings, siding, stripwood, sheetwood and laser cut trims. Also dollhouse for your dollhouse kits. Custom laser cutting services to manufacturers. pp. 59, 97, 98, 104, 110, 258

O

OLDE MOUNTAIN
MINIATURES

366 Starkville Rd., Fort Plain, NY 13339. Manufacturer. Catalog, $2. Pewter hardware and fireplace accessories, 14th-18th Century furniture kits, authentic Navajo needlepoint rugs, leaded stained windows, by IGMA Artisan, vignettes, room boxes in kits and finished, and commission structures in explicit detail. See your local hobby dealer. pp. 66, 95, 178, 186

OMNIARTS OF COLORADO

498 S. High St., Denver, CO 80209. Mail order. Catalog, $5. Items for castles, palaces, museums and fantasy settings. pp. 64, 174, 189, 205, 208, 255, 268, 272, 275, 291

OPENING SCENE REPLICAS

4356 Falcon Crest Dr., Flowery Branch, GA 30542. Wholesaler, manufacturer, retailer. Combined Silver Screen and Prime Time catalog, $5. Manufacturers of famous fictional houses in miniature, dollhouses and roomboxes designed especially for the hobbyist. For realism, accuracy and ease of assembly, choose an Opening Scene Replica. pp. 24, 32, 37, 46, 55, 59, 67

P

"PANNIKINS" BY M.E.

M.E. - (Mary Eccher). 199 Laurel Ridge, South Salem, NY 10590. Mail order, retailer and manufacturer. Price list $2.50. Hancrafted foods and beverages including fruits and vegetables, seasonal, international, regional, ethnic and period favorites. Also, supplies and "empties" for the do-it-yourselfer. p. 248

PARKER HOUSE MINIATURES

783 Sunset St., Banning, CA 92220. Artisan. 1/4" scale handcrafted Victorian houses and furniture. All houses (shells) are center-split and electrified. Catalog $3.50. Price list available. p. 298

PAUL'S SPECIALTIES

3880 Grape Vine Rd., Huntington, WV 25701. Manufacturer of electric and non-electric collector's turntables and glass domes. p. 63

PERRAULT MINIATURES

27609 Loyola Ave., Hayward, CA 94545-4224. Manufacturer, wholesaler, retailer, and mail order. Price list available free of charge. Send for descriptive price list. Retail at shows; more than 50 sizes or styles of unfinished miniature wood frames from which to choose. Dealer inquiries welcome. p. 266

PETITE PEOPLE PLUS

16 Teed St., Huntington Station, NY 11746. Manufacturer, retailer, mail order. Doll catalog $4. Fine porcelain dollhouse dolls and fantasy creatures in 1" and 1/2" scale. We handcraft over 190 varieties of dolls and animals that are dressed or available in kits. Other hancrafted items are landscaping, small scale fantasy houses, ceramics, and whimsical toys. Look for us at shows. p. 218

PRECIOUS LITTLE THINGS

The Fieldwood Co., Inc., PO Box 6, Chester, VT 05143-0006. Wholesaler, manufacturer, artisan, retailer, mail order. Catalog $3.50. Handcrafted moderately priced furniture and accessories in 1", 1/2" and 1/4" scales. Roadside stands; produce in bulk, Mason jars, bowls or baskets; stoneware; handblown glass; holiday accessories; medical and dental furnishings and much more. pp. 59, 248, 262

PRECISION PRODUCTS

763 Cayuga St., Unit #2, Lewiston, NY 14092-1724. Wholesaler, manufacturer, retailer, mail order, distributor. Catalog, $3, includes samples. Price list available. See your local distributor. Manufacturer of 1/2" and 1" scale plastic veneer sheets and of Spincaster (casting) machine and manual. Distributor of glues, mold rubbers, casting materials, fillers and dyes. pp. 74, 79, 108, 110 121, 174, 244, 290, 305, 311

PRESTIGE LEATHER

810 Laroche, Grand Prairie, TX 75050-3435. Wholesale, manufacturer and retailer. Wholesale catalog available. Brochure, LSASE. Price list available. Fine handcrafted leather goods, saddlery, western wear, sporting goods, doll accessories, and carved pictures. pp. 219, 259-260, 263, 266, 270, 272-273, 276

Q

QUAD COMPANY

49 Dublin Drive, Ballston Spa, NY 12020. Manufacturer of "tiny turnings" line of finely detailed, easy-to-assemble wooden furniture kits and turnings with a unique interlocking design. Send LSASE for product brochure and order form. pp. 100, 304

R

R & N MINIATURES

458-C Wythe Creek Rd., Dept. M, Poquoson, VA 23662. Retailer, mail order, crafter. Specializing in quality handcrafted dollhouse accessories in 1" scale, made by our own artisans and top artisans across the country. New, not shown is our instant garden. Write for: GPLI price list, "Gardens by the Inch," and APLI price list, "Accessories," $2 each. pp. 219, 248-249, 251, 254

REAL GOOD TOYS

10 Quarry Hill, Barre, VT 05641. Manufacturer, wholesaler only. Catalog, $4. See your local miniatures dealer. We produce the broadest range of dollhouse kit designs available anywhere in the world. Only the finest quality materials are used and every kit is handcrafted with care by Vermont craftspeople. pp. 19, 24, 26, 27, 28, 29, 32, 35, 37, 47, 50, 51, 55, 60

REIS MINIATURE ART

PO BOX 3182, Newport, RI 02840. Mail Order. Free brochure. Price list available. Original oil paintings in a wide range of subjects: landscapes, seascapes, botanicals and assorted animals and insects. Range in size from 1" x 1", to 3" x 5". Works are available framed or unframed. p. 280

ROYAL MINIATURES

5907 Noble Avenue, Van Nuys, CA 91411. Wholesaler. Catalog, free to retail and trade only; price list available. Enormous range of miniature dollhouse accessories, including glassware, kitchen and household items, baskets, brass pieces, musical instruments, porcelain, food and much more. More than 1,300 different items. pp. 197, 245, 249, 251, 252, 257, 265, 273, 275, 278, 282, 286

S

SANDY'S LACE AND TRIMS

7417 N. Knoxville, Peoria, IL 61614. Mail order. Large selection of antique and new lace and trims. Six sizes silk ribbon, silk

pleating, cottons, silks, wools, batiste and wide variety of mini-prints. Also bunka, crystals, dolls, patterns, hair, watch cases, straw, bear fur, knitting and crochet needles, brasses, trunk kits. And much more. Catalog $2. p. 305

SCIENTIFIC MODELS, INC.

340 MC Snyder Ave., Berkeley Heights, NJ 07922. Catalog, $1. Miniature furniture kits and accessories. pp. 95, 187, 193, 194

SHENANDOAH DESIGNS, INC.

PO Box 313, Brookfield, CT 06804. Manufacturer, wholesale only. Send $1.50 for complete literature. 1"-1' scale furniture kits, assembled furniture, kitchen kits and assembled units. Porch and patio kits and assembled pieces. Porcelain doll kits. Some 1/2" scale pieces. Turnings and hardware also available. pp. 186, 202, 206

SIR THOMAS THUMB

PO Box 1093, Anna Maria, FL 34216. Mail Order. Catalog $3 refundable. We specialize in exquisitely handcrafted, collector-quality, early Americana, crafted from wood & metal, carefully hand polished to a soft patina. Our line encompasses garden, woodworker & farm tools as well as country kitchen furniture & accessories. pp. 188, 251, 257, 275, 276

THE SMALL DOLL COMPANY

7117 Beechwood Dr., Urbandale, IA 50322. Wholesaler. Price list available with LSASE. See your local hobby dealer. Exquisite miniature dollhouse people. Imported fabrics and laces. Dressed with attention to detail. Real leather shoes. p. 218

JUDITH SOKOLOW

4030 Cherokee Drive, Madison, WI 53711-3059. Mail order. Rosemaled wooded oval "tina" box, $25. Norwegian painted furniture, upon request. p. 277

SPECIAL SELLERS

5826 Macinness Drive, Memphis, TN 38119. Manufacturer. Handcrafted quality accessories including designer candy gingerbread houses in 30 styles; elegant gift baskets; candy trees; party platters; assorted holiday and food items; toys and dolls. Price list free with LSASE. pp. 271, 278

BARBARA STANTON

PO Box 3516, Livermore, CA 94551-3515. Award-winning artist will custom paint portraits, landscapes, etc., in oil from your photo or mine. No catalog, just price list and examples of work. Original one-of-a-kind pieces also available. p. 266

STEELE MINIATURES
JEFFREY R. STEELE

PO Box 1104, Libertyville, IL 60048-4104. Manufacturer, retailer, mail order. Catalog, $20. Price list available. Steele Miniatures offers custom, one-of-a-kind, handmade furnishings and accessories in 1"-1' scale as well as miniature interiors, settings, and video "how to do's": The Basic Upholstered Chair, The Faux Marble Table and Mail Order: The Steele Collection. p. 308

T'NEE PRODUCTS

1851 W. Berenice, Chicago, IL 60613. Wholesaler. Price list available. Polymer clays and related books and tools. p. 102

TERI'S MINI WORKSHOP

Box 387, Goldenrod, FL 32733. Retailer, wholesaler, manufacturer and artisan. Catalog, $1 and LSASE. Handcrafted sporting goods, medical supplies, nursery items, contemporary dolls, pet supplies, beauty parlor pieces. pp. 207, 218, 242, 257, 262, 273, 276

THREE BLIND MICE

pp 207, 274, 275, 292

TIMELESS IMAGES IN MINIATURE

8863-C E. Black Point Rd., Syracuse, IN 46567. Mail order. Catalog, $2 (refunded with first purchase). Your family photos miniaturized in B&W, sepia, or color. Quality hand painted frames and "instant ancestors," too. p. 269

TITMOUSE COLLECTIBLES

PO Box 286, Pomona, NY 10970. Manufacturer. Artisan-created floor and table lamps and chandeliers. Custom orders and dealer inquiries welcome. Brochure $3.50. p. 160

TREASURE WORKS

1650 Limekiln Pike, Suite 434, Dresher, PA 19025. Manufacturer and mail order. Price list available. Designer and manufacturer of 3-D miniatures. Mostly sterling - mostly jewelry wearable. More items 1"-1' scale are coming soon (by August publication). Wholesale available. pp. 254, 260, 278

UNIQUE MINIATURES

16 W. Main St., Isanti, MN 55040. Wholesaler, manufacturer, and retailer. Catalog, $3. Quality architectural castings from polyester resins of several styles and of many items. pp. 74, 75, 81, 105, 170, 263

VICKI'S MINIATURES

PO Box 142407, Anchorage, AK 99514-2407. Manufacturer. Specializing in handcrafted, detailed exercise equipment. We have more than 22 different products available. Send for free brochure. p. 274

THE VICTORIAN CRAFTSMAN

Dept. C, P.O. Box 234, New York, NY 10276-0234. Please see display ad page 13.

VICTORIAN TRIMS & LACES/DOLL FAIRE MINIATURES

2310 Monument Blvd., Pleasant Hill, CA 94523. Retail and wholesale. Catalog, $4. Many narrow trims and braids including soutache, tiny picot, six sizes of silk ribbon with bunka dyed to match. Old and new English and French cotton laces, beautiful Swiss embroideries and hat straw, three sizes of tiny pleated laces, many dollhouse doll dressing books and patterns. Also available are glues and special mini glue dispensers, pleaters, dollhair, books and patterns. p. 166

JEFFREY W. VIGEANT

PO Box 414, Williamsburg, VA 23187-0414. Artisan, wholesaler, retailer, mail order. Creator of the Nursery Novelties Collection lamps. Unique collector-quality 1" scale chandeliers and accessories in gold-plated brass. Color brochure, $4 ppd., no charge to dealers. pp. 137, 160-161, 163, 169, 267

WALMER DOLLHOUSES

2100 Jefferson Davis Hwy., Alexandria, VA 22301. Manufacturer. Catalog, $2. See your local hobby dealer. Full range of wooden dollhouses, Designer Home™ architectural building components, decorative hardware, architectural accents, children's furniture kits. pp. 19, 24, 28, 30, 33, 34, 49, 50, 51, 52, 53, 56, 57, 68, 75, 76, 77, 80, 90, 91, 95, 96, 101, 112, 113, 121, 122, 128, 129, 189, 214

WARLING MINIATURES

22453 Covello St., West Hills, CA 91307. Artisan. For price list send LSASE. Our specialty is Victorian to modern wicker furniture and accessories in 1" and 1/2" scales, available completely finished or in kit form. Sealed, signed and dated pieces are available in natural or white and are upholstered and/or dressed in the color of your choice. Wicker kits contain natural color waxed linen cord that can be left natural or sprayed white when completed. p. 208

WEE THREE

516 A Opa Lane, Stratford, CT 06497. Mail order. Catalog, $2. Needlework supplies — for scale knitting, crocheting, tatting, etc. pp. 265, 307

WENZEL MINIATURES

PO Box 584, Ventura, CA 93002. See your local hobby dealer. We offer a variety of fruits, vegetables and food in preparation. Our specialties include aged painted or stained tables handcrafted by Jacob with food made by Kathleen and some vegetables which can be sliced open to reveal "botanically correct" interiors. pp. 249, 255

WHAT'S NEXT?

1000 Cedar Ave., Scranton, PA 18505. Manufacturer. Catalog, $1.50. The fastest, easiest, most beautiful roof you can put on your building. Thirteen super colors. Our varnished paper tile floors are unique and beautiful. pp. 97, 108, 175

ROSALIE WHYEL MUSEUM OF DOLL ART

1116 108th Ave. NE, Bellevue, WA 98004. Retailer. Dollhouse dolls, dollhouse accessories, books, miniatures; antique and contemporary. Please call, FAX, or write for details. pp. 218, 219, 254, 280, 300

WILLO MINIATURES

RD1, Box 55, Walton, NY 13856-9709. Mail order, shows. Brochure, $1. Superior construction material. Performance features include rigid and durable, excellent strength to weight ratio, moisture resistant, easily cut, lightweight. Thickness available from 3/16" to 1-1/2". p. 77

WISCONSIN CRAFTS

W6407 - 20th St., Necedah, WI 54646-7503. Mail order. Price list with SASE. Lengths of wood, measuring 24" long, come in basswood, maple, walnut, cherry, red oak and butternut. The pieces are available in 2", and 4" widths and come in various thicknesses for building to scale. Both sides of each board are pre-sanded. p. 101

THE WORLD'S SMALLEST CO.

1398 Oregon Rd., Leola, PA 17540. Manufacturer and Mail Order. Brochure, $1 in stamps & LSAE. Specializing in pet birds, wild birds, rustic and traditional birdhouses. Flintlock and modern rifles, fishing rods, bows and arrows. Every item is carefully handcrafted. Collector-quality 1"=1' scale—you will be delighted. pp. 224, 274

ALICE ZINN

1498 Kirke La., Pt. St. Lucie, FL 34983. Wholesale, retail, mail order and shows. Catalog, $4, SASE. Pet and wild birds and animals, hand-sculpted original dolls, oriental food and accessories, sporting goods, leather goods and shoes, hats and clothing, audio-visual equipment, holiday accessories. Custom challenges welcomed. Alice Zinn is available for workshops. pp. 216, 222, 258, 267, 272, 275, 301

PRODUCT